TROUBLE
THE
WATER

*A Young Woman on the Edge
of Living and Dying*

IDINA SANTINO

Printed in the United States of America.

Library of Congress Control Number: 2019909711

ISBN   Paperback   978-1-64803-325-4
              Hardback   978-1-64803-326-1
              eBook   978-1-64803-327-8

Westwood Books Publishing LLC
11416 SW Aventino Drive
Port Saint Lucie, FL 34987

www.westwoodbookspublishing.com

I dedicate this book first and foremost to my daughter, who had more courage, fortitude, and dignity in her twenty-one short years than I would have in five lifetimes. To my son, who, similarly, lived with courage and integrity, I owe more than I could ever repay in missed opportunities for mothering him as I would have chosen, had leukemia not inserted itself into our lives. And to all those who believed in and encouraged me as I mothered, taught, and wrote, I am humbled and grateful.

Contents

Preface

A lthough the events and situations described in this narration are real, names of people and many places have been changed to respect identities. In writing this narrative, I drew from memories and impressions, and notes and journals both I and my daughter kept over the course of the years included. Though I have tried to approximate the style and capture the voice of my daughter's writing, I am the author of the diary/journal sections ascribed to her. This narrative is my attempt to honor the spirit of my daughter and to fulfill her request to write her story.

Introduction

~~I want to thank my mother for~~
~~All I ever wanted was to be able~~
List of points

- listen to me
- I know my own body
- I know what I can handle
- it's my body
- I wanted to be normal
- it's not right to make someone do what she doesn't think is right

MHC, home, or die

December, 1989

"It's not life at all cost for me," she says, regarding her audience with lucent blue eyes.

In her camel skirt and black blazer, she, like the others, is suited, tied, and polished, poised to take her place among the assorted mature panelists. In reversed chronology, though, she may be the oldest one here. I like her best in blooming pastels that tenderly compliment her fragile coloring. And even as pink is her favorite color, she images herself in a slinky black spaghetti-strapped sequined dress by night and the neat, tailored, ready-to-conquer-the-business-world suit by day: clothing with a future in mind.

I have arrived just in time to the hotel hosting the conference, thanks, in part, to the weather, Minnesota's, acting like a displeased two-year-old throwing a tantrum. Snow has covered Halloween pumpkins of other years, but this year's November had whooshed in between the cracks, trying not to alarm us too soon for what surely follows. Today, as I waited for the bus, the sky a sloggy gray batter, the wind more than once sliced open my coat, spiked icy glimmers at my face from the ghost drizzle that haunted the afternoon, a murky distraction.

Amid the customary scrapings of chairs and tappings of papers before the speaker stepped to the microphone and announced the last of the agenda, making introductions for the panelists, I survey the audience, heads strung out like fishing bobbins, a few clumped together here and there where the current drew them. The back of Arnold's head, thin sand-colored hair with an undertow of orangey

1

red giving way to gray, drifts alone, vacant seats radiating from him like ripples in a lake. His freckled hands would be knit together in his lap. When you've known an actor for twenty-four years, you can't discount his presence, even in low theater light. He wears a suit. The glare sheds a ray of light on his staged persona: he knows how to find the babies in the crowd. And when to wear a suit.

As if I were a noxious gas seeping through the vents, he turns to sniff out the source, squinting his eyes as when he sips his coffee. He flees every room in which I appear, though not today. There is a body to impress.

I exhale as if expelling an undissolved aspirin. Whatever differences, we had two children in common. That Dom isn't here is to his credit: no senior in high school wants to give up his classes, his friends, his sports, and his jeans to sit in a stuffy auditorium to hear his sister say what he's witnessed. Ever since the beginning, which to him is almost half his life, he has watched one sacrifice after another, been sacrificed himself. For all I know, he blames Jada, or at least her disease, for what went wrong with our family. I admire Dom's tenacity and have long since forgiven his means of self-protection; he needs them to hang on.

We are all hanging on. Arnold took two days from school to be a spectator to this conference of professors, doctors, and nurses, an outsider looking in. Maybe I am caught in another ploy. Maybe I am the one missing out, showing up for only the one panel discussion my daughter initiates. Maybe in my journey with Jada, I have too singularly narrowed my focus.

Too many maybes. Too many should haves on their heels. And not enough tomorrows on the tips of their tongues.

I had no difficulty envisioning Jada, a twenty-one-year-old math major in her senior year at Mary Hillyard, talking about the ethics of organ transplantation. We'd spent the last eight-and-one-half years and the last two nights distilling her experiences into fundamental truths. When I was Jada's age, the only aisle I looked at was the one leading to my husband who waited at the altar. I follow my daughter's form down the auditorium of the Sibley Midtown

Hotel where she will contribute a voice from a patient point of view to the professional community. Twenty-two—nearly 23—years ago, I blubbered up to my destination. Today my daughter stands confidently, her posture straight, her step purposeful, her dimpled chin raised. I sidle in a few seats, watching her as the panelists assemble on stage.

"I want to thank Dr. Lourde for inviting me to speak about my disease and my decisions. I was diagnosed with leukemia when I was twelve years old. I didn't know what was going to happen to me. And every time I thought I was going to get better, something else happened to me. I had two relapses. I had infections. One of them ruined my arm. I had reactions to treatments. I had operations. I had both of my hips replaced. I had diabetes. I got sick a lot. It was very hard for me to live a normal life. And that's what I wanted. To live a normal life. To go to school, to have friends, to have a job, to go to college.

"Every time something happened to me, Dr. Lourde tried to help me. Everyone said to try, to keep on trying, do it their way, not what I wanted. I didn't want to keep trying something else because every time I thought I might have a normal life things got worse. You all want to save life. But what good is life if it can't be normal? I decided not to have a bone marrow transplant. I decided not to because I wanted to have a normal life. I wanted to go back to my college and be with friends, not spend weeks and months in a hospital. I wanted to save *my* life."

Poisonous as he thinks I am, I take no delight in making Arnold run, rising and swinging out the aisle to an opposite exit after she steps away from the podium to applause and seats herself at the table on stage with the panelists. The conference drawn to its close, Jada bounces toward the foyer, in her black-slippered feet, the air whispering through her feathery golden hair, the blue in her eyes gathering light and refracting it into sparkling sapphires, the color of cold, the color of winter, her favorite season. I came to the tail end of this conference to take Jada home, not to taunt her father. She wears the shine that says she is content. I ask in a lowered voice, "You were eloquent. Are you pleased—do you think you made your point?" I think of the missed classes, the flight home, the planning, the build-up.

"It wasn't exactly what I expected. They never talked about what I thought they were going to." Her eyelashes flicker, an acquired gesture that, intentionally or not, averts elaboration. "It was all on medicines and studies and legal stuff, not just leukemia and other cancers. There are psychologists and nurses and oh, a lot of different people. They weren't ready to hear me." Her voice is patient, relaxed. "But I got to talk to people at breaks."

Two tall men approach, and Jada swivels to introduce them, Dr. Adam Martens and Dr. Paul Whitington. Another Adam in her life, I mentally remark. Standing with overcoats draping their bent arms, they wonder where they can get a table for dinner in Nokomis. I am about to recommend a place in Sibley when the doctor with shorter blond hair suggests that they should be watching for the cab. "Are you ready, Jada?" he asks her.

"Adam and Paul invited me to dinner," Jada informs me, pulling the car keys from the open-mouthed purse at her hip and swinging them toward me like a rattle.

"But don't you need the car? I can take the bus home. It's no problem."

"No," Jada says, in two syllables. "I'm going with them."

"Yes, I gathered that, but... Do you want me to pick you up?"

"No," she repeats. Her eyes say, "Don't you get it?"

Dr. Whitington explains, "We're staying in Nokomis."

"But if you're going back to Nokomis...."

"It's no problem to take her home."

"Mother, I'll be all right. I'm just going to dinner." I feel my color growing along with my tongue, which seems to be blocking a reasoned utterance.

"We better get out there," the other doctor says. "The cab must be here by now." Jada dips over the table, grabs the manila folder containing her notes and the program, and hands them all to me. I say good-bye as the three aim themselves at the double glass doors that the two gentlemen hold open to her. I feel like a missing puzzle piece lying just beyond hand's reach behind the skirt of a couch.

"Hi, Mrs. Petersen?" The tailored voice interrupts my self-absorption.

"Well, I was," I say, turning to face her. Instantly I see how well matched her appearance is to her voice. "Ms. Santino now."

"Sorry. I'm Pat Crisham. I teach graduate nursing students. I thought you were Jada's mother. You carry yourself just like her."

"How do you do?" I gather the folder into my left arm and reach out my hand.

"I'm not going to tell you what a remarkable person Jada is because you know that already. I've had the opportunity to speak with Jada, and I want you to know how important it is that my students hear what she has to say. They come back to me after they've already been in the field, and they grapple with these issues. I'll carry Jada's message back to them. You must be very proud of her. You've done some remarkable work."

"She deserves the credit, not me. She's had to fight for herself and put up with all the garbage, make her own decisions and test my own beliefs—at least what I've said I believe. She has a lot to teach all of us."

Pat's easy-care hair clings to her head as she tilts it, her eyes holding mine as she continues in disarming tenderness, "Yes, but she's learned from you, too. I can tell by looking at you both. You must be a wonderful mother. I wish you well," she says, half-smiling, and lays her other hand on ours, as if sealing what passes between us.

"Thank you" doesn't seem adequate, but I have nothing else to offer as she releases me and walks away, leaving me alone in the hotel hallway, neither staying nor going, gathering the parts of myself together into, if not a neat package, at least a transportable bundle. Whatever similarity between Jada and me, real or concocted, it is not poise. My bag rests against a table, the kind that isn't noticeable except as a prop. On a nearby chair is my coat. I check for the car keys and start for the rest of my belongings. As I lean over, the papers inside the folder slip out and zig-zag to the floor like drunken sailors straggling the pavement back to ship. I berate my clumsiness aloud to myself. "Here I am, everything falling apart around me. I must look like a goon."

With one arm in a coat sleeve, I stoop to scoop the papers into a pile. Underlines and exclamation marks move my eyes around the pages, some still blank, others with pencil notes in Jada's script, a combination of sturdy lines and carefree loops as I look for order so characteristic of her. A cluster of lines crisscrossing into a star catches my notice. As I read, "I want to thank my mom for her true and loving support," my hand clutches the cloth at my chest as into a bouquet of prickly-stemmed roses. Whatever notes follow, I can't see them, can't even look at them on the paper, and bow my head to emotion.

Hastily I put everything together, no longer worrying about its organization and make my escape to the parking lot under a broken-hearted sky. A misting of tears scatter themselves over the evening, but that isn't why I am relieved to find isolation in my Mazda. I need time. No, not really. I have time, time enough to think and think over and wish I could bolt from my mind's chamber, as Arnold does the room when I enter it. What I need is quiet, the quiet of not thinking. I need the quiet to listen.

She's right. Baring private passions to rows of impersonal faces? There is so much more to her story than the cold hard events of disease, the succession of debilitating infections, tumultuous mishaps, unsettling complications, torturous procedures, and the mind-boggling treatments for all of them, and then chains of unforeseen reactions to all of those, her chances of survival, diminished from a bettor's 50/50 at the outset. And though I was present for her story's unfolding, I can't piece the journey together by myself. The bumps are just too many and too jarring. I need the quiet to pay attention to Jada's story.

The windshield wipers slap intermittently, and as they clear away the tiny droplets that blur the edges of objects ahead of me,

I look for a starting place. Tonight isn't the first time I've been caught in transit, pondering the future, questioning the past. Red lights shine double in the sheen on the asphalt. As I work my way home, the distorted reflection of my passage shimmers alongside me: somewhere the real and the unimagined are one, but I can't separate the two, and I arrive home at a 1918 converted hotel, in which Jada and I share a sixth floor condo, without awareness of driving there. My headlights, at cockeyed angles, spray uneven halos onto the garage door as it starts open with a jolt. I park my car under a flickering fluorescent light that stutters, l-l-look, look, n-n-now you see it, n-n-now you d-don't, ride the rattly elevator and walk the long corridor strung with glass blown into segmented bubbles, oversized flies' eyes, spraying yellow splintered spotlights along the moon-colored walls, casting shadows like corners.

Making a grand entrance, I swing the wide door to our unit open and flip light switches as I move inward. Glass tulips surrounding four hundred watts of light spray the foot of Jada's brass bed, our first purchase when we moved in. I wanted her to have her own suite and papered her bedroom, hallway, and bathroom with dusty rose and cream wallpaper. Jada chose the Victorian love seat and matching chair that I planned to refinish and reupholster; I had blue fabric to pick up the flowers that splashed in petit-point dabs on the walls. So many things left to get done. She found the old cedar chest—among other things—and an antique marble-topped bureau with a tall mirror attached by two wobbly wood slats. We are still on the lookout for a roll-top desk that isn't too big or too masculine.

Jada's stuffed animals, usually spread about the smooth bed, are heaped together on the cedar chest as if they are sleeping off a night's carousing. A curled-up lamb whose metal knob I wound up to play a tinkly lullaby the night before lays tilted backwards on her bed quilt, rumpled from being casually released from service. Hambone's head, almost the same creamy color, peeps from beneath her blanket.

7

"Oh, Hambone," I say, extracting the smushy fleecy pig from his warm nest next to the pillow. "You've been through it, too. Imagine the story you could tell." Enfolding him within my arms, I draw in a huge breath and let out a surrendering sigh. "I'm going to need a lot of help telling Jada's story."

April, 1981

"What's the matter with Jada?" Punky asked. She was named Lucretia after my mother's mother, but, being the first-born, I supposed, she was Punkins—"hot stuff"—to my aunt, and, when her two younger sisters arrived, out of the mouths of babes came Punky. That's a guess. My mother could not tell me how I was named—or would not? Once, as I stood a shying pipsqueak at her side, she fabricated an origin not heard before or since, an offering that not only belittled me even more but also would have required more imagination than my imaginative name that I forever refused to repeat it even as a mistake. Nor was my father, who didn't talk about any of us except to call Domenica, the skinny one among us, a toothpick running around with no clothes on, a source even to consider. In high school, Punky shortened Lucretia to Lucy, and, as she grew older, Punky instructed us to call her Lucy, too, a new inductee into the family. Domenica continually corrected me, as if I was uninformed that Punky had chosen a new name, which was ironic, since Domenica still called me Dee Dee. Families. Doesn't every story start there?

We sat at Punky's dining room table, the growling sound of her dishwasher flushing away scraps of our Easter dinner. "Jada hardly ate anything," Punky said.

"Oh, she's not too crazy about ham, and sweet potatoes are still exotic. Besides, she's been wanting to lose weight."

"Really?" Fred said, shooting a playful glance at his wife. "Lucy's been trying to talk me into going on a diet, but I told her

9

that it would upset our shopping routine. She'd have to skip the aisle with the Oreo cookies. It would throw her off entirely."

"Yeah, look at us," she said, patting the rounded protrusion at her lap and burping a belly laugh out of it. "It looks like I'm hatching a basketball. It's those damn cigarettes. Ever since I quit smoking I've gained twenty pounds." Punky turned back to Fred and smiled deceptively. "You should quit, too."

Fred's exhaled smoke clouded the table. "Lucy has this funny notion that as long as she's on the wagon, she may as well reform other people's habits, too. She's always surprised that other people don't appreciate her generosity."

"Oh, Freddy, boy. You think you're so funny." We all laughed, recalling perhaps our memories of the Punky of our growing up. She smiled along with us; where Domenica and I had never been able to fight back, Fred had met her eye to eye. A long time had passed since our neighbors' father called us DeeDee, DoDo, and DumDum, but we hadn't changed much no matter what names we were called.

Coming up from downstairs, Dom looked to me for salvation from his boredom. Like his grandfather—Dominic, for whom he was named and with whom he shared the same rich coffee brown eyes and thick crooked nose—Dom had automatic entertainment as long as there was a sporting event on television or a ball in his hands. Being the only two males in the family—not counting those who came in by marriage—my dad and my son were outnumbered and misfitted in a world of females who had little sympathy for the frivolity of play, especially when there was real work to be done. Grandpa Pope lay on a couch downstairs, his large open hand covering his forehead and eyes, and Punky's teenage girls had no basketballs or baseball bats for Dom, only just turned nine, and me to go out and play with.

I sat at the table with my sisters and our husbands and our mother. Jada usually sat beside me, sometimes climbing onto my lap, for Punky and Domenica always told stories, oftentimes retellings of pivotal incidents, sometimes revelations of long-kept secrets like the time Punky was walking home from the neighborhood movie theater on her first date having to pee and then being asked in for hot chocolate and being too embarrassed to ask to use the bathroom. She shuddered as she remembered how the wet corduroy froze cold between her legs when she walked home—with *him*. Domenica got going about our moving to Pine City and how little notice we had and how at fifteen she had to drive with a trailer attached to the car. "Can you believe it?" she laughed and coughed, "Me? I never drove a trailer before!" She coughed again and ran some air along her throat like a vacuum cleaner.

"Well I found out for the first time when I came home from California. There was a note on the door saying, 'We moved'; not even directions how to get there." Punky was not laughing.

"Those were hard times, and if you had known," defended my mother. On rare occasions, she listened in silence, expressing a wonderment as if hearing these family sagas for the first time, though they'd been a part of the after-dinner talk every time we got together, which was pretty much only at holidays.

"But I'll tell you, we were on our own a lot and it made me strong and independent," Punky summed up. "That's how I could get these promotions without a college degree." To Jada, our lives were an adventure, at times comical, mostly pitiable. More than several times Jada marveled at how I, her mother, came out of *that family*. Over liquor-spiked coffee, Arnold worked his jaw, curiously silent at the opportunity for sarcasm while Dom hovered at my elbow, his head of silky brown hair and long black lashes brushing my arm.

"Dom," I coaxed, "why don't you go out to the living room and see what Jada's doing." Dom slid off. In minutes he returned and leaned on my arm. "Didn't Jada want to play?"

"She's sleeping."

"Sleeping? That's a first," observed my mother. Everything about Jada was a concentration of energy, intensely consuming. From birth, she took half-hour naps, and not many, at that. At 3:30 in the morning she was starved for play. As late as ten or 11 p.m.,

11

I rocked her, kissing her fuzzy head and singing soft lullabies into her ear.

Sometimes it was enough—for a while; but she woke up crying for more.

My mother had warned that I was spoiling her. "Let her cry, Idina. She'll get tired out and fall asleep. That's what I did when you girls were little. If you didn't go to sleep right away, I left you in a basket or a dresser drawer and shut the door. Babies need to cry. That's how their lungs expand. It's good for them."

A young mother in desperation, I took my mother's advice. After feeding and rocking, rubbing her back and proffering her pacifier, I shut her bedroom door and walked away, which is not far in a two-bedroom apartment. Jada cried. I paced. Jada cried. I counted. Jada cried. I lit another cigarette. Then came a knock at the apartment door; the man said he was my neighbor. Arnold was out with "the boys," so latching the chain, I opened the door a crack. Immediately a foot thrust in between the door and the frame. "I want to know what you're doing to that baby. I'm trying to get some sleep, and that crying's keeping me awake!"

"She's supposed to cry herself to sleep, so that's what I'm waiting for."

The man spewed back with convincing menace, "I'm going back to bed now, and if that baby doesn't stop crying, I'm calling the police."

Arnold arrived home to find us in the rocking chair, Jada's sticky head nuzzling my neck, just under my ear. Arnold would tell the story from his point of view, chuckling as he summed up our situation: she had to be with me.

I can name the event that forced my acquiescence. On this night I'd been routed from bed four times and comforted her, I'd hoped, to sleep. She cried again, and I decided to let her fuss long enough to irritate Arnold into getting up himself. He didn't stir, and I gave in, quieted Jada again. Seven times I got up to Jada's wailing; at the time I brought Jada into bed with me, I'd lost track of numbers. I considered my transgression as merely caving: my mother's voice, Dr. Spock's, and Dr. Freud's, too, chided me. Jada cuddled under my arm drowning them all out.

Jada was spinning a bowl with clumps of cold oatmeal around on the high chair tray when Arnold joined us in the narrow apartment kitchen with its pocked linoleum floor tiles. Walking across to the percolator on the counter, he beamed with the authority of being the reporter first to the scene. "Jada had a good night last night, didn't she?"

"You mean you didn't hear her or me getting up all night? She slept in the bed between us and you didn't even know it?" The stove burner I was scouring clattered and spun unevenly in its orbit as I faced a man who would not face me, and feeling rutted myself, I spurted, "I stay up with her at night. I get up with her in the morning. I get up with her all night long. And then when you come home from school, you take a nap while I make dinner. Why can't you take care of her at least once in a while?"

He stopped, his face a TV screen just turned off and taking all the life into the diminishing hole. "Well, you know she only wants you." While he waited for his toast to pop out, he poured coffee into a stained olive green Melmac cup.

"That's because she only gets me."

"Uh, uh, uh!" Jada squirmed and knocked her feet against the wooden footrest. She had been ignored too long and wanted out.

"All done!" I said in high voice, raising my arms in the air.

"A' dun!" she copied, a smile consuming her face. The spoon dropped from her grasp as she threw up her hands. Her hair hung in straight wispy shreds, matted here and there with pasty globs of dried cereal.

"All done," Arnold joined in, tearing a corner of toast. Jada pushed against the wooden tray and drew up a knee while I washed her clean. Arnold lit a cigarette, alternately inhaling and tipping his coffee cup to his lips, then tamping out the burnt-down stub and clamping the cup on the Formica tabletop both at the same time, before driving off to school. Arnold would defend his version if recalled: it's exactly the kind of story we remembered differently.

Like I said, we don't change much, and eleven years later, Jada and her brother, four years younger, still clung to me. During the conversation around Punky's dining room table, Dom asked, "When can we go, Mom?"

"Can't find anything to do, hunh? Pretty soon. Let me see how Jada is, and then we'll play a card game or something." Dom's hand lay on my arm, and I ran my palm back and forth over it, explaining to everyone else, "She's been awfully busy lately, getting ready for her piano recital, orchestra rehearsals for the spring concert and all the ice show practices on top of her early morning lessons. Not a lot of sleep and a few too many falls on the ice. Too many things going on all at once." My mother and sisters had no idea about our getting up at four in the morning for skating lessons, having to make every ice show practice or be cut from the performance. I didn't bring up the possibility of our not having enough time to find a new dress for the orchestra concert, what with the frequent trips to the doctor's office. "She's been sick, too. I took her in to Dr. Silverman again this week. Whatever it is, she can't quite shake it. Dom's been okay, haven't you, Darlin'?"

Dom walked alongside me to the living room and watched me put my hand to Jada's forehead. Usually her skin turned red and hot when she ran a temperature, but her face was blanched of color. Born with my dad's full face, as she grew older, Jada's lips and eyes, though bluer and deeper, resembled my mother's side of the family. Her eyelids lifted to my touch, revealing gray shallow pools.

"I have a funny feeling," she complained.

"Where? In your stomach?"

She squinched her eyes. "Mmm, no."

Crouching, I searched out symptoms. I had learned that complaining elicited an "Eyh, it's nothing" from my mother. As a mother myself, however, I couldn't wait out the mystery of sick: my children got sick visually and dramatically, teaching me that sick was unpredictable and always including a series of visits to the doctor. As Jada and Dom grew, manila folders holding records of body temperatures, hemoglobin, and white blood cell count readings from routine finger sticks, grew taller with them. I slid my hand along the side of Jada's fragile face, along her arm, careful not to place pressure on the bruise that stained a patchy blue. "Dom and I are going to stay with you for a while; then we'll go home pretty soon. Do you want anything?"

Spikes of laughter and an occasional retort from Arnold in the dining room reminded me of juvenile cravings to be part of the card games at my Aunt Winnie's house after the holiday dishes were washed and put away. "Dom," I said, "why don't you ask Punky for a couple decks of cards and we'll play a game of Pounce."

His face worried slightly, and I acknowledged his shyness with a smile. "Okay, then, I spy something that has two syllables in its name." While Dom's eyes roved the room, I contemplated the clues to the puzzle that confronted me: since the winds picked up autumn's scent and launched Jada into the season of seventh grade, budding breasts like acorns ripening seeds within, Jada revealed other changes. Her once wiry body grew pudgy. She knocked into things, fell while attempting figure skating moves, bruising her arms and legs. Increasingly, her patience with my opinions grew shorter. And now, like my sister Punky, as she turned toward adolescence, it appeared that Jada was turning into a sleeper. I would never have dared to say it to her, but I wondered if maybe we were all more alike than we wanted to admit.

"Here's the next clue. It has eyes but it can't see."

If this were my story to tell, I'd start with the days my two children were born. Three months after the assassination of Martin Luther King, Jr., and one month after that of Bobby Kennedy, and amid riots and protests Jada was born. Arnold came to the hospital during designated hours on Independence Day carrying a miniature flag on a stick. He was going on to his mother's for a picnic; I was going nowhere, waiting somewhat apprehensively for a nurse to bring Jada to me. For two days, nurses delivered my firstborn to the crook of my arm at appointed hours; I thought she was the most marvelous creature in the universe and I wanted her to know how much I adored her, but I couldn't hold her without her crying.

I tried placing her in different positions, and after Arnold left, I walked with her in my arms, on my shoulder. The nurse, finding us both out of bed before the end of our five days' recovery period, reprimanded me, trundling my screaming baby off to the safety of a plastic bin behind glass and replacing her with my lunch tray. I cowered back into bed, taking comfort from the lukewarm pool of gravy in the potatoes under the stainless steel dome on the tray.

My mother came into the room; a dented pea dropped from my fork onto the folded bedspread when I asked, "Have you seen Jada, yet? She looks a lot like Dad, doesn't she? She's got the cutest dimple in her chin, just like that picture of Rocky." I knew Rocky, the baby of my dad's family, from one encounter and an 8 x10 framed photograph.

My mother dragged a chair next to the bed and sat. "Oh, no, I didn't notice that. They've got them pretty well wrapped up, you know." Her aquamarine eyes studied the mounds of food in their flat compartments. "I haven't eaten all day," she said, the skin sagging under her eyebrows, draping her eyes.

"I wish I had known before I started eating; maybe I could have saved you something. Now it's too late." My fork hung in the air, shreds of skewered beef dripping from its prongs.

"I'm always too late," she said, looking at the food but hinting at a medley of missed opportunities. I opened my mouth and took the meat in and tasted the sourness of pity. That was the second painful reflection I'd heard from a woman who didn't much feature reflection, preferring instead to act urgently and to make the best of the results. She was always quick to smooth over discord or contentious stirrings like she was making up a crisp-looking bed after a night's wrangling in it. A flick of the wrist, a swoop of the hand, and nothing looked like it had ever been disturbed.

My mother lived by a very simple and unyielding rule: work first, fun, later. She toiled for long hours, at the businesses that she and my dad owned and operated. According to my mother, my dad had lost a job for being seen walking into a bar during working hours, and whether that or his struggle with mental illness precipitated their enterprises, no one can answer. She and my dad lined up ventures like fish on a stringer, opening new ma-and-pa businesses, one upon the other as they got a new strike, never revealing the reason for their entrepreneurial spirit until after it died. "No sense crying over spilt milk," my mother often said, the consequence being the loss of a story, however much truth it evaded.

"When we get home, you and Dad can see her," I offered, ashamed to admit to my failure as a mother. Last-born, I was the baby. When I asked questions about how things were as they were, what made my aunt Rosie not go out of the house, or why was my mother all balled up and groaning in bed, or what happens when you go to sleep, my mother's blue eyes cast shadows over my curiosities, and through her rigid lips she answered, "Oh, Idina," and I guessed I was just supposed to know.

But I didn't, so the thought that the cause of Jada's crying was not mine could not cross my mind. Someone else thought it out. Jada was born with a subdural hematoma, a bruise of sorts, that bumped out of her head, giving her face a lopsided look; on the top of her head was a red open sore that shimmered like red coals surrounded by white ashes. An X-ray revealed nothing wrong with her head, just a bump from resisting the hard bones and pulsating muscle tissues separating her from the sloshy warm pillow of my insides and an unhealed catch of skin in the skull as the bone came together. The day before we were released, the radiologist re-examined the original X-ray. At eight pounds fifteen-and-one-half ounces, Jada was large for a pelvis but small under a camera, and the source of her crying was discovered: she had a broken clavicle, another sacrifice in Jada's soft and supple bone to claim space in the world. Nurses who had disapprovingly snatched her from me now adjusted a tiny diaper into a sling to hold her arm in place and smiled benevolently as they watched us cooing. Jada left the hospital scarred from her voyage into the world, an ominous admonition that counting five fingers and five toes wasn't enough.

We were home one full day and Arnold had driven back to Oneida for his summer job, and I readied Jada for the first bath I was to give to her. Unwrapped, she shivered and cried as I dipped her tense body into the water. I dipped my face close to her trembling body and sang to her, all the while sponging her with soft caresses. "What are little girls made of, made of? Sugar and spice, and all that's nice, and that's what little girls are ma-a-de of."

Gradually Jada's tight red fists and rigid legs loosened. Her mouth, a red siren, became rippling water. I lifted her out of the water and onto the towel, enveloping her with warmth from my hovering body and told her how pretty she was, all soft and powdered and warm in my hands. Her eyes, black orbs, searched, recognizing my voice, my touch, me. Her body drank in the pleasures like they were the milk of my breasts. Jada and I had found each other. Jada stopped crying.

No, that's not true. Before Jada's sling, she cried when I picked her up. At home, she cried when I didn't. I stacked her on top of the laundry and carried her downstairs in the basket. There was no vacuuming, no washing dishes without her hitched to my shoulder, for it was not just my physical presence she craved, but my attachment. Arnold nicknamed her Tag.

Though I learned a lot from Dr. Spock, Dr. Ginott, and parenting magazines, everything I knew about babies I'd learned from Jada, so I thought I was ready for Dom, who also, it seems, came into the world with the same conflictions as Jada and caused the nursing staff to eye me as suspect.

It was eleven o'clock, I in my hospital bed, seven hours after giving birth. Dr. Silverman called. "I'm sorry to bother you late at night like this, but I'm afraid that your son may have a malfunctioning heart and I don't want to waste any time. I've already sent the boys to pick him up by ambulance to go to Ramsey Children's."

"I want to be with him. Can I go, too?"

"No, no, no. You stay there; you need to rest." "Let It Be" played on the radio speaker clipped to the bedside. Days later a nurse lifted Dom out of a little nest of white flannel inside a see-through cubicle where he had been hooked up to every modern device for complete monitoring and testing. Nothing showed up in the tests, run backwards and forwards, and whatever hadn't been rightly formed at birth had righted itself in this world's time. Still, hospital protocol wedged its way between Dom and me. A nurse stood by to watch me caress my son and feed him before releasing him to my care. A social worker made a home visit the following week.

Maybe I felt singled out as only a temporary mother, watched and judged for worthiness and, loving my children fiercely while I had them, readied myself in case they would be snatched away without warning or understanding. For years to follow, I alternately mused that either my babies wanted to get busy living in the world so much that they pushed themselves out before they were fully put together or that they resisted leaving my womb.

My mother, of course, believed I spoiled them, not agreeing with me that it was charming that Jada colored the bottom of her potty chair bowl with crayons. To my female colleagues in the lounge at the school where I taught, I delighted in my admiration of Dom's attempt to decorate an empty space on his wall, newly-stripped of nursery wallpaper, by drawing a smiley-face. Jean, with a stiffness to her mouth, exhaled cigarette smoke through her nostrils, and curling her upper lip, shook her head. "I hate to see the day when your kids grow up; you won't be able to let them go," as her lips stretched in a strict line. "You're too attached to them to release them."

"I'll let them go because I am attached," I defended.

Petra Jackson, purposely dubbed P. T. because it cut an edge to her that she proudly used to slice away at people, was short and slight and a little humped right below the neck, but she was not timid, and her chipmunk cheeks, always looking filled with nuts, twitched as her beady brown eyes darted back and forth. She sat hunch-shouldered in her chair by the refrigerator. A cigarette between two fingers, Petra used two others to lift an errant strand of hair that had strayed from the tight little bun on the very top of her head. She was not pretentious, boastfully washing her hair in Ivory Liquid dish soap and daubing red lipstick to her tawny face.

"When children come into this world," she proclaimed, the words vaporizing with gray smoke, "God entrusts them to us. You've got to find the fault in their spirit and break their will." She broke her oldest son's will by dragging his stereo equipment to the river and tossing it in. All ninety-eight pounds of P. T. Jackson.

"Mmm," I mused. "I think children have individualities that should be developed, and I think my job is to help them make the most of who they are, and that includes getting them ready to leave me." Jean and Petra exchanged a knowing glance. Jean's long hooking nose flared, her diamond-shaped face spreading wider as she spew smoke through slightly parted teeth. "Yeah, we'll see."

I would be tested, about five years later beginning in Dr. Silverman's office.

Easter occurred late, on the 19th of April, in 1981. On Wednesday, Jada woke with a fever and severe pain in her chest. I called for a substitute teacher and sent Dom off to catch the school bus that stopped in front of our house. I made an appointment with Dr. Silverman and sat next to Jada on the couch waiting for the morning to disappear, the spring sunshine dappling through the yellow sheer curtains behind us. She held her fisted hands on her sternum as if there were a precious pendant hanging inside. I searched her face for the flush that went with a fever but saw only eyes flushed of color, swimming in a sea of water, squeezed to block the light.

"Jada, I'm not going to let you go to the ice show practice today. I can see how weak you are, and you've got a fever."

"No, Mom. I have to go." She released the words with effort, leaving spaces between each as if the sentence could abort at any one. "They won't let me skate in the show."

"I understand why they have the rule, but it's impossible for you to go." Anyone, and that meant everyone, no matter their part in the annual figure skating club show scheduled during the first weekend in May, who missed a rehearsal lost their part. "If you get some rest and some medicine, we might change plans, but right now, I don't think you could even stand up on skates."

20

"Can't I just go? I'll be okay. I wouldn't have to skate." Eyes closed, she pleaded with me.

Knowing how hard she had worked to pass each level of the international tests, knowing how huge an event this was, I put my hand gently on her thigh, "No, I'm sorry. I'll call and explain. We'll have to take our chances." Nothing from a willful fiery child? I had more than once placed my hands on hers to practice the piano. Nothing from a child who felt herself all-powerful, climbing up to the rafters in the garage to hang upside down, like they did in the circus? Nothing from a child who wasn't afraid to defy me? I wrestled her flailing and wailing body, hair tangling in the tussling, down the street from her friend's house because it was time to go. Nothing?

Jada looked like the whole inside of her was broken and needing to be glued together for the car ride to Dr. Silverman's office and moaned as the bumps and stops and swerves jangled the shattered pieces. Memories of driving into the unknown nagged at me like a child pulling my pants' leg for attention. We'd had other alarms—high spiking fevers, projectile vomiting, a finger slammed by a door, a call from daycare that an arm could be broken from a fall—missions clear and immediate. Jada and Dom received enough shots of penicillin in their butts to cure a schoolful of kids. Like a kiss on a boo boo, the shot offered reassurance. Hot reddened skin would cool, recovery would refashion listlessness into impatience.

In the waiting room, Jada leaned her head against my breast, my lips close to her head; I kissed her hair, telling her how brave she was to wait so long. A nurse arrived in the examining room with Jada's folder, a compendium of her medical life. As usual, the nurse asked what brought us there and stuck a thermometer in her mouth. Then, as sure as the lollipop that was to follow, the nurse unwrapped a sharp pointed razor and, holding one of Jada's fingers, made a quick stab to draw blood. After squeezing a tiny rosy pool onto a glass stain, she wrapped Jada's finger in a bandage.

All that over, we waited for the nurse to enter the figures from her probings, and usually during the interval between the recordings and Dr. Silverman's appearance I paged through entries in the folder. Over the years I learned to read the formula. A temperature reading wasn't as reliable an indicator of the severity of the infection as was the white blood count. Written like a fraction, underneath WBC was Hgb, the abbreviation for hemoglobin.

We waited and waited for what usually happened to happen, but instead of the nurse returning to fill in the blanks, Dr. Silverman appeared at the door, and instead of the injection, he left behind an apology. Something about counting and being certain. I stood by Jada, who lay, knees bent, holding her hands to her chest. Dr. Silverman returned, extracted a pen from his pocket, and wrote on his prescription pad as he talked. "I want you to go over to Ramsey Children's Hospital and take this with you. We need to do one more test, and they can do it better over there." He scraped the paper from the pad and held out a maze of Latin scrawl.

Time's passing was beginning to worry me; my evening school class began at five, and Dr. Silverman insisted that Jada not walk. "Put your flashing lights on, and when you get inside, take a right by the elevators and go down the hall to the outpatient lab. They'll be waiting for you." Dr. Silverman put his hand on Jada's forearm. "This won't take long, Jada. Hang on just a little more."

Jada appeared laden with a heavy cowl that bent her head down; her eyes were talons picking out clues about what was going to happen to her in the outpatient lab. Gray metal bins lodged against each other at the end of a raised track that came from the inside of a wall and ended in the middle of the room. Out another door was a row of chairs and a cutout wall to what looked like a pharmacy. Another smaller rectangular room jutted from my left. To my right were two walls with continuous counters on which were instruments with small white-faced gauges and metal clamps reaching out like pincers ready to tweak anyone who came too close. A woman in white held onto a sheet of paper that jumped line by line out of the top of a machine that sounded like it was nibbling it, not growing it.

"Okay, what can I do for you?" asked the woman, shoveling aside a clump of hair from her forehead as if it were the discarded product of another machine run amok.

I unfolded the paper. "Dr. Silverman sent us for some test."

She looked at the paper and at Jada, dropping into the nearest chair. Wooden slats running lengthwise down its back, it stood next to a table cluttered with racks and glass tubes, a box of what looked like crystal toothpicks, a notebook and a pencil. "Oh, yes. You must be, um, Petersen, right? Jade?"

"Jada, yes," I corrected her.

"Okay, Jada, I want you to come over here with me." A lab technician, I assumed, she motioned at an old-fashioned brown oak school desk, the kind that began as a chair with a paddle attached to it by a square peg on the right side for taking notes. Dullness revealed areas where the varnish had been worn away, a relic from a lecture hall, stuffy and dry. I pictured the hospital staff hand-carrying this desk as if it were a priceless antique to the hospital, newly built and replacing the building that still stood behind it. "You need to remove your jacket," the technician instructed from behind the cupboard door. Pulling the sleeves off Jada's arms, I also watched the technician fill the plastic tray on the counter.

"What are you going to do?" asked Jada.

From behind her glasses, the technician's eyes made a sweep across the room and landed on Jada's arm. "We need to take some blood. Put your arm on here," she said, stretching a yellowy snake of latex.

"Why do you need that?" The strap lay coiled, ready to strike, next to Jada's arm while the technician tore apart an alcohol pad and began scrubbing the inside fold at Jada's milky elbow. "Ouch!" Jada pulled her arm back, worry spreading across her face. "Wait a minute. Aren't you going to do a finger stick?"

"No. This is the way we do it. This doesn't even hurt." After tying the strap, the technician closed Jada's fingers and held them to the table. She rubbed Jada's skin. "I'm trying to make the vein pop up. Make a fist for me."

"Eyow!" Jada wrenched her arm back again, and I smelled fear, tensed myself. "Why are you telling me that? Don't! Make her stop, Mom!" The words rattled from her chest, while tears formed in her eyes.

The technician released the strap; its venom spent, it fell to the floor, flaccid.

I stepped in closer. "Jada, the more you fight this, the longer it will take. Take a breath. Do you want me to hold your hand?" Jada guarded her arm.

"No! I don't want anything," Jada shrieked. We towered over Jada, one of us on either side.

"This is serious, Jada. Now, we have to get this done." The technician was stern, maybe vexed.

I coaxed in a calmer tone, "Jada, can you try one more time? It's worse to think about it."

Streaks of tears made jagged tracks down Jada's drawn cheeks; her fragments of breath caught on her panic; she was choking, drowning, hanging. The technician went to the telephone, speaking furtively into the mouthpiece, and Jada's chin slumped to her chest. Rejoining us, the technician said, "Come on over here where you can lie down." She reached her hand under Jada's armpit, and together we lifted Jada from the chair and to a table in a little room to the side. To me the woman said, "I'm expecting another technician to come down here to help. I don't know when she'll be able to get here."

"I'll help. What do you want me to do?"

She considered. "There's nothing to keep her from falling from this table. Can you stand here and hold her while I get my things?" Falling or jumping? If Jada left the table, it would not be an accident.

"Let's just go ahead," I said when the technician returned. "I'll hold her."

Banked against Jada's legs, I held them and her right arm to the table. The technician tied and scrubbed and warned. "Hold still, now, Jada. I need you to hold perfectly still. Ready?" With the prick of the needle went up a yowl of protest, Jada's head beating side to side.

"It hurts! You're hurting me! Stop! Mom, help me! Why are you doing this to me?"

"Hold still, Jada. I can't find a vein if you don't hold still." The technician's voice sweat.

Jada shrieked again. "What are you doing? It's not working! Stop!"

"Got it, Jada. Just a few more seconds."

"No! No! Now!"

Now for me, too. Sights and sounds of blood and pain and torture made me woozy. I cried for Dumbo and Bambi and the bison that were driven over the cliff in a massive kill, and even though my dad told me that what I watched wasn't really happening but only made to look real for a movie, the feeling was real. I felt sorry for the bison for being tricked and scared and humiliated into their fate. I wanted to get Jada off her cliff, take away the indignity of giving up her blood; I wanted to take away the shame of being held against her will even while it was I who held her. The story had been written, the movie made, and there was no changing what was going to happen to the elephant, the bison, my daughter.

The technician put a cotton ball and a bandage on Jada's arm and folded it up, and I slid over next to Jada's shadowy green-gray chin, lying in the creeping blotches of tears on the crinkled paper. "Why did you let her hurt me?" The words were thin, bled.

"Would you like to put this on your forehead?" the technician asked, returning with a wet cloth in her hand. "I'm sorry it took so long, Jada. We're done now."

Arnold's clunky green Pontiac was waiting in the parking lot near the fountain, the sculpture standing dry and naked. I waved to Dom standing on the hump in the back. "Bye bye, Sugar Plum; I'll be home in a few hours," I said as I delivered Jada to the front seat. She slumped into the cushion, and I bent down and kissed her forehead.

Dom popped his head around Jada and said, "Mom, Mom, baseball's on tonight!"

"Oh, good. Get your homework done first, then. And be really nice to Jada. She doesn't feel well, and she had a hard afternoon. Okay? I'm counting on you." Dom leaned forward, and we plunked a slurpy kiss on each other under his San Diego Padres cap. "See you later, Alligator."

"After while, Crocodile." Dom stood at the headrest and called out through the open window. Then I backtracked Lyton Avenue to the west side school, once a combination seven-12 high school and my first contract teaching assignment, with one, and then a second baby, a killer fourth hour English class with Sparky, who'd rather have parsed a person than a sentence, and a student with the surname of the man my uncle allegedly disappeared, and where I was playfully dubbed Mama Pete. Now I taught at an alternative program, where I was Idina by day: we were supposed to be more like advisors than teachers for the students who had been booted from their former school and often ordered by court to this last chance; and then for two hours a night, two nights a week, I went back to the west side to teach the 5 p.m. shift of evening high school.

Folders of materials in the crook of my arm, I headed down the steps to check in. "Hi. May I have the key to 306?" I asked as I heaved my load onto the counter in the office.

"Mrs. Petersen. You're here," proclaimed Blanche Dvorak from the back desk; diminutive with a voice of the same size, she swelled it with urgency. "We've been calling all over the building for you."

"I've been up in the workroom; I didn't hear anything."

Two other women bent over desks while Blanche brought forward a message on the familiar yellow paper, Form E-40. "Your husband called. You're supposed to go to Ramsey Children's Hospital immediately."

"Oh, no. It's something serious!" The words had been crowding my brain to find voice, and they were out of my mouth before I was aware I'd been storing them. The panic that erupted in Jada were temblors in me. *I should never have left her! She'll be wanting me and I'm not there!* Nowhere is far away from anywhere in a city the size of Sibley. Ramsey Children's Hospital sat smack in the crux between the two schools I taught at, only ten minutes apart in the worst traffic. Still, *all that time, how much time was it? Twenty minutes? Ten? All that time. I could have been there by now!*

A red traffic light. *We're wasting time. Can't you see we're wasting time?* Memories of other crises muscled their way underneath cloud-spun skies, between blank headlights, and into my idling car. Jada was two; we were coming home from her cousin's birthday party. Seven, 7:20; the day smelled old, like charred wood in a fireplace, too late to start anything, too early to call it over when we turned onto Lambert Lane, a winding paved street of the suburb where we had just built our house. I was still painting the trim on the windows. Gritty sand and dirt stuck to the creases of my skin under my denim hip huggers. A hot Friday in late July: I should have worn shorts. And taken off my shoes, like Jada. There to the left was our house, caked brown dirt waiting for a front lawn and tall leafy trees to protect it from the flaying heat of the whole day's sun. "Take me on a bike ride, Mommy," Jada asked from the back seat.

I considered what I might be doing instead and consented. "Okay, but just a short one. Mommy's tired." I backed the one-speed bike out of the garage. On it was a metal-framed baby seat screwed in place atop the back tire. Jada hopped about the sizzling black asphalt on her tiptoes. "Jada, where are your shoesies? You know you need to wear your shoes." She peered at her bare feet. I pushed the front seat of the car forward, looking for her red tennis shoes. Arnold must have taken them in, I thought, lazily rejecting the effort of going into the house, up the steps, and on a shoe hunt. "Well, I'll let you go without them this time only. We're just going around the block."

I pedaled hard to get enough speed to climb the first rise around the corner on Rutledge. The suburb added blocks of houses like rings of a tree as it grew over the years; branches from older growth along this boulevard reached toward each other overhead. Cool air whispered past me, drying the perspiration on my forehead. "Faster, Mommy," Jada squealed from behind me.

Nearing the end of Rutledge where it ran into Oakcrest and ended in a "T," I felt energized by the physical activity after cake, ice cream, and sitting, and said, "I can add on another block or two." Then I felt a jolt, a momentary resistance, in my pedaling. Jada yelped.

"What is it?" I locked the brakes and jumped to the asphalt. I had the same dread that I felt when she was a toddler and tumbled from the couch, hitting her head on the heavy wooden coffee table, wondering if I'd have the courage to scoop up a dislodged eyeball. Jada held onto her knee, looking stunned, and followed my worried eyes down her leg that hung by the back tire of the bike. The inside of her heel revealed layers of white flesh, as if they had been chiseled out. "Okay, Jada, okay," I said. "We're close to home. We'll go take care of that. Hold your legs out carefully, now. We're gonna go real slow."

Each push of the pedals made me cringe. "Remember, keep your feet out. Almost there. See? There's our street. You're doing just fine! When we get home we'll get all cleaned up. I wonder what Paddington's been doing all day. Should we ask him? You can tell him about the birthday party you went to."

"Pooh, too," Jada whimpered, restrained cries interspersing her words.

We slowed into our driveway. Jada wrapped her arms and legs around me and rode on my hip into the house. As she sat on the kitchen counter, Dr. Silverman's soothing, salving voice over the phone made the words sound healing. "That's a common injury," he said. "Rarely is the leg broken. Just be sure the wound is clean and come in around ten tomorrow morning."

In the familiar cool air with the astringent smell of abounding alcohol wipes of the examining room, Dr. Silverman stood at the door, pens and sticks and wands jutting from his breast pocket. "I don't think you have anything to worry about, but we'll take an

X-ray to be sure." A nurse reached for Jada, and she shrank back, clutching my neck.

"It's okay, Sweetheart," Dr. Silverman assured her. "The nurse is just going to take you to another room so we can take a picture of your foot."

Jada loosened her hold and let the nurse take her, wonderment opening upon her face. "Foots don't smile," she said to Dr. Silverman.

"You're right, they don't," he chuckled. "But you can. When we're all done, I'll show you what I mean."

Dr. Silverman returned shortly after Jada, her even teeth gleaming between cherry cheeks as if she'd just taken a twirl on the teacups at Disney World. "I'm afraid I have some bad news. Her leg is broken. I'm going to send you over to an orthopedic specialist."

Signs, misunderstood, rode a phantom passenger with me again, to the new hospital. It *was* just a broken leg, just a handle broken from a cup: with a little glue, a little pressure, and a little time, no one would ever know the difference. Events as that were alarming, but they were repaired, and in almost no time, unlike the ones that no one suspects, the ones that are part of the story before you know how to tell it.

Shakily I pushed open a door through green tea-colored air to a single light shining down on Jada, laid out under blankets that had snowed white upon her. Arnold and Dr. Silverman stood around her like a fence and parted when I approached the bed.

"Mom!" Through little puffs of air on which wafted a little voice, she cried. "I was so afraid without you. I wanted to wait for you." Another shallow breath. "But Dad said I had to go right away."

I leaned over and slid my arms under her. She had already been banded, uniformed, and assigned to a chrome-barred bed. "I'm here. I'll be with you, Jada."

"What's wrong?" Her eyes shifted to a space behind me.

A female voice said we had to go to another room for a conference. I released Jada, and a large woman with long-hanging hair appeared in my wake to raise the rail on the bed. "We don't want you to fall out." Jada and I looked at each other through bars.

"I'll be back as soon as I can," I told her.

"Hurry."

People carrying trays and sticking things in their pockets darted through doors along the corridor; everyone had a mission to accomplish. I felt like a new kid moving into the neighborhood, watching them before they tested me. We stopped just as the hallway angled off into darkness and into a closed-up room with fermented smells of former inhabitants. A few light bulbs were a weak opponent for the darkness seeping through closed window blinds at the end of a long table where we sat, Arnold to my right. Settling across from me was the woman who took us from Jada's room. Her bosom lay weightily on the flat wooden surface, but her head zoomed forward, focusing on me. I tensed to catch her. "Your daughter is seriously sick. She has leukemia." The words came suddenly from her moving lips, like a gush from a fire hose, mowing me down before I could run. I understood then why Arnold's hand lay on the table, a guard dog. He had already been told.

What was the expected reaction to such extraordinary news delivered with such ordinary words? When there was no sound its memory repeated itself inside my head and pounded me with equal force at each remembered strike. I had trusted the signs, the ones I could see. Whatever was wrong, it shouldn't be the worst, it wouldn't be as bad as my stomach told me it was; it couldn't be the awful that it felt inside.

"No, no, no!" I pushed back my chair. *How long have you known the name to this fear? And what else do you know that I don't?*

But the woman resumed speaking in a steady stream, as from a sprinkler set on a lawn to provide thorough and even coverage, a contradiction to the firestorm of words that deluged me. "There have been many gains made in the treatment of cancer, especially among children. The diagnosis of cancer is not a death sentence. The sooner we start treatment, the greater her chances."

A minute ago this room was empty. A minute ago this woman had a secret, was eager to release it. Her voluminous breasts inflated like water balloons, a white laminated name tag inscribed with "Helen" riding the heaving flow. My arm stuck to my side. Old sweat. That's what I smelled, sweat soaking the fibers of tired clothes. Arnold. I felt him next to me, as if someone called "Freeze" and he was waiting for the command to move again, and I was relieved I had not panicked. After all the years of our not touching, his hand on me now wouldn't offer the solace or support it never had. "The roof fell in," he said, the skin around his mouth dragging the lines of his lips down.

"Things are going to get hectic for you the next few days. Testing, setting up treatment. There'll be a lot of people calling, wanting to know everything that's going on. I suggest you ask someone else to answer questions. You're going to need a lot of strength. This is not a time to be bothered. I'm Jada's nurse, and I'll be here all night and tomorrow morning. If there's any questions or anything I can help with, just ask."

The talking stopped and I felt stared at. "I've got to go in there; she's all alone." I rose from the table, knocking my shoe against Arnold's chair in my haste to get out. I'm trapped by gawkers and good intentions, I thought. *I've got to get to Jada.*

By the nurses' station stood Dr. Silverman. Waves of other people's comings and goings lapped upon me, a pitted shoreline, ever receiving, ever changing, yet holding the place. "I'm sorry, Mrs. Petersen. I just hate these things to happen. They're starting to work right now. It's a real hard one," he lamented, shaking his head.

"Jada has to be told what's going on."

"Come on, we'll do that now." His brown eyes peered over the rectangles of glass that straddled his nose. He looked so gentle, so fatherly, a real-life Marcus Welby, M. D., with all the answers. Arnold trailed me and I trailed Dr. Silverman, to where he sat, bending his head closer to Jada's.

"Jada, you have a disease that's called leukemia. Your body produces a lot of white blood cells; they're the ones that fight for you when you're sick. But the white blood cells in your body are young and don't know how to fight off an infection, so you stay sick, and there are so many of them that there's no room for the red blood cells to get oxygen to where you need it, and that's what's making you tired. What we have to do is get you going on chemotherapy that will stop all those white blood cells. It's going to take a while, but we'll do everything we can. I'll be here to check on you tomorrow, but there'll be other docs here at the hospital who'll be taking over. The main thing is to get started right away. Okay, Sweetheart?"

Jada was stretched out on the bed, an ironing board on which Dr. Silverman was creasing a fold, steaming a wrinkle, flattening her future with a weight she was too young to uphold and too old to submit to. I listened as if he were reading her a scary story but leaving the gory details out, not naming the monster that hid right there under the bed. Helen could tell me anything she wanted about how things have changed; this was still a verdict. I wept for Jada as I watched her watch Dr. Silverman. I wept as I did when I pictured Jesus being nailed to the cross during the Stations at church. I wept for Jews being branded and separated, watching their husbands or mothers being herded toward the death chambers, or worse, their children. I wept for me.

As soon as Dr. Silverman stood, Jada's watery eyes pooled in an uncertain face. "Mommy, don't leave me." I sat on her bed, wanting to take back the day. Behind us, Dr. Silverman told Arnold, "It's enough to make you drink." Abruptly he added, "I didn't mean that seriously."

"No, I know what you mean." Arnold shuffled his feet. To me, he said, "I'd better go. I left Dom with the Redmonds. What are you going to do?"

I looked from wall to wall for a clock through the gray; the only pool of light from a thin tube on the wall circled around Jada's head. A large window beyond Jada's bed framed a world that was voided by the darkness of night; behind me was a gray accordion-like wall, the folds unable to cast shadows in the dimness; a television hung from the ceiling, its huge blank screen staring like the murky gray eye of a whale. I'd been here before and let my heart lead the way.

"Tell Dom I'll call him in the morning." I said.

A barrage of people began filing through the door, moving our crisis into the public domain. First was a house doctor. How did she come there, what was wrong, when did things start, who else was in the family, and what was the family medical history? Did anyone have cancer? Silently, except to tell her to breathe in, he dabbed and peered and listened through his stethoscope. A nurse followed with a clipboard. She made clatterings on the ledge between the bathroom and the bed and above it taped a chart to the wall. After a blood pressure reading, she made marks on the chart with her red and black pens taped together like the feet of prisoners in a chain gang.

Helen was next, pushing a burly brown chair in front of her and stationing it to face Jada's bed. "You'll find this much more comfortable; I assume you're going to sleep here." In the seat of the chair was a white plastic bowl with two wings extending from the lip and a clear bag that she tore open while heaving about the room, placing a box of tissues in a drawer, toothpaste and toothbrush in the bathroom. "This is a shared bathroom, so you have to remember to lock both doors," she said from the doorway.

"What's that for?" I looked into the bathroom and took a step back from the deep royal blue walls and apple green cabinets. Helen was placing the flying bowl on the toilet and bringing the seat down over it.

"This catches Jada's pee. We have to keep a record of what she takes in and what she puts out." I nodded dumbly. "Here's the nurse call cord." She moved, revealing a small, lighted square in the wall. I nodded again and backed away. "Is there anything I can do for you before I go?" Like a wounded cat fleeing under the bed, I could think of nothing except for a place to hurt in private. Helen pulled up the guardrail, turned the light off over Jada's bed and closed the door to the hallway after her. I sang huskily as Jada accepted sleep, and I eased into the chair, which, I discovered, opened out, pushed parts of me up, denting others. Filtered through the darkness in the room, fluorescent brightness of the hallway gradually dimmed, and I was left in a twilight of voices inside my head.

The orphaned boy diagnosed with leukemia deciding to spend the remainder of his life hopping trains across the country, dying peacefully in the arms of two girls who befriended him. On television, death was sad but somehow sweet. Helen's announcement of the miracles of progress. *But they don't have to die now.* The leukemia I learned about isn't the same as it is now. *Now we have chemotherapy that conquers leukemia.* Dr. Silverman said they had to start chemotherapy. Chemotherapy a hundred years ago might have been only a bottle of whiskey or ether or a bullet to bite on, the end resulting in death. Helen said the sooner they start, the better her chances. *Right away.* Dr. Silverman said right away.

The door opened; two women in hospital blue scrubs over turtlenecks bustled into the dark room, silhouetted by the light from behind. The woman on the right, looking very somber and very hurried, motioned me toward the door while gruffly whispering assurances. "We're doing everything we can to find out the cause of Jada's sickness. We'll let you know as soon as we can."

"What? I thought we already knew."

She made a quick sideways nod to her partner, giving me enough time to notice the strands of honey hair that sagged over her right ear and the conspiratorial knowledge between them. "We don't know for sure. These things are hard to diagnose. We don't want to make a mistake."

"When will you know?"

"We'll tell you as soon as we know anything. We're here all night. Right now we just want you to know we're working on it. When did you notice that Jada was sick?"

"That's hard to say because the first few times you don't think anything of it because, you know, kids get sick. Dr. Silverman has all her medical history. Why don't you get it from him?"

"I'm sure. Would you say it was recently, say within the last month?"

"No, before that. She had fevers, I took her in, then went back for a check-up, oh every few weeks for the last couple months. Until lately; then it was more often. She'd get better for a while, but then a week later, she'd be sick again."

"Has anyone else in your family had cancer?"

I started to tell of my dad's father who died when I was too young to be told the details and my mother who had two mastectomies and a hysterectomy that were all labeled as precancerous, all before my adulthood. I stopped with a petulant sigh. "Can't you get this information from the other doctor? I've already told him this."

"No. He's the house doctor. We're residents, and we're gathering information on our own."

I shifted feet and crossed my arms in front of me, irked at the thought that Jada was like an archaeological dig, everyone plotting his or her own square of her. The women scurried out with their collections, promising to return soon.

Plopped in my chair, I dreamed of sleep. Though it was the nearest to me, it was the farthest. My stomach burned with too much instant coffee from the machine in the waiting room around the corner and too many cigarettes that went with it. Crying had left my eyes swollen and dry. Instead of pulling a soothing shade, my eyelids scratched my eyeballs like fingernails on a chalkboard when I shut them. "Mom?" Jada called. Helen came in for vital signs. I tortured myself with my fears of the disease that, like a burglar, broke into our family. What could we offer to spare her?

The time card clock outside the room thumped through the wall at the turn of the hour. Somewhere in the dark between thumps, a lab technician swooshed through the door and set her boxy tray on the ledge. She lowered the rail with a jerk and bent over Jada. With a stumble, I hoisted myself out of my zig-zag position.

Groggy, Jada asked, "What are you doing now?"

"We have to take some blood for tests. I'm just feeling for a good vein."

"Ick!!! Why can't you do a finger stick?"

"We have to do a blood culture to see what's causing the infection. We divide the blood up into...."

"Stop! Don't tell me that! You have blood already. Why don't you use that? I'm not a faucet you can turn on!" In the dim light, Jada's protestations cast shadows.

"That blood is being used. The doctors order tests, and we need to collect the blood to do them. Now hold your arm still. It's hard to find a good vein on you."

"Of course. You used them all up!" Sympathy for Jada wrung me dry: technicians came for blood the way doctors came for answers. How many doctors were running tests independently, duplicating orders? How many different people came in to take a part of Jada?

"Here, let me look on the back of your hand," the technician continued.

"Oh, no, you don't! You're not going there." Jada's face cast an iridescent glow under the bed light.

The woman straightened up, sighed. "Okay, let me see your arm. I'll try again."

I heard the rip of packets being opened, the strap squeak as it was fastened around Jada's arm, and I reached for the chair. The world seemed to require my stepping onto it, but I couldn't lift my foot. "Get down on the floor. Now." Disembodied words floated around me.

My head felt frozen, as if it had been left out on the back step all night, and I buckled to the floor. I stretched my eyes as open as they would go, while shapes began to emerge first in little crystals, then as recognizable forms until I saw the technician standing, looking down at me. "Mmmm. I'm sorry. I just couldn't stay up."

"When was the last time you've eaten?"

Heat flowed upwards to my head; I was being pulled back. "Lunch. No, we didn't eat lunch."

"Don't get up. I'll send a nurse in with something." Feet stepped around me.

"I'm sorry, Jada. I'm supposed to help you, not get in the way."

"Take care of yourself, Mom. I need you."

While the technician collected blood, a nurse came and knelt down with a large cup in her hand. "I hear you got a little dizzy. This is orange juice. Drink it before you get up. And do it slowly. You know how to call if you need help, don't you?" She stood and eyed the nurse call light glaring like an eyeball in the middle of the wall above Jada's head, positioning the gray control piece beside Jada's pillow. Then she checked the chart on the wall. "I may as well do your vital signs now while I'm here." With the whoosh whoosh whoosh of the air pumping into the band around Jada's arm, I grabbed onto the chair and began my slow ascent. "Okay, you better get some rest now," the nurse told Jada. She raised the rail and pulled the light cord above the bed.

"You better, too, Mom," Jada told me.

"Don't think I wouldn't like to. I feel like a cartoon character on that torture rack they call a chair. I can't stretch out." I reached over the rail. "You sleep, too."

"I would if they'd stop coming in and bothering me! These things make me feel like I'm in jail. Do they think I'm a baby?"

"You do like your freedom." I released the barrier between us and tumbled into the chair, unable to toss or turn into a comfortable position, my back aching with the weight of both the top and the bottom halves of me pushing on it. The clock thumped. Voices grew louder and gradually disappeared. A crackly hum picked up overhead, and I tried to identify it. Inside my mouth was a pasty coating. My teeth grew fur. A siren soared. I imagined it on the high bridge: a police car with alternating tones, back and forth, high and low.

I felt the light before I heard the sweep of the door opening. Even if I wanted to, I couldn't turn around to see that it was the pair of residents again. One behind the other, the one who did the talking stopped at the chair and looked into my face like a cat studying the person who feeds it. "Are you asleep?"

"No. Just trying," I whispered back.

"I think it's better if we go somewhere we can talk."

Again I pushed myself awkwardly upwards, more cautiously this time, and followed to the open door, rubbing my itchy eyes and raking my fingers through my hair. I tried to swallow the bad smell in my mouth and draw in clean air. The light stabbed my eyes.

The women sat side by side on the blue couch, their knees lined up like slats in a gate. On their thighs lay thick bundles of papers clasped in hardcover binders. The resident nearer to me put her arms on her notebook and leaned intimately toward me. "We still haven't found what's causing Jada's fever."

"What difference does that make?" I asked, lighting a cigarette and folding my legs under me.

"We want to make the correct diagnosis. We don't want to say it's leukemia if it isn't."

"But everyone's already said that it is. How can one test say it is and another say it isn't?" Irritation poked into my words like holes in smoke rings.

"Well, there are different kinds of diseases that look like leukemia; and there are different kinds of leukemia. We wouldn't want to prescribe the wrong treatment. And we want to start treatment as soon as we can."

"I don't understand. What are you telling me, that we can't start anything? But they are already, aren't they?"

"We're just trying to help," the first resident said defensively, and added with a hint of condescension, "We knew you'd be worried, and we didn't want you to think we weren't working on it."

"Oh. Thank you." The two gathered their papers and slapped them to their chests like armor and disappeared around the corner, their assurances to keep me informed hanging in the air with the stale smoke. The night had all the markings of a nightmare— floating faces and events slamming against each other, making no story but feeling frighteningly real.

Daylight brought no relief: another shift of nurses and technicians, a repetition of procedures, questions, and fractured explanations. Before the light from the horizon peeked through the crack of the drawn curtains, a lab technician walked in and set her tray down on Jada's bed. The grab of Jada's arm woke her. "Do a finger stick," she said, instantly alert.

The woman threw a gust of impatience out of the side of her mouth. "It hurts more on your finger. Everyone else prefers it in their arm."

Jada countered, "I'm not everyone else. I think it hurts more in the arm."

"I've got everything set here and other patients are waiting." The technician's eyes bore through a face that hung gray like the droopy April sky, waiting for her reasoning to fall like a steady rain and soak in.

"It's a finger stick or nothing." Jada's chin was as set as her eyes, a cold green cast to a resolute visage.

The technician's head jerked away and began an appeal to me. "We have to get this blood; the doctors have ordered it."

"She's not refusing; she's just telling you how she wants it. Why not try it her way?" The technician's face muscles seemed to flex and twist, wrenching her lips into a tight fist and pushing her eyebrows together over narrow eyes like she was playing out a massive military maneuver; she slid her shoes back to the wicker tray for a new set of tools. I thanked her as she left the room, but she did not acknowledge me.

"Well, good morning, Sunshine!" Not much of the morning was left, but not much daylight had passed, either. After wracking through the night and the early hours, Jada dozed, I went to the cafeteria for coffee, and, browsing the gift shop, bought a journal and a pen for her, then waited bedside for her to reawaken. We had time to wobble into the bathroom, and it was while we were coming out that another staff—there seemed to be a new person for each new job, second appearances by the two residents only— pushed through the door.

"Hello, Jada. I'm here to take you for a bone marrow aspiration." She had before her a wheelchair.

"What's that?" Jada asked.

"It's a test to see what your blood cells look like. It feels just like a shot in the butt. You can stay here if you want," the nurse—who knew her title?—told me.

"No, I want my mom to come with," Jada stated.

We both assisted Jada up to a long raised table where she was instructed to lie with a pillow tucked under her stomach. The nurse disappeared, and Jada shivered in the cold basement room. No covering available, I stretched as much of myself across Jada's shoulders as I could. Soft footsteps squeegeed like wet sponges around me. Voices, one man's, one woman's, made brief exchanges intermingled with rips, clicks, and snaps as two people approached us. Blue lettering etched the doctor's name in a white plastic rectangle on the man's right chest. From peaked brows, long gray hairs curled downward over small dark eyes. The woman scooted to his side holding a tray filled with instruments and supplies while he pulled open Jada's hospital gown. Then he lay folded towels across her buttocks. He rubbed the skin at the top of Jada's hipbone and stabbed fingers at it.

"Ouch! Why are you doing that?" At the jam of his fingers, Jada jumped and grabbed my hand. The tension flowed between us and she pinched into my skin. This doesn't look like a shot in the butt to me, I thought, not with that razor.

"I'm looking for the best spot. Here, get on your knees and push the pillow down more. Okay," he continued, resuming his probe. "Now, I need you to be very still so I don't lose my spot."

"Ow! Do you have to be so rough?" Jada's fingernails pressed crescent moons in my skin as the hairs inside my nose tingled. The doctor scrubbed Jada's skin with a sponge dipped in a cup of brown liquid. Then he mopped up with alcohol pads.

"We have to be sure to get the area perfectly clean. Now don't move. I'm going to make a little poke. Okay? On the count of three. One, two, three."

"Stop!" Jada cried.

"It's over. No, don't move." Blood sprang from a slit. The nurse took the pointed blade from the doctor in exchange for a large-barreled syringe while he pressed a wad of gauze to the bleeding. Then he held the skin apart with two fingers as he brought the syringe over the cut and thrust the thick needle tip into Jada's back like a spear, punching the plunger down.

"Don't look, Mom." Jada's knuckles whitened as she tightened her grip. "I don't want you to see it! Stop. It hurts! Stop! NO!"

"Hold still. It's not coming. I have to pull harder," he said quietly, and I felt the pressure of his body on the other side of the table as he forced his might against Jada, drawing nothing.

"Mom, don't look!" Her tears soaked the paper, shredding it underneath her cheek.

Jada's hurting flowed through me with burning pain. I was furious that he had tricked her. The doctor sighed that he'd finally got it and left the room without a word.

Apr 25, 1981

The last three days have been DISASTER!! Mom took me to Dr. Silverman's office and I just wanted a shot of penicillin. Then we had to go to the hospital. A lady wouldn't do a finger stick and I started crying! Mom tried to get me to calm down but the lady was trying to stab me with a big long needle! I just wanted to go home. I was so tired I couldn't move but then Dad said I had to hurry up and get to the hospital without Mom. I didn't know what was happening to me. It's not looking good. Everyone, except mom, just shows up and thinks they can help themselves to my body. Even when I'm sleeping, someone tries to take my blood (YUCK—I hate blood! My tummy does back flips just hearing about it!) even when they just took it! But, no, all day and all night, someone grabs me and says oh, I have to get blood for a culture, or I have to get blood for Dr. so-and-so or the lab wants another gallon! I'm still tired mostly because they keep waking me up for more blood. And they don't ask, or anything, they just think I'm here for them to do whatever. I don't like being a guinea pig. That's what I feel like, ever since I came in here. They call it a hospital but I call it a zoo. They lock me up and use me! Dr. Silverman said I have leukemia, but everyone else says they have to do a test to see what is making me sick. They better find out lickety-split so I don't hurt any more. I've been hurting long enough.

They gave me some medicine, and now I hurt because of what THEY'RE doing to me! Especially that hack of a doctor who lied to me. You won't even feel this, he said. HAH! How do you not feel a stab from a javelin? I screamed and told him to stop, but he kept jabbing and pinching and punching. Don't I know what hurts me? Maybe if I could jab HIM he'd know what hurts! And mom should have made him stop, like she did the VAMPIRE who wouldn't do a finger stick when I asked. I need Mom because they don't listen to me, but then she has to help me ALL the time. No one cares. No one asks. No one even tells me what's going to happen to me. No one apologizes. No one remembers what happened an hour ago. I have to go through a whole explanation over and over again with everyone who attacks me. I feel so helpless! I would never want to work in a hospital where they treat people like this! I just want to get out of this torture place and go home. I don't think I will soon, though. Mom says I should write, but it hurts so much. I don't think I can for long.

I greeted Dom at the front door, hugging him tight and long before releasing him to his after-school snack. I paced the kitchen floor talking to myself, talking to him. My future was collapsed to a few hours: get Dom to basketball practice, bathe, change into clean clothes, pack a toothbrush. Questions and fears overflowed, dribbling down the sides of my courage, drowning me in a pool of pity. Dom jumped down from his chair, winding his arms around my waist and burrowing his head into my belly and said, "Don't cry, Mom."

"I can't help it, Dom. Seeing her and seeing what they're doing to her; it's awful!"

"Don't think about it. I don't like to see you cry."

His request, so simple, was also commanding. "You're right, Dom. Crying won't change anything. And it won't get things done. Do you have any homework? I want you to do it before basketball because I'm going back to the hospital."

"I'll do it later. Will you play a game of Yahtzee with me?" Wiping the milk from his upper lip, Dom took his plate and glass to the sink. "I'll go get it." He skated over the scarred yellow linoleum floor in his stocking feet, as eager to delay his schoolwork as Jada was to get hers done. Though they shared the same gene pool, they were near opposites. He liked cooked carrots, she raw. He reveled in teams and packs of boys, she was loyal to one or two friends. A toddler, she mixed potions and designed board games; he played hockey using a yardstick and making his own play-by-play announcements on the kitchen floor, a two-year-old skating and checking and scoring, while I readied dinner, making a buzzing sound to call time out so I could cut through from the sink to the stove. Having a facility with numbers and their operations and an immediate need for a snack when they came home from school seemed the most they had in common.

The diagnosis of leukemia spawned a new pattern, doing all the busy people things that wove us together as a family and splintered us apart: I left the hospital to greet Dom's arrival from school, to feed him supper, take him to games and practice, while Arnold stayed with Jada; Arnold came home for dinner, and I returned to the hospital, sleeping in Jada's room. Dr. Silverman paid daily visits, but care had been turned over to Dr. Malley, a hospital and clinic doctor; as far as I knew, the whole hospital was involved, a mass of nameless, faceless experts all sending emissaries of nurses and technicians to take from or give something to Jada—chemotherapy and beyond.

In the flurry of our activity at keeping ourselves functional, I felt a blanket thrown over my head. Leaving for home, I ran into Dr. Malley. "What's going on?" I asked, hurrying the steps to beat Dom's bus. "I never get to talk to you and wonder what's happening."

A smirk broadened Dr. Malley's long face as she looked down at me. "Well, I come around every afternoon. Your husband is there." Her words stood in haughty single file, making a barrier to where I wanted to go and scrambling for the code. "You might want to be there tomorrow. I'll be bringing Dr. Lourde with me. He'd like to meet with the patients and their families."

Dr. Lourde's introduction could have taken place without my knowledge or presence, and would have, but for an accidental meeting in the corridor. Who had been the keeper of this secret?

In a crowded examination room on Jada's floor, the resident who worked on Jada's diagnosis the first night waited as Dr. Malley introduced Dr. Joe Lourde and described his qualifications to us. He sat on the edge of a stool, the heel of one loafer hooked on the upper rung, the other planted on the linoleum, paging through a notebook of Jada's hospital history, while Dr. Malley explained to us that she would, in fact, defer to Dr. Lourde's judgment, if we chose to retain her services, as he was a specialist in oncology and hematology.

I crossed my arms, waiting for Dr. Lourde to talk. Instead, the resident produced the report of Jada's bone marrow aspiration, counting out T-cells and neutrophils and naming the diagnosis, Acute Lymphoblastic Leukemia. She straightened her posture and turned in my direction. "Jada's mother accompanied her for her bone marrow aspiration. It was very difficult." In an accusing tone she continued, "We feel that your presence for the bone marrow aspiration was not good for Jada. She was screaming uncontrollably."

"She was afraid, she was in pain." I countered. "No one prepared her for what was going to happen."

Dr. Lourde's face revealed nothing as the resident persisted, looking back and forth between us. "You were crying, too. That reinforced her behavior."

My throat rasped. "Are you telling me I'm not supposed to feel anything when my daughter is in so much pain?"

"Your show of emotion overexcites her. That makes it harder for us to do what we have to. We feel that it is better that Jada have bone marrow aspirations without your presence."

Arnold took a step forward. "Idina and Jada are very close."

I breathed, deep. Arnold chewed his cheek. The folder gaped open in front of Dr. Lourde, and the resident seemed to be waiting for his command. I spoke instead. "Jada wanted me in there. I'm not staying out unless *she* wants me to. Are we done?"

"I'll be out at the desk if you want me," Dr. Malley concluded.

As the week lengthened, Jada requested items from home, items to make her at home. I brought her bed sheets and pillow, her telephone book, stationery, her clock radio to a room teeming with her presence, get-well cards hanging on the walls and vases of flowers on the ledge in front of the window that by day framed a familiar urban scene: streets, traffic lights, billboards, and stained irregular-shaped buildings constructed to fit as close to the curb as possible. Across the river was the brown bluff of spring in Minnesota. Buds were still forming and received no encouragement from the cement colored skies and scratching raw winds to blurt out green and juicy. My bed was there, too, on the slick cushion under the window, and at night I drew the striped curtains on the city closed up and gone home, waiting for someone to turn off its lights. In the morning I folded and stacked my linens in the corner, next to my toiletries bag, and opened the curtains to another day. We had moved in.

And Arnold had moved his mother into our house. On the first warm day of spring, I pounded up the steps. Grandma M sat in the wingback chair in the living room, both wrinkled hands on the wooden arms.

"Hi," she said in sweet melody. Never had I heard a tone less sugary from her, she who remained silent if her silence avoided discord. "You look tired. I don't know how you can keep up with this."

I flopped into the love seat and locked my fingers behind my head. The house needed a sweeping of fresh air, but I felt welded to the cushion. Budding lilacs, the sound of a breeze whisking through waxy new leaves: I was awake to sensory details. "I'd like for Jada to come home so I can sleep and not have to run somewhere all the time."

"I know it. Spring isn't the same not seeing my own flowers coming up." Grandma M's eyes bobbed in limpid water. She never cared much for travel, even across town, not holding a driver's license since her marriage to Hank fifty years ago. Arnold joked that before she and Hank got somewhere, they were already making plans to leave. Since her husband died, she had an excuse to not even start the journey.

"Why don't you ask Arnold to take you home? I appreciate your vacuuming and keeping the house neat, but you deserve to be at your own home."

The loud whine of Dom's school bus and a peek of its orange nose through the window drew me up. In came the dusty smell of exhaust fumes and the screech of dry brakes through the open door while I waved to Dom, whooping up the driveway, his backpack hooked on his arm.

"Hey, Mom!" Inside the door, he dropped his pack. "I'm changing into shorts! Can I go to Jerry's and play baseball? I have to call him up and see if we can come over. Whoo-ee! It's hot."

Grandma smiled, but her eyes belied her. She stayed in the chair while we went to the kitchen. "How was school for you today?" I asked.

Dom dipped a cookie in milk. "Oh, yeah. There's a note for Jada from Miss Davis. It's in my backpack." He lifted the cookie and caught it with his mouth before it splashed, milk-soaked, back into the glass.

"Anything else?"

"Just some math sheet. I'll do that when I get home."

"What if you forget?"

"Then I'll do it in the morning. It's easy; I have time."

A soft warm breeze whiffled through the screen door, and on it rode the scent of the earth's evaporating moisture. "When I call tomorrow, I'm going to ask you about it." He looked to the plate of cookies and then to me, his long eyelashes curling over beseeching eyes. I nodded my permission.

"Can you drive me to Jerry's?" Jada ragged me that I disallowed bike riding on Lyton when other parents didn't; on that and crossing the busy street, I held my line, even if I was lax about sugar-sweet snacks.

"Fine. How will you get home? Am I picking you up?"

"I'll find out when I call him. Is that okay?"

"Sure. Why don't you get that note for me before we forget."

The note from Miss Davis, Jada's former fourth grade teacher, meant that news of Jada's illness had traveled among the schools' staffs. I'd been in that situation, having heard of a cancer afflicting someone receiving chemotherapy as if it was a commodity, a one-dimensional something to be obtained from a server. "I'll have a chemo, please, but hold the mayo," not the impersonal multi-syllabic names that bullied the tongue when pronounced, but when absorbed into the very personal being of the body, bullied it with its occupation. Now that we were akin to the beast and coping with every significant as well as insignificant detail we learned that chemotherapy could not be tamed just by giving it a nickname. Chemo wasn't the friend it was touted to be but a gift horse containing bottles and vials with labels and purposes and life spans, unending intravenous intrusions, repeated injections, a series of pills and elixirs, and then throwing up and feeling sick all over, eyeballs to toenails.

There was Methotrexate and Prednisone, given orally. Jada ingested other colorful pills, too, but their effects were shrouded by time lapses. IVs produced instantaneous results, the first being the method of delivery. If searching for a vein, first by pinching and prodding with fingers, then with a needle tip digging for just the right entry spot, IV delivery scared up a bloody protest in Jada. Added onslaught was the prolongation of tenderness with the needle taped to her arm, and the duration, the slow-dripping substance burning through her vein.

"Mom! What are they doing to me?" Jada lamented.

How could I argue? For or against? Remission was the supreme goal, and the road to remission was paved with Ara-C, Vincristine, and any other human-unfriendly-named stringent scientific substance suspended in bags of bilious saline hanging from metal-footed poles and tethered to Jada in her bed. "I wish I could make this easier for you."

"Make them stop! They don't even tell me anything! They just come in and dig in me like I don't have any feelings!" Jada screamed and cried while the nurse, or whoever she was, administered the drug, then cried and sobbed after she left and pleaded for a way out.

"So what you're really asking for is a little kindness and consideration."

Jada's sobs calmed to a whimper. "No. I want them to stop. Or at least not be so hurting. She just pushed on; when I asked her to wait she didn't listen to me. I need you to tell them."

"Okay, Jada, I can do that. This is all so new to us. I'd like to know more, too." Like how many hours it would take for the bag to empty out, sometimes getting clogged because of the slow pace. Or how to handle the vomiting and retching that followed the drug's flow through Jada's system, coming not immediately after the removal of the needle but during the night, after a wretched day.

There were no palliatives to chemo, though one was offered. Dot, a current night nurse, brought a plastic medicine cup to Jada and waited for her to drink it. Jada held the cup and sniffed at it, crinkling her nose with the skepticism of a twelve-year-old. Jada tipped the cup, emptying half the thick liquid into her mouth. "Yuck!" she gasped. "What are you trying to do, poison me?" Jada scraped her tongue against the roof of her mouth and reached for the cup of water on her nightstand.

"No, no," Dot corrected. "You don't want to rinse the coating from your stomach. I really think it's better if you drink it all at once."

"Do I have to take this? What does it do?"

"Don't you like it?" was Dot's incredulous response. Dot was short, short and sweet. Her height was short, her hair was short, and her utterances were short; to extend an explanation dragged her down until she tweezed the syllables of her words into pert uprightness. "Your meds work on fast-growing cells like the ones that make your hair grow and the ones that line your mouth and stomach. After you eat, the enzymes that work in your stomach also make your stomach lining hurt because it's more tender from the meds. Finish it up now."

On my mother's visit to Jada in the hospital, she sat stiffly on the blue vinyl chair, watching as another nurse, Mandy, set the plastic medicine cup of chalky pink Maalox on the bed tray as if she were serving an after-dinner liqueur.

Jada greeted the vile liquid with a sneer. "But what if I don't want it?" she asked.

"You wouldn't like it if you *didn't* take it. We wouldn't give you something if it wasn't good for you," she chirped, sweeping the blankets smooth and checking the chart on the wall.

"Do I have to take it now?" Jada asked. "I just brushed my teeth."

"Leave it," I said. "I'll see that Jada takes it. Would you empty the toilet bib, too?" I asked. Somehow the nursing staff did not feel as strictly accountable to that standard order as they did to others and let the contents accumulate. We heard the flush and rinse.

"Okay, sounds like a plan to me," Mandy agreed over the crush of paper towels between her hands. "Anything else I can do for you?"

Behind Mandy's departure, Jada brushed her hand at the tiny tub, coagulating into a curdled clot, the smell clogging my nostrils like the dusty residue after erasing a chalk board, and ordered, "Get rid of that!" I dumped the Maalox into the sink and splashed water to rinse the evidence.

My mother's eyebrows arched in surprise. Though she broke rules here and there to her advantage, she loved them nevertheless, as they could be used to substantiate a righteous position and disallow nuance, uncertain territory for my mother. "Don't you have to take that?"

"That? Do you want it? You could use it for ant poison."

My mother, swayed enough by Mandy's authority to build a fort on, brought it up to chew again. "She didn't even see you take it. Up at the hospital we have to watch the patient swallow everything we bring them. Otherwise they might hide it in their pockets and not take it at all."

"Well, this is a little different," I said, muffling the hardness in my response. "Jada's a cancer patient, not a ward at Deer Lake." Her Martin mouth setting firmly, my mother could be trusted to keep the secret, for, though as an aide at the state hospital she was trained to follow regulations, blood was thicker than water, or at least thick enough not to risk "upsetting the apple cart," a phrase my mother used whenever raising a question might ripple what she believed to be placid.

One day shy of one week from diagnosis had passed. Remission, we were told, was the goal. And how would we know if that goal had been met? A second bone marrow aspiration would tell.

"We have to get ready for this next one, Jada. Now that you know what it's all about, we have to work out how to get through it."

"You mean 'make a plan.'"

"I don't have to be in the room with you if you don't want me to," I prompted.

"Yes, you do! I need you to hold on to." The electricity in Jada's reply turned the room hot; melting, she said, "Don't you know? I can't make it without you. You have to stay with me; you promised."

"And I will, for as long as you want me and as long as I can. But you have to be strong inside by yourself. There could be times I can't be with you; there could be a pair of orderlies at the door barring my entrance. I could be in an accident; I could die."

"You can't. I have to die first." Her face had grown longer, thinner; her chin and her mouth seemed remote from her eyes, and I noticed that each could communicate without connection to what the other was transmitting. Right then, though her lips quivered, her eyes were cold, black ice cold. "I couldn't go through this without you."

"Jada, I don't want you to die!" Leukemia and medicine's response to it spattered me all over the place: wisdom came from no source, and direction had no clarity. I added, "Maybe I should be saying something, doing something."

"You do! They don't listen to me. When you tell them, they listen." I envied Jada's assuredness. "I need you to stay and help me. If you're not there, I won't go."

"Okay, then, how are we going to do this bone marrow? You know it's going to hurt."

"Just let me have your hand. I need to hold onto your hand."

Upon delivering us for the bone marrow aspiration, a new floor nurse stood for a moment, looking around, as if someone might be lurking in a corner, then bent down to take Jada's slippers off.

Jada pulled her feet away. "No, I'm keeping them on."

"You can't when you're on the table."

"Am I going on the table now?"

"No, we have to wait for the attending nurse. I can't leave you here until she arrives."

"Then I'll wait for the other nurse with my slippers on. It's cold down here." The nurse looked up at me from her genuflecting position.

"It is cold in here," I answered. "She'll do it when she needs to." Looking around for something on a counter to reveal its secret, I found nothing in this dull gray room to yield a story about it, spare of all but cupboards and table. A stuffed-cheeked woman entered from an unseen door behind a curtain, crossed behind the bare operating table to open a cabinet door and vanished just as mysteriously as she appeared. Was she the magician or the magician's assistant? I looked down at Jada and shrugged my shoulders. In a few minutes, presto, she was back and turned her attention on Jada.

"Hi, I'm Peg. Are you Jada?" Her smile crowded into a bulbous face surrounded by short dark hair that sprang out in tight curlicues. "Let's get you onto this table, okay?" Her belly bumped out her white jacket as if it were inflated with helium, and like a hot air balloon, would carry her up to bob against the ceiling, but her movements were oily, not those of some adipose persons. I moved to the opposite side while Peg reached under Jada's arms and spread her out on the table, plumping and patting her along each side as if fluffing a pillow. "You have beautiful hands. I bet you play the piano."

"Mm-hmm."

"I love the piano. I wish I could play, but I've never learned how." Peg came back with a tray covered by a folded white towel.

"You can," I joined in. "I started taking lessons this year." Jada slid her eyes to the side, and a beam grew on her face.

"Okay, I know there's a difference between playing notes and making music. Jada makes music; she doesn't have to think about it. So far, I'm just playing notes, but no one's said I should stop yet. Well, not to my face anyway."

"You sound okay, Mom. You just have to work on learning your key signatures."

Peg's nimble fingers rubbed against each other as they tucked Jada's arm under her head. "I guess I don't want to play unless I can make music. Are you cold, Jada? I can put a blanket on you until Dr. Wagner comes in. I know it's hard enough waiting."

"My feet get cold." Reflexively, we looked the length of the table at Jada's white feet. Though she was born a baby Santino down to the cleft in her chin, her skin coloring and her hair lightened as if her father's Scandinavian blood were the cream northerners like to add to their coffee. Now her feet were the color of milk. I began to rub one, then the other between my hands.

Tall and straight, a woman joined us, walking briskly from behind the curtain. "Hello; sorry it took me so long. Someone sees you walking down the hall and it's like adding weights around your ankles. Hi, Jada, I'm Jan." Jan bowed to talk to Jada face to face.

"I bet you're not too crazy about this." She covered Jada's shoulder with her hand. "I'll let you know ahead of time what I'm going to do, okay? Let's get this show on the road." Dr. Wagner bobbed up and looked over at Peg and the tray. "All set?"

"Ready to roll," Peg replied.

"Mom, get up here."

Dr. Wagner scrubbed. Peg bunched up a pillow beneath Jada's hips. "Tell me if it gets too uncomfortable, Jada."

"Why do you have to have that pillow there?"

"That's a big bone there. By scooting you up like that, we can change the angle and have less distance to get to the marrow inside it. Okay, now, can you lay like that for a while? And keep your arms raised, there, that's the way."

Dr. Wagner snapped her gloves on and began to press and pinch at Jada's back.

"Oh, good, you're doing the other side," Jada said. "I'm still sore where the other doctor did it last week."

"I see you have a bruise left. We like to alternate sides when they're this close together. Okay, here comes the scrub. It feels like I'm doing the kitchen sink, hunh? I'm going to let it dry a little bit; that way it won't sting so much when I give you Novocaine."

"I get Novocaine? I didn't last time." Jada brought my hand up under her nose.

"Don't you want it? It hurts a little, but I think it's worth it not to feel the poke."

"Yes, yes, I want it." Jada squeezed my fingers.

"Okay, here goes. There. Now we'll wait a minute for it to work." Dr. Wagner raised her hands as if giving benediction. "Oh, did you hear that? My stomach just growled. I'm on a hunt for the best egg rolls in town; got any recommendations?"

"There's a Chinese restaurant on Rice and Larkspur that I always go to." I offered.

Dr. Wagner's deft hands worked, and without looking up, she said, "Oh, you mean the Princess Garden? Okay, Jada, you should feel a little pressure is all." I swiveled my head to see the blade make a red gash in Jada's skin. With her other hand Dr. Wagner dabbed the blood and parted the incision. She placed the blade onto the tray and precisely picked up a large-barreled syringe. Just as she was aiming the needle, Jada tugged my hand. "Don't look, Mom."

"Okay, Jada. You're doing very well."

"You're going to feel this, Jada. It'll hurt, but I'll work as fast as I can."

"Owie, owie, owie" Jada's fingers dug into the web between my thumb and pointer.

"I love the Princess Garden. Have you had their egg rolls? The owner went to Chicago for six months to apprentice with the best Chinese chefs," Dr. Wagner continued as she worked.

"I'll have to try them some day," Peg joined in.

"Do you live over that way?" I asked Dr. Wagner.

"No; I live way across in a suburb on the other side of town, but it's worth it to drive there for those egg rolls. I go anywhere for egg rolls. Okay, Jada, I'm done." She stepped away, holding a gauze pad to the bleeding until Peg took over.

"Now don't take the bandage off for twenty-four hours, and if you take a bath, don't get it wet," Dr. Wagner told Jada, again bending over, looking into her eyes.

"That didn't hurt as much as last time. You're the best bone marrower, not like that other guy."

"The best bone marrower? Well, that's a new title. Thank you." Dr. Wagner chuckled, her twinkling eyes revealing her pleasure. "Actually, the Novocaine just numbs the skin. Bones themselves have no feeling. Your marrow was packed with white blood cells last week. What hurt so much was the pressure of trying to get them out. After a week of treatment, those cells should be gone so the process is a lot less painful. But I'll remember that, the best bone marrower. I like it. Good-bye, Jada."

"Thank you," I added. Peg's right hand reached over for a bandage while Jada released mine.

Remission was the supreme goal. Remission signaled success. Remission meant future. I asked for results like a child waiting for

Santa and expected that when remission was achieved, everyone would rush in to whoop the jubilation of our granted wishes. I was tired of the hospital, the doings and not doings, the non-questions and the non-answers; the wrestles over IVs, looking for and not finding veins; everyone's insistence that Jada lay like a rubber doll while they jabbed and stabbed at her. I wanted to get out of there, go home and get on. My time was eaten by traveling back and forth, rushing to be places. Bathe, get the laundry in the washer, get Dom to a game or a practice or a birthday party, bring a fresh set of sheets to Jada, give her a bath, buy a raspberry Mr. Misty for her, help her to the bathroom or convince a technician or a nurse to work with her, not on her as a mindless, unfeeling mannequin, put some time in at school—I returned to teaching, adding another stop in the cycle of my day, once stopping on the way home to buy a pair of corduroy pants; it took less time to buy them than to wash and dry what I had. Time, precious time, appeared as the only remaining hurdle; my objective was to get over it.

Numbers were posted daily, numbers of neutrophils, hemoglobin, platelets, T-cells, and who knows what else, numbers in the hundreds, thousands, and fractionals that changed like odds before a horse race, and the lingo the hospital staff used to report the numbers was uselessly detached from our daily interactions. I gave up trying to keep up with electrolytes and cultures and whatever it was that was keeping Jada in the hospital regardless of assurances that remission was easy to accomplish in just a few days and maintenance a thing of minor consequence, almost unnoticeable. None of Jada's activities would be curtailed, Dr. Malley promised. Ice skating, piano, viola, school, anything and everything would reappear, as if nothing more unusual than a head cold had interrupted Jada's life, once she got out of the hospital. Oh, sure, Jada would have to come in to the clinic for blood counts, shots and IVs, and examinations, but life would go on as normal as soon as she got out of the hospital.

Dr. Silverman, in his avuncular voice, made all the sympathies no one else would. Up early with the crisp spring morning sun making white columns of light along the curtains' edges, I stepped out of Jada's room for breakfast. With a roll and a cup of coffee hot in my hand, I came in upon Dr. Silverman sitting at the side of Jada's bed, asking her questions about the peculiar feeling she was describing, a dizziness and a compelling urge to urinate. Though the sun's light brightened the room, a dreary spell could not be dispelled, giving the scene murkiness not unlike the colored but tasteless coffee I carried. Dr. Silverman pushed his chair back to give Jada room, and as she rose, she sagged forward. Her movement, appearing to happen frame by frame, took less than a second. With his strong left arm, Dr. Silverman interrupted Jada's fall. With his right, he caught her onto his body and set her down on the mattress.

Dr. Silverman and everyone else who asked knew that my mother's mother was diabetic, but they didn't know the story, how after twenty-five years of marriage my parents closed the restaurant they owned to use it for the celebration, the only real party they'd ever thrown for themselves. My folks were bursting with fun bubbles, floating higher and higher as each of the Cold Duck bottles popped its cork throughout the night of their party. They had spent days cooking a bunch of food, lasagna, pizza, rigatoni, braciole, spiked with cayenne, oregano, basil, pricking the hairs inside our noses, chicken and shrimp, lettuce and pasta and potato salads, creamy and bountiful with vegetables, breads, cakes, and, of course, pies. My dad loved his pie. Banana cream. My Grandma Santino's was a legend. We ate, we laughed, we drank.

The tables cleared and the able dancing, someone noticed that my Grandma Martin—my mother's mother—was not in her chair next to my banana cream pie grandmother. She was found on the bathroom floor. Blame was placed on an elevated sugar level, though no emergency interrupted the party. She could just as easily have felt a little tipsy and a wee bit sleepy, as I did hear my dad say something about two drinks and a limit.

My mother asserted that diabetes ran in the family and warned us to keep watch. How could I not include the disease when asked my family health history? Dr. Silverman read the signs and surmised that the stress of one disease, leukemia, stimulated a genetic latency of the other, diabetes. He ordered another blood test immediately. Which turned out to be more than one.

Along with Jada's other possessions from home, I had brought her Easter basket of yellow, pink, green, and purple woven balsa still brimming with a lustrous cherry nut cream-filled egg, baby silver and gold foil-wrapped chocolate eggs, like little moons reflecting the light, winking "eat me first," oversized speckled malted milk eggs, machine-pressed chocolate bunnies and duckies, every one uniform and indistinguishable, like septuplets, except for tiny air bubbles that hid, like birthmarks, in unexamined places, and bright crusty jelly beans with gummy centers. At first Jada was too sick from leukemia and then from chemo to eat even one confection; with the diagnosis of diabetes, the basket mocked her rejections of these candies, all nestled on green cellophane grass, the sweet temptations replaced by litmus papers and insulin and Sweet'n Low packets.

Apr 29, 1981

    There must be a hex on me! Just when I think I can get out of this horror house ZONK! Dr. Silverman says I have diabetes! Another blood disease! ICKY! I think it's because of all the poison they're filling me with. Now the Draculas have to suck more of my blood. AND give me insulin. They're going to show mom how to do it. NO!! Moms are NOT supposed to hurt their babies! I don't think I will ever have a life again.

    I think they made a mistake and put me in a mine field, not a hospital. They say I should trust them, but how can I? Not once has anyone got an IV right the first time. Your "veins went into hiding" they say and poke around until they find one. Get it right the FIRST time I say. Maybe then the veins wouldn't hide on you! And let the alcohol dry first! Do you like to be stung by a bee? I have to tell everyone how to do it right instead of preparing myself. I feel like a pin cushion. What did I do that I'm stuck here? I think all they want is someone to stick pins into so they're never going to let me out of here.

Medical dictum declared leukemia a family disease. Now our family had two. We were assigned to learn about the pancreas, the way sugar is processed, the role of insulin. We, being Jada and I, sitting drowsily at the end of the long table in the same stuffy conference room where her leukemia had been announced to me. How Arnold had excused himself and Dom from this family disease had not been explained to me. I looked down the length of the dusty brown table as I would an afternoon's detention with a dotty old schoolmaster, feeling wrongly accused and made to pay bitter penance watching a grayish hand pointing to words on a flip chart at the other end. Jada was angry. Too bad we got caught. I was bored and resentful. Too bad the others got away.

The drone went on. Jada slid onto the table, lying across her outstretched arm; I blew at the fine blanket of specks beside her, the weight of my eyelids pressing as heavily as my gathering feelings. Secretly, silently, I cursed Arnold. "Well, someone's got to do it," he'd always said when I was the someone doing it, unloading kids and groceries, making dinner, cleaning the house, getting the kids ready for school, bed, outings, while he was not.

I put my hands to my head in this room that shrank tighter as the afternoon pressed and I felt sorry for myself. My back bowing, my shoulders leaning toward the table, I glared glassy-eyed at the insulin bottle the pharmacist set on the table. He wanted us to know about the difference between oral insulin and insulin by injection and why Jada could have only the latter. He was pointing to dates and chemicals, running through the history of insulin production. I was running through the history of us as a family. I wanted to know when and how we separated, for being here with Jada as the only other family member of this family was undeniable recognition that we had. I flipped through memories like the pages of a telephone book, not quite sure what I was looking for; I couldn't remember way back to the beginning, but I remembered one day, an incident, like people remember Pearl Harbor because it was concrete, divisive. Probably, though, we divided the family gradually, and my looking for one incident was like blaming World War II onto one attack.

Lambert Lane was growing with families. The four-bedroom vinyl-sided houses attracted people like us, people past their first apartments and looking for a neighborhood and a school system that would flatter their young families. Just within four houses from our front door lived Jonny and Ty and Itu-be, all the same age, for Dom to play with. At the end of our block was a patch of land dedicated as a park. Lake Jeannie Park had a metal tube swing set with black wide strips that slung under a child's bottom and reminded me of my dad's razor strap used to spank us, except the park swing was attached to chain links that left hands feeling dirty and smelling like they were coated with iron. Two wooden planks with T-shaped handles screwed on them to make them into teeter-totters, once painted but since worn gray and etched with crevices, cracked and widened from rain and wind and sun and snow, and a slide were the only other attractions because Dom and Jada were forbidden to go near the shoreline of the grassy-lined hole someone generously christened a lake with a correspondingly diminutive female name.

Sometimes Jada and Juleen or Katie rode their bikes to the park, or they played at one of the girls' houses. Jada and Katie set up laundry and housekeeping for their dolls in her back yard across the street. Juleen, two doors down, seemed as happy to play with either Jada or Katie, maybe because she was the youngest of her family and the newest to the neighborhood or just because she was the kind of child who showed up, running, her blouse hem flapping freely from one side of her skirt, the last one at the corner in the morning for the school bus, with a milky mustache from breakfast drying above her lip.

Katie was programmed with an auto-alarm inside her; at the sound of her buzzer, play ended, no matter what was going on. Juleen depended on anyone else's deference to time and sometimes had to be told to go and accompanied home because it was too dark to send her up the length of two houses alone in the street. Jada's sense of time had to do with some universal order to which she expected others to subscribe, sacrificing their private concerns to the higher law. When she and I were not in alignment, Jada saw to it that the gods be tested to reveal their favoritism. At eight years old, Jada believed it would be she.

Jada was playing at Juleen's house on a mild summer day when everyone threw open their windows and front doors to capture breezes that fanned through their houses. Three o'clock, to me the edge of the sinkhole of the day, I walked to Juleen's to fetch Jada. Frank welcomed me in. "Jada, your mom is here. Juleen, put your things away and wash up now," he called around a corner. Even giving directions toward a distant audience, Frank's voice was soft and gentle. He and his wife Jane and their children had moved here shortly after he was awarded his Ph. D., being a certified pastor and counselor. This house was their first fruit of middle class living after years of schooling and four children. They added an Alaskan pup that soon grew large and bounded down the street, being restrained from taking off in a full lunge only by Frank's stumbling weight. Arnold wrinkled his nose at the sight of Frank jerking behind the dog, saying that anyone who kept a whining barking dog in the back yard all night and couldn't control it for a walk must not be very smart, doctor or no doctor.

"I'm not going," Jada announced as she emerged from the half flight of steps to Juleen's bedroom. Her hair straggled in tangled vines about her head. Only for special occasions did she let me pull her hair away from her face and bind it. She preferred to let her hair fly wild.

My eyes ricocheted off Frank's before I reasoned, "But, Jada, they won't be here. We have to go back to our house."

"No, I don't. Juleen won't mind."

"Well," said Frank, only his thick black eyebrows hinting at what "well" meant from behind his equally thick black-framed eyeglasses, "there's only one thing to do."

"I guess so," I agreed. I encircled Jada with my arms, and by virtue of my willpower and size, pulled her across the floor.

"No! I'm not going! You can't make me!" She challenged, trying to weld her feet like metal posts into the floor. Frank held the door for us to wrestle to the outside.

Jada and I wrangled our way off the Gandara's stoop and across two driveways, past the other doctor's house, the "real doctor," as Arnold had proclaimed, she screaming, whipping her head, her hair, her spit and her tears of indignation, lashing at the street, at me, at her betrayal by the universe, all the way to ours.

My jaw clamped tight on a dry mouth, and my hair feeling like someone had just dumped a jug of syrup on it, I tussled with Jada up the one and only step before our front door, where Arnold stood inside it. "What's going on?" he demanded with his grainy voice. Begrudgingly, he held the door open for us, keeping himself well-hidden within. "The whole neighborhood can hear you! What is the matter with you?" he lobbed, curdling the words as if he were clearing out phlegm and working his jaw to roll it around in his mouth.

I shut the persimmon metal door and let go of Jada into a slump in the corner. "Nothing is wrong with her, nothing!" I countered amid the squall. "She's angry and hurt, and there's nothing wrong with that." Arnold tightened his temples and his jowl shook like a slab of jello, then humphed away, punching his fists like jackhammers toward the ground, returning to his station downstairs, either to the black Naugahyde chair with his paper or television or to the couch for his nap. Bending down to Jada, I squared her shoulders, looked her in her crying eyes. "Nothing is wrong with you," I said to her. "I don't like your screaming, but there is nothing wrong with you."

If Arnold were telling his story, he wouldn't be able to articulate the reason for the tantrum, for he hadn't been interested to find out. What mattered to him was that I allowed the public spectacle that reflected unflatteringly on him. But since I was remembering the event, I processed it, partner in an audience of two, in that stifling gray hospital room, steaming through the oppressive diabetes lecture. What mattered was not the principle but the persona, that faculty of his to know to do the dishes when we had company and to leave them for me when no one was watching, to smooch the baby in a crowd but to leave me with the dirty diapers in private. Arnold was right: someone had to do it.

The four of us lived in the same house; we made a family. But what kind? Our comings and goings and doings as transparent as cellophane wrap, we probably fooled ourselves anyway. Arnold had been tacitly exempted from this family event and I alone was there in the hazy hot conference room with Jada, slouched in her chair.

Weary, we dragged each other back to Jada's room, dull even with the dashes of blue and green paint. Rain-gray skies brought dusk early and everywhere as we settled in. The inundation of blood work, measures of vital signs, checking IV drips had given way to regularity, and we had agreed that I would go home at her bedtime. "Jada, do you think it's still a good night to try being alone or do you want me to stay?"

"No," she said confidently. "I want you to get some sleep. Go, unless they come up with some other weird thing. Maybe I'll get a new disease tonight." Soft squishy animals, some old companions, others sent from friends and relatives, crowded the room and surrounded Jada, robed in a new nightie and slippers, on new French sheets with blue and white narrow stripes. The garland of pink-petaled flowers running along the borders of the pillowcase made a halo for her head, delicately nestled in the center.

The air heaved sandbags on our feet, our shoulders, our spirits. At the conclusion of *M*A*S*H*, a silvery glow from the television screen cast a blue shadow on Jada's face as I lowered the mattress and fluffed her pillows. A pull of the chain erased light from over her bed, and the only illumination came through the door to the hallway.

"I'll be back before you even wake up in the morning."

"Mm-hmm. Can you sing slow?" I sat between her and the light from the hallway; her sculpted face and thinly defined eyelids compelled me to stroke her silky skin.

"…Pigtails and petticoats, where have they gone?…with babes of your own." Jada reached for my hand and brought it up under her warm cheek. "What are little girls made of, made of?…"

I finished, humming "Rock-a-bye, baby," and Jada said, squeezing tighter, "It's too bad you can't take your hand off like a glove. You could leave it with me."

"Yes. But you know, you always have my heart. I love you, HonBun. You're my baby."

From under my shadow, Jada's skin radiated cherubic, and my hand was warm under hers. I wanted to stay just like that, the two of us together all night, and closed my eyes.

"You're too good, Mom. No one else would do this," she said.

"Yes, Jada, they would, when they love someone. Love makes you responsible. Do you want me to wait for you to fall asleep?"

"No, if you wait, I won't fall asleep. Just stay here for a little bit. Then, go."

Minutes are longer in the dark, and the longer I sat, the darker it seemed to be. Jada's shoulder rose evenly, and I felt her warm breath on my wrist. My own breath came quickly as I anticipated the scurry to my car, the ride home. I tugged my hand away, at first feeling a reflexive resistance, then sliding it from under hers. Slowly I rose from the bed, hearing the crackle of a protected mattress.

I tiptoed to the plastic bag, packed and ready to go, its cotton drawstrings drooping along the side like unused lariats. Noise is noisier in the dark, too. The slick plastic brushed against my jeans and bumped the door as I opened it. I listened for Jada to call me back, waited a second outside her door in case, maybe hoping, she changed her mind. Then I crossed the hall to the stairwell and, through the dark empty lobby, I swung the bag, twirling and twisting its cord around my wrist until it burned.

Home, I tiptoed into Dom's room and kissed his head through thick dark hair and slipped into bed without the sense of luxuriousness I had expected. Arnold sputtered beside me, while I lay stiff-legged, looking upwards at the ceiling. The next thing I knew, I was driving to the hospital to be there when Jada woke up. Or maybe just to be there; I felt strangely out of place at home.

My call to Dom made, the morning yawned lazily, stretching its paws out before curling up in a feather pillow. We had more diabetes education, this time with a nutritionist who told us about carbohydrates, measurements, and all the no-no's ahead. When we returned to Jada's room, her lunch waited obstinately on the two arms of the chair like a bill collector for Jada to pay up. She refused to open the lid.

"Why not just pick out something you like, like the bread?" I urged.

"I'm not hungry."

"Jada, you have to eat or you'll get that funny feeling again."

"I don't care. I don't like this food and I'm not eating it. I'd rather die, anyway."

"If you're going to die, shouldn't it be over something more important than a vegetable? Let me pick something out for you." I lifted the lid, and sure enough, crumpled like a dog's chewed rawhide that'd been left in the dirt was a mangle of sliced roast beef; and the mixed peas and carrots that were there yesterday were there again today, boiled and blanched of color. Jada might have eaten corn; too much starch was not allowed. The censors substituted peas and carrots. I grabbed the waxed carton of milk. "At least drink your milk while it's still cold."

"Why are you doing that?" Jada's voice shrilled, and she whipped back the layers of blankets from her bed and surged from it, the power of her anger like spinach to Popeyes's bulging arms revving up to blast Bluto out of this world. "I'm not eating and you're not giving me any shots, either! I'll kill myself!" Then, grabbing the corner of the sheet with Miss Piggy in her voluptuous dress, Jada pulled it and wound it around her neck, falling backwards, all of Miss Piggy's buxom weight pressing against her throat. With her hands tugging the sheet crisscrossed at her neck, her head wobbling about the bed as if it were trying to squeeze itself out, she seethed. "I hate this! I'd rather be dead!"

She released her hold and shot up, her hair matted, crowning a face filled with color she hadn't had in months. She sprang to the bathroom, and like a punch to the midsection, slammed shut the door. I heard the lock catch. "Just try and make me!"

"Jada, I know you're angry. And you must feel helpless, too," I said to the gray metal as a troupe of people, Dr. Malley in the lead, stopped beside the entrance to the room.

"Get away from here! I don't want you here!" she shouted through the barrier. Dr. Malley continued to address the band that crowded in front of Jada's room, and as her lips moved, her eyes swept past mine. Jada cried out, "This is all a bunch of shit! I won't do it and you can't make me. Why can't I just die? Just get out of here and leave me alone!" I turned from Dr. Malley to the door and back again. Dr. Malley's speech hesitated, she shrugged, a look of disapproval sliding down her long bony nose, and netted her entourage to amble down the hall.

Dr. Malley could have provided a fencepost along the path I stumbled over in the dark, but she was cold, aloof, without even a spark of compassion when I needed a flicker. Maybe that was what Arnold liked about her, that pellet in her eyeball that always struck the fault of things. She, my mother, and my husband. It was the inside out of pleasing that linked them. Jada, overwound with emotion, a wind-up doll dialed to spin around and perform tricks, was put into a toy box, her unspent energy pulsing, coiled up, with no way to release it, except on me. Jada was a difficult patient, and me? I was the cause of her difficulty. After all, we had a family disease.

I sat down on the only chair in the room, listening for danger signals from the bathroom. As time passed, I heard clicks, first the unlocking, then the unlatching, and then Jada emerged, thin blue lines radiating from her eyes as if they were electric currents engraved in her chalky white skin. I tried not to notice that her cheeks were beginning to hug her jaws like she had a sour ball stuck on the back of her tongue, and it was sucking the rest of her in.

Why did I cater the lunch tray outside the room, saving the milk and crackers? "You never know when you'll need it," my mother would say. She saved twist ties flattened and bundled up like a miniature wood pile, bound neatly with another twist tie, a 6-inch beaded wire chain, rubber bands that snapped when you tried to stretch them, a silty brown light switch plate, among other found and salvaged oddities in the end drawer of the kitchen cabinets for when they might be needed. Many times in my frenzy to compile a paper for a college class, I plunged my hand into the drawer to feel around for a paper clip. What I needed was never available, for nothing that wasn't rescued was saved, and what wasn't saved was never purchased by its own merit. Items in the end drawer were the currency of survival in my mother's thrifty household: you never needed what you didn't have.

That night an evening nurse poked herself into the room and invited Jada to the playroom. A four- or five-year old cavorted among Fischer-Price play people; etch-a-sketch and coloring crayons spilled onto the floor like wildflowers in a vacant lot. Either a man in a suit chased her or she pulled him close behind her; it was too soon to tell. Neither the child nor the man used words, although I did hear a kind of squealing. Jada and I stood at the entrance to this open space, the nurse behind us, blocking the doorway. Another woman greeted Jada. "Would you like to come over here?" Jada followed, and they sat at a low table. The nurse beside me was saying something in my ear, but I was paying attention to the vibes from the room. Dim lighting and the dark night sky outside the window created garish shadows, not fully formed and permeating each object.

At the table, a naked doll lay between Jada and the woman. Beside it were two-inch square foil-lined packets of alcohol and Betadine, thin plastic syringes with orange caps protecting the needles. Gray wisps of hair like electric bolts shot out from the woman's head as she held in her one hand a bottle of insulin. With calm and steady movements that belied the unsettled hair around her face, the woman injected the doll. Then she presented the doll to Jada.

"Why? I'm never going to do this." Jada's voice carried back to us amid the clacking of the plastic four-wheeled vehicle making a circle in the corner of the room with the little girl pushing the pedals.

I felt the nurse standing next to me move, her arms still crossed. "You have to be able to give yourself insulin when you're out of the hospital," she said.

Jada turned sideways. "No, I don't. My mother will do it." Learning how to triple prep the bottle and the skin, first alcohol, then Betadine, then alcohol, how to fill a syringe and tap the trapped air bubbles out, and inject a knobby-skinned orange, I bent the needle every time I stabbed. "Don't worry," the nurse had reassured me. "Nobody's skin is that tough. You'll learn."

"She won't be with you all the time," said the nurse with the doll. "You'll be at school, away with your friends."

"I don't care. I'm not ever going to give myself a shot."

The nurse stopped short of Jada, her hands falling, her body rocking. "But, you have to." Her voice wheedled like the plastic parts of the three-wheeler rubbing each other. "You never know when you'll need it. You…"

I waved my hand like a truce flag and cut the rest of her sentence off. "Can we go out here to talk?" Standing in the hall, I used my most conciliatory tone. "She'll learn to give herself shots when she has to. Right now she has a lot to handle. She's feeling pretty bad about not being able to eat what she wants and having to have more blood tests and the whole thing."

The nurse shook her head sympathetically. "I feel so sorry for these children with diabetes. They have such a bleak future; so many with blindness and amputations. It's got to be the worst!"

"Yeah, if they live that long. I'm more concerned with getting her through this leukemia."

"Oh, that? That's nothing. There's a cure for leukemia; diabetes lasts forever."

I wanted to tell her what uncertainty felt like, how it tasted, metallic like the barrel of a gun at the back of the throat, how it smelled, cut flowers rotting in jellied water, how it smacked us right in the middle of the chest when we were faced with changing the most normal routines, like saying good morning or good night, nights that Jada claimed were never good, singing verses of lullabies that promised wifehood and babies and the beatification of every feeling I had for Jada and hoped she'd have for herself. I wanted to tell her how it felt to have those simple wishes drawn and quartered because there was a maybe kind of a cure, a tomorrow cure, a horse race, a roulette wheel—yeah, someone wins—a no attached to every yes, yes a crippled yearning within each maybe. "I'll work with her," I promised. "Just not today, okay? We've still got today's problems."

Jada remained sideways at the table, the knobs of her knees knocking the edge of the top. "Let's go," she said when I returned. She grabbed my arm and hoisted herself up, ignoring the doll and the woman on the other side of the table. Together we left the room and the little girl who pedaled the tricycle, the man still following.

"They call this the adolescent floor," I said casually in the corridor, "but where are the things for people your age?"

"They shouldn't lie to you," she said. "I hate it when people lie."

I was learning what it felt to be manipulated, a knowledge Jada had been trying to articulate but I was just beginning to hear. We reached her room.

Jada sank back into her bed and into herself. Unfurled pages of magazines were pressed together under a growing tower of books she rejected. She reminded me of long Sunday afternoons when I was a kid and had nothing to do and no urge to do it.

Two days later, Dr. Lourde caught us by surprise, Jada in her bed, her spindly arms two gates atop the sheets stacked over her, and I sitting at the ready, the ins and outs of our breathing ticking and tocking while the rest of the world kept its own time. His step paused like the dot on a quarter note. This was his second visit, the first official. He held the door open. "Hello, Jada. May I come in?"

"Mm-hmm," she answered, almost imperceptibly. Through horn-rimmed spectacles, his eyes followed the rows of cards sticky-tacked to the wall while he pulled the chair out for himself. I shifted on the cushion next to the window, brushing against a hanging frond from one of the flowers. "Looks like a zoo in here," Dr.

Lourde said. It was impossible to know if we should apologize or beam with pride.

"I know," I said. "I don't know how we'll ever get them all home."

"This looks like it *is* home. Have you been getting out much?" He directed his question at Jada.

Jada's eyebrows crouched together to give him a hard look, the blue in her eyes icing over. "I go for X-rays and to the tub room for a bath."

"I don't mean the things you have to do. There's no reason for you to stay in bed. When you first came in there was because you were sick, but now we're just waiting to get things regulated. I'd like to see you get out and mingle a bit. Things happen to people when they stay in a hospital too long. They start thinking they can't do anything anymore."

"I'd like to get out, too, but you won't let me go home."

"Well, no, we can't let you go home yet." Until then, the only part of Dr. Lourde's face that held animation was his mustache, bobbing gray strands amid the brown coarse hairs as he formed his words. A hint of a smile creased his cheeks. "But that shouldn't stop you from getting out of this room, maybe going for a walk down the hall or down to the main floor." Jada shifted her eyes downwards. He pushed on, like some rock that tumbled into new territory and had to make room for itself. "I think they sort of frown upon you taking meals in the cafeteria, but, as long as you're not contagious or too sick to move, you could go down to any of the visiting places or the lobby. There's an outdoor deck on the top floor of Sibley. If that's not being used for a function, you could go there. Just tell the nurses at the desk where you're going. If nothing's scheduled for you, you can just go; you won't need a pass as long as you stay in the hospital."

"Could she go to the gift shop?" I asked.

"I don't know why not. I'm sure they don't want you just hanging around in there, but...."

"No, no," I said, leaning forward now. "There's that money from Uncle Rob, Jada. You can go downstairs to the gift shop, find something there."

"Maybe. But it's hard to walk. I get tired."

"Get a wheelchair. There's at least one on the floor." Dr. Lourde's lips shut firmly; he looked steadily at her.

Jada reached toward the foam cup of water with a straw, bent like a reed by the wind, on her bed tray. "Oh, Jada, I can't wait. You'll like that." She gave a little shake of her head, like a filly who knows how much her beauty gives others pleasure but loves to run on her own anyway.

"The other reason I'm here is to tell you to expect a visit from Heidi soon. She's been meaning to make it up here during her lunch break, but that hasn't worked out. Heidi is the clinic nurse who will care for you when you come in as an outpatient. When you're ready to go home, Heidi will take you through the clinic."

"Sure. Do you know what time?" Jada sipped through the straw.

"That I can't say. She'll just try to slip out when she can." Dr. Lourde uncrossed his legs and lay the palms of his hands on each corduroyed thigh. "Is it all right that I just check around your neck?" Dr. Lourde rose and slid his fingers up and under Jada's ears and chin. She stretched her neck long like a cat being stroked.

Satisfied that all was well, he released Jada and said, "Okay. See you later."

"Bye."

"Thank you." Then to Jada I asked, "How about a story?"

"Maybe later. I just want to rest a little bit." She closed her eyes. Through Jada's bath, I described the wonders in the gift shop as if it were a magic carpet ride away. While I dribbled warm water over her shoulders, I filled in a picture with shimmery glass figures, translucent porcelain teacups, bright gems and pastel slippers as delicate as colors in a Monet. I patted her dry and smoothed creamy lotion along her arms and legs. She might buy a scented talcum.

The flurry of starting the day in the hospital blows through like a squall. Lights go on, breakfast trays clatter, voices ring with shared family stories, scales get rolled in and out of rooms, doctors and nurses and technicians go round and round. Her Cheerios delivered, Jada munched her cereal watching *I Dream of Jeannie* on the television awaking to the day while Jeannie's efforts to help her master ended up in another blunder he had to fix before his commanding officer could figure it out. Arnold labeled this program junk, nary a one of its genre having a new plot since 1952. He was right. But, I reminded him, I had read and reread *A Cat in the Hat* and *Chicken Soup with Rice*, a laudable practice, and he watched football games, and there'd been no new plot there that I knew of. With the music for *Bewitched!* fading into its first scene, I went off to work.

On my return to the hospital, I looked around the room and felt the inertia of walls. The neon colors thought to brighten the curtain, break up the span of surrounding drab, only tightened the room's grip. Like the window to the city streets outside it, the contrasting bold colors set boundaries, like No Trespassing signs. Our excursion to the gift shop was at hand.

We crossed over the clattery divide between the metal edges of the elevator car and the hospital floor, twice, but not without a few near misses. The wheeled apparatus seemed to roll like a grocery cart with at least one independent wheel skidding along sideways and veering us off on a contrary course. We were just beginning, and already the sounds of life moving, women in pants and jackets and shoes, real shoes, shoes with color, shoes that made noise as they clicked on tiled floors, excited my senses. Jada popped out like a Jack as she rolled the preciously narrow gift shop aisles; her wary eyes researched our path, made even more crowded with protruding drawer knobs, metal brackets, and unsteady reed baskets overflowing with odd-shaped doodads that rolled away when nudged. "Watch where you're going," Jada warned.

"Okay, Jada. You look at the shelves; I'll be careful." I rolled her along slowly and kept my eyes to the boundaries of an imaginary conveyor belt.

"Stop. Up there!" A ceramic blotchy peppy-eyed dog, eternally blooming glazed flowers sprouting from a shapely vase, an angel with broad gold wings and stars stamped on a white flowing gown, two porcelain hands formed together in prayer; these? Then I saw it and knew by the way their eyes were locked on each other that it wasn't inappropriately placed but waiting out of everyone else's sight just for Jada. My hands went up for it, a crushable stuffed pig sitting on its haunches, all four round stubby legs reaching out for her. When I delivered it to her, they seemed to breathe together the air of a new life. I lifted the tag that was tied to a pink curlicue tail sticking out from Jada's embrace. "Oh, look! Its name is Hambone!"

"*His* name is Hambone." Jada held out his creamy nubby body. His head leaned a little to the side from fitting beside her neck. "Look at his eyes. And his ears!" She rubbed her hand under his pink ear and let it bounce. "I know I have a lot of stuffed animals, but...," and she squeezed him closer.

"He's pretty special."

"Do I have enough money? I'll pay you back my allowance if I don't."

"Don't worry. He's yours." I rolled Jada and Hambone around the corner to the glass case glistening with jewels as I counted out the change in Jada's coin purse.

Hambone rode on Jada's lap back to her room and into bed with her. She doted on him, seeing that he did not fall off the edge or get caught in the sheets like Albert, a snowy white stuffed dog, that was hauled off by mistake with the laundry by housekeepers at a Rapid City motel. From that day on, Hambone was Jada's ever-present companion. When Jada got an X-ray, he got one, too. His pink-tipped snout poked out from her sheet or his rotund body balanced bravely, a stout beacon atop Jada's pillow.

Arnold and Jada in the front seat, I in the back, we drove toward home with a pass in strained silence subdued by the sounds from a music station. A hot dry wind picked up the surface layer of dust from the gutters and tossed the particles about like brown confetti on a Sunday in May; the cotton pants that sagged from Jada's hips billowed like wind socks around her wobbly legs. I imagined her being swept away in a strong gust, she and Hambone soaring up and away into the sky between the car and the front door.

Jada took each of the seven steps up to the living room, Hambone clutched under her armpit, as a goal in itself. Grandma M stood wearing a sleeveless blue housedress and a ready face that could break into a smile if someone made a joke or drop her brows and lips into pitiable sympathy if the action called for the reverse, her hands spread-eagled on the railing overlooking Jada's climb. "Do you guys want some coffee? I'll put a pot on if you have time," Myrna said as Jada made the crest and plopped onto the couch.

"No, not for me," I said, trailing Jada with hawkish eyes, setting a plastic gallon milk jug on the floor. "Hi, Dom!" I hardly needed to bend to hug him.

"What's that for?" he asked when we let each other go. Given the jug while signing Jada out of the hospital to go to the ice show she was to have skated in, I decided that hospital care had not advanced far, after all. Nurses were charged to carry out orders, and they had to make do with what they had. They trimmed and carved Dixie cups to make protective tents on attachment sites for IVs. They filled latex gloves with hot water or ice to use as foot warmers or ice packs. Nurses, like teachers, had to scavenge their own belongings to supply usable equipment, and finding this, a gallon milk jug, decided it would do.

"We're supposed to save Jada's urine in here."

Jada jerked as if poked by a pin. "They expect me to carry my pee around with me? I'm not doing that. How am I supposed to get it in there, anyway?"

"I wondered the same thing. And look at how big it is." I held the jug up for display. "I hope they didn't think you'd fill it up."

"Get rid of that," Jada said regarding it with the same disgust as she would have for a dead rat. Dom's hair smelled of shampoo as I nuzzled him, my arm itching from the wool Afghan, out of season on the warm May day.

"Okay," Myrna chirped, carrying her purse, coral lipstick glossing her lips and round coral buds blooming on her cheeks. "I'm ready."

At the announcement we started up, all except Jada. "Help me get to the bathroom." I picked up the jug along the way. "I told you, get rid of that thing!" Arnold, stood, his hands clasped beneath his belt; Myrna, wanting all her ducks lined up in proper pecking order, froze; Dom, the peacemaker, remained in the background.

"I have to bring it back with me."

"No, you don't. Just leave it here and throw it away." Jada pushed forward beyond the stairway. I set the jug down, and from behind the bathroom door I felt the vibrations of people moving in unison. We were on our way.

Heidi had come into Jada's room almost without making a sound and introduced herself, a smile opening her face like a hot bath at the end of a cold day. Jada jumped in. Brown wavy tresses swayed around Heidi's freckled face as her mouth seemed to croon. "Before you go home, I want you and your mom to come down to tour the clinic where you'll be getting treatment for the next three years. And I want you to meet Marilyn. She and I will go out to your school, meet with your teacher, and explain leukemia to your classmates. You've been gone a long time, and after radiation, you will lose some hair; your friends will have a lot of questions."

"But I have eight teachers and different friends in all of my classes."

Heidi hesitated; her liquid brown eyes stopped swimming and she paused before resuming in a melodic wave. "I'll talk it over with Marilyn and let you know." The hospital routine had become so natural that I had lost imagination for a different life, and now Heidi suggested its possibility. I began to bag up animals and magazines to take home, lighten the burden of the promised day. Like the last night of summer before the first day of school, Jada and I laid out our feelings as if they were the new clothes we were going to wear.

"I don't know where we're going to put the rest of these," I said, talking aloud to myself while gathering a befuddled looking stuffed floppy-eared dog, a cat that was already curled up and sleeping, and the black and white dolphin, nestling them side by side in a plastic bag. The rigid handle on one side ripped away, and animals spilled out, a reminder that they were not meant to be penned in. I set the bag on the floor and looked back at the window ledge, where a little lamb and the gray Husky remained, along with a stack of magazines, journals, and notebooks, and three vases of cut flowers, and then to Jada, watching from a half-sitting position. "Your bedroom is overstuffed as it is. It's been so long; it will be good to be home."

"I don't know if I want to be there," Jada said quietly.

"What do you mean?" I grasped the Husky in a stranglehold, dangling him above a gaping bag. "Are you scared of getting radiation treatments? Dr. Malley says that most people get them and just go off to work afterwards."

"Yeah, where am I going?"

School was the obvious answer, jumping onto the blank screen of our new lives and nearly escaping before my mind surrounded the whole picture that encompassed Jada's life, extending through the night like the old test patterns before tele-broadcasting ran around the clock uninterrupted, hour after hour, year after year ad infinitum. "Are you worried about missing school?" I counted days: by the time she was finished with radiation, school would recess for the summer. Time, precious time, had been swallowed by disease.

"I don't want to go back to school. I mean I do, but I know I can't handle it. Is that what it's going to be like for me? I'd rather stay here than go home and not be able to do the things I'm supposed to do."

I released the gray and white dog I'd been clutching. The light from above the bed shed itself on Jada and muted the paint on the walls, melding them into the ceiling. "I think I know what you mean," I began. "Sometimes I have to remind myself that I've made it through a bad time before and can again. We have to start up again."

"It's not just starting up again, Mom. For me it's starting over."

The change of that one word revealed a truth that isolated Jada: leukemia might be a family disease in the books of medicine, but it was a disease owned by one life, one and only one person's life. The rest of us, our choices were relative. Jada's choices, she discovered, had been transformed. She was on a new journey that required a new set of tools. "We'll start over together. I'll start over with you."

"You better. I couldn't do this without you."

"You could. And you would if I wasn't here. But I am."

"But, Mom, how can you keep doing this? You're always here, and you do everything for me."

"Jada, I remember when you were a baby. I wanted to take you back inside me because I couldn't get close enough to you even though you were right there in my arms. My mind and my heart were so filled with you that the only way to feel complete was to fill my body with you, too."

"I wish you could have taken me back. Then I wouldn't have to go through this." Faint freckles sprinkled across her nose and cheeks like a dusting of glitter faded to shadows the color of butterscotch pudding.

"True. But then, you would never have been able to be you. I'm glad you're alive and here. You'll do this, Jada; I'll help you."

"Promise, you've got to promise me you won't leave me."

"I promise, Jada. I'm sorry I can't take things away, take them myself. I've had a chance. I've had two beautiful babies. I wouldn't want to leave the two of you, but I've been able to sing lullabies to you, hold you, kiss you. I want you to have that chance, too."

I flipped over page after page of gritty pink duplicates, all of them dated and edged in the same smeary blue ink imprinted in blurry lines of instructions. At last, after three weeks in the hospital, Jada was going home, and with us we were taking a script for our lives. Dr. Silverman would regulate Jada's insulin dosage, increasing by hash marks on the syringe barrel with each test. She was given a list of how many servings of starches, sugars, and fats she would be allowed at each meal. She had a prescription for insulin, boxes by the gross of needles, litmus sticks, Betadine and alcohol pads. She was to take three green pills all at once every other day as a preventative against pneumonia, little white pills five days in a row, then two days off, yellow, pink pills every day, and one and one-half oblong goldenrod pills one day alternating with only one the next.

The medications she received worked well, reputedly, on what circulated through her torso; her spinal column and her head, the control centers for her body, however, were mysteriously separated, perhaps for security reasons. Beginning on Monday, in addition to weekly spinal taps, Jada was to begin a two-week round of radiation therapy to her head. Dr. Lourde had carefully reminded us that leukemia was a very pesky disease and loved to hide out in protected places, like the spinal column and the area in the brain connected to it, a kind of island in the body with its own set of rules and regulations.

A section of the kitchen counter was appropriated for holding supplies to manage Jada's diseases. In a bin were vials of confetti-colored pills, foil pacs of cleansing pads, needles, and happy-faced bandages. A kitchen scale, its measurement varying according to the tilt of the bowl, jutted from beneath the overhead cabinets, crowded the toaster. The insulin needed refrigeration, and the urine test strips logically stayed near the toilet; the encapsulated cannabis—brown jellied balls that looked like mouse turds in a brown glass jar—I kept on the very top shelf of the cupboard out of reach. The telephone numbers of the hospital and clinic were taped to the wall beside the phone.

Mornings I called Dr. Silverman, then drove Jada to St. Barnabus's Hospital for radiation treatment. Glazed-over saggy eyes watched us walk through the lobby and followed us until we entered the narrow hallway to the technician who measured and marked and X-rayed Jada's head. I waited in the outer area with the other radiation patients. People changed with every morning, but faces of blue-haired grannies and stringy-looking codgers with miniature brown craters on the ends of their yellow teeth didn't.

Having raised their families and made their mark, these old-timers were hoping to steal one more day to add onto their lives. We sat together in a room as contestants, eyeing each other jealously, though afraid to give up what we had. I drove Jada home again and then drove to school to get another day of work in myself.

Heidi and Marilyn's visit to Jada's school turned technical rather than practical; Jada had missed too much and was assigned homebound instruction. Two afternoons a week I brought Jada to either the hospital clinic, a designated area beyond the general lobby, or to Dr. Silverman's office. With the risk of infection, Jada was permitted to bypass the waiting rooms of both. It was another one of those defensible nonsensical practices that epitomized the irony of this disease. Jada was encouraged to roam the hospital halls, but lounging in the clinic's waiting area was off limits. Jada entered through the back door of Dr. Silverman's clinic, like an unseemly character in a melodrama come to make a sleazy deal with the rich baron, and sat in a lint-filled room with a dust-covered desk; a bookshelf hovered, its sagging board crammed with journals and notebooks and layers of papers leafing out like fronds of an untamed palm tree. In the corner were boxes of paper towels stacked upon each other. I hurried our steps for fear of being attacked by any germs that picked up our scent.

May 18

> *Gimp is me! I can hardly walk without falling. I fell twice at the mall on Saturday and bruised my knee. And on Sunday at Grama's I fell on the sidewalk. Then mom stayed so close she stepped on my shoe and my foot got wet from the grass. And then I fell again. I scraped my knee and hurt my hand. Mom helped me but I fell again anyway and stubbed my toe. Blood was on my nose, too. Grama was waiting at the back door and I just couldn't stop crying. It was like a balloon bursting in me and gushing out tears. Mom washed the blood and put bandaids on my owies, but I was shaking and crying. Mom held me and*

said I was hurt more inside than I was outside, and I felt a little better. But I was so thirsty and hungry! I didn't feel good at all!

My tummy is still rumbling and tumbling, like there's a bunch of rotting worms squirming in there and trying to escape. I was hungry again today, though, and I made a peanut butter sandwich and ate potato chips. I can't tell mom because I want her to trust me. I think I should be punished. She stays home with me tomorrow because I go for a spinal tap. I need Hambone to be there for me. I hate the way Dr. Malley does them! I'm scared I'll get sharp pains that shoot all over my back and pounding in my head. Dr. Malley says I shouldn't. She says I shouldn't be falling, either. But I do! I fell again today. I get so mad at my back and my foot and I am tired and my tummy feels TERRIBLE. It must be the season for shedding. My hair is falling out by the pound. This is god damn SHIT!! I'm sick of living with it. I should just die. Then I won't have to care anymore.

"When can I start skating again?" Jada asked.

Dr. Malley raised her eyebrows. "You can do anything you want to; what's stopping you?"

"I can barely walk. Look at my foot. How come I can't lift it up?" Jada put her hands under her knee and raised her leg from which her foot dangled like the tongue of a sweaty dog. "My whole leg feels weak, and when I walk, I can't lift my foot up like I'm supposed to. It just drags along. I can't skate with a foot like that."

"Just start when you can." Dr. Malley glanced over at Heidi who was tearing away the paper seal to the package for the lumbar puncture called a spinal tap. My nose wrinkled at the smell of Betadine.

"That's what I'm asking. When will this go away?"

Dr. Malley looked over the contents Heidi had spread out onto a tray as if they were confections from which she could choose. "It's hard to say. It's probably just a consequence of one of the drugs; I'd say Vincristine. You'll just have to get along as best as you can."

"The thing is," I interjected, "we have to buy ice time and pay an instructor. If we give up our slot, it's harder to get another."

Dr. Malley's angular face sharpened at the eyebrow. "I don't know what to tell you." Heidi was done arranging and stepped away from the tray. Dr. Malley turned on the faucet.

"I get headaches, too," Jada added. "They're worse when I stand or sit up."

Quickly, and not without a hint of impatience, Dr. Malley spoke to the tumbling soap in her writhing hands. "There's nothing that shows you should be having headaches from leukemia. Take some Tylenol."

"I do," said Jada in a voice the size of a dime in a jewelry store. "It doesn't help."

"Are you back in school?"

"No; I'm on homebound. I get sick every day." Jada curled up, Hambone tucked into her chest, my hand in her firm grip. We fell silent as Dr. Malley rubbed between Jada's vertebrae and poked with the needle. One slight movement botched everything. Collecting spinal fluid took time as it dripped through a needle into an attached syringe. Today the fluid flowed slowly. Jada waited, hunched, part yoga pose, part ball of yarn. "Aren't you done yet? It hurts."

"Bend over more tightly, Jada. Maybe that will help." Heidi guided Jada, pushing Jada's neck downward. Jada's fingers dug into my skin.

"Just another minute." Dr. Malley eyed the clear fluid that filled half the syringe and nodded to Heidi, who let go of Jada and reached for another syringe filled with the anti-cancer drug. Dr. Malley detached one syringe and reattached the other to the needle in Jada's back. "I'm going to put the medicine in now." A wince wrought Jada's face as she felt the cold fluid creep up inside the center of her back. As soon as Dr. Malley withdrew the needle, she also withdrew from the room. We breathed. Where she had placed a cotton ball, Heidi pressed her thumb and stripped a bandage across it.

"You were brave, Jada," I said.

"Yes, you handled that very well." Heidi agreed. Her voice sounded slippery, like it had been lubricated to speak the French language, sliding in one sentence from a deep throaty sound to a high trill at the end. Her full freckled face surrounded by silky wavy hair looked French. Instead, she was German, from a small German town in southern Minnesota and having a German last name to verify it. But she didn't sound German. She spoke in sounds that joined each other like sisters in a circle holding hands. "That's too bad about your foot. You must miss skating." The words poured out and flowed together in a pool of honey.

"I used to do it just for fun; but I was just starting to work hard at it before I got sick."

"I don't like getting up at 4:15 to get her to the rink, but it's worth her doing something she likes."

"You can stay here as long as you like. Just remember to get up slowly," Heidi cautioned. Disturbing the equilibrium after a spinal tap caused headaches; balance had to be restored gradually. She put her hand on Jada's head. When she lifted it, hair came away and clung to it, as if Jada had been a frightened animal and released hair to escape. Heidi shook the strands off to glide lazily to the floor.

"It's falling out in droves," I said. "We use a lint pick-up on her pillow every time she gets up."

"You know, there's a place in Nokomis that you can get a wig free. A woman who had cancer donates them. Usually people get one and bring it to a hairdresser and have them style it. I'll get the number for you."

With one hand, Jada shielded her eyes from the glaring fluorescent light, and with the other, pinched my sleeve until she met with the brown table, covered by a strip of rough paper, and lay down with a groan of relief. Dr. Silverman arrived in unusual speed and asked, "What's the matter? Do you feel sick?" He reached for her wrist and peered at her face.

"No. The light hurts my eyes, and I have a headache."

Dr. Silverman reached into his breast pocket for a wand and aimed it at Jada's face. "Open your eyes, Sweetheart. I have to take a look." Leaning over and peering into each eye, he asked, "Have you told the doctors at the clinic?"

"Yes," Jada covered her eyes. "Dr. Malley said I shouldn't have it, but I get it after my spinal tap. I don't feel as bad when I lie down."

Dr. Silverman perked his head up. "Does the pain last for about a week?" Jada took her hand away and squinted at Dr. Silverman, nodding.

"I know what that is," he said. "The same thing happened to me when I was in the hospital a few years ago. It's from doing a spinal tap too high. It doesn't have anything to do with what they're doing, just *where* they do it. Somehow it upsets the balance." He turned to ask me, "Do you have a girdle?"

Jada asked, "What's a girdle?" Dr. Silverman pressed. "It doesn't have to be a girdle. Just anything tight that you can wrap around her middle, right about here." With one hand, he scored a wide band below his chest. "The pressure helps to relieve the pain you feel in your head. I had to wear one every day."

At home, I dug through the top drawer of my dresser while Jada lay on my bed. There it was, at the bottom, with the wrinkled nursing bras I saved because, well, they weren't worn out yet. Holding it up, I stretched an old girdle for Jada to see. "Did you really put that on yourself?" she asked. "How could you stand having something so tight on?"

"That was the style then. No one was supposed to have jiggles. We were all supposed to be smooth and flat, except for our pointy bras."

"When was that?"

"The fifties, and into the sixties. Everything was, oh, contained, I guess you could say. No bouncing allowed. You were supposed to show only the edges, the contours of a sleek form, not the real body. I had a hard time with that, as you can see." I poked my finger into my belly and it sank into soft flesh like the Pillsbury Dough Boy on TV.

"I know it," Jada slid her hand down and let it rest on her abdomen. "How come I had to inherit that from you? Look at my legs, a couple of sticks, but I still have a belly bulge."

"Sorry. Well, at least you didn't get my nose, like Dom did." I slid my pointer down my curved nose to accentuate its right turn toward the end. "That affects his air passage, like mine does. So, want to try this girdle?"

Jada looked like she was being asked to walk on nails. With both hands, I stretched the elastic, placing it next to Jada and observing, "He must have had a real old fashioned girdle that came down over the thighs."

"If I have to stay up for a while, I'll wear it, but not when I don't have to. Is that okay, Mom? It looks too uncomfortable." The girdle in one hand, I towed Jada with the other back to her room. The sun carved a parallelogram out of Jada's dingy yellow rug. Once all the toys and papers and animals were picked up, the indelible stains of childhood remained lonely and neglected under the spotlight. In the corner, dogs and bears, whales and cats and monkeys tumbled from a heaping pile. The room was crowded with too many unclosetable things. It needed a girdle.

Aimlessly, I picked up a pen and journal from the floor. Where to put it, that was the question. Her nightstand, with a lamp, a brush, a clock radio, a box of tissues, and last night's glass of water on it, was the logical choice, since she did her writing in bed. I opened the top drawer: full. I removed the glass and set the journal under the box of tissues. The brush belonged on the dresser.

"You can throw that brush away," Jada said. She put her hand to her head and caught clumps of hair between her fingers. I winced in sympathetic pain as I watched her pull the hair from her scalp. "It doesn't hurt," she said, holding out a bunch like a bouquet of flowers that had lost the blossoms and only the wilted stems were left. "I hate all this hair on my pillow. I'd rather just get rid of it." I held out the wastebasket as she dropped one after another fistful of hair into it. Grayish white scalp showed little patches among the fine strands of hair that remained. I held onto the brush and said, "I'll just clean it and put it away for now. Your hair will grow back. Maybe it's time to go for the wig."

"I don't know why everyone wants me to have a wig. It's like they think hair is the only thing I care about. Why don't they care if I can eat what I want to or walk like everyone else or not get sick? No one wants to talk about that. Just hair."

"Maybe they don't see all those other things so they don't know what's really been taken away from you."

"They just want me to be like everyone else. All they ever talk about is how other people don't like to lose their hair, so I'm not supposed to either. It doesn't matter what I say, if I want more time to get myself ready for treatment or if I don't like how long they're taking to do an IV. They do what they want, not what I want."

"You must feel that no one is listening to you."

"They aren't. Otherwise why talk about my hair?" Jada closed her eyes, and I went to the bathroom to comb the hair from the brush, and while I was at it, wash both it and the comb. I wondered what people thought when they grew old and discovered that their lives just didn't need things anymore. Were they sad or did they celebrate their liberation? I shooed the question from my mind like it was a black cat crossing my path. Likely the loss was real before it was recognized, like this brush, swishing through the suds. But Jada's not old, I said to myself, and she's already losing hope. I reaffirmed my promise to her. *Yes, Jada I will start over with you. I will hope.*

Jada had concluded radiation therapy and looked about as white as the paper on the table at the clinic. "Do the spinal tap as low as you can," she said to Dr. Malley, explaining why that was necessary. Dr. Malley hesitated, and Jada pressed. "Is it harder for you to put the needle in lower?" It wasn't, she admitted, and scrubbed Jada's back.

I found the address for the free wigs, a nondescript storefront with plate glass windows and turquoise panels beneath them. Inside, a young woman with dense brown hair, white pants and a white shirt stooped over a mound of brown hairy balls that looked like they could have been road kill bulldozed and heaped into a pile pushed up against a wall. In another pile were yellow creatures. She dug her hand in a ways and tossed a few, splat, to the cement block wall and then down they tumbled. She turned around and thrust out her fists covered by curly little balls of hair; along her arms she had tucked others and she hugged them to her body like a mother nursing her brood.

Jada's face showed nothing, and I guessed she'd have refused all of them, so I said, lifting one off and spreading my fingers to stretch it open, "This one, I guess. Do I need to sign or something?"

"Nothing." She pitched the other wigs, carrion, not looking back to see how they fell, and we followed her away from the piles.

Outside, in the sunlight, Jada observed, "Well, now I have part of my costume for Halloween."

"It will take some getting used to," I said, politely. "I'll bring it in to Deb and we'll get it cut."

"Cut! You'll have to run a lawn mover through it. Nobody has hair that thick."

I admitted that Jada's face would look shrunken inside a big brown helmet of hair. "Actually, I think your face and head have beautiful features. I'd like to see the hair you have left cut shorter. Your face doesn't need hair to be pretty."

We jolted through traffic and arrived home, and inside the garage, I reached into the back seat for the wig. "Feeling all right?" I asked, meeting Jada rounding the back end of the car. The skin about her mouth tightened as she continued toward the front door. "What I mean is, you don't look like you have a headache."

"Nope. Not yet." She went on ahead, and I saw her from the back the way she might appear to others, sharp-shouldered and straight-spined; her neck rising from the center like a standard on top of which was balanced an orb as pure as a crystal ball. From the back, she could have been as old as last night's sunset or as young as tomorrow's morning. At the stoop to the front door, she waited for me. She needed a hand to raise her leg.

June 4

    I still have diabetes and I had to get 4 units of insulin. I threw a fit and then I was sick. I had to go to the hospital but it was just an insulin reaction. I don't care anymore. I'm going to eat what I want to and don't care if I test sugar in my urine. I hate having diabetes. I hate the puke sleeping medicine. It makes me want to throw up. Nothing is good! Well, going to school last week was fun. After we went to the hospital for radiation, THAT took forever, I went to school and got my yearbook. I was super nervous. I have almost no hair on my head, and a few kids avoided me I think because I am practically bald. I have a wig, but it is JANKY. It might look good on Miss Blanco, but not on me. It looks like shit and I won't wear it. I miss being in school and orchestra and seeing my friends. My whole body hurts and all that walking and climbing stairs tired me out! But it was worth it. I had fun and laughed with some friends. I got my yearbook. It has really good pictures of school life.

    I should be happy, or at least feel normal because I am in remission, but I hate how I feel. I have a million emotional ups and downs. I hate how I look, what I can't do, and I want to bite or kill something! I have a killer headache, and my stomach hates me too. It wants to send back everything in it. I'm sore around my tummy, my legs and arms are weak and they hurt to touch. I can't fight anymore I'm so tired! My first vincristine IV bled and I had to get another poke. My hemoglobin has been dropping and was 6.7. That's why I couldn't do my school work. Mom said I'd like A Wrinkle in Time, and she finished reading the last part to me because all I could do was sleep and rest. That's all I got done. My teacher comes tomorrow.

    GRRR! I HATE everything. I'm mad at me for putting up with this shit and I'm mad at mom, too. I'm mad that I feel that way because I need mom to help me and hold me and kiss my boo boos. I'm mad that I throw tantrums but I don't know how to stop. Talking about my feelings is hard because I feel I need my forces to fight this battle and it's only going to get worse. I have many different feelings and it confuses me! Hambone is the only one who understands what I'm going through. Hambone knows how tired I am of my life. I want to feel normal! But instead I think I want to just DIE. It's too much for me to handle. Everyone else's lives would be better, too. I don't know. I don't care. My arms are about to drop off and my head is exploding. I tore into my wig.

Clouds of bilious fluid threatened to vomit their churning contents, smearing the sky green. Jada slept in her bed while the siren atop the Church of the Good Shepherd blared its warning. I refused to believe the alarm was real. Oh, the siren keened loud enough; I just couldn't feel the fear it signaled. The threat of tornadoes was usually earlier in our spring. Spring tornadoes tore up Brighton Lake, north of Nokomis, with some regularity, and they sometimes traveled an arc to sweep over Englewood, our adjacent suburb. Coming as late as June 12, this warning didn't stand a chance of frightening me.

Arnold called up the steps that a tornado was sighted in downtown Nokomis. On less than a clear day, I could see the upper outlines of the tallest buildings in Nokomis from the window above Jada's bed. I went into her room and sat on the floor, my ears straining to hear even a leaf ripple above the rhythmic ins and outs of Jada's deep breathing. The room dulled in the late Sunday afternoon, and trees swayed restlessly, even in the quiet. As afraid of falling prey to a tornado as I had used to be, next to Jada, I wasn't even curious at my tranquility.

I was making supper when news broke that a tornado ripped into the Rossmore Theater—the Rossmore, where I took Jada and Dom to see movies—tossed cars into the air, and then traveled right up the streets that fanned from the church with the siren attached to its steeple, taking roofs off houses just a mile from us. Monday, the first day of summer school, I drove through the next block around limbs obstructing passage to Lyton Avenue. Halves of trees split down the middle and fallen like slain soldiers in the streets presented hurdles. Volunteer crews brought hot food and water to families who tried to patch their houses with plywood and tarp while I drove away to work. We could have been in the path of the worst tornado that hit us since 1965. This one tornado that I ignored cut right through us. We were lucky to have been spared.

Jada finished her cycle of radiation, school let out, and on Thursday, on my 36th birthday, we had an appointment with Dr. Lourde, now the full-time hematologist oncologist at Ramsey Hospital, and Dr. Malley, to set the course of another new routine. I could no more prepare for the imminent changes to our lives now than I could in April, when Jada was diagnosed. We had been tossed into two diseases, to life in a hospital, to radiation. Once mere observers, still noticing ourselves noticing a place, we had got used to them all.

Neighbors lined the boulevard with stacks of branches with browning young leaves, monuments to their proximity to tragedy, anxious to display their meticulous lawns again, to erase the reminder of mortality. We passed through the hospital lobby, somber with our pending decision and self-conscious of our conspicuousness: we were no ordinary people coming in. I led the route through the clinic corridor, a familiar turn here at the blue line that ran along the wall, a stutter at the yellow. In the heart of the clinic we stopped at the counter, a gray wall that rose to my shoulders, hiding anyone who sat directly behind it. I scanned the forms along the wall for a familiar person. Heidi's voice from behind greeted us. "Hello," she said, raising the second syllable and letting it flutter like a flag in the breeze. "Let me check and see which room is open."

She peeked into a room and motioned us in. Arnold went for a chair, one of two crunched closely together against the wall, while I lingered in the doorway, listening to a mother holding a full-faced, bald-headed child just outside the room next to ours. She shouted over the counter to a nurse as if they were hanging laundry in their backyards.

A tall blonde woman collided with Heidi at a narrow gap between the counter and the wall. "Oh, excuse me," the two said simultaneously. They backed away one from the other until they realized that each was going in the opposite direction of their original destination and to reverse their course would lead to another collision. Heidi's eyeteeth dented her lower lip before she broke into a broad smile that spread the freckles across her square face.

"Just like home," the other said in a voice that sounded distant, from a ventriloquist lurking somewhere.

"Barb," Heidi said, as the other woman came into the corridor, "have you met Idina Petersen? She and her husband have come to see Joe. Jada is just starting maintenance therapy."

"Hi, I'm Barb. Heidi and I will see most of Joe's patients." Barb continued toward the woman and child in the doorway, Heidi disappeared around the counter, and I felt misfitted to this bustling culture into which we had been jettisoned by one blood sample, blotches blossoming in my cheeks under a light bulging from the ceiling.

Heidi held a gray page torn from a tablet advertising a drug for one malady or another. "I don't know where Joe is, but I'll tell his secretary to let him know you're here."

Inside the room, I studied figures painted on the wall. Oversized coppery pennies and gray nickels were frozen in a tumble from an open coin purse into a smiling piggy bank, the front legs of which were hidden behind one of two maroon molded chairs backed against the wall. In the opposite corner was a striped hot air balloon painted on the ceiling and the two adjoining walls, surrounding anyone who stood in the corner, suspended forever in space, never to finish the flight.

The door opened, and I swung around, nearly falling into the place that seemed to have been saved for me, the chair I was avoiding. Dr. Malley followed Dr. Lourde into the room barely spacious enough to accommodate us. Her features characteristically stern, she hoisted herself onto the counter top.

"Mr. and Mrs. Petersen," Dr. Lourde began, "thank you for coming in today. I want you to think very seriously before you decide anything. Take all the time you need. Everything that happens from now on will be determined by this decision, and you will not be able to change it.

"First of all, you don't have to receive treatment here. You may elect to receive treatment at the university hospital instead."

"How would I know which is better?" I asked.

The stripes of the shirt on Dr. Lourde's shoulders seemed to slacken, as if, after loosing the first burst of air, they could hang naturally. "The treatment of cancer has set patterns to it based on what we know from past studies. There's really little difference between the recommended treatment options here and at the university. It's not unusual for us to share professional practices and opinions to treating cancer patients in hospitals all over the nation."

"Why are you asking us to choose if there aren't any differences?"

"Some patients develop a relationship with their doctor and follow him, or her," he added, dipping his head to Dr. Malley, "wherever they practice. I have a patient who now comes here even though she's 20 because she didn't want to change doctors. But since Jada's a new patient, you have that option to choose both a hospital and a doctor."

I said to Arnold, "I don't see the point of going elsewhere. The trips would take longer, especially with traffic."

There was a knock on the door. Heidi eased through in the same manner of her speaking, as if she were oiled for sliding between the partially-open door and the jamb. She remained wedged behind the examining table, standing with her arms crossed behind her as a sort of spring between herself and the wall.

Dr. Lourde turned back to us. "Then there's the issue of who will treat Jada. I'd be happy to be her doctor. But I would certainly understand if you wanted to continue treatment with Dr. Malley. Before I was hired, she treated all the childhood cancer patients."

Arnold venerated Dr. Malley and perceived a kinship with her that I did not. "Charlotte this" and "Charlotte that" he said in conversations. At our first meeting, I was introduced to Dr. Lourde as an obstacle in the way of Jada's well-being. But he showed no signs of holding that vision. On the contrary, he addressed mostly me, and I intuited that, regardless of his opinion of me, we had a chance of starting on more level ground by choosing him instead of being tossed into a slot, remaining locked up in the chamber beneath it, like the coins on the wall. "If it doesn't matter to you," I said to Arnold, who moved his jaw as if he had a wad of chewing gum tucked in his cheek, and then back to Dr. Lourde, "I'm fine with Dr. Lourde." Dr. Malley dropped her feet to the floor, and Heidi sprang to open the door for her unceremonious departure. I felt shed, as toxins flushed from a system.

Dr. Lourde waited for Heidi to close the door, and, crossing his legs, continued. "Now for the most important decision, and that is if you want to participate in a study treatment of leukemia prescribed by what they call a protocol. I report everything about Jada's case to a central research center, and they in turn use those results to determine the best way to treat cancer in the next study group." Dr. Lourde spoke slowly and carefully, rolling each word in a tight spiral, delectations aligned on a deli tray of information.

"The protocol I would follow calls for an intense induction period followed by maintenance and then observation. All that means is that we discontinue treatment but watch for signs of recurrence of the disease. They've found that if the disease is coming back, it usually happens in the first year after treatment has been stopped. Just recently the plan has been revised down to a shorter maintenance term."

"So are you saying that if Jada doesn't participate in this study she gets a different treatment? I want the treatment with the best chance of a cure."

Dr. Lourde stroked graying strands sneaking in at the edges of his mustache, as at his temples, and put his hand back onto the manila folder in his lap. "It isn't quite that simple. All treatments are experimental in nature and have about the same success rate. The main differences are in the frequency of administration and the combinations. I like this protocol because early indications are showing some remarkable success with adolescents. The older a person gets, the harder it is to knock leukemia out, but using this protocol, I think we have a better chance. Belonging to a study group helps to further research. Once you're in the group, you follow the protocol; otherwise we can't find out how well it works. Now, that doesn't mean that if something comes up we don't treat it. We report all the variances so they become factors to consider and we adapt treatment if we need to within the guidelines of the protocol."

Arnold shifted in his seat and cleared his throat, a habitual prelude to his speaking; hairs on my arms stood at attention. But Dr. Lourde stopped only for a breath.

"Right now, we say that Jada is in remission because there are no signs of cancer in Jada's bone marrow. That's because during the induction phase, we bombard the patient's system with high doses until there isn't a trace of cancer cells left. We can almost always induce remission in patients. What's tricky is maintaining remission. If all we did was to induce remission, the cancer cells would reappear within a few months and the patient would need to be induced again. Early cancer treatment looked like that until someone experimented with maintenance. People were dying because with each new induction, it became harder and harder to achieve remission. Cancer cells are pretty smart. They learn to hide from drugs, or they change so the drugs can't work on them anymore.

"The idea behind treating cancer is to extend induction drugs with less intensity so cancer cells have no place to breed. They're fast-reproducing cells, so the trick is to kill off those cells without killing off too many of the non-cancerous cells and allowing the patient to recover. Actually, we come dangerously close to killing the patient because good cells are eradicated along with the bad.

"Now, the reason for the observation period is that we don't really know if we've gotten every cancer cell. Jada is in what we call drug-induced remission." Dr. Lourde smoothed his mustache, bringing his thumb and index finger to the center and parting the hairs until he reached the ends and pulled his hand along the sides of his mouth. "We take samples from her blood and her bone marrow, and if there isn't the presence of cancer, we can say she is in remission. That doesn't mean that there are no cancer cells in her body; it means only that we don't see them. Cancer is funny; it can hide anywhere for the longest time, and all it takes is one cell. If the cancer shows up during the maintenance or observation periods, we believe that the cancer was never eradicated in the first place, and we have to try something more powerful. The danger, again, is how much can a body take if we've already tried the most powerful combination. So it's important to try to get the cancer the first time."

"Dr. Malley said Jada has a 50% chance of being cured of leukemia, the same as being hit by a bus." She'd reacted to my disappointment with a cloudy look as if I were a greedy child wanting more dessert instead of hope for a future for my daughter. "Exactly how do you know her chances?"

"One of the factors we must consider is surviving treatment itself. When we inject all these chemicals into the patient's body, we're leaving it without some of its own defenses and it becomes susceptible for a whole host of complications. For instance, a kind of pneumonia that commonly attacks leukemia patients is hard to treat, and we may have to interrupt treatment to fight it. More patients die of other diseases or complications while being treated for leukemia than they do of leukemia itself.

"We can come up with that number because we do have a study group. It used to be that leukemia in teenagers meant a grim future, but more and more are surviving. Now, I'm not talking about AML; there's almost no hope for a cure there. Those poor folks' best hope right now is to improve the quality of their lives, but in Jada's case, we looked at her age and her gender and how quickly we got at the disease. If she were older or a male, we wouldn't be able to say a number like 50%."

"Idina and I are both in education," Arnold said. "We believe in supporting a study and would gladly be a part of it. And if you ever need anyone to speak about it, we'd both be available. But I have a couple questions. We were planning a trip to San Diego this summer, and now with Jada having leukemia and being in this study, will she be able to travel?"

"I don't see why not."

"Is it okay for her to be so far away? What would we do if something should happen?"

"Just what you'd do if she didn't have leukemia. She shouldn't have any restrictions placed on her just because she has leukemia. I think traveling is good, and if something comes up, go to a hospital, and they'll treat her. If they need to call me, they can.

"That brings up another issue. I understand that Dr. Silverman has been your doctor for a long time. He's very well-respected, and I don't want to interfere with your relationship with him. However, now that I'm in charge of treating Jada's leukemia, I will also be in charge of her other health concerns. Dr. Silverman knows a lot about diabetes, and I won't change what he's doing, but in Jada's case, I would have treated the diabetes differently. He disagrees with me on that, but there's some research to support that high doses of Prednisone can bring on diabetes-like symptoms. It's my guess that, as the dosage of Prednisone decreases, so will the high count of blood sugar."

Arnold moved his jaw and rasped his throat, pulling out a collection of papers from a folder. "Jada has had to stay in the house more now and I'd like a letter from you saying that because of her leukemia she needs to be comfortable, so I can take the cost of installing an air conditioning system off our taxes."

"Sure, I can do that. Heidi, why don't you get a copy of the schedule of treatment for Mr. and Mrs. Petersen, and then set up a time for Jada's first appointment. If there's nothing else, I'll leave these papers here for you to sign. They're stating that you agree to follow the protocol and that we may use all the data on Jada's treatment for study purposes. Heidi will be with you in a minute, and she can answer any other questions you have. Good-bye."

Heidi glided out the door before Dr. Lourde finished his leave-taking, leaving Arnold and me to each other. He lifted a page and signed his name on the second. How easily reduced to a page and a half was Jada's life. My shoulders slumped with resignation as I signed my name, the second time I'd autographed her future. Weeks earlier I signed a document releasing the hospital, the doctors, and the pharmaceutical companies from future litigation should Jada become unable to produce children. The reproductive system is very delicately balanced, and what was going through Jada's body could corrupt it. Arnold shot his arm up in a kind of salute to look at his watch. "That's all this was? He made it sound that it was going to take hours."

The door opened to the sound of swishing cotton on Heidi's marshmallow thighs rubbing together. She set a black notebook on the counter and opened to a page blocked off into squares. "This is the schedule Jada will follow. She'll come in to the clinic for all examinations and procedures, including IVs." She pointed to the first block. "We'll start with ARA-C; that's the orange colored one." Her pointed finger moved falling hair behind her ear as she turned from the page to my face. "You'll probably want to come in early in the day for these. Some patients don't get sick at all; usually when they do, they get sick a few hours after the drug is inside them, so it's easier if they get sick before going to bed. We send patients down to the lab for blood counts and Dr. Lourde will do an examination. Then it takes a couple hours to run the IV. Leah Cantú is our Child Life Specialist. She'll come by with some games or things so you have something to do while you're here."

I stepped back; Arnold tucked his hands together between his knees and craned his neck to see the open notebook. "Dr. Malley said that kids come in for treatment and then go to school afterwards," I said. "Now you're telling me that Jada will be here for a pretty big chunk of the day."

"Well," Heidi drawled, "that's true for some of the younger ones. They don't get as much because of their size, and it's not so stressful for them. Once the IV is in, they forget all about it, and when it's out, they're on to the next thing. For the older ones, it varies. You'll just have to see what's best for you. Have you met Debbie? Once in a while she'll check into the hospital for treatment in the afternoon and then lets the hospital staff take care of her during the night. She goes to a community college and doesn't want to miss classes."

I nodded, knowing I didn't understand, but also knowing that I didn't know enough of what I didn't know to ask about. "Do you want a copy of this?" Heidi asked, pulling apart the metal rings. "Then you'll know which drug is next. There was a longer period of time between induction and maintenance because of Jada's radiation, so we'll adjust it for that." I nodded again. "Can you come in around 1:00 on Monday? We have lunch by then, but we don't always get it on time, so it won't matter if you're late. Just come in and someone will be here." Heidi gently brought the cover down, closing the notebook as if she were in a room of sleeping babies.

Heidi, whether she was aware or not, had given us a warning, but we would not know, ourselves, how profound was her understatement. Jada indeed wasn't "a little one" who could be distracted by a dangling doodad.

Summer was anything but a vacation. I did teach Summer School, and we did fly to San Diego, and Jada did make maintenance therapy her own. She wasn't able to adjust dosages or rearrange spacing or mode of administration. Not that she wouldn't have if she had had the power. No. She exerted her power in ways only she could. Clinic visits were preceded by a blood draw in the outpatient lab, which she resisted and delayed by walking the hall. We came in upon another patient receiving a draw, and Jada darted out. Every time after that, I was sent as a scout to assure her that the lab was clear. The technician, new or familiar, needed a reminder of how Jada wanted her blood sampled: a finger stick only.

Then, afterwards, the intravenous administration of a drug, the most careful probing for her vein almost certainly caused a tearful and venomous reaction. As did the size of the needle. If a smaller one would deliver—or extract—fluid, she asked, why would a doctor use a larger one that hurt more as it was inserted? And, since alcohol left wet on the skin caused more stinging as the needle punctured the vein, she repeatedly requested time to let the alcohol dry. Too many probes, difficulty making a clean insertion, swelling at the point of insertion: nothing, except for the occasional spinal tap, seemed to go smoothly, not that any part of chemotherapy could on the most placid of patients. Certainly not the whole-body sickness and the vomiting it caused when everyone was way-long gone home. And placid Jada was not. That she voiced definite opinions about how she wanted to receive treatment, directly, or indirectly through her reluctance to proceed until they were addressed, or to viscerally react with revulsion to them, made her appear to be, if not just difficult to treat, downright unpleasant.

Jada withdrew her hand when Dr. Lourde had trouble finding a usable vein for the IV, leaving him with a needle in his. "Jada," he warned, "I'm not going to wait here to do this."

"Then do it right," she retorted, with piercing blue eyes, extending her arm.

"I admire your insistence for competence, Jada. But you have a way of making people nervous when you demand perfection. When we get nervous, we don't do as well. Heidi, get me another alcohol packet, will you please?" Heidi tore open the foil pac and went to the other side, bringing her hand down to Jada's arm as if she were resting it on a feathery pillow.

Dr. Lourde swabbed again. Then he fanned the alcohol dry. "I remember, Jada. I'll be as careful as I can."

"Ow, ow, ow, ow, ow! Hurry. You're not being very fast. You said you'd hurry!" She jerked her knee upwards. Heidi hovered, one hand on Jada, the other cocked to act.

"Almost done, Jada. Be still so we get it done right," Dr. Lourde said. "Okay, tape, Heidi? It's in fine, but watch the angle; it doesn't want to set the way I want it to."

"Ow, ow, ow! It better be right 'cause you're not doing it again!"

"It's okay, Jada. I just like to be careful. I'm sorry we have to do this, Jada." Dr. Lourde whispered some last instructions to Heidi as he released the tube hanging out of Jada's hand like a snake whose fangs were locked in its prey, and examined the large syringe of cloudy liquid Heidi would inject into the plastic cylinder. He washed his hands and stood at the table long enough to say, "Okay, Jada, see ya." Heidi began trimming and slicing lengthwise into a paper cup to fashion a cap over the hump of needle and tape protruding from the back of Jada's hand.

Jada wrinkled her nose and clucked her tongue, swallowing noisily. "Want some gum to get rid of that metallic taste?" Heidi offered.

"No, it doesn't work."

"Some 7-Up? Are you warm enough? Leah should be around pretty soon."

I dragged forth a plastic chair. "I brought a book. Want me to read it to you?"

"No. I just want to rest."

Leah, whose acrylic badge was labeled "Child Life," knocked at the door, and cradling a stack of magazines in her arm, pushed the door all the way open. Her knock on the door was supposed to mean fun. "Hi, Jada. Want a magazine? Let's see, I've got *Seventeen*, *TEEN*, oh, some others I don't suppose you'd be interested in."

"Are they the same ones as last month?"

"I'm afraid so. Sorry. I can get you a puzzle if you want."

"It's too hard to do that stuff with this." Flat on her back, Jada looked at Leah over her arm bound to a splint, the cup atop the needle like a fish house on a frozen lake. "Do you have any kids' toys?"

"I can see what's around. Most of the stuff is pretty basic. Dialing and pushing buttons."

"It's too hard to think with this, anyway. You should get some things for older kids."

"I haven't seen a whole lot for you older ones. But then, my training is for the littler tots. Maybe Meg will know of something. I'll go scouting around for something, Jada."

Heidi returned with a Dixie cup and handed it to Jada. "I know, kinda small, isn't it?" She rounded the table and twisted the cylinder of medicine, checking the settings. "Are you doing okay?"

"No, of course not. How long is this going to take? It hurts."

"I'm sorry, Jada." Heidi said thoughtfully, "I can't really speed this one up because your body wouldn't react very well if it got too much at a time. But I can try to increase the drip after it. It's a little more uncomfortable, but it's faster." Heidi gave a sincere look of sympathy to Jada, who lay stone-faced. Silence filled the room like a paralyzing gas, numbing our senses and power to help each other. Heidi swayed and left the room, closing the door behind her. Yes, she could leave sorry behind; but I didn't begrudge her that. It was sorry I hated for its sorry aftertaste.

Mid-summer, we had met Debbie, and by the time we did, we suspected that what prompted Debbie to be admitted to the hospital for treatment was less for convenience and more for aid. After a day at the clinic and before the drug's expected effect, I drew Jada a bath. We both luxuriated in the moistness and the celebration of privacy after the exposure of examination and manipulation. The ringing of the telephone brought me out of my reclusion.

"That was Heidi," I said, bringing a puff of cool air back in with me. Jada lay in the bathtub, swishing soap bubbles over her body. The toilet seat creaked as I sat on the lid. "She's trying to get you to go to the group tomorrow night."

"You know I don't like that. I wouldn't do anything with them if it weren't for this disease," Jada replied.

"That's the point. They want you to feel you're not alone. They want you to be able to talk to others who have the same things going on with them."

"Most of the kids are little. When Debbie isn't there, all I do is sit around while the younger kids play. What do I have to say to a six-year-old, anyway? Why do they think that just because we have a disease that makes us alike?"

To meet Debbie, a thin young woman with a gaunt face and hard eyes behind large-framed glasses, was the reason Jada agreed to go to a support group for children with a life-threatening illness, while a similar support group met for the parents and caregivers to these children. Nineteen, maybe twenty, Debbie had relapsed treatment of leukemia; and for her to discuss the consequences with such obvious novitiates as we may have broken the skin of her own perseverance. She knew the one bandit cancer cell that hid out on her and her doctors like an outlaw in the canyon and waited with wily patience to ambush her system's posse at the pass. Debbie had been new once, herself, and if she could remember what it was like to be us, then we could be in her place, some day. I was stepping into a mirror, knowing the only passageway out was through more mirrors.

"I don't like those parent meetings myself," I commiserated. "There's something about flaunting your problems that disturbs me. I also think that Heidi wants you to go because of your anger today. If you talk about how you hate treatment to others, you won't take it out on her and Dr. Lourde."

I crossed my legs and leaned back against the sweaty tank, and it felt cool through my sticky shirt. Jada squeezed the washcloth between two hands, the fingers closing around it like a spider trying to get its legs around a wide-winged moth. "You're a very strong-willed person. I like that, but it makes it hard sometimes to get you to do things, and sometimes you gotta do things even when you don't want to."

Jada grabbed the side of the tub and sat up. I filled cups of warm clear water and poured them, the water cascading over bones bumping out of her papery thin skin in a waterfall. Although much of the hair on her scalp had fallen out, she was growing fine wisps of soft pubic hair. Her nipples looked like brown caps of little mountains dripping with melting snow. She had not begun to menstruate, and she was warned that she may not follow a regular pattern. I wrapped Jada in a large towel and blotted her warm skin. She resumed, "I like Heidi and Marilyn, but they don't really seem to know what to do with the group, either. I'd rather be with my real friends."

"You know, Jada, I think you're right. There's a lot of talk about how adolescents with diseases are such a special group. But what do they do for you that's specialized? They lumped you together with babies and little kids in the hospital and now it's the same in the support group. Looks to me like they're saying one thing and doing another."

"When I grow up—if I grow up—I want to be the person who runs the hospital. I could run it so much better. Do you see how much stuff they waste? They don't even need half the stuff they pack in those spinal tap kits and then they throw everything away, even if it hasn't been used. That's terrible! No wonder the world is in the mess it is. All those chemicals. Where are they going?" She balanced, holding onto the vanity top while I lifted her foot and dabbed between her toes. "Maybe I don't want to grow up. The world will be so messed up, I don't know if I want to live in it."

"Jada," I said, clenching the towel, "that's exactly why you *do* need to live. We need people who care and who think about what we do and how it affects us and the next generations. I hope you grow up. You ask good questions and seek solutions." I squirted lotion onto my hands and warmed it to swathe her neck to toes in the slippery pink film.

"But you're the only one who listens. Even Dad doesn't. When he came to the hospital after school he went to the cafeteria and got a cup of coffee and then sat in the big chair and took a nap. When he woke up he read the newspaper, and then he had to go home and have dinner." The last of the bath water gurgled down the drain, leaving behind an island of weak bubbles on the floor of the tub. Muffled by the nightie being pulled over her head, Jada said, "Why don't you just get a divorce? You don't love each other, anyway."

"My mother put up with more than I knew, just to keep the family together no matter what, so she said. I guess I'm like her in that way. Besides, I wouldn't want to leave my children, so I think it would be hard for your dad to leave you, too."

"See? That's your own fault. Jada rolled her eyes. "You and Grandma Pope. I don't think you're like her at all. You're always worried about other people. You don't talk back to Grandma so you don't hurt her feelings. Dried, soothed, and dressed for bed, Jada opened the bathroom door, the cool air raising goosebumps. "When they're wrong, they're wrong. I'm not going to stay quiet," she said as she left.

Rinsing the tub and hanging the washcloth on the bar to dry, I felt the front door slam, rattling the wooden crossbars inserted into plastic brackets, creating the illusion of panes in the front windows. Dom was home.

"What's the score?" he called downstairs to his dad. After a pause, he yelped. "Awesome!" Thump, thump, thump. We met at the top of the steps. "Hey, Mom. Are there any cookies left?"

"Yes. You just made it in time. I was beginning to worry about you. How many have you had already today?"

"Only one. Remember, Jerry called and I didn't get to finish my whole snack. So that means I can have three." He looked at me askance, his long black lashes batting coquettishly.

"How do you figure that? New math?"

Somebody once said his eyelashes were much too beautiful to be wasted on a boy. "Two?"

"Sure. Go wash up. I'll pour some milk. Want it in a cup or a glass?"

"A cup. Two big ones. Thanks, Mom. We're gonna win, we're gonna score; da da da da da, watch that baseball so-AR!" Dom sang from the bathroom.

"Don't you know the words to the song, yet, Dom? You watch baseball enough." Jada shouted from her bedroom at the end of the hall, to which Dom rang out a louder second chorus.

"Okay, we get the point. Now, remember, you're just washing up to eat. Are you taking a bath or a shower?" He had never liked food on his face and insisted on a washcloth even in his highchair, but he never seemed to mind sporting the dirt he accumulated from playing outdoors, and getting him to bathe required several warnings and some negotiation. He looked crestfallen as he came out to his spot at the table. "Oh, Ma. Do I have to? I could shower in the morning. I promise."

"No, Mom, don't let him. Dom, do what Mom says."

"Be quiet, Jada. Mom and I are talking." With wide eyes Dom admired the cookies on his plate and doused one in the pool of white milk.

"Yes, we are," I added. "And no, you can't wait till morning. You're all sweaty from playing outside. Do you want to find out what inning it is and then decide? A shower is quicker. You could get one in right now and be done with it." I let the idea linger with Dom, though probably he replaced it with his own.

"You shouldn't let Dom go downstairs," Jada said when I joined her in her room. "He knows how to get what he wants." Because she was here first, Jada was not about to allow him room on her blanket, categorizing him as a spoiled little brother who made wrinkles in the smooth operation of life as she spread it out.

"What, my little Dommy? He's so kind and gentle."

"Hmph! He's not as sweet and innocent as you think. There are a lot of things about Dom you don't know. Don't forget, you left us together in the morning, and he's not so kind and gentle then."

"Maybe it's because of the way you treat him. "Dom might not do what you want him to do, but remember, he doesn't like to be bossed around any more than you. He has one mother; that's enough."

"He wouldn't do anything if I didn't make him. You let him get away with too much. And Dad! He doesn't even try to make him do anything. Dom says no and Dad just walks away. If I didn't make Dom take a shower, he wouldn't."

I was sympathetic for Dom, a teddy bear, and defended his easy-going ways. Though different, neither child was more tractable than the other. Every one of Jada's outrages was out in the open, displayed with equal brilliance, like primary colors reflecting the bright sun. As awful as it was when Jada fought treatment in the hospital, I feared how Dom might respond were he a victim of such a formidable disease. Dom would probably brood, turn as dark as his skin and hair color, make us have to dig.

My head bobbed as the fluid from the sac dripped into Jada's vein and Heidi came in noiselessly, checking flow, releasing more until the bag was empty. We had begun the spring with numbers to drive us: 50-50 chance, three years of treatment, 9.8 hemoglobin, one and one-half white pills everyday, two green ones three days a week, one yellow for five days only, four ounces of skim milk, wait two hours, decrease three ccs of insulin and call before seven with the blood sugar count. We were enfolded, routinized, not yet veterans, but no longer new when the school year started. I thought about Debbie, how she had changed in appearance over the summer. Hollows rimmed her eyes, sinking them further into her face. She stood hunched, as if a boulder had been placed between her shoulder blades. The hump pushed her head down into a landslide to her chest, making her angular chin into a spear. What numbers did she have to juggle?

Sometimes we were done and out of the clinic by two, other times not until four, always a full school day. At eight or nine or ten, the cramping and the vomiting started. My arms around Jada's middle, I held Jada as she knelt over the toilet and spewed into the bowl. She tried a patch behind the ear and still retched. She didn't like the way the marijuana beads made her woozy. Besides, she still cramped. IV nights all ended the same.

Mornings after, no matter how late we'd been up or how light-headed Jada felt, or how queasy was her stomach, she and I reappeared at our schools. One of Jada's classmates remarked, "Oh, you're so lucky. You get to miss school. I wish I could." An assistant principal asked me if I enjoyed my day off.

We were sucked up and swallowed into chemotherapy, and whatever bands looped about us when Jada was diagnosed became more taut. When she took a breath at the clinic, I breathed. When she threw up, I gagged. Our friends and families sent flowers and cards and then went on with their lives, regardless of ours, just as Jada and I went on, regardless of Debbie's. And then, one day, because we hadn't seen her, we asked about Debbie, wondering how and where she was. Heidi's answer came like a warning, like the tornado that just missed us: Debbie had relapsed again and died. That kind of news was not circulated at the clinic. If it happened to Debbie, couldn't it also happen to Jada? To another little girl, someone else's daughter?

Nov 23

I've been sick for a super duper long time. I wasted half the summer lying in bed! And now this fall I still haven't felt good. My counts were so low Dr. Lourde took me off meds for a week. That was like a vacation. No headache or stomachache. I still can't walk right. My foot will be bad as long as I'm on maintenance. I think the medicines keep me from being able to play the piano, too. I tried but I didn't have the agility. I wanted to start volleyball, but it would never have worked. I can't even run. I hate that I can't do anything or if I do it looks funny! I hate that I'm sick all the time. My stomach hurts all the time, worse than the 6-MP kind. I have a cold and cough. It keeps me awake hacking at night. Yuck! Yuck! Yuck! Well, one good thing. I went to the ballet Swan Lake with Kathy Davis, my fourth grade teacher. The dancers were amazing, especially the swan. She moved her arms like they were wings.

I read The Pistachio Prescription and I liked it as much as The Cat Ate My Gym suit. My French teacher gave me a Toblerone for speaking French to our visitor. Mom and I help at the Eucharist program and I ran the projector but she left me there and I wasn't sure when to play a song. Sometimes she asks me to do too much and it makes me want to scream at her! She does so much for me but I still get an urge to hit her and I don't know why. I know I wouldn't get through this without her. I must have something wrong with me. It's hard to get older. Mom says that a lot. Maybe that's all it is. I think something is wrong with me though.

I go for Cytoxin tomorrow. That I.V. is the worst one. It takes a long time and makes me throw up. Last time I threw up everything in my stomach and tried to throw up three more times but there was nothing left. I detest that feeling! Ne vomir plus! I dread going. Last time they stuck me four times before they got the I.V. right! I was furious and could have killed them and everyone else! I feel that way now. Never again! I've had all I can handle. Hambone is the only one who helps me through. I'm tired and scared and sick and mad. Another thing that I'm mad at is I have to go to the clinic and get sick when Jill is having a birthday party sleepover. Meds always ruin my life!! I'm missing three important tests and some painting and an assignment in science. I worry about missing school and getting bad grades. I hate getting behind and then I have to get everything together when I come back. HORRIBLE describes this disease!!! I detest this disease and I hate that it's ruining my life. I'm sick of being sick and I'm sick of living. It's just not worth it!!

"Bitch!" Hambone bounced off my raised arm, the red ribbon with black-hatted chubby snow figures springing summersaults and holding onto upended brooms through the air flying with him. Jada had thrown him at me and now he tumbled end over end like the little figures he wore for the Christmas season. We were ahead of Christmas. We had made Christmas cookies. I mixed the dough; Jada decorated. I signed the Christmas cards; she addressed them. I licked the envelopes; she licked the stamps. Jada cross-stitched ornaments and wrapped lollipops in calico to hang on trees; and I sewed paperback book covers and Christmas mouse doorknob covers. We sold our crafts at gift shops and a craft fair. I purchased the supplies; she kept the books.

We worked better together. Mostly.

"Get out of here!" she screamed at me in the examination room with the sheep painted white and black on the wall, a riddle about their getting a hair cut at the baa baa shop swirling around their hooves. We were waiting for Dr. Lourde, waiting for chemo; and waiting gave Jada time to think of what was to come.

Hambone had hit his mark, and I stood holding him next to my stomach, my mouth an open till waiting for someone to dig in and pull out the exact words in change. With all the words in the English language to choose from, I could find none to make the right combination. "Why did you do that?" Heidi watched, stiff, eyes holding steady.

Outside the clinic, Jada acted as any other thirteen-year-old daughter would, I thought. I bought little surprises for her; she wrote me notes of affection. I sewed for her: I selected the pattern, she picked the fabric. She tidied my records; I advised her writing. We went shopping together, she choosing the clothing, I granting approval. I slept in her bed, like a sleepover companion. We went to movies together, maintained our ritual when she bathed.

We were melding, mixed together and poured out into two equal portions; even as she grew apart from me and tested her adolescent independence, she grew back into me, and together, we completed each other. She had the vision, I had the mission; she had the dream, I had the determination; she had the picture, I had the words. Our shadows of each other became more difficult to determine. But when we went into the clinic, it was Jada who lay on the table and I who sat in the chair. It was Jada who got punctured and I who stood by the side. It was Jada who had leukemia and I who did not. That reality severed us not only from each other but in some ways from our selves who had become like the other. Once whole with each other, we became in the clinic not even whole with ourselves. When Jada was in the clinic for treatment, she was a part and I was a part; apart, we magnified each other's missing parts.

Walking me out of the clinic and into the lobby of the hospital, Heidi began speaking, her voice gaining resonance as words bloomed from her lips. "Jada is a very willful person. She has a right to be angry, but I think she's manipulating you when she screams and gives orders to you."

I was bundled in my winter jacket, on my way to bringing the car to the other side of the large windows that grew white mountains of frozen moisture condensed with the sunlight, illuminating the panes of glass like a smeared movie screen. "I can't make her stop being angry."

The sun glinted in Heidi's eye, turning it into a kaleidoscope of brown and gold and green, but she looked squarely at me as I went on. "I think Jada has to be angry; it's her self-proclamation. Her disease is forcing her to change her life, to change it unnaturally. She doesn't see that all these chemicals are good for her. It all just hurts. It interrupts her life, makes her sick. It takes away her feeling of control. It's no wonder all the anger in her explodes. All month long she's pretending to lead a normal life, and then, wham, she gets here and what happens tells her she's not normal and there's nothing she can do about it. At home at least she could slam a door. For you or for me, finding out we have no control may not be such a revelation. We're asking a thirteen-year-old to accept a pretty mature idea. She doesn't believe she's going to live through it all anyway. So, yes, you're right, her anger has rein."

"But, she's too willful; she has too much freedom. Her belligerence gets in the way of treatment. We can't help her if she won't cooperate." Heidi's silky voice contrasted with her sandpaper words.

"What do you expect when you say, 'Go ahead and be angry' to her. But you want me to make her cooperate. She's not seven or eight, sitting at the piano refusing to practice. Laying down the law to a 13-year-old getting painful and sickening medication is quite different. I can't hold her legs and her feet and her head and her arms and make her put her hand out for the IV needle.

"Jada is forced to be dependent on me at an age when she is supposed to be growing into independence. One day I'm encouraging her to have a voice and then when we get here, she's supposed to be quiet and compliant, keep that voice underneath the surface so you guys don't have to put up with it? She doesn't plan to come here and make a scene. But then we get here, here, where she hates what's happening to her, and she acts out her anger."

Heidi tilted her head, and the wry line of her lips remained unchanged.

Water slithered down along the bumpy bone of my back and tickled my skin. I tightened my shoulders, would liked to have told her what it was like for a child asked to grow old and not grant the old person the right to say no, "don't do this to my body when I don't want it"; and what it was like for the youth in her to be pushed back into childhood, to believe in myths, good over evil, happy endings. "I have to go; Jada will be wondering what happened to me."

Heidi returned a steady gaze before touching the sleeve of my coat. "I'll go get Jada. Take care." That was Heidi's signature, extracted from the peace-loving flower generation of the 70s. Take care. Of what? A second earlier she was telling me to take charge. It was all too hard to figure out what I was supposed to do.

Walking out to my car, I categorized each person in the clinic, trying to figure out how to deal with them so they'd deal with Jada. There was Bethany, enigmatic Bethany, who seemed to be separate from the rest of the nurses. Her shiny, lacquered-looking straight black hair cut to fall in bangs to her eyebrows and to the tips of her ears, swung in rhythm to her movements. Each strand seemed to come back to where it belonged, framing a porcelain face, effecting a severe look, Chinese style: white face, deep brown eyes and red lips. She moved differently, too. Sure of herself, rhythmically. She said hello, but she didn't talk like old high school friends.

Other nurses treated our visits to the clinic as if we were neighbors, dropping over for a cup of coffee. We never really made appointments with Heidi. She told us to "just come in" if Jada needed to. We picked a day for treatment, but she gave us good times and bad times, not *a* time. Sometime during our visit, Leah, the Child Life Specialist popped in to say hello; as soon as she found out I liked to cook, she spent more attention asking about recipes, especially for kids to cook in the clinic than on finding activity for Jada.

Marilyn specialized in home care visits, and it was through her we met Amy Kill before she died of a brain tumor, though only Marilyn used the word dying. Marilyn knew what people needed. Not just TVs and videos and hand-held games, but inside things. Marilyn listened to what Jada didn't say, understood when she called me "Bitch" in one breath and in another clutched me for dear life. On a rare occasion, it was Marilyn who brought in Jada's counts. "I miss seeing you, so I thought I'd bring these in and see how you're doing," she reported through a smile. It was a smile I trusted. Marilyn gave Jada's knee a little jiggle as she bent her head.

"I'm okay. Except I gotta get Vincristine today. I don't like that stuff."

"Pretty bad, hunh?" Marilyn's crinkled yellow hair fell forward, hiding her eyes and freckled cheek. "How's school for you? It's a big place."

"It's okay, except for phy. ed. She expects me to do everything everyone else does. I tell her I can't do those things, but she says to try anyway. She's mean." Marilyn smiled. "If it weren't for her, I'd have all A's. I can't run. My legs aren't strong enough."

"I didn't like running, either. I wish I did, though. Maybe I wouldn't look like this." Marilyn stepped back and spread her arms out to show a figure softly padded around the hips and waist. "My daughter is only nine, and they've already got her on a swimming team. You have to start young."

"But, Jada, you requested regular phy. ed.," I interjected. "Now she's holding you to her expectations."

I exchanged a knowing look with Marilyn, who sighed. "Gotta go, Jada. Want me to tell them anything out there?"

"No, just that I'm tired of waiting for Joe. Where does he go off to?"

Marilyn sobered while retaining her smile. "Oh, he's very busy. When he has patients upstairs, he gets called a lot. He's very thorough. If Chelsea were sick, I'd trust him, and believe me, I've worked with some people I don't know if I would. I'm going that way by his office. I'll see if anyone back there knows where he is, okay?" With a wink of her eye and a twink of Jada's jeans, Marilyn was out the door.

"It's about time," Jada said to Dr. Lourde when he and Heidi came into the room. "Did Marilyn find you?"

"Marilyn? McKuen? No. Was I supposed to see her?" He looked quizzically at Heidi as he lathered his hands with soap under the faucet.

Jada shook her head in bewilderment. "And the other thing is," she went on, "how come the faucets are funny? They're all missing a piece. I looked. Here this is a brand new building and something's wrong with it already."

While drying his hands, Dr. Lourde dipped his head to look. "I don't know, Jada. I never noticed that."

Heidi, locked in the center of the room, said, "Those were taken out by maintenance before you came, Joe. They explained it to us, and I'm trying to remember it all. Um...I think germs collect in the washers, and when the water goes through there, the germs grow and...." Heidi spoke with bumps, not her normally wrinkle-free flow of words.

"I didn't notice that up in the rooms," I questioned. "Why do germs matter here and not there?"

"There's no explaining what goes on in hospitals," rejoined Dr. Lourde. "Heidi, did you order a size 22 needle for Jada?" He visually riffled through the assortment of equipment on the turquoise tray for the hair-thin needle Jada had requested to replace the larger one.

"It should be there. I can get another one if it isn't." She crowded in and began searching the packages, each filled with sterilized cellophane-wrapped objects. "Here it is."

In the silence of Dr. Lourde's probing under Jada's chin and down her neck, Heidi splashed water over her lathered hands. She had explained to us how she washed bar soap before even using it to remove the germs on its surface. Over and over and over the soap revolved in her hands as it produced fluffy puffy mittens of large foamy bubbles. "Have you noticed any changes or have any concerns, Mrs. Petersen?"

"No." I turned to Jada for verification, "Jada hasn't mentioned anything different." Heidi and Dr. Lourde, their preparations made, gathered about Jada.

"Do you want to move your bear?"

"It's not a bear." Jada pushed Hambone's head from under her chin, proof of his species.

"Oh, that's right. What is it? I can never remember."

Jada pursed her lips. "You never remember anything. It's a pig."

"That's right. And what's its name? Jawbone?"

"Hambone. And do it low."

"I am starting to remember that. Okay, I'm ready; hold still, Jada." I held my breath as Jada squeezed Hambone. I was silent by agreement, Dr. Lourde by concentration. As Dr. Lourde waited for the fluid to drip into the vial, he said, "I've taken the liberty to talk about you to Dr. Drake Bradley. He's an adolescent psychologist on staff. I think he can help you manage your pain."

"What do you mean, manage my pain? If something hurts, it hurts."

"Well." He continued quickly. "Pain is just as much in the mind as it is in the body. Your mind is a powerful tool. You're letting your body tell your mind what to do; that's why all this hurts so much. You don't have to let it control you if you can get your mind to take control over your pain." He turned to me. "Have you heard of Dr. Bernie Stein? He's beginning to get a following for his work on the power of the patient in a doctor-patient relationship. I think, Jada, that's an issue you're concerned about. Heidi, do you remember the name of his book?"

"Mmm, Love? *Love Medicine*, I think."

"It's probably not in our library because it's so new. I understand, Mrs. Petersen, that you've taken some materials from the library, so I gather you're interested in reading as a way to get information. I'm sure you could get it from the public library or a bookstore. Okay, Jada, done." Dr. Lourde capped the vial and set it in its nest for the lab while Heidi tore tape and he readied for the IV.

The needle securely in Jada's vein and her teeth ground together for the first flush of fluid, Dr. Lourde tossed the used gloves into the trash container and said, "Heidi will set up the appointment with Drake for next time. Anything else?"

Jada looked beyond him, seeing perhaps a spot, perhaps nothing, and I nodded my head in agreement to Dr. Lourde's departure as Heidi dropped the used syringe into the plastic receptacle. Large orange print warned that it contained bio-hazardous waste, suggesting nuclear reactors and underground storage sites. I imagined mounds of dead needles and syringes coated with lethal chemicals, the contents of one enough to kill for a month, buried about the countryside, contaminating the water, being sucked up through roots. The implications for saving one life were daunting.

Heidi returned to Jada's side, laying her hand on Jada's upraised knee, and seeing Jada make a little shiver, asked, "Are you warm enough? I can warm up some blankets in the microwave." Jada's chin nodded up and down in nibbling movements, sending Heidi off on her mission.

Heidi returned with folded white blankets draping her arms. While she opened each one, spreading them over Jada like layers of whipped cream, Jada asked, "Have you ever been on his boat?"

Heidi straightened. "Whose? Joe's?" Jada nodded.

"No."

"Have you ever seen it?"

"No, I haven't Jada. But I understand it's quite nice. Why?"

"Oh, I was just wondering what he was like outside the clinic."

Heidi's eyes turned upwards in thought, and spoke with characteristic care. "Joe doesn't socialize with us or do things like go to the doctors' lounge. He really likes his boat, and he goes out on it whenever he can."

Jada nodded. Heidi waited, not seeming to be in a hurry to get somewhere else, though, certainly, she had places to go, until a sufficient time had passed for her to ease out of Jada's need. Jada and I waited for the slow drip that I hoped bought her another month.

And so the bargain had been made; we walked through November as guests. November, when the wind wags its finger in admonition to get the winter wraps out. Courageous brashly painted leaves of October, finally vanquished, are yanked away by brawny-fisted gusts and banished to decay to moldy mush. Bare, brown, battered. Poor November, a strip-mined month wedged between two intensities. A month of mortality, before pure white newly-fallen snow covers it up and brings Christmas with it.

Christmas and Jada were made for each other. Every year I added to growing a tradition, setting shoes out for St. Nicholas to fill, baking fruitcakes, cookies, breads, and pies, leftovers stored in the freezer almost as long as the brittle wind-worn wreath on the front door, leaving extra cookies and milk for Santa. Stockings hanging near the mantel overflowed, and boxes of games and books and jewels lay at the edge of the fireplace as if it were a giant marble piñata burst of its goodies. All this preparation was done with joy and given with joy. Christmas brought joy to the face of leukemia.

But Christmas brought no relief from the dreaded treatment of leukemia. After our Christmas celebration, we waited for Drake Bradley in a hospital room. The psychologist brought a faint musky scent with him. "Hi, Jada, I'm here to help so it won't hurt as much next time you get an IV."

"What are you going to do? Make the needle go in right the first time? Make the stuff not burn?" Dangling her legs, she sat on the examining table and stared back at him.

"No, I want you to learn some things so you don't have to feel the pain. Here, let me show you. Where are some special places you like to be? By a lake somewhere? At a beach?"

"Ooouu," Jada made a disgusting face. "All those bugs. Ick."

Dr. Drew considered. "What kinds of things do you like to do?"

"Well, I used to like skating, but I can't do that anymore, not since I got this disease. They said I could, but they didn't think I needed my leg muscles to do it."

Cinched tight, Dr. Drew's necktie danced when he spoke. "What else? Do you have a collection? Something you like to read about?"

Jada looked at me and scrunched her nose. "I don't really read a lot. My dad has a stamp collection for me."

The doctor paused, suppressing a sigh. "I'm looking for something you do that takes your mind off things. Something you do that gives you pleasure. What do you do when you have time to yourself?"

"I bug my mom." Jada smiled.

"What do you do with your mom?"

Jada thought. "We talk, go places. She takes me shopping."

"And you like that? Where do you go shopping?"

"Northpointe, mostly."

"So Northpointe must be your favorite place to go shopping, and when you're shopping you're so engrossed you don't think of anything else."

"No, my favorite place is Baker's in Nokomis."

Dr. Bradley shifted feet. He appeared fit but somewhat square in build, or at least bottom-weighted, like one of those inflatable plastic figures you bop with your fist and it will rock backwards but come back upright again. "Okay. When you go shopping, what's your favorite floor?"

Jada shrugged and brought one corner of her mouth down. "I don't know, what floors do we go to, Mom? Fifth? Where's the Oval Room?"

"Um, second? Third?"

"We go a lot of places. Shoes. They're in different places."

Dr. Bradley felt for his watch; he would never make a good shopper. "All right. Now I want you to close your eyes and imagine you're at Baker's."

"Why?"

"It'll be easier for you to do this with your eyes closed. Okay? Close your eyes. Your mom can do it, too. Do you take the escalator or the elevator when you shop?"

"Both. It depends."

"Okay, put yourself on the elevator. You've just come into Baker's and you're on the first floor. You get on the elevator. Can you see yourself in the elevator? The elevator door opens and you're on the second floor. What do you see when the door opens? Do you want to get out? Then the door closes and you go up to the third floor." He paused at each floor, gave us time to envision the scene. Every time the elevator doors opened for me, I saw the same display shelf, two white drawers at the base and glass shelving stacked with folded baby garments. I wondered if Jada saw different images as the doors parted, or if she, like me, faced a frozen picture that blocked rather than invited me into it. He continued, "The door opens; imagine all the things on this floor."

We rode up and up, stopping at floor four, then 5, 6, and still Dr. Bradley invited her to step out of the elevator. He might have met with better success if he had learned to call out departments on each floor, like the operators who ran the elevators before they were replaced by buttons. "Tell me when you see something and want to get out of the elevator."

"I don't know what's on every floor."

"Maybe as the doors open you can see something you came to buy. Can you picture it and go toward it?"

"I don't always have an idea of what I want to buy when I go shopping. Sometimes I just go. This isn't working."

I sensed I was the only one left with my eyes closed and opened them to the fluorescent glare of the examining room and two stubborn people. "She's right. We don't always go for something in particular, and there are lots of departments on every floor." Imagine the money a store could make, I thought, if they paid attention to the shoppers' first sights as they stepped onto a floor. But to Jada I said, "But maybe you can make something up from somewhere else. It doesn't really matter where you are, right? Aren't you just trying to get her to put her mind somewhere else?"

Dr. Bradley repeated the process he wanted Jada to practice, promising that if she found a place that gave her pleasure, going there in her mind at IV time would take away her pain.

Jada's back straightened. "But I don't want to think of something else when I'm getting poked. I have to make sure they do everything right. They'll do anything they want if you let them. If I don't pay attention to what's going on, I won't know if everything is okay."

The psychologist's tie bounced as he stepped away and said. "You can try this at home with Jada when she's more relaxed. You don't have to be so concerned with...."

"She's not going to try this at home," Jada shot, "because I'm not doing it."

Dr. Bradley continued to look at me, not registering Jada's refusal with the courtesy of a glance or a nod. He didn't read me any better if he thought I was going to participate in his collusion. "She has a right to want to know what's going on," I said, wondering if he had always been pompous and stubborn or came off that way because he was just young and naive. "I don't know why everyone thinks that's so bad."

The doctor's face hardened. He wasn't the type to be wetting the armpits of his shirt, and I doubted that he considered any of what transpired besides writing his report. Without saying goodbye, he left the room, and I decided, in addition to being arrogant, he was also pouty when he didn't get his way. "Jada, I think there's a lot to be said for self-talk and self-confidence, you know, like thinking positive thoughts and all that. But I am getting tired of their getting angry at you and me for using our minds if it isn't the way they want us to use them."

"See, Mom? That's what I keep trying to tell them. That's why I need you. You understand; they don't."

My chin jutted, leading a shake of my head. "I have a ways to go, but you have to help me understand without getting so mad at me. When you yell and scream and call me names, I don't know how to help you."

"I try not to. Every time I come here, I tell myself I'm not going to do it. But when I'm here, I can't help it sometimes."

"T'ain't easy being two people at the same time, yourself and what others want you to be. Well, looks like we've been deserted. Let's go." Jada eased herself off the table, and partly to her, but mostly to myself, I kept talking. "You know that book that Dr. Lourde said was so good? Thank God I got it from the library and didn't waste my money on it. I don't want to interfere, but I have to ask Dr. Lourde if he really believes in all that."

"You don't interfere. If you could just do what you did today, that's what I need. I need someone to listen. And help me explain. You're good at that because you always want to analyze."

"Yeah, too much at times."

"Sometimes I get tired of it when you do it too much. Just listen to me. I'll tell you when to stop."

"Oh, thank you! Just what I need!" I circled my eyes, wind-up doll fashion. Jada smiled, nudging me with her elbow.

"No chance, hunh? You should have been a psychologist. Then you could just analyze everyone else and they'd have to listen to you, not me."

"Yup; I'm afraid you're stuck with me."

"My mom, the goofus." Jada grabbed my arm and squeezed it along with Hambone. We jostled each other down the hall, like we were the scarecrow and Dorothy holding Toto. If we could have just gone on and on and on and not stopped at the lab and not gone back to the clinic, maybe we could have reached the Emerald City.

By the time we got to Dr. Lourde, our rose-colored glasses were far behind us.

"Tell me, how did it go with Drake?" Dr. Lourde asked, his eyes eager. Usually Dr. Lourde kept to the middle, moderating extreme emotion—with us, anyway; this uncharacteristic show of excitement made him appear a husband someone could nuzzle, a father whose jokes spawned laughter from his kids.

"I don't think you're going to be very happy," Jada said. "I'm not riding an elevator at Baker's."

Dr. Lourde's face looked like he had just opened the wrong package and couldn't yet figure out why the contents were given to him.

I explained. "I don't think the guy worked very effectively with Jada. He came in and just started an exercise with her. He wanted her to imagine shopping, and Jada picked Baker's…"

"I love Baker's"

"…so he had her imagining herself on an elevator, and every time the door opened she was supposed to want to get off and shop, I guess. But she never got off and he gave up and left."

"Like I'm supposed to want to go shopping in my head. He gave me the creeps."

Dr. Lourde's face muscles let go their anticipation. "Dr. Bradley came highly recommended. I'm sorry if he made you uncomfortable. I was hoping you'd find something you could use. Some people actually need fewer drugs when they train their minds to concentrate on other things."

"I don't want to deny the mind's power and all that," I reflected, "but I think we have to be careful not to misapply that concept. Have you read the book you told me about?"

"No; I just heard a speaker who interned with him. He's got quite a loyal following."

"Yeah, well, so did Hitler. I read research, and this guy didn't quote any studies or get any other support to make his conclusions. He just walked around the hospital—*his* hospital because some places wouldn't let him practice his way—and 'discovered' that a woman, for example, who had a hysterectomy was also sexually repressed. So he made all these connections that whatever goes on in the mind shows up in the body; he concludes that whoever is sick chooses to be sick and could be well only if they wanted to! I think that's pretty dangerous! What about babies? You can't tell me they choose to have an ear infection!

"Worse, though, than his 'Patient, heal thyself' message is assigning shame to those who do not. It's hard enough dealing with a disease; now you're going to heap blame onto the person for having it? How can you explain progress in medicine? All of a sudden when Salk developed polio vaccine everyone wanted to walk? I think you'd better read the book before you recommend it to anyone else."

Silence echoed in the room. I folded my arms back in again like an eagle that had just landed and, after surveying the ground, decided it was safe to rest. Dr. Lourde stroked his chin as if taming a goatee, and murmured faintly. "Well, Jada, do you want to get started?"

"No," she answered.

"I know you don't want this, but I'm just asking if there's anything else you want to talk about before we begin."

"Then say that because I'm never going to say yes to the question you asked."

"Okay. Anything else been bothering you since last time?"

"No."

"Good. Then let me just do a quick exam and we'll get this thing going."

"Look what I got, Mom." Jada reached into her backpack. One after another, she birthed two- and three-dollar gifts. "This one's from Ann Skelton." She held onto the little drugstore rabbit slightly longer before setting it down for display with the others on the two hand-made Valentines I'd created, one each for Jada and Dom.

"Who's that from?"

"Kimby."

"Really. She decided it was okay to have you for a friend?" The sweet smell of fried sugar clung to the air in the kitchen. Tulipe shells, waiting to be filled for dessert, lay stacked under a sheet of waxed paper. Jada's Halloween party was where I first met Kimby. She, along with four other 8th grade girls, was invited to our house for brain soup and other ghoulishly appetizing food to eat and games to play. Tall and straight-backed, Kimby stood in front of a fake spider casting a blobby shadow among the thready spikes of a crocheted spider web taped in the corner of the dining room. With her hands clasping the back of her chair, she looked like she was holding onto a scepter, carefully and premeditatedly executing measured moves, quite opposite to Jada's flamboyance and irreverence.

An hour on the telephone it took for Jada and Kimby to negotiate the terms of their first official visit. I could drive Jada to Kimby's house at 2:00 on Saturday and at 3:30 pick her up. I knocked on the door and met Kimby's mother and their dog, a jumpy little bit of a thing that yelped while it ran back and forth between the kitchen and the front door. "Be quiet, Skippy," Roberta admonished. "The girls had a very nice time," Roberta said, holding the door open for Jada.

"Thank you for having her." Kimby was nowhere in the background, and Jada was halfway along the sidewalk to the car. I joined her, locking myself into the seat belt, automatically now, because Jada would not let the car roll an inch without beginning a lecture on the risks I was taking if I didn't. "Did you have a good time?"

"Mm-hmm."

"What did you do?"

"We looked through her yearbook from the school she went to last year."

"Ohh. That must have been…. What school was that again?" After a series of questions, though it wasn't clear to me when Kimby's parents got divorced and how that affected where she lived and went to school, I pieced together a story of a lawyer who fooled around with his secretary and exchanged his wife and children for a new life.

We walked into the house and Jada sniffed around for something to eat. "It's kind of close to dinner for a snack," I said. "Didn't you have anything at Kimby's house?"

"No. We stayed in Kimby's room the whole time. It was cold in her room, too. We couldn't sit on Kiimby's bed because it was already 'neatly made up,' she said."

"She looks like she'd say that."

"You know what else she said? When we were done looking at her yearbook she said it was time for me to go. She said, 'I think it's better not to spend so much time together so we don't get tired of each other.' Don't you think that's kinda strange?" Jada asked.

"She's either self-centered or she's been trained well by her parents." Silently I predicted the incipient friendship would pan: a couple visits before one of the girls decided she really didn't like the other enough to say they were friends. But who could tell; there was, after all, that adage about differences bringing people together and similarities keeping them together. Or was it the other way around? Whichever, in February, Jada and Kimby were still in the bringing together stage and exchanging Valentines.

I was willing to bet that in Kimby's house there were no leftover tulipe shells for after school cookie treats. Kimby's mother was probably the type who had empty space in her cupboards. My shelves sagged with cans stacked two high, monuments to the house of plenty and fortifications for the urge to bake something sweet during a snowfall. That year we had plenty of huge snow dumps and extra visits to urge Dr. Lourde to do something for Jada's perpetual cold. She walked around sniffling, one end of a tissue screwed into her nostril, the rest of it hanging out like the flag on the end of an overextended pickup truck.

"I have to apologize for Drake Bradley," Dr. Lourde said when he joined us in the examining room. "He and I talked about your visit with him, and I got the same sense you did. You're a discriminating person, Jada, with high expectations. I should have taken more care in sending someone your way." Jada's chin tightened as if to nod, or maybe she had stifled a sniffle. "I have someone else I'd like you to meet. This time I was more careful in who I selected. Her name is Beverly Parks, and she just joined our staff in the Social Services Department. Her job is to act on behalf of patients. Is it okay if I invite her in here to meet you? Now would be a good time, since you're not here for treatment."

"Are you sure?" Jada asked, narrowing her eyes.

"Well, I'm fairly confident. But you're a tough customer. Why don't you see for yourself?"

"Okay. But I don't want any hocus-pocus."

"No, she's not that kind at all. I'll tell Heidi to call her." He ducked out of the room and reappeared, closing the door behind him. "Now, what did you say was bothering you?"

Jada explained her symptoms, and Dr. Lourde made all the routine leukemia checks. Claiming ignorance to colds and rashes if they weren't connected to leukemia, he disappeared again, this time to ask Dr. Murthy to give his best advice. Heidi, in the meantime, had slipped in on soft feline feet and stood near the door at ready dispatch. When Beverly came, she hesitated at the door. "Is there room for me?" Her mouth was a smile, but the blue rings in her eyes were ethereal with a tinge of sadness. We melted away from Jada and welcomed her. Heidi vanished; behind her, the doctors left.

"Do you want me to leave, Jada?" I asked.

"No. Stay in here."

Beverly held Jada in her gaze as if she were a fragile soap bubble. "I won't stay long." Something in her voice made me wish she would. I was hearing her as through an old telephone receiver, the sounds taking on the fizzly crackle of the filter but all the more reassuring because they were strong enough to survive distortion. She told Jada she could come to see her every time she came into the clinic, and the hypnotism in her voice drew me to her; Jada accepted the invitation.

Driving home in the last bright light of the late winter day, I wondered aloud to Jada. "Don't you think it's strange that her name is Beverly?"

"Why?"

"Well, remember when we were at Domenica's? And the Ouija board?"

"Come on, Mom; you're such a wacko. It's just a coincidence. And don't tell Domenica," Jada warned.

Near the end of Jada's eighth grade year, her social studies teacher announced a three-day trip to Washington, D.C., and the parents of a friend called me for advice. The way Jada told it, Joanna's parents were strict; if anyone could convince anyone, Jada assured me with a hug and a grin, it would be me.

Joanna's father spoke apprehensively through the telephone, wondering about our commitment to the trip in June. "If it's all right with you, maybe we could look at the papers together. Say at your place?"

Our living room, stuffy from a hot sun during the day, hadn't cooled by the time Mr. Jeter and his wife arrived without Joanna, who, he explained, was staying home with her younger sister. Arnold beckoned our guests to a love seat while I spread out the papers describing the itinerary, the cost, the accommodations, right alongside the plate of brownies and the pewter coffee pot my grandmother gave us as a wedding gift. "You've seen the itinerary, haven't you?"

"No, I, ah, Joanna's brought...we haven't wanted to commit ourselves until, you know.... Kids these days. There are so many influences. If I just knew...."

"Yes, there are, but there really isn't much opportunity for mischief here. The way I understand it is that just about every minute of the day is taken up with something to do or see."

Mr. Jeter wasn't convinced. "There doesn't seem to be any control over what goes on at night."

"You mean when they're sleeping? It looks to me like they'll be pretty tired when they get done for the day!"

"A lot can happen; you have to be careful about other people. There's a lot of trouble with drugs these days." Mr. Jeter set his cup down and quickly shot a glance at his wife whose tight shiny skin was painted with bright colors of pink and violet and green. Behind her glowed yellow orbs from neighbors' windows.

"Well, yes there is," I agreed. "But I think there are reasons people get involved with drugs. I don't think it just happens."

"Idina and I are both teachers. We see some of that with our students." Arnold's lower lip made a pouch as if he were incubating a story.

"But again," I jumped in, "I don't worry that Jada's going to try anything. She can't even stand smoking around her. Or drinking. She's about as anti-drugs as they come."

Mr. Jeter's whole body seemed to recede, and his face lengthened as it withdrew. I sipped from my cup, waiting for his response. "Good," he exhaled. He glanced again at his wife who looked nothing like the teetotaler Mr. Jeter projected. She sat stiffly, out of place and uncomfortable on the puffy cushions. If I could match her with a fitting environment, it would be at a local bar on a Friday night; I could see her perched on a stool, her thigh almost, but not quite, touching the man's beside her, while she threw her long tousled and streaked hair back, her neck a long white arch full with laughter. Mr. Jeter's plaid shirt and clean fingernails said nothing about his occupation, but I became instantly curious about not only what he and his wife did for work but also about their relationship.

"Kids can get into drugs just by trying them when they're around. They might not mean to, but if you aren't careful, watching, it just takes one time."

"Well, I don't have to worry about Jada. She doesn't like taking the drugs she has to already." A tiny flicker, like a tic, jerked through his face.

His voice lowered. "But if they got in the wrong hands, I mean, someone else might like to try...."

"I don't think so. The ones Jada takes can make a person sick—do, in fact." I looked alternately between Mr. Jeter and his wife, but I couldn't be sure if she was even listening. By the looks of things, she didn't need to be. Except for her greeting when she arrived, she'd said nothing. "Can I pour you more coffee?"

That brought her eyes back. She shook her head.

"We really should get on now; the girls are home alone," Mr. Jeter said, making a lid of his hand over his cup. He shifted in his place and Mrs. Jeter responded immediately by rising.

I also rose and said, "I think Jada and Joanna would have a good time. If you want more information, I suggest you call the school." Arnold, too, got up, but he stayed behind while I walked the Jeters to the door, refreshed by the abrupt flash of coolness outside. The cold evening reminded me it was just May and that we had a long way to go for summer. One last goodbye, and I shut the door. Arnold and I crossed on the steps, he going down, I up to Jada in her room.

"Jada! I think Joanna's dad came here to grill us! I felt like we had to pass an inspection."

Jada got up from her bed and pinched the fabric of my sleeve to pull me along with her to the bathroom. "I forgot a towel. Will you get it for me?"

Facing the open closet door, I went on, "They must have had some problem, or else they're super strict. Sometimes the two go together. What have they got to be afraid of? Imagine, you on drugs."

"I am!"

"Yeah, Prednisone. Who would want your drugs! You don't suppose they're afraid of that, do you?" The thought made me laugh, but I clapped one hand to my chest, shocked at the possibility, poured Mr. Bubble under the running water with the other. Jada steadied herself on my shoulder as she stepped into the tub.

"Can you make this a short bath; I have to take one yet, too."

"Why don't you get in with me?"

I considered: which mattered more, time or comfort? "Only if I can add a little more hot water."

"You want everything hot. Okay, but you have to be at that end." I crowded myself in near the faucet and turned on the hot water.

"Okay, enough." Jada and I may have shared a lot, but we had different ideas about a bath. I heated the water for an intense short singe; she liked to lie and soak, dribble water over her skin in a tub brimming with tepid sudsy water. I chose the thin and worn cloth, she the thick, so that when she squeezed it, she had to roll the cloth into a ball and press it between her hands, her spindly fingers pushing over and over, drip, drop, drip, drop, water slipping from the wad as much from its own weight as from her pressure. "That's what I like about you," she said. "Kimby's mom wouldn't do this. You're more like a friend than a mom."

"I'm not so sure that's all that good. Maybe I close the doors for other people in your life. Turn around; I'll do your back while I'm here."

While I rubbed round circles of suds over Jada's back she said, "You can't count on other people, anyway. I'd really like to talk to my friends about what's going on with me, but they don't understand. Kimby says she wants to be my friend, but as soon as I say something about how I feel, she has to go and do her homework or something."

"Maybe you have to tell her what you need from her as a friend. She doesn't know. I mean, who does? My friends, my *family*, don't know what this is like."

Jada turned around, and I quickly began to swab myself. She watched carelessly. "I do tell her, I try to tell her, but it's like she forgets and doesn't change. You're the only one who really listens. I know I can count on you."

"We're really a pair, aren't we? They must wonder about us at the hospital. Okay, you can have the tub to yourself now. Man, it's cold."

Jada stretched her legs out in the tub, herself just getting comfortable. "You take the fastest baths. I don't care what they think or what anyone else thinks. You're my bestest friend. People even ask me if you're my sister."

"They better get some glasses then," I said, drying myself in front of the mirror. At 18, I tried to imagine how different I would look when I reached my sister's mature age, 21. But all I could see was me, and I wondered when I'd see myself change. Twenty-some years later I still saw only me, a gray strand here and there in my brown hair, the same crooked nose and too-big mouth, not very different than when I was 18, but I suspected other people saw a me I didn't. Apparently, the Jeters, that is, Mr. Jeter, perceived me, Jada, in a way I would not recognize. Like steam receding and gradually unclouding the reflection, I realized that it wasn't just Joanna or just us tonight. In unenlightened times, people with cancer were shunned as if they were contagious or morally responsible for their fate. Times hadn't changed all that much.

"Okay, time to redecorate!" Dom sat on his knees at the kitchen table, his summer baseball schedule before him, he glued to it as to a movie screen. He probably saw himself standing at the plate, bent at the hips, ready to launch the ball beyond the fence for a home run. He thrust his fist into the palm of his leather mitt as he would a ball, letting his fingers relive the ecstasy of that brief union before hurling the ball to its final destination, "You're out!" ringing in his ears as the sting of the ball lingered in his hand. The star in every role, he plucked the visor of his hat and wiggled it into place.

Down came the picture Dom colored in school for Mother's Day, wobbly blue letters spelling his name across the top. Jada's orchestra schedule, Dom's field day events, a spelling list with two red blotches, one a big circle, an A in the bull's eye, and the other a shot by some bubbling brew we would be having for dinner one night, those I tossed into the garbage; the math paper, ruffled at the edge where it was torn out of a notebook I set aside with the picture for the cedar chest. A cookie's fortune promising comfort and wealth held in place by a magnet with two red cherries and the epithet "Dieting: it's the pits!" I considered superstitiously.

Summer proclaimed itself through open windows and doors. That tuff, tuff, tuff had to be claws on a set of scampering squirrels as they clutched a tree trunk; erh-eh-erh the bobbing bough under their weight. Birds chittered, making coded cries to their own kind. We could always tell when it was 5:00 by listening to the birds that flocked the trees in our back yard. Sometimes I thought I heard the whistle of air as the birds zoomed through it.

"How was the baseball game?"

"Good. I hit a home run and I almost had another one, but the coach said I should've stopped at third but Jason, he was at third, and he was waving me on and I thought I was okay but then I was running up to home plate and I couldn't slide in, and I started to run back but the catcher threw the ball and I ran back to home plate but he didn't really touch me with his mitt but the umpire said I was out anyway."

"Wow! Sounds like you're really working on those skills. Sliding; that's the big time. When you're ready, we'll hang your schedule right here." I pointed to the center of the golden door of the refrigerator. What a trap the 70s were. We'd been so eager to add brightness to the uniform white kitchen appliances that we didn't see how drab our harvest gold, avocado, and muddy brown really were. And now the cost was too great to replace a motor that hadn't given up just because our excitement for its shell had. "We'll have to have something special for breakfast tomorrow because Jada will be home. Shall I make some pancakes?"

"Yum." Dom fixed the tape on the corners of his schedule. Above it were the swimming and tennis lessons, maps of our lives for the next two months. He took no notice of them but stood mesmerized in front of his baseball calendar. His voice would crack soon now that he was between his eleven years of childhood and first year of adolescence, and stood as tall as I; when I looked at him I wondered in disbelief that I could have carried him inside me. Though he weighed less than Jada at birth, he had a heftier look, and I heard the nurses say, "Oooh, he's a big one. I can't wait to see how much this one weighs." As he grew, he looked more and more like his Grandpa Pope. And acted like him, same affinity to play or watch sports, same dark Italian face, same hands running down from his forehead over his twisted nose.

"What position did you play, first base?" He wiped his fist across two pink crescents that stained his upper lip.

"Third. Coach wanted me to pitch again, but Dad said no. Coach says I might be able to go to the tournament in August if I pitch."

"What do you think about that?"

"I guess I'd try pitching, but Dad won't let me."

"Pretty excited, aren't you?" I gave Dom a squeeze. "How do you like your coaches?"

"One's cool. Dad had an argument with the other one. He wants me to pitch. Dad said we're not supposed to pitch in Little League because it ruins your arm."

"What do you do then? The ball's got to get to the batter."

"He says the coach is supposed to pitch."

"What do you want to play?"

Dom's brown eyes blinked, his long black lashes fanning his cheeks. "I could play either first or third. The only ones I don't like are the outfield. You have to run too much."

"I don't suppose at your age the ball gets out there very often, either. I know you have to be good in every position, but runners don't always get to second or third."

"Yuh!" he said, but he was already two home runs and three triple plays away from me. Dom's finger moved along dates, stopping at game days.

"Is it okay if I go out to the church lot and play baseball?"

I looked at the clock. "It's almost lunch time."

"I have to call and see if they can play."

"Okey-doke. I'll make lunch as soon as I go down and get the wash in the dryer." As many times as I'd complained at having to take care of all the mundane chores of running a house, this summer I hoped to find those the most challenging of my daily life. No summer classes, no summer teaching, so summer writing curriculum. This summer I was going to concentrate on Dom and his baseball schedule, Jada and her passage into the world of high school, and washing the clothes.

For the rest of the summer, Jada and I ignored how the plot of our lives was playing out and instead enjoyed those playing in the movie theaters. We shopped, too. We went to the malls, to the downtowns, to the suburbs, the small towns, and to the city streets, as if they were all little candy shops with an endless array of sugary sweets we had never seen. Jada learned folk painting, embellishing everything from sweatshirts to five-gallon ice cream containers to wooden trinkets, sold them along with my paperback book covers and doorknob covers. Together we labored and out we went peddling our creations.

Every week we drove to the bank with the money we earned and deposited into an account exclusively for Jada's travels, and Jada and I made plans to stay with my aunt in San Diego. We shopped for one new swimming suit and bought two. We bought shorts and sandals and straw hats. I sewed a jacket and sundress. We stocked lotion and lip smackers. We spread open the suitcases and watched our treasures mount. We had the airplane tickets; we had the okay from Dr. Lourde; we had the cash. All we needed was to have the day.

Five days before we were to fly, Jada developed a streak of red on her back, accompanied by both pain and an urge to itch. A corresponding streak appeared on the other side of Jada's back, just behind her armpit. As her temperature spiked, she grew sicker, and streaks flamed along her skin as quickly as licks of fire spread by a gusting wind. Anything that touched her sharpened her nerves' exposure. Jada was admitted into the hospital with shingles, the name of the affliction evoking a vision of scales instead of skin. There was nothing silly about it. The illness flared like a brush fire. Jada's temperature soared as she sank deeply into pain, and gradually as she lay drugged in the hospital bed, the heavy doses of pain medication blocked her awareness of anyone's presence, including mine.

This disease seemed sickly ironic to me. Jada was popping pink, white, yellow, and green pills in various combinations daily; she was given toxic chemicals to save her from her own natural cell division gone crazy and non-toxic chemicals to save her from the toxic ones. She was poked and prodded and invaded to keep her from slipping out of stable compliance. But her body got back at her anyway. No matter what anyone did do, there was nothing anyone could do yet to prevent shingles from searing itself in any body. Every body carried its own potential for shingles, and all that could be done was to let it run its scorching course.

It was those titers getting back at her, with poetic revenge, her first bout with an invasion of an opportunistic condition just waiting for its chance to scavenge an open wound. In the cool hospital room, refrigerated air swirling about, feeling as ashen gray as the linoleum floor while everything outside blistered with white-hot yellow August sunshine, I finally accepted that we were not going to San Diego.

The plane had days ago taken off when, gradually, Jada's eyes opened and semi-conscious times frayed into lucid moments. Wincing, Jada began to recognize her surroundings, asked for water, drank juice. She was released and sent home with Benadryl to wait out the dying embers along her nerves. I called Dr. Lourde for a refill on the prescription, but was told that he was gone. I soaked Jada in tubs of water thickened by baking soda. She took Tylenol by fours. She gritted her teeth and slowly she tolerated sheets, and the red streaks faded. She had made it back, and she had made it on her own.

She had lost a fistful of time. The school year was about to commence. Dr. Lourde's eyes flashed curiosity to see Jada not on the examining table, as usual, but sitting in a chair next to me, Hambone's stubby body nestled in her lap. "Hello, Mrs. Petersen," he said in a voice as crisp as his striped shirt. "How are you?"

"We're fine. Now," I added. "I didn't know shingles could be so bad."

"It's variable. Some people get a mild case. For others, it's insufferable. You had a rough go of it for a while there," he said to Jada. "Your counts are good; you're here for treatment, aren't you? I see you have ah, um, what's his name again?"

"You can remember white blood cell counts and Prednisone amounts and the size of my spleen. What's so hard about remembering his name?"

"I know it's a pig, but I can't remember his name. Is it Jawbone?"

"Hambone." She lifted and pointed him at Dr. Lourde as if printing his face onto Dr. Lourde's memory.

"That's right, Hambone. Sorry. I'll get it. Does he go everywhere with you? You don't take him to school, do you?"

"No, I don't need to. He comes with me to the clinic because he and my mom are the only ones who understand. If it weren't for them I couldn't have got through that shingles thing."

"There's not much we can do for that except let it run its course."

"I'll say. We called for more medication, and were told you were on vacation. Even Heidi wasn't around or I would have talked to her. If I had known that both of you were going to be gone, I would have checked things with you before you left."

"Didn't I tell you I was going on vacation?" Dr. Lourde jerked his head, his upper teeth biting his lower lip. "I thought I referred you to Dr. Malley and gave her everything I had on Jada's condition. So you got no more Benadryl after she went home?"

"No. And, let me tell you, it was hard. Jada was very strong."

"I'm sorry. It wasn't meant to be that way." To Jada he asked, "How are you feeling now?

"Okay," she answered, definitely differently than ever before, at the threshold of a new season.

If seasons could be bottled up, all the things growing, living, and dying, scenting the air, captured and sealed in a bottle, just by opening it and smelling its fragrance, I would carry autumn with me and sneak a whiff when I needed to alert my senses. I would dab fall's perfume about me when I wanted to feel vibrant, seductive. Fall has fire in it; you don't need to burn leaves to smell its passion.

In fall, Jada and I both were at new schools. She was a ninth grader in high school, and the alternative program for administratively transferred or court-ordered teens I taught in moved to an unused elementary building a few blocks west of the hospital. Jada wore new clothes, and I dressed up a new room. She made new friends, and I ordered books for the tiny library in my room. Adolescent literature had made its latest venture into real-life issues, including books about young people with cancer. In Lois Lowry's *A Summer to Die,* Meg's twin sister has leukemia, but the only thing she witnesses is a nose bleed that stained the bed sheets, the nearest thing to real in a story, which ends with the birth of a baby as the young woman dies.

In another, a teen boy and girl from different small towns meet in a faraway hospital as they await their separate treatments. Over time they correspond, mostly about their fears of relapsing; alas, he learns that he has relapsed and has little time left. He drives to the young woman's home, picks her up, drives them both to the hospital, where they decide "it's now or never," and spend a honeymoon night together in a hospital bed. Maybe I was too practical, but I wondered how they kept the IV tubes from getting in the way. In yet another, a young woman drops by the hospital for treatments as if she were stopping for a measles shot. She, like the young man in the other story, discovers she has little hope, and a kindly hospital orderly takes pity on her by closing the door and having sexual intercourse with her, a sort of Make-a-Wish for older teens.

Television programming followed the same sappy flow. Every week *The Love Boat* focused on two or three people who came onto the cruise liner confused, unhappy, aimless, looking to find what was missing in their lives. In one episode, a radiant young woman boarded with an equally pretty young man. Their problem was that he wanted to marry her, but she refused him because she had leukemia and didn't want to burden him with an uncertain future. "Leukemia!" Jada burst. "Look at her hair! It hangs down to her butt! And her face—it's not all puffy! When are they going to show her throwing up?" The ship's doctor does a blood test while they're in the middle of the Caribbean and delivers the bad news that she has only six months to live, which finally convinces her to marry. So while tragic, the story was really about a happy ending. No wonder we were unprepared, we who knew so much, for what could happen.

Filled with fall and all its expectations, Jada and I began the school year with hope and a cautious energy that nagged us, urged us on. Beverly had been true to her offer, popping into the clinic while Jada lay receiving her medicines, a blanket after the storm. Jada cross-stitched Beverly a seashell for her wall. We met Beverly for an ice cream sundae. School underway, Beverly visited Jada at home.

Just as Beverly was leaving Jada in her room to her homework, I arrived home, and the school bus emancipated Dom. He piled up the steps, dropping shoes, jacket, and backpack along his upward climb toward the kitchen for his snack. Beverly and I sat opposite each other on the yellow love seats in the living room with coffee; the sun filtered in weakly through diaphanous yellow sheers that stopped short of breath at the coffee table.

Arnold took a seat in the wingback chair by the fireplace, and said, "You have to understand Jada. She's a high-strung child, so anytime a doctor tells her to do something she's going to rebel." He bounced his bended knee, swinging his top leg outward to underscore his infallibility.

Beverly held the saucer under her cup while Arnold went on. "Terrible thing, cancer. It changes people, breaks up families."

"Oh, I don't know," I said, my voice an even simmer. "I think people act out naturally, no matter the circumstances. If we didn't, we would never be accountable for who we are."

Arnold persisted. "Studies have shown that there are more divorces among people in families where there's cancer, especially in children." Arnold's foot kept time like a metronome.

He had a way of relating information with uncheckable absolutism, and I had no data to refute his claim, but I redirected. "That may be, but aren't we getting off the point? Beverly and I were talking about Jada's last clinic visit."

"She has such a hard time. All that confusion; everything's always so rushed there. It's always hurry up and do this and hurry up and do that. It excites her, makes it harder for her."

My eyes rolled, marbles in a sand lot. "That's not true. Sometimes we sit in that room and wonder if anyone knows we're there. She sends me out to the desk to find out where Dr. Lourde is. She, and I, too, would like them to be more responsive."

Arnold'skneepumpeddoubletime."Oh,I-know-it-I-know-it."

"No, you don't. You don't know what goes on there when you've never been there. You don't even know that she didn't have treatment Wednesday because her counts were bad and that we have to go back to try again." I wanted to go on, to say, "You're downstairs watching television when I'm either getting her ready or settling her down. You don't know if she's sick or isn't sick or when I get up in the night when she is." I wanted to tell Arnold all the things that had been stewing for years, but Beverly's presence made us public, and there were rules about that, rules that I still honored. Arnold, not saying goodbye, got up from the chair and descended the stairs.

Beverly sipped coffee. "Jada is such a lovely young woman. So poised. I enjoy our visits."

"Yes. I wish I could be half as."

Beverly smiled forgivingly. "We can get together, too, if you want to. I love girl talk."

"I never told you, but my sister has séances, and when Jada and I were at her house last summer, she asked, 'Who's Beverly?' She pressed her fingers to her temples and said, 'I'm getting a really strong message from a Beverly. There's a Beverly who's really important in your life.' The only Beverly I know is my mother's sister, and I haven't seen or heard from her since I was a kid. It must be you. Thank you."

Throughout the fall Jada was in and out, back and forth, to the clinic for blood counts and blood cultures, only to be sent back home, unable to tolerate chemo, and unable to regain strength, and without answers. Without a cause, there could be no remedy.

A day following a clinic visit, I was called to the school office to answer a telephone call. To the shuffling feet and scuffling banter of students making their way outside for their break, I strained to hear Heidi's tentative voice. "I'm sorry to bother you at work, Idina, but I thought you'd want to know. Jada's counts don't look good. Her disease might be back."

"Oh, no. How can that be? You just saw her." Hot tears broke forth as I asked in disbelief, "How can that happen?"

"We don't know for sure. Sometimes a cell shows up and sometimes it doesn't. We'd like her to come in for a bone marrow aspiration tomorrow. I wish there was something I could say to help you."

"You can say it isn't true."

Heidi's silence strangled the air from my throat. So it was true; shingles, relapses, anything could happen without warning. I felt like a rat in an experiment being zapped and unable to fathom why I wanted to behave as I did, bouncing my nose into walls and taking turns in blind pursuit of an unseen but anticipated promise. Scrawny lights feebly brightened the dark hall for kids excluded from the mainstream. Some of them were sure to get shot, get caught in a crime and be imprisoned. Maybe some would scrap along at the fringes of living, inflict on their offspring the horrors they endured, and others would find their way out. I would meet them in a grocery store, at a movie theater, their past lives shadows of the color of their presence. Who chooses? What will they do that the others won't? And will it matter? We tell them it does.

And there I was. There were the rectangles of wallpaper Jada and I pasted to each pane of glass on the French doors between the hall and my classroom. There on the desk was the chart she made for me in her never-ending attempt to arrange my life into a neat day planner, sequential and zip-uppable. School pictures of her and Dom smiled arrestingly from the frames we'd made. A dizzying wave overtook me, and I held onto the ledge of a bookcase. Leukemia ran in siblings like weak knees; Dom's chances were greater than other boys'.

There were only two hours left to my day. What difference could it possibly make, I wondered, that anything I did for these students could last when a bullet or a blood count could mean the end to anyone's life, theirs, Jada's, Dom's? I felt overwhelmed trying to drop and cultivate seeds of joy and wonder and curiosity in thinking and feeling and wanting something more and better than what these students saw in themselves now, knowing what a serious and tenuous business it was for them to stay alive. They needed too much from me, too much when I had to keep my own life from falling off the tightrope, for if Dom and Jada and the taking care of them were not my life, I would be stepping into space, unbalanced, unwilling. Sometimes, now, when everything I did seemed pointless, I wanted to jump off, free-fall into oblivion, not have to live and think and feel the life I wanted for others. Then, like a safety net that appears when I thought there was none, Beverly walked into the room. "Can you leave for a cup of coffee?" she asked.

"No, I've got students coming. But I'll ask Patti to cover." The school was old enough to maintain a living boiler room that doubled as the teacher lounge, which is where I might find Patti on her preparation hour. She holed down there to grab a cup of coffee and puff hungrily on a cigarette, the entrails of the building growling in protest against the strain of having to keep the rest of it alive and running. Patti snubbed out her cigarette and went upstairs to my classroom. Beverly sat at the round table some people used for their lunch. I paced around her, a wary eye to the floor, on the lookout for creatures that might scamper underfoot.

"There is nothing to do," I said in response to her question. "Something doesn't feel right about this. I can't get my brain to imagine it."

"From what I've gathered, Jada's been a fairly accurate barometer; I wonder how she'll react."

"That's just it. She hasn't been *really* sick, not like when she first got sick. Well, if it is, I'll know what to do then. But right now, I just can't believe it. I can't believe I'm standing here; I can't believe I'm going home to make dinner and go to bed and get up in the morning. I can't believe anything. I can't believe in medicine—how can I? She's on medicine and look what's happening. And people praying for her. What do they mean when they say that? I don't believe God has anything to do with this. Oh, I don't know. It's bullshit! It's all bullshit! And we're standing knee-deep in it."

Beverly's eyes lured me, but I couldn't accept, not here, not now, not until I knew for sure. All I could think of was a fire drill. How many of them had I done in my life? They'd done their job training me, done their job so well I couldn't get panicky when I heard it; something inside told me that the cause for alarm wasn't real, but was that because of the excellent training? Still, you could never tell. The thing is, the place doesn't have to burn down to qualify for an alarm. How long it took to think and to think about my thinking, I didn't know; Beverly continued after a second or a minute or an hour, "I'm still going to South Dakota to see my father every other weekend. It's almost like he wants this all to end so he can find the answers to the questions you're asking. But he keeps living, against his will, even." Beverly rubbed her eyes; she looked tired.

"I'm sorry, Beverly. I'm feeling sorry for myself. But mostly I feel sorry for Jada. I can't even imagine facing my own death. And here I am, healthy and with every chance of living to 95. It's all wrong. She shouldn't have to think about dying. But she has to and I get to go on living. It's too awful. If I could believe in something, maybe it would be easier to think about. But I can't. I can't believe."

A door latched. The stooped figure of the custodian rounded the corner to the stairway. It was rumored that he kept a bottle of bourbon in a drawer to keep himself going while his wife was slowly dying at a local beer joint. By the looks of his weepy eyes and purple-veined nose, he was barely hanging on himself.

"I have to get back up," I said. "Will you be at the hospital tomorrow?"

"I'll stop in and see how you're doing." Beverly pushed her chair away from the table and gathered her purse like it was a medical bag. "No one should have to do this alone."

"Imagine all those people who do." I thought of the kids upstairs.

When I told her about the necessity of a bone marrow, Jada did not believe that leukemia was causing her malaise. Dr. Lourde reported negative results of the bone marrow aspiration the following day. "See, I told you," she said.

"Yes, Jada, you did. I'm sorry to put you on this roller coaster, but we had to find out." Dr. Lourde looked earnestly at Jada as if deep down underneath her skin and her capillaries and her nerve endings and her bones, way deep, he could find the answer. He was still worried, but I breathed relief: no relapse was good news. But news, as we had learned when she was diagnosed, was rarely purely good. Counts can appear to be good if you don't look at percentages and relationships among T-cells, neutrophils, and platelets. A negative bone marrow aspiration can mean the absence of leukemic cells but not other serious causes for low counts.

"Unfortunately, while we've eliminated the worst, we're no better off than when we started. I can't tell you why your counts are so low and you're not gaining strength." Jada's eyes beamed a blue light of challenge as he continued. "I'm going to wait another week for treatment. I think your body needs a little more time to recover. There's really no danger of relapse with a short delay," Dr. Lourde said, assuringly. "We could skip a whole month or even cut the dosage if we had to. Sometimes the residual effect is too much for the body to handle. Is that all right with you, Jada?"

"You can skip as many as you want. If I never get another treatment, I'll be happy."

"I'm sure you would be." Dr. Lourde instinctively smiled, and I liked him for that. He wasn't like the mushy punched-in beanbag that lay squashed on the floor; like me, he probably avoided cushions and pillows and marshmallow-puffy chairs and went right for the hard-surfaces and sharp angles of the Quakers and Shakers. He had principles and ethics and standards and boundaries, and he protected them. We may clash one corner with another, Dr. Lourde and I, but I trusted the form.

And, as jealously as I wanted to keep Jada for myself, I wanted to give her to him. He would save her, not me. But for that to happen, my daughter would have to trust him like a mother. The thought came noble and petty at once. I had borne her, nurtured her, prepared her. After all that care and all that push, someone new, someone male, someone quite by accident, was going to take my place. Revelations come in the most embarrassing places: I realized my undoing in the sight of the undoer. Giving her up to Dr. Lourde was going to be hard; but nothing worth saving is worth giving up unless you love her so dearly that her salvation lies in your relinquishing. But if I had to give her up, I wasn't going to dump Jada into some shapeless amoeba-like blob that made her feel good when she hit it but had nothing to support her when she lay in it. I had to, wanted to, give her to a man who didn't squish and fold and collapse like the beanbag chair.

The four walls of the examining room with bright colored paintings of stamps and mailboxes and nursery-rhyme figures and riddles swirled around Jada and Dr. Lourde like the spinning of a merry-go-round; I would have got dizzy if I didn't focus on her. "So now what? I don't get treatment and I don't get anything for what's wrong?" she asked.

"We'll just have to wait and see. Either the condition will correct itself as your body gets stronger to fight it off and we'll never know what it was, or it will announce its presence. This is not uncommon for leukemia patients."

"This is a pretty dumb disease. And you think you're doing us a favor by making us live through it."

"Well, I wouldn't have said it that way, but I do think the progress we have made in treatment is a benefit to people. Twenty years ago, you wouldn't have survived the first three months. It's just recently we've been able to keep people alive beyond that. Now people are surviving the disease itself."

"Yeah, and look at all the chemicals they're putting into the ground. When I die, I'll pollute the earth."

"We can do worse things than that," Dr. Lourde readily replied, sincerely, too. I was beginning to hear him hear her: he didn't once stroke his gray-streaked mustache, as he often did when selecting his words. "You know, Jada, you're a very intelligent person. I'd like to see you grow up and do the things you care so much about. You could be that hospital administrator and make the changes in the ways things are done. You could be a researcher and find the one last key to curing this disease."

"If I ever get rid of it, I don't want to have anything more to do with this disease. But I won't, so it's all a big waste anyway. You have all this trust in cures and chemicals and you can't even find out what's wrong with me."

"No one ever said that medicine had all the answers. There's a little science and a little art and a little luck in getting them to work together. I couldn't do this if I didn't believe there was hope."

"Well, you better have enough for all of us." Jada dropped her eyes and leaned back on her hand, as if, like the weathered gray wall of a shed under the pressure of a too-heavy roof, she might slump into a rubble of boards and rusted nails if she didn't have a prop to keep her upright.

The room was filled to bursting with the urge to address the letters and postcards painted on the wall to heaven, if, indeed, there were such a place; Dr. Lourde broke the silence. "I'll send Heidi in. See you in a week, Jada?"

"Do I have a choice?"

Twisting the doorknob, he swung the door toward him, stopped, the muscles in his face working at a response. Then he left us to interpret his thinking on our own.

"They're afraid," Jada said. "They're afraid that if they asked us, we might say no."

"I'd be afraid of that, too. I wouldn't want you to say no."

"Why is everyone so afraid of dying? I don't want to die, but it's natural, and everything they do is so unnatural." Heidi came in as on a stream of air, and before she whisked through, on a mission to sweep us out, Jada asked, "Heidi, what would happen if I refused to take treatment?"

Heidi chuckled, baring her sharp eyeteeth. "Is this a trick question? You *do* refuse."

"No," Jada waved her arm, wiping away Heidi's teasing smile like a smudge on a window pane, "I mean, do I *have* to have treatment? Or what if I never came because I didn't want anything?"

"Then Dr. Lourde would file a suit in court and you would be ordered to have treatment."

"How can they do that?"

"You're a minor, and the State would act in your best interest."

"That's so unfair. They even take that away from us. It's my life."

"Yes, it is, Jada," I said, "and I don't think it's time for you to give up on it yet. We'll be back next week."

"For more poison. And I'm going to get you guys a new poster for the door."

"Why?" Heidi's chin stretched to the picture of a giant-sized black cat next to a cut-away house and a profile of a bird atop a green tree. A rabbit crouched in mid-air in an upper corner while large black letters printed that May was Be Kind to Animals Month. "I like that poster." Heidi said.

"Doesn't that look weird to you? Look at the cat's leg. It's all twisted. It bugs me to see it like that."

Heidi shrugged in bewilderment. "I don't see anything wrong with it."

"No one around here ever sees anything wrong with anything."

One week went by, then another and another. At first, Dr. Lourde delayed chemo. But he ran out of reasons to do so, when he said, carrying a written copy of her blood counts, "I'm going to go ahead with your chemo, Jada. These counts are good enough for us to get back on schedule."

"But you still haven't found out why I feel so tired and sick. I can hardly make it through a day at school." Her skin color, having grown sallower through the month, paled to the white protective paper she lay upon.

"I can't treat what I can't see, and what I see is that you are strong enough to get a dose of chemo. Some kiddos get into a state of mind where they don't get so much attention anymore, and they find a way to get that attention."

"You think I'm making this up, don't you?" Jada challenged, though not with force.

"I wouldn't say that you're doing it intentionally. But, your leukemia is not making you sick, and your blood counts don't show that you are sick. I've already ordered up the pack from the lab."

We waited alone in the dim room for the chemo to drain into Jada, and just as darkly, she said, "He should keep looking. He should know by now that I know when something's wrong. Do you think I like feeling like this? I don't like coming back here all the time. How would he like it if no one believed him?"

"I agree, Jada. You know he's thorough, and, he's your only hope. What should we do?"

"We keep after him. Something's wrong, I know there is, and I don't care what he thinks of me, I'm going to bug him till he finds it." And she did; we came back and we came back. Dr. Lourde's patience seemed ragged by Jada's tenacity, but he said, "You know I don't like to do more testing than I need to, but I've done everything I can think of except this one last thing. And it is the last thing I will try, but I've scheduled you for a chest X-ray."

Heidi called us in to the clinic, and Dr. Lourde walked stridently into the room. "Jada, I read the results of your X-ray, and

I was more surprised than anyone. In fact, I almost rescinded the order to keep you from unnecessary exposure to radiation." But, there, on black was the white haze, evidence he needed, evidence of great concern. Way way back, or so it seemed, when all the pills were dumped into Jada's lap, we learned their names and their purposes. White was Prednisone; a steroid, it was the modern day wonder drug, given for everything from poison ivy to asthma to cancer. Yellow 6-MP, tiny white Methotrexate—some drugs she took on faith. Septra or its green generic prevented a dreaded form of pneumonia, pneumocystis, so we were told. And here it was anyway, pneumocystis right along with the green oversized oval-shaped pill, right here, he said, here in Jada's lungs.

"How can that be?" How could it not? Just ingesting chemicals did not spare a body from disease, whether it was shingles or pneumonia or leukemia. So what did that say about a life? What killed cancer patients more than cancer itself? Over and over I'd heard it, but every day Jada lived, and every day she took something, and every day that something or combination of numbers and sizes and colors, arrayed in ever changing kaleidoscopic form, and every day I had been lulled into falseness. Warning after warning failed to alert me, like practicing too many fire drills to believe this was not just another one.

We were on that roller coaster again. As fervently as Dr. Lourde had been skeptical and resistant to respond, dismissing the cause that he called critical, he rushed Jada into the hospital Intensive Care Unit and doubled his efforts and the speed of ministration. The slow pace of deterioration had speeded up to a struggle for life— within minutes! The fast-forward change forced us into a drama we had no forewarning of.

Again, the second time in three months I lived at the hospital with Jada, standing in the way of death if it made an appearance at her door. And if that sounds melodramatic, I can only repeat how surreally events flipped, not so much that I was informed as that I witnessed. She was heavily drugged with whatever could knock out the infection and with whatever would knock her out of consciousness. Beverly brought Jada a white rose bud, each petal laced at the edge with an aching pink, like the quick of skin where a fingernail has been peeled too far. It reminded her, she said, of Jada's innocence afflicted by pain.

"How are you doing? You have to take care of yourself, you know." The words rolled out of Beverly like a carpet we were supposed to follow. I slowed down to keep pace with her as we walked the sidewalk on the perimeter of the hospital. She added, "You're no good to her if you get sick."

"I can handle anything. She's the one I'm worried about. What if she doesn't come out of this?" The words sounded other-worldly, unfamiliar words I should have rehearsed, tested to hear if they were the ones I was supposed to say. The tip of Beverly's nose reddened by a November wind. She stuck her hands into the pockets of her trench coat.

"I had a dream," came out of me as a gust from around the corner of the hospital. "I was standing on a hillside. There was green all around, green grass, green trees; I was struck by the fullness—it was lush. And there was a gazebo right there in the middle. It's not clear if I was in it or near it—you know how dreams are. But Jada was walking up the hill, walking and climbing, walking beyond me, yet the distance didn't increase so that she got very far away. I don't know why, but I was being left behind; I couldn't go with her and walk with her, but I wanted to.

"It was cold, or she was cold, and I wanted to give her a sweater; I knew she'd need it where she was going. I held it out to her, but she kept walking; she was always out of reach, kept going without being able to get the sweater. I don't know if she could even take it because she was being pulled by some other force. Something else was making her go along her path, and when I looked at her there was light all around her, a brilliant light. I was so sad! I felt so separated from her. I called to her and reached out with the sweater, but I couldn't get it to her. Somehow I knew she had to go without me, but all I wanted to do was give her the sweater, and I couldn't.

She kept going. It was awful! I have the same anxiety now just remembering it."

"Sometimes people have those dreams when their children are growing up, especially at adolescence. The children are separating from their parents and don't need them in the same way anymore."

"Mm. Maybe. I'd be glad to let her go into adolescence. Maybe subconsciously I want to hang on to her, but consciously, I keep trying to nudge her away, to do more with other people, to make decisions without checking everything with me. It's hard; how do you prepare for tomorrow when you know all the time you might have is only today? There are no books or guides to tell you what to do."

We walked in silence, not hearing the cars or trucks that rolled along the pavement beside us, just the rhythm of our falling feet on the sidewalk. Beverly reflected, her frail face, her thin lips bluing in the wind. "I see mothers with their small children, and it's easier, somehow, when they're younger. Their needs are so simple. What you do for a small child isn't quite so different whether they have cancer or not."

"I know people think I'm controlling Jada or she's controlling me; they all have solutions for us, don't they? There are times I try to protect her, but how does that get her ready for life, especially with this disease? But I can't just push her away, either, and say, well, it's your disease, you deal with it. That's what people want me to do. My mother, some of those ding-dongs who come in and want her to be a potato they can dig into. She's fourteen; and I'm not done being her mother."

Beverly's stubby heels stopped clumping against the concrete. On the rise of the hill was the old hospital; to our right was the entrance to the new hospital, a red brick face with decks like watchful eyes overlooking the front doors. Suns and flowers and smiley faces were painted on one side of the acrylic panels. Beverly looked at her watch. "I wish we could talk longer. I admire you for your courage and for what you do for Jada. It's lonesome finding your way, but you're doing it."

"You know what they say about hindsight; I guess I'll know someday if it's the right way or not. Thanks, Beverly."

Inside Jada's room, I sat and waited and hoped I would know what to do next because, for sure, as I'd been learning, there would be another opportunity to figure out something new.

Touch and go; that's what Dr. Lourde said it had been when it wasn't anymore. He said it with a sigh of relief. Reflecting on the past days, I prickled with growing sensations, like when the feeling disappears from the fingertips after being out in the cold too long: they keep operating, doing what they're supposed to do even though they cannot accept feeling through their nerve endings. They hurt in a self-protected kind of way, the cause of their pain coming from inside themselves. So, too, their relief, a different burning pain as feeling is restored. I prickled with that.

Jada, released from the hospital, was expected to resume her visits to the clinic, which she did, preceded by the customary blood draw in the outpatient lab. We waited in the examining room for Dr. Lourde to make his appearance, a slip of paper with symbols and numbers holding the code to Jada's future in his hand. The breakdown told him where she was on the cycle of decline and repair and whether she could tolerate another treatment. Up until the onslaught of shingles, neither she nor I had thought to fear the reading. And up until this visit, neither she nor I had experienced the lab technician coming into the examining room. Her arm balancing the wicker tray, she surprised us with her appearance.

"I'm sorry," she apologized, "but Dr. Lourde needs another sample."

"What, again?" Jada asked. "Don't you guys get enough?" Around Jada's eyes, gray rings spread, radiating storm-laden clouds throughout her face. The technician set her tray down and brought out a container, the one used for cultures. "Why do you need more?" Jada asked suspiciously. "What's wrong?"

"I don't know. I was just given the order." She stretched the latex band and said, "I can't do a finger stick this time, Jada." Jada's muscles stiffened and her lips compressed thin and straight. "Make a fist now."

"No, I don't want it!" Jada shot, but her fight came out only in words and her body lay rigid but limply inactive, as if she'd used up all the energy she had.

The technician shut the door and our connection to life outside the room, a little cubbyhole blueprinted for efficiency. Cupboards, lights, a long metal fork with a funnel-like contraption at the end that came out of the wall, a pouch to hold the black arm band and black rubber bulb to pump air into and then, pshsh, out to measure blood pressure, a sink, chairs, toys, and an examination table, everything, had been thoughtfully positioned. And thoughtfully omitted, too? When the planners drew up their sketches, who decided to leave out the clocks? Surely money wasn't the issue. I didn't know how long we'd been waiting in the closed-up room, only that it felt like a very, very long time.

"What time is it?" Jada asked, weaker looking, so that I wondered if even the surrender of a small vial of blood could cause such a noticeable depletion. She lay on the clinic pallet content not to move, yet discontent with waiting, the first fish strung through the gills trailing the boat, last on the line. I opened the door to find out: almost 6 o'clock. The clinic seemed unusually empty, not bustling with nurses and doctors crisscrossing the intersecting corridors as they did earlier in the day. Even Heidi and Barb were gone, taking their comfort with them. Bethany stood near a counter, her head aimed at an open notebook she was writing in. She was apparently the only one left in the clinic, head bowed so that her black hair skimmed around her cheek into a pirouette at her chin. Fluorescent lights bounced starkly bright from her white face. She moved her finger to the tip of her nose as if to kiss it. I felt like I was left behind in my seat, and awakening hours after the auditorium lights were turned out, spied on a performer practicing alone. She must have sensed being watched; minutes after I shut the door, she came in. Behind her, distant corridor lights were going off.

She breathed intensely, and after a deep breath, her words came amazingly soft. "I'm sorry you have to wait like this. Has Joe been in here to talk to you?"

"No," Jada said with a hook at the end of it.

"It's really his job to tell you, but I think you have to know that whenever Joe sees a set of counts like yours, he orders a transfusion."

"A transfusion!" Jada's head jerked slightly, the first sudden movement I realized she'd made in a long time, and I gasped, the insides of my mouth feeling hot and red like skinned-up palms after a fall onto the pavement. Too soon to feel the hurt or even the embarrassment, I looked back to find proof that the cause for my fall actually existed.

Bethany's face was a mask, emotionless, direct; but I trusted the softness in her eyes. "First they have to do a cross and match, and then it needs to be radiated; that's going to take a long time."

"What's a cross and match?" Jada asked.

"That's when they check your blood cells to find compatibility so you won't reject the new cells. One thing you don't want is an allergic reaction to new blood!" she said, clearing the tray on the counter by the sink, picking out the unused needle and dropping it into the plastic box, tossing Betadine swabs into the gray/beige rectangular cupboard. At the door she said, "I'll be right back."

Jada lay on the table as if knocked out waiting for the count to get up. The flat light in her eyes told me she wasn't going to, and I pieced the past few days together. Her tiredness, the gray-green set around her lips, the drive to keep up, her missing giggle. Even now, she could not sustain her astonishment, but lay, half in, half out of caring, and shut her eyes.

With a sure and purposeful gait, Bethany returned and repeated, dimpling around her lips in disapproval, "I'm really sorry. I just don't think it's right that you weren't told. Usually we do transfusions in here, but it's very late, and everyone's gone home, except for Joe. The only reason I'm here is that as head nurse I have to stay until everyone is out of the clinic."

"How long do transfusions take? I'd better call home."

"Actually, I've called admissions and ordered you a room. You can stay there for the night and go home in the morning. Some of our patients do that anyway. Why don't you go out there and sign the papers, Idina; I'll stay here with Jada. When you get back you can call home."

We were tired, more than tired, of the needling insinuations of the day—and the waiting. As it turned out, the day's doings were a mere prelude to the night's. A team bearing packs, trays, and bags came into the hospital room and clustered near the bed. Among the shadows cast by a singular over-the-bed light, an anonymous figure bent a knee and flicked his finger at Jada's arm. "Your vein won't pop up," he complained to Jada. Then, shifting from personal to omniscient, he directed the chorus of people behind him. "We'll have to use the back of her hand," he said, turning Jada's arm over, merchandise he was examining for a flaw. "I think there's a usable one here. Your vein went into hiding."

"It's not my fault. Stop talking and just get on with it!" The fire in Jada's eyes could have ignited the room, while around her were aides ripping open the tools of their trade, including the needle for the transfusion. "You'd better get it right 'cause I'm not giving you another chance. Hurry up, you, you…. Ouch, stop pinching me!" Jada flinched as the technician tried to coax the vein into service, but he caught her fingers and held on.

"Whoa. I don't want to fight you on this," He rubbed the alcohol vigorously across her hand.

"Then don't! Mom, make him stop!"

"I'm here, Jada. Let him try once more." I stood at the foot of the bed and the crux of a decision, and for an instant she shot a fiery look at me. And that's when he did it.

"Aaugh! It's burning! You didn't let it dry!" Jada's eyebrows pulled together, and like a drawstring, brought the rest of her face into her rage. And then, just as quickly, she turned hard. "You should have stopped him, Mom."

When it was all over, the thick silver needle transporting thick maroon blood lay lodged beneath her skin like a toothpick under a fingernail, white cloth tape keeping it in place. When a nurse returned, I asked for a reclining chair. She admonished me, saying that an item as precious as that had to be reserved. She came back pushing a sandwiched rollaway bed that screeched in agony and told me how lucky I was to get it, especially since the closet was supposed to have been locked up.

"Is this supposed to hurt so much?" Jada asked. She winced when the nurse pulled the light chain and looked at the plump burgundy bag, ran her fingers along Jada's arm above the needle, and pulled half of her mouth back as if she were about to cluck.

"It's running a little slow." She grabbed the end of the bag and gave it a wiggle, then gently massaged it. "Sometimes the blood starts to clot. I'll get a warm cloth for your arm; that should help." I unlatched the bed and opened it out, the mattress flopping thin and wobbly on the metal springs. I wondered if that was how flop houses got their name.

Jada moaned long and low. I should have known that the night begun that way could get only worse. "This hurts too much. How long is it going to take for all this to go in? I'm not going to make it."

"Sure, you are. Here's another warm cloth. Do you want to watch television, Jada? It might help to pass the time, get your mind off it."

"No, I can't. Don't talk to me, Mom. I can't." Her voice flowed like sap at the end of the season. Then, she shrieked, "Something's wrong. Call the nurse again." To the nurse she said, "Can't you speed it up, make it go in faster?" Jada kept her eyes averted from the sac that hung heavy above her. Instead of flowing into her arm, the thick brownish sludge seemed to be caught in a clogged pipe swelling her arm into a giant blister.

The nurse dabbed at Jada's puffy arm. "It's going as fast as it can. You can take only so much at a time, which is why you're swelling." She felt the cloth. "Are you keeping this on?"

"Yes, but it doesn't help. Can't you stop this now? It hurts."

The nurse reached up and squeezed the bag, "We're doing the best we can," she said before leaving.

"Just take it out, Mom! Me, of all people! You know how much I hate blood! Look at how long this is taking and it's not getting any better. I'll be like this all night! I can't do it. Help me, Mom." Jada whimpered, her eyelids thick in her sunken sockets. I wished for strength and hope and an end to the night, and most of all I wished for sleep; I sat by Jada's bed and sang lullabies, over and over. She tossed her head, side to side, the wispy strands of hair crackling with electricity against the white pillow. We were in silence a time; I flopped onto my flattened mattress. The bed screeched and stretched under me, its coils even more tired than I; a thick metal bar jutted through the center and poked my back. "Yank this thing out of me, Mom!" I was half glad to get off the bed.

All night I just wanted to know when we'd get to the *Love Boat* part of this disease where there's a beginning and an end and everyone disembarks having no unanswered questions about right and wrong and purpose and worth. No wonder people turned their glassy eyes away from Jada. Who's to be entertained by the dirty parts of living with leukemia when someone sells you the romance of dying from it? Cranky and groggy at 2:21 in the morning, neither sleeping nor waking, being gouged by a pole or nagged by pleas to release my daughter from her misery, I began to wonder at what else I had not known, and if I had known, if I knew before what I knew now, if I could have glimpsed into Jada's future, what?

"Can't you see what's happening?" Jada said in the dark. "I'm getting deeper and deeper. The more they do, the worse it gets. I never should have started. I'm going to die. All you're doing is dragging it on."

"But, Jada," I pleaded. "We wanted you to live."

"That's selfish. You're making me do this just so you can have me around."

"No, I'm doing this so you can live for yourself. You don't belong to me, but I'm responsible to you, to love you, to keep you clothed and fed and healthy, to help you grow strong and good, to safeguard your life and your future, to have a future. Everything they tell us is that you will live. I have to believe that even if you don't, especially if you don't." And I did believe that at 2:21 and all night long until the sun rose and all day long until the next long night. I was Jada's mother, and I was going to get her through because I knew she was worth life and I knew the names of the boys she liked and what she talked about on the phone, and I knew that she liked to dance, to play the piano, to learn, and to run her life, not to mention mine and everyone else's. Kisses and hair and a brave cruise into death held greater appeal to a television audience than veins and clotting blood and a nagging crying voice, but that was *Love Boat* love, not my love.

The night plodded on, and finally even the blood in the bag wore itself out and gelled motionless in the tube unable to squeeze through the hole in the needle stuck in Jada's arm. What had gone in would have to do. Sometimes, we would learn, a transfusion holds, and sometimes it doesn't. Sometimes the bone marrow is on such a downward slide that one transfusion isn't enough. And sometimes, the bone marrow starts to exert its territorial rights and rejects the new blood, sensing a takeover if there are too many transfusions too close together. Instant knowledge; Jada's next transfusion followed in a week. That's the other thing we learned from this disease. Some things come and go without explanation, and other things can be touch-and-go for a long time.

Nov. 16

I can't write when I'm sick, and of course I've been sick a LOT! I went to school the first week, and then I started getting sick again. My WBC was down to 4,000, and before that it was 880 and the differential was 6%! Dr. Lourde thought leukemia was striking back. I'm always scared that it's coming back. I can't go through HELL again. Well, I had a bone marrow, and it turned out that what was making me sick was not leukemia. So why was I so sick?! Finally they said I had pneumonia, and

I had to stay in the hospital. I am so fed up with this shitty life. My stomach is always giving me sick feelings lurching to throw up. They said my headaches were from radiation, but I still get really bad ones. I miss too much school. It's hard. I feel left out. I have to worry about getting a transfusion or having a relapse. This is SHIT!

Living on this earth is unbearable. I want to get off. When I had pneumonia, I think I did get off. I felt like I was above by body, like I was just hanging in the air. I was so cold! Well, I want Hambone to be buried with me. I'm depressed to the lowest I can go. If they don't find a cure super fast, I don't know what I'll do! I had a blow-up and made a scene about having an I.V. again. But I didn't get very sick because of the THC. They're rubbery brown squishy balls, actually quite cute. I don't like how they make me feel, but I also don't like sending up everything from my stomach!

Joanna kissed and did a bad thing with a boy. I don't know anything about that stuff. I'm furious that I don't, and it's baffling, too. A read A Summer to Die and cried. It was a really good book, which I could relate to. Am I bad for wanting my hair back? I do. I want it back NOW! I also hope Cheryl and I go to San Diego.

Jada's skin color took on a silvery sheen making her face appear cast in metal. What little hair that remained on her head had finally dropped away with the slightest breeze, replaced by fine stubs sprouted fine and smooth. People, mostly children, stared at her "crew cut." We could feel their eyes wondering, their lips wanting to ask questions. Angular nose, chiseled cheekbones, fading lips, the tiny scar appearing larger in her thinning eyebrow, Jada looked more like a sculpture than a living body wired with nerves and blood bearing vessels and feelings.

She missed school for chemo and when she was hospitalized, but she never asked for extensions or special allowances. This was her life; I was busy being in the middle of it, and to draw attention to it made us more like a circus than a drama. I had learned, hadn't I, that I didn't know one thing about cancer and its treatment before Jada was diagnosed. I had also learned that one cancer is unlike another and every patient is unique with his or her own story. And I learned, too, that nothing could be explained that did not have its deeper more private underside dredged and flipped belly-side up for public view, not hair, not skin, not pain, not fear. Let the people stare, let them wonder, and let them ask if they care.

In some ways I pitied Arnold in the same way I hated him for not getting up in the night with the babies, for not considering ever staying home with them and allowing me to work my job, for taking the typical man's role and leaving the woman's for me. He never had to clean up the mess made by diarrhea or vomit or blood; he never had to sit up and hold a hot body next to his throughout the night and still be ready for the other one at breakfast. He never took Jada in for treatment or took the abuse for doing it or took her home and took care of her after. All those things he didn't have to do kept him clean. All he had was a shadow of our experience, the mere image in darkness that proved we were there. It must have been hard for him, he who loved the stage, not to be a part of the rich drama of our lives, knowing only the surface, little more than the people who didn't know.

Christmas was rounding the corner. Arnold made an appointment to photograph Jada and Dom for Christmas giving. The bell over the door of the photography shop jangled as we filed in, first Jada, then Dom, and a gust of cold wind coming in behind Arnold and me. "You may have to use special lighting," Arnold advised as the photographer seated brother and sister against a bland backdrop. The photographer looked back and forth between Arnold and the scene with a puzzled wrinkle at his eyes. "You might need to adjust the light for my daughter's leukemia," he explained, motioning to Jada.

The photographer ran his fingers through dark hair that was inclined to fall onto his forehead and squinted at Jada, then back at Arnold. "Can't she tolerate bright light?"

Arnold cleared his throat and shifted his weight. "I mean her skin is so white from her leukemia."

The photographer's lips groped. "Oh, sure." He returned his attention to his composition, lowering a shoulder, nudging closeness. Leaving the sitting, Jada clutched my arm. "My moo," she said playfully, Tinkerbell voice, light and high, prancing on air. "Isn't that a good name for Mom? She likes cows. And she's like a cow, you know, in a good way."

"Sometimes I feel like a cow, but I'm not sure about being called one."

"I'm not calling you a cow, just Moo. You're like my moo. It sounds like a mom should be."

Arnold's voice came gruffly. "That's enough, now, Jada. Your mother said she didn't like it."

"No, she didn't. You always want to act like you know everything. You don't have to get in this. You didn't have to say anything about 'my leukemia,' either. You always butt in when you don't even know what we're talking about."

"Jada! Don't talk to your father that way."

"Well, he's always butting into somebody else's business."

"You may not always like things, but it's not okay for you to use this language with us."

So on Christmas Eve, Arnold did not come up from the lower level when Beverly visited Jada. She and I waved her out the door to a carful of friends, most a year older and all of whom played in the school's orchestra, off to an afternoon Prince concert. Just being in the car with Mark probably was good enough for her. She had graduated from infatuation with a boy dubbed City Fox to an admiration for the prototype of the boy next door. Mark was a serious student, a talented musician, a strong believer, and a safe date, which she pined for. Beverly looked longingly after Jada when the door closed behind her. "She really has grown up, hasn't she?"

I smiled. Any girl who would wear a green and black wool skirt her mother sewed for her to see Prince in concert had to make her mother sleep easy at night. Dom, hearing the door shut, hopped up the steps and plopped next to me on the couch. "What time are we going to Grandma's?" We had to wait away the long hours before opening presents at Grandma M's.

"As soon as Jada gets back. 'Bout six, I guess. Getting nervous?" I patted Dom on his thigh. He put his hand over mine and together we did a little dance with our fingers.

"No. I just wanna know if I have time to play with Jerry."

"Oh, Dom, this is a hard day for that. A lot of people are busy getting ready for things, and you'd get all sweaty and have to take a shower."

"Can't I just see?"

"Okay. But if you do make plans, you have to be home in time to get cleaned up. We don't want to be the ones who are late. Especially not with the big fuss made over Roger every year."

Dom bounded to the kitchen phone, and I heard him dial as Beverly's lips widened into a smile. "He sure doesn't let any of this bother him, does he?"

"Apparently not. And it shouldn't. After all, he has his life to lead." Then I heard the phone click back into its cradle and Dom step gingerly down the stairs. If he were going to Jerry's, he would have run to his room or the closet or to me to ask for a ride.

"Got a busy day tomorrow?" Beverly asked.

"Oh, yeah. My family comes here. This Christmas stuff is crazy. And it just keeps getting bigger and bigger every year."

"But you like it, don't you?"

"I must."

Leaning forward, her eyes limpid and large, she said, "You'll know it when it's wrong. I'll be on my way now."

"Here, take this fruitcake home with you. It's chocolate, and there's no fruit in it, so why it's called a fruitcake is a guess." Beverly thanked me and opened the door, walking out into a billow of sunshine.

At Jada's next monthly IV, Beverly's head peeked through the half-open door; she smiled, fixed her eyes on Jada, and asked, "How was the concert?"

"Do you two want to be alone?" I asked.

"No, you can stay." Jada closed her eyes again. "It was good," she answered. "He played extra because it was Christmas Eve."

"You're pretty tired, aren't you? I just wanted to say hi. Is it all right if your mom has a cup of coffee with me?" Beverly glanced at me before getting an answer.

Jada opened one eye and looked at the tube of orange-colored fluid in the cylinder hanging above her left shoulder. "I guess so. But only a cup."

I nodded to Beverly. "It's already 12:30; do you want me to bring back anything for you?

"No. Just find Heidi and ask her to bring me a cup of 7-Up."

Beverly and I walked to the cafeteria, and I sat facing the clock. "Jada looks so innocent lying there; I just want to pick her up and hold her. Was it hard again today?" Beverly asked. If Dr. Lourde had thought Beverly could make Jada's clinic visits less stressful, he had to be disappointed.

"Yes. Very. I just do all the wrong things."

"I don't think there is a right thing to do. It must be harder with an older child. I was just with a little one with a brain tumor. His mother dangles some toy in front of him and he forgets what's going to happen next."

"That's the thing," I observed, setting my cup onto its saucer. "Jada is so aware of everything. And everyone else wants her not to be. It's like she's being punished twice. I think she's all the stronger for wanting to be so mindful."

"I'm always amazed at children's resilience. They have a very strong will to live."

"People always say that, but I'm not sure what that means. If I really let Jada have her way, she may not have treatment at all." The thought out loud begged elaboration. "It isn't that she doesn't want to live. She doesn't want to live *this way*. She doesn't like the pain of the treatment, she doesn't like the side effects, she doesn't like the, um, artificiality, the effects on nature, she doesn't like being different. So for her to say yes to treatment means for her to say yes to all the things she hates. She lives a contradiction. It's like she's fighting herself.

"And then there's me. I want her to live. And I want for Jada to have her dignity. Puts me in a rough spot, doesn't it? I think she puts all the bad stuff on me so she can save her dignity. She knows I won't let her not have treatment. But, she's so bound up in this mucky mess; there's no straight line for her. Maybe there isn't for any of us."

Beverly rubbed her eyes. "It must be hard doing all this alone. You really don't have any support, do you?"

"I learned a long time ago that I'm on my own. It seems when I count on someone else, I'm left to find my own way, anyway." I became aware of the tables around us and sensed that I had said more than I had meant to say, but I was curious, like a listener nearby, to hear what I had said, and why. I wanted to replay the sequence, but Beverly kept looking at me through blue eyes with tiny black dots in the center and rings around them.

"Do you think you and Arnold would have made it this far if Jada hadn't got sick?"

Her question, so natural, so knowing, startled me. "It's hard to say. In some ways I've become stronger, more self-confident because of the circumstances, but...." I dropped my eyes, embarrassed at her knowing.

"How does Dom fit in all this?"

"He's the type who doesn't want to dwell on things. He doesn't sit well with ripples in life. All this fighting and getting sick and time away; he's a peacemaker—just keep everything running smoothly. I want him to have a normal life, do the things he likes to do; I try to be with him as much as I can. When he's older, an adult, he can look back and tell me."

"You really are a good mother. What you need is a mother yourself."

"Too late now." The hands on the wall clock rescued me from saying more than I'd already felt was too much. "I better be getting back; she'll be looking for me."

I returned to Jada feeling as if I'd just come from soaking in a warm tub, relaxed and reflective, the bubbles of thoughts bouncing, erupting, swirling round and round, moving but going nowhere, out of and back into myself.

Snow fell in fat gobs during our spring break, and all the delicate green buds being pushed against their protective covering by some birthing drive layered deep in the roots and stems felt the burning ice of the unwelcome cold. Maybe some were afraid. Maybe their curiosity spurred them on to find out for themselves what was so great about breaking through moist dark earth. After the school bus picked up Dom, I went out to shovel the driveway. Arnold was in Hawaii. Arnold and Jada and a plane load of other chaperone teachers and seniors from Jordan High School had departed on Saturday. After I shoveled the driveway, I met Beverly for lunch. "Here's a little Russian coffee cake I made for Easter."

"You really like doing these things, don't you?"

"I like to try new things. And I want to have some traditions. This year we're having an Easter egg race."

Beverly smiled. Though she shared nothing of her own personal stories, I felt parity. A you-tell-yours-and-I'll-tell-mine would have closed me down, made me suspicious, not honest. "You look relaxed. This week must be good for you."

"I can't get over how much easier it is without him in the house. I miss Jada, but I'm happy for her. She called and said she wished I were there with her. But she needs a break from me, too. I thought Dom and I would have all this time together, but he's still in school during the day and then off with his friends. He's happy."

"Jada just went to San Diego and now she's in Hawaii. You're investing a lot in her."

"I'm trying to give her experiences and things, too, to balance what's being taken away. My mother wouldn't think that was right, but she also believes that the family should stay together, no matter what. I used to think that I could sacrifice my own happiness for the sake of keeping the family together. But now I'm not so sure it's a good thing to live with this much tension."

"Do you ever talk to Arnold about it?"

"I used to try. I remember way back when I suggested we get counseling. He said he didn't want anyone else knowing his business."

Beverly's mouth scrunched up against her nose; her eyes winced.

"Anyway, I stopped asking, and then I just stopped talking. Now he talks about wanting to get help. It's like Hawaii. When I wanted to go he said, 'that's not seeing anything but a beach.' Now that it's cheap as a chaperone, well, there he is." The sun sparkled on the freshly fallen snow heavy with water as it melted and I could almost hear the cars slosh through it in the street outside the restaurant window. "It would be worse being there knowing what I missed. I just want to get through the next seven, eight years and get out."

"I'm not sure he's really going to change anything, anyway. It sounds like he's afraid he's lost you, so he'll say what he thinks will keep you there."

It seemed like Beverly's words had been in me forever, and at that moment I realized he really had me trapped, and I felt like banging my head with a mallet. "He refuses to even acknowledge how far back our troubles go. He keeps blaming Jada's leukemia for our breakdown, as if it just happened. Poof, she's diagnosed and we fall apart. Sex was a once-in–a-year event until it became never since Dom was a baby. But Arnold forgets that."

"I'm convinced that men have a funny way of distorting the past to inflate their egos."

"There was a study of how genders accounted for their successes and failures. When men succeeded, they took credit as if they were entirely responsible, but when they failed, they looked elsewhere for the reason. Women, on the other hand, didn't take credit for success but thought there were external factors that made their success possible. But, of course, when something failed, they blamed themselves. Is that true or what? I also read that the probability of divorce for people my age is 50% and rising. We're in a phenomenal period of time."

"Can you imagine how different it is for women growing up today?"

"I think of that, too. How Jada, and Dom see me. Will they see me as weak for staying? Will they blame me for their growing up in a family that doesn't work? Would they want me to do what is right for me and see that, ultimately, it's right for them, too?"

"Most children survive divorce quite well. The strain of a poor marriage can sometimes be harder on children than the struggle of managing alone."

"Yeah, I believe that. I wonder if I've waited too long already. Life should be an adventure. The only way it is is if you take control of your decisions."

"How old are you?"

"Thirty-seven. But I feel like I'm as smart as about 13. When do you ever start to feel like you know what you're doing?"

Beverly's short even teeth cut a smile. "It's always hard at the beginning. No matter what the process is. But you have to go through it. You sound just like you should sound."

"All I can say is that I have to believe. I have to believe Jada will be okay, that she'll have a good, long life. I know there's a possibility that she won't. I also know that she or Dom could be hit by a car this afternoon. I don't want regrets for them, either. I want them to think that life is an adventure, too."

"Back off!" I recoiled, a wounded animal that doesn't trust anyone or anything, even the hands of a healer, Beverly's. Spring had finally arrived in Minnesota and its bitter disappointment permeated the corridor of the hospital. Covered with gray, the windowless corridor, lined with close-up photographs of water beads rolling on green foliage and hummingbirds poised, their sharp beaks extracting sweet nectar from willing flowers, retained winter's chill, which in spring was all the more insulting.

Spring was my least favorite season because it was, like North Dakota, always carrying the burden of absence, nothing glamorous, no mountains, oceans, deserts. No one defends the flat blanket of grasses waving mellifluously as the wind asserts its way, uninterrupted, across the plains. No one praises the mounds of clouds in unending sky. People are uncomfortable in the even horizon, element to element. Like spring in Minnesota: no color, no flair, no sweet scents; as if birth wasn't a lot of dirty work.

And death. Unlike autumn, when people, animals, and even leaves create warmth by layering and scurrying around to store up for winter, in spring there is a shedding too soon, and we are left bare-armed and vulnerable, unprepared for the dangers like the plump worms coming out of the thawing squishy ground and being smashed underfoot, not by frolicsome antics, but by mean-tempered ploddings of people swept into shelters by blustering winds. When Jada was diagnosed I had new reason to dread the coming of spring. It reminded me that we had about as much chance as those worms.

So when we encountered Beverly in the hallway, her eyes still warm with greeting, Jada slid her hand beneath my arm, as if a show of fortification against a formidable force would dissolve it if we kept on walking toward the lab. Beverly's Cheshire cat smile remained as I said, "We come here for Jada's medical treatment. What goes on in my life is not Dr. Lourde's domain. I am not one of his patients." Beverly could piece together what led to my outburst.

Jada was there with me when I opened the envelope addressed to me from the hospital. In it were photocopied articles, "On Saying Good-bye Before Death," "Childhood Leukemia: The Emotional Impact on Patient and Family," "The Availability of Insurance to Long-Term Survivors of Childhood Cancer," and more about families and illness. And a letter from Dr. Lourde, which began,

Dear Mrs. Petersen:

I have thought alot about you in recent days, and as you know Beverly and I have spoken at length. Amidst the major responsibility of caring for a child's medical problems in the best way possible, we also feel we must take a major role in trying

to assess families' emotional adjustments and try to help them when necessary and when possible…."

My face flamed as I pictured Beverly and Dr. Lourde hunkered over a desk in the late evening hours, the hot light of a lamp spotlighting her notes, bleaching my confessions from them. I understood that Beverly and Dr. Lourde had the best of intentions and that they wanted to help. In one article I read that divorce in families with childhood cancer patients was high, around 70%, but that discord characterized the marriage before diagnosis; in another, that divorce was no higher in families with cancer than in others.

"…I quite strongly believe that most of the difficulties you and Jada have (and that difficulties her dad and brother have, if any) are either due to, or made substantially worse by, the tremendous stress of having a child with leukemia. Your position is not easy, to say the least, but it is not hopeless or helpless. Many, many families have gone through it, and many have learned to cope fairly well."

Judgment reeked from the page. In the dark rooms of my mind I thrashed through my humiliation, quickly turned to anger. Why wasn't the envelope addressed to both Mr. *and* Mrs. Petersen? Why did Dr. Lourde state that Jada and I had difficulties but gave Arnold and Dom the benefit of the doubt? I knew, I knew, I knew, but instead of offering the elixir of satisfaction that I craved, knowing surged through my body with an electric pulse that blew the circuit of understanding; I wanted to punch, crush, scream, squeeze out the poison of womanhood at the very time that I wanted Jada to inhale its perfume. Be strong, independent, assertive; support, nurture, teach. Which part of womanhood was not violated?

Sitting on the side of Jada's bed at night, I said, "He has no right to meddle. It's not his business what goes on in my life, just yours, and not even that, really."

"It's like I told you, Mom. We don't need anyone else."

"Maybe you feel you don't, Jada, but I think it's still a good idea to talk to Beverly."

"Why? I have you. You won't leave me the way she did." The lamplight sprinkled golden dust drops around Jada's head. I squinted my eyes, running them along Jada's steady jaw, sharp-edged even in the dusky light, across her cheek and up to her eyes, themselves half-closed and gray, hoping to sift out her meaning. "You stole Beverly away from me. She was supposed to be my friend."

"But, she is your friend. When I talk to her it's about my stuff. You can still talk to her."

"Beverly? Not after what she did to me. I can't trust her anymore."

I tilted my head and stared at Jada's pencil drawing of Henry hanging on the wall. Though cast in shadow, the outline of the floppy-eared stuffed dog gradually took shape and I could almost make out the eyes and the nose, but not her signature. Threesomes never work. But I didn't see this one. Instead of my leaving Beverly and Jada to be alone, Beverly and I left without seeing what was happening to the one left out.

The letter from Dr. Lourde gave Jada a hook on which to hang a hurt she'd been feeling for some time. "I'm sorry you feel I stole Beverly away from you. That's not what either one of us wanted to happen. I don't think. I don't know. I get the feeling that everyone there is trying to fix us."

"Now you know how I feel." A small kitten of sadness crept over Jada's face, too precious and innocent. Understandings came too young to Jada, understandings that were not meant for fourteen-year-olds. She did not have the years to study and learn, as I did, that mourning such losses of trust and faithfulness and simple friendship makes a softness inside for compassion and gentleness. She knew only that she had to give them up, and their loss left a hardness that could not produce tears.

After our encounter in the hallway, Beverly kept an honorable distance. Jada no longer made appointments to see her. Nor did Jada let on that she missed her. I did. Jada may have thought we could make it on our own, but I felt that parts of me were running out.

The fresh chill of a new-born day seeped through the walls of the clinic as we began the summer of 1983. School was out. Jada and I had gone new-car shopping. It was the first car I picked out and bought. By myself. Well, except for Jada. She was taking driver's training, and being behind the wheel of a bronze-colored car was like coming face-to-face with her image on the cover of *Seventeen Magazine*. We were planning to baptize the golden car with some road trips to bed-and-breakfast inns. We waited in the clinic for Dr. Lourde and chemo. He sprang into the room, a smile budding under his bristly mustache. "Well, Jada, I suppose you're happy. Looks like I won't be seeing you anymore."

"What do you mean by that? Are you going on vacation again?"

"No," he said, his smile limping. "You're done with your cycle of treatment."

"But, I thought I had another year." Jada looked to me.

"Yes," I agreed, my face heating from the chin up, my eyes beginning to boil over. "You told us, somebody told us, that Jada had three years of maintenance therapy. Remember the chart Heidi showed us when she first started?"

"Do you have it?" Dr. Lourde sat across from us, his hands clasped prayer-like between his knees.

"It was in a black notebook, a 3-ring binder. When we chose the protocol, Heidi counted treatments."

"I'll be back in a minute," Dr. Lourde left, shutting the door behind him. The room was getting colder.

"How do you like that? Well, it's not that I mind. But I don't like the way it's happening."

"Neither do I. I'm supposed to have a party. Everyone else does." We'd been invited for cake, hand-churned ice cream in the summer to celebrate the completion of a cycle of a patient's cancer treatment. I'd probably supplied the recipes if they had strawberry and rhubarb in them.

"You know, I wonder if it's Heidi who made the mistake. This wouldn't be the first time we've been caught in the middle of what she said and what he said. And she would have been in charge of the party. I just want to get this last treatment over and get out of here."

"I want to have a party. I'm cheated out of that, too."

"We'll just have to have our own party. Say, how about having lots of them? Let's think of people who have done something for you or been supportive—Beverly, Phyllis and Ann. Heidi; Margot. How does that sound? It's summer; we can have little luncheons on the weeks we're not going put of town. We'll make foods especially for them, have themes. Where is he, anyway? We'll be here forever if he doesn't get started with your IV." I stepped outside the door. From our room toward the end of the hall, all I could see were the tops of the backs of computer monitors behind the clinic counter. Voices rose like smoky clouds without clarity or definition. I returned and waited with Jada.

Dr. Lourde finally opened the door and came in. Not all the way, just from his hips up, one hand on the doorjamb, the other on the knob to stop him from pitching forward. "I've had Mary look all over for that chart you say you saw, and she can't find it anywhere. I'll have medical records do a search in...."

"Why?" I asked. "Jada could be having her treatment instead of sitting here waiting."

Dr. Lourde took a step forward. "There isn't one scheduled for her today. Her counts are excellent."

"Then why did Heidi make an appointment for one? I don't get it. Just tell me when she has to come in again."

"She doesn't. She's through. Jada?" Dr. Lourde walked toward her and reached out his hand. "I hope you take this the way I mean it. You can visit anytime, although I don't imagine you'd want to. But I hope I don't see you in here again. Have a good life." Jada lifted her right hand to his. In my day, people took females' hands, not shook them as males did. I read a description of how much a character could tell about the other fellow by his handshake. Jada made firm and mighty contact.

"Mrs. Petersen?" I rose to meet Dr. Lourde.

"Thank you," I said, and he reached his hand toward the door. "Well, Jada," I asked, "want to dump some pills?"

July, 1984

*T*ears glazed Jada's eyes, and an aura of golden light emanated from her, radiating to those who encircled her—a halo of admirers. For sixteen years I'd begun singing lullabies with verses from "Turn around...," and on her sixteenth birthday, I could think of no better gift than to hire a handsome young man in a tuxedo to serenade her with this song. Half of it, anyway; I'd stopped singing the second verse when we learned that she might not grow up and have babes of her own.

But she had grown up one whole year, and Arnold wanted a big party, her sweet sixteenth birthday party, he called it. I celebrated one year's anniversary from chemotherapy, one year's anniversary of waiting, watching and waiting. Waiting for Jada's hair to grow; waiting to get it styled and permed. Waiting for her periods to commence. Waiting for every little pain to subside and not be a sign of relapse. Waiting for the end to the waiting. Three years; that's how long it took to declare a cure. One down, two to go. I celebrated this one year and reserved space at the hotel, planned the food, ordered the cake, invited the guests.

And now, the first full year of observation ended, she returned from a chaperoned trip to France, on the threshold of taking her driving test and starring in her sixteenth birthday party. The plane safely off the ground and out of sight, smiling, I dropped into the mailbox a letter addressed to the hotel in Paris. I didn't know how different Jada would be when she came home, but when I said good-bye to her at the airport, I knew she would be. And I was happy for her.

Jada came to me smiling, and I put my arm out to encircle her at the airport when she returned. "Did you try to call one night? I answered the phone and thought it was a crank call because they didn't talk, and so I hung up."

"Yes," she answered, eyes sparkling, dewdrops reflecting the morning sun from soft-petaled flowers. "I wanted to talk to you so bad. I was so disappointed when the operator told me the person didn't know me. I couldn't call again because we made a special trip out of the way just to make the call, and it takes such a long time. You can't just make a call there the way you can here. I really wanted to hear you."

"Did you get my message then? I felt terrible that I hung up."

"I thought that's what happened. The operator had trouble understanding me, and I was speaking to her in French. Then we left Paris the next day to stay at my family's house. I was okay. I was having a good time. I just wanted to talk to you then. You know how you get that feeling, and it's so strong then? That's how I felt."

"Yes, I do know." Her body felt sturdy, full of rich red blood, and I wanted to feel we would be all right, if only we could be together like this, but already we were where we were headed, and I had to release her.

"You're sixteen years old," I answered to myself as the messenger at her birthday party recited the lines I'd sung throughout Jada's sixteen years of life. "You passed your driver's test; you're applying for a job. Turn around and you're a young woman going out of my life." One year down, two to go.

Arnold and Dom went on their own vacation to St. Louis, where there was an amusement park and a baseball team Dom liked, and I made my decision to move Arnold out of the bedroom. Jada had just come home from work at Target, where she stocked and sold McGlynn's bakery, and sitting at the kitchen table, filled out a deposit slip for her first paycheck. I breathed big and pronounced, "It feels good, doesn't it, to make your own money, to have something that you earned? Here with the music playing, I feel so relaxed."

Jada stopped writing. Her response was as simple as the sum she added on the paper. "It's because you're away from Dad. You're not the same when he's around. You don't even talk the way you usually do. You should never have married him. You wasted all those years, and look what he's done to you."

"Oh, I wouldn't say those years were wasted. There are you and Dom."

"Yeah, you better tell Dom to watch out. Look at me. It's because of the two of you that I have this disease." Jada clucked her tongue against the roof of her mouth, and with a flick of her sleek pointer finger clicked the pen. How she had been endowed with such beautiful hands was a marvel to me. Then, just as gracefully, she inserted the check and deposit slip into an envelope. "I'm glad that I'm different, though. If I didn't have leukemia, I wouldn't be like this, you know what I mean? I don't want this disease, but I look at Kimby and other people my age, and I'm not like them. It's like I know more. I've had to think about other things, important things, like having to get through things they take for granted, and dying, and I just can't get excited about the same things they do. Like when Kimby says she couldn't call because she was sooo tired." Jada continued, bitterness biting into her words like coffee grounds in the last swallow. "But *I* should call *her* when I was the one who was at the clinic all day and barfing all night."

"I know. It's hard for me to listen to some other people talk about their kids not getting the right classes or something that they make out to sound life or death. But you had to go through what you did just to be different. That's why I don't think I've wasted all my years with your father. We don't like what made us get here, but we don't want to go back to being dumber. That's why I like teaching, so people can change. But, you know, they have to be unhappy first. Maybe that's not the right word. Umm. Unsettled. Yeah, you have to be unsettled—in a conflict with the status quo—to change."

"Oh, Mom, there you go again, always talking about teaching. Come on, we're on vacation." Jada tossed her white jacket and pants from the bathroom. "These have to be washed and dried for tomorrow," she said. I waited for her to finish brushing her teeth. She was so proud of how she cared for them. Dom didn't like to put in the extra time to floss and brush. Yes, he did take a different approach. Definitely different from Jada's. I wondered how he would take the move.

"If we get a television set for you and Dom up here, then all we have to do is share the kitchen and the laundry room. Then I'd be free." I said, following Jada as she bounced down the hall, past the photographs of her and Dom hanging on the walls, into her bedroom. They were cute children, even when they didn't cooperate for the camera. Dom cried sitting on Santa's lap.

"You could be free anyway. Just tell him to leave."

"I missed my chance. Why do you think he took Dom on vacation? Now he's acting out of spite. He'll put up with anything. I'm beginning to see why women stay in battered relationships. By the time they start to figure it out, they're hooked. But I can make it if he moves downstairs."

"At least you don't want us to be like you." Jada's head popped through her nightie, her caramel-colored hair beginning to cover the tops of her ears. "I don't mean that in a bad way. You can't help the way you were brought up, but you try not to be the same way. And one thing I really like about you is that when you don't like the way things are for you, you tell us we don't have to be the same way."

"Thank you, Angel. But I'm afraid I'm more like my mother than I thought." For a second I wished I hadn't quit smoking; it was a perfect scene for taking a deep pull of smoke and hurling it out in a plume of revelation.

"I won't put up with anything, but I pity the woman who marries Dom. Look what he's learned already. He's going to be just as selfish as Dad and get away without doing anything."

"What do you mean?" I sputtered, "First of all, you're his sister." Growing up with two older sisters, I learned that they could be both wise and protective, cruel and demanding. With children it's not easy taking sides, and maybe not with parents, either. I had an instant image of my father, his white apron dusted with flour, mixing up and rolling out pizza dough. *Ahh, yeast, that's what I smell.* I had always felt sorry for my father, who must have had a gentle touch to roll out that dough so thin and so tender. "I think Dom's pretty agreeable. You're too hard on him, poor guy."

"Poor guy, nothing! All those Sunday nights when you used to go bowling, I had to drag him into the shower. You should have heard him." Jada's words came incongruously from the image of her slipping so blithely into her bed. I sat next her.

"He would have taken his shower when we came home. I don't let Dom get away with everything you think I do. There are people who think I let *you* get away with way too much."

"Well, they're wrong." Jada swept her pointer finger across the bottom of her nose. Habit or not, the gesture seemed purposeful in its indignation.

"I guess it's a matter of perception, and time. Dom's still learning." I turned the bedside light off and sang.

Arnold and Dom came home, and Arnold cleared off his dresser top. He and Dom began the transfer, first carrying his organizer and my brown Schenely bank bottle from my parent's liquor store days, then taking drawers to the lower level. Jada and I removed the screws from the headboard, releasing the frame for transport. Finally I took one end of the heavy queen-sized mattress and Arnold the other, and we shared the burden, making the final trip down; it was our last family effort and my only trip to Arnold's new room. Having my own closet, I wouldn't have to store Arnold's dirty clothes any more, and small as that circumstance may have seemed, I felt like a window was opening up for me and letting in a cool fall breeze.

The next day my own daybed was delivered, and I pulled out and raised the trundle for Dom. The evening had the feel of a sleepover, both of us falling asleep dreaming, he perhaps of a long drive out to center, I of the exhilarating work of stripping the walls and uncovering the windows. I was going to paint the room white.

Aug 16

 Dom and Dad are home from their trip to visit Des Moines, Arkansas, and Kansas City. They said they had fun. So did Mom and I. We had a whole week without them. Tonight Mom and Dad were talking about Dom's school meeting and started fighting. They were yelling and Dom took it really bad. They said they needed to be separated. Last week I told Mom to divorce Dad, and she asked what I thought of her wanting to leave. I told her I wasn't mad at her, but now I'm not sure who is to blame and who I should be mad at.

 They measured me at the clinic. I have grown one inch (5'3") and gained a pound (103 and ½). Mom says I look good. Wow. But I don't think so. I look ugly and feel FAT. I do NOT want to be a tub like I was. Moo is still losing weight and will weigh less than me if she doesn't stop. She walks six miles a day and looks skinny. Her bones stick out. I wish I ate what Mom does or just quit eating for about a week. Maybe Mom is right and I'll lose my pot now that I'm maturing physically. Well, my hair is growing thicker. I want to get a small curling iron and start to curl it. I still have itchies and have a prescription for Benadryl and Novahistine for my allergies. More pills to take! I think some of my drugs have affected my mind. I forget things. Sometimes I don't remember what someone said to me a few minutes ago. Mom says she has noticed it and says she doesn't like what's happened to me. I'm scared I'm losing my mind. I'm reading a very good book, The Best Little Girl in the World. I passed Classroom Drivers' Ed (BORING), and I've finished the range class. Boiling Hot! We couldn't run the air conditioning while we drove. (???) Mom took me out to practice twice today. She says I am a "marvelous" driver. I like driving.

As we ended the second summer of observation, I forgot the waiting for a day once in a while, then for a few days in a row, and as the year lengthened toward winter, forgetting the waiting spread itself out like a tablecloth waiting for the food to arrive. I was teaching in a new assignment, back to a traditional setting when I received an urgent phone call from Jada's school nurse. Jada, she reported, was sick and needed to go home. I fought the urge to panic as old memories flared. Colds, sore throats, spells of fatigue belong to everyone.

Jada lay on the cot in the nurse's office. She rose to her feet unsteadily and I studied her face. She was wan, but the color seemed drained from the surface only, and her eyes were still a vibrant blue in the light. She walked to her locker as if weightless on the moon and forcing each step to make contact with the floor. In the still-warm car stranded outside the bank of heavy school doors, I asked, "Do you want me to take you to the clinic?"

"No, it's not like that." She paused. "I feel so dumb leaving school for this. But I didn't know why I was feeling so sick until she already called you. I finally started my period."

"Jada, that's wonderful! Not that periods are wonderful. But, after all the grim things that have kept you from school, don't you think it's fitting that something normal, good, and right should get just as much attention? How do you feel now?"

"Not so bad, really. That was what scared me. My back hurt so much. I have cramps now." She sat stiffly, as if the pain would not be jarred from her hips. "I took some Tylenol when I found out it was my period." She had entered another passage.

Jada talked on the telephone to Dale and Scott and Mark, and when she went out at night, they were sometimes with her. On a Sunday afternoon while the muffled roar of a crowded football stadium rose from the downstairs television and mingled with the sizzling juices of ribs rendering their fat in the hot oven, Jada wrote secrets in her journal. It lay tantalizingly unguarded, her increasingly private life ripening within its skin. I still sang to her at night; I still sat with her through her bath; I still dried her and soothed her with

176

lotion and powder. But she was reseeding her mind as her body budded seeds of sexuality. When other mothers might have locked their daughters up hoping to restrain them from temptations, I had mixed dreams for her spurt toward womanhood.

May 19

> *Mom took me to a really good modern ballet. We both enjoyed it. On the way home I heard a song that gave me chills because it describes how I feel about Mark. I hope I didn't take us too seriously going to the Video dance at the YMCA. We danced almost all of the slow dances together. We've had other numerous occasions together having a fun time. Like when he asked me to help him make orchestra folders. Or when we went on a bike ride together. It was hard keeping up with him, but he waited for me. He invited me in for lemonade. He has a cute poodle that gurgles "MaMa." He called to invite me to a concert at Sibley Chamber Orchestra on Friday but no one was home. I'm happy he thinks of me, but bummed I wasn't home. I hope he'll ask me out again! He's such a polite guy and super nice. He told me I was a nice person and a great friend. But I want more for us. I'd love to kiss him and dearly want him to WANT to kiss me, too, and hold my hand. I hope he likes spending time with me. We get along great. We like the same things and have many like interests, especially school related. He said that he went shopping for orchestra awards and got mine. That will make it even more special! Maybe I have my hopes up too far. I really REALLY want a boyfriend!! But maybe I'm too mature for them. Maybe I scare them. (Except for Dwayne. I went to prom with him but I am not comfortable around him. He asked me to a movie, and I didn't go.)*

May 21

> *I am taking piano lessons again (and viola, I have a new teacher and I like her better). Naomi treated me like I forgot key signatures and stuff. It took me a while to get back, and I*

think I was getting better until I did awful at a piano exam at Stassen! I was so nervous my hands shook while I played. After I finished, I had a nosebleed and almost fainted. The blood came gushing out and wouldn't stop! Terrible day! I am nervous by all the red dots on my legs, too. I'm scared to think of all that could go wrong.

I have to go on a blucky retreat, which I don't look forward to. I have to be away from Mom a whole weekend. We have a friendship that I don't think others have. We can talk about important things I have trouble talking about with my peers, especially religion, which I don't think is too important to me. I don't have beliefs in a certain faith, and I don't do or not do things because of religious beliefs. Maybe later in my life I can "get something out of religion," but now I'm doing this confirmation program for "social service." We have to list the gifts that God has given us, but I think we have interests and develop them ourselves. I don't even think a God exists, and that's one reason I can't talk about religion with others.

Well, this is what my interests and talents are: I love cute things, Hambone and my stuffed animals, stamps and stickers. I am intelligent, creative (artistic), and musically talented (piano and viola). I also have a good ear. I am a nice person with other people and I have VERY good taste (I should be rich!)

My dad said he has compassion. Mom said she has the capacity to learn and change, and she can speak well in front of people. Dom said one of his gifts is his intelligence.

I sort of agree with all of them except Dad's. We had another big blow-out yesterday. He says one thing and then contradicts himself! I hate it when he does that! GRR!! He makes me so mad! So we were yelling and he was sputtering! And then I pounced on Dom. Mom calmed me down. I love her and am grateful for her, but our relationship could get better. Both of us have to work on it. She says I'm leaving her, and I feel bad about that! But I won't ever leave her. I love her toooo much! She's my Moo!

I dribbled water down Jada's rounded back. The steam in the bathroom dampened my forehead and my dry nostrils. Yet, I loved October best, especially because of the dusty heat and lusty smell of browning leaves. Still imbued with their colors, autumn leaves scented the air, and I could smell the red turning a rich cocoa brown, yellow veined with green, a savory tea against the blue porcelain sky. I had spent the day painting my bedroom, and my body wanted to enjoy the rewards of its stretching. Jada helped, slapping the roller back and forth, drinking up and applying color in her own patch.

"I need the car again tomorrow, Mom. I have to stay and work on the yearbook, and then I have to be at work at 3:30. Is that okay?"

"Sure, if you drive me to the bus stop."

"You know it would be easier if I had my own car."

"Right. It would be easier if your dad could help out, too. But I don't mind taking the bus. In fact, I get some work done, and I like the walk home." I sat back on the toilet seat lid as Jada slumped into the water and poked her knees out. "What time do you get off?"

"Nine." She groaned.

"That's a long day."

"And it's hard, too. I'd quit, but I like the money." Her back rubbed the bottom of the tub, making a belching noise followed by the pata pata beat of water slapping about on the surface.

"Will you get your homework done?"

"I'll do some on break, and then if I have to, I'll finish when I get home. I don't think there'll be much; it's Monday, confirmation night."

"Speaking of, how can you miss that?"

"Don't you remember? We're not meeting to make up for our service hours."

"Oh, yeah. Well, just so you're not getting into too much and falling behind in your school work."

179

"I won't. You know me. I couldn't not get all my work done. That's one thing you taught me." Jada contorted her face in mockery of one who's been cursed. "You're such a perfectionist."

"I suppose we all are about some things. I'm not about cleaning this house. And yet, how am I judged? I like that you like to learn. You don't do things just because you have to. You think and you make connections."

"You taught me that, too. You're always reading or working on schoolwork. It's because of you that I wanted to go to kindergarten so bad. I thought we'd sit in desks and be doing work because you always had papers and stuff. I was so disappointed that all we did the first day was color."

"You ran a tougher play school than the real thing. Poor Dom and Allison! All those worksheets you made for them."

Jada laughed. "Dom hated them. I had to make him sit there until he finished."

"I'm not surprised. He still puts things off. You two are so alike and so different. You both are good in math and with language, and neither particularly likes to read. The first thing you do when you get home from school is your homework, and the first thing he does is go out to play. You practice your viola without being told, and he doesn't touch his bass. You're a lot like my mom, and he's like my dad."

"Oh, don't say that. Grandpa Pope walking around rubbing his forehead all the time. Why does he do that?" Jada paddled water across her belly. "I feel so sorry for you growing up in a family like that. Are you sure you weren't abused?"

I drew my eyebrows together in denial. "Things were different then, Jada. Anyway, Grandpa Pope is sick. My mother says he always was. But then, she thought I was sick, too." I made my finger twirl circles at my temple. "Thinks it runs in the family. I was always a little different from the rest of them." Jada had stirred up some questions in me as I pondered the secrets in my family. "Sometimes I want to understand everything, and sometimes I just want to accept and forget. Okay, ready?" Jada balled up the washcloth and set it on the tub. I eased her out of the tub, and wrapped her in a towel.

Jada dropped me off in the parking lot of Cheslock Heights Elementary to catch the first run of the bus into the city still in the dark. Running myself to catch the bus, I tripped on a parking barrier and landed splat on my knee. The bus driver wore surprise as I looked up through the open door. Later that morning, I learned that I'd broken a bone and would miss a whole week of school.

My dad avoided people, sleeping the day away when he wasn't pacing. Yet, he'd invited the whole family, including his sisters, to a day of bocce, a party my dad planned for the weekend. Stranger than that was his call to me: my dad couldn't have known my telephone number nor made a long distance call without my mother's help. "I really want you to come up," my dad said to me. "Everyone else will be here."

"Arnold says we can't; he says I won't fit inside his car and I can't drive by myself," I answered. "Besides, I'm not supposed to stand. We'll come up later this year."

My dad insisted, strangely, as well. "I think you should be here."

That admonition should have been a clue. And it was: on Sunday night I had a case of the jitters, and when I answered the ringing phone, my mother said, "I have some bad news."

Voices from the television news broadcast plumed up the steps as through a chimney and Jada waited in her bedroom while I requested another substitute. As soon as I hung up, Domenica called. "I didn't get to say goodbye." Domenica's voice wavered, and, I envisioned, tears streaked her cheeks.

"You were there; that was your goodbye."

"But I didn't know. If I'd known, I would have told him stuff. I would have said goodbye."

"You say goodbye every time you see someone. He had a nice party after a bad life. He called me and wanted me to change my mind; he had to know."

"Idina, you must feel awful!"

"No, not for me. For him, yes. No, I take that back; he finally gets some peace now. That's all he wanted, that and a good time." I wondered when my dad stopped having a good time. A black and white photograph of him and my mother and another couple at a restaurant flashed before me. They each had a drink—a highball, my dad called it. They used to travel to football games in Iowa, Illinois. And they had poker parties, went dancing. My mother wore a silky blue print dress with a full skirt. I begged my dad to polka and schottish with me at the barn dances in Finlayson, but he never stomped his feet one-two-three the way he did with my mother. I think that's when he stopped having fun, somewhere after we were born.

"Dad wanted to be cremated," I told my mother two days later. The rest of the family sat around my dining room table. My mother's and Punky's faces were plastic, hard and glossy where yellow light hit and lay like discolored shellac on the surface of their skin; they were exhausted from making funeral and burial arrangements. Picking out the casket. Ordering flowers. Bickering, I was sure, over money. I expected an arched eyebrow, a folding together of skin above my mother's upper lip. Her face remained flaccid.

"It's too late now. He never said that to me; I wish I'd known about it before."

"I figured you knew. I mean, if he told me...." I trailed off, knowing before I got there that I had taken the wrong turn.

I felt Domenica's eyes sear through the thick air like the ends of two car cigarette lighters crackling with tobacco newly lighted. Punky spoke out, "It's going to be real nice. We're getting the priest from Our Lady of Mt. Carmel, and we got matching sprays of flowers, one from wife and the other from daughters. Then inside the casket will be a heart of roses from the grandchildren. Real nice. But, man, I'll tell you, it's a lot of work. I'm so tired. How you holding up, Freddy? He had to drive last night and then get up early this morning." Punky reached her hand over to Fred and patted him on the thigh. Fred's elbows squatted on the tabletop, immovable stumps to his sagging cheeks.

"Just let me know how much I owe you." I didn't really care about the details and couldn't imagine my dad would even have wanted a funeral. Dust swirled and settled silently around us, and I felt that when we all stood, we'd leave behind our imprints.

"He just collapsed," Punky said, remembering. "Everyone had just left and I was helping clean up, and he fell to the floor. Mother called 911 and I tried CPR on him until they came."

"It was his kidneys," my mother said, her nose pinched and her eyes searching a small area of the table. I bet she wanted a cigarette to accompany her vision; the smoke would help to cloud unpleasant memory.

The house cleared of my family, who left as they came, touching down and skipping out like a squall, I crutched my way to Jada's room. I pulled the blankets over Hambone, huddled within Jada's arm, up to Jada's chin, and sat on her bed. "Poor Grandpa. I just hope he'll finally get some rest."

"How did you come out of that family? You're so different."

"Jada, I have been and am one of them. And you're part of me. We have to try to take the best of what we get and make it better. You say you want to live in a mansion with a little cottage for me out back. The day will come when I'm not going to fit into that little cottage the way you want me to. I'll want to be who I am and you might not like all the parts of me."

"I don't already," she said.

"That's the way it's supposed to be. We're supposed to separate. We can't be the person the other wants just to please each other. You deserve to have your own life, and I should have mine."

"I know. I can feel it already, and sometimes I like it, and sometimes I feel sad. Why can't we just stay the way we were? Just you and me? We don't need anyone else."

"You wouldn't like it for long. You have wonderful things ahead of you, and I want you to have them, just as I wanted to have them for myself. It's your turn."

"Grandma Pope didn't even care that Grandpa wanted to be cremated. She probably just worried about how much money it would cost."

"What felt weird about tonight is how careful they were. I've been a champion for my dad; maybe they thought I'd put up a fuss. It must have been hard for Punky to try to save him. She's always taken my mother's side, especially when they fought and he beat her. I woke up to him belting Punky, too, calling her names, my mom looking on. She had dreams of carrying a gun to protect my mother, and there she was, breathing mouth to mouth to save him."

"I want to be cremated, too. Remember that." Jada's voice skimmed the room's peppery darkness with a hawk's outstretched wings, its tips seemingly relaxed and letting the current support them.

"Me, too. And burn my journals, too. Put them all in there with me. But not my rings and jewelry; you can have them."

"Mom, do you believe in heaven and hell?"

"No, I don't. I don't believe in an afterlife, either. People have been believing all kinds of explanations to help them understand the world ever since the beginning of people. I believe in the spirit and memory of people, though. I believe anything is possible, so I don't disbelieve. We don't know, so how can I say what is or is not?

"I'm pretty sure your Grandpa's spirit came into this house once after he died. Your dad was gone for a night, and I heard a door shut downstairs and felt him here. Now you and Dom have no grandpas left. Dom never even knew that grandpa. Too bad Grandpa Pope was sick. He could have liked Dom."

"I feel sorry for him and everything, but whenever we saw him, he was either sleeping or walking around rubbing his forehead. Did he even know who we were?"

"He did. But even if he had been well, he wouldn't have been much different. That wasn't his way. The only time I remember him playing with any of us was when my folks gave me a softball and bat for my birthday."

"You? That must explain why you like to walk so much. I hate to walk."

"You like graceful things, like skating and gymnastics. Dom's the one who likes team sports. My dad might have gone out with Dom and hit a few balls with him.

"I think if my dad had had his way, he would have played his life away. But he did care. My dad hated hospitals, but he came to see you. Out in the waiting area he asked about 'all those people walking around in jeans,' and I told him they were nurses.

"'They let nurses wear them kind of clothes?' he asked.

"'Them and the doctors,' I said. And you think you hate blood; Grandpa also told me that if you ever needed blood, he'd give it. No one else ever offered theirs. He knew what was going on. I think he was just trying to survive in a very unfriendly world. I don't know what ran through his head all night, but it kept him awake and moving, and then when day came, he was exhausted and slept. Maybe he couldn't bear to face what he could see during the day." Jada's eyelids fluttered sleepily.

"I have to get Dom to bed, yet, too. Ready?" After the last lullaby, I bent down with a kiss to Jada's forehead. "Good night, Jada; I love you."

Mary Lou's voice up close and personal could shatter a plate glass window. Amplified by the microphone she spoke into, it came a bolt of lightning cracking the quiet of my empty classroom. "Mrs. Petersen, someone's here to pick you up. Shall I send her to your room?"

"No, I'll be right down." When I arrived in the office, Mary Lou ran to the counter and leaned over it as if to leap in a one-handed swing over a gymnastics horse, a highly unlikely event, given her size. She was short, but she was also wide, but not as wide as she was before "The Diet," which, she told me, shimmed her to what she considered manageable proportions. "She went into Thomas's office. Who is that, your sister?" she asked hungrily, smacking her bloated breasts this way and that until there was no more room for them to spread, to get closer to my ear.

I laughed. "Thank you! That's my daughter."

"Oh, I didn't know. She told me her name was Jada, but I thought she must be your sister. She's so pretty. She looks just like you."

"Well, thank you again!" I swung my leg between crutches and turned the corner into the assistant principal's office. Jada may never have known Thomas, except for, pushing our grocery cart around the neighborhood SuperValu one winter Saturday, Jada and I nearly bumped his. Thomas, in his surprised manner, ricocheted stiffly backwards as if our appearance in the same aisle had been a shot at close range. "What are you doing here?" he asked.

"We come here to shop," I answered, instantly self-conscious of my Saturday clothes, my Saturday hair. When he learned how closely we lived to him, he and Sheila called Jada to babysit their two boys. Later, out of convenience or necessity, I rode to and from work with Thomas instead of taking the bus, and we fused a friendship. Morning conversations in Thomas's car, black and slick and fast—he sported speeding tickets as another would mounted game—left me at a disadvantage. With a ready wit, incisive as a snake's fangs, and especially current with popular culture, he plied the machinery of world events as one would a sexual toy: by itself, objectified; for himself, manipulated for pleasure.

Both he and Jada stood overlooking the irregularities he had been sorting, one of the duties of his position—dealing with the human fallout of public schooling, students and teachers not seeing eye to eye. Reasonableness and decisiveness, both, made him the assistant principal people could count on. Thomas's ease with language made him appear arrogant, and teachers looked askance when they speculated on his private doings, but they balled a fist and banged it down hard expecting a bottom line when they wanted action from Thomas. They got it fair and square; he documented everything, though not always to their liking. He was short and slightly built. On a bad day, I weighed as much as he.

"Come in and sit down," Thomas said, half rising. He motioned to a chair next to the wall. Jada walked to the same chair and sat on my lap. Thomas, who shook anything like it was a rattle to hear what was funny in it, gestured toward another chair and asked, "Didn't you see that chair next to your mother?"

"Yes, I did. So?" she volleyed. And scored, if you count last words. But they weren't in competition, so Thomas withdrew his hand and sat down.

"I hope you didn't come all the way here just to pick your mother up. I could have given her a ride home," Thomas said.

I peered around Jada and said, "Thanks. We're not going home yet. We're off to the clinic."

"Oh, is it time to get that thing off your leg? It looks like a modern day version of a chastity belt."

"No, not yet, unfortunately. Anyway, I don't need a chastity belt. There's nothing to be protected from."

"That's too bad." Thomas's eyebrows shot up into little arrows. His lip kissed his front teeth in one of his facial gestures that looked like he was taste-testing the information. Thomas paused, swallowed that tidbit. "Well, then, I've got a question for you. Sheila and I are taking some friends out, and they like Italian food. You're Italian and appreciate the penultimate in cuisine as in other things; where do you go when you want to savor the fine spices of Italian cooking?"

"When I want good Italian food, I make my own. Everything else is all watery with no seasoning."

"Not even Luzzi's? They have the reputation of being authentic. Surely there are other Italians in the city who know how to cook."

"Nope, not like my mom," Jada popped.

Thomas reared his head, raising his eyebrows again, but dropping his lids to make his face elongate into seriousness. Dropping his tone as well, deeper than was meant to travel the distance between us, Thomas said, "I bet you like everything you get your hands on to be hot and make you sweat." He bound the irregularities into two piles and placed them neatly, like two cairns, in the center of the blotter on his desk, shifting the mood into business as usual. Anyone walking into his office would know exactly what Thomas planned to do the following day, and indeed, that was Thomas's greatest gift to teachers: to follow through on their complaints, large and small, in one day's turn-around time.

While Thomas gave one his full attention, he observed his limit, and you knew when you had used up his allotted time. He put his pencil in the center compartment of his top desk drawer, which I also knew, would be as uncluttered as the surface, and shut it. At my first teaching job, Arnold advised me to keep neat appearances for the custodians' sake. "Line up your shades before you leave," he counseled. My initiation into how one gets a reputation as a teacher, good or bad, was how you take care of the little things. Thomas closed his drawer gently and locked it, not because he was concerned with censure from custodial staff, but because Thomas was neat and tidy and meticulous about everything. I wouldn't have been surprised if he had opened the drawer to check that the order he had imposed hadn't been disarranged by the sliding of the drawer, except that Thomas was also self-confident.

When we cleared the parking lot, Jada asked, "Does Thomas always talk like that?"

"Yes, he feels pretty sure of himself."

"I think he likes you."

"Thomas could 'like' anyone. What saves him is that he's transparent. The things he says are casual invitations. What I think he wants most is for someone to make a pass at him."

"Dale Williams's like that. He's been with a lot of girls. When he makes a move on me, I don't know if it's because I'm a girl or if I'm someone special."

"Whoa. You haven't told me about anything like that."

"I don't have to tell you everything." Her tone was identical to Thomas's. "But what would you say if I did want to have sex?"

"I'd say, 'Be careful. Be careful of who and why. Remember, it's your body. And use birth control.' Are we talking that now?"

"No, don't worry, Mom, Cerise and I have made a vow to be virgins." Cerise and Jada advertised their pact, each wearing a white sweatshirt, the numbers 69 painted in alternating tantalizing pinks, one baby, one hot, above their French names on the back, "Une Vierge" above their softly mounded breasts.

"I'm a six, and she's a nine," Jada asserted when I raised my eyebrows at the suggestive number. "So together, we're sixty-nine. We're not going to give up our virginity until we turn twenty-one." Of Jada's sincerity I had no doubt. I had an uneasy feeling about Cerise, though, and it wasn't just that her "girlfriend-assigned fruit" was a cherry. She had long honey-colored hair that could have fallen, like Veronica Lake's, over her right eyebrow, and plump wet lips bursting with cherry juice that seemed, the way she bunched them together, to invite sucking. To a young man, Cerise's flirtatious eyes and sexy badge were more of a come-on than a put-off.

"It's a noble pledge," I observed.

"I don't even see what's so wonderful about sex. But Dale, he kind of makes me feel like it."

Settling into the car, I said, "If I could choose, I'd want you to wait. I'm glad for the excitement you feel, but I'd advise you to make your choice to have sex on more than that feeling."

We arrived at the hospital, and this time, Jada dropped me off at the main entrance. "What happened to you?" Heidi asked. We caught each other up on our lives. Heidi paged through Jada's album of pictures from France and told us that Dr. Lourde and his wife had a baby boy and that he was an awful patient when he was hospitalized with appendicitis surgery. Heidi and Barb still shared an apartment, and Marilyn was nursing on the floor.

Dr. Lourde came into the room with a lighter step than I remembered. He looked lighter, too, though he hadn't changed his costume; he wore the same crisply colored striped or plaid buttoned-down and open collar shirt and the same taupe, navy, or black corduroy pants, and brown loafers, not the kind he could wedge a penny into but ones with tassels. His hair was newly cropped, a rim of white scalp receded into the curls that clung close to his neck.

"Well, Jada, long time no see! Mrs. Petersen, how are you? Looks like you should be here, not Jada."

I assured him that I had no complaints. "I used to say that if you're going to have an accident, there's no better time than on a Monday morning on your way to work. I don't say that any more."

Dr. Lourde considered. "And how are you, Jada? Your counts look great."

"Good, 'cause I don't feel so great. I was a little nervous because I've been tired a lot lately, and I don't know, just kind of weird feeling."

"Have you had a fever or any sickness, like a sore throat, or lots of headaches, soreness in the joints, anything you can name?"

"Have I, Mom?"

"She has a job now, and there're some physical demands, lifting, and things like that."

"No, I don't lift anything anymore. A guy who works the early shift does that now. By the time I get there, everything's out."

A hush descended while Dr. Lourde examined Jada as if he were lining up to swing for double birdie on the 18th hole. He stood focused still, the only movement detectable from the rear was the flexing of the muscle in his right leg as it tightened to keep his torso unmoved. That patience to be still enough to detect signs on which to wait, signs on which to act, that had to be taught. Or at least learned. Then, as if the ball had dropped in, he broke the silence. "You look healthy to me," he said, replacing the ophthalmologic instrument into its cradle on the wall. Dr. Lourde gave Jada one last look and said, "Call me if you notice anything unusual. Nice to see you again, Jada, Mrs. Petersen."

"Thank you. Okay, Jada?"

Heidi's liquid voice poured honey on Jada's departure, and Jada lapped up the sweetness of Heidi's interest in her life, namely school and boys. She promised, to Heidi's saccharine smile, to bring in the pictures of herself and Bill from the Sadie Hawkins dance.

Jada quit her job selling bakery at Target. She was feeling the pressures of going to school and going to work, feeling a little more tired. The hours were a little long and a little late. She had a little more schoolwork and a little less time to do it. Then the holidays were approaching, and she was a little busier. Confirmation classes, piano lessons, the orchestra winter concert; she had a little less energy.

Winter's ice-cold jaws bit into our bones and locked us indoors. Hawaii: the perfect antidote to aching backs and cold extremities. And, as much as Jada loved Hawaii, she was just too tired to go. But Dom? Now that didn't take too much time to lean up against, and more tempting than getting away from the cold and snow, which Dom definitely did not like, was getting away from seventh grade.

Dom and I negotiated his keeping a spotless rating at school, and he went downstairs to tell his dad the good news. "What's the matter?" I asked as Jada rummaged medicines in the cupboard.

"It's my back again. I don't like it." She dug the cotton out of the plastic container. "I don't see why you don't take this stuff out of the jar."

I shrugged and snatched the white fluff from her before she threw it away. "I can take fingernail polish off with it."

"You don't wear fingernail polish."

"I used to." I had bottles, each partially filled. Now and then I opened one, hoping the rose-colored syrup had thickened to a gooey sludge so I could justify throwing it out, but luck was on my wrong side, and I set it back to grow more feathers of dust. "Is it your period?"

"No, it isn't," Jada said, clapping her open hand to her mouth and throwing her head back to swallow. She had gotten very good at taking pills without water and would, sometimes, swallow them dry voluntarily. "I think we'd better go in to the clinic for some blood counts."

"You think it's leukemia?" As if that thought weren't alarming enough, the telephone rang as I said the word. Watching Jada's face, I tried to make the picture of her sick, but I could see nothing other than how she looked there before me, the same as yesterday and the day before, short light brown hair, thin, like everyone's on the Petersen side. Fair, fair skin, white almost, but it was February, and anyone with as much as half Scandinavian blood in her was bound to look a little like the color of snow when that's all there was outdoors. Jada didn't wear lipstick much, so I was used to her lips natural; I could still see the two points of her upper lip, rounded like the top of a heart. And she still had freckles, little, and I mean little, not the big blotchy ones that looked like hand-torn confetti, but little motes dusted along the crest of her nose as if someone had just jogged by and splattered the sandy beach into the air and she, a bystander, caught a smidge from the wind. Still blue, blue like the ocean with the sun shining straight on it so you can see through the blue to the bottom and all the sparkling rocks and pebbles that glimmer upwards, were her eyes.

"That's probably for me; Kimby's supposed to call me when she gets home from work." Jada was halfway down the hall, and my picture was gone. I was left alone with the fullness of a thought for which I had no putting place. The next day I called for an appointment. The report from the lab contained no ominous figures, Dr. Lourde made an examination, and we were sent home with the assurance of lack of evidence—again.

But Jada gobbled Tylenol like they were M & Ms. And, for weeks, she insisted that it sure felt like leukemia, but her blood cells passed inspection every time they were counted. As nothing after nothing turned up, Dr. Lourde became less and less receptive to her unexplainable symptoms and suggested that her fears of the return of the disease could cause the mock beginnings of leukemia. He assigned a doctor who specialized in less traditional medicine to Jada's case.

Jada asked, "Mom, do you believe me? Do I sound like I'm making this up?"

"No, but I think it would be to your advantage to go along with the suggestion, not because of you, but because of Dr. Lourde. You have to trust him as much as you want him to trust you."

"I better not be going up in an elevator again!" Jada assented. "I'll see her, but only if you stay with me. I want you to see that

I'm doing everything right. I might be afraid of getting the disease back, but it's only because what I feel is real."

Dr. Cleary didn't promise miracles. Two weeks passed. Two weeks of meditation instruction and practice. Two weeks of more pain in Jada's lower back and a growing malaise. "Can't you call Dr. Lourde again? I've tried; hasn't it been long enough?"

"Yes, it has, Jada. I'll take you in for counts the next time we see Dr. Cleary." I looked hard and long at Jada for a sign, any sign that made her look different. Was her skin always this faint, or had I only imagined it was once painted with vibrant colors? She did sound different, her speech winding down like a record on a slow-moving turntable, like too much inflection infused into her utterances would cause her to break out in a sweat. The brightness in her eyes dulled along with her excitement. But the counts continued to come back as normal.

The snow was still tall but getting wetter as each day in March the mercury stretched upwards towards the freezing point and new snowfalls were heavy and swollen with their own demise. From a vacant counselor's office I phoned Dr. Lourde and requested that he return my call within the hour. Locked away from the heat of human occupancy, even for a few days, the room held onto the hard chill of emptiness. Shivers ran up and down my arms like the little Scotties that were knitted into my sweater vest, and I turned my face up to the overhead lights as if to the sun. The phone rang an electric current, shattering the air into little crystals that scraped against each other, sending them into a frenzied cascade against my nerves. "I know I've bothered you a lot, but really, Dr. Lourde, you've got to find some way to help Jada. She's tired all the time. She's sick, and she's sure it's leukemia."

"Mrs. Petersen, it seems unreasonable," he answered in his reasonable voice, "to suspect leukemia. She's just been in for counts, and there's nothing to indicate that her disease has returned." I could almost hear his muscles tense to listen patiently, another behavior learned.

I stood my elbows on the desk, one hand holding the phone to my ear, the fingers on the other feeling cold and stiff as it clamped, a standard bearer for my forehead. "You know she has complained of pain in her lower back. On top of feeling she has the disease, she feels no one is listening to her."

"Jada is a very bright young woman. But that intensity might be what is clouding her perception. She focuses so intently that she may be creating a situation that has no basis in fact." Dr. Lourde took breath in quickly and loudly. "I know of a young social worker who works well with young people. This is out of his usual field, but I think he'd be able to connect with Jada. I think it's worth getting hold of him and seeing if he wouldn't see her."

I felt myself grow colder, the girders in my body stiffening, and stalled at his authority. He had it all figured out, probably already talked to the guy. "You know what happened last time."

"I don't know what else to suggest. I don't think it will serve a purpose for me to see her again. I've done all I can do except a bone marrow. I just don't think that's something we should do without some concrete reason. Medicine isn't 100% accurate, but there isn't anything more we can do until we have something to go on."

I imagined going home and facing Jada with Dr. Lourde's response. I saw her face, grown long and thin, her cheeks hollowed, as if the wind of long suffering eroded the color from flesh, her forced exhalations, her sagging shoulders, weighed down by the suspicions she'd been bearing alone for so long, her limp legs, tired, too tired to make long distances worth the effort, and flecked with red. Her legs. "She has red spots. How do you explain those little red dots all over her legs?"

Hesitation hummed in my ear. "What do they look like?"

"Like tiny little ink dots, not even the size of pin heads."

"They could be petechiae. Those are tiny breaks in the capillaries." Another silence. "I have a conference this afternoon, but you can bring her in tomorrow. In the meantime, I'll get the information about the social worker for you. If you don't like him, you don't have to go back."

If Jada didn't see this new wonder social worker, and my gut told me she wouldn't, what would be Dr. Lourde's response the next time I called? Tricked, caught in between, damned by one if she refused and damned by the other if he wouldn't see her, and damned either way if she knew the truth. A rivulet of water slid down my back, moistening my waistband, as I switched off the light and shut the office door.

"Hmm. They're hardly there, but I do see them. I don't see any bruises. Had any fevers?" Jada had Dr. Lourde's attention. He breathed intensely as he examined her.

"I told you something was wrong." The words were the air waiting to be breathed as when emerging from under water, except they lacked the robustness of one's return to the surface.

"Well, Jada. I don't know what to say. Your counts don't show leukemia. I even asked for one more test to be done on them. I don't know what's making you feel the way you do." Dr. Lourde stepped back, and in the same clinical tone, said, "I told your mother about someone I want you to see. I'd like to go ahead with that. I'll see about insurance coverage." The remark was for me, or for time. "But I want you to watch for any unusual marks or fevers. I don't like the looks of this either." He peered again at Jada's polka-dotted leg. Then he straightened his back. "Okay, Jada? Will you do that?"

She had been watching him all along—she always did. Their conversations, or consultations might better describe them, belonged to the confidential category. Jada looked away from Dr. Lourde to me, nodded, and I felt an unnamable feeling crawl along my skin and burrow into my sense of prediction; I did not trust what I saw.

We said goodbye to Dr. Lourde on Thursday and on Saturday to Arnold and Dom, flying to Hawaii for the spring break tour. School was still in session for Jada, so the days were mine until Good Friday. On Monday, I made my trip to Regina's for Easter basket candy and stashed it in the closet just before Jada arrived home from school. Her face was squeezed of its juice, and she raised her feet to climb each step as if cement blocks encased her shoes. Tuesday and Wednesday were no better, but Jada did not ask to go to the clinic, so I waited, too. *Tomorrow, though; if she's the same tomorrow, I'm going to call.*

Thursday morning Jada called me from her bed. To humans, all seals might look alike, but mothers returning from hunting in the sea can find her own just by sound; I could tell what was wrong by the way Jada sounded, that morose undertone that comes from fear and knowledge, and submission to both. Deep sadness fought against jumping out of my bed. Her teeth chattered; the pupils of her eyes so deep and hollow, I was afraid I'd fall into them. And all the knowledge she had in them she had given to me when she called my name.

The entire hospital wanted to be on vacation during the week preceding Easter. The clinic was closed, as was the outpatient lab. I had my pick of parking spots and boarded an empty elevator to the second floor to the inpatient lab, where Jada, Hambone, and I went for another blood sample. As we waited, Jada was being pulled into a possession, a sleep of submission, of what I imagined happens with hypothermia, when body functions slow down, and a false warmth comforts it. I felt I had to talk her awake, watch her breathe, keep her from freezing to death.

"Sorry," a voice broke the air like a pick the ice. "This won't take too much longer. You can leave as soon as we're done." The starched woman eyed Jada, whose head slumped on my shoulder, and turned to her work counter. "It'll take a while for the test to be processed," she continued crisply, and I wondered if lab technicians were trained to be cold, their sharp surface harboring grim secrets about people's futures. Jada's spirit resisted the snapping of the band, the flexing, the final piercing of the needle, cringing as the syringe drained her of truth serum, but she didn't fight while the blond-haired technician performed her rituals, four years from the month and holy season of the initial diagnosis, when her enemy appeared to be conquerable by brute resistance. Maybe her surrender was payback to her blood that had turned on her. Or maybe she just wanted everything to be over, the mystery, the hurting, the waiting; all that was worse than the inevitable.

"I'll forward the results to Dr. Lourde. He'll call you." I could see that the tube the technician held in her hand lacked richness.

Jada rode with me to a Polly Berg store where I set Jada on the brocade couch and began piling up nighties, pink or white or the faintest blue, soft, like powder. Jada's skin shone luminously, as if nothing were there underneath the thin layer of tissue that held her together except for a faintly glowing light. She breathed in short gasps, her whitened face drooped to her chest, a wilting innocent flower. "Two pairs of slippers, one pink and one white," I requested.

The penitent thing would have been to go to Maundy Thursday services to keep vigil before the betrayal, to pray for redemption and salvation, or just to pray. We did neither; asking for favors just because times got shaky seemed no more honest than the hokey manipulation of statistics and success stories of the religion of medicine. It took all of our faith to boil eggs and roll them around in cups of colored water because, late in the afternoon, Dr. Lourde called and wanted us to meet with him the next day— late the next day, 4:00 o'clock on Good Friday, after Jesus had been raised on the cross and for three hours suffered to his death while the skies gathered all of God's fury into a massive darkening gray thunderhead that retaliated vengeance, when the skies, according to the nuns who taught me, should have cleared. We were going to discuss Jada's options for treatment. Officially, her leukemia was back, and it had taken her five months to convince them, five months of knowing it was back before they did.

The rest of the night, Jada sat next to me, in the corner of the couch, resting in a half-upright, half-lying sprawl, her legs and feet spilling from her torso in a lifeless tangle like used clothing carelessly tossed and fallen in disarray. There were better things to do than to watch television; but, we cared to do no other thing than not to disturb our numbed state, and we were not really watching television, for that would take at least some imagination. I heard only the thudding of Dr. Lourde's message and the beating of my heart, made palpable by Jada's head leaning against my chest.

I kissed the top of Jada's head, and for a long time we were silent until she said, her face turning up, her words coming as after a rock lodged in her heart had been tippled, upturned, and bared to the sun, "My body's dying." No matter from which angle it was approached, and no matter how many times she tried to give her fate back, it offered no soft spots, just hard truth.

"I want it to be different. I want you not to have to go through all that agony again. But I also want you to have more phone calls and more chocolate-frosted custard-filled doughnuts, and I want you to fall in love, and I want to kiss you at night and tell you how good you are and how much I love you." I began wishing my words back, scrambling my thoughts, making them unknowable and, therefore, prayer-like. But if I can take words back, why not her? What if I could take her back, just pull her back inside me, keep her from this night, this wrathful cloud that hovered above us like a stone too heavy to remove? What if there were no drugs and no X-rays and no telephones or boys with leukemia on *Little House on the Prairie*? And what if nothing mattered?

I had called Dom, who that day, that Good Friday in Hawaii, turned thirteen and to whom I wished a happy birthday and promised a birthday cake on Sunday. They were just leaving for breakfast; we were getting ready to go to the hospital.

"Hang in there." Arnold's encouragement caught me up short, and like a noose, it cinched me inside it. But what was I to do? Change the test results? Change my life. If I could just believe, I could turn over my burden, be rid of it, ride on the wings of the eagle, hang on, hang tough, hang in there.

Bath water lunged into the tub, and bubble bath under the thundering spigot grew foam. I bathed Jada with knowing hands and thought back to those bath times at the apartment, when I discovered how to turn a convulsive event into one of pleasure, her infant feet kicking with uncensored delight. A few years later, in this blue tub, I wreathed suds around her child's face. "Look," I had said, holding up the mirror to her face, "who let that lion in here? Did you?"

"Roar!" She tried to sound ferocious, but the fury she manufactured gave way when the giggles overtook her. "Do another." Soap bubbles hanging from her ears and chin transformed her into a goat; coaxing pointed tips atop her head, I made her into a dog. Her favorite was the crown; she looked at her fantastic self in the mirror and stretched her lips so wide her straight, sturdy teeth could have jumped right out and done their own little tap dance of pleasure when she saw she was a princess. I rinsed off the lather, and soap bubbles drooped and fell into flat little pearls that floated on the surface. Then she went to work herself and concocted potions of flaky bath water and mushy bar soap; Under the spell of her own incantations, containers perched along the lip of the tub, each one holding a secret only she could divulge, while I sat, ever watchful, on the damp ceramic floor. She was a darling child with glistening teeth; when she smiled a whole row of stage lights lit up. I watched her progression into young girlhood. When she saw the page with the ballerina in *Someday,* by Charlotte Zolotow, "someday" became a theme.

And now, what could one hope for someday? No one's someday dreaming should warp like a book left out in a spring rain. Jada's disease back, I was not ready to let it take her, not yet. *I'm going to stay with her, bathe her and love her, keep her someday alive.*

I felt like a heathen trespassing sacred ground as we walked the hospital corridors and met no one and heard no sound on Good Friday. Four years earlier I anticipated the conference to determine Jada's treatment with somberness and felt ironically like I had come to the wrong masquerade party disguised as Godiva, having already bared my ignorance. When I left, I knew little more, except that the clinic and the hospital were the heartbeat of Jada's existence. I never got over the feeling of being misfitted with that hospital culture, and though I learned signs to worry over and nicknames for chemicals and doctors' timetables and nurses' dispositions by the turn of their heels, and though I ate meals there, napped for minutes and slept for hours there, cried there, dreamed there, brushed my teeth there, I never once felt that I belonged there. It was a place where we lived, but it was not home.

Four years later, Jada and I were returning to that place different; the hospital had not changed and the people there had not changed; we had. We did know a little. We knew that Jada had lost the 50-50 wager of four years ago: she had not survived cancer at all, even though none showed up for almost four years. We knew that Jada's chances of surviving this round were significantly reduced, since what had been prescribed to cure had not. We knew that there was only one worse fate, and that was for cancer to rear atrociously even while the host body was receiving anti-cancer drugs. Those were just the mind-knowing things we knew. We also knew that if we were committed to living we were committed to each other. We knew that no matter what anyone said about helping us or supporting us or caring about us, we were alone, each alone, born alone and dying alone. We knew this was not a fire drill. We breathed the smoke and felt the heat of the flames that consumed the way of our living.

This time when we met with Dr. Lourde, we knew that the decision to be made, like all decisions, had been made already, ineluctably bound to its origin, through time before Jada was born, before even I and all the other mothers and daughters that came before us and came down through us to this moment. We gathered, Dr. Lourde, Beverly, Jada, and I, around a large long table in a central conference room of the clinic with lights dimmed to an all-enveloping shadow. Good Friday. It was four o'clock now, and it was dark; this must be what the word umbra describes. Dr. Lourde's eyes appeared equally muddied by the silt from too many lives passing through his vision and slipping through his hands.

"Again, I have to tell you how sorry I am that Jada's leukemia is back. I don't know why it hasn't shown up before this, but now it has. I guess Jada was right all along." He waited, and I wished someone would come rushing in and shout, "Release the accused!" like Monsieur Madeleine being unable to allow a wrongful guilty verdict for an innocent person in his place. But no one stopped the sentencing. Beverly sat in her chair, her eyes brimming eternally sad; if tipped, they looked to spill forth wars and famine and disease and cry every mother's lament to see her child leave her. Jada slumped at my left, leaning into me, the perfume of newly washed skin sweet to my nose, Hambone huddled in her lap. I brought a tissue to my eyes to keep tears from dripping onto Jada's hair.

"I'm sure you know that we'll have to try a more aggressive therapy this time. For one thing, we know that the cancer in your body was able to 'hide out' from the cycle of treatment that was prescribed already, and, once a body has relapsed, it is no longer eligible for participation in the original study group because of its ineffectiveness. The folks who study cancer know that cancer cells are smart. They learn about the medicines we use and how to change just enough to resist them." Dr. Lourde paused again, sucking his upper lip between his teeth, and I thought, smart: the bastards could wipe out a whole universe before being found. "I've done some research, and I think there are very promising results coming out of a treatment regimen that is currently in use in some European countries.

"If you're wondering why we didn't try this the first time, let me explain that, at the time of your original diagnosis, we did follow the recommended protocol for your type of cancer based on your age and gender. The drugs in this treatment plan are the same ones we used. It's the combination of the drugs and the dosages that make it more aggressive and, I must emphasize, apparently responsible for a high survivor rate. I say apparently because there haven't been enough people who have completed both the program and observation period to constitute valid and reliable statistics."

Dr. Lourde had speeded up and began to sound like a barker selling snake oil, leaving no space to feel all the memories of pain and sickness; to ask questions, such as how researchers can come up with their statistics of a "high survival rate" without the many survivors. I felt the maimed officer in Hemingway's "In Another Country," who sat passively receiving therapy on the experimental machine while surrounded by posters of limbs they restored, proof that the untested promises could be trusted. But we had nowhere to go, nothing to hope for without Dr. Lourde, with or without his promises, and it didn't matter that he didn't want us to remember pain and fear, to raise doubts about out confidence in a plan that was written on paper and treated people as if they, too, were just phrases and abbreviations and measurements on paper themselves.

"Now, I know how much you hate all the details and the pokes and the tinkering around with blood and hospital routines." Jada shriveled a little further into me. "This round of treatment demands heavier and more frequent dosages. There will be two very intense phases plus recovery times. You'll not do as well as you did the first time, so I propose that we put in a Hickman catheter. That will virtually eliminate all pokes and also provide us with an easier port for drawing blood." Dr. Lourde reached into his shirt pocket and withdrew a pen. Click. In front of us he sketched lines on a pad of paper with a drug manufacturer's name in brown italics printed at the bottom. "We make an incision in this vein at the base of the neck and insert this tiny catheter all along just under the skin until we bring it out right about here in your chest." He pointed to a place at the bottom of his shirt pocket. I winced and rubbed my neck. Beverly looked on, emotionless, the shadows exaggerating the roundness of her eyes in the pouches that encircled them. How many gruesome things had she listened to?

"There's a clamp at the end of the tube that allows us entry to inject medicines or blood products you may need, as well as to take blood when we need it." Dr. Lourde looked up at Jada, retracted the tip of his pen and replaced it in his pocket, rested his back into his chair. "One of the bad features of this program is its high dosage of Prednisone. You had trouble with high blood sugar, and when we cut back the Prednisone, your blood sugars stabilized. Now, I suspect you're going to have more trouble as before. It's rare, but one of the side effects of Prednisone is that it can produce diabetes-like symptoms. I propose that we treat it as a side effect, not diabetes. You'll have to have insulin injections, but we'll manage that so we won't have to be precise, just so that it's within a safe range. You won't have to worry about your food intake, as that shouldn't have significant bearing on your sugar levels.

"Your catheter will allow us to sample blood for sugar tests, too. It's very important that your catheter be kept free of infection as well as free-flowing. You know how fast blood clots. Every time we access it, we have to flush heparin into it, or it will become unusable. That's pretty serious business for two reasons. Any time we operate or go into the body we run the risk of infection; and once we use that vein, it forms scar tissue and can't be used again. You have only two to use; we don't want to hurt our chances by risking the other one if we run into trouble later on."

Dr. Lourde stopped talking, and it felt like a hurricane had blown through, torn everything up, leaving only a shambles and an eerie silence. I felt a tug and Jada's face rose small and trembling from under my arm. I felt the heat of her fever as she brought her lips to my ear and whispered, "I don't think I can do it. I'll get sick and I'll fight and I won't want to do anything. Why can't you just let me die? I'm just here taking up space. Think of all the people you can feed and help if you don't spend all this time on me. It won't do me any good anyway. And then when I die, I'll pollute the earth with all those chemicals in me."

My tears rolled. "Oh, no, Jada! It's too soon to know that it won't work. No one knows what's ahead, but we have to believe you have a chance to live a wonderful life and to add to this world. I have to believe. I love you!" I held onto Jada, trying to keep her afloat in the wall of water that was tugging at her, pulling her from me and swallowing her in a raging sea.

"But what if I can't go through with it. You have to be there with me, you have to! I can't do it without you; you know I can't."

I held my breath and waited, waited like I imagined mothers must wait for their stillborn babies to cry, make any sound to breathe life, feeling somehow that I had failed. A flurry of words skittered and screeched across my brain like static jumping across electrical wires, and I could make no sense of any of them, just that I needed to say something else to make her want to, to, what? Do I want her to fight or do I want her to submit? I want my daughter to live a life of integrity. I exhaled a flutter of silky thread, fragile and translucent like the trail of a jellyfish, "Jada, I'll be there with you all the time. I love you; I won't let you do this without me."

Jada lifted her chin higher, nuzzling closer to me; her words came to me in a quivering whisper, throbbing like lips in a kiss, "I'll do it for you, Mooie." The rightness of her living seemed indisputable: she was my baby. The depth and the breadth of the morality of the sacrifice she was making was not. Beverly slid a box of tissues toward us, for she noticed that Jada, shrunk back to my breast, was crying, too.

I raised my head and bravely pronounced, "Okay. We're ready."

In the same trained manner with which he delved the depths of Jada's eye or sensated her spleen, Dr. Lourde said, "Jada will have surgery at nine on Monday morning, so she shouldn't have anything to eat or drink past midnight, including Tylenol. We may as well do a bone marrow while she's under. I'm hoping to get Dr. Graham to do the surgery—he's kind and gentle. You'll need to be here at eight." I nodded agreement. "You know where to go for admitting. You can stay here as long as you want," he said pushing away from the table.

When Dr. Lourde was out of the room Beverly moved into his chair and watched us with her perpetually sympathetic eyes, laying her hand just at the edge of my arm, the round fingernails with a slim crescent of white extending beyond her fingertips. "I'll be here whenever you need me," she said in a voice husky with the shadows of the room.

"Thank you. Will you stay with Jada while I go to admissions?"

Beverly smiled her assent. Purportedly, in some indigenous languages there are as many different words for snow as there are snow conditions. In this language, we should have as many different words to represent how we use a smile. Papers signed, I said, "Let's go home, Jada." On Monday we would see if Jada could rise from the dead.

A handsome young blond, among many people surrounding the gurney in the pre-operation area, leaned over the railing, telling Jada what he was going to do. "You'd better be good at it," Jada said.

His head cocked back, about to fire, and he said, "I'm very good at it; I do these all day long. I'll have you out in no time." He looked around his crew with a boastful smile and landed a wink on me.

A woman wearing a white paper cap and two white booties answered the jangling telephone. "Okay, they're ready in there," she said, the corrugated fabric mask scraping her chin.

"See you in a little bit," I said, watching Jada who was watching how she was being steered out of the room. She was gone. She was gone for a long time. In the waiting room, the television clanged with gongs, bells, and buzzers of game shows no one watched. Children tugged toys from each other. I lugged my bags to the cafeteria; there were people, there was noise, but there was space and anonymity. Ten-thirty. I returned to the waiting room, not knowing how to know when the operation was complete or if anyone knew where I was, a ticket holder without a ticket number, watching how the others knew when their numbers were called.

A telephone rang. No one sat at the table and no one stood to answer it, except for me. "Jada Petersen has about 15 more minutes in the recovery room. Do you want to call the floor and find out what room she's in?"

"I don't know how to do that. I'm Jada's mother, and I just picked up the phone."

"Oh, no one's working today. I'll call. She's doing fine; we're taking her to her room in a few minutes. We'll stop by the door and you can go with us."

Jada opened her eyes momentarily, first seeing me, then following the tube from her arm up to the bag which swung like a cow's full udder from the pole which a nurse rolled alongside the gurney. I smiled at her and joined in the journey to the third floor. The three of us, the nurse on the floor, the nurse from the recovery room, and myself, took the corners of the sheet underneath Jada, and on the count of three, lifted it and transferred Jada to her bed. The floor nurse scampered around the room like a rabbit, checking the IV bag, marking the clipboard that clattered onto the counter, scraping open the drawer of the bedside table and dropping into it the patient package: toothbrush, toothpaste, and comb. Jada opened her eyes again and murmured, "Can you bring me something to eat?"

The nurse looked surprised. "You can't yet. You just had surgery."

"But I haven't eaten since yesterday. I'm thirsty and hungry."

"That's unusual," the nurse said to me. "The anesthetic makes people sick to their stomach. Food just makes it worse. We don't even offer meals on the first day."

"My stomach feels fine. I'm not asking for lunch. I just want some juice or something."

"I'll watch so she doesn't overdo it," I added. "Can't you get some Jello or something from the patient kitchen?"

"We-ell, if you start out with water, just sip it, mind you, see how it goes. I'll see what I can find." To the sound of her receding footsteps, I released the catches on Jada's bed rails.

Dr. Lourde wasted no time starting drug therapy, and in days, I drove off from the hospital to teach. With the catheter, Jada's main concern was how careful the nurses were to triple prep, a swipe of alcohol, then Betadine, and a third cleansing with alcohol, and to heperanize the catheter between medicines and fluids. We knew, or thought we knew, what to expect. Radiation to the brain was deemed unnecessary, but everything else repeated itself: same metallic taste when a drug surged through her bloodstream, same orange color to the drug in the bag and the urine in the toilet, same spinal taps, same admonition to do them as low on the back as possible.

What wasn't the same was that Jada had engaged a different part of Dr. Lourde. He had seemed to hold her in comparison to a former patient of his, she a fine work of art, who battled a brain tumor valiantly and met death courageously, while Jada was seen as a velvet pillow of Elvis hawked on street corners. Her intelligence, that he admired; her irreverence made him uncomfortable; and her resoluteness got in the way of business as usual. But he listened. And this time around, I thought, he listened differently, more respectfully, to Jada the person.

L'Asparaginase had a short life span. Within minutes of its release from the pharmacy it had to be plunged into Jada's thigh to do its job. Timing was everything because, not only did it open the window just a crack for its use, it had to be administered at specified intervals. And this injection was no little poke, like insulin. The needle and the syringe were both large, requiring almost 5 minutes for the contents of the syringe to empty into body tissue.

She asked Dr. Lourde, "Can you give the shot to me in the afternoon when my mom is here?"

"I can't give in to you on this one," he answered matter of factly. "I'm not in control of the release of the drug."

"Well, I won't do it without my mom." Jada scooped her unflinching gaze off Dr. Lourde like she would a dollop of ice cream and landed it on me as if I were a piece of cherry pie. "What time in the morning do you call me from school?" she asked.

"Between 9:45 and 10:00. That's my prep," I added for Dr. Lourde.

Jada's attention turned back to Dr. Lourde. "What time does L'Asparaginase get here from the pharmacy?"

"'Bout 9:00."

"Can it wait until 10? Because if it can, my mom can come over here, can't you, Mom?"

"As long as I can get back by 10:40."

"Then that settles it. That means you have to be on time," Jada said to Dr. Lourde, who agreed to be called when I arrived. Then, as an afterthought, while Dr. Lourde concentrated on the tubing between his fingers, Jada asked, "What do your other patients call you?"

"Most of my patients are pretty young to handle Dr. Lourde, so I tell them they can call me Dr. Joe."

"That's different from before," Jada observed, her eyes on his work. "You said you didn't want to be called by your first name."

"A lot of things are different from four years ago," he said softly, not with the raised pitch of surprise or defense, and I started to see him more forgivingly. We had both been new at what we were doing four years ago. He was what I wanted him to be—Jada's doctor.

As Dr. Lourde predicted, Jada's blood sugar levels soared, even as she spurned food, and she and I were assigned to another round of classroom lectures about the feeding and control of diabetes.

"But we've done this before," I told Dr. Lourde. "Why do we have to waste our time sitting through hours of monotony about glands and cells, and carbohydrates and pigs and weights when she isn't diabetic? And, doesn't it strike you as odd that we're told how to control the intake of food that Jada won't take in?"

"Hospital rules and regs," he said. He actually said more, but we were all plugged into an institutionalized system, and like a string of Christmas tree lights with male lightbulbs and female sockets, the whole system wouldn't work if one was not in place. Arnold, again, was forgiven for not fitting in.

From school I went to the hospital, where Jada and I were marshaled from her room on a sleepy Tuesday afternoon, to sit at the end of the conference table. To Jada's protest, the pharmacist said, "I'm just doing my job," and then proceeded to pointing to drawings propped on an easel, as if his job required no imagination. What the history of diabetes had to do with treating it made no sense to me, and I felt sympathy for all the teenagers in the world who had to sit through dry lectures dining only on what the teacher chewed up and spat out, not something fresh and tantalizing, something they could bite into, like a rosy-skinned peach, and let the juice dribble sticky from their chins onto their hands and shirts, attracting bees and flies and all manner of critter and creature because they were so sweetly scented.

And I felt sorry for us for witnessing the parade of horrible implications of this disease in later life when it was all we could do to usher Jada through this week. On the second punishing day of "school," a nutritionist labeled the food groups as if we had just emigrated from Mars, and my head nodded and jerked every time I fought with sleep. I shifted in my seat, changed my posture, studying Jada, who set her head on her arm as if it were a buoy, cast out across the table, like a lifeline, hoping to be roped in and rescued from the sea of swollen purple feet and blindness and lost sensation. The nutritionist had to find it just as tiresome to listen to herself as it was for us.

One week in the hospital had multiplied itself to two. Each new day dawned a new complication for Jada, a reprise of her first diagnosis. She was bleeding in her stool; she had been dehydrated but then she retained too much fluid and in the wrong places; her sugar had been down but then soared unexplainably high, even with a maximum dose of insulin; she had a fever that refused to moderate, her hemoglobin was low, and she was in severe pain, none of which had anything to do with leukemia. An infection was brewing in her left arm. And, I reminded Dr. Lourde, she wasn't eating. Was anyone paying attention to her steady shrinking? Each complication warranted a new test to figure it out, and treatments to untangle the causes piled up on their back sides like a ten-car collision. It looked like Jada would never get out of the hospital, and there was not the tiniest prospect that she'd return to school. Urgency and gravity both kept me from finishing my school year; I took a long-term absence.

Jada's catheter was in constant use, with lines waiting to be installed like calls to the New York Stock Exchange on a bullish day. Technicians came and came, and, unable to wait for a turn on the catheter, pierced her veins for one blood culture after another. Each one stung Jada with Dr. Lourde's promise of the catheter's utility. The door creaked open and hesitated as, I imagined, the interloper's pupils widened for the advance into darkness. I sat up from my vinyl slab, both irritated by the interruption and relieved to stretch my back from its unyielding pallet. I saw a figure stepping stealthily toward Jada's bed, first setting down the woven tray on the ledge.

The technician didn't set about waking Jada, just nudged the overhead light on and helped himself to her arm like it was a turkey drumstick. Jada opened her lids to halfway and eyed him menacingly. "Not again," Jada objected. "Someone was just here."

His hair lay flat to his head in rows, like it was planted. He peered closer, snorted, and moved to the other side of the bed. "The veins in your arms have been used so much, I can't find one I can use," he announced with a hint of accusation. Stepping back, he looked up and down her arm, drumming on the inside, then slid his hand down to her wrist, turning it over, a slab on a spit.

"Oh, no you don't." Jada jerked her hand away. "Not on my hand."

"Your doctor has ordered a culture." First-timers' irrelevant edicts to Jada bounced flat off the issue like a ping-pong ball off the edge of the table.

"You know," she retaliated, "it's not my fault that you guys have used up all my veins. Do a finger stick."

The regulars gave in, finally, to the reality of Jada's veins, collapsed like clams digging into the bottom of the ocean, and pricked a finger to get the needed blood. But as the days of Jada's unidentifiable malady drew on, even her fingers recoiled from the hunt for blood. Technicians soaked Jada's hands in warm water and kneaded her fingertips to get red blood to flow to the white ends. It could have been comical. But, when in came another unlucky technician for yet another sample, Jada held up ten bandaged fingers and said without humor, "You've used them all! Guess you'll have to try another day."

That fiery flash of reality infected Jada's tone with every brusque ministration. And while technicians came and went, the head nurse had assigned Vera with Jada's care, possibly thinking she would be for Jada what water is for fire. Put Vera in any position, secretary, crane operator, baker, lawyer, sergeant, and she would perform her duties competently, swiftly, dependably. She was, though, a nurse; gray- and white-haired, Vera had the demeanor of an alloy of metals, unflinching as steel, impervious as iron, unflappable as nickel. Vera was dedicated to serving her patient well and efficiently. On that level, Jada admired Vera.

They were, however, two positive ends of electrical current, and Dr. Lourde warned Jada to "shape up, or she'll be gone." The warning might on the surface have looked to bode a better trade, but, as I saw it, once Vera was on your side, the rest was gravy.

If everyone gave up on Jada, they would be letting her win at her own self-destruction, and I pleaded with her in the wake of Dr. Lourde's admonition. "Give people a chance. They're caught, too, you know, having to do what they've been told to do."

"They don't have to be so insensitive about it. Do they think I'm a little baby? That I don't think? I know things have to be done, but why can't they come in and ask me instead of acting like I don't have any feelings? It's my body."

"They're trained to do, not to accommodate," I offered. "They're not used to dealing with anyone other than children who they're used to telling, not asking."

"That's what I'm saying. Can't they see I'm not a child? Can't they for once listen to me and remember how to do things so I don't have to explain everything all over again?"

"I agree," I conceded. "But, you know, sometimes they may not hear the point you make because all they hear is your tone."

I talked to gray; the gray from the walls of the hospital room she had been in so long had slid under Jada's skin and dyed it gray, swam in her blood, churned in her stomach and turned to lead, washed the color out of her eyes and leeched her heart. If Jada stayed here like this much longer, she would be hard like the gray walls, too. "Jada, I think you're capable and smart and mindful. I think Vera sees that, too. Use what you have. Don't let them win. Think about how you can get things done your way."

"I try sometimes. Really, I do. But it all comes so fast and I can't stop myself." I nodded. Damn this disease. That was her problem—she matched its will.

"I'm not going to tell you that it's a matter of mind over body. I just want people to see the Jada I know. The Jada I know is also full of love, love that is worth mining for. I want people to know that Jada."

"That's the worst, you know. I'm just a disease to them." A smell of rusted metal filled my nostrils as I took in a deep breath of awareness. She did appear to be rusted in place, never moving, her spirit corroding from neglect. "I want to do things. I want to make decisions. I want to be who I am. They won't let me be me here."

"If only your body could do what your mind does, you'd be out of here in no time."

"That's another thing. How can my body do this to me?"

Struggling to control my face, I looked down at my hand, smoothing a snag on my fingernail and rubbed the end of it. Nothing I could think to say would ever answer that question, so why should I pretend? I wrote, instead. When Jada drifted into sleep, I sat in a vinyl-covered chair that sounded like a cellulose floor sponge being squeezed of dirty wash water and wrote our days in my journal, hoping to archive the meaning behind this betrayal, if there were one.

One afternoon, I opened my journal and Jada cried out, alarming me to action. At first I didn't know that the curse of drugs caused Jada to slip in and out of two worlds, until I witnessed her living in both worlds at the same time. Impatient with words having to appear linear one after another, a slow development of an instantaneous picture, I recounted the event in a flurry:

"Are they sticking me?" Jada's voice shrieked like a hungry baby bird. "Jello." I jumped to fill her request. "Put me down, Dad! Don't drink my Tang. You can have some if you want, but don't drink my Tang. You can't use three." Padded with blankets neatly folded back under her arms, Jada turned her head to me and raised her torso like a mummy reentering the living and burrowing her unseeing eyes into unsuspecting victims to keep them from escaping. "Am I going to the bathroom?" Her head swung to the opposite side, as if on command by some other demon, and her eyes closed. Click, just like that, a flick of the light switch, and she was gone. Whatever she asked for, whatever she said, came from somewhere else. Jada lay as still in her bed as she had animatedly sat up. I watched for the rise of her chest underneath the blankets.

Visitors were few. On another afternoon, Mark and Cheng made a visit. Cheng sprang into the room on sprite-like feet and landed close to me on the apple green settee. Jada sometimes teased how Cheng liked me about as much as she. But it was Mark who Jada wanted to want her. Mark, tall and stringy, compared to Cheng's slightness of build, stood reserved, gentle.

"Mom, please don't leave," she asked wanly. "Don't mind me if I don't talk," she told the boys, both in orchestra, in Jada's estimation the flint of the school. "I don't have much energy, but tell me what's happening in orchestra."

Mark stood at the foot of Jada's bed, his arms folded as they might be when he finally reached his goal of being a doctor, and in a moderate cadence, continued, "and you know how the percussion section likes to get a rise out of Mr. Moldenaur; so they just kept on missing the beat." Cheng and Mark both held elite seats in the string section, which gave them license to look down the hierarchical ladder with tolerance at such clownish pranks. It was a tough call for them to know with whom to side in situations of chicanery.

"Old Moldy's bald head just got redder and redder. You could see he was trying to figure out how to get back at them." Cheng punctuated his addition to the back-and-forth account of the latest tragicomedy starring the orchestra instructor as the man who would tame his crew, no matter the number, by swabbing his hand over the crown of his head with animation.

Mark waited patiently, his lips eased into a comfort zone; I always thought Cheng would be the statesman, though Mark had the stature. Mark opened his mouth to continue the saga.

"Hambone!" Jada jerked up from the bed and screamed. "Hambone's face is on fire!" She thrust her arms forward, straight rifles aimed at blank space. I jumped up; Mark jumped back.

"No, Darlin', no! See, here's Hambone, safe and whole." I took Hambone from above Jada's pillow and showed him off as if he'd just won a blue ribbon at the fair. Jada's eyes looked, but they were an abandoned house before the mice and the squirrels found out. "See, Hambone's okay, he's here with you." Jada's shoulders fell with the weight of her arms and her eyes came slowly back, as a childhood memory that had been lost was found by walking into a familiar room. Slowly she leaned backwards, and I caught her to ease the way.

"Poor Hambone," Cheng said, pushing his glasses upwards with his pointer finger.

A mole the size of a carpet tack stood out brown and nascent to long wiggly hairs of old age in Mark's paling face. "I think we better go now," he said.

Jada's eyelids fluttered, tremulous signage, I thought, to an unnamed power that could release her from one world and put her in the other. Unaware of the last moments, she said, "I'm not very good company tonight. I'll feel better tomorrow; we can talk then. Mom, say goodbye to them for me."

The three of us walked to the door and formed a huddle. "Do you think she'll remember we were here?" Mark asked in a whisper.

"I don't know. Don't let that stop you from coming; the more she's connected to life outside the hospital the better."

"We're supposed to go to the prom together." The skin on his face quivered with little domes of doubt.

"Don't worry. Jada wouldn't miss that." She's looking for a kiss, too, I wanted to add; why don't you get that going so she doesn't miss out on that, too?

"You must be um very tired yourself," Cheng consoled. His deep brown eyes were moist behind his glasses. "Take care of yourself." Cheng set his hand lightly on my arm.

"Have they gone?" Jada asked as the boys headed for the elevator. She brushed her teeth in bed, and afterward I ran the lint pick-up roller across her pillow. Hair that shed freely beneath her head formed a tangled mat as intricately webbed as a crocheted doily. "Mooie, I don't think I can keep up with this. I won't even get back to school. They'll forget me."

That knowledge hurt me as much as hearing her cry in pain. "What can I say to them for you, Sugar?"

"Tell my teachers that it's not just that I'm missing their classes. They have to know what it's like for me to have to think through the work. I can't concentrate. I don't want them to think I can do the same things as I could before. Even if I do go back," she added, a mixture of sadness and longing in her tone. I swept her blankets so they made a protective berm around her, her own little house. I started for her pillow; she liked it plump. "No, write this down. You have to tell them."

I set Hambone back on his haunches at Jada's head and opened my journal.

"Tell them…tell them it's not like being out with a cold. I bet they've already forgot who sat in my chair." Her eyes looking beyond the room, Jada might have been seeing another body already sitting there. "Tell them I can't keep up with them; they have to be the ones to call. I want to hear about all the things that are going on. Tell them not to be afraid of me." Jada dropped her lashes, closed her eyes. "You have to tell them."

"Yes, Jada, I will." In the silence of her breathing, I remembered when my kindergarten teacher led us along the park across the street from school and then across the next street to visit a classmate at his house. She gave us a stern warning not to make a sound. I felt hot standing inside the kitchen door, looking in wonder at the boy who sat straight-legged on the floor, one leg bound in white. I remember waiting for him to return to school, for a while, anyway, and like a scrap of paper that ignites and is consumed by its own flame, a thought came to me to wonder why I never saw him again.

I shut my book and then lowered Jada's bed. Hambone I left above her. When Jada's body hurt this much, even Hambone could not touch it. Dr. Lourde could have saved himself a lot of questions and got a more accurate read on Jada's overall condition if he had made simple observations such as that.

Dr. Lourde found me in the waiting room the next day while Jada talked with Kimby on the telephone. He sat on the edge of the chair and began in an even voice to detail what he thought was not causing Jada's fluctuating imbalances and pain and what he feared could be. I listened as delicately as Dr. Lourde elaborated technicalities. Each familiar fact and old consideration became a new obstacle to clarity as it changed in relation to the present set of conditions.

"The good news is that Jada's total body infection is now localized. It's no longer life-threatening, but what concerns me about Jada's arm," Dr. Lourde went on, his eyes piercing his glass lenses, "is that we're not finding the bug that's causing the infection, and I'm afraid of the damage it's doing to her muscle. We've changed the antibiotics to see which ones are helping and which ones are getting in the way.

"She has a staph infection in her mouth and nose, and on her skin, but it's not in the bone. Her sugar is down, and that's a strange one because it should be up with the meds she's taking. I'm cutting the Prednisone, not because of the sugar level but because it interferes with her neutrophils—she needs those to fight infection. We've given her a dose of Vincristine, but no Daunomycin today, and we're still monitoring her fluids. I know how much it irritates Jada that we have to come back so often for another blood culture, but, unfortunately, until we find the cause, we're only guessing at how to treat it. I've been talking to a doctor who specializes in infectious diseases, and he's putting together a combination of antibiotics that should cover just about everything. Jada is in no condition to handle this on an outpatient basis."

Dr. Lourde's hands, loosely clasped and remarkably still throughout his speaking, now opened up and came together, each finger tip touching another in an apex, like the beams of a cathedral ceiling. His thumbs opened when he said, "I'm more concerned about the cause of Jada's leg pain. Even though we can't identify the source of the infection in her arm, we can see it and keep it isolated. I'm afraid that's not the case with her leg." He spoke methodically, placing every essential word where it belonged. Even when he caught his lip under his bottom teeth, it seemed to form a natural bridge between the sentences he lined up, each tailgating the other. "There's a side effect, a very rare one, to Prednisone, that deadens the bone tissue at the joints and typically shows up in the legs first. That condition is irreversible and has very serious implications. I hope that that condition is not the case with Jada, and I'm not going to bring it up to her unless it shows up on bone scans. That's a nasty one," he added, casting his eyes downward. Did Dr. Lourde pray, I wondered?

After a moment's silence, I asked, "When will you know that?"

"I want to move on this right away. The radiologists said they'd squeeze her in this afternoon."

To Jada, Dr. Lourde described the bone scan, assuring her that she would feel nothing, lying essentially undisturbed on a bed that rolled through the huge metal-clad tube, and then mapped out the circuitous route through the hospital bowels and underground to a different building.

Action after a long spell of languishing electrified the air. A gurney arrived at Jada's door, the bump of its hitting the wall like a knock of an unexpected visitor, and then Vera charged into the room. While I can't say I ever saw her waste a movement, she seemed to have come in with the sole purpose to say, "We're short-staffed this afternoon. I'll be back as soon as I can to take you."

"Oh, Vera!" Jada gasped, too late to stop her; she was already out the door.

Metal banged against the doorjamb, causing the bed to backlash into Vera's steel chest. She recovered before she knew she'd been hit, and with my help, she steered the bed next to Jada's. Jada gave me beseeching looks, and not for a minute did I feel envious of

Vera's position as head engineer of this operation. Too many times I was the designated driver of Jada's wheelchair and been watched like a bug making its precarious movement on the wall at risk of being splatted. I had to admit that the contraptions were a bit unwieldy, but, I thought, I'm not foolhardy, not like Vera.

Jada and Vera and I started out like pilgrims on a voyage, me at the helm, Vera providing the power, Hambone tucked securely at Jada's chest, restrained from flying out. "Vera, can you please slow down?" Jada asked in a conciliatory tone. But by the time Vera registered Jada's request, we were at a corner, an elevator, our first destination. I speculated that she might have a history of speeding violations, a possible reason for her and her husband to buy a residence in the converted former hospital building, close enough for her to walk to work. The thought of her going to sleep every night in a place she had worked every day was otherwise too poetic. When she got behind Jada's gurney, I had to jog to keep the front end on course. Jada returned my reassuring glances with wide white space surrounding shrinking blue beads for eyes. "How can such a ponderous device move so rapidly?" they asked.

Out of the elevator, Vera revved up again. Jada made another request to slow down but was outchimed by the clank of the glass bottle hanging from the IV pole, the revolving metal wheels on uncarpeted floors, and the whir we created as we whizzed down the hall. Vera was like one of those drivers who hug the rear end of your car until they make a break for it, and you watch them dart in and out, between and before all the vehicles in front of you; for them it's one speed—fast. We would travel about five floors down, two city blocks on a level plane, through a tunnel, and up and down two more elevators to get to the facility. "They should put seat belts on these things." Jada's remark went up in gusts into the lights that zoomed above her, white streaking blurs of a fast-forward film. Vera didn't hear; she was already mentally at the elevator.

Having just started our journey, Vera nearly collided with Arnold, who had just arrived at the hospital, having made his stop at the cafeteria, and balanced a lidded foam cup of coffee in his hand.

There was no stopping to explain. He reversed his direction and instinctively latched onto the long metal bar. Watching out for my toes, I parlayed as much information about our journey as I could. Boarding another elevator, necessitated by the fact that we were in the adjoining hospital, another nurse gasped as she just missed losing the hem of her jacket to the closing door. With her belly as anchor, she embraced two metal-clad volumes between folded arms. They groaned as she lurched with the forward movement of the elevator. "Oh, I'm so glad I caught up with you!" she exhaled. "I was going to dinner anyway, so I said I'd bring down the records. You'll need these." She had no choice but to grab onto the rail to help get the gurney off the elevator when we reached the bottom floor of the second hospital.

We turned the corner at the hospital credit union service desk, nearly running over Beverly, who, by the look of things, had just finished doing business there. "What's going on?" she asked, lips parted and eyebrows arched. She couldn't stay, she said, as if having been invited to go on tour with us, but she, too, found a bare spot on the aluminum rail. The heels on her shoes tip-tapped the rhythm to our procession.

"Now here's the tricky part," Vera said. I suspicioned that she was trying to rid herself of the hangers-on, much like the slogging barnacles on the hull of a once-fleet ship. "This is a very small elevator; I don't know if all of you will fit." We did. There was even room for jangling tambourines, flowing ribbons, chains of tinkling metal coins to lace our ankles. If we wanted to add them. And Dr. Lourde and Barb. They were there, too. They backed themselves into their corners, temporarily joining our traveling troupe of jesters.

All journeys find place, somewhere, and we reached ours. Dr. Lourde and Barb were the first to peel away from us; there were other patients to see. Beverly was on her way to pick up Dante; she was running late. As usual. The other nurse was only delivering records, charts, orders; she had to get her dinner before going back on shift. Arnold, well, who needed two people to sit here in the catacombs, he said before he excused himself, coat hanging from his arm like a dressing room curtain, coffee still in hand. Vera had to get back to the floor—they were, after all, short-handed.

We were alone, Jada, Hambone, and I, as we had started, in the cool dim room where shadows clung around artificial lights and voices sneaked out from hiding places. Unless you count the two silvery bound histories of Jada's hospital life and the ghost of a receptionist. Maybe she didn't like it down here either and went up for air. I looked around the spacious room that entombed us. No one had lowered the metal rails on Jada's gurney. I traveled up the rows of rail, from toe to head, first reaching out to the one ahead of me before letting go of the last, looking for my daughter. I found her alive and whole, magnificent and dignified, no matter how foolish we had made ourselves appear in the name of medicine.

"Don't even wiggle your toe," the man warned Jada before he slid her like a tray of cookies into a cylindrical oven. "Don't worry, we're watching everything. You'll be able to hear me, but don't talk. I'll tell you when to breathe." Then he clamped the door shut. It looked like a berth at the city morgue to me. I held onto Hambone and remembered that I could breathe in and out, in and out; but I had to think about it. Just as Jada had to think about not.

We waited, Jada flat on a bed in the middle of a waiting area in what I called the catacombs because it was so deeply embedded, a canister within a canister within an ever larger one, made secretive by a route impossible to remember, while the radiologist made a preliminary reading of the report. Jada, like a plate of food under the warming light, waited in the more public area near the receptionist who called for a nurse from the floor to come down, sign for Jada, and take her back to her room, ready to serve. The return trip would seem anti-climactic, just the four of us, counting Hambone, and two clattering volumes of records, percussion pieces in our recession.

Results of the scan sang an all-too familiar chorus: nothing. Relief that the feared bone disorder was not the cause of Jada's leg pain and weakness was followed by the frustration of unanswered questions and an unlabeled perpetrator. "I can't treat what I can't see," one of Dr. Lourde's signature lines, came like a refrain. That and "I guess you've gotta bite the bullet," which he said more frequently now. Jada seemed to be glued to a seesaw. What should have been up wasn't, what was normally low was elevated, what should have been working backfired. Dr. Lourde, left with his own bullet to bite, kept coming up with new combinations of old remedies, but nothing seemed to have any effect: Jada's condition worsened to its own tune.

Jada quipped that I should be put on payroll for all the nursely duties I performed, supporting Jada on the bed pan, changing her sheets, keeping her cup filled with fresh water. I watched how the nurses pushed the buttons and checked the digitals on the blue machine that regulated the flow of Jada's medicines through the tubes and turned them off when they'd beeped too long. Every bath Jada had in the hospital, I gave to her.

Whereas I had been the assistant to some nurse's duty, now Vera assisted me. She helped me get Jada in and out of the Jacuzzi safely because Jada couldn't support herself on her legs without both of us to help. The Jacuzzi was in the mother bathroom, the bathroom large enough to hold a brood of bathtubs like bassinets in a nursery. A full-grown person could lie down in the tub, and the edge of it came to Jada's waist. The only way into the tub was up a ladder, reminding me of a pyre from Greek writings.

For someone with use of both legs, getting in would require some forethought; both legs still had to hurdle the side of the tub from a narrow top step of a ladder. I climbed the two steps, my arms lugging Jada under her arms as if she were cargo being hurled into the hull, while Vera put her strength under Jada's legs to lift them over the edge. From there, theoretically, it was easy for Jada to let her legs drop to the floor of the tub and make a landing of sorts on her butt.

We shooed Vera out of the room, water still running into the tub like an old math problem through my brain—if water flows from the faucet at the rate of 4 gallons per minute and drains at the rate of one-half cup per second, how long will it take before the water overflows—Vera had opened the spigot before we began our trek down to the bathroom.

Bathing Jada completed, I yanked the cord for Vera. Vera standing helplessly by, about a foot and a half too short to grab onto anything, me included, at the top of the step stool I grasped Jada under her arms and pulled her up. To make room for Jada's feet to stand at the top of the stool, I had to move backwards and down a step. Jada weighed but 100 pounds, but she had the force of a falling object in my direction, and I absorbed her, falling downwards myself. It was a miracle I landed on two feet, my arms still holding Jada upright. Vera couldn't have stopped the two of us if she'd been twice her size and twice as quick, for it was over before the sheet of white horror flushed color from her face.

In her room, Jada sat stiffly, her legs stuck out bare from a pink and blue polka-dotted cotton robe of thinly spun cotton, perfect for a mild summer day, breezes lifting curtains at open windows, not for an air-controlled hospital. Her lips washed out of her face, a grayish green in the unevenly lit room. I cleared off the linens down to the mattress cover and spread fresh sheets on her bed. Jada's eyes lay flat in their sockets, the fun punched out of them, and I roamed memories. "Here, Jada, some nice clean blankets." Unfurling a blanket, I pulled in the smell of disinfected cotton. Tiny lint specks flew like salt from a shaker tossed over a shoulder for luck. The substance of life had been scattered, it seemed, with just as much superstition. "Remember how you and Dom used to help me fold the sheets? It was kind of like a little dance, meeting each other with our corners," I said, guiding Jada into bed. "Feel better?"

"No. How can I? They lied to me. They said they were watching me closely. You call this watching me closely?" She looked down at her reddened swollen arm, the heat from it radiating like an electric coil atop the bleached white blanket. "Why? Why am I doing it? I'd rather just go home and drink poison and die."

"I don't want you to die! You have to learn things and try things and go places. You haven't gone to the prom yet. I want you to live because I think those things are worth living for."

"But I'm not doing those things. Fifty-fifty chance. I don't even have a fifty-fifty chance of going to the prom! Do you want me to live this way?"

"No, not this way," I answered carefully, "We didn't choose life this way. But we can believe that it won't stay this way. It's easy to have dignity when everything is going along fine. The hard part is having dignity when things are rotten. Until this way of living changes, you have to find a way to get through it with dignity."

Closing her lids she said, "Yeah, they don't let me have it here. They won't even let me have water. They let this happen to me." This, the infection in her arm.

I wanted someone to blame, too, as if by assigning responsibility for this evil deed I could also give orders to fix it. I said nothing, neither agreeing nor arguing the folly of turning to science and the medical profession to rescue her. We can manipulate chromosomes in a mosquito, send rockets to planets at the edge and into the next indescribable space, and receive pictures through the air waves, but it means nothing because all the art and all the science of medicine cannot find the magic we need to manipulate the puzzle of our own bodies, our lives, our luck because some spoiled sport kept breaking up the puzzle and we had to start again looking for the pieces that hinged together.

What a beautiful being Jada was, even in sickness and despair. High cheekbones were wrapped with unblemished skin so clear you'd think you could look right through it to see the ugly invader that ravaged her body. She closed her eyes, the blue seeming to sear through her lids, silver now that I moved away and sat down, reaching for my journal. My brain jumbled ideas up and about like number balls colliding with each other in an automated Bingo machine. "Are you writing about me?" Jada asked.

"No, not yet." Snippets was all I wrote, snippets that I couldn't add up because I didn't understand them. "I can't yet."

"You have to. You have to write about me." Her eyes remained closed, but I could feel them on me.

"I will, Jada. When I can, I will." I opened the grain-colored book. Tiny flowers pricked their way through the fabric. When I ran my fingertips across the nap, it felt bristly, like it had been shaved. Random notes hung out like thirsty tongues, dripping ragged edges. A section of pages had loosed themselves from the binding and slipped to my thigh, strings dangling like leashes on runaway dogs. I replaced the clump of papers, leafing through until I found naked lines. Click.

April 28, 1985, I wrote. Already I smelled the ink of my favorite pen. I called it violet not because it smelled like violet, which I doubted I could identify. The color of the casing was violet, and when I rolled the tip along paper, smooth violet figures were planted along the lines, like flowers along a fence. As the ink grew on the page, its color darkened and sometimes I just liked looking at the shapes made from my hand making words. I didn't use the pen carelessly because other pens weren't as wonderful to hold.

April 28, 1985, I read. Three weeks after Jada's diagnosis. I looked back among the pages to see what had happened. Pieces of dialogue, mostly. A record of what she'd eaten in the last four days: half-bowls of cereal. The infection in her arm: why aren't the antibiotics working? Or are they? There is her mouth. The contest of learning to communicate well. When Dr. Lourde heard "why," he went to the clinical, analytical reasoning part of his brain, whereas Jada's motivation originated from her deep-rooted query of the universe and life's value. She waved her hand, sweeping the air of his rational words.

My journal closed when the dinner tray was delivered, a meal she would not eat. She no longer filled out her menu cards, except for cereal in the morning. I crossed out the dinner choices and wrote "raisin bran and skim milk only." I lifted the salmon-colored cover to see if my request was honored. Peas and carrots. Sliced beef. Dinner roll. Jello. Whole milk.

Getting home was nearly crossed off my menu, too. Once or twice a week I drove to school, doing enough to keep my substitute going, then left, as students arrived. Sleep came, but it wasn't restful, regular sleep. I didn't really miss that, except that when I was awakened, I couldn't find sleep again. Food, there was plenty of it. I ate more than enough to gain weight. I didn't even mind the mediocrity; a person can get by on institutional coffee and SuperMom's bakery, canned green beans and baked chicken. I didn't miss a social life either. Why go for a walk if it was only a block? Why go home if no one waited there for me? Why go to a movie when I had a drama to live?

One morning bled into another, and on this morning, lights in the hall went on, a hospital's way of calling reveille, on schedule. Jada's door swooped open, and a nurse delivered her breakfast tray. Announcements twittered from the hallway like birds outside the window. "Dr. Blue, please report to room 352; the meeting for Team A has been delayed until 9:00." Down the hall female laughter erupted. I missed the time clock, its thumping like the lid of the letterbox when the carrier dropped in the mail; it had been removed since Jada's first diagnosis. The nurse returned, pushing the scale ahead of her, the wheels rolling over the linoleum like percolating coffee. Jada opened her eyes to another day in the hospital. She went through her morning routine of testing her blood sugar, taking her temperature and standing on the scale. Missing was her water—she loved having water from the jug on her nightstand—but that was restricted, and she could sip from only little baby cups. White lips. Dry, peeling.

By the time everyone was done with her, she was exhausted. She lay back into bed, her left arm lying uselessly by her side, her right hand, tender with pin pricks, collapsed to the mattress, too tired or too bored to reach for the remote control for morning television programming. Books required what Jada had long ago lost.

I threw my Styrofoam cup away, another excuse for what I was calling exercise, and nearly bumped into the nurse, who scurried into the room and lifted the cover to Jada's breakfast tray, still on the seat of the chair where she'd put it, and whisked it up, turning back toward the door with it gripped firmly to her uniform, as if she had a half-Nelson on it. She stopped and threw her head backwards in Jada's direction. Then she stepped closer to the chart on the wall. "When was the last time you had something to drink, Jada?" she asked.

"Last night. Why are you taking my cereal?" she asked, now alert.

"Your salts are way out of whack," the nurse said with a hint of reprimand, "and if your blood sugar doesn't come down, you're really in trouble. Dr. Lourde has left orders that if you don't get this under control, we have to change your diet."

Jada bared her gums and sucked in air. "Now what? I didn't get to eat my breakfast!"

"Here." The nurse swooped in again carrying a jumbo-sized cup. Beads of water dripped from the rim. "I want you to drink all of this within the next half hour. It's very important that you get clear liquids into your system." She held the cup to Jada, a straw poking at her nose. Jada raised her chin and took a sip. "You'll have to drink more than that." She sounded like an inquisitioner, itching to issue torture at the stake if Jada didn't perform adequately.

"I will. Just leave it here. But it's hard, you know, when your mouth hurts."

"It doesn't have to be water, it could be juice, although, that has sugar, so you don't want to drink a lot of that. I'll be back in half an hour, and I want to see that container empty."

When the nurse returned, she carried with her another covered tray and set it down, rolling the table across Jada's bed. "How you doing on that water?" she interrogated, walking around the bed and peering into a partially filled cup. "You have to do better than that. Do you want a fresh cup?" She gave the IV bag and tubing that sprang from it an up-and-down look; maybe that was a suspect she had overlooked before.

"No, my mom will do that," Jada said. A bleating beeped loudly from a far-off place, and for once I was glad for the alarms on those damned blue boxes. If a patient weren't already in some kind of danger from the irregularity, the incessant irritation of the repeating beep would take care of that. The nurse clucked her tongue and removed herself.

"Are you hungry, Jada?" I felt like a cheerleader for the underdog, fiercely chanting for the impossible, a fickle following to stay till the end. "You know she's going to come back and do the 'you've got to eat routine.'"

"You eat it."

"Really, Jada, I won't bug you about eating everything, but I'd like you to try."

"Okay," Jada agreed after a heartbeat. Or two. I pushed the button that raised her to a sitting position. I rinsed a cloth with warm water, folded it, and put it next to her tray. I brought a towel to catch spills and draped it over the front of Jada's hospital gown. I positioned the bed tray, made sure the height was just right. If she had been the queen bee pampered by a hive of drones, she would have settled for less. I plucked the lid off the tray and quickly upended it to avoid drips.

"What's this?"

Before Jada were harvest gold-colored insulated mugs. No grapefruit. No raisin bran. Not even the daily dose of dried toast. Under the lid of one mug was an amber liquid. I sniffed: broth. Under another floated a tea bag, saturated flecks of chopped tea leaves bloating the paper sac, with brown printing on its tag hanging upside down, dead out of the water. Dull orange gelatin cubes that didn't wiggle, even when shaken, lines imprinted on their surface as if they'd been quarried, not cubed. Apple juice in a plastic cup sealed with foil. One plastic spoon. Even that was beige.

"Mom," Jada ordered, her temper surging, "get this away from me. Now get out your book and write this down." Fiercely she dictated before I opened to the first blank page. "You wake up. And then they make you go to the bathroom. Your lips are dried shut because they won't give you water, but they tell you to wait more so they can take your temperature. You can't hold the thermometer in your dry mouth."

I wanted to go back and cross a "t," but her staccato pace had no mercy for conventions. "Then breakfast comes in, fine and dandy, but then the nurse runs back in and that gets whipped away. She's about to leave the room carrying my tray and gives me a big long speech about water. After a while she runs back in with another tray saying I have to have clear liquids. One hour ago they were giving me just about anything but no water. Now I *can* have water and they bring me some slop liquid I didn't even get a chance to choose! And all of it's 'cause of some sugar problem and some sodium problem and I want to do it on my own!"

I was almost caught up. Then, like the slow silky stroke of satiny strands on the strings of a violin, her voice released a soft, sad, sigh, "I was dreaming of cereal last night."

"You love your cereal," I said, my pen down, my eyes up.

"That's why I ordered two cartons of milk."

Jada's sadness was trapped in a stalled elevator. Words, I thought, delivered us to the place we want to be. What if they were just threads by which we hung, threads worn and frayed by use and overuse, words like I love you, and I wish and I want and you can; what if one tiny little movement, a cough, a sigh, a tear trickling over a cheekbone, were enough to snap one, then another, all of the threads. Then we, both of us, would fall surely and finally down the shaft to land in nothing more than a crushed heap, and those frazzled flimsy words I'd been trusting would lay broken, nonsensical sounds, like wreaths above our shared tomb. The day droned on with no words to lift us.

Dr. Lourde walked past Jada's untouched lunch and asked, "How are you doing, Jada?" He always asked. She always told him. More or less. One look at her needn't much elaboration. "Ahh," Dr. Lourde sighed, in response to her question. "I don't know about your leg, Jada. I don't think it's related to your arm. At least, it doesn't look like your arm or feel like your arm. You know I'd like to find out what's going on with that as much as you, but I just can't risk treating something without knowing what we're fighting. We'll just have to keep up with antibiotics. If it's bacterial, something in there ought to get at it." Dr. Lourde gestured upwards to the gelatinous sac hanging from the pole from which the best of modern medicine drained a steady stream. "I suppose we can order another bone scan, though I don't know if it will tell us much. Last time I was looking for something specific. Maybe we need to ask for different readings."

Dr. Lourde stood and asked, "May I?" before pulling back the stack of blankets. His fingertips tiptoed along Jada's right thigh while she grimaced, and he cocked his ear slightly as if listening for the infiltrator to whisper "boo." He shook his head. "Let me see that arm again."

He checked the settings on the box that was clamped to the IV pole. The machine was a wonderful invention: by threading a tube through a tunnel, the operator could program the flow to precise specifications over a continuous period of time. One knob was the only thing that held it in place, the only thing that kept it and Jada's tubing from crashing to the floor. The picture of its disconnection from her was gruesome. But the machine's main drawback was its alarm system. Meant to free the staff from making repeated checks and adjustments to a manually regulated bag, its warning system blasted bursts of shrill rings that could be heard by nurses working elsewhere.

If the machine was in good working order, it emitted only one or two false alarms for every setting. Like a fire alarm, once sounded, it could not be stopped without authorization. Nurse responses were erratic; they sometimes swore under their breath at the machine's capricious habit of sounding for its own aggrandizement, like a rooster, waking everyone up during the sweetest time of sleep or, more than once, neglected the signal altogether. Or for as long as we could tolerate the incessant bleeping. We learned how to turn the alarm off but were worse off when we acted: for if someone were slow to come when the alarm rang, who'd we expect to find and correct the cause of the alarm when it did not?

"Careful," I cautioned Dr. Lourde. "This one's temperamental." He made no response, and I guessed he had never been captive to the torture the machine wrought.

"Anything else?" Dr. Lourde asked.

"Yes," I answered. "I'm concerned about her coughing—she's had two episodes. And how long is Jada going to have to stay in the hospital? Maybe you can't say exactly, but she's planning to go to the prom, and we need time to shop for a dress and get it altered."

His eyes circled in thought and he raked his mustache with his lower teeth. "The only thing that's keeping Jada here is that we have to give her these meds. I don't mean that to be a trivial thing. What I mean is that we know she has an infection and that there's no other danger to her by her being elsewhere other than that we have to watch closely to keep it localized. Now, if her fever doesn't fluctuate and if she keeps up her body fluids, I can ask Dr. Craig to adjust the cycle to allow Jada to get unhooked for a period of a few hours. Would that help?"

"When?" she asked.

"Well-ll, I don't want to promise tomorrow, but, I'll put a call in to Dr. Craig yet today. Maybe the day after, what's that? Thursday? Stores are open then, aren't they?"

We had from eleven till two to get our shopping done. My car waited at the main entrance of the hospital like a coach transporting Jada on a fairytale journey. It was only a couple miles up Franklin Avenue to The Wedding Shop, and a parking place near the front door appeared just for us, a sign of luck. We hadn't anticipated the steps. Five of them loomed before Jada, plus one inside the porch which we didn't see until I held open the aluminum door. Many shops on Franklin Avenue had once been two-story homes. Only the contents changed.

We crossed another threshold; a bell rang. We stopped at a sample wedding book, white clad and propped open to a large glossy photo. Jada leaned against the case, her face bent into the pages. "Tell me when you're ready," I said. Stained wallpaper crept up to tall ceilings in a room that had once been a front parlor. "Here are some garters and nylons." I pointed to a metal rack. Floorboards creaked from what would have been the kitchen. The clerk's dark eyes studied us as she approached. I had become accustomed to the flatness of Jada's pale skin color, the green undertone that, in this lighting, grew bolder. Hardly a strand of hair survived, making the scar in the middle of her skull, ironically, the only pink spot on her marble-white head. Leaning against something, she hid the wavering way she walked, head pushed forward and legs that dragged. "We're looking for a prom dress," I said.

"They're upstairs," the clerk answered. "This way." Jada and I read each other's disappointed faces. The clerk stood at a wooden newel post; behind her was a narrow opening, the end of which was not in sight.

"I could bring some down to you," I offered.

"No, I'll try."

"Go ahead," I said to the clerk who looked like her prom wasn't very long ago. "Maybe if you have a chair up there, you could bring it out?" Her short dark hair bounced against the top of her neck as she disappeared up the steps. Jada began her ascent at a much slower pace, every step beginning with her left leg, pausing to regain her balance when the right one joined it. At the top, Jada dropped into a stuffed chintz chair. We were, apparently, the only customers in the shop.

The young woman had gathered a few dresses in what she guessed to be Jada's size and displayed them before her. "I don't know what you're looking for, but this will give me an idea," she explained. I went back to the racks for more.

"I'll try on that one," Jada pointed to a white dress with a full skirt flowing from a fitted bodice. Pink ribbons trimmed the edges of the flounces at her shoulders and at the hem, along the low sculpted neckline. Wearing it, she looked like the rose Beverly had given her when she had pneumocystis.

231

Every hat Jada tried on wobbled over her ears. Padding the hat emphasized the gap between her skull and the brim, looking even more ridiculous. A child's hat, though it fit, miniaturized Jada's head. The clerk proffered a bride's maid's triangular headpiece. With a pouf of white netting, a bundle of pink ribbon, and an elastic band, we had the perfect crown for Jada.

Everything was written up, the headpiece was marked for sewing and the dress for alterations. The frilly white gloves and a pair of white nylons with sparkly rhinestones at the ankles were packaged and lay cradled in the crook of my arm while I balanced Jada with the other, a proud escort. The clerk smiled at Jada, and at me, and I was as proud of her as I was of Jada. Taking in the spongy May air, I could feel Jada's eagerness to get back to the hospital and into bed. The hour and a half in the shop seemed a day's work.

When Dr. Lourde thought Jada could manage at home, he authorized her release form the hospital. The release became a punishment. At home, her temperature climbed, and Dr. Lourde readmitted her. Then repeat, and repeat, and repeat, in and out without enough warning to launder the sheets. I could understand why Jada was safer in the hospital, but I could not see that anyone was doing anything I couldn't do at home, especially on a Saturday evening, this Saturday evening, the evening of the morning she came home again only to be back in a hospital room. Weekends at the hospital were never-ending: no one's around and nothing gets started, an eternity of holding; it was easy to lose tomorrow.

Jada waned in the dusky light of early evening, waiting for the morphine to transform burning pain to simmering ache. Dr. Lourde said it was pneumonia, not life-threatening, but, as he also said, she was not out of the woods yet. I sat by her bed and let the little dots of darkness crowd into the room. We were in one of the worst rooms on the floor, the other one being the room on the other side of the push-pull accordion wall between the two. A bump on the wall could send it bowing out the other side. The television, mounted with its back to the adjoining room, annoyed no matter how low the volume was set. Boisterous neighbors meant a miserable stay. The wall intended to divide us from the people in the room next door only symbolized how inseparably bound we were to the patient on the other side.

Huddled next to Jada, I wandered in the rhythm of quiet until I heard the commotion of a patient arriving in the room beyond the accordion wall. At once, I sensed a clumsiness, a hurriedness that permeated this place we were. Bodies went in and out of the room, the sound of shoes scuffing the floor in short strides, almost running pace, but I heard none of the babble of welcoming nurses, sounding somewhat like tour guides, "Hi, my name is Pam, and I'll do everything I can to make you happy. Here's the call button, and to your right...." Instead, hushed voices and secretive exchanges seeped through the thin membrane between rooms.

Jada's eyes were closed; she made no movement except for her breathing, but her face had not the relaxed look of sleep. Then I saw Dr. Lourde skim by her door. It's late at night, I thought. Ten, eleven. He's never here at this time of night. I heard his voice join the others in the room. A nurse closed Jada's door to the corridor, trapping uneasiness inside.

I listened against my will to the darkness where no babies cried, where no machines screamed, where no call lights lit, to a wrestling of breathing, weak cries, shuffled footsteps that moved without haste. Beverly floated by. Now I knew what palled. At the sobbing it was over. Burning with embarrassment that we should be witness to something so private as the passage of life, I rose as quietly as I could in the corner of the blackened room and pulled the thin cotton curtain around Jada's bed, as if that could keep us from what was not ours, and hoped that Jada was asleep.

For a long time I sat in the chair, a wooden slat at my back, the cushioned seat my only comfort. I dared not leave the room for sheets to make up a bed on the window seat lest I swipe a glimpse at what others had to admit to themselves and I did not. I felt devastated that I should feel lucky. When no sound was heard from the next room, vacant, as if no one had been there at all, I lay across the settee. My cheek smacked cool vinyl.

"We're going to have to get into that arm," Dr. Lourde said on Monday. "I've been talking with a hand specialist here. He's excellent in his field, and I think you'll know what I mean when I say he's especially good with young people when you meet him. He has a daughter himself who has a similar circumstance to yours, so he's sensitive to what you're going through. Surgery with anyone carries a certain amount of risk, and in your case, surgery opens up a whole realm of possible complications, but I just don't think we can wait anymore, not with your fevers."

"Good, it's about time," Jada said. Dr. Lourde went on to explain that Dr. Randolph would clean out the infection but that they would have to continue with a course of antibiotics, which was under the supervision of the mysterious Dr. Craig. Jada listened patiently. "Just get this over with and get me out for prom."

"We should have plenty of time," he reassured her. Then he sprang up from the chair, like a Jack-in-the-box, and looked at her right arm.

"What are you doing that for?" Jada asked, her eyes narrowing suspiciously.

"Well I just wanted to see how the veins are in your arm. You know we won't be able to use your left arm, and I'm concerned we don't overuse these veins in your right. After a while they collapse and then..."

"Yuck! Don't tell me that!" She jerked her arm away from him.

"Jada," Dr. Lourde said, releasing her. "I don't get it. I was just talking about surgery and you didn't bat an eyelash, but all I do is mention the word vein and you practically have a convulsion."

Jada shuddered. "I don't mind that you have to do the things, as long as I'm not awake when you do them. I just don't want to hear about all the grody stuff. You guys think that just because you can do such gross things that they aren't gross to us. Do you want the guys who work in sewers to tell you about their work?"

"That's quite a comparison, Jada."

"Just tell me what you're going to do," Jada said, "not all the details. If I want to know, I'll ask."

When Jada's nurse heard Dr. Randolph was coming, a look of adulation overtook her. "He's the one who rebuilt that little boy's hand after the bear mauled him in Yellowstone. They flew all the way here just for Dr. Randolph." I nodded, trying to remember which month, which bear, which boy I'd read about.

Dr. Randolph stood tall in a large frame, disproportionately diminishing his recessed eyes. I could see why the nurses called him a big teddy bear. His voice was small, too, another contradiction to his size, though he didn't say much, just told Jada who he was and that he wanted to see her arm. I stood like a camera taking shots at the whole scene. He left without ceremony.

Dr. Lourde, at his next visit, asked how things went between her and the venerated Dr. Randolph. Jada shrugged her shoulders in response. The air clung awkwardly about us as we all waited for someone to speak. "Anything else, Jada?"

"Yeah. How about my leg?"

Dr. Lourde shifted. "We'll have to wait and see on that. Maybe after tomorrow we'll have a better picture of what's going on there."

"Tomorrow, why tomorrow?" I broke in.

The expectation in Dr. Lourde's face froze into bewilderment. "Well," he sputtered, turning from me to Jada, "after the operation. Didn't Dr. Randolph tell you he's operating on your arm?"

"No. He didn't say anything to me."

"Oh, I thought you knew." Dr. Lourde was back in control again, though I still felt like we could be bruised by bumping the air. It was a crowded room anyway, dark with little sunlight and dark with memory. He went on with pre-operative instructions and assurances. "I'll see you tomorrow," he said as he left.

Early the next day, swinging doors from the operating room opened, releasing the team who would work with Jada. They rimmed the gurney and hovered over her like she was a wounded bird that couldn't get off the ground. A man in blue spoke up, chewing his gum, "Hi, there, Pumpkin; I'm Jim, and I'm going to be with you all the time. Who's that bear you have there?"

"It's a pig," Jada twisted Hambone's head for proof.

Jim snapped a bubble and made an exaggerated face at being corrected. He took Jada's hand away from Hambone, letting him tip over. I moved Hambone to Jada's other shoulder. Jim stretched out Jada's arm and slid two fingers up the inside of her elbow. "Do you have to do that?"

"I'm just checking out your veins. Nothing pops out at me."

"Ick!" She tugged again, harder. "Can't you just do it without saying it?"

"Okay," Jim said, opening his grip as if he'd just dropped a rotten fish. He slid down the length of the rail and reached for her ankle.

Jada kicked at the groping hand. "You aren't using my foot!"

"All right, just looking. Jim picked up Jada's hand to examine it and made a subtle grunt. She kept her eyes on him. When he lay her hand down, he said, "Okay, you won't even feel it," and started back for the swinging doors. The others cast reassuring smiles down at Jada, and at the receiving nurse's nod, pushed Jada toward the same doors.

I signed in at the waiting room and listened for as long as I could to the account of a swimming accident that was being repaired in another operating room. As one by one people joined the teller, the woman went through the tears and rips, lingering on a new detail, how long it took to fetch the youngster out of the water, what repairs the doctor was going to make, enlarging the story into an epic. I wondered what it was like to have so many people who felt that close that they would come together at a hospital and decided that it would embarrass me.

Jada exuded self-sufficiency, and I think people sensed that she didn't need them. But she preferred company to being alone and craved support from others. More often, others let her down. There was Steph, loyal; she wanted to be a best friend, but Jada felt she had to do more taking care of Steph than enjoying her. Kimby said she was Jada's best friend, but they could never agree on the terms of friendship. Kimby set up time frames and conditions for their visits. She stood tall, always properly dressed with the right color of lipstick and conservative earrings. Jada experimented, changing colors and whimsical baubles and jangles. She wanted to be more spontaneous instead of always checking with some interior rule that determined the right thing for the two of them to do. Even now, while Jada was in the hospital, Kimby measured her time with Jada, doling out a phone call only when Jada pressured her. Jada could no more conform to Kimby's stringency than I could tolerate all those people in the waiting room around me, chit chatting about this and that. Easy for me to say; I could get up and walk away. I did.

Jada and Hambone both wore splints when I saw them again. Jada's was wound many times around and bulged like Popeye's mummified muscle. When Dr. Randolph came to roll away the gauze the next day, he was unwrapping my hope to get out of the hospital for good. "Jada, I'm here to change the dressing," he said as he walked into her room.

"Just a minute, I'm on the phone." Jada glanced back to the wall and resumed her conversation. Dr. Randolph moved closer into the room and stood at her bed, looking a lot less like a comforting teddy bear than he did an angry father who had given her ten seconds to do as she was told or else. I could mentally hear him counting down, "...eight...seven....six...."

Jada's voice iced over. "My doctor is standing here waiting for me to get off the phone. I have to go now." Jada's marble eyes glared, and her lips cut a straight line. "You've made us wait; you can wait a couple minutes."

I expected bellowing reverberations from a man of his stature, but he spoke so softly that he almost mumbled; yet he used his dominance to threaten in the time-worn tradition of knowing what's best for 'the little bit,' saying, "Have you ever been spanked by your doctor?"

237

Jada still hadn't blinked. "Have you ever been hit by your patient?"

Then there was silence. But not for long because Dr. Randolph was unwinding the gauze, and, as he got closer he slowed, handling her arm more gently and studying it more intensely. The gauze grew pink, then red. "What are you doing?" she cried out. A muddy yellow soaked strip of cloth trailed like a fishing line that Dr. Randolph reeled out of Jada's stuffed arm. The outraged red edges of her skin were parted along Jada's entire inner arm and gaped open to raw meat. "Don't look, Mom! Don't look!"

"I cleaned out the infection. But I didn't want to close your arm up in case I have to go back in, so I'm keeping it open and packing it with a dressing."

I didn't count, but that utterance contained the most words I'd heard Dr. Randolph speak at one time. "I want to know what's going on, Jada," I said.

"No, I don't want you to see it!" Jada's order was like a snap of the fingers, and I stepped backwards, dropping into the safety of a chair while the room burned with Jada's fury. I could hear her teeth cut each word. "What have you done to me?"

"I couldn't close it, Jada. This will heal up just fine." Dr. Randolph was wrapping Jada's arm again, and, when he finished, promised to return the next day.

"Mom, what's happening to me?" She simmered with anger. "You're selfish for making me go through this. People should have a right to decide about their lives."

Thin glimmers of light poked holes in the shifting clouds outside. I got up from the chair and moved toward the window, hoping to be in the right spot for just one second. "I agree, and I disagree. People should have a right to determine what goes on with their bodies. But sometimes they aren't in a position to make a good judgment. At 80, I'd say let the person decide, no matter what. At 3, no. At 40, it's different. Sixteen must be the hardest. It's too late: you already know too much; and yet, it's too early to know that you don't know enough.

"Yes, I'm selfish if I want you to live. Remember when you broke your leg and we were at Grandma Pope's and that butterfly landed on your cast?"

"I have no memory."

"You should have seen your face. It was the biggest butterfly I've ever seen." I spread my hands to recapture the image for myself. "You were in a wheelchair, and the butterfly stayed on your leg, its wings pointed up toward the sky, and your eyes were just as wide as its wingspan. You were a little scared, but your dad talked to you and made you know it was really a wonderful thing to have a butterfly on your leg, especially one so grand. You stayed still, except for your mouth; it opened wide, too.

"Stuff like that, Jada, little marvels of the world. Butterflies, talking on the phone with a friend, getting all dressed up for the prom: they have to be worth even this thing that happened to your arm."

"It won't work out anyway," Jada continued. "They won't make me better for prom. I'll end up like that girl in there who died." She motioned to the wall.

"Not if I can help it!"

"No one else cares the way you do." Tremulous utterance. Wings of a butterfly.

"No one else is your mother." Well, if I couldn't hide death from Jada, I'd not deny it and steeled cold with determination: the inconvenience of living in a hospital shrank next to submission to dying. Because there was no warning, even when the warning signs were everywhere. We stand fumbling with a key when the door is already open. We refuse to see the signs.

Every night I asked myself for a second chance to make good on my affirmation of life; as I drove the empty streets of Sibley, through dark-masked Lyton Park, and up the Lyton straightaway, I vowed that tomorrow would not be the day of yesterday's regrets.

Living followed a routine outside the hospital; inside as well, which is why, when I arrived at Jada's empty hospital room, I was surprised to find Jada gone and not knowing where she was gone to. Carrying clean blankets, Brenda nearly collided with me in the hallway, smiling her girl-next-door-smile. "I bet you're wondering where Jada is. Dr. Randolph ordered a therapeutic bath and we needed to get it started before a new patient arrives tonight. We're a little short-handed."

Only one tub room was closed, so I made short raps, then turned the knob, swished in and shut the door swiftly. My next breath felt like I was a fire swallower who'd made her first mistake, and my eyes felt the burning of hot peppers in them. I wanted to shut out the prickling poison in the air, better yet, escape from the firebombing to my nose and throat and eyes. But there, in the oversized tub, was Jada, buried up to her chin in brown billowing bubbles.

"Oh, Mom, thank God you're here! Help me!" She gasped over the roaring motor of the Jacuzzi and the roiling water it created. She swiped away huge blobby sheets of red-brown bubbles that multiplied about her with greater speed than she could bail them out of the tub, cascading down the side, bounding magnetically to each other and onto the floor in ankle-deep bales that surged ominously toward the door.

"How do you turn that thing off?" I coughed, realizing that if I didn't join her in batting at the reddish-skinned mounds, they would be climbing up Jada's nose. She must have discovered the futility of fumbling for the hidden switch herself.

"I don't know!" she shouted over the rumbling Jacuzzi motor. Each breath had to rake her throat more than mine. She had had the swiftness of mind to reach for the nurse call button; the square light on the wall was lit. But where was the nurse? Even if Jada were fully capable of rising and hoisting herself over the edge and out by herself, I thought it a dangerously long time to let a call from the tub room go unheeded.

A cool draft of air swept up my back, and I turned to see the shape of a body coming in through the haze. First she reached her hand through the foam and turned off the loud machine. Then she released the call signal and stood back to wonder. Brenda, an endearing nurse with a fresh country manner of caring, stood, blinking her watering eyes and crinkling her nose. "What are you trying to do to me? I couldn't get it to stop!" Jada demanded, coughed.

Brenda remained dumbfounded at the scene. "Are you all right?" she choked out. Together we lifted Jada out and onto the slippery floor, and Brenda hurried away.

Jada wore a bronze hue except for her face; the one part of her body that was not submerged in the billowing foam was almost pink by comparison. The big white towel I wrapped around her did not towel off the brown tint. "You have to see yourself in the mirror. You look like an Easter egg that's been dipped in brown dye."

Now that the water was draining and the bubbles had stopped bursting with the pungent smell, the hilarity of the adventure remained like the foam that crusted the tiled floor. Jada recounted the sequence, her eyes still smarting. "I knew you were on your way, so I let Brenda start the bath. When I got in, she poured Betadine in the water and turned on the Jacuzzi. She said she had to get to another patient but that she'd be right back. But the bubbles kept coming and coming and no one was here and I yelled for help and pulled for help but no one came."

"And when I came in, I was nearly strangled by the fumes and there you were, up to your earlobes in bubbles, and you furiously sweeping one batch away after another. It was awful!" I laughed, and coughed. "You should have seen yourself! And then I just jumped right in there, like Ethel finding Lucy in a jam. I mean, that's what it was like, an episode of *I Love Lucy*."

"I couldn't get them to stop," she laughed. "They kept coming and coming, and all I could do was try to keep them from drowning me."

"Somebody turn off the bubble machine," I mocked, refreshed by the surprise of laughter.

In Jada's room, Brenda was making up a clean bed. She turned around and sheepishly confessed to misreading the directions. Dr. Randolph had prescribed the disinfectant as a guard against topical infection to her arm. But instead of measuring in grams, Brenda poured ounces into the bath water. The rest was just a misadventure.

Lucky for Dr. Randolph, too, that it was the nurse who botched the treatment. He was in enough hot water with Jada. As her arm wove itself together, it carved a deep red jagged scar, like a young angry river running through a craggly ravine with hard, knobby bulges on either side, elbow to wrist. Extending her left arm, straight from the shoulder to the palm and fingers was impossible. He repeated adamantly, however, that the damage to her muscle and tendon fibers—and, thus, the ugliness—was due to the infection, which perhaps was the grosser insult to Jada. Dr. Randolph promised that, with rehabilitation, Jada could regain full extension, but he had no remedy for the deformity of her taut and supple skin.

Localizing and removing the infection in Jada's arm was an illusory remedy to what necessitated her repeated hospitalizations; she was home for two days, then back in for one—or was it three— all blurred by the sameness of her condition. When she was released to home care, Dr. Lourde warned us to be on the lookout for the slightest sign of a change; the nature of the change counting not as much as the speed at which that change could lead to disaster. Without a moment's indication, Jada spouted a nosebleed that gushed a flowing stream of blood, blood from so many transfusions that what flowed through her was less hers than others', and a binge of lower blood counts, numbers so terrifyingly low they couldn't be counted. And not just whole blood: Jada's platelet count sank so low as not to even register. And there was nothing Dr. Lourde could do about it.

"We can't risk a platelet rejection," he explained, leaving few blanks for me to fill in. "She might need them later. And when she needs them, she will really need them." In this state, if she were to have a nosebleed, or begin bleeding from anything, it wouldn't matter where she was, in the hospital or not—that Dr. Lourde stated outright.

Early on Saturday, Jada was released from the hospital, and I coaxed her to let me stop at the school to update my plans for the substitute before it closed for the day. Fire doors closed off the stairwell leading to the third floor, leaving them eerily dark and empty. "Can't I just sit on the steps?" she asked, and then, thud, she fell forward. I had neither strength to carry her nor volume to reach a hearing ear to keep my daughter from bleeding to death right there on the steps of Parkview High School. Her face shriveled, fear terrorizing her widened eyes. The image froze: would this be her last vision of the world, smudged walls, one phlegm-colored light fixture, me reaching down, too late to stop either the fall or every decision that led to it and living with the consequences that we were sure would come from it? Yet nothing did, and shakily, like a leaf hanging onto the limb after a severe frost, she painstakingly took the remaining steps, no gash, no blood, no end.

Such high drama should have led to a climax, but most of our days were spent with Jada's either being admitted—with great speed—or released from the hospital. Plastic identifying wrist bands that could have been pieced together into a story strung themselves out, distilled into simple exhaustion, and the collection became a gluttonous growing entity without plot. Keeping track of Jada's hospital ins and outs was as foolish as keeping track of rotini bobbing in a pot of boiling water. There were too many, and they all looked the same. I remembered not when we went in or came home but only to keep a freshly laundered set of sheets packed and ready to go and placed by the bedroom door, and to sleep in my street clothes, even at home.

Except for transfusions and blood cultures, the catheter ran a repetitive course of morphine, dulling her senses. I suspended bags of fluids from the curtain rod above her bed and injected morphine into the port, 15 cc over 15 minutes every four hours, followed by a flush. I could recite it by heart, do it in my sleep; Lord knows I had to, every four hours every day and night; too fast, I had been warned, and it would kill her. I bought a foam slab that folded up into a chair and unfolded into a bed and stayed in Jada's room, on the slab on the floor, not unlike the slab at the window in the hospital. The toilet, twenty feet away, was too far: she had trouble standing up, and walking was troublesome past suffering.

I kept track of Jada's temperature, 104.2, 103.4, 104.4, and called in to Dr. Lourde, who decided if she could stay at home another four hours or if we should hit the road again for the hospital. At a loss for how to respond, Dr. Lourde discontinued the antibiotics and Tylenol. Whatever culprit was making her sick would, sooner or later, come out of hiding and name itself. Jada kept saying it was her leg. It was weak, it was painful. But Dr. Lourde found nothing. No bumps or lumps on the surface, no bumps or lumps that he could feel in deeper tissue, and no bumps or lumps on CAT scans. Examinations ended in frustration and the same advice: "bite the bullet."

Jada's fever reached too high for too long, and the upswing of the seesaw jerked her into the hospital—again. She sank more sullenly. I had promised her undying support; now what did that mean? Was I supposed to let her choose her way in this deeply entrenched moment, or was I to hinge on the future, no matter how far-flung it was from reality? My mettle was being tested, whatever that was. We had cut to the bone a long time before this, and Jada now challenged me to gnaw away with her at the hard stuff, within which nestled the sweetest softest jelly, the most vulnerable juice, the nectar of life. I started talking in my sleep, answering the pithiest statement, the profoundest question, the $64,000.00 question without the tick-tock grace of the minute hand to force a decision. We were back again, back to the hospital long enough for Jada to notice her surroundings had changed, but that they hadn't really. I looked in the closet: the cereal round I noticed on the floor from two days earlier was still there.

Beneath the white bedspread, Jada looked at a shadowy wall in the sunless afternoon, her own features disappearing into the blankness of fading light. The stripes on the curtain were lost in the folds as they were pushed into a bunch near the wall, providing a brackish-white backdrop to Jada's head. I tired of sitting on the one non-gray in the room and stood up, a test really of my ability to act, for I had nowhere to go, and moved my chair closer to Jada. "Do you want me to get you something?" I asked.

Sometimes so blue they made your mouth water, Jada's eyes on me turned rheumy, as if the question had driven a stake in her and drained her of the only color she had left. Looking back at me, flatly she said, "When dogs get this sick, they put them to sleep."

For all I knew, I was being overtaken, too. Is that how it happens? Does everything lose its color and just turn into a blur, more like a shadow, an eye becoming blind? I had never watched anyone die and had not considered death by degrees. Now I envisioned it as an energy in itself, one that could gain strength by wrenching color from the world and making the void of color more attractive. Death was not, perhaps, a calamitous strike on unwitting prey but an ingratiation to a welcoming host. I answered, "But that's only when they're ready to die. People love their dogs; they don't put them to sleep just because they're sick."

"But some people are ready to die." Jada's face looked to be made of putty, not just like the old school paste that the teacher slabbed on a paper square in the corner of our desks, but also in its void of animation, so that each feature had been put there and arranged by some other's hand. She had always been right about the condition of her body.

"I don't think many people are really ready to die," I said. But there was Grandma M, and her mother before her, both old and alone, sitting all day long, waiting, they said, to die; and you could see them turn time into their enemy as the world turned monotonously gray. I wasn't sure that dying wasn't a state of mind, but I didn't want to believe that we willed ourselves to die. "I think we get ready to die because we face death. But we aren't ready in advance—we get ready only at the time."

"No, I disagree. Some people are really ready. I've felt that way for a long time." There is a time of day that brings apprehension. It begins somewhere in the late afternoon when the sun loses its buttery color and blue seeps from the sky. It's a restless time, a time without resolve, a time of ambiguity, neither light nor dark, day nor night, a time of passing, a miasma of time. We were in that time, and it was soundless, that time, because it was not either in the world or out of it. It was just time, unclaimed, a vapor. "You know," Jada said, her voice neither loud nor soft, passionless yet clear, "I could do something about it."

"I wonder if you're being realistic. I can understand why death appeals to you now; it offers an escape from your pain and uncertainty. But do you think that just stopping will not require pain? Do you think that dying will be easy? I've seen glimmers of your enjoying something. It makes me believe that when you feel better, you will want to be better. I want to see you better; I want to see you at seventeen, eighteen."

"I won't get there anyway, so why go through all this?"

"There's enough hope that you do get there. Let me be your hope."

"I had a dream one night," she said. "I dreamt that I was outside my bedroom window and wanted to come in. I called to you, but you couldn't come to me. Then I stood at the front door, but three spiders were on the screen, and they kept me from entering, and you stood at the top of the steps and you couldn't move. You couldn't get down to the door to get the spiders. I kept calling you, but you didn't answer."

"Oh, Darlin'; you must have felt so sad! I won't abandon you. Let me hold you!"

Every part of Jada's body seemed set, placed, a still life. The curtain hung from its track without a ripple; the machine behind it was turned off, the buff tag wired onto the pole jutted like the flag that was planted on the moon, stiff and board-like without gravity to let it drape; the ring of cereal shaped like a miniature life preserver that had been swept away to the corner, lay unclaimed behind the closed door. It was so clear to me; why didn't she reach out and grab on? Maybe it was the difference between being the witness and being the drowning person. I couldn't sit still in the stick-like chair and watch her go down. "Say in a few weeks you were told that there was no hope. I believe you would be somewhat disappointed, wouldn't you?"

"It depends on what's going on then."

"Okay. Then what if you heard that tomorrow? You know what's going on now."

"Well, I guess I'd be a little disappointed," Jada said, pushing the words just past her mouth so that they stopped there, and, if they were painted wooden letters, they would have dropped and tumbled from the bed onto the floor, chipping off the edges. I strained to hear them. "All I want is relief. I don't want anything but painkillers. I can't do anything. Why can't they put me to sleep for a long time? No, I don't want to go to sleep because that means I have to wake up. My head hurts. My teeth hurt. You know why my teeth hurt? I've been biting the bullet too long."

Dr. Lourde recommended she see a woman in social services. "When patients are in the hospital for extended periods of time, sometimes they get what we call hospitalitis. It's psychological, but sometimes it's harder to treat than a real disease. Whatever is causing Jada to be so sick is not her leukemia. Trudy specializes in adolescent counseling. I can see her getting along with Jada very well. She's extremely intelligent and sensitive. She'd respect Jada's integrity."

Beverly peeked her head into Jada's room and invited me down to the cafeteria. I took a cup and let the steam rise to my nostrils. She spoke glowingly of Trudy and offered to set up the appointment for me.

"I don't want what happened last time to happen again. If I never see Trudy, I think that's what's best for Jada."

Beverly thought for a moment, her cup poised at her lips. "I'm really sorry about that. You were my first assignment. I knew at my first visit to your house that it wasn't a simple case of a disease in your family. I made a mistake. But I do think you should have a talk with Trudy first. If Joe or I talk to her, she'll get only our opinions. She really should know as much about Jada as she can, and you're the one who knows her best."

"Maybe that's the trouble." Beverly started to speak, and I held up my hand. "Okay, but I want Trudy to get to know Jada on her own."

I always walked the steps, used to. By new habit, I sluggishly boarded the elevator. When the doors opened, a blank beige wall spread itself in front of me. I looked right and left for a sign, but saw only a dimly lit continuous corridor without, it appeared, an end. No brightly colored mural or series of photographs of flowers in the woods and sunlit leafy trees as on the first floor. The basement was unnaturally quiet, without faces or voices or bodies of people anywhere. What an irony, to hide the social services department in the bowels of the hospital, away from the action. The symbolism piqued my irritation.

The smell of newly sawn wood and fresh paint reminded me of someone's new family room as I opened the door: the carpet, the walls, the furniture were meant to be durable—industrial strength gray and beige and scratchy. And no natural light. All the tricks in a decorator's repertoire could never camouflage the feel of a basement—dim, dark, and dank.

A woman in a white and blue two-piece dress came from behind a newly-installed wall and greeted me. Shaking my hand, she introduced herself as Trudy. I followed her blue and white pumps down the row of apportioned cubicles. Inside hers were a few posters framed in silver, like the silver streaks that ran through her short wheat-colored hair, and a table lamp casting a cone of light on her desk. We sat, I on the edge of the wooden-armed guest chair, she at the desk facing me and able to reach out for paper or pen without disturbing our union. She sat back comfortably and crossed her legs, the pleats of her skirt rippling away from her knee in waves. "So, tell me," she began, her hands clasped in her lap, "about Jada."

I stammered. I had books to write about Jada. "She's very strong-willed, resolute, pragmatic. Some people think she's uncooperative because she insists on things being a certain way. But, she doesn't ask for something unreasonable. She's been on morphine for pain and Halcyon for sleeping, and she wonders why she has to ask for it when it's prescribed. The nurses get all tight. One said, 'We don't want you to get too dependent on it.' Jada sees right through that; she has leukemia, and they're worried she's going to be a drug addict.

"She hates incompetence and thoughtlessness. It's her body everyone is playing around with, but sometimes people act as if she wouldn't know the difference, or she wouldn't care what they do or how they do it. She wants people to see her and treat her as a person, and she's aware of all the little things they do that treat her as a rag doll who can't think or can't be trusted, or...like she's a baby, like putting the bed rails up. I know it sounds trivial, but it's the symbolic gestures; she is not one to do things just because of tradition, but questions practices on an individual basis.

"She's also a teenager going through all the teenage things— or not going through them. Just when she's supposed to become independent of me, she becomes dependent on me, on all the doctors and nurses; imagine what that does to her to have to be submissive. The wound on her arm is ugly, grotesque, and it embarrasses her: she wants to be pretty. She doesn't have any hair, which is not as important as the other things that are yanked from her. Like her arm: people dismiss it, ask her if she's right or left-handed and think, oh, no big deal, you don't need your left hand, anyway. But she does. She plays the piano and the viola. And even if she didn't, she wants her left hand, you know?

"She really wants someone to respect her, to listen to her. And care. Besides me. She wants me with her all the time—I want to be with her, too, but I try to get out of the way. I try to let her be with her friends, to have her time with Dr. Lourde. Once I intentionally kept busy with a task during his visit to extricate myself, to force a conversation between them without me.

"Sometimes..., sometimes I have to be careful to separate us. I can feel her, I flinch when they touch her. I know there's an explanation for it, but I breathe when she breathes. Even when we're in different rooms, I can tell... Sorry."

"No, that's okay," Trudy said, her voice mixing the crispness of a tart apple with the creaminess of a thick caramel coating. Her eyes were a warm gray.

"They tell her that it's all right to be angry, but then when she shows it, they tell her that she's not cooperating. She can tell you this herself, but she gets so mad at me. I don't know if she's angry at me for her having the disease or if she's angry at me for making her have treatment, or if she's just plain angry and I'm there.

"Well, anyway, now she's stuck here in the hospital, and I think she thinks nothing is being done, no one believes her. She's got a fever and no one is doing anything about it. Maybe she thinks we're all trying to hide something from her. I just think she needs someone besides me to believe her. Someone who'll listen and empathize. I haven't told her yet about you because I didn't know if you'd be willing to see her."

Trudy smiled serenely. "I'll give it a try, but I don't want to come in now when things are bad. The last thing I want to do is to disappoint her. Do you think she'll be out of the hospital next week? We could meet somewhere on neutral territory, away from the hospital. There's too much negativity here."

"Fine, but from now on, I don't talk to you, okay? You're seeing Jada, and anything you know about Jada will be between you two. Has Beverly told you about that whole thing with us?"

"She mentioned that she had been involved but that there were complications." Trudy's voice was clear and deep and honest. I liked the way she responded without giving me sad-eyed looks or tsk-tsks. An hour had gone by.

"Well, Jada," Dr. Lourde began, his eyes round with conviction; he had an urgent demeanor today; something was up. "I can't find the cause of your infection. It's clear you have something going on in your body, something that is causing you to be sick, although I'm concerned about just how sick you really are and why something doesn't show up. I've been holding off, hoping for something else so I wouldn't have to do this. Sometimes an undetectable microorganism gets trapped on the end of the catheter where it connects with the vein. It just sits there, and in your case, with your suppressed immune system, you can't fight it off. The chemo we've been pumping into you is making you vulnerable to anything and everything. Unfortunately, the only way to remove the culprit is to remove the catheter."

"Now, we could put another Hickman in on the left side, but I am reluctant to because what's making you susceptible on your right will be a threat on your left, and I would hate to take away our only chance at that vein. We may need it later if you get into trouble. I know this is disappointing news. You have an inordinate amount of fear of pain and intolerance for IVs, but the heavy-duty therapy for this round is over, and the next isn't for another eight months. In between times, there's only your monthly IVs."

Jada grimaced and said, "Yeah, and how about all this?" She motioned to the antibiotics strung through the blue beeping machine.

Dr. Lourde nodded his head. "I'm proposing that we implant what we call a subclavian catheter and see how far that takes us. The tube attaches just below the clavicle, hence the term subclavian. It's not meant to be permanent, such as the Hickman, but it's worth a try. We can install that catheter at the same time we remove the Hickman, which, though it worries me to do so, requires another operation."

"When is that?" Jada asked.

"Tomorrow, if that's okay with you." Jada assented with a nod so imperceptible her head did not rustle the pillow. I would like to have felt relief, but everything about this relapse so far did not come without a price. I felt like we were on a demented game show where people gambled everything they had on a prize hidden behind one of three doors, except that each one was a booby prize.

The next morning, a nurse and I brought Jada to the pre-op room for her third surgery since her relapse just weeks earlier. The nurse-in-waiting looked at Jada's wristband. "Why do you do that?" Jada asked. "You should know who I am by now."

"We have to make sure. We don't want to perform surgery on the wrong person."

"If I were the wrong person, do you think I'd let you do it to me?" The nurse released Jada's hand. Through the swinging doors came three more nurses, and one by one, they surrounded Jada.

"Hi, Jada," said one nurse, softly. She gave a little wave of her hand over the raised railing. "I see you've brought your friend." Hambone sat, his tilted head leaning to the left, above Jada's pillow. A man wearing a white paper cap joined the women and introduced himself as the anesthesiologist. How curious: every anesthesiologist was new to Jada, and every one of them was male. I studied him, and I saw that he worked with Jada the same way the others had: authoritatively, condescendingly, conceitedly. He began by sweet-talking her, promising her a rose garden if she'd just leave everything to him; he knew what he was doing, and he was good at it. Others said that with a gloating smile; this one verged on a sneer. He ran his hand along Jada's inner arm, flicking his middle finger at her vein once. Jada pulled. Twice.

"No," Jada said. "You can't use those. Use the back of my hand."

"This is really the best spot," he said in the familiar patronizing tone. He jerked toward her as he tried to hold onto her hand.

"No! The veins aren't good there, and I don't want you poking around. And don't even think of going down there."

He checked his movement toward her foot. Jada stuck her hand out, palm down. "I told you. Use this, or I'm not going!" She dropped her hand and waited. He looked at it suspiciously, then back at her arm. The telephone rang, and the nurse reported, "Dr. Graham is waiting. They're on a tight schedule—we have to get going."

"So, tell him to leave me alone and do it the right way." Eyes darted about and met.

"Okay, Jada; let's go."

Hearing the clatter of television noise from outside the doorway, I didn't bother to check in across the hall. I roamed toward the chapel, which was usually empty, a quiet place. Today several people sat inside, whispering among themselves as if what they said could be kept a secret from their god. I backed away and stepped almost magically into a skewed square of bright sunlight. A green spiky plant at one edge sprayed its leaves in open praise, sunning as much surface as it could. I looked up to a skylight and squinted. All our worries and questions and disappointments had locked me in solitary confinement for so long that I had forgot how glorious it was to feel the sun. I pulled a chair from the chapel into my solar alcove and prayed. I didn't address any deity. I didn't ask for anything, nor did I confess any sin. I didn't heap sympathy upon myself. I didn't think ahead, and I didn't remember what was past. I didn't take out anything to read, to write, or to embroider. I closed my eyes but I did not sleep. I dreamed no images. I emptied myself of every sight and every sound, and let the sun fill me.

After surgery, we went back to wait and see. Not a very satisfying way to live life. Especially when life as it was seemed to have little to wait for and not much to see, more backing and forthing between hospital and home. Dr. Lourde clung to the belief that Jada's failure to respond had more to do with her mind than with her body. Stimulus starvation, he conjectured; she needed more stimulation.

"It's all your fault, Mom. My body's not supposed to do this. You should have let it die. It was meant to be." Jada lay in her own bed, a whisper of a breeze, heard but not felt, passed through an open window. Night was knitting itself together outside, obliterating the dainty pink and blue and yellow pattern on the wallpaper, and I could hear Dom and David banter as they bounced a basketball on the asphalt driveway and shot it against the backboard. Thunk! It hit the rim.

Nothing's easy. "Even if I had foreseen everything that has happened to you, I still wouldn't have given up, Jada, because I'm hoping for a future beyond this. You're feeling the short range, and I'm looking for the long range."

253

"Do you know what it's like to have needles in you? To get sick, to throw up, to have IVs, to have cuts in you?"

"No, I don't." My stomach turned at the memory of cleaning up the curds strung together in a slimy slough of vomit.

"Then you can't make me go through all this. You're mean to want to put me through all this. I'm not Jada any more. I feel awful. I'm tired and I'm ugly. I'm all scarred, and I have a coat hook for an arm. I have no hair. I can't do anything. They're doing all the things I hate. I *like* to look good."

"Yes, you do. You aren't the same. But you're not ugly. You just look different from what you were." Her skin was so fragile and her eyes so deeply open that I felt I was seeing her thoughts as I spoke. "Right now you're not feeling pretty, but with or without hair, you'll *always* be pretty, no matter what. It's you inside that makes you pretty."

"You know what bothers me the most about this? I can't dance. I love to dance. And I can't move."

"I cry sometimes when I think of what you can't do," I said.

"So do I. Did you hate me that much as a baby?"

"What? Why do you say that?"

"You make me do all this."

"I loved you so much as a baby—that's why I want you to live. I loved you so much then, and I love you so much now, and I want to love you so much tomorrow and always."

"Oh, Mooie. I need you to kiss me." Yes, and then what? It was easy to kiss her, easy to give in, give up, give away, but I couldn't not try, even in the face of despair. That's what it was that April and May, the season of can'ts. I used to want easy, until easy presented its awful image.

Holding Jada close, I said, "There's a woman I want you to meet, Jada. Her name is Trudy. You'll love the way she dresses: she had on a dress that looked like a Lanz and her shoes could have been Bandolino. I thought you'd like someone to talk to."

"I don't want anyone else now."

"Remember, you have a long two years and eight months ahead, and things will change. You may want someone to talk things over with."

"Why would I need someone to talk with? I have you."

"You might be angry with me, you might want to say something about me."

"Then I'll tell you."

"Yes, I'm sure you will. Still, there could be a reason you'd want to see someone more qualified, someone you can talk to especially when I won't do. And I promise. I wouldn't ever ever talk to her."

The front side of the house shuddered with the slamming of the door. I slid to the floor, my back leaned up to Jada's mattress. Her non-answer was not a no, and I turned my attention to Dom. "I'll be back in a minute, Sugar."

In the kitchen, Dom turned on the T.V. I bought a small portable and put in on a cart in the kitchen to get Jada out of her room without having the stress of steps. Dom was overjoyed because this TV unbound him from watching his father's fare; he flipped the station. "What's on?" I asked.

"I just want to check the score of the hockey game."

"Hockey, in May?"

"Yeah, Mom, it's the Stanley Cup playoffs."

"Oh. Who do you want to win?"

"The Nordiques, but they're not going to. Philadelphia's too…. Yes!" Dom's arm shot upwards in victory. "Show me the score, why don't you? Good. They're tied."

"What period is it? You better hop in the shower before it gets too late."

"I will. Got anything to drink?"

"Some juice. Want me to get some for you?"

"Naw, I'll get it." Dom shoved away from the table and leaned his head into the open refrigerator. "You know what we need? Some chocolate milk. Doesn't that sound good to you?" He pulled out a carton, poured a glass of juice, and returned to the table. "After my shower, can you play a game with me?"

"I'll see, Dom. It might be too late." I said the last part from the hallway. Jada was tweaking her little rubber pig, aptly named Squeaky. One of her collection of pigs, she squeezed her thumb and fingers around it to summon me to her room. I knew the urgency of each squeak. I learned a lot that spring—to see the beginning signs of convulsions, a reaction to a blood transfusion; to make a cover of my body over her shivering; to wrap her head with a gray flannel cap. I learned what not to say to her. So many nights began or ended with pain, uncertainty, trauma, despair, and after singing good night songs, I said good night.

"It's never a good night," she'd responded, "so don't say that." I learned to keep a suitcase packed, like an expectant mother, who could be having a conversation one minute and be off to the hospital the next, stealing away during the night while Arnold and Dom slept.

Driving to the hospital, when there was little traffic to contend with and the lights shimmered in black puddles on the asphalt and the forms on either side of the street lost definition in the darkness, I began to imagine what I fought so hard to deny: what if this is the last time I drive Jada to the hospital? What if, as she sits next to me, jaw set firm against the jostling of riding, her mind is telling her eyes to take one last look? What if two years and eight months has no more meaning than the 50-50 chances she had been given? We assumed it meant life.

What if, just what if, Jada would die? What if she would be like the memory of a gust of wind dashed on exposed flesh, gone? What if someday I would find Squeaky wrapped up somewhere in my closet and remember when Jada was as suddenly felt, alive to the touch? I squinted my eyes tightly to keep myself here, in this car, on this street, with Jada beside me. Two years and eight months seemed like a long time. Maybe it was too big a swatch at one time. Maybe I was asking for the wrong stakes. If I bargained for less, I'd have a better chance of getting it. Graduation from high school was only a year away. Jada could live with the disease to do that. I declared her graduation from high school a finish line and everything after that a winner's victory lap.

In the morning, I went to Trudy's office. "Jada's back in the hospital, and I think she thinks she's dying. She's asked to see Heidi alone. She said she wanted to talk about something with her. Ever since Tracey's death—that's a girl who died in the room next to hers one night—she sounds so hopeless."

"Beverly told me that she's having a real hard time. What does Joe say?"

"He says he can't do anything more for her. I don't think we can wait for Jada to get better for you to see her."

"I can't really do anything," Trudy cautioned, swinging her appointment book around. "But I think you're right. Who knows how long we'll have to wait if we don't start now."

I had read every card in the gift shop, and there's only so much coffee a stomach can tolerate. Wasting time in a hospital is no exaggeration. There were no more unfound nooks for me to hide in, no more anonymous crannies I cared to discover. I stood, plastic bag hanging from my wrist, at the intersection of two hallways. Arnold arrived with a cafeteria coffee cup in hand, and I told him he couldn't go in yet; he walked away.

Trudy emerged from the elevator and stood, slightly less tall, with me. "Heidi's in the room with Jada now, but I don't think it will take much longer." Arnold walked toward us, and without introducing himself, hovered at my rear as I concluded. "This is the last time you and I will talk. From now on, I'm out of the picture." We stood silently, as three strangers waiting for a bus, until Heidi passed us, she leaving the floor, Trudy and I, with Arnold following, turning to go into Jada's room.

At first Trudy stood beside me as I introduced her, but I quickly shifted away toward the foot of the bed. Arnold staked out his space in the far corner of the room and resumed his stance, right hand over left arm. He cleared his throat, said "Hi, J," and remained cross-armed and silent thereafter.

"Jada," I said, "I'm going to leave so you two can get acquainted."

"No, Mom, I don't want you to go." Jada hardly got the words out before she convulsed with sickness. I grabbed the blue kidney-shaped dish and held it to Jada's chin, catching the vomit. Then I pulled the nurse call cord. Trudy retreated toward the door, and I liked her even more. Jada continued to retch, and close on the heels of a nurse came Dr. Lourde. The nurse measured the liquid material and held another container to Jada, while Dr. Lourde looked on.

His calm posture, he placing most of his weight on one foot, giving rest to the other, contrasted to Jada's spiraling panic. She leaned over the bowl, perching herself for each convulsion and pulling herself back as if bound in conflict with her own will, and Dr. Lourde said, patiently, quietly, "Jada, I can't think of any medical reason for you to be throwing up. I think you've talked yourself into it. The lab reports that nothing is growing in your culture, and there's no reason to believe that your leg pains or even your fever could cause you to die now."

The pupils of Jada's eyes shrank smaller and she fell back to the pillow. "What's making my body do this?"

"I don't know, Jada. It could be hospitalitis, but you have been in and out a lot, so I doubt that. I think what we have to do is let Dr. Craig throw everything he's got at you and get you out of here. When's prom again?"

"Next week-end." Jada looked weary, about to drop off to sleep—no, drop off a cliff.

"I'll get on the phone with him right away. We're going to get you out of here." Always Dr. Lourde talked about Jada's disease, about the treatment, about her reactions. He seemed to hold his emotions somewhere else, kept them packed up in some hard-sided suitcase that he could open later, taking out whichever one he wanted to wear for the occasion at hand. I did not fault him for that. That day, though, I heard him talk to Jada's fears. That day I saw a compassionate man. If I could pinpoint a time when she relinquished her trust to him, when she let him touch her vulnerability, I would choose that day, that time that he did not separate her feelings from her being.

Jada responded to the treatment plan laid out for her and was sent home—again—with the obligation to come into the clinic for antibiotics. On prom night, Jada wobbled on her feet, but she was standing. She paled in the delicate white dress. We dotted rouge around her face, but there was no pink glow beneath her skin. Still, she was gorgeous. I served canapés, took pictures. Jada posed like a marble statue, an ideal of beauty of spirit and determination. She wouldn't fly about tables to giggle with her friends, shimmy her hips and rustle her dress to the beat of the music, but maybe she could dance a slow tune, and maybe, with a rest in between she could dance another. I knew she'd try. She'd packed her painkillers.

At exactly 7:00 p.m., a car appeared at our door. Thomas stepped out of the driver's side of the sleek Lincoln Continental, the low evening sun laying on it like a coat of wax. In a dark suit, Thomas needed only a chauffeur's cap to look the part he volunteered to play. He practiced every amenity, mechanically graceful. I snapped more pictures and went back into the house. Jada's absence was a hole in my pocket. I opened a bottle of pink champagne, bought especially for this night, but a feeling of accomplishment could not be coaxed even with the bubbles that burst as they trickled down my throat.

"You're home early. How was it?"

Jada stood, one hand on the railing, the other clutching her dress as if she depended on it, not it on her, from crumpling to the foyer floor. "Help me up, will you, Mom? I've got to lie down." I felt heat as I neared, her forehead pressing hot like an iron on my shoulder. "Mark has to go to work tomorrow morning...and I'm so tired...we decided to come right home," she said at each rise of the steps. "He's calling me tomorrow...then we're going...to do something."

"And dinner?"

"It was good, but...I couldn't eat it all.... Mark and I split a dessert. He's so dreamy.... He's such a good slow dancer, too." In her room we continued to talk in whispers. "Mom, I have to go to the bathroom, but I can't walk another step. Both my legs are killing me." I brought the pan to her, and laying her down, I took her temperature.

"104," I announced, though I could see the red had crept beyond. "I'm giving you some Tylenol; I don't care what Dr. Lourde says." I pressed cool cloths to Jada's skin and set Hambone, looking dapper in a black bow tie he wore for the occasion, to rest on Jada's arm. Together they drifted into sleep while I sang. Whatever visions danced in Jada's dreams, they were locked inside her, a private performance for an elite audience of one. I prayed for my own dream state and unfolded the blue blob. Worry, my bed partner, preyed on me instead, and I listened with every nerve ending I possessed for breath, counting, one thousand one, one thousand two, waiting for her signal to breathe.

Had it not been for prom, it seemed that the only places Jada knew were her room at home and one in the hospital. And the car that transported her. Mid-morning, she lay in a hospital bed. Mid-afternoon, Jada held her breath, as Dr. Lourde showed off to the surgeon the two bulges he had found. Two probing eyes followed the path that Dr. Lourde's fingers traced under the scrutiny of an intense ultra-violet light. "Here, you can feel a lump right here in her right leg. And there's another one in her left." Dr. Lourde gave up his place to the surgeon, who, his eyes skyward, continued to read Jada's leg with his fingers. The next morning the surgeon operated.

Old age must feel something like this, being confined to floors, and rooms within; the physical confinement was not as restrictive as the constraints of imagination. If my life were to pass before my eyes at those moments of waiting, it would have been as indistinct as a smear on the gray wall I leaned against.

Late in the day, Dr. Lourde came into Jada's room with the animated face of a man with a story to tell. The surgeon, he said, removed two cysts of green gluey poisons from each of her thighs. No wonder she couldn't walk, he exclaimed. Then with a grimace he said, "You wouldn't believe what some people do! There's a guy whose job it is to take pictures of stuff in the operating room. He's a medical photographer, and before they send the stuff down to the pathologist, this guy has to get up close and take shots of what they remove."

"Where are they? I want to see them" Jada's face brightened, even in the blank dark of a sunless afternoon.

"You don't want to see them! They're grody! One looked like a long green bratwurst. Yuck!" he expelled in gleeful distaste. In a more professional tone he continued, "The body is very protective. There was an infection and your body enclosed it in a sac, like a cocoon. All the antibiotics you've been taking couldn't get through the sac to fight the infection, and it kept growing and growing."

"See, I told you something was wrong," she murmured, sorrowfully. "You guys never believe me."

"I'm changing my mind about that, Jada." Dr. Lourde bowed his head toward her, and I felt a kind of victory had been won. No longer a boss, Dr. Lourde began talking in earnest, as a coach. "Now we can get back to treating your leukemia. You have six more weeks of intensive antibiotic treatment, and we're resuming high doses of chemotherapy. You've been through a pretty rough patch, but you're going to need to dig deeper to get through this intense phase. I can try to help you out if I know of anything you're counting on doing for the next six weeks."

Jada's eyes roved the room, muddied for lack of color. "I've got tickets to the Madonna concert next weekend. And some of my friends are graduating. I'd like to get to their parties." There was Jada's confirmation, too, but if it wasn't important to her, I didn't mention it.

"Well," he considered, "I can get you to the Madonna concert. You may have to get a pass from the hospital, but I can arrange that. I'd like to keep you here for a bit, just because you'll have to be monitored while we see how you adjust to the meds, which will be running pretty much around the clock. Dr. Craig is readjusting his part of the treatment plan to fit in with the chemo—some things just don't mix well with each other. I'll bring him with me tomorrow and I'll tell him about the concert. I'm sorry it took so long, but now we can get on with things." He patted her on the shoulder and smiled benevolently.

"Maybe it's just a mother thing to fret over food," I interrupted his leaving, "but I'm concerned about her not eating." Dr. Lourde lifted his chin.

"Before, she was being weighed every day, and then, with all this," my arm flipped down, palm open to Jada's legs like a pan handler's upturned cap, "I let it go."

Dr. Lourde looked back at Jada, and that guilty feeling for bringing up something that didn't connect with the drama of leukemia crept between my shoulder blades like a wood tick in the middle of a deep sleep. Perhaps it was better to brush off those distractions so that he could remain focused. I, unable to find the menace, however, felt it crawling on me everywhere. He nodded. "I'll write that note in her book."

"I'd like to see my book. Look at all you've done to me. I bet I take up the most space on your shelf."

"Not quite," Dr. Lourde answered and left the room.

Dr. Craig and Dr. Lourde made an odd couple, jocular, quipping together. Jada fantasized about Dr. Craig. Like a paper doll to her, he became more animated as she named his children, planned his dinner party. His wife, she mused, did volunteer work and their two children, one girl with dark ringlets tied up in blue ribbons and a younger brother wearing spiffy saddle shoes, went to private school. Jada and I judged, by Dr. Craig's navy blue double-breasted sports coat and cocky way of standing tall for a short man, that he drove an expensive sports car, lived on a grassy knoll in exclusive suburbia, and played tennis at the country club. Even though Dr. Lourde owned a yacht, Dr. Craig seemed more fitted to the imagined lifestyle of the rich and social upper class. And, either he knew more about Madonna than Dr. Lourde, or he cared about appearing to know about her, with a suspicious twinkle of his obsidian hard blue eyes and a curl of his black eyebrow, he agreed to adjust Jada's scheduled medications to allow her to go to the concert. I had the feeling that when the two of them left, they parted worlds, Dr. Craig to a posh office where he expected clients to meet his schedule, Dr. Lourde to another room or downstairs to a windowless clinic, to track down clues for a patient, always on call.

Instead of being jealous about the privileges of money, Jada admired life lived in the upper echelon, and had aspirations to breathe its rarified air herself. Perhaps because she felt camaraderie with Dr. Craig, she never condemned him for the thrush carpet that grew in her mouth and down her throat, caused by the heavy and prolonged use of antibiotics.

Outside the sun beat its palms at the windows, trying with all its might to get in, and I felt spring's restless energy peaking. The leaves had pushed open their buds, engulfing the gray-brown branches that brought them life. Lilacs and honeysuckle clutched deep pink and purple fists, punching the air with their sweet scent.

The blue box, the familiar sidekick that regulated Jada's IV flow, detonated its alarm, jolting Jada. She pushed the nurse call button, saying, "I'm tired of being here. I'm tired of calling nurses to tell them to do things they should be doing. I'm tired of not being able to sleep. Then when I do sleep, they bother me with tubing, or these broken-down machines go off. I thought they were supposed to make it easier for me."

"The irony," I hissed through clenched teeth, "is that the alarm is designed to summon a nurse immediately. Do you know how long one of these was ringing last night? If I could hear it all the way down here, don't you think a nurse could have got to it? Please let me turn it off, Jada." Incessantly it beeped like a barking dog and I paced, waiting, waiting, for the nurse to quiet it, find out what was wrong and reset it to its tick-tick-gruummp-tick. I rubbed my hand over my forehead, my fingers stroking back and forth, back and forth, as if pacing there, too.

"No, they'll forget about me."

A woman clutching a notebook tightly to her white-frocked chest peeked in the door. She looked from me to Jada to the flashing blue machine and teetered on staying. "Do you want me to get a nurse?" she asked, one step forward, one step back.

"If you can," I said. Turning, she nearly collided with a nurse coming into Jada's room.

"What can I do for you, Jada?" Brenda asked over the din.

"What can you do? You can turn this machine off!"

Calmly, Brenda leaned over Jada to cancel the call button, and turned toward the miscreant hanging onto the pole as if shinnying halfway to the top and shrieking for attention all the way. "Now what's wrong here?" she asked the machine, in the same manner as she'd asked Jada how she could help, and bent her body to read the numbers. As soon as she thought she had made the right corrections and turned her back on it, the machine sounded again, taunting her and sending her back into pursuit. The two, human and machine, tried to outshine each other. She made her adjustments, started the machine again and this time did not straighten herself out, but remained in a stance ready to pounce on the red "stop" button. Satisfied that the steady drip pattern would hold, she asked, "Anything else I can get you while I'm here?" Brenda always tried to accommodate.

In Brenda's wake, the other woman opened her notebook and, balancing it with one arm, began lecturing Jada on the importance of eating. My eyes wandered to the identification bar pinned to the smock that rendered formless the body within it, and I couldn't remember if she'd told us her name, just that in the chaos of the noise that ushered her in, I'd heard the word nutrition. Now that quiet reigned, I assumed that she, like the gray slabs of beef, was dispensed from the kitchen. The notebook wobbled precariously on her arm, like the words from her lips, stirring a solution to Jada's steady weight loss. Jada shrugged, tolerating her like a second-rate television show, too disinterested to get up and change the channel. "I'm not hungry, and it hurts to swallow," Jada stated, opening her mouth of thrush as proof.

"But you can get into real trouble if you get into the habit of not eating. You start losing healthy tissue, and that can put a strain on everything else," she persisted, her blond hair beginning to fall toward her eye. I wondered how she would handle that with the notebook teetering between her two hands, and started to feel sorry for her. But then she went on, and I decided she was no different from the priests from church who wanted to come and pray with Jada, assuming that what they brought with them was what she wanted. "If you don't like what's on the menu, you can make a special request from the kitchen. Bland, soft and starchy food might be the most appealing."

The suggestion amused me: Jada's favorite foods were bread, potatoes, corn, cereal, and macaroni. She'd ordered them to no avail. "If you're so worried about it, why not just give me another bag?" Jada gestured toward the IV sacs draped over metal bars looming like telephone poles by her bed. "Don't you give people food that way?"

"That's not an efficient way to feed people. Your body can't get everything it needs through intravenous feeding." She fingered the edges of the pages in her book, strumming them like strings on a guitar, and they curled upwards.

Jada turned her head away. "I'm not eating if I'm not hungry."

Loose hairs caught on the woman's eyelashes and bounced as she closed her book. She brushed the strands back and warned that she would be back in a few days to check on Jada's condition.

The two doctors, who now made their daily visits in tandem, promised to devise a plan to allow medications and antibiotics on an outpatient basis and left us, the steady growl of one of two boxes, one stacked upon another, boasting its victory over the silent one beneath it. Eventually the nurses had tired of its cries for attention and ordered another, leaving the vanquished one uselessly hanging on, not unlike the three television sets, a pyramid of screens each smaller as they sat atop the other, in my parents' home. My mother was angry at my father, setting the third TV on top of the other two nonworking sets, plugging it in, and watching it. You had to sit up close to the screen to make out the figures, which was hard to do because it was higher than our heads, but we got used to the novelty of having three TVs. I guessed that happened in a hospital, too, and it seemed ironic, the cord associated with life disconnected and trailing on the floor.

Jada was to continue both antibiotic treatment and chemotherapy in the clinic by coming in three times a week and spending the day there. At home, I would continue maintenance ministrations. The bargain made, I brought Jada home.

But what a price. Stretching now through June, Jada had been ironed to a bed somewhere, in a hospital, in the clinic, at home. She changed sites, but she hardly changed positions, almost always hooked up to some drug, some blood product, some antibiotic. In that spring turned to summer, we each made our separate resolves. I vowed never to chide anyone, myself especially, for languishing in bed, lapping up sleep. Jada swore that once she could cast off the tethers that bound her, she would never squander any more of her minutes lying captive in a bed.

We were at her bed when outside her window, I heard the passing of a car, a sound that seemed isolated from all other goings on that produced tiny tremors in the airwaves, a sound that came as a long-forgotten memory of a life once led. The car is going home, I thought, yet inside the sound I visualized no people, no magnetism of cells to make bodies with hair or eyes or teeth that clacked together in conversation, just a coming closer of ticky tacky rolling over rattles inside my ear while I stood over Jada, trying to draw blood from the catheter protruding from her chest.

"I can't get it to draw, Jada," I said, having gone to kneeling, as if genuflecting would bring ceremonious power to draw the blood into the syringe.

"Did you heperanize it?" Jada, ever watchful, once had to remind a forgetful nurse, so, too, would she have reminded me.

"But I didn't need to," I said. "I never closed it." Jada considered. Mentally I retraced my steps, and Jada's face appeared as if those steps had trodden on her, hollows around her eyes filling up with alarm.

"You can't leave it like that. Call Barb and Heidi; what if it's not working at all?"

I heperanized, dialed, and immediately the call was returned. Barb's voice sounded wrapped up in a tea cozy, all warm and soft and layered. "We'll come over," she offered. "We're out anyway, having pizza, and our order's in already. We'll be there as soon as we're done."

"I feel terrible making you leave your party." I imagined a booth, two people on each side of the table, maybe three—Heidi and Barb were the type to mingle in groups—in the center a pitcher of honey-colored beer dripping water down the side and pooling around the base; the person to lift it would have to tug a little until whoottsch, it broke suction, laughter bouncing from one voice to another.

"No, no, don't give it a second thought; that's what the pager is for." I considered the time; 8:30, a late hour to be out on a weeknight. I calculated eating and travel time, then opened Jada's curtain, looking for headlights to slow. Arnold and Dom were downstairs watching television when a car stopped in front of the house.

"So, Jada," Barb said, her voice a soft nougat center of a chocolate covered bon bon, "You're holding back on us, hunh?" Heidi followed Barb and smiled so that the tips of her eye teeth, longer than the others, showed just over her bottom lip. She accompanied Barb, knew not to compete for attention nor to let her eye be distracted by her surroundings, the yellow carpet under her polished brown leather shoes, the pastel pin-dot flowers that spattered Jada's walls, even while she took them in.

"It's all this junk you're putting into me; pretty soon I won't have anything left of me to take out."

"You just like to make it difficult, don't you?" Heidi wore a brown leather jacket, not the same as Barb's, but brown. Barb knelt next to Jada and her eyes watered as she concentrated on the tubing and the clamp. The expression "liquid eyes" took on meaning. Heidi looked over Barb's shoulder as she prepped and pulled and siphoned. "Humph! I don't know." Heidi was overhead, examining the translucent tubing, peering at Barb's rounded fingernails, uniformly shaped and buffed smooth. "What do you think?"

For the first time I was seeing them work together; they shared an apartment, they worked in the clinic, but they were separate, and though Heidi was Jada's nurse, Barb led the way in and was the first to tackle the problem. Heidi and Barb bobbed and weaved, exchanging guesses and perplexed responses. "Just trying to be stingy, aren't you, Jada?" Barb had a natural bedside manner, seriously attentive but able also to communicate affably with her patient. Jada looked like a magician's prop, lying still yet ready to jump out of the box whole and smiling after being sawn in half.

"I can't find it," Barb told Heidi, Jada, and me, and by the time she did, we were all one step away from giddy, sounding as if we'd been turned around too many times and set loose blindfolded with a tail in our hands to locate the donkey's ass instead of Jada's tubing and the reason it would not allow us to draw her blood. Everything went in just fine, they assured Jada, so she was not in danger, but she would have to come into the clinic, probably the hospital, to get the kinks out.

The kinks turned out to be the catheter, like the broken blue box left on the pole in the hospital, and Dr. Lourde decided it had to be yanked out.

While waiting for Dr. Lourde in a room where Jada had her bone marrow aspirations, a woman with short black hair nipped at her round chipmunk cheeks came into the room. "Hi, Jada," she said as she approached. We wouldn't have immediately recognized Peg because she looked remarkably different from when we'd met her four years ago. "What are you here for; not a bone marrow aspiration?" Peg's warm eyes looked softer in a face and body that were considerably thinner than when she assisted Dr. Wagner.

Jada pointed to the lifeless tube underneath her hospital gown. "Another thing that doesn't work; they're taking out my catheter. Now I'm back to needle pokes."

"Yuck, hunh? I just came in here to look for some supplies." Peg lingered at an open cupboard door, and I asked her if she had ever got to try the egg rolls at the Princess Garden. She paused, remembering. "No. I had to watch what I ate for so long, and then I forgot."

"You look good," I complimented her. "You've lost weight."

"Oh, this is my normal size." She chuckled, delighted, her watery blue eyes amazingly wide for the amount of space in her face for them. "You saw me when I was having the worst of my troubles. I was bloated with fluids my kidney couldn't get rid of. The only thing that would save me was a transplant. I was waiting for a donor."

Jada raised her head, "What was it like?"

"It was awful! I don't remember the details. It was all a blur. The worst was that I couldn't have any pain medication, nothing— not even aspirin—because of the anti-rejection medication. I was just there and I couldn't tell one day from another; it was just part of one long painful time. I couldn't have visitors, my children, no flowers, no cards, no TV, nothing was allowed in my room because of infection, nothing. It was awful."

"Oh, my God! You mean even after surgery?" I shuddered.

"Nothing." She was smiling, and in her smile was triumph and resignation. "But, without the transplant, I was going to die."

"I'm sorry for what you had to go through, but I'm happy for your success. You look great!"

Peg smiled and thanked me, returning to the mission that brought her to the room. "Take care" she said.

By July 2, Jada's seventeenth birthday, the thrush that had swelled the lining of her mouth and throat was manageable, and her appetite made weak cries for small portions of fruit, a slice of turkey. I made her favorite, Boston cream pie with double filling and dark chocolate frosting that sank the center, and she ate a bite. On her left arm, she wore a brace designed to keep her fingers from tightening into a half-formed fist. At first once, then twice a week before her visits to the clinic, Jada went to the large white building across from Ramsey Hospital to see Mary, Dr. Randolph's peppy assistant, who fashioned a custom-made brace built to stretch the fibers of Jada's arm.

The process began with precise measurements: how far was it between this finger and that one? How tightly could Jada squeeze an object in her fist? Mary cut and boiled strips and bits and blobs of mosking that stiffened and held their shape when they cooled. There were appendages for each of Jada's fingers, attached separately, rubber bands for tension, and Velcro strips that anchored the brace in crucial areas. As the brace was in constant need of adjustment and modification, we watched Mary draw patterns and trace them and then painstakingly shape, fit, reshape, and glue, adding a new extension, patching a strip on the outside rather than on the inside, adding cotton to alleviate blisters. Mary ate Jada's time like it was dessert, taking multiple strength measurements and laboriously spreading the calipers to see if the extension of Jada's fingers had lengthened. The entirety of Mary's work produced one slight improvement, but no more, and Mary quipped, "It'll just take more time." She attached a new strip to the ever-growing brace until, like an ornately decorated cake, there was no more space to add another glop. So she started on a new brace. By late summer, Jada suggested her own design strategies, extending one strip farther, curling another sooner. Mary promised yet a fourth design.

Heavy and clumsy and unwieldy, the new plaster contraption anchored Jada's arm while the other was immobilized by a needle in it, bound by tape, and yoked to the IV pole, "strapped" down for chemo at the clinic. "How long do you think I have to go back to get this arm working?" she asked.

"The question is why," I answered. "I hate to always go back to Hemingway, but he wrote of what you're faced with. The man waiting for his killer, the fisherman dragging home the skeleton of his catch, the officer who'd lost everything: they're defeated, but they don't run. School is going to start soon, and neither one of us will have the time to spend on Mary's fancy braces. I guess you have to decide why you are going. What is it you expect to gain; or, put another way, what is it you don't want to lose?"

"She's a quack, too," Jada said, her eyes preparing a squint. "Dr. Randolph doesn't even see me any more; that tells you how much *he* thinks it's working." Jada's voice had matured, not overnight, but it felt like it had been that sudden, and now the clarity of wisdom in it was a resonating chime of an antique bell. "You know what makes me so mad, though? No one ever asks me what I do. Do you know how hard it is to play the piano with this hand?" She lifted her arm; it looked like a robot's claw. "I love to play the piano. Dr. Malley thought I was a wimp to stop skating, but I wanted the chance to do it well. I didn't have the chance with that leg. I wasn't so good even with two good legs. Now I won't have the chance to be good at piano, either. And I *was* good at that."

"I think I know what you mean. The fun has been taken out."

"Yeah, like orchestra. It isn't just playing the viola, it's being with all my friends. That was my favorite time because everyone in orchestra is so much fun. Kids think it's fun to be out of school. But it's not; that's where all your friends are."

"And you do like to be with people."

Jada brooded under bleached cotton blankets. Behind the closed door, the busy sounds of the clinic were not heard: we would be the last out. "You know, Mom, what you said about supporting me? If I make it through all this, and it comes back again, don't make me do it again. It would be so much easier not to do it."

"It will not be easier for all of us." I stood up and looked down into Jada's eyes. The scar on her eyebrow was shiny. Without hair to cover it, what was left of her eyebrow looked like it had been shaved off just past the arch. "If the disease does come back, you'll be much older and prepared to make that decision. I will not like the outcome, but I will support your decision. It hurts me to watch the life taken out of you. If you'll go through the rest of this, I will support anything you choose."

"Mooie, I need you to kiss me." I did, just above her eyebrow with the scar.

Jada went to the hand clinic less frequently in the fall; not wearing the brace, her hand coiled, like a cat curling up for a nap. All she wanted, she said, was to keep her arm from getting any worse.

Then she stopped. It was her senior year in high school. Her last year in high school. Jada was not going to waste it at Dr. Randolph's clinic killing time. She got a job at Charlene's Cards and Gifts, close to home, just across Lyton and down to the corner in the small shopping center near Thomas's house. The job was more play than work, arranging displays and selling Hallmark cards and Precious Moments figurines and sterling silver charms. She telephoned me to come see them. Sometimes I delivered a lunch to her, and she walked me around the store as if it were her newly decorated room. When she was sick, I thought too sick, Jada went to Charlene's and worked her shift. Jada's refusal to "baby out" inspired my admiration.

Sep. 14, 1985

Mom brought home a book about different colleges so I could compare them. My head is spinning like a tilt-a-whirl! I want to go to Mary Hillyard, but Mom says I should look at others out East and some here. She calls it "insurance." Dr. Silverman doesn't think I should go away because I'd leave my support system. I'd have to leave my mooie and my doctors and nurses. He has a point, but if I stay I'd be just like Kimby. Her class ranking is higher than mine and her dad is paying for everything, so she could be accepted anywhere. But no, she's going to a 2-ranked school that's practically out her back door. Mom could walk to it! We're going to some teas here to see if we like the colleges I'm choosing. Then we'll go out East to visit. Mr. H. says I'll be an outsider if I go to school out East, but I'm not excited about the schools here. Mom says I should try for the schools I want but thinks I should visit Stanton because it's ranked a 4 like Mary Hillyard and has a lot of international students and Marist because it's all female in case I can't go to

Mary Hillyard. I stay awake wondering if I will be able to finish because of this dumb disease. It will cost a lot of money, and I feel guilty wasting it.

But I have to go away from here. Dad poked into my bedroom and said he needed more deodorant. "Why are you telling me," I asked. Then he laughed his fake laugh and said, "I did it again. I get you two mixed up." Why can't he get it himself? No, he tells me because he still expects Mom to get it and he and mom don't talk to each other. I wish she would could go away with me. Well, I don't know what is possible for me. I haven't taken the SATs yet. Life would be so easy if I didn't have a disease that could stab you in the back any minute just like that! And if I didn't have to worry about money, like Kimby. And a boyfriend. I want to have a boyfriend. No! I need one! Maybe I'll have a boyfriend, someone like Mark, at college. That would be soooo nice!

Early in the morning, ribbons of pink clouds streaking the eastern sky, Sibley streets were sleepy enough to tempt speed, and Thomas did not resist. He loved to drive for all the male reasons. With the gear stick in his hand, Thomas let his heart have its way; instantly I understood why video game rods were called joysticks. As we rode to school, I told him we'd attended teas for prospective students.

"And?" he asked.

"I like Wharton's nonchalance; a woman tried to impress us with getting the New York Times every day, but even that snootiness was kind of transparent, and there was something earthy to it, like, we grow hybrid roses, but we still play in the dirt." Thomas made a startled sound, and I thought more carefully. "Jada liked Mary Hillyard; they didn't seem to care where you were from, not like Rhoades. We went up to the party room of some posh place on LaSalle for that tea and had the feeling that if you didn't wear the right clothing, you wouldn't make it there. But I think Mary Hillyard will be the one. It's the oldest all-female college in America, rated four stars and graduating more pre-med science majors than any other female college."

"How about the West coast?" he asked. "If I could choose a college again, I'd choose Pepperdine."

"Why Pepperdine?"

"Oh, you know, California. The campus is right on the beach." We whizzed through a yellow light, his gloved hand reflecting metallic silver, the tail of a comet streaking the black streets.

"What difference does that make?"

"It'd be fun. Say, speaking of fun," Thomas made a slight jerk of his head, like shifting from first to second gear. "Sheila and I had fun Saturday night at the Manomen Dinner Theater, thanks to a gift certificate I just happened to find with my name on it." Thomas accepted gratitude with the graciousness of a millionaire, seeming able to accumulate more because he was used to the feel of it. "You're going out to look at colleges pretty soon, aren't you?"

"Yes, over teacher convention week-end. Jada has appointments at Mary Hillyard and at Wharton, and she has an overnight at Rhoades scheduled for Friday night.

"That gives you some free time. What are you going to do?"

"Eat dinner, go back to my room."

Thomas tilted his head and said, "You don't have to go there alone, you know. An attractive woman like you. I'm sure you could find someone to share your bed." I felt Little Red Riding Hood's uneasiness when the wolf asked to peek inside her basket. "It's a shame to waste a night out of town. Whenever Sheila and I go away is when we have the most exciting sex."

"It's been so long since I've had sex, I've talked myself out of its appeal. What is it anyway? Just a wet sticky mess."

"Oh, no," Thomas said, bringing his lips together in a kind of ecstatic kiss. "Two people sharing their most intimate private selves. If you're with the right person, you get lost in each other. Mmh!"

"That's a bunch of hooey, too."

"Don't give up hope just from one bad experience." The left turn into the parking lot forced me toward the door. Thomas sprang out of the car, and I thought, I've never seen him walk without a spring. His golden hair thinned on top of his head, but it settled into place naturally. So it seemed like all of Thomas, his only desire was to go where he was, and no regrets for elsewhere could be imagined. Climbing the steps to my classroom, I wondered about Thomas and Sheila, according to Thomas, the perfect couple. Or was it according to me? What did I know about their private selves untouched by a brush, flawlessly right for each.

Look at Arnold and me, I thought. Together we...well, no one saw us together anymore. People could think the strain of leukemia separated us. I kept no secrets. What did he say about me? I couldn't imagine him baring his soul; it would be like revealing where he hid his money. I unlocked the door to my room and shook my head as if to a friend by my side.

Room 321 in Parkview Senior High School was double-sized, a demonstration table on one end, laboratory tables in the other half, classroom desks in between. A former chemistry lab with two windows, side by side in the center, it had the best view in the building. I stood looking over the golf course across the street. Through the yellow filter of a fully risen sun were trees, millions of them on the other side of the river, just brush strokes, so far away you could never make out one, yet you knew it was there, maybe as a spot of yellow or a little poke against the horizon in the long, broad canvas of morning.

Voices as thick as trees in a woods spread toward me as students pushed open the two metal fire doors at the top of the stairs. Today had come. You can't teach with your mind on anyone other than whom you're teaching. The hours flew by and no one could tell I had a care in the world, bunched up into myself, sanity inside insanity inside sanity like a wooden doll enclosing ever-smaller and different versions of itself.

Jada and I arrived in Hartford, drove past the city of Loudon, Massachusetts, and around our first rotary. In Minnesota, straight highways divide large expanses of flat plain, bludgeoned by nature and stripped by humans who tried to make it cede to their greedy hands. In summer, green scrub rises from a layering of brown. In winter, the brown rises, too. People who have not given up on the land toil away on the occasional scruffy farm down dusty gravel roads. Carcasses of barns and houses stand on four bowed legs, their ceilings caved in like broken backs. Jagged glass juts from a window frame, an incisor ready for its prey, and doors gape open in a silent wail of loneliness.

My harsh Minnesota image of countryside dissolved when I encountered the lush, lyrical rural New England, where the Mary Hillyard campus lives in Founders' Valley. In the rich valley of Massachusetts were villages surrounding greens, land living graciously with people, places I'd thought were fiction. Parting through, swinging in and out of coves, of orchards, and velvety lawns rising to tidy gardens and satiny white houses with dates in wooden letters posted on them stretching back over 200 years, the land to either side of us rose and fell in a wave like the road we traveled. There really was a carpet of burgundy and chartreuse and amber leaves underfoot. Yet there remained a splendid canopy overhead and far into the horizon, soaring beyond us. Caught in spotlights of sunshine were old brick three-story houses; inside, envisioned wooden floors, radiator heaters, long fabric-draped paned windows, pianos, fireplaces, formal dining rooms with silver service—all beckoned to Jada: "you could be home here."

"Five hundred feet," the sign read. The narrow highway curved, so I had to slow down. A rutted dirt road jutted to the right, and next to it the sign beckoned passersby to visit an amusement park just a few miles inward. "It can't hurt to look," I said, backing up and turning into a road narrowed by tall trees and thick bushes at its edges. I registered the mileage on the odometer. Several yards into the road and behind the amusement park sign was a yellow slice of board with black splotchy lettering. Like the occasional placard put out by an irate citizen over a proposed tax levy, the text was too copious and too small to be read by motorists except for this: "THERE IS A CURE FOR LEUKEMIA. DON'T BE FOOLED BY THE GOVERNMENT." Jada scoffed, but I crept further inward, the road losing its purchase to the encroaching limbs and tangled foliage with tentacles that could at any time reach out and wrap themselves around us. Guiding the car over ridges strewn with rocks and pocked with holes, I juggled up and down. Jada made a plea to turn around, and I promised, "Only three miles—that's as far as we'll go." The road worsened, and my gullibility raised itself like the ridges that rocked us this way and that in our thin-skinned vehicle. Nothing in sight: not a Ferris wheel, not a parking lot, not even another sign to bark our folly.

Jada's forearm braced on the dashboard, and, sitting sideways like a helpless passenger afraid to look over the edge, her eyes wide and begging, said, "Mom, I don't like this."

Stopping at a hollow in the road, I felt a ripple of wariness. The false but convincing sense that escape is possible in movement escaped itself when we stopped. Even locked doors did not protect us from being picked off, captured like Hansel and Gretel into some mad person's lair. No one knew to rescue us.

Sliding the gear lever from one to another, I jockeyed by inches to turn the car around, afraid a tire would slip off the road, sink, maybe, into a pool of quicksand cleverly camouflaged with brambles and heavy grasses. Picking my way back went slower. I feared driving recklessly, getting a flat tire, breaking an axle, or whatever people broke on cars in deserted places. We could be caught in one of those finger traps, so easy to enter, impossible to pull free of. The road dipped and swelled with no physical evidence, no sawed off tree, no slanting fencepost, by which to remember our distance. The odometer read that we should be at the end of our trail as we crested a hill. Then, like the pupil of an eye, a speck of light appeared and dilated as we drove to it. "We made it," I said, braking at the pavement.

"Good. That was really dumb. Do you know what could have happened to us in there?"

Jada looked behind us as the tires spat gravel. "We knew our limits. The thing is not to get caught in the psychological trap of thinking that we had to finish what we started. Some people think it's greed, gambling for more; I think it's desperation, not knowing when to stop."

"Yes," Jada blew out a gust, settling back into her seat. "In church they told us that the only sin is the sin of despair. I don't think it's a sin to know when to stop. Sometimes it can be a sin to keep people alive by chemicals. It's against nature."

"Are you thinking we could have tried something else?"

"No, you know me, all that hocus-pocus about eating certain food. But... cancer is natural. It's a natural way to die. Why does everyone think it's so awful to die?"

"I suppose because we're here. I don't mean that flippantly. But, what do we know? This, and it's pretty wonderful." I made a flourish with my hand to take in the landscape outside our car. Jada's eyes followed like a camera panning the hills making a giant lap in a rocking chair for us.

"But all those chemicals, don't you think they ruin that? If they can kill stuff in me, won't they kill stuff in the environment?" She had put her sunglasses on, and when she turned, a tiny fragment of myself bounced back at me.

"Some of those chemicals are from plants, and they exist in the environment. Yes, everyone has to die, but I don't want you or me to, not yet. We have a lot to do."

"Yeah, like write my book," Jada said. I nodded, pulling the seat belt away from my neck. Some people think the hard part is in the hard parts, Jada in the hospital, looking more like a death kept alive than a life kept from death. If you survive, people call you brave. In good times like these, though, it was hard to let the good be here just as brilliantly as the bad, to get just as lost in them and not to feel sorry for yourself that times are not always good. That's the hard part. Jada twisted her class ring into position on her left hand that curled in her lap and continued, "Death doesn't bother me. It's just not thinking. Everyone thinks it's sadder if a baby dies, but I think it's harder when you get older. Babies don't know what's happening to them. I do. If only I didn't have to think."

Yes, I thought. I was glad for distractions in the world to keep me safe from thought, the same thought my daughter had of her dying, because the fact that she was *my* daughter meant I'd be losing, too. I was glad for the sign that pointed left to Hamilton College and the sign outside Northridge and the massive stone arch with the sign announcing Rhoades College. They reminded me to think about the daughter sitting beside me, setting goals for herself I would have run away from, unsure, unconfident, unable to see myself as anything but less than what I was. She was a miracle, everything I envied but denied myself, standing firmly for her right to live her life, while leukemia, she knew, held the trump card. Jada looked to, through, and beyond the windshield, her eyes like blue lasers beamed into the future, bringing with her the women of her past, and boring through the possibilities with her sisters.

Jada woke up with a fever and feeling the first waves of weakness and nausea on the morning, her last chance, to take the SATs; she had started the second intensive phase of treatment.

The air had the nip of December in it, and an occasional patch of ice could trip people up if they were careless. And they were; they thought they had forever. They were young and cocky, these high school seniors who came by ones and twos from Saturday morning alarm clocks and kitchen tables and borrowed family cars into Archbishop O'Sullivan High School's front door. They were invincible, exposing their heads, leaving their coats unbuttoned so the wind could sneak its way through cotton sweatshirts and fashionable sweaters.

"At least let me walk you to the door," I coaxed as I drove up to the sidewalk.

"No," Jada insisted. "How do you think that looks?"

"Oh, who's here, anyway?" She opened the door and swung her knees onto the pavement. It was fine that she leaned on me in the hospital, the clinic, at home, but not where she was supposed to be "like them," her peers. She stepped cautiously along the plowed sidewalk and up to the heavy metal door. When she disappeared behind it, I parked the car, keeping the door to the school in sight.

While I waited for Jada, the sun burned away the gray that dawn left behind. Jada had to take three extra achievement tests for admission to her chosen schools, and I moved the car closer, as one by one, young men and women emerged from the building. The parking lot was almost empty when she appeared, taking a staggering step. I drove to the sidewalk and stood outside the car, one hand holding open the door, the other to her. She crumpled, limp in the seat, her head dropping to her chest. I didn't know if she was going to sleep or going to vomit, but she didn't appear to have the strength to make an audible response, so I let the crunching snow under the tires and the hissing of the fan blowing heat on her stiff white fingers fill the void.

Jada had scheduled the day off work; I drove straight home, put her into bed, and sat on the soft yellow carpet, a ball of yellow yarn rolling near my thigh. Snickey-snack-snick, the knitting needles snickered as they wove loops into a hat for Hambone until, I, too, felt weary and stopped, enfolding my idle hands in my lap and resting my head against the mattress. The curtains were drawn to dim the afternoon light, weak already by the sun's creeping to close a winter's day but still light enough to work by. Immobile, I stared at the wall, pink and blue and yellow flowers dancing, moving a little to the right and left, up and down, like pinwheels spinning in a breeze, growing larger and smaller, around and around.

I denied the part of my brain that told me they weren't really moving, for I could see them whirl and roll around like fuzzy cottonwood balls being bounced from tree to bush to my nose late in spring. Frightening and mysterious, both, the part that denied reality seduced me, and I wanted to stay under its power, so delicious was my loss of will. I shut my eyes to the dancing flowers, but the dots were still there; they had squirmed underneath my eyelids and twirled about.

When I opened my eyes they disappeared, leaving a blank sheet of white wallpaper. Then, reprised, they appeared, rows and columns of pink and yellow and blue flowers making a curtain call on Jada's wall. If only it were that easy, just close your eyes and open them again and you would know what was real from what tricked you. I had been so emphatic. Yes, treatment was worth it, life was worth it, suffering was worth it.

What was it that I valued so highly that it could be promised as a reward for my daughter's being reduced to near helplessness, she who craved excellence? I wasn't as horrified at the grotesqueness of every convulsion or dangerously low counts, or even to her outbursts at doctors and nurses and me as I was at the corrosion of her spirit. I watched us come into the clinic, Hambone tucked under Jada's arm, me following the two of them like an equipment trailer, hitched behind. I didn't notice new faces anymore, didn't even wonder if they were there, peering curiously from behind half-closed doors, as we had, once, afraid to think that we might be they, an image made possible by our presence. There were no pamphlets or how-to books that come close to telling what to expect or how to cope. We were the story no one wanted to read.

We changed definition as well, and while I wanted the change, I hated what we had become. I hated my life with Arnold. Even more, I hated me for letting myself get caught. I hated how my hatred controlled my thought. I hated that I did the work to produce the source of my hatred.

Just so he could stay. He'd put up with anything to stay. We were each of us waiting to see how much we could put up with and how long we could last. How could he continue to stay where he was so blatantly not wanted? How could I? But we did. Maybe he thought it would pass. Maybe he thought it was love he was showing, or righteousness.

Eyes closed, eyes open, I wasn't sure anymore. *I hope to God there is something at the end of all this bullshit because I have no heart left for keeping on with keeping on. I don't know what I'd say if Jada were to ask me right this minute if it was all worth it, survival for a mess like this. I pulled a length of yarn and picked up knitting where I'd left off.*

When Jada stirred, I was two-thirds to the top of the hat suspended from the needles.

"Let me see it," she asked, and I held it up to the slice of light cutting into the room where the curtains met.

"How are you feeling?" I asked.

"Not good." I set the needles and their growth on the floor. Lifting myself to the bed, I put the thermometer into her mouth and went for a fresh glass of water. She gulped the Ibuprofen tablets from the palm of her hand. "I'm proud that you went through the tests. I know it was a hard morning for you. What do you think? Were you able to do well?"

She handed me the glass and fell back to her pillow. "Not as well as I could have. My neck felt stiff and puffy, and the longer I had to sit, the more it hurt. Get me my mirror." She peered at her neck and rounded cheeks, like plump feather pillows.

"Does it hurt?" I asked as she pressed lightly into the soft tissue.

She crinkled up her face and handed me the mirror, saying, "Not any more than anywhere else. A couple of times I thought I would have to get out and throw up, but you can't come back into the room once you leave it. I was glad I didn't eat much for breakfast."

"You poor darling. I wish all those people who see you only in the hospital could see you in these situations. Tell me about the tests."

"I figured that math was my strongest area, so I did that one first. So, if I couldn't finish, I could at least have a good score there. I could have answered more questions I think, but I didn't think I could last much longer." Jada sniffled and reached for a tissue.

"What were the other tests?" Her hand responded first, a fish attempting to swim on land, a movement of ambiguity.

"I had to choose two essays to write; you know how bad I am at that. There were three topics, one on something about American involvement in world affairs, another about the value of a higher education, and another about some literature I liked and how it affected me. None of them interested me, but I decided to do an easy one about education, and because I couldn't think of any book I really really liked except *A Summer to Die*, I wrote about that, but that's not the kind of literature they were looking for. Almost everyone was done and I didn't want to stay there any longer. So if they don't like it...."

"I think what matters is what you say, not the title of the book. They're more interested in how you write your ideas."

"Then they probably won't like it because I really couldn't think very clearly. But I said how in the book that's what happened when you get a disease, that it's not all glamorous like everyone else makes it and you still have to go on and do stuff like this test. It was probably dumb, but I wrote about how some books and movies give lies about disease, and then when people read about them or see them, they think that's how it is. You know, like that *Love Boat* show."

"All you can do," I said, "is write what you know about. You have to trust that. Well, you did it. The outcome is what it is."

"I almost didn't do it. I had to climb a whole flight of steps to the second floor. I was nearly late."

"See, if you had let me help you; maybe we could have used an elevator."

"I thought of that, but I was already at the steps, and it was too far to look for one. I would have missed the test. So, I grabbed onto the railing and took one step at a time. It was a good thing there was someone's mother there today. I asked her to help me up the steps."

"Next time I complain about being tired, remind me about this, okay? If you're this sick now, what are you going to do about work? You know it's going to get worse."

Jada closed her eyes. Though her face was rounder, the line of her chin was still firm. "I have to go as much as I can. I told Donna about what's going to happen to me, and she said she'd work my hours whenever she can because she's married and needs the money. But I don't know about the others. They haven't been too happy to switch. I just hope I can get through these next two months without all that stuff that happened to me before."

"Dr. Lourde said it shouldn't be as strong as last spring."

"Yeah, well, Dr. Lourde also said I didn't have anything wrong with my legs. Look at me." She held up her arm, letting her hand dangle from its wrist. "I'll probably be stuck in the hospital and this time they'll send me out with a toe tag."

The image blew up in my mind like a balloon too soon too full, exploding before it was released. The picture of a body, long and large and thick without contour, a white sheet thrown over it like a tent, two gray-white feet sticking out, a tag winging from the big toe made a morbid yet comical vision. Seeing her own dead feet that way, down the length of her own dead body being taken away from life, conscious of her unconsciousness, solidified the detachment.

Humm went the air being blown through the vents at the floor as the furnace kicked in. I felt the mattress give next to me and Jada's hand reach out. "I've got some reading to do. Will you read it to me?"

"Sure." We rearranged ourselves, switching the light on, fluffing the pillow, before I sat back on the floor. "On a ship at sea; a tempestuous noise of thunder and lightning heard."

Dec. 9, 1985

I've been out of school for more than two weeks. My last day was Sadie's, and I almost missed that day, too, AND the dance with Dale! I hate missing school, especially during Christmas. I don't get to give people cute Christmas stickers and candy canes. Well, I couldn't go shopping for anyone anyway because I'm really sick and weak from treatment. I LOVE to shop, especially when everything is decorated and I'm in the holiday mood, and there's so many gifts to buy, but I'm really zonked! We didn't go to Grandma's for Thanksgiving, either because it's been so rough for me.

I went in for L'Asparaginase and guess what! Yup! They took out my second subclavian because it was oozing pussy fluid. I'm not getting another one, which is okay because I didn't like the way the doctor who put in it treated me. He didn't remember what he did but lied about it and said he did. And he called me Pumpkin, like I was a baby. They didn't give me enough medicine to keep me "asleep" through the procedure, so NO MORE! But that's good AND bad! It means Mom won't give me Ara-C injections anymore. She says it's better that we don't have to go in when she can do it at home, but I don't want her to do anything that makes her one of THEM! I had to go in for my last Adriamiacin and Vincristine I.V.s. It was an awful struggle for me! There's still a big bruise where Dr. Lourde gave the IV.

My platelets are very low, which is why I have bruises and red spots and bloody noses, not big ones, but they're runny. I had one last night that scared me because it lasted so long. My other counts aren't too bad for me to try to get to school for a half day or maybe two this week. But I have pains in my knees and leg muscles. I have aches in my arms, too. I feel like I've been lifting concrete! Oh, and I have nasty blisters on my fingers from the brace because it doesn't fit right. I can't wear it anyway so my hand is cramped like a claw. My skin is dry and cracked and sore, especially on my butt and the sides of my legs. The alcohol for my insulin makes my skin even drier. (That bothers me, too! I was supposed to be done with that a week ago.) And my ears still bother me. I think the yeast junk in my mouth is making my ears a pain. My body is SHIT!! I'm bloated like one of those big balloons in the Thanksgiving parade. My face feels like it's about to POP and I look like I'm storing acorns like a chipmunk in my cheeks and chin. My tummy sticks out all big and round and looks like it would go FUSSSSH if you stuck a pin in it. But what's really weird is that I weigh 108 pounds and my arms and legs are skinny as straws! My watch slips off my wrist. I have a few skinny hairs on my BALD HEAD. Mom made a flannel hat for me because it's so drafty on my skin head. If I had just a little fuzzy covering, I wouldn't be so ugly! I'm tapering off the decadron and I'm done with the pills that are like prednisone. Oh! When we went to refill them we found

285

out that I was taking 16 extra milligrams a day. I didn't tell them OR mom that I cheated and threw out some pills instead of taking them.

I've kept up with my homebound but I haven't gone to work for over a week because I was so sick. Maybe if I told Loretta I had the flu she would be more accepting. I got Donna to cover for me, but I have to get back so she'll cover for me again on December 20th. After Christmas, too, when I have another round of treatment. I don't want to lose my job!

I told Kimby that if we're Best Buddies, she has to come over and help me and visit me. I think she heard me and she's been here a couple times since. I haven't seen Mark for a while. I went to a movie with him and then to Bridgman's. I offered to pay the tab or at least the tip, but he said no and paid for it all! Afterward, I invited him in and gave him the wooden cherries I bought for him at the St. James with Cerise. He loved them! We went to an afternoon movie so he could go to evening church so he couldn't stay long. But we talked and had a great time together. He confuses me. He says we're friends, but the way he acts with me is like we're more than just friends. I don't want to push him because I might ruin everything, but I do love him and want to tell him I want him for a boyfriend. He would make such a super one! I't's a BUMMER that I'm so depressed about a relationship with him and other friends. I want more from people and I feel like I'm trying to get more involved, but no matter how hard I try nothing is working out. I blame it all on this damn disease! I had so much fun while I was off chemo and wasn't having other reactions! I don't think I'll ever have a life again. This disease just stabs me in the back whenever it can! It breaks me down and then traps me in a cage that I can't get out of. I have to accept the changes and not give in or up. I'm not good at these.

I took the SAT Achievements. Mom had to drive me because I was not able in this condition. I was super worried and feeling sick, but I didn't say anything to mom. She would have *put up a hassle, and I didn't need that! When I got to the door there were two steps and no railing! I asked another "mom" to help me and she wanted to help me inside, too. I was embarrassed but at least there was a railing so I said no. Troy Archer was there. I felt a bit better because he was recently diagnosed with Hodgkins and he has to keep up too. Thank goodness there were no more stairs and I found the room. First we did the ECT essay. I wrote an intro, three supportive paragraphs, and a conclusion. I needed more time to think of a "bang-the-gong" ending. I tried to answer the Math questions I knew and ran out of time to finish all of them. I started out strong in the French vocab fill-in, but the sentences with blanks for verb forms were hard because we haven't worked on them for very long. Then we had to figure out answers to questions on four or five readings, and I think I did them well. I was zonked! And stiff because I had to sit for over three hours. I bloated like a water balloon.*

I think it will be easier for me to take early decision for Mary Hilliard. It won't be easy to leave my moo because she helps me so much. I don't think things will work out for me but I have to worry about so much now that I can't worry about treatment later on. I've already missed out on so much I wanted or needed to do this year and I'm bummed. I know I could handle things better if I stayed here and be a loser and not challenge myself. I can't see myself returning to a normal life without a miracle. Right!! Nothing in my life has worked out. And I need mom to take care of me and stay with me. What if I fall when I am all alone and I can't get up or my nose gushes and I faint. But she says she can't stay home all the time and I know I have to try to keep up my best, but it takes all my energy to just live. I wish she was home with me today. I need her now! My claw is ugly!

A large room across the hall from the clinic had been carved out of the wall, carpeted, furnished with tables and chairs and toys, and made into a combination family room for patients receiving all-day IV treatments. Jada could sit or lie on a couch, sleep, watch a movie, or do homework while I sat nearby. As she grew weaker, I called Charlene's and asked for a week's time off. The manager's voice was strident and firm, like the lacquered black hair that curled about her ears. "Charlene's needs reliable help. We'll have to hire someone to replace Jada," she replied with some impatience.

"What if I took Jada's place when she couldn't come in; I've clerked before," I argued.

"Oh, no, I just don't think so. Tell Jada not to worry about getting anyone to cover for her. It's slow now and we'll make a new schedule until we can train someone else." I hung up the receiver and replayed the conversation, nagged at what could have been said. Jada had already been replaced. It doesn't matter how many pillows are stuck under it, when you get to no, there's nothing to soften the fall. In telling Jada I heard what was missing. No concerns about Jada, how she might feel about being so sick, how she might feel sick about losing the work she liked. I heard only that Jada was not to worry about Charlene's, as if Charlene was at stake, not Jada. I wanted some pans to scrub and bang around in the sink or cupboard doors to slam, some physical conduit for my anger.

Jada hadn't changed position, not her knees, not her hand, not her head, lilting to the side like a wilted lily about to drop off the stem. I didn't really have to tell her something she already knew, but without confirmation, truth is an unfinished river. Sadness mixed with sickness and drained into Jada's eyes, diluting the blue to a thin watery wash. They shut when I finished. When they opened again, they were marbles, blue streaks in the center of milky crystal. "Oh, Mom, I'm so sick." She breathed through her mouth, the draft of air parching her lips, white-edged patches of crust raised on the flat ivory surface. They moved, hardly touching each other, about to crackle and flake away if they did. "Don't make me go through this again. I just don't think I can take any more."

"No, I don't want you to go through it. But I do want you to live. I love you."

"Well, love is not enough." She turned her face to the wall.

Three times a week she went to the clinic, to the family room, for more chemotherapy. Late in January, Jada sat with her white tam on, perched above her right ear and coquettishly draped over her left. Her sleeve rolled up, she might have been holding a paintbrush in one hand and a palette in the other except that attached to one hand was a needle. A paper cup made a shelter for it, and around and around Jada's hand was wound tape to secure it to a board. Her little finger curled over the edge. Her other arm rested on the chair. Low hemoglobin bleached her skin, and drugs bloated her face, making her cheeks round and plush, like rabbit fur ear muffs. She looked composed, more so than the anchorman who sat across from her. A local television station was doing a series on children surviving cancer, and Jada was his first interview. The cameraman moved to the side and said, "Any time you're ready. We're rolling."

"What is...why are... Let me start over. What are you doing here?" With slicked hair and evenly colored skin, the man who had been painted perfectly for the screen was having trouble steadying his gaze and stammering lips.

"I have to come in here to get some drugs for leukemia. This is Vincristine." Jada nodded toward the line that linked the needle in her hand to the bag hanging from above. Other times I get different drugs."

"What do you think of when you are here?"

"Think of? How sick I'm going to be after. I try not to, but it's hard to ignore. I hate getting sick."

"Do you ever have bouts with depression?"

Jada batted her eyelashes, what remained of them; her puffy eyelids made the few light wisps invisible. "Oh, many. It's hard to deal with, hard to be normal.... You know you have to keep up with the other things, keep trying to participate...school, work, activities. I go to school sick. I'm sick when I'm out of the hospital; people don't realize that; they don't know how to deal with it. You can do it on your own, but it's nicer to have people around who understand."

The newsman hesitated, and I sensed he wanted to follow his own curiosity instead of what the program prescribed. He was well trained and continued on script until he concluded. "I see you have a book over there. Looks like you haven't let any of this stuff interfere with your life."

"Let it? It changes everything. But you have to keep trying. You become more independent, I've become more independent. You have to carry on with everything. You just go for whatever you can and try to do, carry on, with what you planned."

"What would you say is the hardest thing about this for you?"

The silence that followed sucked time out of the room. "Being forgotten. People don't care. They say they care, but it's hard for them to keep up."

The reporter looked upwards in a questioning gesture to the cameraman, who gave him the signal and pressed a button. "Thank you, Jada. You're a senior, is that right? Would it be okay if we came out to your school and took some footage?" The cameraman stepped backwards and turned away, looking through the viewer as if filming the wall.

"Yes, you mean of me? When?"

"We'll let you know. We have to have clearance with the school, but the series will be aired in February, so it'll be in the next few weeks."

"You'll have to find out when my treatment days are, so you know when I'll be there."

"I'm sure we can get all that information from Ms. Kellen. She'll call and let you know when we're coming. Nice to meet you." He followed the cameraman to the door and out.

Jada looked my way and said, "He should have got a little background first."

I raised my eyebrows in agreement. "Why do you suppose he seemed surprised? I'll be eager to see what they do with it; you know they have a certain angle and show what they want. It *is* television."

"Yeah, I know. *Love Boat.*"

"I thought you sounded sincere and honest. You did very well." Heidi entered the room, followed by Ms. Kellen, wearing a badge identifying her as Director of Public Relations at Ramsey. The heel of one of her pumps snagged the carpet as she stopped in front of Jada. "Thank you, Jada. Bob left quite impressed with the interview. I want to double-check some information about your school for filming if you agree to it. You're under no obligation or pressure from us, so think about it, and let me know." The color of Ms. Kellen's suit almost matched the beigy gray walls of the room we were in. There should be a name for that color—greige—that, the moment you see it, sets you into a box. She sounded institutional, too; not unfriendly, just standardized.

Winter can freeze everyone's emotions, making them immovable blocks of ice in their souls. With each snowfall and every bitterly cold morning, people begin to tire of the drudgery of cleaning the car off, of being delayed in traffic, of worrying about making it through the unplowed side streets, ice underneath thick ridges of brown snow, rock-studded and rutted, like leftover Malt-o-Meal. We long for the white heat of the bright yellow sun, so hot that to look at it is to see the edges leaping in flames, singeing a hole in the sea of blue sky about it instead of rising to meet winter's cold so cold it sears like a hot branding iron. All winter long, people want summer. Or the romanticism of it. Desolate winter, what you want to go away from.

Winter had put its name on Jada, and that winter, the last winter of her years in high school, seemed to crystallize her polarity—there was no in-between, no moderation, no temperance. She finished the second phase of heavy treatment. She arrived home from school before I, before Arnold walked across the street for the mail after pulling into the garage. Jada received recruiting material daily, and whereas once she greeted mail, she now cursed the signing of her name to every list at the college fair. "Yes, I want a challenging education in a caring environment. Please send me more information."

Traffic bungled its way on Stuart because of the snowfall. It wasn't heavy, dumping feet, or even inches. But it was a greasy kind of snow on the pavement and had been compressed by heavy vehicles before the plows came to scrape the asphalt clean. Slippery surprise patches not completely eaten away by salt divided motorists into competing foes: those who impatiently lurched along, sure of themselves and their vehicles and wanting us to get out of their way, and those whose timidity slowed them unnecessarily and put them in our way. I was glad to be home and heavily climbed the steps. "Hey, Mom," Dom shouted up from downstairs.

"Hi, Dom! Got a friend here?" He said somebody's name, but I was too far up to hear clearly and too weary to step down to find out.

"Is that you, Mooie?" We both rounded corners, each at the opposite ends of the hallway. My shoes I had kicked off inside the front door; I wore my coat buttoned to my chin, my school bag slung from my arm.

"Finally," I said, about to complain about other drivers. In Jada's hand was an envelope neatly sliced open at the top and a sheet of paper winging from it. Both she waved through the air while she came at me down the hall and leaped into me.

"I've been accepted! I got my letter. I'm going to Mary Hillyard!"

"Jada, that's wonderful. See, I knew you wouldn't have any trouble."

"I wasn't sure. Not after those tests!" Jada was standing on her own again. "But now I'm scared." I removed my coat and hung it in the closet. Fallen mittens and old boots heaped themselves atop the vacuum cleaner. "Now I have to go. What if I can't do it?" she followed me into the kitchen, where two long white envelopes lay on the table; I flung them to the counter underneath the telephone where they landed on other envelopes.

"Jada, look at what you've done already! College will be hard, but if I could do it, you can do it. You're so much smarter, you won't have to work, and you know how to study."

"But I don't know if I can go through treatment without you."

I tackled the stack of old mail, got bored, and decided I would whittle it down by one piece a day. "Don't worry about that; you'll be home in November and December. It might be the best thing for you not to have me there. And look, you'll get away from all this stuff at home. Ugh!" I shuddered.

"Are you sure you can't come with me?" Her eyes glistened like a fine misting in the sunshine, every minuscule droplet reflecting sparkles of light. She looked so childlike inside her growing-up body I wanted to pick her up and swing her in the air, listen to her giggles of delight as she made an arc toward the sky and came safely back to my breast and my kiss. We grabbed onto each other, our chins almost level, and I said, "You don't know how much I'd like to. But it's your time. I'll have to miss you."

"Oh, Mooie. I can't wait to tell Madame. She lived in Massachusetts for a while and said she'd come out there to visit me. Kimby said she'd come, too."

"All that ways. I'm surprised. Have you told your dad?"

"What does he care? He's probably too busy sleeping. What time is it? I can't call Kimby until after five."

Jada had made her calls and I the dinner; at the end of the table sat Dom in what used to be my place, across from Arnold. As my children grew, I moved around the table like the hand of a clock ticking time, ending up sandwiched between the wall and the table, the farthest from the stove, the refrigerator.

"Don't you have something to tell your dad?" I said to Jada. Arnold had come to the table and lifted a pork chop from the pan and scooped rice, sticky and wet the way Dom liked it, a lump of starch alongside a slab of fall-apart meat onto his plate. He set his plate down and clanked the cover on the pan.

"I've been accepted to Mary Hillyard," she swallowed and said. I felt Dom's eyes make a sweep of the table before taking position, his mother and father in full sight.

"Congratulations," Arnold said.

"Good," Dom said. "Then you'll be out of here. We won't have to listen to your fake cries and your orders telling us what to do."

"Yeah, away from you and the...."

"Jada, that's enough," I admonished. Dom kept surveillance, his chocolate brown eyes spying through long black lashes.

Jada said, "Look at him. He can't even sit straight." I put my hand on Dom's arm and looked first at him and then at Arnold, his torso facing the table, his legs outside it as if ready to escape.

"Jada, please, enough." She sniffed again. One minute, two. It looked like we had made it. I rose, taking my plate and silverware with me, depositing them at the counter. "Done, Dom? Let's go to your room and find a game. How about Tribulation?"

Shifting places, that's what we were doing, each of us looking for space, rubbing one the wrong way here, finding another fault there, gathering more and more anger as we circled about. I was ever vigilant, snuffing out the small fires caused by our eruptions, tamping my authority over Jada's and Dom's tempers to put them out. Others smoldered, and left alone, they became flame-throwers sprouting like geysers into the pattern of our lives together.

Days later, our morning hobbled along as usual, everybody following his or her own schedule to get ready and out of the house on time. I cut carrot sticks, preparing Jada's and Dom's lunches while Dom showered and Jada sat down to her bowl of apples and cinnamon oatmeal. As I poured hot water on her cereal she proposed that she might save air and cab fares if she had her own vehicle, thus helping her to "pay back" the cost of a second-hand car. "I could drive it out there in the fall and keep it there all year." Jada gave me a squeeze, right around my hip before stirring the water into her oatmeal.

"You don't want to do that," Arnold cut in. I went back to the breadboard.

"How do you know what I want?" Jada challenged. I heard the clink of his coffee cup on the table. "You always butt in thinking you know everything."

I cringed. If there was anything we did not need, it was a fight in the morning. Dom would be out with us in a minute. I took in a breath while pulling cellophane along the toothy metal edge of the carton and wrapped a peanut butter sandwich, putting the bread knife next to the sink. A chair scratched the linoleum. Bending down for a bag, I heard Arnold's uneven step. "Jada, you don't need a car when you're going off to college."

"Why don't you leave?" Jada snapped. I'd heard it so often I stopped hearing it. I reached behind the toaster for my brown bag, wrinkled and crinkled from reuse, then opened the refrigerator door and scanned the shelves for the container of leftovers. Another chair was being slid, skimming the floor as hard-soled shoes on a sawdust-strewn dance floor. "All you do is sit around and drink coffee and read the paper!" Jada's voice trailed like a whistle on an outbound train, at first high-pitched and loud and gradually diminishing as it grew more distant, though there was little distance to travel from the kitchen to where it sounded she was shouting, in the living room.

"Don't be ridiculous; I do not. Help! Jada, you're attacking me! Idina, make her stop! She's attacking me with a knife! Help! I'm bleeding! Aaach!"

Arnold's shouts brought Dom, wrapped in a towel, running from his bedroom and me from the kitchen through the dining room, making a jaw that closed in on them both, except we stopped, locked open to take in the scene. Arnold held his red-fingered hand out before his eyes, running downstairs and up, back and forth on four or five steps, as if his body ran on orders given before his head made them. Jada brandished a cheap bread knife with a flimsy serrated blade, thin and long, its tip a round knob. She stood threateningly at the top of the stairs, knife raised for another attack.

"Jada, put the knife away." I spoke resignedly. She must have followed him to the stairs as he left the kitchen, and when he turned around and backtracked, she swung, catching both of them by surprise. She had indeed drawn blood from Arnold's scalp;

a filament seeped red under a few thin straggles of hair that he combed to the side.

"Idina, take that knife away from her! She's crazy. She's a madwoman!" Watching myself watch my daughter exulting in her power, I felt some bit of detachment from the urgency Arnold invoked. His awful authority to control the appearance of things had deserted him at last. Or no—he could have gone downstairs and escaped the entire scene; instead he made a production, taunting her for more. I went back to the kitchen, Jada joining me, triumphantly laying down the knife. Arnold cried of the injustices done him as he descended the steps. Without a word, we went about our business, Jada back in her room getting dressed, me gathering my school bag. Dom sat on his rumpled bed. "I'm leaving now." I said.

"Can't you stay home for a little bit?"

His eyes, inching closer to my level as he grew, watered with worry, and I sat next to him, wishing I could take away not just this incident but other painful memories with it. He would harden; he would have to. "No. I can't get into their argument; I lose with all of you. The knife is back in the kitchen, your father is downstairs getting ready to leave, and Jada is over it. Everyone is safe. Come on into the kitchen and I'll get your cereal."

It did appear that everyone was safe. That evening we all faced a television, Arnold downstairs in his fake leather chair and Dom, I imagined, stretched out on the couch, his arm underneath the pillow supporting his head, Jada and I upstairs in the kitchen. We had seen another of the four children in the news series, earlier in the week, and on this night Jada was introduced. "If determination could win the battle with cancer, it would be Jada's," Bob Sherman began, and Jada appeared in a red hat and the red sweater I knit for her, walking along the windowed corridor of her school, the bright February sunlight and a fat snow field illuminating her. She appeared purposeful and confident, carrying her books and then taking notes in a class while her teacher asked them to name their heroes. At the closing of the segment, the camera zoomed in on her face while her voice ran behind, and I thought she had to be the closest image to an angel that I'd ever seen, her skin like a pearl, iridescent, her eyes looking upwards, heavenly blue, light skipping about like a star shower. And then a close-up of Jada in a Wharton sweater, her puffy face, being interviewed at the hospital, the image viewers were left with, that and the heart-tugging music.

"What do you think about it, Mom?"

"It looks like they're going for the hero approach. How 'bout you? What does it feel like to see yourself and know you are part of a message?"

Jada's eyes turned up in thought. "I was a little disappointed that they left out the part in the beginning, remember when he came and kind of like, was surprised? That's what I mean about being taken for granted by other people—they want to see you sitting in school when you look like nothing's wrong, not the...the real, when it's really happening."

"That's a good way to put it. Well, remember, they're out to get viewers, not necessarily understanding. I think what you said was clear. You told the truth."

Arnold came to the kitchen doorway and leaned against it, half in and half out, caught in a hokey-pokey dilemma. A small pink bump shone with tenderness as he tilted his head toward Jada. "I just have to tell you, Jada, that was wonderful. You're my hero." He inhaled deeply, his lower lip fluttering, repressing, apparently, an emotion which threatened to set him to weeping.

"And that's Greg," Jada said with a swing in her voice that, if it could have vibrated to her hips, would have shimmied them to the hula. Pointing to a picture of a young man with sandy brown hair just a little darker than the beaches behind him, she beamed a grin full of memory.

"Oh?" Heidi smiled back. "Did he go on the trip with you?"

"No, I met him at a luau." Jada's eyes glistened, filled with glassy grains of sand just washed by the turquoise ocean under the broad smile of the Hawaiian sun. Heidi scanned the rest of the photos on the page while we waited for the results of a bone scan.

Jada knew what she hoped for in Hawaii: hours stretched out on a beach towel, the waves of the ocean rustling an unexplainable desire to lunge into an unexplored part of yourself, shopping the markets, eating chocolate covered ice cream sundaes in waffle cones, evenings with the blazing sun dropping over the water's edge, torches lighting the mysterious night, fueled by desires that something magical might happen. She had invited Kimby to go on the spring break tour and phoned me three days in a row, her words tilted like rose buds too heavy for their stems, flopping downward before they bloomed.

"Miserable! How? You've been looking forward to this for two months."

"Kimby's a dud. She never wants to do anything. It's a perfectly awesome day here, and she has to go inside and rest!"

"Well, where is she now that you can make this call?"

"I'm in Dad's room. I wish I never came. I miss you, Mooie. I wish I were at home with you. Or at least you were here with me. We'd have more fun together."

"Yeah, right. A forty-year-old with a fat belly and sagging boobs on the beach in Hawaii. How're you going to lure bait with me around?"

"I don't care about meeting anyone else. I don't need anyone but you, anyways."

"Promises, promises," I started. "It's easy to say that now. But, remember, you're the teenager, and you're there to do teenage things. You'll be off in college next year, a young woman on your own. You have to practice."

"College, smollege. Maybe I don't want to go to school. Maybe I just want to stay home and do nothing."

"Wouldn't that be a little like Kimby? Not going off and trying things, being daring. Isn't that what you don't like about Kimby now? When you get home, we can talk about next year, but right now, I want you to think about what you can do to make this trip fun for yourself."

Jada released a sigh I could almost feel. My own chest muscles relaxed, pushing out doubt and loneliness, and fear. Grandma M observed that I wouldn't know what to do without Jada.

"Why do you always want to make me independent, always go and tell me to make my own decisions? Don't you know I want you to tell me what to do?" I tried to see Jada in a hotel room with sun streaming through the windows thousands of miles away, but I felt the warmth of her breath to my ear saying, "I don't want to grow up; it's so hard."

"Yes, it is. But it can be wonderful. That's why you went through treatment two times. You go back to Kimby and see if you can't compromise. If you fight, you both will be more miserable. Call me again if you need to. Otherwise, I'll see you Saturday night. Love you, Darlin'."

The photo album rested against Jada's thigh while Heidi gasped at the brilliant colors. "I've never been to Hawaii," she said. "These are just gorgeous! Even these night shots are clear and bright." Photos of grass hula skirts and loopy leis and flower crowns on long black hair cascading past narrow brown waistlines that fanned into luscious hips danced on the page.

"Tell her, Jada, about the luau," I coaxed. Everyone rode to the luau on a bus. A young man sat with his mother a seat ahead; Jada engaged the man in conversation and they agreed to sit together at the luau. Men with daring gathered upon the stage for hula lessons. Then the women were called, and Jada joined, while Kimby sat back like an octogenarian with a rusted pelvis, as drums pulsed and women's skirts made circular sweeps around their bare feet and their hips spun on the ball bearings of the night's rhythms. When the lesson was over, the women greeted the men in the kissing line. The guide on the bus kept the party spirit alive, telling jokes and leading the passengers in song, adding verses, and jubilantly the passengers clapped their hands and stomped their feet. The final verse called for kissing. On the last picture in the photo album, Jada attached a sticker with the caption, "Ready, set, go!"

When Jada returned to Minnesota, we were into April. In contrast to pictures of a pink sun-splashed hotel, our spring skies were mud-splashed. The snow had finally relented to the last cool sprinkling of rain that nudged it down the gutters. Heavy winter parkas too conspicuously warm were left behind in the closet, and we shivered in our spring coats. The sun wasn't shining, but we persevered because it wasn't snowing, it wasn't so cold that it was ice cold. It was spring. That was enough to make up for the hanging drab clouds. It was April, the month of mistrust, cruel skies, washing out our bridges, smearing us with dread.

This April, Jada had stepped off the school bus, and landing on first one, then the other foot, she felt a collapse within her body, like two ends of a vise squeezing her together at her hips. She heard a crumpling that was not unlike the sound of compacting an aluminum can. Every step since was painful.

We waited for Dr. Lourde, Heidi admiring Jada's album. She was going to show it to Trudy, too, at their appointed time, which followed. It was getting to look like she would be late; I, too, getting Sheila's car to its cozy home. Thomas was going to a workshop and his wife wasn't driving hers. They handed me the key: five minutes it took me to figure out how to remove it from the ignition. Then the key buzzed at me and I looked around for a flying insect. A colleague clued me in to the built-in mechanism for locating keys. I guessed everything, animate and inanimate alike, longed for a warm hand to hold onto them. Now anxiety churned inside my stomach like an idling motor. Should Jada call and postpone her appointment with Trudy, or should she skip out on the chemo and come back for that another day? We were pondering when Dr. Lourde opened the door. Behind him was Beverly. It had been a year since Beverly sat in a room with us; the last was another April day, Jada's relapse.

"What have you got there, Jada?" Dr. Lourde asked, pulling a chair into the circle.

Jada tilted the book and answered. "Pictures from my trip to Hawaii." Heidi exited, and Jada, perched on the table, offered the book. Dr. Lourde looked down at his hands, his fingers spread open as spokes that met and connected into a tent between his parted knees. The dance in Jada's eyes disappeared.

"Jada, I have some bad news to report to you. About the pain you feel when you walk." Dr. Lourde talked in pauses, and I held onto the first bit, a corner piece of a jigsaw puzzle.

"The scan shows that the tips of your bones where they fit into the sockets have deteriorated. That sound you heard when you stepped down was literally the crushing of bone." He stood and went to the table where she sat, took a pen from his shirt pocket, and drew on the paper. "Here in the center where it should be rounded, it is crushed, and what remains is this cup-like edge. Technically, the name for this is bilateral necrosis of the femoral heads." He backed up and sat down again. Jada's face turned to stone; in it were carved two holes, her eyes following him.

"It is not uncommon among older people to have this wearing away of bone tissue," he continued. "But in your case, it is caused by an interruption in the blood supply to the tips of your bones. It's a very rare side effect of Prednisone; and it's irreversible. We're going to have to discontinue Prednisone."

Prednisone, though just a tiny white pill to swallow, packed a wallop to Jada's body. Prednisone produced the diabetic reaction, and its dosage had already been slashed. Even so, it caused chronic queasiness and the loss of hair. Small, small matters. I thought back to Debbie's hunched back. When we first met her, she stood straight, but as the months trudged towards her death, something grew between her shoulders and stuck out like a miniature mountain, not unlike the hump seen in some very old women. That's what this disease does best, this disease of young people; it makes them old. Jada maintained her statue-like form, her face cemented in defiance of emotion, her album discarded to the edge of the table, a collection of disremembered faces and names and days, as if the trip had happened a long, long time ago, in her youth.

"Now, what does this mean to you in terms of your leukemia?" Dr. Lourde forged further, feeling his way tenderly. "We say we know about the combination of medications, but we don't know how each medication affects the whole treatment. Because the effects of the drug are residual, taking you off Prednisone will not put an end to the problem, which is in the blood flow and the eventual death of the extremities of your bones. In all likelihood your arms suffer the same condition, which is that shoulder pain you feel, and we cannot say how much more damage will occur. We'll just have to watch for the next few months. In the meantime, we don't want you to put undue weight on your hip joints, so we want you to use crutches from now on."

"Crutches!" Jada yelled with accumulated energy. "You expect me to get everywhere on crutches? How does that help?" I could see the picture of herself forming behind Jada's eyes. The last thing she wanted was to be identified as helpless. No, the last thing she wanted was to live a life without freedom. Already she felt she had given up too much, and I couldn't disagree.

Dr. Lourde persisted, making a fist and fitting it under his other cupped hand. "When you walk, your leg swivels in your socket, and a lining inside the socket naturally cushions the bone." Then he went back to the drawing and drew a line through it. "But when this part of the bone is not healthy, every time there's weight put on it, little pieces crack and the surface becomes ragged. The rough edge then scrapes away at the lining of the socket and that's what makes the movement painful."

"What about my arms? If the same thing is wrong with my arms, how can I put weight on them?" Jada spat out. Behind her was a board with black Velcro patches to catch darts thrown at it, darts that were never to be found: a curious contradiction, to tempt people with the things denied them.

"Your arms don't bear as much weight as your legs. How much of the sockets are involved or how extensively your legs are damaged we won't know for about another six months, so we have to be extremely protective of your legs. There's a special kind of crutch, ones that reduce the weight-bearing stress to your arms."

"Well, I'm not going to have crutches," Jada said, shooting her words, each one a bull's-eye hit. Then she placed her two palms on the table beside her hips, making a dent in the hollow space of Dr. Lourde's drawing, and landed on the floor. Each step she took toward the door was made with effort, like learning a new dance. She left the three of us in the room cluttered with a baby play board with dials to roll, rubber buttons to push, and plastic rings to spin, a mustard yellow beanbag in the corner, the door hanging askew like the cat's leg in the Be Kind to Animals Month poster. And the dart board.

Dr. Lourde's job was done. I picked up the abandoned photo album while Beverly made a discreet phone call. Then I followed her to the cafeteria as if attached by a lanyard to her sympathetic eyes. "I can't imagine what it must be like for Jada," she said. "You or I might be devastated by something like this, but we'd go on with our lives in somewhat the same pattern. But this changes everything for her—her decision to go to school, her whole life in one instant faces her as a totally new person. What are you going to do next?"

Coffee steamed toward my nostrils and my stomach sickened at its smoky smell. I could no more foresee the future that convulsed before us than I could go backwards and say why I took the coffee I didn't want. So much of my life seemed to repeat dire consequences to that question. "She's going to be furious, blame me for this. What happens next between us will have a lot to do with the rest of her life."

"I think you're right. Jada takes a lot of her direction from you. I remember the time last summer when Jada was having some operation, I can't remember what it was for, but it was in the day surgery and she was refusing to do what she was supposed to. Remember that?"

I nodded. Beverly, who had moved in closer, surrounded her slender fingers like the silken threads of a spider's web around her cup, the way she spun a story to contain me. "She was locked in battle with herself, and you recognized that and stepped in and as much as said, 'That's enough. This is what we do.' And then you pushed the bed toward the nurse. It was what Jada needed, a way

303

to know what to do. The more I watch her, the more I admire her courage. She looks to you as a model in these tough situations. That's why she can blow up with you, isn't it? You're the one and only firm anchor in her life that's changing so fast around her that she doesn't know what to do."

"Oh, my God! I don't know if I can take all the anger this time." Like there's a choice, I wanted to add. Once, just once, I'd like a choice. Jada would say I had one every time. Of course she was right, and the guilt for bringing her down with my choices sank in me like the *Titanic.* "I never know what to expect. It's not something I can rehearse for. I always feel so beat up; yes, that's what it's like. I'm afraid that some day she'll stop listening, give up. Or that I won't be able to hold more of her anger. Then what?"

"I don't envy your job tonight." Beverly glanced down at her watch. "I'll call Trudy and see if she made it down there before I go."

"Yes," I said, grateful for the suggestion and, with it, the anticipation of getting on with the terrible job of getting it over with.

"Quiet Hospital Zone" signs used to admonish people to slow their speed around hospitals. I imagined cars and motorcycles and taxi cabs gearing down to a mild purr as they approached the tall brick building, while mothers in hats turned from the front seats, holding up their gloved index fingers to puckered lips making the "shhh" sound heard in the eye of the storm. I felt I was in one of those quiet zones as I paced the corridor outside Trudy's office. June's keys, cached in a pocket of my bag made muffled gurgling sounds, being shushed themselves.

I waited on the couch, and when I could no longer sit, I waited, standing, in the cold, dimly lit underground hallway, alone, except for my companions, Hambone, Jada's coat, her school bag and photo album, and my own bag of schoolwork, all untouched, and thought that while friends were working at jobs, reading books, talking on the phone, shopping at malls, Jada and I were at the hospital facing a showdown.

Jada appeared and stopped, her slender form a staunch barricade. Her arms stationed at her sides, she was poised, as in the final moment before diving from the very top cliff into the narrow stream below, or before taking aim at a deadly foe. Her steel blue eyes shot at me. She spoke void of volume, inflection; yet her words were so passionate, they drilled holes in my heart.

"I hate you." She sprayed me with her wrath. "All along I've been right about my body and what would happen. But you didn't want me to make 'such harsh decisions'. Now, just as my small life was finally getting a bit livable, it's ripped from me. My life's been fucked over way too many times." Her lips moved with syncopation, programmed not to waiver until her jaws locked tight bars around my conviction: guilty as charged and sentenced for life.

"Yes, Jada, you have been right all along. If something wrong was going to happen, it did. I made decisions with the hopes that your life wouldn't be this way. I kept believing what we wanted for you, not what you feared."

"Now that it's too late you admit that I know what should be. I'm so goddamned stuck I can't believe it! This extended life is not worth it. Just when I'm coping with my horrible situation I get another stab in the back!" My eyes were afraid to move from hers, as if breaking the magnetism would also break us. All the other bouts Jada had with her anger, with the disease, with me, were like the preamble for this climax, and a misstep tonight would leave a scar on our relationship as red and knotty and irreversible as the one that ran down her arm.

"I'm sorry," I dropped into the universe that separated us that night. "I'm sorry that you have more pain, anguish, frustration. I'm sorry that it gets harder and harder for you. I'm sorry that our vision is not always clear."

"I hate God, people, everything." Once erupted, Jada's emotions flowed, sliding downward like lava, words of desecration being carried along with it. "I hate myself for going on. My spirit or body or whatever continues the living in me won't die out. I feel it pittering but it just won't give out all the way. It's gotta make me suffer a long time, too. I don't believe in treating cancer, especially relapsed cancer. It's destroying the world."

Borne on the wave of loathing and filled with the cargo of our past, her words engulfed our existence. The transaction seemed complete, my having taken the anger, not for keeps, but perhaps as freeze-wrapped and "put on ice" for a later date to thaw, when Jada could work with it, chunk by chunk. I felt filled but not weighted. Though the words ended, I could not paint them pink and send them out as pleasure rafts, for their passion for battle was only just launched. We would carry these killing things with us wherever we went. Jada's shoulders settled. Her stance shifted. I breathed. Simultaneously we moved, and silently we walked out into the musty spring night to separate cars, each finding our own way to be home together.

Aug. 8, 1986

I leave for MHC in 26 days. I have to admit that I do want to go, but I'm also very worried how much my medical situation will affect my first year. I feel defeated! I'm scared that my shoulders and hips will get worse and handicap me more. I'll probably have to be in a wheelchair with scars and brain damage. If I don't get better, it won't be worth it. I'm so fucked over! I have chills and sweats and fevers. My bones hurt, my head hurts, my belly hurts! I'm sick and dizzy and I can't even sleep because it hurts to move! And I can't DANCE! It's not worth living with all these restrictions and abnormalities. Others think I am just feeling sorry for myself, but damn them! I don't care if other people are thankful for living and put up with their pain and handicaps and I don't think they should be admired just because they do. They're not ME and I DETEST it all! I want to live life the way I want, not this way with the struggle I've been going through for five and a half years! And my condition is deteriorating, so I don't think it's selfish for me to want to DIE! I wanted to die when I relapsed in 84, but I was trapped and NOW WHAT! I knew it would be a terrible time ahead and

*NOT WORTH it for me, but Mom made me feel sorry for her.
She tries to convince me that no one is to blame, but They're
ALL to blame! My body can't tolerate drugs and my body is
crumbling apart from this shit! My luck I'd go on living if I quit
treatment. Like this! No, I can't win. This battle with pain and
keeping my life together is breaking me down. I feel so alone and
worn out. I have to do so many things but can't and I am SICK
of waiting for when I can. I feel like I've lost everything and I
am a failure! Nothing will work out for me so why the hell go on
living? I hate living like this and I hate doctors and nurses and
their flubs and the whole world for making me go on! I'm not
going to add anything to the world except more pollution with
cancer drugs in my body. The world is too crowded already with
people starving and dying and killing each other and destroying
the earth. I am STUCK living when I should be granted death.
If God existed he would change my life or let me die. I thought
of committing suicide and telling everybody what I think of
them. Like Kimby, you just "forgot" to come over last night?
Will you be able to take off work? And Chris, I know you're
sorry you forgot my birthday. Mark, you're in college and are
so busy with your schedule. I'm dead—can you fit me in now?
Say you're sorry for me for killing myself, Mom! Give me a tad
more "support" Dad, and don't take credit for killing me this
time even though you really should. And get an ugly suit on sale
to wear to my funeral. And everyone else, we love you, but we
have very busy lives and we can't come visit you. Then they can
all say wonderful things about me and brag about how I was so
NICE!*

*My counts are really low—7 hemoglobin, 800 WBC,
2500 platelets. They even shocked Joe. But I have to go to the
clinic for a spinal tap tomorrow and he'll probably say I have
to have treatment anyway. More poison! I am sick enough! I
can't remember when I haven't had complications or drugs! I
don't have faith in God or medicine or doctors or nurses or the
WHOLE profession! They've ruined my life and I don't see*

why I should want to go on living a life when I'm not even ME anymore. SHIT! Let me out of this world!

Aug. 11, 1986

Well, one more delay to get on with my life and reason to want to just get out of it! Dr. Randolph says he won't do what he calls elective surgery on my arm. He didn't want to "interrupt" my treatment for three months and said the problem with my hips and right shoulder were another reason not to operate! I can't walk without pain or even open a jar and he wants me to live with this muddled up life! I want to go away and get rid of this crap but it's so damn scary to go so far away and have to deal with treatment, hip and bone pain, and meds. I'll have to turn down the things I've dreamed of like work and fun and travel because all my time will be taken up with my wretched condition. And if there is no miracle—and there won't be!—I'll probably be stuck with handicaps, medical treatment next summer, too! It's so hard to psych myself up to keep living and hoping for a life of no pain, no, even a month! Pretty high goals I set! I have to hide my struggles and fears about what's happening to my life and this whole shitty situation. Not Trudy or mom knows how much I hope I die or how much the unknown future scares me. But I DON'T want to miss out on my freshman year at MHC!

Less than one week from Jada's first night in her dorm and home from shopping for what she absolutely needed to bring, I drew a bath, and Jada let the soothing ripples wear away the edges of another hard day. Dr. Lourde was right. Walking was becoming more and more of a strain on her; she had pushed her anger at her brittle and shattering bones deep inside her, and underneath an unyielding exterior of hard will power, the bottled up emotion gnawed at her confidence as if it were brittle bone, too.

As I trickled water over her shoulders, peeping out of the soap suds like two white stones, smooth and velvety, in a burbling stream, I felt her begin to untangle the ribbons of fears that tied her up. I had learned a lot since giving Jada her first bath eighteen years ago, how to touch her and calm her fear, and I was again careful of damaged bones and fragile feelings. Odd, how the act that had caused us pain had been transformed into the act that forgave each other. In a voice small for the bathroom, I suggested, "You'll need a new telephone."

She balked, feeling guilty about buying anything when she hadn't earnings from a summer job.

"That little bit of money?" I asked, blowing it off with a whiff of air through my teeth and reaching over to release the trap on the drain. "You've earned a scholarship and you have a work-study grant. I have to take a loan anyway, so what's a coupla hundred dollars more? I'll make up for the difference you'd earn in a summer job if I get hired again for evening high school. Buy what you need and don't worry about the cost."

"But what if I don't need these things for very long?"

"That isn't even part of this situation." I answered, as if nudging a cork out of a bottle of champagne in a room full of crystal. "You're going to college now, and we're getting what you need." I helped Jada from the tub and patted her dry. The summer night breeze sopped up the steamy air. "We forgot your powder, Doll. I'll get it."

"Why didn't you let me die?" Jada followed me into her bedroom, padding barefoot, landing flat on each foot as if she were a mechanical toy that moved forward mainly by rocking back and forth, and let the towel slide open to expose her ivory skin. Her pubic hair had thinned along with the hair elsewhere. She never denied the benefits of chemotherapy: not much left of a period, and no need to shave her legs or under her arms.

"Because I want you alive," I answered, standing in front of her dresser, facing her mirror.

Playfully, she swatted her bath towel at me. "You Boofus. Selfish, selfish, selfish." She swatted again, a venomous snap to make her line hang true.

"No," I refuted, turning around with the powder in my hand. "I didn't want you for me. This thing, this disease, is a part of life; no, it's a part of your life. And I want you to have your life. It's like an antithesis." She smirked, the change in her eyes, brilliant enough to light the night just a minute go, now clouded like April skies. "What you must go through is so awful, I suppose it's like a birth for a baby; somewhere in the awfulness is the good that it leads to, and you can't get there any other way. But, like a baby, or maybe like the lame man who can't be healed because no one is there to help him get into the curative water, someone or something else is in control." Lost, I tried to defend the ugliness, the chance for beauty. "I wanted to help you into the water; but I cannot justify anything. I'm sorry that you must go through treatment, especially when you don't want it. But it may be that the drugs will work this time because they're so much stronger."

"But they didn't work before," Jada said, cold and hard and big and loud and heavy, a goddess not to be outthought with ordinary power.

"So if that is the case, that they didn't knock out the disease then and won't now, you will have had four, six more years, and you know all the opportunities and advances time holds. That's a hope and would make this second attempt worth it."

"But breathing, taking space, eating. You could feed a whole country."

"Well, now I will be selfish. I like to have *you* doing these things. Besides, the little room you take up, the world can afford."

"It's still not right. The leukemia was there all the time. It's prolonging the psychological stage of flipping the switch to life-saving machines. But it's worse because the choice is mine—it should be mine. I don't want to go through treatment; it's not worth it." I slipped a nightshirt over Jada's head. Her arms emerged, and smelling baby-powder soft again, she said, "But I don't want a long and painful death. If it could be instant, I'd say okay. Yes, I wanted the prom, the school things, but had I known how they'd be, I would not have chosen treatment. It just wasn't worth it."

"You know, I needed to hear that. I wanted you to know your choices and I hoped for those 'one mores' for you because I felt they had purpose. I'm sorry you had to go through pain to have them, but I didn't think giving up them and all the other life things you do was a worthy tradeoff to avoid treatment. Do you see what I mean about having to go through the awful? Life isn't avoidance; it's meeting every bad and awful and ugly thing, and in some twisted way, the beauty lies not in beating the foe but in the courage to say to it, 'You fucker, I count, I matter,' because not to fight back means you don't. Who was it said, 'Don't run away from a battle you cannot win?' I wanted you to own these decisions.

"Well, maybe you have known all along that treatment wouldn't work for you, and it's me who has had to come around to see things as you do. But it isn't just that you turned eighteen or something magical like that that turns the decision over to you whether to continue or not. It's that you make the decision to live that gives you the right to decide to die. And I want you to know that, as much as I want life for you, I will support your decision, no matter what."

The next week's days spirited themselves away like helium-filled balloons released to the sky. With a sense of light-weightedness, Jada gathered about her, one by one, the things she couldn't live without at school. Two suitcases already jammed and locked up tight, a line drawn through everything on Jada's list; she was eager to leave, and the days ticked slowly by. Jada sat on top of the last suitcase while I clamped the latch shut; I zipped up my carry-on bag and stuffed Hambone into Jada's new tote bag; we put on as much clothing as we could, including our coats, even though it was seventy degrees, and boarded the flight to Hartford, Connecticut.

Dr. Lourde arranged to transfer Jada's treatment to the clinic in a hospital in Loudon where we were to meet with Dr. Cartwright, who would deliver IV chemo three or four times during the school year. We waited in a cramped ocher room, old men and women pressed to straight-backed wooden chairs against the walls like figures in a pop-up book. When someone came into the room, no one looked up, pretending to be involved in a magazine or thought or prayer, wishing, perhaps, that they wouldn't be noticed either, while the newcomer scanned every face for a place to fit in anonymously. Yet, even with such guardedness, everyone in the room would know some secret about someone else. I could feel eyes stealing glances at my shoes, noses sniffing at my perfume, skin sensing the blouse on my back. *Jada will not like this.* When her name was called, she passed through the door, me following.

Dr. Cartwright greeted us stiffly in her starched white coat, though she was small and wiry and appeared to be spry underneath the uniform's veneer. Very simply she stated the procedure: the patient comes in, the doctor punctures the vein, the patient goes off into another room while the anti-cancer drug runs into the body, then the patient gets up and leaves. What more could a patient want to know? Yes, she was a firm believer in a patient's taking control of her treatment. She was very busy, as we could plainly see; if there were no more questions, she would like to get on with her work.

Walking to the car, I remarked, "Maybe that's good she's so businesslike. Just go in, get it over with, and get out," like an assembly line for automobiles, or cows down the shoot for slaughter. "You're with adults now; maybe you'll find a more mature strategy on your part."

"You'd think that here in the East they'd have better facilities. Did you see how old everything was?"

And dirty, too. Everything here felt like it had a coating of coal dust on it. "Yes, but haven't you noticed that all of Loudon looks old and run-down? The name sounds so charming and bucolic; I guess I associate it with the college, not the city—and it's a big city."

"Will you use normal words? What does bucolic mean?"

"That is a normal word. It means like the country, you know, pastures and farm animals and quiet. The other thing I notice out here is the smell of the air and the water. It tastes like iron. After my shower, I couldn't get rid of the smell, like I'd doused myself in eau d'ore." I drove a narrow lane of the one-way out of Loudon toward Founders' Valley. Originated as a women's seminary, Mary

Hillyard was about to celebrate its sesquicentennial. It was in the shadow of the famous Mt. Loudon that towered the valley in which the campus made a verdant cloistered nest. "When are you going to make an appointment?"

"I have to wait and see how my schedule looks. I don't want to go when there's a lot to think about. I'll do it, if that's what you're worried about. But you said you were turning everything over to me, so don't start bugging me about it."

"Sorry. I didn't mean it that way." She sat back on the contoured seat, her left eyebrow arched in my direction. "Now, watch for the sign; the rotary is coming up pretty soon." Jada read the directions to the college one more time, and we looped the rotary, a miracle, I thought, given its reputation as a knot rather than just a circle.

Once inside the dorm room, Jada discovered a meeting for new students, the first of many. I unpacked, stacked, and folded what I could and went back to my motel room.

At 9:30 a.m., I searched for a familiar door tucked away down a hallway just past the showers. A legendary charm of Mary Hillyard was its splendid campus; quaint dormitories in old houses, with nooks and corners, high ceilings, flowing draperies, windows towering over the people who lived there, old knocking radiators. Her door was open, and I sat in a desk chair. One window, two females; what would they decide? An adage warned against rooming with best friends. These were awfully small quarters for new acquaintances, as well. Her roommate's sheets had bright splashy flowers climbing all over them; Jada's had colonial blue and white stripes, long-necked geese waddling across the border, their beaks carrying a ribbon along with them. Hambone lay cozily on her pillow. On a desk worn beyond the finish, the *American Heritage Dictionary of the English Language* and a paperback thesaurus stood staunchly between two teddy bear bookends. If I had opened the drawer, I would have seen bright paper clips, pencils, a mini tape measurer, shears, all partitioned neatly into their own bins.

A shuffle of heels on wooden boards softened by years of traffic announced Jada's coming. "You're here! I'm sorry; there's so much for me to do! I didn't know we had all these events." Jada set down a notebook and dropped a pen in the pink plastic cup, then leaned against the desk.

"As long as we get everything done I came here for, I'm fine. Are you ready?"

She reached behind her back for another small notebook, one with wire coiling through the top edge, and flipped it open. As she tore out a page, she handed it to me, making one seamless movement, with authority, and said, "Here's a list of the things I need at the mall. Do you mind going to get them? I've got to go to a dorm meeting, and then there's a rugby practice I want to see."

"I don't mind, but I thought we'd be able to spend some time together. How about the other things we have to get?"

She sank to the chair and softened her voice. "Can you go to the Zayre for those? And pick up another pillow," she added, her eyes widening. "I'm sorry, Mom. You know how hard it is for me to walk all over and get in and out of the car. I didn't know they'd have so much for us to do!"

"It's okay, Jada. I'm happy that you are doing these things. You belong here. It's me who has to let go." My voice cracked. "This is your home, and I'm a visitor. That's new for us." Once the words were said, the sting in my eyes brought tears. My nose heated with the pressure to hold them back. "You know, on Sunday we'll say goodbye, but it's already happened."

"Oh, Mooie." Jada rose to me and we caught each other. "You know you'll always be my mooie! Here! Let's take a picture of us!" Jada swirled around the room for her camera and aimed it at me before setting the timer. Then she scampered toward me and draped her arms from my shoulder, leaning her forehead to my cheek, her glimmering blue eyes and brilliant wide smile facing the lens. I held her around her waist, smiling but wanting to cry.

"Now Hambone and you!" Jada squealed, reaching down to where Hambone lay, one eye staring at us from under his cocked ear. Nuzzling my face next to Jada's wobbly pet pig, I surrendered my daughter to her new life: she and living were made for each other. Before driving to the mall, I stopped at the florist shop along the highway and ordered a rose to be delivered; at the same time, I hoped, she should receive the welcome card I mailed from the Founders' Valley post office.

Jada's door was closed when I, the doting mother from nice Minnesota helping her daughter get all the right things to go to one of the twelve sister schools in the Eastern states, arrived the next morning. She had donned a college lifestyle in just one day. In her nightshirt, she answered my knock, looking haggard, eyes swollen, and creases along her face showing a need for sleep. Jada tumbled back onto her mattress, scooping Hambone out of the way of her rolling body.

Sitting quietly, I took a third look around the room. From where I sat, the green bursting through the window was like looking at the reverse of an impressionistic painting. Instead of seeing the shape and shadow and form from a distance, I saw bundles of strokes overlapping each other, green on green on green.

Jada's mattress screeched, not unlike the tightening of a wooden screw in an old-fashioned nutcracker. Her eyes opened halfway in a vacuous stare, and yawning, creeping toward being awake, she rolled in her bed, landing on her back to face the bottom of the mattress above her. "How late were you up last night?" I asked.

"I didn't get to bed until after two. I was so tired, and then when Jill got up this morning, she made so much noise. What time is it?"

"Almost 10."

"I have to get up if I'm going to get breakfast." She sat up, placing her feet on the floor and stopped. She yawned again and rubbed her nose, rising cautiously, the first flower of spring slowly unfolding its petals, and moved tentatively about the room, collecting her gear for the bathroom. I drank a cup of tepid coffee while Jada ate toast and jelly across from me in the nearly empty dining room. At another table sat a young woman in floppy slippers, one dangling from her toes as it flapped like a paddle, the ball of her foot tapping against it.

It was Saturday, slow-starting, still-sleeping Saturday. Jada dragged her feet through the discount store, on her legs too much and too long, as I pushed the clackety wheels of the metal shopping cart up one aisle and down another for remaining necessities.

After hoisting the last of the shopping bags into her room, we rode silently through the countryside, our car rustling leaves, to Goodrich. Jada reclined her seat and pushed herself back. About 20 miles separated the towns, each with its college campus. During the school day and up until midnight, a bus shuttled back and forth along the highway. On the weekends, traffic was sparse. I couldn't remember just where we had made our turnoff to the phantom amusement park and a promise for a cure to leukemia, nor did I see the sign. When I reached the edge of Goodrich, I felt that the drive into the woods in search of some magic had been dreamed. "It's not there any more," I said.

Jada must have looked for it, too. "Good. It shouldn't be. Telling lies like that. There'll never be a cure for leukemia, at least not for me."

On Sunday, Jada and I hugged each other and parted, stumbling a little with our feelings, wanting the relief that would come with having crossed a border, and for myself, feeling a little guilty for wanting to get across. It meant a change that took my daughter away from me and said to the world, to herself, and to me, that she was a young woman in her own right. She seemed content to get out from under me, too, and if that urge for independence didn't nag at her, I wished it would, just a little bit, just so I could feel I had done my job.

Yes, yes, all that is true, I said to myself as I retraced my way to the airport in Hartford. Almost everything I had done over the past five-and-a-half years had been either to, with, or for Jada, and now I was driving to the airport by myself. I would fly home alone, a single person. I had concentrated all my thought on preparing Jada for our separation. What I hadn't done was prepare myself.

September, 1986

"I can't live like this anymore," I said. The twenty-year mark of our marriage loomed before me, and suddenly reaching that meant failure, not success.

"It's not easy for me either. But I'm not leaving. I have just as much right to stay here as you have." The muscles in Arnold's jaw bulged, like a ping pong ball shot from cheek to cheek inside his mouth.

"Technically, yes. But don't you think it's selfish to stay when it's clear that it's not healthy for Jada and Dom for both of us to be here?"

"You're the one who's poisoned everything. I said I would be a father to Jada and Dom, so I'm staying."

"Don't even start on that. What has staying in a house got to do with being a father? Now you're going to get interested after I've done all the work of caring for them and disciplining them and seeing that they get places and have things and do well in school?"

"You wouldn't let anyone do anything. You think you're always doing something for them. It's easy when people ask you. Last spring I could have done a lot for the all-night party, but no one asked me to do anything."

"No one asked me, either. You could have done the same thing I did. You could have volunteered when the notices came out. But you didn't. You never did because you were too busy taking care of yourself and *not* being a father. You did the same thing when Jada made her confirmation, too. Who signed her up?

Who got her there and saw to it that she did her reading and service work? But then, when it was time for the show, you showed up for the ceremony and acted as if you played some part in the great accomplishment. And now, now you show up at Dom's school, when you have never done so before, because now maybe you stand a chance to lose something—or maybe you think there's some glory in holding down the fort—and you say it's because you want to be a father. You're making Dom a battleground when all you care about is what everything looks like. Well, it looks like a house of cards to me!"

"What about you? I saw you after Dom's teacher asked me if I was Jada's father. You went right over there and wanted to be sure she knew who you were."

"What, Madame? That's how much you know. Kathy's been Jada's French teacher for years; Jada was her assistant! I've driven Jada to her house at her invitation, and Kathy's planning to visit Jada this fall. This is exactly what I'm talking about. If you think staying together is good for the children, you're not only selfish, you're blind. I can't do it to them. What do you think they learn by seeing us like this?" The lever on the dishwasher jabbed into my back, just above the divide of my buttocks.

"That's your fault. You've poisoned Jada against her father and her brother. You and your women's rights." Arnold snickered at gender neutral words, chairperson or waitron. He had no problem with my making equal pay, of course, because it went into the family checkbook, which he controlled, but he snorted at the thought of answering to a female administrator. "You say you want me to leave for the children, but you won't admit your own selfish reason; you want me to leave for you."

"How can they be different? They're acting out us. If everything were okay for us, it'd be okay for them, and I wouldn't need—oh, I just can't do this anymore. I think I'm going to have to leave, get out, get my own place."

"See, you admit it. You want to leave for yourself. I think you'd better leave, too." How did that happen so naturally, so effortlessly, as if we were peering into the refrigerated case and deciding whether it would be the ground beef or the porterhouse steak.

Dom sat at the table, the television, a permanent addition to the kitchen, across from him. "Who's playing?" I began. His back to me, I thought of how much of his life the past few years had been as difficult as Jada's. Only nine when she was diagnosed, Dom had to grow up to be older before he was ready. Too many nights I wasn't there to read stories to him, to tuck him into bed, to sing to him as he had been used to. The disease was a thief not only of time: Dom knew when Jada was on my mind. Dom had grown up, and as much as I wanted to be to him what I was to Jada, I couldn't plug in all those times when I was away—and would be.

Jada and Dom, for all their differences, each possessed the same strong drive to be themselves, and I loved each for who they were, even though I did not love how they were with each other all the time. In time they would be able to spread their sibling differences out between them as a tablecloth at a picnic and let the food and the carefree spirit take them away from the present, this situation. If they had time. I knew they had something stronger that would outlast how they saw each other using life, he so effortlessly, she under such a strain.

There Dom sat, almost grown up. He was tall, dark, and handsome in a fourteen-year-old way, features strong and promising to develop classic character with maturity. There was no wholeness to a family life anymore, and I couldn't hold the life he made against him, only wait for time to stretch over our being through this part. "Your dad and I—you know we can't get along. It's just not right for the both of us to stay together. What would you say if your dad and I separated?"

I sat in his former spot, which, at one time had also been Jada's and mine. Odd that we three did all the shifting of places, adapting, in our family, while Arnold, his back to the sliding glass door, never budged. I felt like the table beneath my elbows also had our future served up on it. "Good," he said, his breathing relieved, as if finally his nasal airways were opened up and all the pressure of having to push in and out were suddenly eased. "It's about time."

"You know both of us want you to be with us, but one of us will stay in the house, and the other has to leave. I just don't see how we can all live here together and stay alive and sane. Jada will stay with me, I'm sure, and I want you to stay with me, too."

Dom was also impatient with deliberations. "I don't care who stays and who goes," he said, gathering up all the concerns into a knot. "I just know that I want to stay in this house. This is where I grew up, I have my friends here, I go to school here. I don't want to move to another place. I don't care who I live with, I'm staying here in the house."

"Your dad has said over and over again that he won't leave the house. And you know Jada couldn't possibly stay with her dad."

"No kidding. You know Jada and I'll be the ones who'll kill each other."

"Well, she'll be away at school most of the time, but not if she gets sick." I waited for a change of mind, a slight reconsideration. But that would have been out of Dom's character. I guessed I hadn't been the first to say something to him. I guessed I might have been the last to know some other things as well. "What will you do with me away?"

"Simple; I'll just pretend you're on vacation."

"You know I love you, Dom. You know if I could have it any other way, I would. You can always change your mind."

"I know. It's okay, Mom. I'll be all right. It's not like we won't see each other or anything like that."

I sorted feelings, thinking back to when I returned to teach when Dom was almost five months old. I felt a stab of guilt leaving him at JoJo's in the morning, crying as I drove away; my swollen breasts ached with fullness and leaked milk onto the blouse stretched tight against my nipples as it neared time to pick him up. I pondered why fathers didn't cry when they left for work. Why was it so acceptable for men to leave a child when couples divorced but so shamefully unacceptable—selfish and unloving—when mothers had to go?

I wondered, too, how Arnold had manipulated me again, for surely he had; but, I admitted to myself, I really didn't care. The guilt I felt for leaving now was little different from the guilt I felt when leaving for work, leaving my children with another. I would have to live with it, but I didn't have to die from it.

I sat at Jada's desk in her bedroom as she sat, I imagined, at her desk in her dormitory room, and as the red numbers blinked 9:30 on Jada's clock, I dialed her number. "I think I might have got the last seat on the plane. That was pretty lucky," I announced. "And I finally found a motel room in Chicopee. Everything's set. I'll go right to your dorm when I arrive and check in later."

"Good. Parents are invited to eat dinner on Friday night in the dorms. I've already signed you up. And I've got tickets to the Mark Russell show in the theater and a dance afterwards at the Alumnae Center. Thanks, Mooie, for doing that. It still makes me mad that Kathy didn't come."

"That's quite a lot of money to spend for a weekend visit to a former student."

"She's the one who said she wanted to come. She said she had a place to stay with friends."

A back yard hammock over a cushion of fallen leaves, crisp apples hanging from a tree filled out a vision of a perfect house in Founders' Valley. "Yeah, well, it's easy to agree to something when it's off in the future. It all worked out. Say, what does a person wear to a dance at Mary Hillyard? I don't think I have anything decent."

"Oh, don't worry about it. You'll find something. I'm wearing what I have."

"Yeah, but look at what you have. I might have to go shopping. When was the last time I put on something nice to go somewhere?"

"Don't spend money, Mom. Just look through your closet. You'll be fine."

We both paused. Nothing flashed from the hangers in the closet of my mind's eyes. I knew when I actually went to finger through, there would be no surprises, either. "Did you get to the hospital?" I ventured.

"Yes."

My back straightened, and I pressed the receiver closer to my ear: there was something not to be trusted in the flatness of her response. "How did it go?" Prickly crackles crossed the wires, sounding like a brush going through hair.

"I went, but I didn't get treatment. I'm never going there again."

"Hold on a minute and explain to me what happened."

"I made an appointment, and I psyched myself up to go and everything. I tried, I really did, Mom, but when I got in there, she just said, 'Sit down and do it now or get out.' She didn't let me have any time to make myself ready."

"Jada, how are you going to get your drugs?"

"I have to come home to get them."

"I can't fly you home every month. Besides, you'd have to miss classes to get here on a weekday." Even as I spoke, I realized that it didn't matter how many reasons I listed. The decision had been made, and I had only to accept it.

"Well, I'm not going back. She's a bitch."

I considered options. "I'll talk to Dr. Lourde and see what we can do."

"When you do, get my prescription filled and send it to me. I need some more Motrin." We paused again. "I gotta go now."

"Okay, Jada; love you, Doll." My lips puckered, and I made the mooch mooch kisses that stood for the Xs at the ends of our letters. She did, too.

Dr. Lourde was writing in a notebook on the ledge, high and protective, a Great Wall, surrounding the working space at the clinic when I passed through on my way from the pharmacy. I stretched up on my toes, hoping to spot Heidi behind the counter. He looked aside to me. "Hello, Mrs. Petersen," he said and went back to writing.

"Hello. I have to get Jada in here, hopefully the Wednesday before Thanksgiving. She's changed plans; she's not getting treatment in Massachusetts, so she's coming home for treatment from now on." The Motrin rattled in the plastic container as I put it into my pocket.

Dr. Lourde lifted his pen from the paper and poised it for its next stroke. He was taller than I, so he looked down at me and spoke, slowly, as if writing the words as he said them. Even so, they sounded more like an accusation than a report. "I spoke with Dr. Cartwright. She said that Jada's behavior was abominable; she told Jada she needed to grow up and act like an adult."

"And do you call Dr. Cartwright's impatience adult behavior?" I retorted, my eyes burning cold. "Usually when people say 'grow up,' they have a superior attitude and really mean 'do it my way' because they don't want to be inconvenienced. Or they don't care. She's not the right doctor for Jada. She'll be in the Wednesday before Thanksgiving, and the two of you can work on a new plan." I released the Motrin and felt relief as I took my hand out of my pocket and walked away from Dr. Lourde, who, I noted to myself, may have been about to say something more, the rest of his face wide open.

More than two months had passed since Jada's last treatment— she was overdue. From my window seat on the airplane, I looked down upon a carpet of crimson and gold leaves that sheltered the valley. Two months ago, we landed when night had already enshrouded the city. Now through a clear window in this huge metal vessel that was bringing me to Hartford I saw bundles of treetops burst their jewel colors of autumn's tapestry. Tears streaked my cheeks, each for one reason or another. One by one, they made small stains on my jacket like puddles I could hop across; pooled together, they spread before me a sea uncontainable and unfordable.

I was looking at the place where I had left my daughter not two full months ago. Yet since I'd departed, we'd each birthed new identities. As the plane banked and Hartford's tall gray buildings winked at me in the setting sun, at least one tear fell to honor Jada's sovereignty, others for the consequences. I packed a lot of emotions with me on this Parents' Weekend trip to Mary Hillyard; that they spilled over and onto my lap was a natural occurrence.

I was later than I was expected, later than the dinner that would be cold and packed away by the time I arrived. Passing motorists flashed their lights at me, but I couldn't figure out how to turn off the brights. Others followed closely behind, repeating a routine and impatient with me in their way.

I rolled the car onto a heap of leaves and bumped the tires into the curb. Lights spread on the front porch of Sarton Hall like a marquee. The front door was ajar, and a young woman at a desk asked, "Are you Jada's mom?"

"Yes, I'll just go back there..." I answered, pointing to the inside of the house.

She rose, exclaiming, "Oh, good; you're here! Jada's been checking. I'll go get her." She turned and said to another, "Go tell Jada her mom is here."

"Good! You're here! We've been waiting for you." She took me by the arm and repeated, "Jada's mom is here."

"Oh, good; she's been worried. Do you want me to tell her?"

"Here, I'll bring you in," said the voice at my side.

"I'll tell her," said another who came and darted back like a hummingbird.

Jada came winging to my side, joining the whirlwind of females fluttering about me.

"Hurry up; what took you so long? You're missing dinner." She pulled me with her, her eyes sparkling as if sprinkled with glitter.

"I'd like to wash up first. Can you show me where I can quickly freshen up?"

"Well, hurry up. They're waiting for you." Splashing my face, I wondered if when I got out of the dwarfish visitors' bathroom—the one and only one males were allowed to use—I'd hear that mournful voice she used on the telephone. It didn't look like she just couldn't make it any longer. I didn't feel like the mean old hag who forced her daughter to go away into a hell on earth.

One table was full, except for a single empty chair and an untouched place setting. Jada sat beside it. Jada made quick introductions. "This is my friend, Anna, and this is her mom. These are Houda, and Mary, and...well, you can finish up while I get some food for you."

As Jada pirouetted with plate in hand, a young face earnest with perfectly shaped gleaming teeth leaned toward me and offered her hand. Her greeting slid from her mouth like icing melting on a warm cinnamon roll. "Hi, I'm Rachel Franke. I'm so glad to finally meet you. Jada's been worried about you!" She raised her hands and clasped lacy fingers under her chin in a pose magazine-cover worthy. "I appreciated all the information you gave me on the telephone. I feel I'm really getting to know Jada and be sensitive to her needs."

She looked too young to be the first-year students' dean. "Thank you for calling me. I'm glad to know that someone here is aware of Jada's situation. Jada keeps up a brave front; she may never ask you for help, which makes it all the more important that there's someone watching out for her."

"Here, Mom," Jada chirped as she set a full plate before me. "I got some extra vegetables for you." Sitting down, Jada burbled about how I was such a freak about vegetables, which launched us into a discussion of food and cooking, my Christmas dinners, the next day's itinerary, and the respective careers we adults had followed. Anna's mother, who had done some work as a librarian, listened with curiosity as Rachel and I ventured into the teaching of writing. Rachel stated that writing was more like a journey of discovery than an end product to a predetermined plan, charted and outlined and neatly packaged, to which Jada nodded, adding, "That's what my mom says."

"She's gained greater control of her writing." From Rachel, that was high praise.

Jada squeezed my arm, affirming her proclamation. "My mom has taught me more about writing than any of my teachers in high school."

After drinking cups of lukewarm coffee and bidding a good evening to each of the departing table guests, I followed Jada down steep narrow steps to the labyrinthine basement that, like all basements, lay hidden and mysterious beneath a grand structure. When we reached the bottom step, Jada led the way beyond a corridor of dormitory rooms and past an unlit fenced-in storage space. There were pop machines somewhere around one of the corners, but I was too concerned to mark my path to notice the one Jada pointed out. "Don't leave me here alone," I begged.

"It's not scary. The only thing I don't like about it is the steps. I can't keep going up and down. If the machines are being used, it's really a bummer. See, it's not so bad." We had reached the end of the dimly lit hallway that opened into a square room surrounded by rough plaster walls. Two bare bulbs hanging from the ceiling shed light onto a cement floor. Along the far wall were the washers and dryers and laundry tubs. I dropped the basket of soiled clothing to the floor and opened the lid to the washer while Jada skimmed items from the top.

"These things I want hand-washed, so don't put them in. I usually do these upstairs in the sink, but since we've got them, you can do them down here." I loaded the washer and filled a tub with cool water while Jada dragged a high stool near the ironing board and hitched herself atop it. I swished suds out of the nylons and a delicate-looking wine-colored bra with cups hardly ample enough to cover her nipples and matching panties as scantily cut. Two discolored camisoles hung upside down from a thick cord anchored across one wall to another. "Okay, now what; do you hang them on this line?"

"Don't leave anything down here. People take things," Jada warned. "I let them dry in my room. It's so hot up there they dry in no time. Okay, now you can start ironing. I've been saving these for you." A smile twitched the corners of her mouth.

"Not too bad, having your own personal maid," I quipped.

Jada tilted her head to prove that her intentions were misunderstood. "You know how hard it is for me to stand, and these are so hard to iron. Besides, you do everything so well."

"Jada, I was just teasing." I filled the iron with water and pushed the dial to its highest setting for the brown corduroy Girbauds. "What else am I going to do anyway?" My nostrils, tingling with the smell of Tide, twitched as vapors of a jillion other fabrics were rekindled by the steam that spurted through the holes of the iron's hot surface.

"Remember that paper I talked to you about? This is what I have so far. I brought it down here so you can help me with it." Pushing the iron along the leg of Jada's favorite pants, I listened to her rough draft. In it she was building an argument against the morality of treating her cancer.

"Wow, Jada, this paper is much better organized than your others, even when they were finished."

"I tried to do it just like you said. You and Rachel say the same things, but in kinda different ways. Now, tell me what I have to do to it before I take it to her for our conference."

She had set up a contradiction between the so-called cure for her cancer that was supposed to restore her to "normal" life activities that had in fact just the opposite effect by excluding her from ordinary activities. "Get your reader to side with you. Bring in your real-life experiences, ones that your readers share. Provide concrete examples, like going to school and shopping and socializing. They will help to convince your readers that what is keeping you alive is keeping you from living. And there are the usual rough spots—you know, when your sentences get tangled up with wordy expressions."

"Find those for me. How do I fix them?"

"I'll find some now, but you will begin to find them yourself as you rewrite. The best advice I can give is to go back to what you wrote and be the reader. I think the hardest thing about writing is that our brains 'get it' whole, and we don't realize that our reader hasn't gone through the process we have. Just saying, for example, that you have to get your mother to do your washing and ironing isn't enough." The ironing board creaked with pressure. Jada's chin jutted toward me and her eyes locked. "Okay," I said, shrugging a shoulder, "wrong example. But you know what I mean. They don't know what you don't get them to know or feel for themselves."

"Okay, Mom, I get it. Here, find a sentence or two that I need to fix." She handed the pen to me as if it were a magic wand, and I read over the first page, dutifully underlining and writing, 'say more,' or 'do you mean…' and correcting the spellings of several words. Precision and clarity she could develop with time, but she'd always be off a letter when she wrote words.

The washer rattled as it began the final spin cycle and water gushed out of the rubber spout splashing its chorus in spurts against the fiberglass basin. Jada eased herself from the stool and said, "When you put those things in the dryer, don't dry them all the way. And leave the light on when you go. It's supposed to stay on all the time. I'll be in my room when you come up."

I had grown so used to Jada's gait that nothing about the way she placed her toes down first and shifted the fall of her weight through her hips to the forward motion of her torso seemed any more unusual than the crooked fingers on her left hand. Her jerky ambulation, thrusting herself forward as bone ground against bone, dominated her presentation. She could have translated her pain differently: she could have demanded a wheelchair.

Late Saturday afternoon the setting sun's energy couldn't stretch all the way to warm us. Earlier in the morning, picking up kazoos, washboards, pots and spoons from a bucket, we held band practice in the stands of the playing field for the upcoming rugby game. Mary Hillyard had its stables and its riding paths, but they were tucked away, back along a narrow road for more sophisticated students. It was the 80s and tough ruled. Rowing and rugby let the aggressor out of these very competitive women. The teams wore their school names, but the games were unofficial; women arrived by vans, unloaded their gear and their beer and played by the rules of the tough colleges: work hard, play hard. We arrived back in Jada's dorm room cold and worn.

I hadn't planned on spending the day outdoors, driving up to the top of Mt. Loudon and walking about the site of the famous painting, the old hotel, and President Lincoln's address and then returning to the playing field. Instead, I had dressed respectably, proper shoes, proper coat, without regard for warmth. Like the sun, I was worn out from shining without heat and wanted to sink behind some cover. Jada slouched onto her bed to give her legs room to stop screaming, and I remained standing, my shoulders tensed with cold, my coat still buttoned, wishing a bucket of hot air to be dumped in my face. "I'm renting an apartment in November. I can't stay in the house any longer."

Jada peered up from the mattress. "What about me?"

"When you come home you can stay there with me. It's just an efficiency, but I can pull the bed out. There's a pool and a courtyard, and even a little putting green for Dom, in nice weather, of course."

"You should have left him a long time ago. But now I don't think it's the right time. I don't think you've thought about how this affects me."

"Jada, if I don't go now, I'm stuck forever. Remember when we talked about your coming out East? You could have chosen the safe route and stayed close to home. But you would always have been unhappy not knowing what you could have done. I face time limits, too. I don't want to be an old lady when I start to live again. I know it's the right thing to do."

There followed a giant silence, a silence in which one could have flashed a whole lifetime, after which Jada sat up and sighed, "Oh, why can't you just stay here? Can't you get a job as the cook? You said you'd always support me."

I took my coat off and lay it over the chair. "That's the last thing you need is your mother hanging around." I took my wedding rings off, they were a set of three, lusterless in the yellow-lighted room, and filled a plastic bucket with Ivory liquid. "I'll do those dishes now. Here, Jada, it's not me, but it's a part of me." I wriggled my finger out of a ring, and with my hands dripping soapy dishwater, I handed forth the ring, two milky white studs nestled on either side of a pearl, my birthstone, in a platinum setting. "This is yours to keep so that you'll know you'll always have me."

Jada placed the ring on her index finger and held out her arms for me. We held each other, I blinking back tears, she brightening with her new prize. "You'd better hurry up with those dishes if you're going to get back in time for tonight."

I left Mary Hillyard on Sunday, carrying home out-of-season shorts and shirts and the feeling of having not left Jada with enough warmth and protection to stay without me. How different from September when the year spread before her like a new wardrobe. I left an old body that didn't fit the new style.

Back at home, my new home, my experiment in sovereignty took root while I listened to Jada's fretfulness; her grades, she forewarned me, would not be what she was used to; all the other women did these great things, like climb Mt. Louden on Mountain Day, that she couldn't do; no one cared. "And I don't want to hear how everyone else is homesick or how awkward it is to make friends. It's just different here," she lamented. "And it's not going to be any better when I get home, either. I don't have any friends there; nobody ever writes to me; and how can I make plans to do anything when my whole time is taken up with doctors and IVs and CAT scans, and X-rays, and you, you're in an apartment. I'd rather have hell at home than go home and have you not in it."

I listened on Jada's doughnut-shaped telephone, her telephone in my apartment with the variegated shaggy carpet and the area rugs I scattered about, bandages on ugly wounds. I borrowed the vacuum cleaner—I had bought it, and now I borrowed it—Saturdays to comb the strands and make them stand up, but nothing could smooth their rough texture. A flannel sheet covering the walk-out door that had no walk out to walk out to was slung open, and I listened to the roar of swiftly spinning wheels on freeway pavement while the flannel sheet rippled and trembled. I had moved into the apartment to be near my son in the quiet suburbs; and what did I have but whrr-yun-yun-yun-yeen-yeen of vehicles, the tire treads thrum-rm-rm-rm-rm-thwaping as if microphones were strung along the freeway, the speakers posted in my one room. I told Jada I'd pick her up at the airport.

Convinced that the only way I could pay rent, child support, tuition, and Jada's airfares, I took another job. That made three, teaching day school, teaching night classes, and sewing visors and curtains at a van conversion company. Still, I had taken the whole Thanksgiving weekend off while Jada was home. Walking into the apartment, Jada valiantly overlooked its sparseness; I hadn't a kitchen table or even a chair. My daybed was the couch in the living room, adjoining the kitchen, wide enough only to open the oven door while standing behind it, and scarcely longer. She and Dom put on their swimming suits and I sat at a poolside table while they slapped at the water. We played a game, and I drove them both back to the house.

I drove Jada to the airport on Sunday and waited for the calling of her seat number. "Maybe there'll be a bomb on the plane," she mumbled as the line of people dwindled.

Walking up to the ticket-taker, I brushed a kiss on the side of her head and slid my arm down her shoulder. She bent a little, her hard body moving against its will. "It's only for a month, you know. You'll like it when you get there."

"No, I won't. Mom, you just don't understand." I released her, and she held out her ticket, walking onto the ramp while I watched her go away. *You can come back, you know.* But could she any more than I could go back to Arnold and live a life forever caged, like a circus bear? The month between Thanksgiving and her winter vacation, I felt as smothered by her dumping anger and grief and bitterness on me as my car after a night's snowfall.

"Jada, maybe that's not the place for you," I suggested into the phone. "You could take a semester off if it's really that awful for you. No one is making you go there or anywhere else."

"What would I do there if I didn't go to school? You don't have a place for me."

331

"If you did come home, I'd get a place for you. I just want you to know what you want."

"Oh, I don't know what I want." Jada had the luxury to vent in privacy, alone in her room. "Why did you have to make me like this? Why did you make me want to go to school? To be independent?"

"I never told you you had to go to school."

"No, you never told me, but I always felt you expected it. I always felt I had to get good grades. I had to be perfect, just for you. You have such high standards."

"I'm sorry, Jada. I didn't mean to make life hard for you." Apologetically I added, "I expect a lot from everybody. Me, too."

"Yeah, that's why you can't ask for anything. Not everybody can be as strong as you. Don't you know I can't do it? I don't have what you have."

"Jada, just look at what you have done already! I'm a wimp. I was too afraid to go away to school. All the time my counselor was telling me about this scholarship, all I could think of was, how will I get there? How would I get home? How will I get to a job? I've been dependent all my life up until I moved out of the house. And you know what? It was you who showed me the way. For the first time I said to myself, I don't want to die not having lived an adventure. I had to be forty-one to say that. You're living an adventure at eighteen."

The space that separated us hummed with suspended breath until broken with a voice in a bucket of tears. "Mom, you've got the wrong person. I'm not what you think I am."

"Maybe, but...but, maybe you don't see yourself for who you really are. You have people who believe in you. Well, you have a couple weeks to think about taking some time off. You can hold on a couple weeks, can't you?"

"I have to go now, Mom. I promised to help someone with her French."

"Okay, Sugar Plum. I love you." The phone clicked; I had said all I could without telling her what to do and spent the next few minutes preparing for my first guest, a young colleague from school. With the Thanksgiving turkey, I made soup and spread a dishtowel on the floor for Jessie and me.

Dec. 7th

I've been here for almost a whole semester! It's been fun and productive and hard, also. I judged a debate round, and I think I did it well even though I didn't know what to expect at first and want to judge another. I also held old books from 1869 and a songbook from 1917 in the history room of the library—it was fascinating. I love those "oldies" and want to do more research. I went with eight others to Princeton and stayed with Eric and other guys. We dove to NYC and went up and down Madison and Columbus Avenues and some other streets. NYC and Boston are my favorite cities! I knew I was meant to live here in the East. It is so exhilarating! We also stopped at a bar near Columbia University. I wasn't on a date or anything, but still je me suis amusée. Traveling to other schools helps me feel more "collegiate" even though it takes away time from doing my schoolwork. I love going to places and seeing things and being involved with more than going to classes. I have a hard time keeping up with what I have to do and with doing things that attach me to what brings me happiness. I have to keep trying to get my life together and not let uncertainty control me.

Some people here make it hard for me to feel I can connect and survive another semester. They can be inconsiderate and just NASTY! I don't have real friends here, just acquaintances. I miss Moo! She said I "looked good here," but I feel so lonesome. Sometimes I get a warm fuzzy from someone, but mostly I feel that no one here cares about me. I need someone besides my moo who loves me back the way I love them. Like a boyfriend! I liked going to the concert with a bunch of women who invited me, and I need more friends like that who keep me going and hype me up with hugs and companionship. I write to everyone but I get a piddle of mail back. I think that's why I'm so depressed. Mom says she's proud of me, but maybe I shouldn't be here. Maybe I shouldn't come back.

Dec. 9th

I have been studying hard for days, and it's tiring me out but I don't have to think much about how hard it is for me to survive here. I got a lot done for calc and French while I worked in the library. I don't have the drive to excel in French which worries me because I heard French 221 has a lot of writing, and that's the worst for me, especially at this level. I have to get some garbage about Northanger Abbey on paper so when I go for a help session I have something to improve on. Mrs. Smith says I am analytic and express good ideas but writing for classes causes fear in me. I need mom to encourage me. I wish she could be with me forever and give me strength.

I really like Susan Allan Toth. No man could write like she does. I can relate to how she tells about sexism and oppression in her life. The opposite of Kimby. In her letter she sounds just like the passive girl-servant to men's expectations. I can't think about how women's roles have been affected by men and how they get all the benefits from limiting us. In Politics of Patriarchy we looked at how women's language is different, We can't speak aggressively or else we are called bitches. But men? When they are aggressive, they're showing their strength! Uggh! The world is a horrible place and I have nothing to look forward to. No purpose. No goal. There must be some reason for me to be here and to go on and take challenges, but I just feel like a jerk who can't take responsibility. If I had a friend, or a boyfriend! who could help me feel positive and intelligent and charismatic, we could do things together on a regular basis. I really don't feel I'm up to the challenge of college life here. I just want to go home to be with my mom. We belong together. We're a team.

Dec. 11th

I want to be done with this semester and be home! It's not long but it's still ten days until I sleep in my own bed. I'm excited to be there but worried about not having a base to return to. Dad is trying to bribe me to love him and pity him. I do pity him but it's because he doesn't ever change. I think that's the main reason Mom separated from him, and he doesn't get what's really going on. Well, I'm not giving in. Still, I think Mom has changed and I worry that she won't be there for me. Maybe it's me, too, because I hate that she's getting old. I don't like the thought of old age and don't want to be old myself. Well, I don't want to grow up period! All I have gotten is more pain, problems, and disappointment. I think I was supposed to die and keeping me alive is against nature and making it harder and slower for me to die. I like to feel energetic and accepted. What's the use with trying to stay here in this condition? All I feel is lonesomeness and behind in everything and depressed. I am in so much pain emotionally and physically that it's hard for me to keep up. Mom says that it's "normal" to feel weary and behind in everything but that just makes me madder. I don't care what everyone else feels. I want sympathy and help! I think that the love-hate relationship between mother and daughter in "Somewhere, Belgium" by Jamaica Kincaid is a lot like mine. She wrote about how she wondered if it was worth it to live like she did. But also I want to live, as she did, too! It's too confusing, and all I can say is I'm two different people! I'm confused and torn apart with wanting to be normal and wanting to die. I need help with my many many problems and my depression. I have no one! Why can't I just go home and die? It's all horseshit!

Dec. 20th

This is the next to the last page in this journal containing some new thoughts and some old continuing ones. Reasons to commit suicide and some thoughts about why I don't. Most of the ways are gross. They probably wouldn't work anyway. Are my expectations too high? Having a boyfriend? Not to depend on but someone to give me a little support and to love me back. People say I'm "wonderful," so why not? Having a solution to my hip and shoulder pain? It's so hard to fit in here when I can't do physical activities like ride bikes or take a dance class or even walk up steps! My body has turned against me! The world has restricted me enough, and now my body is restricting me physically and psychologically even more! Maybe there'll be new joints to replace these pained and grinding hacks. They are killing me! That's what would really make me happy. Shit! The world is so confusing and unpredictable that I can't make plans for myself. I hope the vacation break—no, I don't hope for anything anymore. So what's ahead for the next three weeks? Mary Hillyard, home I go!

I had a small flocked tree, decorated with ornaments Jada and I had made over the years, propped on an overturned box. She and Dom bought me a wooden chair, which made two for my two knives, two forks, and two spoons to set a borrowed card table.

Not knowing what to recreate of all the Christmases past, nor wanting a harbinger of Christmases of the future, this Christmas became a hinge between what was known and what unknown was to be. Arnold wanted the pretense of a family on Christmas, and unable or unwilling to understand, I agreed to sign our names to the gifts and to live Christmas Eve and Christmas morning as we had for nineteen years.

Riding home from Maureen's, I complimented the gift from Dom's aunt and uncle. "They know what you like, don't they, Dommy?" Christmas carols played on the radio, and we arrived home cocooned in the shadow of tradition, its nostalgia having power to mythologize it even as a new tradition grew in its place, like a new cactus growing in the protection of a tree it will ultimately outlive.

I sang, first to Jada, then to Dom, and sat in the kitchen sipping syrupy Amaretto, allowing them time to fall asleep, surveying the plates on the wall, porcelain figures, some bought for me, or for me in mind, at least in pretense, denying myself a snoop through cupboards and cabinets for things I used to handle; some I had made myself. Arnold stayed downstairs, out of tradition, until he heard the crackle of paper bags.

The carpeting muffled the creaks of his feet falling on the steps and he stood, hovering over my distributions on the floor. "Have you got everything?" he asked.

"They wanted small things," I replied, arranging a Stratomatic game and a golf club next to Dom's stocking bulging with surprises that crowded toward the toe. The two long stockings I latched over andirons, morning signs that Santa had come and left them with his other leavings at the base of the fireplace. Hambone's stocking Santa had filled with a ribbon, and my stocking—Jada had sewn it for me, spelling out "MOM" in glittering sequins across the top band —remained on the mantel for Jada to fill with a surprise note or trinket on Christmas Day.

At the rustle of bags and tissue paper wrappings, I expected Jada or Dom to pad out of their dark bedrooms to catch me hot-handed. They never had. I had no funny Christmas stories starring any of us to tell them when they became adults. Unless, of course, this wry Christmas tale counted, in which I was invited to a sleepover at my family's house. I slept on the blue foam-stuffed pallet, covered by a Raggedy Ann and Andy sheet next to Jada's bed.

The holiday over, we resumed our new routine, and added an orthopedic clinic to the circuit. Open and airy, the waiting room reminded me of a train station, except it was a contemporary building and carpeted in maroon, and we weren't leaving town, just the house on Lambert Lane. Jada muttered in her seat and looked menacingly toward the large circular reception desk, where a traveler might have bought a ticket to anywhere. Every time a nurse came through the door with a chart in hand and called someone else's name, Jada marked passage. "Half an hour," she announced, holding her wrist mid-air as proof, though even up close I could barely read the small, dainty face with only the numbers 12, 3, 6, and 9.

Jada pushed herself out of the wine-covered chair and walked her peculiar way to the receptionist who swiveled about an enclosure; either she had to agree to meet a client where she stood or the client had to skirt the counter in a kind of chase to catch the receptionist head on. Jada stood midway, a political position that put her in the receptionist's peripheral sight; the receptionist glided on her wheels a wee bit to accommodate her. Jada returned to her chair, her face taut, reined in.

"What did she say?" I asked.

"Oh, you know, how busy they are. So I said they shouldn't schedule so many patients at one time if they can't get them all in."

"I don't suppose she liked that. Did she apologize?"

"No." Sarcasm oozed from the word as Jada's eyes rolled upward, her eyelids fluttering like tappings in code. "If I don't get in there soon, I'm leaving."

"Actually, we'd be doing them a favor; let's stay." Soon, relatively, a bustling nurse herded us down a long hall, turning backwards and stopping for us to catch up. Ironic, I thought, that she exuded impatience with Jada's slow pace. After Jada's return from X-ray, Dr. Ritter knocked on the door. "Sit up on the table," he directed. In his left hand was a small black device that I identified as a tape recorder. Into it he said, "Twelve-twenty-nine. Patient Jada Petersen." He looked up momentarily. He used some technical descriptors of the angles of the X-rays and concluded, "condition of the deterioration of the bone mass only marginally worse. Recommend review of case in six months." Deftly he nudged the machine off and put it in his pocket, the process completed so seamlessly that I was not aware it had steps until I had to remember what happened; pivoting toward the door, he vanished.

All of a sudden I could see through his place to Jada, her legs bent over the edge of the table. Between her thighs, where the denim seams would scratch against each other like fire stick on fire stick if she could walk fast enough to create friction, lay her hands. She raised them in supplication, screwed her eyes around like pinwheels. "I don't know," I replied.

We waited in the room until a nurse swung the door open and stared at us, not at Jada, not at me, but at us, a scene. "Is Dr. Ritter coming back?" I asked.

"Oh, no. He's very busy."

"But I had some questions for him," Jada protested.

The nurse clicked her teeth together as her eyes traveled around the room; she had come expecting not to find us there. "Well, I'll see if I can catch him in the hall, but I just hate to interrupt him." I had the feeling that if Jada didn't have some prize-winning questions the gong would sound and we'd be expelled from the temple of the great wizard, never to have another chance at bidding his favor. Not Jada. She raised her chin and ran the middle section of her index finger like a brush under her nose and sniffed. The nurse leaned back into the room, saying, "Okay, follow me." Jada did, in her fashion. I started out, too, but grabbed her coat from the table and straggled behind.

When I caught up to them, Dr. Ritter was running a pointer along the brownish green film attached to the lighted X-ray screen almost as wide and half as tall as a theater backdrop. All along the top border were clasped semi-opaque celluloid sheets with shadows of body parts, images that could and probably would survive longer than the real things they outlined. Looking on, I could make out only some of the words he spoke into his hand-held microphone and I didn't know if he was talking to Jada or the image of her pelvic girdle in front of him. I contented myself with a sideways view of his drawing circles and half-moons with the end of his pointer stick while, occasionally, I heard his voice pause ever so slightly. Jada's eyes stared upwards at herself—part of herself—while Dr. Ritter dictated, and then he made that same closing movement with his hand and let it, along with the device in it, fall from his mouth. Then he was gone, not physically, but gone as in done. His presence was turned elsewhere and the nurse slid between their bodies and hovered at Jada's side. There would be no more curtain calls, it was made very clear.

"You know, I don't think he even knows about me," Jada mused in the car. "He says stuff like maybe I'm going to grow new legs or something."

"What?"

"I don't mean really, but you know. He reminds me of Dr. Randolph." Jada made a face I could not mistake, even from my peripheral vision, as for a bad smell suddenly released. "'We'll just stand here and watch it get worse and worse, it's only your arm or your legs, everything will be okay,' right! Did you see how old everyone was there?" I admitted to stealing surreptitious glances, pretending to be looking beyond heads of frizzy ratted hair to a doorway or down at the pattern of the carpet when really I wanted to see shoes. What people wore and did with their feet told a lot about them. Jada concluded, "I'm tired of being told what I should be happy with. Can't they see I'm not an old hag? It's not worth it to me if I can't live the way I want to live."

In the wake of Jada's statement, the car moved noiselessly through the winter streets, no slapping slush against the underbody, growing brown behemoths that clung, frozen sloths behind the tires. We were lucky this year—I was lucky this year without a garage—that there were very few snowfalls, for Minnesota. I hadn't been stuck in a four-foot snowbank and only once had to set the alarm for 2:00 a.m. to get out from snug blankets and into pitch dark and eye-icing cold to start my engine and run it until the needle on the dashboard pointed to warm. I drove silently over clear pavement, unmindful of ice patches and ice ruts. Before my eyes were images. In one Jada's visage seared the canvas with a passion for living; another scared me with its suffocating heaviness like viscous quicksand being vomited all over it. Something about Jada's smeared face stirred uneasiness in me. She had plans for herself that others did not.

Maybe that's the struggle of life for everyone. Only Jada's fortune was to learn early on, while others sniffed out a smoother course, blaming the devil for messing up their plans and thanking God for working in mysterious ways for things turning to their advantage, smelling their own sweetness. How this struggle came down on me would be my own survival story.

Jada made calls on the telephone while I sat in the kitchen. If her friends weren't available for the evening, she was going to pack a bag and spend the night with me. Arnold came up from downstairs and asked to settle the Christmas gift bills. "I don't know exactly, but make it $400 total and pay me half," I said.

"How do I know you spent $400.00 on those presents?" he accused.

"You're kidding me! Simple head calculations for one thing. But I've got receipts—most of them. It'll probably come out to more." I pulled my wallet from my pocket and dug through the papers crammed in with the dollar bills.

"You must be counting your gifts, too. How can you spend $400 just from Santa?"

"Here!" I unfolded a half sheet of paper, wrinkled from handling, rough where it had torn. "These are the things I bought from us and how much I paid for them."

Arnold cleared his throat. "That doesn't prove anything. How do I know that's what you paid?" My shoeless feet went from cold to numb. I wanted to pelt him for every penny's worth of happiness he'd ever tried to pinch from someone else, resentment for my generosity toward Arnold rising from my stomach like bile, and all I could do was sit in my puffy black down-filled coat like some bloated penguin and try to keep my voice from shaking.

"You really are something! That just goes to show you how much you've bought for them over the past eighteen years. I've done the planning and the shopping and taken care of everything and you've come along as usual at the end and had me sign your name! Four hundred dollars is cheap. I paid over $300 for her college ring alone, and you weren't even charged for that!"

"Idina, don't get so angry. I have every right to ask for proof. I have bills to take care of and things to worry about, too." The creases above Arnold's lip grew deep.

"Question me! After I split my mother's gift with you! That check had my name on it, not yours; I gave *you* more than what I'm asking back. And you think I'm cheating you. You have this house and everything in it; I'm the one with nothing. I'm the one who's working three jobs, and you have the nerve to accuse me of cheating you. Boy, now I know what Patti meant when she said you hadn't paid your fair share in Europe."

"What are you talking about?"

"You've got a funny sense of fairness! Kept telling me I couldn't have anything I wanted, but we sure got things you wanted. And you call my mother cheap! She denies herself along with everyone else. Here I am paying for Jada's plane fares and dorm needs, and you have the nerve to want to see every goddamned last sales slip. Don't pay anything then, return 'em if you want. Get out of my way; I'm getting out of here!"

The sleeves of my coat swished back and forth as I walked the hall to Jada's room, swish, swish, swinging my arms, rubbing one bad memory against another, each one losing another layer of dusty grimy pretense and glowing with new awareness. Jada sat on her bed, her telephone book open beside her.

"What are you two fighting about now?"

"Nothing. If you're coming with me, let's go."

"No, it's not nothing. What is it?"

"Oh, just money. He says he doesn't owe me what he owes me. I have to get out of here before I really get mad and lose it."

"I'll get it for you. I'll just threaten to kill him."

"Jada, I know you don't mean that, so why even talk that way? Besides, I don't think you want to spend your life in jail."

"Good, then I wouldn't have to go back to school."

"You know what I've told you: you can always take some time off. If it's that bad…." Jada closed her book as if swatting a fly, and

I flinched inside my jacket, bunched up around me; I felt like a charred marshmallow. "Did I ever tell you about Totsy?"

"What's that, another one of the books you read?"

"No, he was one of my students. Totsy wanted to be a hit man."

"So why are you telling me that now?"

"Oh, I just remembered him now. Here you are, sorting through pages of a teddy bear telephone book, making cold threats." Jada shrugged. "Well, what's the deal; are you coming back with me or not?"

"I guess. Daniel called," meaning he called Kimby, which is why she wasn't available to Jada, who tossed the book onto her desk, landing with a thud on the name. "She's such a sucker for Daniel; she does anything he says. I don't know why I put up with her. She always says we're best buddies and then she dumps me but not him."

"Why *do* you keep up with her then? Almost every time you talk about her you're mad at her."

"I know it. She asks me to tell her what she can do to be a good friend, and she gets all sorry and everything. I wrote her a long letter telling her what she does that makes me so mad. But still she never calls. She always complains about having no money. But her dad pays her whole tuition; she has a car. And when I come home and I'm sick, I still have to fit in around her schedule, and now Daniel." Squinting her eyes, Jada made her voice tiny. "She has a little time for me tomorrow afternoon." With renewed vigor, she pushed herself off the mattress and plucked clothing from a drawer, dropping a nightshirt, a pair of panties, socks into her bag. "She's so boring. She never wants to do anything fun or spend any money. It's just sit and talk; now, instead of at her house, it's at her dorm."

"Well, I'm afraid it's going to be the same with me tonight, except, I'll be sewing your suit."

We stopped for chicken sandwiches and French fries. In one hand I carried the warm bag; in the other, Jada's tote. We ate our meal at the wiggly card table, covered with a square table cloth with

German dancers along the border and red flowers popping out in the middle; our plates wobbled on the warped surface.

I rather enjoyed my meager accoutrements, especially the ones people donated to me. Another teacher gave me a toaster and, with it, her own story of having nothing but a refrigerator and five small children when her husband moved out of her life. "It's kind of like playing house," she said. "You get to do everything from the beginning." The sparseness of my surroundings reminded me to enjoy my adventure and have what I wanted, even if it was nothing more than a second-hand toaster, not be boxed in by Arnold's choice of stoneware, his porcelain, his desk, his wife, another piece in his collection of things to make his life comfortable. Finished with our sandwiches, I began sewing.

"Let's go out to Albert's together!" Jada blurted above the whir of the sewing machine motor. "Call Akiko and see what she's doing."

"You're not even 21 yet."

"I've got into Albert's before. I bet if I went in with you, no one would ask me."

"I'd say probably the opposite." I picked the pins from my pursed lips, taking time to envision the evening. What if I was asked to dance with someone and she wasn't? The whole night spread itself out, one nasty scene following another, beginning with her being carded and ending with an aborted party. "But it doesn't matter anyway; Akiko is already gone somewhere. She plans her nights weeks in advance. Look at the time. It's way after nine."

"Call her anyway. Take a chance." Her words sounded more like a taunt than a temptation.

I dialed Akiko's number and left her a message. To Jada I suggested a card game.

"I hate this place. How could you do this to me? You said you'd never leave me." Rumbles of thunder rolled through Jada's words.

"I'm sorry you think I've deserted you. I didn't leave you; I left the house."

"Well, what do you think that is? I can't stay here; you don't have anything for me here."

"No, I guess I don't, but what would we be doing at home?" I got up to brush my teeth, and Jada followed; we were almost face to face.

"You should have stuck it out longer. I don't have a home anymore. It's all your fault!"

Her face strained with anger, and the blue drained from her eyes as she narrowed them at me. "Just imagine for a minute what it would be like if we were at home," I said. "Do you think there would be peace and happiness? That there wouldn't be any fighting? No one would be left alive!"

When I came out of the bathroom, Jada was waiting, a pillar of solidified anger. "You're mean to put me through this! You should have let me die."

"No, Jada, I shouldn't have let you die. That has nothing to do with this. And keep your voice down; these walls are thin and we're close to the door." We were in a traffic jam, both of us moving stop-and-go with each utterance. "Excuse me, Jada, I have to move these things." I put my arm between her and the end of the bed, intending to pull out the trundle and make it up.

"Bitch!" she yelled, resisting my attempt to wedge between her and the bed. "You deserted me. You promised! Take me back to the house." Her body had the tension of flight, and I met her resistance, stepped forward. She followed, her arms rising, and we collided.

Jada dropped onto the floor, her arms still aimed at the ceiling, like shooting stars before they arc and fall sizzling through the atmosphere. I could have fallen, too, had the wall not been at my back. "You pushed me!" she cried. I was nearly convinced that I had, for I felt the impact of our two bodies, our two wills. I held out my hands to Jada, but she spurned my offer with shrieks of vilification. "Get away from me! You pushed me. How could you do that?"

"No, Jada. No. I didn't push you. We need help! Look at us. How can we get along this way?"

Jada lay on the shaggy carpet, her elbows digging into the warp, the fibers crawling up her sleeves to burrow into her skin. She sobbed and shouted and wailed, "You're a bitch! You pushed me down! Get away, you bitch!"

"I'm sorry. I don't know what to do." The pages of my telephone book quivered as my shaky fingers searched for Beverly's number. Jada looked up at me, perhaps considering the prospect of an audience, perhaps curious at whose number I dialed, what I'd say, perhaps just interrupted. "She won't stop. She keeps screaming at me, saying I pushed her."

From the floor Jada listened, cried, "You did! You pushed me! How could you do that!"

"Call 911," Beverly said. "Will you do that? Don't talk to her anymore. Just do it. Tell them that she's out of control and that you need help to restrain her. Do that now, and call me back."

Dropping the phone to its bed, but leaving my hand on it as a cudgel, I warned, "If you don't stop screaming and yelling, I'm calling 911."

"What! Why?" Jada's incredulous voice demanded. "Who would come? What would they do?" she asked, her voice gradually decreasing in volume, raising herself to a sitting position.

"I don't know. Maybe they'll take you for help. But I can't do anything anymore." Jada rose from the floor and sat on the bed next to me as if we had just rehearsed a scene together.

"You could have hurt me."

"I'm sorry, Jada. It was an accident. I didn't mean for that to happen. Sometimes I feel like I'm just sticking my finger into leaky holes, and I can't keep patching them up; there's too much pressure."

"That's how I feel, too. You have to get a place for us, Mom." Her face was dry; her voice, too.

"I'm worried. Look at what happened tonight. Maybe it's not a good idea for us to be so close."

"Oh that!" Jada clamped her jaw, a blue vein running like a cold stream over the bone and under her chin. "That's just you and me. We'll always fight." She bounced up from the mattress into the bathroom, the action seeming to flush the incident from her mind. Somehow, I was missing the one piece that made sense of what happened between us, the piece she evidently possessed, a priestess gifted with supernatural vision. I stuffed the incident into my crowded closet of unsolved mysteries. Some day I'd take it out, expose it to the light of wisdom, someday.

Eating was always the first thing Jada did in the morning, her eyes still groggy with sleep, her voice yet unused. She chewed mouthfuls carefully, so unlike the rest of us, her jaws moving in segmented starts and stops as if hooked together by rusty hinges. She didn't seem to mind that her cinnamon toast grew cold. Sometimes her spoon, brimful with milk and woven pillows of Life cereal hovered mid-flight between the bowl and her mouth as she studied a picture on the cereal box. Or she'd stop chewing. She loved breakfast that much.

I poured milk onto the mound of cereal, watching. Dom overfilled his bowl, and when he bobbed cereal puffs with his spoon, the milk spilled over the rim. Jada seemed to know the correct ratio of cereal to milk to bowl. She signaled to stop pouring, for she had the final say. It was her cereal. And it was her morning. She was also slow to wake up to the day, the breakfast ritual being to her what coffee was to me. In between spoonfuls she said, "I don't want to go back on Friday."

I approached, cautiously. "Ever?"

"No, just not Friday. Can't you return that ticket and get another one for a later day?"

"I would have to forfeit half of the ticket's price. Why do a few days make such a difference?"

"I'm just not ready to go back. I made a mistake when I picked the date. It's interim and I didn't know you didn't have to be there. A lot of people won't be, and I can't stand to be there alone. I don't really want to be there at all."

My mother's voice, Arnold's, too, spoke both at once, telling me why I couldn't give in. "Okay, let's say I buy you a ticket for another day. What if you say you don't want to go back then?"

"It'll be okay then. I'll go back."

"I'll see what I can do." After breakfast, I drove Jada to the house and returned with the vacuum cleaner. The unfairness of having to borrow what was mine wasn't nearly so strong a feeling as what I'd have to pay in personal identity to keep it. I had nowhere to store the monstrosity anyway. It was meant for a house, not a one-room patch of hairy rugging. I called Northwest Airlines for alternative flights to Hartford.

In the airport we walked the gold concourse, and while we had left her luggage at the check-in counter, we towed eighteen years of our joint baggage with us and sat side by side, waiting for the call of her flight number. The rows containing Jada's seat were announced, and I shivered waiting for her to stand. As three people remained in line, she picked up her bag with Hambone crowning its contents, and I followed, holding out her coat. "Call me when you get back," I said. My other arm reached around her, a column of poured concrete that I was trying to enfold like a spring sapling.

She zig-zagged down the ramp and crept along the rail, and even after the flight attendant closed the door to the jetway I turned around to see that she wasn't sneaking up behind me. I could imagine her surging into the aisle and hobbling to the cockpit, ordering the pilot to let her off. I watched the plane back up, begin its taxi to the runway. I watched the sky, watched planes climb into a distance until I could watch nothing any longer. Everything outside me proved she was gone, but something inside me believed I had to be there to accept her. Slowly retracing my steps through the concourse, I listened for the announcement of my name on the public speaker.

In a way, I was right. Jada's presence in my apartment, in my car, as I found myself with quiet moments, clotted the air like fog. Everything I saw and heard of her seeped through the filter of her sadness. We talked on the telephone, someone's knock on the door taking her away, some place to go on her schedule. The best of her, the Jada without disease, the Jada who had a future, the Jada with the friendly strong voice greeting her friends, who pretended to act like her college mates, stayed in Massachusetts, while growing inside her like the lump of cancer that refused expulsion, was her sadness that she poured out to me.

"Mom, I really can't take this anymore. They've got to do something about my legs. If you were here, you could help me."

"How is that? You'd still have to get to classes."

"You could do my laundry. I try to ask someone here to help carry it down the steps, but I feel funny doing that. You could drive me to Goodrich so I don't have to walk to the bus. And you could sing to me at night and kiss me and tell me how much you love your baby."

"Well, that I'd like."

"No, really, Mom. You could come here in March when you're on vacation. You could be here at Easter. You know what? You could stay in the dorm. Lots of people sleep over. Okay, Mooie? See if you can get a ticket."

I agreed to investigate and also to making an appointment with Dr. Ritter at Jada's next trip home. She felt relief in doing something concrete, taking another grab at hope.

I savored the sound. "Ma." My dad and Dom each addressed their mothers with the same clipped syllable, not drawn out and nasal like Mom, or sappy and showy like Mumsy, or trendy Idina. Dom was so much like his grandfather, I'd have sworn he was my dad reincarnated, a continuation of his spirit. During the few years they shared on this earth, Dom had little opportunity to study my dad, hardly ever seeing him when he wasn't pacing or sleeping or rubbing his big bovine hand around his speckled brownish face the way he mopped the restaurant floor. Dom looked like my dad, my dad young, dark brown eyes the color of rich newly unearthed farmland set either side of the crooked nose, not my dad's aged skin being dragged away from the bones of his cheeks by the weight of his coarse gray beard. Tall, big-boned and beefy with hair everywhere except for the top of his head, my dad was bald when he married my mother, and I wondered if Dom would go bald, too.

He was only fourteen, and I looked into his future as if he were a spinning image in a crystal ball. I wondered how different he and I would be if Jada hadn't been sick. If he listened to his dad, and I was sure he did, he could blame every ill in our lives on Jada's leukemia, but I gave more credit to Dom. He had to make sacrifices, but his life was all he knew. The fact that he never wanted to talk about these very personal matters meant probably that they weren't very personal to him after all. Or, he was like his grandfather and just plain didn't see the point in using a whole lot of words on anything. Life, down to its barest minimum was a soundless flash, and any words blown at it were like the whoosh of breath that disturbs the oxygen from the flame of a candle.

Dom liked a little warning but not until the details had the firmness of Jello able to suspend fruit dropped into it. I didn't tell him I was looking for a new home, a permanent home; he already knew I wasn't coming back. On a Saturday, a sunny clear afternoon, I gathered the Backgammon pieces from the green carpet in the living room while Dom talked on the phone, putting a game of snow football together at Jerry's. My shoulder and neck hurt from holding a position of the floor too long, and I thought back to all the times Dom and I played in this spot and how Jada didn't think I was teaching him how to deal with competition when I stacked the cards to my disadvantage. I had played cribbage with my mother, and even when I had a good hand, she had one better. She also loved to win, counting out her pegs on the board by fives and tens, cooing to the cards in her crib as if they were puppies. I figured Dom had enough chances to lose when the competition was even, so why lose to me?

I wedged the boxed game onto the closet shelf. "All set?"

"We can't come over till two. I'm getting dressed now."

"Okay, I'll wait in the kitchen" The church parking lot, even patches of Lyton Avenue, were visible through the burly black-barked oak trees, their rusty brown leaves hanging on like the words of a torch song. I had thought this yard big and lush; on a midsummer day, inside the thicket, one could not see outside it. Without the thick brush, there weren't really that many trees, and recently added suburban yards mocked the feeling of isolation. I heard the muffled creak of a step and recognized Arnold's ascent, felt him striding across the living room floor, over the spot Dom and I had just played at, by the sound of his lopsided gait, ever so slightly shuffled without his shoes on. Papers rustled, and then he hesitated at the kitchen, saying, "Come take a look, Idina; I want you to see this. Look what your little job did to us." Arnold held out the 1040 tax form and pointed to one of the lines of pencilled numbers. "That lousy $400.00 you made put us into another tax bracket. It wasn't worth the effort."

Every other year he bemoaned our sorry financial standing, erasing and refiguring the tax until it was whittled to numbers that would steal us a few more dollars. "Everyone," he said, raising his nose and chin a notch, "was entitled to an undefended charitable contribution to the church basket." Now this year, inked in for signing, he said, "Look at how much money we made," sadness dripping from his voice. "We could have been rich."

Popular thought was that a woman married her father. Arnold was more like my mother, but what separated them was this one fine point, and it was everything: she didn't care about appearances; she was just as stingy with herself as she was with others. My dad hated cheapness. Everything they ever purchased was a struggle in which they fought out their basic identities. He bought a flame-red Oldsmobile Delta 88 station wagon and then a shiny gold Impala, both with automatic transmission. He could never savor them. My mother's jibes and derisive innuendoes about those vehicles and the trouble they were, burning oil or guzzling gas, won out: she replaced them with an army green Ford Galaxy with standard transmission and standard brakes and said it was the best car she ever had, bragging of its engine, never once needing or receiving an oil change, enshrining it next to the pole shed twenty years beyond its use.

Snow still covered the ground when I picked Jada up at the airport, home for chemo. The top of her head, a golden sheen radiating from the center, reflected the light of the terminal. Surrounded by a few straggling passengers, Jada came forward, the last through the jetway. She handed over her coat and bag without a word interrupting her thinly drawn lips, lines about her eyes pinching the sparkle out of them.

"Do you want me to pick up some food for you?" I asked, driving from the airport.

"Umm. Is there a Mc Donald's along the way? They have the only French fries I like. I might try to see Kimby tonight, if she's not too busy for me. Maybe I should drive you to your apartment so I can have the car."

"Then you'll have to pick me up in the morning, say seven forty-five." We had two appointments, one at Dr. Ritter's, the other at the hospital clinic.

"Oooh, it's a treat to get into a nice warm car," I said the next morning over Hines and Bergland on the radio. She missed the station, saying that good radio was not available to her at college. We listened, responding to our faceless companions, the rest of the way.

Dr. Ritter stood inside the door, a starched white jacket cropped just below his hips, a cutout character. Having run through his routine, he made his cryptic report to the machine in his hand and rose, saying to Jada, "There hasn't been a measurable change in your range of motion since the last time you were here. We'll have to keep watching to see the extent of the damage. I can save you a trip; you won't have to come back if you can send me an X-ray."

"But it hurts to move. Isn't there something you can do?"

"We can fit you with a brace."

"I don't want a brace. Isn't there some operation you can do to fix my legs?" My head bobbed back and forth between their volley. Dr. Ritter looked crisp and jaunty, eager to bounce away while Jada tracked his muscles, anticipating his move before he committed it.

Dr. Ritter hugged the door. "Why, you're young. If you were older, we could replace your sockets. Many elderly people need new hip joints, but the lining in your sockets is still good. We wouldn't consider such a radical operation on someone your age. We'll wait and see how well the condition reverses itself." A white jacket with a woman inside it squeezed around the door and said in a low voice, "You're late for your next appointment." Dr. Ritter followed her out the door.

I dropped Jada off at the hospital entrance and joined her in the room with the beanbag, one of the three, besides the "family" room across the hall, now reserved for patients like her. We'd seen more than a few changes at the clinic, and it was no longer out of scheduling sloppiness that Jada went out scouting for Dr. Lourde. I think she roamed the hallways like a farmer would her back forty, just because they were hers.

She sent Heidi out in her place, to give her legs some relief, and when she rejoined us, she stopped at the sink. I stepped back, my heel indenting the smiley-face yellow beanbag. "This reminds me of the 60s," I said over the whoosh of running water. "These rooms are small enough without this blobby thing in the way."

Heidi took its side. "Some kids like to come in and sit on it."

"How can they? All it does is squish outwards when you put weight on it; there's no backbone."

"Some kids don't really sit. They just need a place to land." Heidi turned to Jada, and in her feline voice, asked, "How are things out East?"

"Fine. A lot of snow. They think it's cold, but it's not, compared to here."

Heidi's eyes twinkled. "I bet it's gorgeous. When I went skiing in Maine we were snowed in for two days. I'd love to go back and ride my bike. Did you just get here this morning?"

"No, I wasted my time at the orthopedic doctor's office. I'm never going back there again."

"Why is that?" Heidi's hip rubbed the table.

"I don't like the way he treats me. He never wants to stay and listen; he's always in a hurry to get someplace. A nurse is always coming in and telling him he's late," she said, fluttering her eyelids in false urgency. "And then he goes and doesn't even say good-bye. You never get to ask him any questions."

"He is quite a well-known doctor, probably the best in the state. I'm sure he's very busy." Dr. Lourde, looking somewhat preoccupied, walked into the room and glanced toward Jada while Heidi brought forth the black three-ring binder, an open book of Jada's medical life history, a third of it.

"I don't care. He doesn't want to do anything for me. He wants me to wear a leg brace until my legs get better. He says I'm too young to get my legs fixed." Without flicking an eyelash, Jada went on. "He's been around too many old people."

Heidi's face melted, her sympathetic "oh" was just soft and mushy enough to cushion Jada's indignation. Dr. Lourde cocked his head.

"Have you been to see Dr. Ritter?" At Dr. Lourde's question, Heidi backed away and exited the room.

"This morning. I don't know why I wasted my time. He's just like Dr. Randolph. They might know what they're doing with other people, but I'm not like other people. I have enough things to worry about; I can't wait for my bones to change on their own because something else is going to happen anyway, and I have to get around now."

"Is that what he said, that your bones will change on their own?" Dr. Lourde might have made a good teacher, I thought.

Jada paused. "Well, no. He said because my lining was still good I could wait for 'the condition,' he said, 'to reverse itself.'"

Dr. Lourde's gaze remained on Jada a long time; then he looked to me, an unasked question written on his face. Heidi reentered with the small paper with perforated edges with Jada's counts from the lab.

"Yes, those were his exact words," I affirmed.

Then Dr. Lourde's eyes searched the room, over the Velcro dart board, falling along with the painted coins forever suspended on the wall en route to the gaping coin purse, waiting, always waiting for someone to snap it shut, until they descended on Heidi. His forehead creased above the frames of his glasses. "How does that sound to you, Heidi? Reversing itself doesn't sound right, not with bone damage."

"Yes, I wondered about that, too," I said, and Jada nodded her head.

"Dr. Doakes is in the clinic this morning. Do you want me to find him?" Heidi offered.

"Why don't you ask him to come in here," Dr. Lourde said. Resilient and yielding was Heidi, as if she were stuffed with scads of little beans, while Dr. Lourde was as steadfast as a hardback chair. No matter how small a concern, he ploddingly researched any question if he thought the answer mattered. Heidi disappeared as softly as if she were speaking, leaving questions hanging in the air wanting to be released, wanting to fall, wanting to be contained. Dr. Lourde began his examination, listening and feeling for signs only he would recognize.

Dr. Doakes preceded Heidi. She closed the door and stood at it, while Dr. Doakes, with his glistening white hair pouffed, like mounds of whipped cream, and the handlebars of his snowy white mustache curling next to ruddy cheeks, convinced me that he was Mark Twain come back to entertain us.

"Thank you for coming," began Dr. Lourde. "There's a little confusion here about Jada's condition, and if you have a minute, I'd like you to explain it to me."

"Surely," Dr. Doakes said in a sonorous voice, Moonlight Serenade played on slide trombone. He started by putting his fist inside his other palm and enclosing it affectionately, bone in socket. When the bone lost nourishment, it began to crack and crumble, much like a saved tooth, a square nubbin with little points, like mountain peaks with a valley in the middle wrapped up in a tiny pillow of pink tissue and uncovered years later: the corners crumbled away into a fine dust that smelled like garlic powder.

"The brittle surface will chip away and scrape the surface of the other bone it meets," Dr. Doakes continued, rotating his palm on the other fist and at the same time pounding, sending the palm on an uneven orbit. "The more impact on the bone, the rougher the surface. The rougher the surface, the more damage and the more pain." Jada nodded.

"Now," Dr. Lourde baited, "how long does this process take to reverse itself?"

Dr. Doakes, ignoring the interruption, continued with the fluency of a well-rehearsed lecture. "The only way to arrest the creeping demise of living cells is to eliminate the source that prevented the blood from getting to its destinations in the first place. The blood flow continues to be impeded by the use of a drug to after its cessation."

Dr. Lourde prodded. "It was April that we took Jada off Prednisone. We can expect, then, to see some healthy tissue pretty soon?"

"Oh, no!" Dr. Doakes boomed, his eyes jumping as if the stage lights had just turned on; yet he was unflappable. "Once the blood is cut off, the bone becomes hard and brittle, like a wishbone from a turkey. It'll snap just like that wishbone, too, if it gets bad enough. The condition is not uncommon in arthritic patients, and the only way to treat it is by surgery where they replace parts of the damaged bone."

"I knew I didn't like him." Looking at Dr. Lourde, Jada said, "I want you to find a doctor who will do the operation."

Coming home from the clinic, we drove past the new townhouses on Cathedral Way, anomalies, given the age and stature of the palatial edifices that were the essence of baronial life in Victorian Sibley and which still stood snubbing their front porches at the common folk who ogled them while motoring past. In front of a center section was planted a for sale sign as common as if it were on the dog-littered grass of a house in Camden. Doing business was the great equalizer, and the sign caught Jada's eye. "Why can't we live in one of these places?"

"Actually, I am looking around here, but I found out that those townhouses you like so much start at $500,000, a little much for a teacher's salary." I made a left turn off Northern onto Poplar into the neighborhood behind the public eye. "This neighborhood used to be a little disreputable when I was in college, but they've been doing a nice job of fixing some of these houses up." I drove two more blocks to Dade and turned left, being drawn like iron to a magnet, back into the rectangle between Dade and Northern, Lawton and Cathedral Way. I made another turn, up Girard, and slowed. "There," Jada said. "I could live in that one."

"What we need is a part of a house, except I don't want a lower part, and you can't climb steps to an upper part. That's huge. Some of these places have been made into condominiums; that's what I'm looking for."

"You don't have very long," Jada cautioned. "I'll be home in May, and if you want me to live with you, you'd better have a place by then."

"I know. At least I'm in the right neighborhood."

Minnesota in March is white, but a visit from my friend from California also brought an unusually warm week. What little snow we had melted to reveal dry brittle grass scorched under a sun that heated the air to sixty, seventy, and even to eighty-plus degrees. I asked Tanya and Akiko to look at Unit 607 at the Compton Hotel with me. Anyone from Sibley who was around my age had at least one memory of the Compton, most likely of the Deco Bar. Built in 1918, the Compton was a six-story luxury hotel where F. Scott Fitzgerald stayed when in Sibley. Gloria Swanson was rumored to have had kitchen privileges to accommodate her peculiar tastes. Gangsters, too, held rendezvous of some sort in the famous hotel that fell into decline along with the rest of the neighborhood, and rooms were let cheap, until the explosion which made way for the conversion to condominiums. Unit 607 had a cathedral ceiling; oak floors; two original step-up bathrooms; a fireplace; and views of downtown, the Cathedral, the bluffs, a park and the gabled roofs of houses and overtowering trees of the historic Sibley Hill neighborhood. There were underground parking, a security system, and two elevators. Across the street was the nursing home Jada and I drove by on our route from the clinic, the nursing home with the woman in the wheelchair looking out the door, the nursing home I joked about retiring to. I made an offer on 607 just before flying out to visit Jada.

As I was leaving Dom, Arnold appeared at the top of the steps and held out a book saying, "Here, you should read this." I wanted not to accept the book, suspicious that a message was embedded in it, but it was Hemingway. Arnold used to say to me that he thought I had such potential, like Liza Doolittle. In taking the book, I stood in the foyer next to Arnold's ideal woman, one that was embodied by women in three separate prints. Arnold was specific in telling the framer that he had bought them at the Louvre. Framed in red was a fiery woman dressed in a red gown, satisfying a lust for fun by throwing her head back as she danced about the cafe floor, her skirt leaping like licks of flames as she followed her partner's lead. In another print, a nearly faceless woman, veiled by a filmy gauze that billowed loosely from a cylindrical hat sat regal in her posture, sophisticatedly ethereal, a goddess in heavenly blues, surrounded by a blue frame. In the third yellow frame was a soft contemplative woman prudishly buttoned to her neck in black, reclining in a chair with an open book on her lap, light illuminating her downcast eyes. Every time I came into the house, I walked into their shadow.

It wasn't that I was none of them, totally lacking and utterly disappointing; I was all of them in overabundance. I was curious to know what he could not say to me himself, what he entrusted to Hemingway. So I took the book to Hartford. Summer-like sun beat through the glass panes of the airport concourse while I waited to board. The rumor among the waiting passengers was that a bomb was hidden on the plane in the previous flight and no one could board until measures were taken for our safety. Every extra minute of waiting brought up a new worry. I worried about uncertainty, which was probably why I married Arnold, a sure thing. He knew all the places to go and things to buy and if I listened to him I would never be in danger of looking cheap or foolish or stupid. I could just go on and be Mrs. Arnold Petersen and yup-by-golly everything would be all taken care of.

Originally, Arnold had blamed the demise of our marriage onto Jada's disease, as if it were a beguiling lover come to woo me. When I left him, he blamed something more worthy of taking me away from him, another man. Hemingway gave him a different thief: another woman. The same self-centricity that supposed unrequited love for himself at the center of Patti's fabricated nervous breakdown made me, like the female in Hemingway's novel, sick, crazy, nuts, in need of help—a man's, his.

I had traveled a long distance since I left Sibley, and, it wasn't just at Hartford that I landed. My driver took us to Founders' Valley past graceful climbing stems covered with pink and fuchsia blossoms, looking fluid, like they were swaying mellifluously with the motion of ocean water. Whereas this magnificent valley glittered with golds and ambers and oranges and reds last fall, in spring it looked like an unending velvet robe of emerald green studded with gleaming regal jewels, waiting for me to snuggle my body along its soft furry nap.

Jada's room felt familiar. Sheets I transformed into curtains draped the windows, tied back with cloth matching a wallpaper trim. The lamp burned in spite of the afternoon's daylight. I left my suitcase and the Easter basket in the hall, not wanting to clutter an already crowded space. We shopped in the quaint storefronts along the commons. She picked out a purse and a billfold for me, one that had windows for pictures, pockets for credit cards; one side was made to hold paper money (and only that, Jada instructed), the other side my check book, a pen included. Neat, organized; I'd never have to rely on a plastic bag again.

I bought way too many books, while Jada gathered cards for writing to her friends. We ate meals together at the dorm, and while Jada attended class, I walked the campus and the roads leading out of town, out as far as the Captain's Den. She was marking events, my visit one of them, to get her through. I thought of this trip as being on one end of a teeter-totter, a high spot to balance our times at the bottom. It was ending on Sunday, Easter Sunday. In the sitting room, in a wing back chair huddled next to the grand piano, Jada asked, "Do you want to go to Mass in the morning?"

"Mass? I, sure. Do you go to Mass often?"

"No; I just thought it would be a nice thing for us to do. The priest here is okay."

"So you have been."

"Yes, a couple times. I'm not turning into a holy roller or anything. I just thought you'd like to go." Jada looked small and fragile in the chair, man-sized, belonging in the smoking room of a man's club, except for its upholstered print, floral, on white background. It was more than the size of the chair that dwarfed Jada, though, and I studied how she arranged her body in position, as if each of the parts was placed separately, like the wooden Tinker Toy pegs and discs, instead of woven together like strings of beads in a garland, malleable and supple. Her eyes were on the piano, and I thought she must have hurt just to think of moving her fingers among the keys. "I tried playing, but I'm no good anymore," she said, adding, "It needs to be tuned."

Nodding, I wondered if she would want her piano moved to the condo.

The college, originated as a seminary for women, boasted its own reverend, as it did its own doctor. Representative clergy from several denominations also conducted worship services in the chapel, Abbott Chapel, and the bells rang to call young women to their services every weekend.

We ambled across the green, the dew already dry under the dappling sunlight through the trees. The chapel, made of large stones, was overgrown with vines, and trees huddled around it protectively. The entryway, spotlighted by a spill of sunlight, invited us inward. Gray stones, bricks, marbles, dim lights and ceiling peaks reaching toward heaven appeared damp and cold, but the chill of morning was gone, exorcised, if not by the sun's streams through colored glass along the walls, by the past few days of our being together. Jada had not been taken in by the church's ceremony, not been ensnared by the emotional entanglement as I had, suffering Christ's pain and degradation at each Station of the Cross. Neither of us believed in the certainty of heaven and hell, unable to reconcile our human place in a heaven without other living beings, dogs, cats, birds, horses that breathed and ran and ate and slept. Their hearts beat like ours, they reproduced and loved and played; they were denied a place in eternity because they could not read and write about Jesus.

I joined a church and tried to nurture faith in both children, believed in the community of people trying to lead good lives, equalized for one hour of the week, if only by shaking hands and singing in unison, that celebration of conscious examination surrounded by the aesthetics of communal ceremony, that lifting up a layer and getting under it to see how it felt, being embraced. But naive interpretations about good and bad, nonsensical blame of the devil, blind suppositions of forces that drove our world drove me away. Why Jada chose to go to Mass at Abbott Chapel did arouse my curiosity.

The priest began his homily about the Easter promise. "Jesus," he said, "is proof of God's covenant with us. Even when we have given up all hope, if we truly believe, God will keep His word. We might think He forgot about us, we might not know how He'll keep his word, but we know that He will. We have Jesus as His Word. Jesus, like the young woman who was senselessly killed, wanted to live a long life. 'Why me, Lord?' He asked as he prayed for the cup to be taken from Him. Yet He submitted himself to death; He said, 'Your will, not mine, be done.' Why, if God loved His only son that much, did He let Jesus die?

"We ask that question today, of all days, after the tragedy of those two lives. Why, we ask ourselves did that young woman die?" The woman the priest referenced had been part of a twosome who had gone to the Captain's Den, a popular drinking spot on a narrow winding highway. One of the two thought her friend had had too much to drink to be trusted behind the wheel, so she set out for home on foot, perhaps laughing at her adventure while watching the woods for danger, hearing and, maybe, turning around to see the vehicle race up behind her. I wondered if she had conscious time to know what was about to happen. I wondered if she realized it was her friend driving the car that hit her. I wondered if she knew she would die.

Would that woman have been alive the next day if she had not made the decision to walk but rode instead with her drunken friend? I wondered if all of what happened was a part of God's heavenly plan or if it was just a giant irony.

"How can we go on believing?" the priest asked. As I listened to him tell us to pray also for the driver who was just as much a victim and deserved not our censure but our forgiveness, I heard Jean's and P.T.'s prayers go up for me when we disagreed over morning coffee in the women's lounge. P.T. would have prayed for the killer of the woman to get her soul into heaven.

"In the Bible, God says that we will all be united in the glory of His presence and that this life on earth is just a preparation for that," the priest continued. No, in P.T.'s mind, there were no accidents, just opportunities to find the Lord, and she'd snub her cigarette, giving it a final twist in the ashtray like extinguishing the issue from further conversation, before standing up, her plaid skirt falling into straight pleats below her knees, and smoothing her blue cotton smock like she was petting a dog.

Jean defended religious wisdom, adding, "What P. T. and I are trying to say is that what happens in life happens for a reason. My brother went to work as usual, but then he was accidentally crushed. I believe that there's a lesson God wants me to learn from my loss."

We relinquished all responsibility if God were the decider, I countered, "That's human sacrifice! To make him die to teach you a lesson? No, I can't believe that."

So far, the priest's argument hadn't changed much from either P.T.'s or Jean's, and I found no salvation anywhere in it. The woman who died on the pavement, perhaps in flight had a split second to know what hit her, would not rise from the dead, as Jesus purportedly did. Sitting in the chapel, I wondered that if we were to believe that life after death was so peachy, what was the point of living, unless as punishment? The priest turned toward the driver: it was the driver we must pray for. She sat in jail on this Easter morning, and she would forever have to wake every morning, many of them in prison, knowing her part in the death of a human being. Life as she knew it was over, too, but she had the misfortune of having to spend the rest of her years on earth with the excruciating pain of her wrongdoing.

"For this," the priest said, "she has been sacrificed. Here is the greater mystery. Here is where our faith is most severely tested." I studied the Kente sash adorning the priest's simple white surplice and considered the pecking order involved in this thing called sacrifice. I could imagine people whispering Jada's name into their clasped hands praying for her as they would blow on a pair of dice for luck. If they just prayed hard enough, would that change the odds, as if nothing else in the world, like the tilt of the planet, the laws of probability, delayed treatment, forgotten medication, had any effect on her fate? And what if she didn't live?

How was Jada supposed to feel, completely at the will and mercy not only of God but of the thoughts and fervent pleas of other humans? And what if there were one solitary prayer, one, from the inside of a cell where a young woman sat on a bench with a terrible headache that pounded so hard inside her head that it seemed it were going to break its way out, and when it did, she would be able to remember that she didn't have that last Sloe Gin fizz and that that sudden movement in front of her headlight was a leaf being swept up from the wind, not a palm raised as if to stop the beast from charging, and that the bump that made her swerve was not the shattered body of her drinking companion. What if the woman who was spared sat in her cell, and like Jada, prayed for release, the sweet promise of never having to think, every morning and every night, of her senseless confinement to life. The irony of our praying for the guilty along with the innocent made it impossible to tell one from the other. Then the truth was that we were all being sacrificed, only some of us were too inebriated with misplaced hope to see it. I left Jada with a brimming Easter basket that afternoon and the thought growing in me that Jada may have wanted some explanation herself.

When school term ended in May, Jada came home mean. Words came out mean, her eyes looked at things mean, as if just recovering from a flash photograph, and her ungainly walk on the front part of her feet threw her posture backwards as if to warn people behind her to keep their distance: she was mean. People sympathize more readily when they imagine a soft, sweet sufferer. Jada was no perky morning radio announcer, gushing feigned and brainless good humor, the kind of prattle only a half-awake zombie could listen to before seriously staring a day in the face. She was real, she was raw; she was fighting for life—her life.

Dr. Lourde may have warned Dr. Janski, who would operate on Jada's leg, of her temperament, peeled like a banana, just as fragile and perishable. He and she had the briefest encounter, a mere introduction at the Shriner's Hospital, where he had seen a lot of children in conditions much worse than Jada's. The operation sounded gruesome, taking a bone out of its socket and hacking the top off, coating it with Teflon.

June first, after surgery, I left the hospital and drove less than a mile to the parking lot, dark and silent, one light illuminating my path through the clump of trees and bushes, to my new bedroom with the unfurled blue chair. Shadows surrounded three glass-bubbled globes, suspended throughout the long hall. Walking down the hall I went from one circle of light fading into another, expecting Jimmy Durante to shake his head and raise his hat saying, "Good night, Mrs. Calabash, wherever you are," before vanishing from stage.

Inside my condo, all around me was space, five rooms empty and dark except for the reflection on the naked windows and the lights from the nursing home across the street, burning eternally, as a sign of hope, maybe a sign of fear, or both, one without the other being arrogance. I made little noise walking the hardwood floors, peering first out one window at the dark expanse of the courtyard, then out another at the street below. I didn't pull the shades, as I would have on Lambert Lane. I wasn't afraid here.

Had I been a romantic, I would have opened a bottle of wine and danced, alone in my vast space. But my practical circumstances surrendered no wine nor music, and the hour was late—it was a school night; I had nowhere to go except my bedroom, a small room made smaller by a wall-length bookcase; I flipped open the "mattress" onto the floor, avoiding the fly, upside down, its feet curled up, dead. I tucked a sheet over the mattress, set the alarm, and lay down, a few feet from the fly. If you have to die somewhere, I thought, this wouldn't be a bad place.

The day after surgery, I left school and walked up seven flights of stairs to spend the evening with Jada. The air was tight as I walked around the nurses' station, an island in the center of radiating rooms that stemmed from it like arms on a starfish.

Her bed was first in the room, and I could not see beyond the curtain to Mrs. Silver, who wheedled and whined, to her husband when he was at her bedside, to unseen victims on the telephone when he was not, or the window. Jada looked blankly upwards, rigid. From her hip down almost to her knee ran a long cut in her skin, like a bass clef, held together with staples, a ladder across the red incision.

Behind my back, the hub of noise and activity seemed far away, though each of the rooms was equidistant from it. Some of the nurses didn't bother to go into patients' rooms, but rather shouted through open doors in response to their requests, giving the place a familial feel. Maybe the older patients liked the seemingly casual disarray of the center because it reminded them that they were not left out, not yet, sipping each hopeful word, every pat, as the elixir of extended life.

Jada saw Dr. Janski, tall, lean, and topped with a head of thin sandy hair, before I did. "What is this I hear about your not following my orders today? The nurses tell me you wouldn't let them touch you, that you screamed at them and sent them out of here." A scowl colored his face.

"Do you know what they wanted me to do? They came in here, and just like that," Jada snapped her fingers, "they wanted me to get up and start walking around. I just had an operation; I can't do that."

"I wrote orders for you, and when I hear that you won't follow them, I get angry. The nurses say they won't come back in here if they're treated the way you treated them. How do you expect us to help you if you will not do as we tell you?"

Anger gathered in Jada's face like the dust in a tornado. Now the chill I felt coming into the room made sense; poor Mrs. Silver. I bet she hadn't heard language like that in her Upper Stanley Circle. "You're expecting me to do too much too soon. I need more time. They wouldn't even listen to me when I tried to explain."

Dr. Janski stiffened even more. "I just performed an operation on you to help you. I have other people to see and important things to do. I will not listen to you insult me or the nurses who know their jobs and are here to help you." Dr. Janski, true to his word, turned away before Jada uttered another word. She remained silent in his absence and my presence, staring upwards again, her arms locked. The quiet of the room crept about us, only us, I now realized. The curtain, usually pulled to its limit, only partially hid the other half of the room, and even the skinny little sliver of sun that snuck across the floor stopped just at the edge of Jada's bed: it, too, knew how to take a hint.

Not one nurse had come into Jada's room while I was there. She was shunned. Could they ignore her forever? She would require bathing and a food tray; or were they part of the boycott?

The evening promised to drag on like a weight chained onto its prisoner—us. I stood, circled a spot, pulled back the curtain. Dr. Lourde had no official reason to call on Jada. He knocked at her half-open door and came inside, exuding caution and reserve: he just didn't seem to have a mercury, or at least to let it show.

Taking the back of the chair in hand and repositioning it, Dr. Lourde began talking. "People here aren't going to put up with your antics, Jada." He sat, his body pert with candor and talked on without giving room for Jada to respond. "You've mistreated us. I have, and some of the other folks in the clinic and the hospital have allowed that. I've asked people to do favors for me to help you. Now you insult them. These people are helping you. They don't have to. They won't come back. And I don't have to be your doctor, either. You know, we have a choice of who we want to treat, too."

Jada returned an unbroken gaze and rejoined. "I think you're being unfair. I haven't called anyone any names. I haven't made anyone do anything for me. I've hardly even called for a nurse. They're just mad because I won't walk. I can't yet. It's too soon."

"Jada, I've seen you pull through a lot worse than this. I know you don't trust some of the docs—you have some pretty high standards. But you asked for this. And you're going to want Dr. Janski to do a second operation. I don't know if he will."

Dr. Lourde lay one palm on each of his knees, spreading his slender fingers, and rose. This must be what it feels like not to have the rent money when the landlord comes around. We would be evicted, without a place to put our things, without a place to sleep. I had put her hands onto the piano keys when she refused to play. I had dragged her screaming down the street to her home. I had rolled her bed into day surgery. I had taken her blood, given her insulin, chemo, morphine, physically and mentally restrained her and prodded her. It wasn't that I didn't have the power or the guts to try to force her because I had also, every time, kept my vision clear. More than any other thing, more than even my desire for Jada's long life, I wanted Jada to own her life, disease and all, and that tussle between wills—to accept and to reject—played a character in every procedure, every twisted incident, every outcome. Her conflict was with the medical institution—it wasn't the people she fought.

I couldn't know who was right and who was wrong. I knew only that I had to support her, not subvert her by trying to fix what she had done. I could only remain quiet. After a time of quiet, I walked down to the cafeteria. Always, I walked up. Tonight, with a cup of coffee in my hand, I redoubled every flight back up to the eighth floor, where I came upon the back of a nurse and the end of a conversation. "Tomorrow, but only when my mom is here."

The next day, Jada called the nurses' station. "Okay, I'm ready," she said with set lips and steel eyes. A nurse strapped Jada to the bed, explaining to her what she was doing. The bed began rotating, setting Jada into a vertical position, her quavering voice cautioning the nurse not to let her feet touch the floor.

"Don't worry, Jada. We've done this thousands of times. I'll stand here to catch you." She stood ready, and when the bed and Jada were perpendicular to the floor, another nurse arrived, carrying a small step stool. Together, the two nurses coaxed Jada into letting them fit it under her levitated feet. Then one unleashed a strap, another, while holding onto Jada's waist.

Jada, who had been clenching the side rails, was now grabbing the nurse's shoulder. "Let me decide. Don't force me. Just let me do it."

"Okay, Jada. We're right here. Tell us when you're ready, and we'll take the last strap off." At first Jada relied on the nurses to bear her weight, but they were going to step away from her, a picture of pushing and scraping and chasing all her courage into trusting her own strength, bearing the weight of her own will to stand, alone. She nodded, and the nurse removed her hands. Jada lifted hers from the nurse, who edged away, and Jada stood on her own power.

"Okay, okay," Jada said, "put me back," and the nurses quickly strapped her to the bed.

"Good job, Jada!" They sounded like they were smiling. When the bed was rotating back to its horizontal position, one nurse gave the smile to me. Later the same nurse came in and suggested Jada try again, but once standing, Jada was to make a step, a first step. Her feet touching the floor, Jada slid her foot forward and brought the other to meet it, relying on the nurses to steady her, guide her. "Okay, now, raise your foot."

Jada hesitated. She had to get the feel of each part of walking, raising her leg, moving her foot forward, placing it onto the floor, which part first, transferring her weight. Every day after that, Jada practiced, at first with the help of nurses, then with the aid of an aluminum walker and me. Always the goal set for Jada out-distanced her stamina, but she made it to the door of her room, then out into the station and around it. I encouraged my daughter and was proud of the way she faced both Dr. Janski and Dr. Lourde, making amends with Dr. Janski, proving her sincerity, but not excusing her fear. She had done what she was supposed to do, on her terms, and by taking those steps, she had crossed another threshold. She was glad for her life. Not happy-jump-up-and-down glad, but quiet glad, thoughtful glad, wise glad.

On her release from the hospital, I drove Jada straight to our new home, up Sibley Hill and a sharp right to Northern Avenue. The rooms echoed as I tagged behind Jada, her eyes roaming along the walls, peering out a window. At the doorway to a bathroom, she raised her eyebrow and said, "I thought you said there were no steps." Her suite, a large bedroom, a full bath, and a walk-in closet, were last. Approval broke open on her face.

"We'll start here," I said, smiling at her smiling. "What color do you think we should paint it?" Summer officially started the day Jada and I went to the paint store and mixed up a special blend. Over the next month, we bought wallpapers and a brass bed. We ordered window blinds and mattresses. Pillows, sheets, towels; we bought it all—Jada loved it.

Early every morning I woke up in my apartment, hauled belongings and a bag of supplies, and went to my condominium to work. Jada went to Stanton College for a drawing class, and at 1:00, I picked her up and brought her to physical therapy or back to the condominium. It was a summer under construction.

I never wasted a minute, and sometimes I left spattered with paint, my hair speckled with a fine sprinkling from rolling. Paint wedged under my fingernails and dried in the lines of my hands, white alligator skin. Settling into the car, Jada shook her head at me.

"What if we have an accident? What if we have to stop somewhere? You look like you should be walking along with a shopping cart with all your bags and mismatched clothing."

"The accident I don't worry about. If I have one, it won't matter what I look like. Just tell me when you want to go shopping and I'll put on something presentable, but I'm not going to get every little speck of paint off because it's just going to land on me again tomorrow."

"Oh, Mooie, you're such a boofus. Did I tell you I found a new antique store? You'll like it just because of the name. Auntie Quarrie Ann's Trove."

"You hate going to antique stores. How did you get there?"

"That's just because you take so much time. And it's so dusty. Yesterday we had a model and went to the instructor's studio. It's on the second floor of a building on Broadway Avenue, down there by um, oh, it's sort of close to where you get onto 260. The store is just down the block from her studio. There's a big glass window and it has big pink letters on it."

"Oh, so that's why you're telling me."

Jada retaliated. "It looks like they have furniture. We should go there."

"How about tomorrow?" I started out with my sewing machine, my daybed, my typewriter. I added a lumpy antique loveseat and Hoosier cabinet, her bed. The library table from downstairs and the chair given to me for Christmas centered nakedly in the dining room. I could think of nothing that would give me pleasure and bind us closer together more than shopping for our condo.

I pulled into an alleyway alongside the building with the pink letters on the glass in front of a doll's house-sized make-believe bedroom. "It reminds me of the Pink Panther," I said as I splashed and bounced the Mazda through the gravel parking lot and nudged her bumper up to the craggly wall. "I hope we can park here." Sloppy letters dripped like snot on the bricks, suggesting names, a spot for every merchant, a merchant for every spot. Yet, many were vacant. Jada and I zig-zagged our way around the puddles in the rutted lot to even pavement on the avenue and peered through the window at the display.

Walking through this portal was like walking into someone's front room. A flag hung at attention in 45-degree angle salute; an eagle perched on a ledge overhead, guarding the small reception table in the wooden-planked foyer. It seemed utterly appropriate that I should leave a calling card in the blue-veined bowl.

Whatever energy went into this display dispersed as we came into the store proper. A few dishes and knickknacks spotted the walls, unrefinished, unrepaired, unmatched furniture, including a massive chair, springs popping through the blackened leather were bunched together; a long rectangular wooden platform layered with odds and ends served to pen them in. I wandered around, following a chair, a plate, a table. In other antique stores, I got to digging in darkened corners, picking up and holding some tantalizing object, hoping to hear its story by the way it felt inside my smutty palm.

Not so in this store. A once-fashionable lamp stood on the floor like a worn-out lady of the night, a corsage of fabric flowers hanging on by broken threads to the disintegrating shade, ragged at the edge from too much handling. Glass beads dripped from rotting strings and landed on the floor at the slightest shimmy, too hastily shed at the memory of bygone glory. I circled the lamp twice, the filigreed pattern of the rusty base webbed with dust globs, and thought to myself that the sleazy appeal this lamp had for me would be the reason Jada would disapprove and refuse to let it ride in the same car with her. I looked for her. Beyond the glass case in the middle of the store, she trailed behind a man, a tall man with blonde hair and muscular legs that shone bronze from under white shorts. Jada glanced quickly at me and rolled her eyes and as much as smacked her lips with a lascivious grin on her face. I realized that while I was following my desire, she was following hers. His cheeks were high and sculptured above his thighs, his stomach flat.

"How about this chair?" he asked, pausing briefly beside some lumpy brown mass. "Here's a desk that's really nice, warm red color. I finished it myself. It's sort of Deco." They continued their round of the store, she right up behind him, his voice coming backwards as a hum, hers in peaks and giggles. They turned and stopped at the display case. With twinkling eyes and halfway repressing a smile that forced his chin into a dimpled "v" he said, "I don't think you're talking about tables and chairs, are you?" She spread her lips as wide as she decently could, coyly looking up at him, teasing him with silence. I could have learned a lot about flirting by watching my daughter. He must have sensed my watching and disengaged himself, turning towards me, now in search of the desk.

"Come see what I found," Jada said to me as I neared them. She had gradually shrunken as the tips of her leg bones ground away; with one leg repaired, she walked lopsidedly, a gait that crossed a limp with a gallop noticeable mostly when she made a sudden move. I followed her and the man right to the lamp, its cord spiraling up its spine, a foraging serpent.

"But that's the lamp I want! I can't believe you like it."

Jada creased her forehead. "Well, aren't you going to get it?" She leaned closer and said, "For that price?" I squeezed my hand around the stem of the lamp and lifted it from the floor; its shade wobbled and the streams of beads clinked together in a kind of jingle dress dance.

"We'll take this," I said, looking into eyes the blue a child would color the sky in a picture. In the transfer of the lamp, our hands brushed. His were square, big to match his height, square at the knuckles and square at the fingertips. He smiled with square teeth, little bubbles sliding across his white shiny square teeth. Happy teeth and happy eyes. "And I have a few questions about that desk over there."

"Isn't he gorgeous?" Jada asked, the lamp poking its tattered shade between us in the car. We hadn't been towed, as had been threatened, nor had the weather played its foolery on us by wringing out another batch of showers from the clouds.

I stopped at the traffic light, remembering the parts of the man as a book's pages cut into thirds whose figure you can change bit by bit by flipping the parts until the figure becomes a different being altogether. "All right, Jada, don't go nuts. I guess he was kind of cute, if you like blondes. I like the dark swarthy type, myself."

"Who cares, as long as he's built. Olle Seeborg—what a hunk!" If the rearview mirror could talk, it would have said, "Ooh-la-la, look out, this could be the end to the virginity pact." But I was busy watching traffic. I had told Olle I'd buy the desk if I could get it home.

"We'll deliver it," he'd said eagerly. He did smile a lot. "But I can't do it until after six; I have to close up first." Two days later he rang my number, and in three minutes he and another man carried the desk into our unit.

"Just put it over there," I motioned. The two men short-stepped, one backward, the other forward, until the desk landed in the hallway. The other man removed himself quickly; Olle swept his eyes down the floorboards and out the windows that opened to the sky. I handed him a folded twenty-dollar bill.

He eyed it. "I don't want that. I'll just have to share it with him, and he doesn't deserve it." He smiled, tacking on a deep-throated heh heh like a post-it note to his twinkling eyes. "See how he's waiting? I had to make him do this." He jerked his head in the direction of the hallway and silently clicked his lips against his white square teeth.

July 2ⁿᵈ

Today I began my last year as a teenager. After I went to my art class at Stanton, a bunch of balloons from Mom were delivered to me. We shopped for bargains at antique shops for the condo and Mom dropped me off for physical therapy. My surgery went better than I expected, and I felt the difference right away. Now I can sleep without taking extra doses of Tylenol 3 and Legatrin. It's my muscles that bother me now because of the exercises I have to do. But I am getting stronger and have more motion in abduction. I am happy I had the replacement (I have a metal and plastic "ball" in my right hip) and hope the left hip will go even better because it wasn't as badly damaged.

Dad gave me 19 pink roses, and I also got pearl earrings and bracelet, another glass of Fostoria, a cute Beatrix Potter figure, and a blue violin vase to add to my collection. Mom's Boston cream pie was terrific, as usual. So the day was very pleasing. Then Cerise and I went to Albert's. I had fun dancing. Oh, and my ticket to the Madonna concert. It was perfectly fabulous! She is so talented and WOW! she is in absolutely gorgeous shape. She danced and sang at the same time! What a show! And the costumes were dazzling! I admire everything about her! I forgot. Tom Wilcox called and asked me out to The Red Room tomorrow night. I can't believe I have four guys in my life (well four if you count Olle, the guy I flirted with at the antique store. But we talked for about 2 hours, so I'm including him in this fantasy) and they're all hunks. Besides Tom, there's Dale and Pat, who's going in the army, Daniel's friend.

Mom is letting me drive up to Dale's cabin. If he makes another move on me, I might give in and have sex, though I still want to talk about us. I don't know how I stand with him and if I really feel in love or if I'm just desperate. I don't want to do something I don't feel sure about. It's scary to think about.

I'm half way through the summer and still have a lot of paperwork to do and getting everything I need to go back to MHC. I want to be there, but I'm also worried about it. Some good friends will be gone, like Lisa Osborn, and other seniors that graduated. I really liked being around her and her fun fiancé and will miss her a lot. But I will see Julie and Joy and hopefully make other good friends. I know I'll have some fun at school but I am nervous about classes and all the work. I will be a little sad to leave because I don't feel ready for more unknowns. Like what's ahead for me. Will I die soon? I can't imagine myself being too healthy in 10 years. Will I continue to live in bad pain and not be able to do the things I would like to for 20 more years? Thinking I was going to survive the first diagnosis of leukemia was expecting too much. Expecting more and pushing myself is more punishment! So now what's going to happen to me? My expectations are too high!! I think I need help! I think my state has made me act not normal and lose memory retention. I don't want to live with the terrible feelings of this damned disease and I don't want to take responsibility for it! Ever since the beginning it's been cheating me. For a while I had Beverly, but she weasled me into submission, all because of Joe Lourde. Without anyone to support, help, and understand me, I bury my thoughts and feelings deeper inside myself and don't let others know. The only place I express these negatives is in this journal. Maybe that's how I work myself into this state and feel so troubled. I don't think I should be happy or even alive. I wish I could die in a freak accident like that girl did walking back from the Captain's Den. I wonder if she died instantly. Or did she bleed to death? Bluck! I guess I have to go on as I have in the past.

Well, I guess I am more happy about what I am accomplishing this summer. A full credit art class, two major hip surgeries and physical therapy, going out on dates and visiting Dale twice, buying things for the condo and the house. I hope I can accomplish things at school and feel successful there. I have to get there first, and then I can schedule and plan. It is important that I am happy with my classes and succeed in them and that I continue to work on the Parents' Weekend Committee. I think I made good contributions to the group. And I helped with the sports activities. I worry that I wasted last year or did more damage than good. I want a filled social life and maybe find a good boyfriend. I'd like to get to New York again, and maybe flirt with guys like that waiter Nick or meet another Scott Perkins from Princeton. If I could choose another sex partner it would be someone like him. He never pressured me or made me think twice. He held me with his arms or legs for the whole time. I loved the way he made me feel! Maybe I should feel a little shame (I do just a bit because we didn't exchange numbers or addresses!) but I'm glad I slept with him. He was gorgeous—

muscular body from crew, and his skin was so soft. I have to believe I can do it. Every little bit, day by day. I have to try.

I took the parking space near Aunty Quarrie Ann's in the alley lot for granted and plucked my feet around the potholes to keep up with Jada. Olle's face opened up like a shooting star. As we toured the floor, I smiled back at him, noticing his sharp cheekbones. With his chiseled features, he could have been a model. I also noticed Jada having a smiling contest with him and making his face color at suggestions that snorkeled under the surface. I had to hand it to him that he kept his eye on the sale, anticipating my questions, squinting in thought as I hesitated at a plate on the table. "That's a pretty sweet place you live in."

"Thanks," I replied, nearing the back wall. "We just moved in so we need everything. I'm hoping to fill it with antiques."

"What things do you collect?"

"Salt and pepper shakers." Acknowledging Jada, I added, "Jewelry."

"Come on up here." He motioned with his finger to the glass case supporting the cash register. Jada followed, a playful puppy expecting a chase. She was there, almost panting, leaning her elbows on the surface when I caught up. Olle reached underneath the cash register and placed a pair of figures on the counter. "How about these?"

"Oh, aren't they wonderful? Look, they're little globes of the world. They even have the outlines of the continents." Jada took one from me and ran her finger over it while I turned mine upside down. "Don't you just love them, Jada?"

"Yeah, they're cool."

"How much are they? They're not marked."

Olle set himself on the tall stool, lifting his feet up to the middle rung and leaning forward onto the counter. He smiled—actually, I hadn't seen him not smile—and confessed, "I didn't want to put them out because I like them so much. But you can have them for three dollars. And look, they still have the original box."

"No, no, if you want them…." I set them on the counter.

His smile ran like an electric searchlight, bright, unwavering, reaching out. "I wouldn't be running a very good business if I kept everything I liked. I don't have a lot of room where I live, anyway."

"Where's that?" Jada asked.

"Back there, on Colfax Avenue. I'm in one of those apartment buildings. I manage the upkeep and get a reduction on my rent. The guy's a jerk, too. If I don't get out there fast enough in the morning to set the garbage for pick up, he threatens to kick me out." I nodded, looked again at the pins and necklaces on the top shelf. "Say, do you need a carpet? I've got a great Oriental rug at my place. I picked it up just a couple weeks ago and put it in my apartment."

"What color is it?" I was hoping he'd say chartreuse or lemon yellow, but when he said burgundy, Jada's antennae were awakened. "I can't take something out of your place, not something you need."

"But I want to sell it." That smile with a little gilded lining returned. "Then I can pay this month's rent." That's what it was about his eyes. They pleaded, they implored, they laid right on me without shame, apology or excuse. "Why don't you stick around and come over to look at it? I have to stay open until five; that's only twenty-five minutes, and you can see it for yourself."

"It doesn't hurt to look," Jada said as if she had been invited to the prince's ball and knew just the shoes she was going to wear. "You need a rug."

"Well, I suppose. I don't have anything going on tonight." I looked again at the trinkets in the case. Olle reached in and brought out a brooch.

"How do you like the display case?" he asked like a dog that'd just done its trick and waited for its treat. "Pretty nice, hunh? I think it's the best-looking thing in the store. And it was easy, too, I just went to the store and bought a piece of fabric. Karen wanted to put stuff out there." He pointed to a board on concrete brick and made a face. "Bor-r-ring! She was supposed to be here this afternoon, but she called and said she had stuff she had to do. I've been here since I opened this morning."

"Who's Karen?" Jada wanted to know.

"She owns half of this store, which means she's supposed to work half of the time, but she just sits around on her fat butt and complains all the time. You saw her husband," Olle looked at me. "He helped me deliver the desk. Did you see how much he hated doing it? I had to make him do it, and then he was halfway down the hall waiting for me. They both don't do what they're supposed to, except eat." He looked at his watch. "Oh, that's close enough. Wait here, I have to go downstairs and turn off the lights."

"I don't know how smart this is, Jada, going over to some guy's apartment."

Jada's face puckered as if she'd just bitten into a sour apple. "Oh, Mom, live it up a little; what can happen? There's two of us. And he's so cute."

"How old do you suppose he is, 27?"

She shrugged her eyebrows. "So?"

"Don't you think that's a little old for you?"

"He's not too old for you."

"What? Me?" The door latched shut in the back of the store, and with light footsteps, Olle gamboled back toward us, lithe, like fingers along the strings of a harp. "Here," I set three one dollar bills on the counter. "How much with tax? Olle looked from the currency to me and back.

"Cash. In that case...." He put the tablet back by the register and pocketed the money.

"How do you know I'm not someone who you shouldn't do that with?" He stopped short, surprised, his hand holding onto one of the shakers he was putting into the box.

Olle finished boxing the shakers and locked the register. "Ready? You can follow me." Jada walked ahead onto the sidewalk. A woman bearing a large flat package between two outstretched arms, nearly colliding with Jada, said, "Jada, what are you doing here?"

"We're shopping at the antique store." Locking the door Olle watched us. "This is my mom; Mom, this is my art instructor at Stanton."

"How do you do. I would shake hands, but it looks like your hands are full."

"Oh, don't worry. But you can't be her mother; you look much too young!" She spoke hurriedly, leaving no spaces between her thoughts, just as her feet wasted no time on the sidewalk. Beaming, Jada hooked her arm around mine as if to show I was already spoken for. It was one of those compliments for which I took no credit because I'd done nothing to earn it. Olle came into focus again, looking at us, smiling, and I waved good-bye after the departing woman, who said, "Nice meeting you, but I have to run." And she did.

We walked around the corner of the building into the alley. Olle pulled his garnet-colored Honda before us, and off we went. "Well, Jada, I said life should be an adventure; here we go." His apartment was small, cramped with a few pieces of furniture, not antique quality, but neat. No dishes sat in the sink, and as I ran my eyes along the walls I noticed no cobwebs. He'd hung pictures on the little wall space he had.

"Well, what do you think of the rug?" he asked.

I looked to the floor. "It's nice."

"It's perfect," Jada corrected me.

"It's dark in here, and it needs to be cleaned. If you buy it, I'll clean it first."

"How much do you want for it?"

"Umm, how's three hundred dollars? I think that's pretty cheap. You won't find rugs for that price. It's in great condition."

"I think you should buy it," Jada said from the couch. Her next operation was scheduled for the following week; she had to be tired from standing at the antique store.

"Okay. But I didn't bring that much money with me."

"That's okay; I have to clean it anyway. In a week or two?" I was the only person standing and looked for a chair. "That's my table. Everything else in here is just junk I picked up." A snaky light overlooked a slanted white drawing table.

"Did you do the art work on the walls?"

"Naw. I studied graphic art in college." *Did this man ever stop smiling?*

"Where was that?" I asked, sitting down next to Jada.

"I went to a little community college up north where I lived, up in Biwabik."

"Biwabik, I've been there," Jada chimed.

"Yeah, pretty small, isn't it? I grew up in a trailer there. When I graduated, I applied to Stassen Law School." He must have expected surprise because he added this unsolicited explanation: "It's not that hard to get in there; it's just a small school, not like Mitchell.

"The professors didn't think I'd make it. There was one class, near the end; we had to build a case and try it in a mock court. That was a hard class because they're doing everything they can to pick your case apart. My partner and I worked really hard on it. And you know what made us win?" Olle laced the pause with gentle laughter, his eyes twinkling, enjoying the telling. "It was my artwork. I made drawings to support our evidence and we used them in the trial. My drawings convinced the judge, and we won."

"What? You have a degree in law and you sell antiques?"

"Yeah." Olle smiled some more, his blue eyes playing, and Jada looked ready to get inside his smile and just cuddle. "Then when I graduated, no one expected me to pass the bar exam. My friend, the partner who I worked with, offered to help me study. She was smart and didn't have to work as hard as me, and even she said I'd never make it. But you know what?" He laughed. "She didn't pass. I did." Jada listened delightedly, while I gaped, stunned at the disparity between the professional life he ostensibly planned for and the life he apparently lived.

Olle screwed up his face. "I can't see myself sitting in an office all day. When you get out of law school, all you can do is work for a firm, looking through books, or maybe you work for the county, like Ann, and all you do is put together information. When you're done after a whole day, you don't have time to do things; you can't play tennis when you want to. I like to repair things, and I like to refinish. I knocked out the front wall of the shop and put in that plate glass window. It looks nice, doesn't it?"

"Yes, it does."

"And I put the lettering on myself. I'm going to paint a sign on the door, too. It'll look a lot better."

"When," I stammered, still trying to integrate this whimsical rejection of the suit-and-tie life for tennis shorts; the thread in one of the darts in back was broken. "When did you open your antique shop?"

"Last week," he chuckled. Jada and I turned to each other like magnets. It was possible that we had been Olle's first customers. Possibly his only customers, based on his desperation to sell his rug. "So, you put in all that work and time in law school, but you found out that you want to be an antique dealer."

"No, I'm not going to do this forever. I just thought it would be a way to make some money. People will pay anything for a piece of furniture if they like it. I can get stuff cheap and fix it up and charge a lot of money." His smile broke. "What I'd really like to do is sell my t-shirt designs." Olle sprang from the chair and extracted an onion-skin colored paper from a folder. "See, here's one I did a while ago. And here are some drawings that I want to put on shirts." He handed me the folder and turned to a closet door. "I had some samples made up of some other designs. Want to see them?" Folded clothing were neatly stacked as if they had been molded and plotted out to conform on the shelves. From the uppermost shelf he grabbed a few shirts, shaking out a blue one and letting it drop open in front of his chest. "See-ee?" he beamed. "Pretty silly, hunh? I actually sold this design to another guy. He bought some others, too. I wanted to sell the shirts to him, but he wouldn't buy unless he could print them himself. Now he's making money on my designs."

Underneath giant mosquitoes with boxing mitts sparring each other inside a ring were the words, "Minnesota's official state sport." Olle smiled at them and then at me.

Jada arrayed the shirts. "I like this one the best," she said holding up the big-schnozzed male figure in a parka. "Discover Minnesota" was written in white letters, from which snow, apparently, fell and gathered about the man in a massive drift.

"It would be cooler if I could add color. Do you know how much money it costs to have just one made up?" Olle stopped smiling. The look on his face could wring sympathy from a rock. "I've got the ideas. But I don't have any money."

I looked snobbishly at the shirt with the two outhouses, ice fishing houses in the "Land of 10,000 Lakes," listening to the falling story, every sentence a stone that, tumbling down the hillside, nudged another, generating momentum, not sure where was bottom.

"How much money do you need?" It was Jada's question. She was looking at me.

"Oh, five hundred, a thousand, maybe. It all depends on how many colors you use and what kind of a deal you get from the printer." Olle pulled the shirt away and clutched it in his hand. The room was full with his tall muscular body reaching to pick up a paper design.

"Mom, you've got some money; why don't you lend him some?"

"Well, um, wait a minute, Jada. I can't just jump into something without knowing what I'm doing."

"What's there to know?" You said you wanted adventure. Come on, Mom, take a chance!"

"Who would buy these? I mean, how would you sell these? It's not the kind of stuff I wear."

"I don't wear this either," Olle chimed. "People at the lakes and that—they like this kind of stuff. It's Minnesota; they get a kick out of making fun of being Minnesotan." He tossed the shirt with the others; it landed on the mosquito aspiring to be the state bird.

"You'd get your money back because you'd get part of the profits. The other guy saw how it could work for him and wouldn't let me share in the take. But I've got it figured out that everyone could make money…if I just had some money to get started."

Jada exuded sparks. I worried. This adventure wasn't a ball with a bell inside, at some times fun to play with, at others, better hidden under a dark and dusty cabinet. But, if I always gathered dust, I'd never hear the ringing. "Okay," I heard, and Olle grinned so wide a ship could have passed between his lips.

After her second hip surgery, I drove Jada to physical therapy where she was instructed to swing her hips side to side instead of lifting them up, thrusting them like slingshots and rocking her weight forward to her tiptoes. Business-bound, we made frequent visits to Olle's antique shop. Always there was something he had saved and set aside for me. Mostly we stood at the display counter and talked, he about what he didn't have, decent food to eat, rent money, and a hard-working business partner. Karen was always "sitting on her fat fanny," while her no-account-good-for-nothing-free-loading husband was not to be seen. I listened with a mix of sympathy and aloofness, in about the same proportion to the smile on his face and whine in his story. And our conversations always concluded with the working of his plan.

August had the cinematic reputation of being unbearably hot and humid with everyone's fleeing the city for fresh country air, such as the wife and kids in *The Seven Year Itch*. The truth was that we lived quite comfortably without the insufferable sunspot of New York; August nights in Minnesota often cool to autumn lows, trees begin to yellow, and the sun has sidled over to the rim of the sky and can't raise itself high or long enough to bake a person's skin. Late on a balmy morning in August, breezes spurted through my open windows and flitted past Jada who sat in the dining room on one of the chairs I bought from Olle. In the basement of his store, he showed me how to nail down a mat of caning with a wooden cord set into the groove along the perimeter, warning me not to whack the nail too hard, and then watched me chip the wood with a hefty swipe of the hammer. I answered the ringing telephone. "Oh, hi!" I said to Olle's laughter, then, covering the mouthpiece, said to Jada,

"It's Olle." Into the phone I said, "I'm sure we can. Jada and I were just making plans for this afternoon."

"What is he saying? Ask him if he's put any food in his refrigerator yet."

"Get on the phone," I mouthed. In the meantime I was getting directions. Hanging up the receiver, I announced, "He wants to look at the silk screens before the shirts are printed and then get some lunch."

"Did he include me?"

"I made it clear that we'd all go. Why didn't you take the phone when I motioned to you?"

Jada retreated, settling her weight on the chair back and then straightened her arms and legs to a standing position, still looking somewhat clumsy, a driver accustomed to an automatic transmission driving a vehicle with standard. "He wants you, anyway," she answered.

"What would somebody that young want with a woman my age? Besides, listen to what he talks about, the things he does. We don't share the same interests. I've got a lot of things to take care of, and all he wants to do is play."

"Will you stop saying that about 'you're too old?' What difference does it make that you're older? Look at Chris Cantor. She was eighteen when she started seeing that guy, and he was in his forties. There's nothing wrong with playing around."

"You have to be careful with people's emotions." I sounded like I was giving a lesson in streaming hot milk into egg yolks so they wouldn't cook solid when mixed. She walked to her room with unaffected confidence while I lagged in some earlier epoch. "He'd be like a toy. I don't treat people that way."

Besides, we were now in business, and everyone knew that in business, affairs should be restricted to business. We had made ourselves equal partners, so to speak. Olle would do the art work, get the shirts to the printers, collect them; Jada, going back to college in a few weeks, would keep records, and, of course, since I had the money, I would order the shirts wholesale and pay for them. Jada and Olle both assigned me the job of selling the printed shirts, a job he said was a natural for me. Selling was not natural, not for me, I said, and when school started, I wouldn't have the time. Nevertheless, I filled out the application filing the name of our infant company with the state and sent it with the registration fee. And so was spawned JIOgraphics: J for Jada, O for Olle, and I for Idina, right in the middle.

We held board meetings, as we called them, around the table in the dining room, Olle brought me to a salvage yard in search of any old thing that could be fixed up and added to my condo, and we went to lunch. The school year started for me, and on Labor Day weekend, it was back to Mary Hillyard for Jada and the arrival of our August heat. Olle was excited about playing in a tournament and smiled, "You gonna come and watch me play?"

It was a long stretch of a weekend; Sunday's breakfast with Dom left the rest of the morning dragging itself over noon like a rake over simmering coals, restlessness the ashen remains. I drove to the tennis courts.

Standing against the fenced-in court in the prickly yellow and green grass, I recognized Olle's white shirt, white shorts, his brown legs, his ratty-looking tennis shoes. They took a lot of wear and tear he told us. To be really good, a tennis player had to keep himself in new tennis shoes. He asked, in his half serious smile, if we knew how much a pair of tennis shoes sold for. So he played in the ones he had, weak at the seams, worn at the soles. I watched the back-and-forth of the ball, the swoop of the rackets, the rock and the lunge until finally the two men stopped.

Olle sauntered to me at the edge of the court. "It was a tough match, but I won. The guy I played, he's got an unbeaten record at the club. Now, he *used* to have an unbeaten record." Olle's chin pointed as he smiled and laughed with his new glory. He detached himself from the real things and worked at the fun things because he could get away with it. Olle added, as if he were still talking victory, "He asked me if that was my significant other watching us play."

"What would make someone say that? I thought there was a big tourney here."

"It didn't work out; too many people went out of town. We're going to look for some water and then we'll play another set. Not too smart, hunh, to come without water?"

I looked around and saw only stubble leading up to the brick walls of a school building on one end and a row of houses behind us. He was right about the holiday weekend: not one person, besides us, was out on the street.

"I guess I'll go, then. Jada's gone, I drove her to the airport yesterday."

"You're lonesome without her!" Olle watched me through the metal diamonds of the fence wires, his straight teeth showing. "What are you doing later? Want to go to a movie and get something to eat?"

"Sure. What one do you want to see?"

"Let's go to the place you keep talking about on campus. Movies usually start about 7:30. Why don't you pick me up at around 6:45?"

We were friends; no, we were more complicated than that. He sold furniture to me; well, he found things for me to buy. He needed a place to store an unusual chair—the back of it was attached by hinges so that when raised, it was transformed into a table—and he needed to borrow money for car insurance; the chair was collateral. We went scrounging together, and afterwards, we ate lunch. We were going to a movie, plain and uncomplicated.

Olle smiled even as he opened his mouth to bite into the pillowy brown bun sandwiched between his fingers and talked about Karen and business, how he knew the area around the U because his mother had had a hip replacement, and he wondered why Jada had the larger of the two bedrooms and bathrooms, and why I was spending money on her furniture instead of mine.

"She needs privacy, a place where people can visit her without my being in the way. Besides, she'll graduate in three years; I don't want her to move out just as we're getting her room together." He pulled half a glass of chocolate malt through his straw, silvery blue eyes sparkling across the table.

"So you're pretty good at tennis," I observed. He laughed. "I have a friend who plays tennis."

"Why don't you arrange a game for us? It helps my game when I don't play the same people. You get used to their style and then you don't have to work at the game."

I nodded. Olle pulled out his wallet and I shook my head. "No, let me. You'll just have to borrow from me later, anyway." He smiled.

Jada had moved to Walden Hall, a larger dorm, and going back as a sophomore, she acted as if she'd grown an inch taller. She almost had. When measured at the clinic, the top of Jada's head had risen a quarter of an inch for each replacement operation. With rounded femoral heads and released from the grinding pain, Jada rose to the challenge of her sophomore year.

I told her I'd gone to a movie with Olle and asked about her new dorm. She reminisced. "He's so cute! Did he ask about me?"

"He wondered why you get the big beautiful bedroom. He thinks you're something of a princess."

"You didn't tell him, did you? Just a minute; someone's at my door." Jada's gurgling voice came through alternately clear and muted. "Mom? I'm sorry. We're trying to get some stuff together for a Parents' Weekend Committee meeting. It's going to be so much fun this year. I might have to get sweatshirts for the committee from our company. This year's color is red. I also need new curtains. Those old ones don't fit."

"Maybe some lace panels or something?"

"Whatever you think. Oh! Can you send that blue fold-out thing to me? I can use it here. Oh, Mooie, I wish you could be here to take care of me. You could kiss me and hug me and...."

"And do your dishes and your laundry and ironing. And maybe a paper."

"No, you wouldn't. You'd make me do it better. You never let me get away with anything. You made me the way I am, you know."

"If that were true, I'd be proud because I'm proud of who you are, strong, confident. But you've become yourself. I was just there to help you along."

"You don't know the real me. I'm not strong."

"Are you kidding? I think your telling the doctors what you want shows you're strong; I think your getting on the plane to a school away from everything you know shows you're strong; I think your dedication to your studies shows you're strong. Lady, you're strong."

"I don't feel so strong."

"We shouldn't be fooled by other people who are cocky and look confident on the surface. Maybe they have something to hide—or nothing, really. Maybe it's a big front to cover up their insecurity. I know you, Jada. It's not easy being strong. There are no arrows pointing the right way; there'd be no moral decisions if there were."

"I don't know what you're doing being a teacher. I hope your students appreciate you."

I winced, wondering what my daughter thought I should have been better than a teacher. "Anyway, so Olle's waiting for me to get out and sell those t-shirts. I'm bringing some up to my mother's next weekend and see if I can sell some there, and I thought I'd try that novelty shop on Franklin. You know, selling is not my style."

"Just go in and pretend you're teaching, and don't apologize for the price."

"I was suckered in. I don't know the first thing about who to see or what to say."

"They want to make money, too. If you talk to them like that, maybe it'll help. Gotta go now, Mooie. I have a lot of things to do."

"Okay, bye; love you, Angel."

My life on the telephone was just beginning; when the need to talk hit either one of us, it came on like a craving for chocolate.

Time of day didn't matter, except I was usually in bed and asleep by ten, which didn't mean anything by Eastern standards, to which Jada adapted easily, enthusiastically honking the car horn at another driver's slow-poking ways. When the phone rang, I expected to hear Jada's voice.

"Hi, it's me, Olle. It's not too late to call, is it?"

Bluish-green ones and two other digits not worth mentioning illuminated the face of the clock like a miniature neon searchlight. My elbow slid into my pillow as I sank to the mattress. "No, that's okay," I said crisply, alert, not just awakened from sleep.

"I just got back from playing tennis at the club. I picked up a bag of burgers on the way home and I'm having them for supper. Probably not too good for my diet."

"You don't need to worry about a diet."

"You know what they call...."

I didn't, nor did I know what lame-brain thing Karen did to irritate Olle that day. I laughed and sighed and agreed with his narration and reassured him that I was going out with his t-shirts. Yes, I would come into his shop, later, after he closed. But now it was time to say good night.

I hadn't made any sales, but I had made contact and proudly reported my initiative to Olle who didn't like the terms the shop owner presented, taking only samples, not orders. The sports shop in Willow River sold mostly fishing gear and did not cater to tourists. My mother suggested that we advertise as a mail-order-only business.

"Jada, I get the feeling," I reported, "that he's pushing me; he doesn't say it, but... there's no business to talk about, but he called a board meeting. Here, tomorrow."

"Without me? Is he still all tan?" Olle's image materialized for me, as it must have for Jada. Probably not the same.

"I guess. He keeps talking about going on a diet, but he sure doesn't look like he's got any fat to me. Do you know, he likes to drink whiskey sours? Besides beer, of course. Dos Équis with lime." These preferences he revealed when we went for dinner at the neighborhood place, and after the tennis match between Thomas and Olle, when we stopped for drinks.

"Oh, I should just give up." Jada sighed voluminously. "He's there and I'm here. I need someone here. But I'd sure like to have him."

I took her last comment at face value, assuming wistfulness, like having a crush on a distant and unattainable movie star.

I came to expect Olle's 11:00 o'clock phone calls so was surprised early one night. "This is unusual," I said. Olle laughed, said he wasn't able to play tennis, and before he could continue, my call-waiting signal warned me that Jada could be calling. I made it a rule to interrupt for Jada; instead it was Mike asking me to cover a night school class. Olle waited, and as we—he—jabbered, another signal interrupted. The blind date Thomas owed me called for the date.

"Busy night," Olle said when I returned again.

"Three men on the line at one time: a woman's dream."

"I could make your dreams come true."

"It sure isn't like the movies, is it?" Olle always caught me off guard.

"Speaking of movies, remember that friend of mine I went to law school with? She and her husband have been bugging me about getting out and doing something. They think I'm becoming anti-social. They want me to go to a movie and get a bite to eat with them. Do you want to come along?"

"Sure, why not?" Olle said the three of them would pick me up on Saturday night.

Conversation about the movie waned quickly—there was little to say about a mediocre film. What people did for a living ran thin; everyone thinks they know about teaching in a school, most having had years of experience in one. I offered no stories, no explanation, no confessions, though I felt Ann picking for them. Her birthday was the occasion for the outing, which prompted her to ask Olle about his birthday. He answered that he would have a birthday soon. "I'm getting to be pretty old to be just foolin' around," he added.

"Yes, you are. How old are you?" she asked.

Olle smiled. "Thirty-one."

"You are?" I sat up as if someone had come up from behind and poked me in the ribs.

"Don't you believe me?" Olle's smile widened, the sparkles in his eyes making little leaps and bounds, like he had released in them a mob of fireflies. Out from his back pocket came his wallet. "See?" he said, pulling out his driver's license and handing it to me. "How old did you think I was?"

"Oh, 27, 28."

"I wish I was. I'd do a few things differently."

Ann's husband made to study the bill, and I placed a twenty on the table. After a cordial parting, I shut the car door and let myself into the Compton.

Olle's laugh through the telephone became more subdued, his voice lower, after that dinner. I imagined him lounging on the couch, half lying down when we talked, the TV screen flashing whites and grays and blacks a few feet away. He laughed at the ridiculous late-night commercials aimed at lonely men. He watched television a lot; I watched it not. I announced my Parents' Weekend trip to Massachusetts, to which he replied, "Have a good time."

Things had been going well for Jada. She had found her niche, using her talents and organizational savvy. She would make a good field marshal. Her room was crammed with a helium tank, cardboard boxes of markers, brochures, and tape; poster board slabs leaned against her desk. On her bed were red sweatshirts, some plain, some laid out, the white lettering, "Parents' Weekend Committee" above the right breast repeating as shoulders overlapped other shoulders, and she knelt painting the letters on a new shirt. "I'm really busy," she apologized, stroking the bristles of her brush. "I have to have these shirts finished by tomorrow. And if someone says thank you for making these, just say 'you're welcome.' I told them you were doing this."

"Why?"

"It's a long story, and I don't have time to tell you now. Here, put this on the chair to dry." Jada capped the jar of white paint at the knock on her door. "Just a minute." She presented the brush to me and stepped outside. Female voices laughed. "Oh, thanks! Have a good week-end!" She returned with a key. "This is for you. You're going to stay in Liz's room."

"I thought I was staying in here with you."

"You were; it's too crowded in here. I'm going to be working on stuff all night and people will be in and out getting things." She was painting again. "You're not going to see very much of me until Sunday. This was more work than I thought it would be."

"Ask me to do something. I've already painted these shirts, I may as well do something else." I laughed.

"They look okay, don't they?" she stood back and tilted her head. "Did I tell you? I joined the Friends of the Art Gallery. We'll go over there tomorrow. As soon as I finish these last two, we can go to supper. Then you can do my laundry."

"Oh, good. I've been waiting for that."

"You said you wanted to help." She beamed a grin at me, wide and twinkling.

And so I did. Dinner was a medley of arrangements and checkups with other young women, also on the committee. Jada and I saw each other in brief encounters, once at breakfast, once at the President's address in the amphitheater, once on the green, near the children's face-painting table. I waited for her outside her door and read the messages, magazine pictures and cartoons, and a postcard, a silhouette of a palm tree sprouting its fronds over a lavender and orange horizon—Hawaii—posted on her bulletin board. We were to meet in her dorm before the evening show—Lionel Hampton playing in the auditorium. Shadows lay across the strip of green and the narrow drive that circled the back of the dorm. Living in a place where it was drizzly and rainy would be hard, not feeling the underside of the sun.

"There you are!" Jada came as a sprite, swift, light, her teeth glittering through her smile as if the sun were reflected from them. Keys jangled as she unlocked the door, and inside, the helium tank was gone from the corner; so were the boxes. Jada tossed the keys onto the desk and tossed herself onto the bed, her arms spread out as airplane wings. She bounced when she hit, the red sweatshirt ballooning like a parachute.

"Someone thanked me," I said, shutting the door, "I said it was nothing. Tired?"

"You should have come on another weekend so I could have more time for you." She raised her torso, forearms propped on the bed.

"Actually, I like seeing you like this. You'd be good in business."

"Speaking of business," she sat up and brought her feet up too. "How is it?"

"Not very good. This selling thing just sort of fell on me and he thinks that's all I should do. He calls and finds reasons for me to come into the shop, and I think Olle is disappointed."

"Why don't you tell him to call the pres?"

"He can't afford to pay his bills now. I suppose he was thinking his shirts would take care of all that." I pulled the chair out and sat, adjacent to a poster of a man with an open trench coat facing a nude bronze sculpture taped to the wall. "Expose yourself to art" was the caption. "He didn't like the idea of mail order advertising, either. Actually, I'm not sure what he wants. Sometimes he says things that I don't get." Jada wore a look of impatience, her eyes rolling skyward when what was obvious to her went over my head. "Do you know anything about phone sex?" I asked.

"What?"

"Olle was saying something about phone sex the other night. He talks so quietly on the phone that I don't hear everything. And he said something about making my dreams come tr...."

"Oh, Mother! He's waiting for you to make the next move." She stood, daring coming back into her blue eyes. "So, what are you waiting for?"

"There's nothing worse than an old fool. Besides, you're the one who wants him."

"Yeah, so what? It's okay if he plugs us both."

"Jada! I didn't expect you were going to finishing school, but is that how you women talk?" She shrugged her shoulders and got up as scenes from *The Graduate* rippled through my memory. "We've been through an awful lot together, Jada, but I don't think we could survive that. I like him, but as a friend; we're business partners, and I'm your mother. Can you imagine the debacle?" She reached into a desk drawer and took out her camera, aimed it at the bed and pressed a button, then pulled my sleeve. Together we landed on the bed, my arms around her, her arms around mine, her head tilted back in Isadora Duncan wantonness, slicing the wind in the front seat of a convertible, scarves flying like banners advocating free love.

Returned to Minnesota, I brought Olle's t-shirts with me to the regional convention of the International Reading Association in St. Cloud and showed them to a woman working at a novelty shop. Alternately scanning the shop for thievery and running her eyes over the shirts, she agreed that the owner could very well be interested in selling them but that, being t-shirts, they would not be a good item to stock on the next to the last day of October. Next spring, though, she assured me, would be a good time to bring them back.

I left a message on Olle's machine, the good news and the bad news, as I saw the situation. I had showered, finished my schoolwork, and sat on a hardback chair with a book. The ghost of Jada, convinced that I liked to torture myself by denying my body the amenities of padding, shook her head at me. I answered simply that I was equipped with enough, and I liked to know the boundaries of a chair—and what was in it. I trusted nothing with cozy nesting places. Give me hard chairs and hardwood floors so I can see what's crawling on them.

Olle returned the call early enough to be interrupted twice to hand out treats. It was the tail end of Halloween, and if he got another bunch of rug rats to come knocking on his door he was going to give them a dose of their own medicine. Like I believed him. "You must get them all day long there," he said.

"Not a one. I bought candy to give out, but they can't get in because we're a security building."

"You mean you've got candy left? Why don't you bring it over? They're nasty here; I see 'em come outta cars from everywhere else."

"No, you don't." He was a victim, I thought, of having to hide his soft inside.

"I could use some candy, though. I bought enough so I could have some and now it's gone, almost. And Dracula's on tonight. Have you ever seen Andy Warhol's *Dracula*? Best movie ever made. Why don't you come over and watch it with me? You'll love it. It's in black and white. I don't like black and white, but this one's good because it *is* in black and white, just what you like. You have to hurry, though; the movie starts at nine."

"You rearranged your living room," I noticed, walking in as Olle stood smiling at the open door.

"Yeah, when I took the rug out I decided to change a few things. I made some popcorn. Want some?" I sat cross-legged on the couch, the bowl between Olle and me.

"Watch this," Olle encouraged me. "This part's funny."

"I never thought of Dracula as being funny before," I mused. "Just an old-fashioned scary story."

"That's just it. He makes it funny. See, look. Where he's supposed to be drinking her blood, he rips her open instead and massages her organs." Dracula moaned. "He's reaching orgasm, only it's not with his instrument." Men, I was learning, made up names for their most precious part as if it had an identity of its own, a tool, or a neighbor: "Instrument, Johnson, Dick, Wallace, Wally." "One-eyed snake" reminded me of a tube forced down the toilet to unplug it. Maybe the movie was a work of art; Olle laughed an appreciable amount. The movie ended, I stifled a yawn. "I better go; I've got to get up for school tomorrow."

"You should have a job like mine," Olle grinned, "so you can do really important things, like watch the late movies. They have some pretty bawdy ones on at night." Golden light from a floor lamp glittered in Olle's eyes, sprinkling minuscule specks of gold dust amid the blue. "But then you couldn't buy my antiques. And you'd have to live in a place like this. And not have any food in the frig." He leaned forward, and thinking he was about to stand up and show me to the door, I stood also.

"There's a trade-off for everything. Thanks for the popcorn. Good night."

"Don't let the bed bugs bite." He smiled; actually, he had been smiling, but this smile was silly, so it was a noticeable smile. Smiling back, I closed the door behind me.

In between our telephone visits, I visited Olle at his shop, buying salt and pepper shakers, a pin for Jada, or he and I, both with nothing planned, planned supper on the spot. "If you're not going home to Biwabik for Thanksgiving dinner, why not eat with us, Dom and Jada and me? I won't be fussing much; I'll be teaching night school on Wednesday night. Speaking of, Jada wondered if you were available to pick her up at the airport. Her flight arrives while I'm in the classroom."

Before leaving for school, I taped a poem, "My Daughter's Coming Home," on the door to unit 607, Jada's home, our home, the home I wanted her home to be: a place where someone waited for her, a place where she gathered strength, not dissipated it with clinic visits, retching jags, and frantic, furious face-offs. And on Thanksgiving, I felt rewarded.

Steam from cooking dishes clouded the kitchen windows through which the sun made its feeble attempt to stave off persistent November gloom; I'd have been happier with gray in all its splendor. The turkey was on its platter, the gravy bubbled in the pan. "Okay, everybody ready?" The table, full with four people surrounding it, was dwarfed by Dom and Olle, Dom's broad shoulders alone nearly taking up the length of the narrow end. Olle's yellow sweater draped his torso indifferently, making him less defined except as a giant happy face. We cleared the table for games and played until, like all holidays, the togetherness became a cramp and we were ready for pie, pumpkin flecked with cinnamon, and sweet potato cheesecake, cherry.

The only light at the kitchen windows as I stood before them, washing dishes, came from an occasional yellow window across the courtyard, some becoming muted as people drew shades to keep their light from escaping. Dom had driven himself back to his dad's, and the essence of bantering voices and occasional laughter made Jada and Olle's locations bleeps on a radar screen as they moved from the dining room to the living room and into her bedroom. They emerged; Jada announced, "We're going to Olle's to watch a movie," as she was getting their coats. Accompanied by Olle, Jada walked with confidence, as if her body was starting to fit her better. The cast of her skin glowed warmly, too.

A week passed since Jada's return to college when Olle and I sat at my favorite table, against the wall, near the back stairway at Zander's. Above my right shoulder was a massive oil painting of a robust woman reclining against a boulder, bolts of white gauzy fabric dripping from her shoulder, catching in her crotch, her large creamy white bosom bursting through, begging for tender lips and a warm tongue to lap them. Across the marble-topped table, Olle made conversation, the forgettable kind, while I was attracted to the affair of a couple sitting in the adjoining dining room, behind Olle, who nursed a whiskey sour.

"Mmmm. I forgot what we were talking about." His hand slashed the air next to his glass. "I talked to Jada today."

"Oh, yeah?" Olle's eyes glittered through his golden eyelashes. "How is she?"

"Fine. A little down. She'd like you to write her a letter."

"Write a whole letter? I don't even write my folks. I hate to write." He was sucked back into his chair.

"It doesn't have to be long—just a note to cheer her up. She likes to get mail. Anybody does when they're away."

"I bet you keep the U.S. Mail in business writing to her." Olle's chin pointed with his smile.

"And Ma Bell. Some people make house payments; I pay the phone bills and Northwest Airlines." I dipped into my jacket pocket for a pen and pulled the napkin from under my cup, cold cappuccino foam dried along the lip, and inked out Jada's address. "Right now I'm making up a finals' survival kit to send her. You don't know where I can get a beanie, do you?"

Olle looked down at the scrap of napkin before folding it and tucking it carefully behind some bills in his wallet. "A friend of mine's got one with a pig and a propeller on top of it, but I don't know if he'd part with it."

I considered. "Well, I don't have a lot of time. Actually, I decided to make her a beanie—her thinking cap, right? I'm going to machine stitch 'Jada Flyer' on it."

Olle nodded his head. "Why don't we make a spinner for it? I'm pretty sure I've got a piece of plastic in the trunk of my car. I think I could make it work." He laughed when he saw me smile. "I've got a lot of stuff in the trunk of my car."

"What would you cut it with?"

"I've got that, too. Let's go; we'll do it now." He rattled the ice chinks in his glass and swallowed what was left. Two men sat coddling their drinks; at the great mass of a bar, an antique, laughter erupted, spiking like timpani after an interlude. It couldn't have been very late, I didn't think, but the bar was almost empty. In December, unlike June or July when the night sky turns lazily from yellow to blue to pink to purple, once the view of the sun has been cut off, the sky is dyed a deep indigo which bleeds through so many layers that even the moon loses its whiteness, lasting from late afternoon into night, making time not so much a measurable quantity as a state of interminable disgrace, and we walked the two blocks to my condo in near darkness.

Olle lifted the trunk of his Honda, parked near the light post, and rummaged the contents: a tennis shoe, its laces dangling from the uppermost holes; a rumpled shirt which he flung by the sleeve into the darkened interior; empty Mountain Dew cans that rattled as if they were tied to the bumper of a car and being scraped over the pavement; a sock, no, two, balled up from when taken off; a sack. I shivered. "Aha!" he said triumphantly, holding up a rectangular piece of milky plastic. "Bet you thought I didn't have it." His square teeth made their customary appearance in a smile. He shook his head and resumed searching; soon he produced a slender tool, the instrument he would use to carve the propeller, and held it high, like a torch, then trudged behind me, at first balking, up the flights of steps to the sixth floor.

On the breadboard, Olle's strong squarish hands, the tips of his fingers poking out from his coat sleeves, began to work. The palm reading book identified hands like his as belonging to artists, a shape I considered more earthy than creative. He drew and carved. "Nah, that's not right," he snickered. I looked on as he carved another, wider spinner and held it under hot water until the two ends twisted in the middle like a propeller blade. "Have you got some paint?"

"Acrylics."

"That'll work." When the spinner cooled, he tapped a nail in the center and painted the spinner red. Then he added white strips to the tips. "See-hee?" He laughed. "Cool, hunh?"

"Very," I admitted. "But how do I attach it so that it spins?" Olle explained the process as if he'd made dozens.

It was late. Olle stood at the door, as I held its handle. "Now I have to go out where it's cold. I hate the cold. This coat looks good, but it sure isn't made for cold weather." He held the right side of his coat open. "See, it's got just a thin lining." I nodded, and he continued, a wry twist of his lips making one of his eyes wink. "But I can't afford another one, so. Well, good night."

"Good night, Olle. Thank you for helping."

"Any time," he said, backing away, smiling, his coat flaps open.

I told Jada how Olle and I had made her cap. "You know he calls almost every night, well, when we don't see each other. I'm making a Santa outfit for Minnie Holiday to put in his window display." Minnie was a large stuffed mouse I'd sewn and dressed in different costumes for each of the holidays. I agreed to make her into Santa Mouse at Olle's request. Jada listened, and I gave in to the luxury of the pause that followed, my eyes picking out the pock mark in the table, glazed over with varnish and begging to be picked like a scab, the beginning squeals of "LoveSexy" on the CD player in the background.

"I can't wait to see him again. I got a letter from him," Jada said. "Not a real letter. He cut a sliver from a dollar bill and glued it to the edge of paper so that it looks like he put real money inside an envelope. Then he wrote on it, 'Use this when you're shopping.' And then on the other side he wrote 'Ha ha. Fooled you.' He did, too. It made me laugh."

"I'm glad he wrote. I think for someone who doesn't like writing to write to you is pretty nice."

"Yup, I'm writing him back," she said cheerfully. "I need a man. Almost everyone here has someone who comes to see them on the weekends. Or they go to see someone somewhere else. I don't have anyone anywhere. None of the guys here want to get serious. Anyway, I haven't met anyone I want to get serious with."

"You know the saying: 'No man is better than any man.'" In the meantime, I thought with self-recrimination, I was accepting blind dates and had, as a matter of fact, agreed to meet Thomas's barber, an "any man" in anyone's book.

"I guess. But it gets lonesome. Too bad Olle doesn't want to get serious."

"I thought you didn't want someone so far from where you are."

"I don't. But he is pretty cute." Jada's tone changed, sounding like it had been trimmed with twinkling lights. "And I'd have him there when I came home. That's better than nothing."

"What about that Pat you see, Daniel's friend?"

"Oh, he's nice, but I can't get excited about him. I don't think he cares that much about me, either. It's just something to do. Do you think it's okay to tell him?"

"That's up to you. It's probably a respectful thing to do."

"Will you do it? It'll sound funny coming from me, I mean, like, I can't just come out with it without a reason. And I don't want him to ask me any questions."

"Sure. If I see him before you come home."

"You will. You know he likes you."

"Yeah. He likes my money. Too bad I don't have any; I think it'd be fun to run an antique store."

"No, Mother. You have enough junk already. Besides, you don't have enough time. You already spend too much time on your job and not enough on your baby."

"Well, then, that does it. When you come home, we'll have plenty of time for each other. That's only in a week and a half. Can you believe it?"

"This will be the best vacation. I'll get rid of this arm thing and I'll be on my way."

The table under the bosomy female occupied, we took one at the far end of the bar, near the railing, where the view into the intimacies of other couples in the dining room was obstructed. I sighed in honor of the ideal, a tip of the hat to F. Scott Fitzgerald in his old neighborhood, and settled at the table for two.

Olle squinted, as he sometimes did when he wasn't smiling, and it caught me in wonderment at how he was in constant entertainment of his face; the little lamp set between us in the darkly-lit room wasn't bright enough to reveal anything less subtle than a show of blatant emotion. Franklin nodded to me as he slid down to our end of the bar, a white towel in one hand making a swipe after the glass he removed with the other. Franklin, white hair groomed along his chin and up to his earlobes, a distinguished contrast to his black vest and bow tie, made bartending look like a gentlemanly thing to do, and the romance attracted me to it. Waiters at Zander's changed, but Franklin was always there, a staff, a candle in the window, reassurance that everyone, no matter what travails strained their relationships, could part on congenial terms, the warm glow of an hour or two spent in a days-gone-by setting guiding them home with temporary blindness. He was a comfort.

Acknowledging Franklin's greeting with a smile, I directed the end of it to Olle. A half-empty beer bottle before him and cappuccino froth sinking in the cup between my hands, I said, "Thank you for writing to Jada. She said your trick was funny."

"Yeah," Olle laughed. "Real funny." Unexplainably I felt sorry for him. His childhood in a trailer home caused him some discomfort—not unlike my own embarrassment living behind a fruit stand on a busy street, with laborers for parents in a storybook world of doctors and stay-at-home moms. We weren't very different, Olle and I, except his growing up made him smarter, mine made me dumber.

"She said it made her laugh; isn't that what counts? You know she's quite smitten with you."

"Oh, yeah?" The chuckle was shallow, like it came from the roof of his mouth, and I wanted to bet that he blushed, but the color of his face was overshadowed by the lamp.

"You know why I knew about that leg operation your mother had? Jada's had two of them, one on each leg." Olle looked up, and his lips sucked in close to his teeth. "She wants you to know that she has leukemia." Olle swooped in a mouthful of air and rocked a little in his chair as if bracing himself for a turbulent ride. "She was diagnosed when she was twelve, got through the first treatment phase, then relapsed. She's on drugs and comes home for treatments. At Christmas she's having surgery on her arm to loosen some tendons that were damaged by an infection during the relapse.

"So, I have another favor to ask of you." The waiter revived my mug with coffee and, after dumping a container of cream into it, I cupped my hands around its warm body. "The prospect of a cure is supposed to be there, but Jada doesn't count on it. She plans for a very intense future. She wants to finish school, have fun, get rich, date guys, and get married. She also wants a condo of her own, an executive job, and a BMW. Those I can't do anything about. But…."

Olle hadn't touched his beer. "I sent away for this genuine zircon imitation diamond ring." Extracting a box from my pocket, I opened it. "I got it free, except for postage. Will you give it to her for Christmas? It's just for fun, and that's what she needs as long as she can't have the real thing."

A smile just tickling the ends of his mouth, Olle accepted the ring and transferred it to his own pocket. I took my coffee seriously, scraping the spongy white foam from the walls of the cup, swirling the caramel colored liquid, and downing it before it cooled. Olle squeezed his lime and took a swig of beer, letting the bottle anchor his hands to the table and stretching the quiet space awkwardly between us, not the stifled hush of a crowd before a diver's plunge into the pool, but rather the diver's residual deafness as she issues from under water, not hearing the thunderous applause for victory.

Just before Christmas, the day after Jada came home, she underwent surgery with a prognosis for uncertain results. I decorated the pole by her bed with a plastic tube of red and white carnations and roses tucked into a red and white Christmas stocking.

She, her dad, and Dom went to Maureen's for Christmas Eve, I enjoyed the newness of the experience of aloneness. Andreas Vollenweider's harp played from the dark living room while I painted a Christmas tree ornament at the table, my all-purpose work area where I'd just rolled out pie dough and we'd eat dinner the next day. Atop the cathedral, lights cast their green halos into the night sky, and across the courtyard, a window blinked tiny sparkles of red and gold and blue and green. The Christmas decorations and the tree that festooned my living room provided a continuity of tradition in a changing life.

Just as happily I prepared for our Christmas Day meal; seeing Jada and Dom in the white noon sunlight that scoured away at the jungle of fern-like fronds frosted on the bottom panes of the windows, I liked Christmas belonging to us this way. On another cold and sunny afternoon, Olle, Jada, and I made our gift exchanges. Jada, sitting in the rocker, holding the package steady with her heavy cast and picking it open with red-painted fingernails on her right hand, opened her "diamond" ring. It would be tempting to say that gift precipitated the change in our relationships with each other, but like all changes, they creep along making you ready for them even when you think you're not, and when you finally find things different, you want to isolate one event, one day, one thing someone said as the cause.

But from that day when Olle gave Jada the ring, things *were* different. The phone rang the next night, around eleven, as usual, but when I picked up the receiver, Jada was already on hers, announcing through the hallway, "It's for me, Mom." Jada and I did not go together to Olle's after that, nor did we have board meetings. I hadn't seen or talked to Olle alone since Jada had come home.

Jan. 21ˢᵗ

I have spent a lot of time with Olle. Tonight we planned to go to a movie but we stayed at the Camden Diner too long. So we rented two movies (one of them was my favorite "About Last Night") and brought them to his apartment. Well just as we were getting cuddly, a woman knocked on the door and wanted to talk to him about something that was bothering her. Olle and I were surprised and it looked like he and she were embarrassed, as I was. But finally she left and we got comfortable tangling up together on his bed. Those were seven of the most desirable hours! He has the most sensual kiss I've ever had—and his touch sends tingles all through me! I think I could have had sex with him—I know I wanted to! I love how sweet and compassionate he is. Leave it to me to start analyzing and wishing we could talk and I knew just how he feels!

I'm having fun, though, even if I'll probably ruin it for us. He's going to call me later today (it's 2 a.m.) and I am excited to talk to him and see him again. Maybe I'll help him with his laundry again. It's weird that I enjoy doing things like that with him. But I don't get tired around him and actually enjoy folding his clean clothes. When I go over to his apartment in the morning, he gets me into bed with him. Oh, I care about him so much and want to know how he's feeling and what I should expect about us! If I could, I'd ask him what he thinks of me and if my leukemia makes a difference. I'd want to tell him about my special love for him and how much I enjoy being with him and ask him if I am special, too, or just another woman in his life, like the woman who came last night. I also want to know if he can be serious or if I can't plan on anything serious from him. I like planned things because they are stable and I know what I can hope for. But I don't get so hurt when things are not planned because I didn't count on things working out and feeling to blame for it. Oh I think too much! Not just about Olle and my love life but that's a theme of my life in general.

Living in a state of hazy gray is driving me BONKERS!! School, operations, relapse, boyfriends, my loss of virginity, going on trips and vacations, the condo. I could go on forever about uncertainties in my life! I wish I could live in a world of black and white. It's worse at school. I don't have a close friend there, not Patrick, not Olle, not Mom (though she's been acting funny). I think why I don't like to be at school is that I don't have someone to hold me tight. I don't feel like I belong there because of the loneliness I feel there. I think I am doing things because other people want me to and my spirit is floating somewhere else, not knowing what I want, just what I should want. I am happy to be home and want to feel settled and stable. That's why I want a boyfriend out East. He would take away the loneliness when I'm there.

January lived up to its reputation with snow, below-zero temperatures, and laborious travel. School resumed for me, but Jada was home until the end of the month, her only obligation to take care of her arm. Jada took the car at night, if not to see Kimby, I presumed to see Olle. During the day, she got up early and, without changing out of her nightgown, drove me to school.

Driving home one afternoon, she described a cedar chest she wanted and asked me to come to Olle's to see it. "Were you at Olle's today?"

"Yeah, he's got some new stuff you should see." She steered the wheel with her right hand and looked like any other young woman, fair-skinned, pink-lipped, and nubile except for the scar, red and jagged down her left arm, as if a lightning strike had burned its path in her flesh. Traversing the bulges of her papery white skin, the streak exaggerated the cleavage it made.

"Oh, I don't think so. If you want the cedar chest, go ahead and get it; I'll just give you a check. It's your room, you can put anything in you want. Do you go to Olle's a lot?"

"Sometimes."

"What do you do there? He doesn't even get up till noon or so. At least that's what he says."

"I watch him work on things." A piquing curiosity grew unexplained, like Jada's abbreviated statements and her face, so inexpressive as she watched the outdoor scene from behind the driver's wheel.

The cedar chest arrived while I was at school, and on another day, she had two throw rugs cut from the same gnarly fabric, heavier than upholstery weight, lighter than carpeting, in her room.

At night I sat on the floor by the one and only heat register in the living room and restrung beads onto the recovered lampshade. Jada came home and dropped in the rocking chair, another purchase from Olle. "Olle likes what you're doing to the lamp."

"Oh? When did he see it?" I was suddenly too hot and inched away from the blast coming from the wall. I was finding the flaws that show up in the perfect place, the ones that wait to make their appearance after your heart has been stolen. The room was too large and tall for the radiant ceiling heating system, prompting me to nuzzle within the circle of warmth that flared from the register, a grate that covered an electric space heater.

"He stopped by today. He likes the love seat, too."

"Hmm. Do you see him a lot?" I asked, the heat now enveloping me.

"Not much. He asks about you. He always says, 'How's your mother?'"

"Well, he could find out by himself, couldn't he? I haven't done anything differently."

Jada gave herself a little shove backward and the chair tipped on its rocker, the movement an ambiguous evasion. "Have you ever thought about how much time you spend doing that?"

"What, these beads?"

"All of this." Light glared from exposed bulbs, making harsh shadows beyond my workspace.

"I guess when you're doing something you like, you don't think about the time. It's therapy, like aerobics."

Jada shook her head and out of her throat came something as close to a whinny that I could imagine, and the rocking chair creaked forward. "I couldn't do that. You're so creative."

"No, Jada, not creative. I'm productive. You're creative. You aren't limited by shoulds and obligations. This lamp shade is fashioned after the old one; I just added a row of lace."

"Oh, Mother, you're so hard on yourself. You're always working too hard at school and expecting so much of people. No wonder I think I have to get all A's."

I stopped, pinning three beads to the needle with my index finger. "Jada, when have I ever said anything to you about getting high grades? In fact, haven't I told you that grades don't matter? You're the one who thinks a B isn't good enough."

"That's what I mean. It's like going to college. I always knew you expected me to go. I'm always trying to be perfect because I know you want that."

"Does that bother you? Do you think you'd like it better if you didn't have high standards?"

Jada tipped forward again, the metal clasp on her sling knocking the wooden chair. I wondered what Dom, the procrastinator when it came to school work, would say if he were part of this conversation, and I secured another line of beads in place. Did he feel the same push from outside himself, or was it only their individual personalities that created their feelings? Jada admitted, "I like doing the best I can, but sometimes I don't like the pressure."

"You're in control of that. We all are. You should talk to my sister about that. She was the first-born, too, and she always felt she had to do things for my mother."

"I don't want to talk to your family; your family's nuts."

"Now you're sounding like them—us. Careful," I teased.

"Oh, Mooie. At least you almost laughed. I wish you two would patch things up. We used to have fun together. You've lost your giggle glands; you know, you don't even smile any more."

"You mean Olle? Yeah, well, his choice; think Beverly."

Jada got up from the chair, finalizing my sense of emptiness, which, somehow, I felt I had brought on myself.

The last Friday of her last weekend home, Jada went out with the car. I heard the key in the door before I woke up; then the door latch caught with a gasp as if surprising even itself. The green numbers on my clock read 2:30, but I rose and met Jada in the dining room. "Just getting back from Olle's?"

She stood at the refrigerator door and frowned. "Have you got something to nibble on? You know he doesn't have anything."

"Hot chocolate. Shall I cut up an apple?"

"Hmm. Bread, I want bread. How come you don't have bread here?"

"I do. There's some Toast to Bread in the bread drawer."

"No, not that kind, the good kind, plain old mushy white bread you get in the grocery store." She gave the door a nudge; the rubber lining made a smooching sound as it hugged the frame. Picking up the bread and turning it around in her hand, she dropped it back into the drawer at her shins. "No, I'll just skip it. I shouldn't eat anything this late anyway. How come you're up?"

"I heard you come in." Jada shuffled around to the table and sat. She didn't like cats—they made her eyes water and her nose sneeze—but she reminded me of one the way she slunk down into the chair. On Jada, the sweater she wore looked silky smooth and inviting to touch, white mohair sheep knitted in a meadow.

"You're getting pretty serious with Olle. I don't want to tell you who to see or how to run your love life, but I don't think there's sincerity with him."

Jada cocked her head, and the overhead light cast an earthy hint to her cheek. "You take things too seriously. Even Olle thinks you should lighten up."

"I can't take this any other way than seriously. I feel something's missing."

"Yes, you can, and something is missing; I miss our board meetings."

"I do, too, but we've gone beyond that, and that's the point. I mean, how would that be, you and him and your mother."

"Oh, Mother! Can't you just play? You're always worried about everybody else and what they think. He misses you. He still wants to see you." Her scowl turned upside down as she jumped from her seat. "Oh, I'll talk to him tomorrow. I know he wants to be friends again." Her words trailed behind her and I heard the shriek of a yawn from the hall. "Come put me to bed."

Jada arranged for our "peaceful resolution," and Olle stood at the open door with stern attention drawn on his face. Foolishness crept in between us, as if we were two naughty children who had to be shown how to take turns. "Okay," Jada began, "let's get this thing patched up. Who's going to start?"

"Okay," I said, rolling a crystal ball around in my hands, opening them like petals of a flower to reveal the clear orb resting in the nest of my palms. Jada drew in closer, her elbows a fulcrum on which her face tilted. Olle stood beside her, a cockeyed slant to his face, definitely not smiling. "I see a tall light-haired man. He's worried about something. He's at a junction, like a fork in the road, and he's wondering which way to take. One pathway is arduous but worth the effort by its reward. The other is easy, and he is tired. He stands uncertain and struggles with the decision. We never know what gets bargained until the deal is done. I foresee...."

Olle's voice came down, a fist upon the table, a jolt that braked Jada, halting her forward inclination. "I'm tired of you looking for the meaning in things and that stupid ball you have. Do you know how hard it is to work and work at something? It's not easy, you know. I'm behind on my rent. And then there's that crazy Karen and her freeloading husband telling me what to do. I don't have time for your forecasts and monkey business."

Olle's thin angry lips broke sharply as words shot out like a geyser. In his outburst, he had moved farther away from the table and Jada sat back in her chair; we made a skewed triangle, I cradling the ball that centered us. "I've been waiting and waiting for you to sell the t-shirts. You took the shirts to one or two places. You think that's enough? I'd call you and you still weren't selling any shirts."

"I'm not sure I can sell those shirts, and I said that from the beginning. I did what I knew I could do, and that's providing financial backing. I'm sorry I disappointed you, but nothing is lost. You still have the shirts, and *you* still can sell them. You don't need me for that. And I'll still finance JIOgraphics, if that's what this is all about...." The hard lines on Olle's face melted and his eyes cleared. Jada broke the silence. "So, will you shake hands and be friends again?"

"I want us to be friends," Olle said immediately. "I don't know why we can't be. I just wish you'd not try to control everything."

"I'm not sure if we can be friends and still do business, but...." Leaning back toward the center of the table, I said, "I'll check my crystal ball to see if it's in our future." Jada laughed and insisted on our shaking hands. Olle held out his hand and smiled.

Jada wore a sweatshirt with Aunty Quarrie Ann's Trove lettering around the head of a white-haired head, Olle's high school letter jacket, and her genuine imitation diamond ring to the airport.

I had accustomed myself to not answering the telephone ring. Olle's familiar sheepish laugh startled me when I did. He wondered why I didn't come into the store. He had some new items I might be interested in seeing. It was a good excuse to pick up Minnie Holiday. He had changed the entryway: not as inviting. Olle smiled from behind the counter and closed his book, a novel, thick with hackneyed plot and overwrought story. Snowy white sweatshirts with Auntie Quarrie Ann's withered face in the center were piled on an overturned crate. Olle put two plates on the glass counter. "I was saving these for you," he said. "I knew they were right up your alley."

I admitted they were, a rocket ship in flight from the orbiting Earth, and bought the pair. His smile broadened. "We're in business again." I wanted to smile and think that all I had to do was to throw away January and pick up from December, but I couldn't force it.

"I see you've made some sweatshirts. What else is new in here?"

"Not much. January is slow, and I'm having a hard time buying more stuff." He stayed seated while I made a ceremonial tour of his shop, coming back to pick up the plates and saying I had to get somewhere by 5:00. Really it was six, but I couldn't find a reason to hang around. "Do you have Minnie Holiday?"

"No, I took it to my apartment," Olle smiled, surprised. That I named Minnie probably seemed laughable rather than endearing to him. "I'll get it over to you," he added, sobering.

"Okay." I picked up the plates he had wrapped in newspaper. "See you."

Olle called again, wondering if I was busy on Saturday night— there probably was a movie showing someplace that we could see, and I agreed to check the listings. "I'll pick you up at seven, okay? Oh," he said before hanging up, "I have a different vehicle. It's a van."

"How do you like it?" Olle asked, leaning toward me, smiling. Some things never change. It reminded me of riding in an old pick-up truck. It sputtered as Olle put it into gear. "It's not too reliable," he said. "I hope we make it there and back."

"Why did you get it, then?"

"Because I needed something to haul furniture with. And it's cheaper than my Honda." So business was worse than not good. It was possible that the only sales he made had been to Jada, and then to me after she left.

We did make it to a movie and back to Zander's. In the cold, the van coughed its resistance to service. "Fun, hunh?" He turned halfway in his seat and shone his face on me.

"Yes, it was, but I don't think this works. I have no problem doing business with you, but I just don't think it's a good idea to see each other socially any more." Grabbing onto the door handle, I jerked it, making it screech like fingernails dragging on a chalkboard. Cold air gushed through the crack.

"Why do you say that? I don't think that's called for."

"I don't compete with my daughter." I stood on the pavement in front of the door to The Compton, hearing my decision as it was unfolding. Olle, almost never without a smile, strained his lips into a meek imitation. The van's overhead light, which worked, I noted, caught in his eyes, and I said before shutting the door, "You did what I asked you to do; let it go at that." Olle's van wheezed as, I assumed, it rolled toward the street and I toward the door. I would have to give up the table-chair, the bust of Chloe on the mantel, but they were only things, not people.

"I left your phone number on my answering machine for Jada," I said to Jessie as I arrived at her door on a February Saturday morning. "She broke her leg yesterday and she's supposed to call me when she gets back from the hospital." My task was to help Jessie with her new fixer-upper house. Len was there, too, in the basement; he was clever at repairs and remodeling, reconstructing the kitchen, for one thing, while I ran a scraper along the wood of the bathroom window, swollen with stripper fluid. Jessie, her deep brown, almost black hair pulled back in a braid, looked more like she should have been trolling the beaches, not doing grunt work under the sink in a slap-dash house, rooms added on by hook and crook. Isaac sized up a 4-foot fence that Jessie had gerry-rigged at the top of the steps to prevent the cat from getting into the basement and into trouble. Jessie whooped as he leaped effortlessly over it.

"She was sitting in class and when she stood up to get out of the desk, wham, there she was on the floor is what she told me. How crazy is that; she has two 'new' legs, and she's broken one of them already."

Len, who had been lost to the basement, along with Isaac, called up to Jessie for something I couldn't discern from my niche in the bathtub, ruminating Jada's confession of helplessness. As much as Jada criticized me for my selfish sufficiency, she was not much different, knowing that being an imposition on someone was worse than being a wasp at an open soda can. Nor did I want to make her appear to be a whiney mosquito by repeating her complaint, in effect, that good help was hard to find.

A clatter knocked its way up the stairway, adjacent to a wall in the bathroom, and voices accompanied it. Len gave Jessie directions for maneuvering the ladder around the corner when the phone rang. "Where is it?" Len asked, a chuckle underlying his question.

"It's gotta be here someplace." Amidst rustling papers and the sound of one thing bumping against another, Jessie searched. When Jessie's voice breathlessly said hello, I breathed, too, and, after a pause, she said, "Sure, she's right here."

"Mom, I have to come home," Jada blurted into my ear, loud, a pealing bell.

"Okay, Jada, calm down. Tell me all about it. But settle down."

"I'm in a cast, and they gave me crutches! How do they expect me to get to my classes? There's snow and ice all over. And steps. I have to get up to the second floor for some classes. How can I carry my books?"

"At school, some kids carry books for kids with crutches."

"Mom, I can't be on crutches! How about my shoulders? And how am I going to ask someone to help me with my books, anyway? They don't have the same schedule I have. It's hard enough now asking for help." Each sentence came down like a pile driver, hard, piercing, and penetrating.

"Would a wheelchair help? I mean, then...."

"This is not Minnesota. They don't have elevators and handicap curbs like we do. And who'll open the door? Or help me down the steps in front of the door? They're tired of me now! I can't stay here. You've got to get me home!"

Sometimes I forged ahead, giving more importance to day-to-day trees and losing sight of the forest Jada was in. But, hadn't I learned that it was the little things that could do the damage; not them so much as what could develop from them? Nosebleeds, for example. Falls, for another. Yes, leukemia patients had colds and nosebleeds like non-leukemia patients, Dr. Lourde said again and again. They also break their legs, as he told me the night before. "Let me talk to Dr. Lourde again, see what he has to say about this. If I don't call you back, you call me here, okay?"

Len had disappeared, back to the basement, where, I gathered, he was working with a caustic chemical. Jessie didn't hover, but she didn't vanish, either. I dialed Dr. Lourde's pager number and stepped back into the bathtub, picking up the scraper and resuming my task.

The window was as clean of varnish as it would get, and we were hanging paper on the bedroom wall. Jessie slathered thick gobs of paste down the strips; I hung and trimmed. And called Jada. "Dr. Lourde says not to worry about damage to your shoulder sockets because they're not as severely affected as hip joints."

"No, I have to come home!" Jada insisted tearfully. "You don't know how hard it's going to be for me to get around here." Tremors of panic rippled through her protestations, and I wanted to hold my hand out and help her up. I also wanted her to climb up, push herself, test her stamina. "There's snow right outside the doorway. I almost slipped and fell again. Who'll help me get up? What if I break the other leg?" For every obstacle Jada claimed, I countered. Jessie's house was small. She heard my every response. She heard my reasoning. She heard my calmness, my steadiness. She might have thought I was strong, but I was just scared.

Somewhere in her insistence and in my resistance niggled an unnamed bone of contention. I had a feeling, a strong maternal feeling to protect my young, that allowing Jada to come home now was turning her loose too soon and unprepared. She hadn't yet learned how to use her cover; she hadn't had, I didn't think, practice in intuiting her enemy, sensing him, which, in the world of predator and prey, was too late. All it took was one swift swoop, and she'd be meat before she felt it. Did I make Olle too cold and calculated and harsh? "No, you do not need to come home. Coming home would ruin everything you planned, everything you went there for. You'd lose credits and you'd lose your status in the class of '90. Give yourself another day; then we'll talk again."

By the afternoon's end, I had scraped and sanded only one window frame and papered a small bedroom, but I felt as if I had hollowed a mine. And I had at least got Jada through the day; the night might be another challenge.

The sky thickened with darkness as the night gathered around the city like a wooly cloak and I shed my jacket and my gloves. Every time I walked into my home, I made prayer-like ejaculations: thank you for this wonderful place; thank you for these glossy smooth wood floors, lines flowing like currents in a river, sometimes curved and lazy, other times in frenetic whorls tied up in their own knots, and sometimes just rippling outward, easy, even, and spreading out cracked-open, egg-like; the lights; the pictures—I had two—one of a couple dancing the tango, she arching backwards, her neck strained, the top of her head aimed toward the floor, his arm a wiry bar that kept her from a death lunge, so thirties, in evening attire, their noses stuck in the air so to keep themselves above the rotting smell of detritus beneath them. My hand felt the brass switch plate in my bedroom, my eyes anticipating the illumination of fluted glass shades on the light fixture I installed after removing layers of paint to reveal its bronze and delicate embossed patterns of pink flowers and green leaves. So much of what spoke to me came from beneath its present condition, a wondrous beauty revealed by effort. The telephone rang. "Oh, lord," I thought, or maybe said; who knows the difference when you're alone? "Here we go."

"Hi, it's me," Jessie said. "I know you've had a frustrating day, and Len and I were wondering if you want to come to the club with us tonight. We're playing wallyball, and we thought you might want to do something where you could move, help to take your mind off things."

"Thanks; I don't think I can handle anything like that." My weary eyes closed. "What I want to do is soak in the bathtub. I'll be fine." I tossed my clothes and drowned my body in the bathtub, Jada's bathtub where she would lie and I would lay my hands on her. There are no recipes for these nightmares, no matter how we rear children.

Feb. 18th

I just had a whopping fight with Mom on the phone! I got a cast on my leg and the doctor said I had to keep it on for six weeks! It better be off by spring break or I'll crack it open myself! I don't know how I'll get through this semester with this cast! I was so confused and depressed that when I got back I took six or seven ibuprofens. That was really dumb of me because that's not enough to kill me. I really need someone to love me because I hate myself. I get angry at Mom and hate myself for that because I love her and want to be with her. I'm still wanting Olle but don't think I can have him. I don't know what to do and should talk with someone so I can deal with my hidden feelings of unhappiness. My life is a lie and I don't know where to turn to find out who I really am.

Last night's "Thirty-Something" was about a father dying of cancer and his son couldn't handle it. The way the show treated cancer was more realistic than any other I've seen. They showed the dad hooked up and tired and vomiting in a small hospital room. The son was having trouble being close to his wife and child because he realized that everyone was going to die and didn't want them to deal with his own dying. He didn't think life was worth living after seeing his father's fight during the last part of his life and then facing death. I related to the show because it didn't have a happy ending after a small conflict. Mom would like the show, too.

I'm still depressed about Olle because I don't think we'll ever be, and no matter how much I wish we could, I know we shouldn't be. I fantasize about him and feel it's wrong so I try to talk myself out of him, but then I get depressed over that! I'm too attached to him and it keeps me from seeing reality! I think talking to him about my feelings would help, but I don't want to look like a fool and goof up our relationship like I have others. I do so wonder if he really appreciates me or if he's using me. I want to tell Mom that we've kissed. She would never approve of us.

I've been stuffing my feelings and hiding them so I don't have to deal with them and others don't have to know about them. Then when I need to deal with something, I want others to take care of it and take the blame. I might look happy, but I'm really a mental disaster. Living with a yearning to die is an example of why they should probably put me away in some institution. To others I show a nice outer side so nobody really knows how unhappy, unwanted, and replaceable I feel. I'm not sure how I'll stay here. I'm going to see Rachel Franke again today, but I don't want to dig up these feelings because then I might have to deal with them.

It just came to me. I am the one who ruins my life. What a stunning realization! I broke my leg, and I can't blame it on anyone else. Just me! Like everything else I've caused to be shit in my life! It's incredible! A broken leg—my broken leg— showed me this reality.

By spring break, Jada's cast had been removed and her leg muscle had regained its shape. There was nothing in her way now. When she came home, she started disappearing again, and Olle festered deep in the muscle of our relationship, like the red scar in her arm.

We were both on vacation for the week, and Jada was dressing to go out. Standing near the doorway to her room with a cup of tea in my hand, I spoke. "Jada, if it's Olle you're going to see, you have to know that I am concerned."

"Oh, Mom, you're making this an obsession. We're just having fun."

"That's what's wrong. You're getting into some serious stuff. I don't trust him. I don't trust someone who claims to be a friend and ignores me when you come home. And I don't trust a person who messes around with my daughter and then comes around me when she's gone. And he says I'm controlling. Just who is using whom?"

"Mom, you're taking this too hard. Here, put out your hand." I dutifully thrust my arm out, but as Jada brought a red and black woven band to tie around my wrist, I coiled my arms tightly about me. "You're supposed to learn on your own, I know. You can carry on and get your heart broken; I'm not trying to stop that. But, you two want to act as if I'm not a part of this."

The wristband dangling from her hand, she turned toward a stuffed bear and tied the braid around its paw. I took my teacup back to the kitchen.

"Okay, Mom, I'm leaving. You sure you don't need the car?" Jada, her skin velvety, ivory petals with a blush of peachy rose, had outgrown cuteness, though an impish sprite seemed just about to pop out sometimes; nor was she stately, fully beautiful. She had within her a paradox of beauty, strong yet fragile features, fairness with rich undertones, a long straight nose with an upturned end, not full, but well-defined lips, and one large dimple in her chin; she had all the markings of classic Roman. She looked proud.

"No, go on."

Her hand on the doorknob, she hesitated, as if waiting for something, making a mental check. "Okay, then, I don't think I'll be late. Bye." Like a dancer, her body readied to come forward, but then she twirled and crossed the threshold.

Restlessly I roamed the rooms, pulling the shades, stashing my book bag, out of sight, out of mind. My eyes roved the books in my bookcase; nothing interested me, nothing that required a commitment. I wanted to finish something, not gear up, and heaved a fat sigh. She's trying to talk herself out of love, but you can't, I mused. *If he had been honest, made a clean break, not called me the minute Jada left.*

Returning to the dining room, I wished I'd not given up smoking. There was a cathartic release in firing up a match, fiercely striking its head against the abrasive strip and dashing it into the ashtray after jerking the flame out with a gash through the air, pulling in a deep gust of smoke and letting it fill my lungs, clog them, drag the air out of them, then force the smoke out, hard, mean, spiteful.

By the end of the week, Jada's bags were almost packed to return to Mary Hillyard. Spring was busting to come out there, but in Minnesota, it was still frosty at night, and while the snow had melted into soggy lawns, flat and brown, we probably had not seen the last of it for the season. The heat register blasted out a mouthful of hot air as I sat on the floor hemming a jumper for Jada. Light from the lamp that seemed to have started everything with Olle shimmered in an oval just short of my toes. The door grazed to a close behind Jada, who shed her coat on the knobs of a chair and, on the balls of her feet, she tiptoed toward me, a cat traversing pebbles. She still hadn't remastered walking, moving with a hybrid of memories of how best to get coordinated. She sat decidedly on the small bench in the corner opposite the heat vent. "I saw Olle today. I stopped by his store."

I felt my face heat up pink, like the color of the sweater Jada was wearing. She clasped her hands between her pants' legs, paused. "Oh?"

"I think you're right about him." I had already stopped sewing; heaven forbid I should prick my finger and fall asleep until someone came to rescue me with a kiss. I pricked my ears instead, tingling with the heat of curiosity and an overworking heater. "I think he was using us."

"Jada, I'm sorry." Whatever happened surprised and hurt her. But I had a feeling it wasn't as easy as a motion or a word or a look. She was putting things together. It was her secret, and she would tell it if she wanted.

"It'll be hard staying away from him," she acknowledged.

"I'm sorry for you, and I don't like what it's done to us."

Jada made an effort not to smile. "Oh, we'll be okay." In stage musicals we would have broken out in song and dance, twirling our skirts, the little hurt feelings and misunderstandings being flung into the air to evaporate under a glittering revolving ball that sprinkled glancing flickers from the ceiling onto the floor. We didn't and sat for a while, neither one of us keen on long empty spaces. Perhaps I missed a chance to do the sorority thing by getting up and giving her a hug, a show of sisterly support, but she seemed not to invite it, pensive to near boredom, eyes drier than teething biscuits. People, by my code, were not commodities to be grabbed and locked into embraces, so I took no liberties, suspicious that when most people hugged another person they did it to fill their own need instead of at the request of the person they claimed to comfort. In the half-light of the night, Jada went to her room. The floors of our condominium might have been six feet thick, but through the walls of our unit, I heard businesslike movements, the slithering of a near-packed suitcase across the floor, the closet door opening and falling to a close, nothing anything like tears on a pillow.

She left behind a note of reconciliation to me, and we resumed lamenting our loveless lives, except I was to have a blind date. "He's a pretty good sounding man, a college math prof, who does theater, not just any theater, but camp theater. Is he my kind or what?"

Jada laughed. "He's a math teacher, Mom. Don't you know what that means?"

"No," I stammered and squinted through the screen mesh to verify that the drizzle wasn't an optical illusion.

"Just look at the math teachers at your school," Jada coached. "They're the most boring of them all. When have you ever met a math teacher who wasn't? That's why they go into math. Everything is orderly and right. There's an answer for everything."

"But he's a college professor," I protested, the drizzle now beginning to pit pat. A whoop of a wind whistled like an overhead train whistle.

"That makes him even worse! Oh, Mother, don't you know anything? He's in love with his numbers and theories and formulas."

"You're a math major."

"But I'm female, and for us that's unusual. A lot of us who go into math are the odd ones, just the other way around from the men."

"That's true. Women study language. Did I ever tell you I was going to be a math major?"

"You would have gone crazy. You can't even stand the routine of what you do now."

Jada was right, and I reported my experience to her the morning after my date. "You were right, Jada. What gave him away was his shirt: his collar was frayed—on a date, and he talked a lot about the value of things which made me look at his leaning toward camp theater in a new way. Tickets to the play at the church were only $10.00 apiece, not like tickets to the Guthrie."

"You're such a doofus. We need to meet some rich guys, right, Mooie."

"There should be some out there. Did I ever tell you about the rich guy I dated in college? He let me drive his Corvette. But I didn't like him, so I had to give that chance up."

"Oh, there's no hope for you. You wouldn't know what to do if you had money, anyway. You'd probably give half of it away. I'm the one who should be rich. I know how to live with money."

"Yes, you do. So I hope it happens for you. By the way, I was hired for summer school. I'm renting a car for the summer so you can have the Mazda to get yourself to and from the U and the Cancer Society and whatever else you need. How's that sound?"

"I'm sorry, Mooie. I cost so much money."

"Yup, and you're worth it, too. That's why I'm working summer school—to do things we want to do."

"I should get a real job, a job that pays."

"Why? I think that internship sounds good. What matters is what's on your resume, not that you made five hundred dollars."

April 14ᵗʰ

I have been SUPER busy all of a sudden with all my involvements. They are

- *Dorm hostess*
- *Parents' Weekend Committee*
- *Math Department*
- *BMW Weekend Publicity*
- *Friends of Rowing Student Rep.*
- *Library work*
- *Student Admissions Rep.*
- *Committee on making MHC more accessible for the physically challenged*

Mom and I just spent an hour talking on the phone. She said she thought I had not experimented with sex and was surprised when I told her I that I have! I don't want to have sex in the wrong situation or with bad circumstances. I have high standards and don't want to withhold having sex if I think love is part of it.

I drank a strawberry daiquiri at Marianna's birthday party and felt a little tipsy, which I didn't like. I like talking to people, especially guys. I can't find anyone, though, who I want to be with other than Pete, Olle, or even Garrett from Dartmouth. I'm feeling bored and lonely and want to be out dancing. I'm trying to get over Olle because I know deep down he's not the one for me. I do miss his sex, though! I need someone who wants to commit to me and show me love. But besides Olle's gorgeous body, he doesn't seem to have anything to offer me. Besides, he's too poor for my taste. I broke down and called him and asked him if he wanted me out of his life, but he said no and that he was meaning to call me. I don't believe him. He's spending more time with Donna. Just like tennis. One scores love and the other one loses. Me. So out of the game I go.

I made it to the Airforce Military Ball in Boston. Karl invited me to the Ball when he was here visiting and he thought we could have a "romantic" time, but I said no. The ride on the train was fun because I met Davonte (sp??), a senior at Rutgers, who sat next to me. We were late arriving but Boston's subway is easy to follow, and I made my connections from South Station to the T and the switch at Park. I was a little confused when I got off at Arlington but figured out where I was and made it to the hotel. Karl wasn't there to meet me. When I finally saw him coming down the stairs, he seemed surprised to see me.

I changed into my black semi-formal dress with the low back in Karl's room and helped his roommates get into their "mess dress," which is their formal wear. I did Pete's cumberbun—he looked really good! We had dinner in a ballroom, which was off from the dance floor because of a conference for airforce people. We had to wait for the dancing to start because the Penn State Staff made nationals and there was a program. But I had fun anyway because I flirted with a three-star general. That's the kind of man I want. He's a comptroller at the Pentagon and in charge of $90 billion! Finally when the dance started we were ready to party! I danced with lots of guys, but mostly I liked dancing with Pete. I liked flirting with him. He kept saying that we went together because we were both wearing black. So all in all I had fun, even if the night started out sour with Karl.

Karl said he didn't want to drive back so I ended up staying the night there—well the morning—it was already 5 a.m.! It was a little awkward because I resisted and kept Pete up talking until 7. The three of us slept in a double bed for about an hour. I suggested that Pete could drive to meet Karl at MHC and then Karl and I left. On Tuesday they arrived at 3:30 and we went for pizza. They gave me their numbers and are planning to come for BMW weekend. I was thrilled! When they were leaving, Pete pecked me on the cheek! I'd love to know him better. He's really hot and such a sweety, too. I'm planning to visit him in Maryland and find out if he and I can be anything together. I'll be happy to escape MHC. I have high expectations for me to be doing something all the time, but right now, there's not much going on.

Gloomy April spread into May, but finally the sun swept the clouds out of the way and we felt like summer. And not too soon. Jada was home, and I turned the car and its parking stall in the garage over to her, while I became the driver of a little box of a baby blue Chevette, and not proud of it, either. The cranky contraption I was driving looked like a toy that had been left out in the sandbox too many nights, its joints loose and its hinges dry; the window sagged crookedly partway from the top. I had to push it up with both hands to close it, and in no time it ratcheted its way down again.

It was a hot summer already, and it hadn't officially started. Home from my final day of the school year, the sun getting lost behind the other wing of our six-story building, I turned up the music and swayed to the slippery sounds of Steve Winwood singing, "Roll with it, baby". His voice sent its tingly fingers to the dip in my back.

"He looks like Olle," Jada said, holding the plastic CD case.

"Hmm; I guess I see his nose and his mouth. Yes, his eyes, too. Olle's bigger though." I turned the volume down, and the whine of the air conditioner drowned out the next cut, a grinding ballad. "Do you miss him?"

"Yeah, I miss him. But I knew he wasn't right for me. He's seeing a woman now. They're pretty serious." I had one chair, a rocking chair, and Jada sat in it, in the center of the room, in the center of the whole affair, as unreadable as a secret code. Some mothers before me, maybe even of my generation, hated their lives while at the same time preparing their daughters to live identical lives, serving, giving up power and autonomy to a marriage partner. Jada was a new generation, a woman to herself first, secondarily a daughter to me.

"Are you still going over there?"

"Once in a while. It's okay," she added brightly. "He's helping me design a t-shirt for the Parents' Weekend Committee."

"Maybe it's time you returned his hero jacket," I suggested, as I had his shirts, records, inventory.

"I can't; it's at school. Besides, he owes it to me." Her eyelids drooped and her voice became plaintive, yet resolved. "I want someone to love me and hold me, someone I can say anything to and he'll listen to me and understand. And I want him there with me."

"Yes. It would be fun to be in love." I sat on the love seat that I should have resprung before I refinished and reupholstered it, but what did I know about inner workings? I simply put another layer of batting on top of what was there, a lump of a seat near the back; the front of the seat dropping off under my thighs.

"What do you care?" She teased. "Remember, you're old. You don't need to be in love."

"Everyone needs to feel loved, Jada. It feels impossible when you're looking so hard. You have to be okay with yourself, and by yourself. You have to accept that you may never find a man."

"Don't say that! I hate being alone." Jada came forward, and the rocking chair creaked under her force.

"Yes, but remember, no man is better than any man. Still, if numbers count, I'm due. How about you? Maybe you'll meet someone at the U this summer."

"I better meet someone soon; I need a man!"

My former mother-in-law, a woman like my own mother who was fortunate to finish high school, picked up an occasional two-bit word along the constricted path through her life. When I received my Master's Degree, she asked if I was going to go on and get my doctor-ette. Whereas doctor-ette may have sounded like coming from the mouth of a Shirley Temple, her use of words like sultry conjured up a more sophisticated speaker, a Dorothy Lamour, and I envisioned Myrna, a young Grandma M squeezing her crinkled billowy skin into a flimsy sarong.

On hot summer days, Myrna wore a waistless cotton housedress. She wore a cotton housedress on winter days, but on hot and humid summer days, Myrna's housedress was sleeveless and she waved a palm-shaped fan before her amply freckled cheeks padded with an extra layer of fat that added bulk without changing the structure, like the extra batting in my love seat; and sitting in her green upholstered chair and fanning herself so that the skin of her upper arms waddled with the movement, she pronounced breathily, "It sure is sultry." Not having traveled to New Orleans or Washington, D.C., or Laos in the drippy hot summer, but having seen *A Streetcar Named Desire* on film, I knew what she meant even if I didn't perspire profusely like Marlon Brando.

Yet, summers in Minnesota could, on occasion, steam for a few days or even a week at a time, and when they did, we commemorated them, elevating them as commonplace as an annual curse that lives on in the record books and daily average temperatures reported on the nightly weather report. The summer of 1988 was the second hottest summer I remembered, not counting my childhood or adolescence, which, in memory, distorts. The first hottest was the summer when the sky turned dark to black in the middle of the day not once, not even twice, but three times, all within a month. I was a summer mother putting a lunch together for Jada and Dom and fought with a toaster that wouldn't keep its bread down, infuriating me so that I smashed the metal beast, chipped the enamel from the stove it was on, but didn't make a dent in the toaster's attitude. That summer in our suburban dream house with only two saplings to make short slender wrinkles in the hot heavy blanket of yellow sunshine, the kids and I ran through the sprinkler sprouting cool water, or, when the air pressed close and heavy, we went to Northpointe Mall to cool down and came home, dragged the mattress down the stairs onto the floor of the basement (excuse me, lower level) and tried to sleep.

This summer of 1988, I wrote curriculum in the sterile climate controlled air at district offices for a week. For six weeks following, I arrived each day at 7:00 a.m. in temperatures that had already surpassed 70 degrees to teach English to two classes each of sixty-seven 9th, 10th, 11th, and yes, 12th grade students in a building not air-conditioned. Our school district designated a modern school site to house us. "Modern" meaning 30-inch high glass windows, few of which opened outwards, none fully, to allow air transfer. "Modern" meaning a large sprawling building with the classroom side exposed to the fiery sun, the opposite a brick wall enclosing a stifling corridor. "Modern" meaning a razed flat plot with a very ample black tarred parking lot, reflecting heat that rose in shimmering waves like bacon ruffling in a hot frying pan, outside the half-closed windows.

Upon arriving to my assigned classroom in the morning, I opened the door as I would to an oven, slowly, to avoid the blast of heat, trapped since the previous afternoon, growing like yeast in the closeted room, cracked open two rectangles of glass, and stared down the baby blue Chevette, usually the only car parked in the lot, looking like it might shrivel up, too. The exertion of starting the day brought out buds of sweat, some pooling to make half moons of moisture under my arms and between my legs; others rolling shamelessly into the crack between my breasts, tickling the fine hairs along their brazen way. It wasn't just hot. It wasn't just hot and wet. It was sultry.

Never had I used the word sultry before the summer of 1988. Never before had I been trapped for two classes of English, each two hours long with a fifteen minute break, in a room without a fan in a school without a shade tree in the summer without a cloud. I wasn't the only fool, having plenty of company in that suffocating overcrowded home economics room. Ambitious brown ants trailed up an outside wall through some sliver of a crack between the cement and the dull gray metal of the windows, across the great wall separating the imprisoned from the freed, down the inside gray blocks, in single file over linoleum tiles laid in an alternating pattern, up one leg of the desk and into the mattery side drawer. Because the desk belonged to another teacher during the regular school year, I was reluctant to rummage through the drawer the ants made their haven; in balance, however, if there was a box of chocolate in there, I wanted to know about it. I used the desk on which to stack papers and supplies. One of my growing obsessive fears was that, sandwiched in between the sheets of the paper and crouched inside my stapler were some swift-legged scouts and, not only would I carry them home with me, but their very loyal troops would also follow. I didn't care what anyone said; I just knew that once a train of ants had been established, the route was indelibly stored in the colony's collective memory and before you could say Leiningen, they'd bury my home.

I eyed the stack of papers from all angles before cautiously picking it up for the second session. Students were out on break, and sorting, I didn't hear the footfalls of a human visitor and made a jump to his mildly spoken greeting. "Hi, remember me?"

"Of course I do," I answered, turning full toward him. "How are you? I've seen you at Parkview a few times after school in the office." But then I remembered, he had a hat on, a ski hat. Now I noticed silvery hair curling undomestically about his ears and neck, looking like it could scour a frying pan.

"I coach some Parkview skiers. Is that where you are now?"

"Yes; I went there, let's see, a year after you were at Life Skills Center. Where did you go?"

"Pierce. Do you have any plans on Monday?"

"Uh," I stalled. I couldn't figure out how he thought I could cover his class when I had my own to teach, unless he thought I had just arrived and that's why I had been staring at my monument to fallen trees.

He leaned slightly forward, one hand seeming to jangle something in a pocket of his tan Bermuda shorts, grayish shadows at the front of each billowy leg; well, not billowy, but the shorts hung loosely from his hipbones, and he seemed eager to move, as if unused to standing still. "Would you like to go rollerblading after school?"

"Sure!" I answered decisively even though ignorant about the nature of this "rollerblading." "What is it?"

"It's like ice skating on wheels. We'll go around the lakes in Nokomis and maybe go swimming afterwards, stop for dinner on the way back." While I listened, I recalled the night after graduation that Patti, he, Bill, and I met for drinks and then eggs and toast before going home. That was the only time I ever had a conversation with the man, and part of the story he told came back to me: a student brought in a roll of film of herself and her boyfriend that she wanted him to develop and he refused. In Patti's judgment, he was good with kids, and her approval of him was good enough for me.

Standing with a backpack on the other side of the desk, Per looked lean, tight, almost as if his muscles and skin had been shrink-wrapped around a metal frame. "Do you have to wear anything special for this rollerblading?" I asked.

He looked at my feet. "I have a pair of skates I'm sure will fit you. Just socks, maybe two pairs, and some shorts—something comfortable. I teach only half-time. I'll come by at break on Monday, okay?" He adjusted his glasses with two fingers, his pointer raised like an umbrella while his thumb and middle finger brought the frame into place with a hint of delicacy. As he left, I noticed the squiggly lines that ran like worn out wire notebook coils under the skin of his legs, at the ends of which were short socks and athletic shoes.

Monday was as hot or hotter than the stream of steamy days before it, and Per and I walked about the grounds during break while we made plans for the afternoon. I caught the eye of one of my students, who grinned slyly at us. "We live in the same neighborhood," he said. "I live in a house on Frey across from the Cathedral."

"Isn't that odd we haven't seen each other around," I added incredulously. "You'd think we'd run into each other somewhere."

Not so odd, really, I thought when I returned for second class: I hadn't seen him at the morning's meeting, but we were both teaching in the same building.

Rollerblading with Per I concentrated on keeping from falling, running into the grassy edge of the pavement or grabbing onto a tree to stop me. Per told me to relax, take things naturally, just like I was skating. I didn't tell him I'd been in skates about as many times as I had fingers; I just told him to teach me how to stop, and not by those stupid little knobs on the toes of the skates, nor by his method which he made look easy, turning sideways and skidding.

The sky's light glinted on the glass of Per's gray Isuzu as we drove away from the sun toward home, Per's fingers trilling the steering wheel to a Sade tape unwinding its voluptuous rhythms. We were sharing our stories. "How did you know I wasn't married any more?" I asked.

"At the staff meeting on Monday morning you raised your hand and I noticed you weren't wearing a ring." I made half of a nod.

"That doesn't always mean anything," I countered.

"But I noticed you *did* wear a ring when you were at the Skills Center."

I lowered the window to mix fresh air into the acrid smell that filled my nostrils, less pungent now than when I entered his truck, as he called it. It was a boxy contraption that seemed to have lost its spring, or maybe its being square in design had something to do with the way we rocked to one side or the other and jostled with a thud stopping for traffic lights as we maneuvered our way from Nokomis to Sibley and into a relationship.

Summer, officially underway, got hotter, more sultry by Jada's birthday. Boston cream pie, two thin layers of golden cake, thick creamy filling, dark chocolate frosting, was Jada's annual birthday request, and this year I poked 20 candles around the circumference. Jada didn't think long to make her wish, and as if it would do any good, I willed all the candles to burn out in one breath. I cut narrow wedges for her and me, a wider one for Dom, and pondered the wish I would have made, in fact, did make.

"Ooh, that's rich," I said, smacking a gob of fudgy frosting. "Makes my eyes water."

"It's so good, though. I'll have to get Kimby up here tomorrow before we go golfing. She probably will say that she won't be able to eat it all."

"I wouldn't blame her. And to think we're going out to dinner. We'll just call this dessert. Oh, well, you know what they say…."

"Aren't you going to finish?" Jada swirled her fork urging me on. Water-blue eyes clouded impatiently. "You do that a lot, you know; no wonder people can't figure you out. Have you ever noticed how people look at you some times?"

"No, what?"

"Right in the middle of a sentence you'll switch the subject. I'm surprised Per can understand you." Fragments of laughter glinted in her eyes like ripples on an incoming wave; she was enjoying watching me wriggle against the wall, my wings flailing. "He probably doesn't even listen to you any more. I've seen him 'zoom, okay, there she goes again talking to herself.'"

"Say, but there's an old Cajun saying, I just read it. I caught myself the other day, you know how they say it's okay to talk to yourself as long as you don't answer? I've had arguments with myself, but I've stopped listening. I was on Lyton Avenue, right by Lyton Lake and I asked myself, 'What did you say?'"

"There you go again! What is it?" Jada's eyes grew wide. And Dom squinted, bringing his broad eyebrows so close together they were one long caterpillar of silky black-brown hair.

"What is what?" I asked. "Oh, the saying. Yes, it's a Cajun saying, 'If you're not talkin' to yourself, you're talkin' to the wrong person.' Don't you love it?"

"Mooie, Mooie, Mooie." Jada made a production of getting up from the table while Dom exhaled, shaking his head like cleaning a dust mop.

Dom, too, had arisen, but instead of setting his plate to the left of the sink to be washed, he stood at the counter, standing taller than I, deliberating. How different they were, Jada and Dom; he, bound to be massive, dark, as unmistakably Italian-looking as my father; she, on the surface, fair, with a faint sprinkling of caramel speckles on either side of her nose and blue eyes, subtly Italian, the green undertone pronounced when she paled.

"Yes, you can have another, but small; you can also take some back to your dad's. Well, then, I suppose I have to send some for him." Dom took the cake out of the refrigerator and ignored my mutterings.

His name was Adam. Jada, back at school, talked almost ethereally as she apologized for her new beau's flaws. "He's not the kind of guy I'd like, Mom. He wears tennis shoes, and he doesn't care about his clothes." I sat one leg curled under my other and an elbow propped on the dining room table, just on the edge of the square of warm October sunlight that stretched from the kitchen window, across the wooden floor, and up to the center of the table where lay the ceramic trivet with the mother hippopotamus and her babies at the decorated refrigerator door. "And he runs."

"Where is he from?" I asked, suppressing my reflections. She was the one who told Per to cut his silver beatnik hair, and she was also the one to ask him, "Do you own any other shoes besides those you run in?" And when Per showed up for our date to a summer concert in a gray squared-off wool knit tie, she pointed out that it was way out of style *and* season. To Jada, Per was hopelessly lost in a time warp. Adam, too, achieved Jada's clearance in spite of his appearance.

"He's from Brookline, which is really a part of Boston, a rich part of Boston. But he's not rich; that's what he says."

"Well, rich is relative."

"He lives with his mother; she's remarried. His father is a professor at Harvard, but he says that doesn't mean he has money. He has to help pay for his tuition; he works at the college, doing research or something."

"Which college?"

"Goodrich. He's a math major, too." That did it. But I would not taunt her with her own judgments. She was nearly in love.

"Will I get to meet him?" Because Jada co-chaired the Parents' Weekend Committee, I was visiting instead on another, and together Jada and I were driving to the coast and, from there, visiting Boston, where we were attending a church union of two sister students.

"I don't know. He's going home that weekend, so if we're in Boston when he is, maybe." Her voice shrank farther and farther away as if she were already on her way there. The thought of her heart fluttering with butterflies of love gave my stomach an empathic jump.

In our rented car, Jada and I exited the arched gate of the college on our way to the coast leaving behind old brick reddish buildings, guarded by ancient trees with intertwined branches and twigs and leaves. Strapped in, suitcases cached within the trunk, map jutting rakishly from the visor, our backs softened into the deep maroon car seats.

"Look at this scenery!" I gasped. The splendor of the leaves surrounded us like an upturned jewelry box, as we topped a rise in the freeway and rolled like Alice down a chute of gold and red and green and bronze horizon. "I feel so small here. Can you imagine how far those hills reach?" This was Jada's third autumn in Massachusetts.

I turned the volume dial of the radio. "Every time I walk into the condo, I say to myself, 'I'm glad I live here.' I would say that same thing if I woke up here with all these trees on all these hills. I imagine that people who live on the beaches in Maine are just as glad."

"That's why I love to travel. People like Kimby who don't go anywhere have such a narrow view of things. She doesn't even want to come out here." Jada sniffled and twitched her nose.

We weren't alone on the freeway, but alone enough so that I could look away momentarily without the danger of getting crunched by another vehicle. Through dark tinted sunglasses Jada's eyes roved the sun-saturated slopes. "Do you know Adam likes to write? He's a math major and he keeps a journal. He wishes he could write things, too. He isn't a very cool guy, but he doesn't care about that."

The trees were thinning, and so were the hills, becoming less like bells and more like overturned bowls. Soon we would be out of the valley on our journey toward the level coastline. Jada's voice rose and fell with the rolling car. "He stops by or calls me just because he's thinking about me. And he has a teddy bear! His name is BJ. And he wears old t-shirts, and socks with holes!" Jada smiled serenely. "And he doesn't mind driving or taking me places. He has this old car. He says he can't afford anything else."

"Driving must be a man thing. Per drives to get the morning paper every day." Usually I squeezed the steering wheel and raced the engine just to get the driving over with. Yet I found myself calm and unhurried behind the wheel on our journey.

"What do you like most about Per?"

"I like that he doesn't tell me what to do or to like. Except for the time in Chicago when he told me to order the fruit instead of the fries. I know he was really going by what I always order, but it reminded me of your dad. Anyway, I told Per not to tell me what to get, and he said, 'You should get what you want, not what I say.' It's easy to be around Per. He's calm. He accepts me. He believes in what I am, not what I could be made into."

Jada looked back through the windshield; the tiny muscles around her eyes turned jelly. "Mmmm," she hummed. "I feel calm with Adam, too. He wants me to call him in Boston." The large square frames of her sunglasses contrasted with her fine-lined facial structure, delicately smoothed over with porcelain skin. Her eyes glistened. Softly murmured the beginning notes of a recent release. Jada turned the dial so the tune filled the car, and we sang the words, "...you came along and changed my life. It's a tre—ue—ue—ue—ue lo--ove."

We had come out of the valley gradually, like a worm that squirms its way out of the water-saturated earth after a long rainfall, and now we breathed unsuspectingly, exposed on the flat crest of a Massachusetts plain. A starkly white billboard stood resolutely in the grass; what had started out as super-highway had shrunk to two-way traffic posting local advertising for the Original Home of the World's First Fried Clams.

The breeze nipped my neck with airborne moisture on its journey from the nearing sea: in the short time of our eastern odyssey, clouds cast their shadows over the sun and sent cool nips like a cat's teeth grazing our skin as it snatches treats from our hands. I was happy to leave the highway, with little to interrupt its narrow incision in the flat earth as we arrived at our bed-and-breakfast inn on the ocean.

The plain two-story yellow-sided home alongside a sign posted to warn me against trespassing on turf uniformly shaved, indicated that the less impressive structure on the street was ours. Around a flight of stairs we were led to our designated room, and Jada's eyes swept the yellow room, a double bed tucked into the corner, covered by a floral printed dacron coverlet.

"I don't see a phone," she said.

"Oh, look, Jada. We have a little porch." I opened the glass-paned door and looked out at the grander houses beyond the trees and across the street. "Let's go for a walk. I want to see where I am." We selected this place because it was on the ocean; yet so far all I could see was that it stood on the edge of town on a paved street. I went in search of our innkeeper and stopped on the small square at the top of the landing. Leafy branches of a tree swayed outside the window to my right. Our host, laden with blue and beige towels, emerged from the door next to ours.

"Do you know of any good places for dinner?" As she identified her favorite, I drew out the contents of my coat pocket for something to write on. "Do you have something to write with?" I asked into the room where Jada was folding her clothing and meticulously placing each piece in either one of two dresser drawers.

Along with her she brought an address book, an appointment book, a calendar, a journal, a notebook. She reached for her purse and plucked out a ballpoint pen.

The innkeeper worked among stacks of linens while repeating directions, which I set to a scrap of found paper. "Okay, I think we'll like this restaurant," I said, coming back into the room and putting the paper, pen, and my cosmetic case next to a ceramic vase, centered perfectly on a crocheted doily.

"Don't put that stuff there," Jada snapped. "That was nice and neat, and now you're making it a mess."

"Jada, these rooms are right next to each other. I don't like to have people hearing us argue."

She continued to align and square off corners of folded cotton sweatshirts and fluffy knitted sweaters like a surveyor mapping out streets in a neatly planned housing development. Her silky soft bikini panties and matching lacy bras she laid in a separate smaller drawer following some hierarchical order that deified the act.

"You're always worried about other people. Just let them think what they want to. You always tell me how brave I am and how much you like my 'deliberateness' you call it. 'Integrity, that's all you have,' you say. Then you say, 'Don't humiliate me.' You take things too seriously."

The sky was darkened by the time we got out to the roadside for our walk. Adam's caution not to call him before six was reason for Jada to join me and, I concluded, her curtness. We strolled along a low stone wall that gradually curved up a growing hill. Somewhere to the left, beyond the wall, was the ocean, but there were no telltale lapping waves, and I expected that if I hopped the wall and kept walking, I might not wade into wetness but rather fall off the edge of the dark expanse. A star appeared to wait for me at the top of the hill, glow growing brighter and pinker as I neared it.

"Just let me run up ahead," I said. "You start back; I'll catch up to you." The light drew me closer until I saw the edge and realized that what I had been chasing was the rim of a neon sign. A few more steps and I could make out the glowing pink words that beamed in the sky: "The Lighthouse Motel and Restaurant." I about-faced and started my descent, before my foolish calling became exposed, immediately missing the presence of the wall. Water misted the air thickly; the image in front of me was like looking at a photograph dot by dot by dot. I looked backwards at the beacon that had guided me toward it, wishing I had one now, the space ahead being densely uninterpretable. At once, headlights streamed the road and illuminated the wall to my right, restoring a guide for my return. Then, as an apparition, Jada's slow-moving form, thin and delicate underneath a thick sweater and voluminous denim jacket began to fade in as she passed through the faint filtered circle from an overhead streetlight. Her small erect head, cradled by the upturned collar, sprouted like a wildflower from the bank of brush beyond her.

"Eerie, isn't it? How you can see around you but not have a clue about what's ahead? We didn't walk that far, and I can't see the house we're staying at."

"It's right over there," she pointed, her arm needle straight.

"You're pointing into the ocean!" Almost magically, small squares of light dappled the area Jada had indicated with her finger. Looking backwards, I felt I was looking into the darkness of an empty closet. "You could have fooled me," I marveled. "Those trees along the side sure do make a difference." We stepped inside, and before leaving for dinner, Jada dropped coins, each one making a ringing noise as it hit the bottom reservoir of the naked pay phone by the stairway, and dialed a number penciled onto a piece of paper. She sagged with each unanswered ring.

"You must be disappointed. You're sure of the number?"

Jada folded the white paper and tucked it into her wallet. "Yes; he didn't say he would be there for sure. Let's go. I'll call later." Her voice cheered with another chance.

I made a few turns into the town of Rockport and followed the darkened doorways until the pavement to the left cut abruptly across and forced me to stop. "This can't be a main street; it runs right into the ocean." We drove another darkened street that looked like it lopped us off into a warehouse district.

"Okay, turn here," Jada directed. "The restaurant is on this street. See it?" For the second time that night, I followed a dead end, and what was nothing became at Jada's command a physical reality. The rabbit pulled out of the hat. A tiny placard swayed back and forth from two hooks attached to the wooden eave. "I'm hungry," Jada announced, as we picked up our feet to stay ahead of a bitter void of cold left by the subtraction of sunshine. Inside, we were greeted by warmth and closeness, fishing paraphernalia caught among knotted nets festooning the weathered planks, and dinner.

Before closing the front door of the house to the gusting wind, Jada had Adam's telephone number in hand. Wanting not to eavesdrop on either Jada or the couple sitting in front of a television set beyond an archway, I studied the wallpaper, searching the corner for irregularities in the match. The clank of the earpiece to the cradle and the metallic tumbling of coins down the gullet of the telephone box signaled the end to the conversation. As we climbed the stairway, Jada lay out, step by step, how we would meet Adam after the union ceremony at a Harvard church.

The light on the nightstand sent ghostly fingers onto the yellow wallpaper, conjuring a ghastly reminder of Gillman's gripping story of madness. Jada took the side by the wall and I propped my head and concentrated on reading my book by the light of the little lamp. But I was tired, and like Jada, nodded into sleep.

"What is that?" I asked the darkness. I had been jerked awake by the sound of a rumbling, which could only be identified as a jet engine or a locomotive, except for being too close and lasting too long. And we were too far from both sky and train tracks. "There's water down there!" I gruffly whispered, folding aside the fluttery curtain. "It looks like it's right up against the house." Jada sat up and looked out the window, and I wanted her to pronounce me half-asleep, making half-conscious sightings of splashing waves and flapping leaves. Yes, the tree was still there, but I could see nothing else through the window, except water, the moon a densely packed bullet lodged deep behind masses of clotted charcoal clouds.

Jada settled wordlessly next to me; feeling her there put a cold compress to my frenzy. The bed trembled, almost unnoticeably, and my senses alerted, as when staring at a spot in the distance, trying to make a visual mark to see if it was really not some small bug on the crawl.

"Mom," Jada's voice tiptoed out, "the bed is moving."

"So, I'm not imagining it!" We laced our arms around each other as the bed jumped up and down like it was doing a soft-shoe. Too much about our stay here portended a mystery. The trembling stopped, and when day surprised me with a burly gray sky showing through the window we had nothing to prove the night's adventure, except Jada's limp arm on me and a groggy feeling.

From the breakfast table, gnarly gray claw-like shapes, whether sky or water, or a mixture of both, teemed outside an enormous plate glass window, an unobstructed and unedited view of the untamed ocean, snarling at the sky and pulling pieces down into it, "Quite a night," I said.

"Yuh, that's a nor'easter." The innkeeper slapped her coffee mug down on the thickly varnished table and glared out the window as if she were daring the tempestuous squall to act up once, just one more time. "I hope no one's out there; they'll be lost for sure."

I nodded, pouring a cup of coffee. Jada silently chewed her muffin. "But isn't it over?" I asked.

"Oh, it might be over here, but the sea is still rough. I just hope no one got caught out there." I made vacuous assertions of weather warnings and ship-to-shore radios and experience.

The salty-haired woman, more coarse than she'd been when laying towels in a closet, squinted her eyes. "Don't matter," she snickered. "Every once in a while we lose one," and she recalled a grisly sea story of a fisherman in a small craft floundering in a storm such as this one. She waited, she added dramatically, as everyone else did, for the physical accounting of every single man who went out. Stretching my vision out to the expansive sea, I searched for microscopic dots of battered vessels and imagined matching eyes were doing the same back at me.

"By the way," I asked, "how do we get the train to Boston?"

We stopped at a wharf that displayed its finery when tourists and sunshine descended upon its boutiques. Birds and boats both were battened down somewhere else, safe from battering posts. The shoreline lost its edge to the gouging sea; reeds and waist-tall grasses flailed each other in defense of their common assailant and themselves, while unseen to the eye they intermingled strong fine fingers into sand and dirt and decay until they encircled each other and made a collective anchor. I hurried back toward the end of the pier and ducked meekly inside the car. Jada wandered slowly farther away toward the water. Another car pulled up to park beside ours, and a woman and two youngsters got out and clutched their hooded green ponchos close to their bodies while the wind tried to spirit them away like kites through an endless gray wilderness, until losing interest, dropping them on the other side of nothing.

My three neighbors retreated to their vehicle, while I cowered in my own shelter and watched Jada walk beyond the frame, conveniently formed by the sidebars of the windshield and the dashboard, out of view.

A sudden wave of isolation enveloped me, and I reached for the door handle. *No; let her go. The course has been set, set even by myself. I just have to learn that this adventure is worthy by its uncertainty, the uncertainty of your own step, your own plunge, your own will. I can no more go on the voyage that is marked for her than I can rescue her and try to hide her away from it as a stowaway with me.*

Rivulets of ocean spray ran down the windshield like the tears on a child awakened by a bad dream, and Jada returned damp and disheveled. She navigated subways, the metro in Paris; if anyone would know how to find the station, she would. The road, once underneath my wheels, had vanished, and I wondered where that had happened. Driving through an apparent open field, we passed a large wooden building to our right, when, to our astonishment, we encountered a slow-moving black train engine. The conductor, who thrust his left arm and head out the window, motioned his arm in a wide waving arc and shouted down to us, "This isn't a railroad crossing, but go ahead, I'll wait for you."

"Are you going to Boston?" Jada's voice sailed upward to the man in the gray and white striped hat that looked like prison pillow ticking.

As he continued to twirl his arm, he said, "Yes. Come on to the other side." Putting us and the car in the direct path of a moving train challenged everything I had been conditioned to do, but I found myself already into the groove without knowing how to get out. There was just too much unknown here for me not to trust. We crossed, the train braked to a stop, and waiting for us near the boarding platform was an open door and a porter welcoming us in.

Passing through the passenger seats, I recognized the green ponchos, now unleashed and hanging limply from two children who divided their gazes, one on the passing landscape outside the square window screen, and the other, a little girl kneeling backwards on the seat, her elbows spread outwards, her chin on her hands, on us. For a moment, a second, a minute, we held each other in our minds. I imagined her imagining me, as if I had traveled backwards through time and could, as a child, see myself in the distance, through unselfconscious lenses.

We stopped and started up again, adding passengers who broke into our visions of each other, and the spying girl jumped across the seat, perhaps enticed by the anonymous flow of trees and highways and buildings that reeled before her sister's gaze. As we lurched toward Boston, the train whizzed us into more populated territory and larger and larger clots of people filled the space between us, until the girl and I were lost to each other.

Jada, sitting next to the window, was unavoidably within my line of vision. Patchy bare spots like craters of the moon made the fine thin strands of hair seem even more sparse and grain straight, except that she permed around them, and they crimped like the fine copper wires inside a telephone line. She, too, searched outside the train window, and more than ever I was certain that her vision would steer her—and me?—through a life she could be proud of.

The storm we had left behind was an echo that reverberated in Boston. Gray, misting, windy, the city seemed to give us a chilly shoulder, and sitting on a park bench, I retaliated, huddling inside my jacket and steeling my face to the sharp slap of wind. I tagged after Jada on her turf, going to her stores, her eatery, depending on her to lead me through the grounds and gates of Harvard campus, searching for the chapel. We arrived to creaky worn wooden stairs and searched for a chair, a bench, anything on which to soak up the musty warmth of the old building. The parents of the two women flanked their sides before walking the aisle to exchange promises of faithfulness, and we joined the small gathering.

Behind layers of gray cloud, the sun would be making its descent, soon to drop off the edge and leave us in darkness. I sat on the cement stoop of a brick building on an anonymous Boston street while Jada made plans in a phone booth. A bus braked at the curb, spraying out people in every direction, everyone with purpose, a place to go. Jada bounced toward me and sat on the top step.

"We're meeting Adam at Faneuil Hall at 6:00. You'll like it. It's an old meeting hall from the Revolution they made into shops."

We walked blocks and cut angles until Jada, looking at her watch, proclaimed it was time to catch the bus. "Now, if we were going antique hunting, you wouldn't have this much energy," I said. Jada went on to cross the street with a spirited gait; we arrived in time for her to lead me up the walkway and to the top of the steps, where stood Adam.

A smile spread upon his face as Jada approached, his hands nesting in pockets of jeans that loosely draped his lean body. I was learning about that—the look of a runner, how he dresses always in jeans that he can't fill, ironically laid back yet cocked for a sprint. Brown frames squared his round hazel eyes that drew Jada closer toward him. So exclusive was his pull on her that I felt like a security camera in a department store dressing room, focusing sharply on his muscle twitches while the doors behind blurred to nothingness. The whirring wind caught his hair that trailed about his face and neck so that he lifted his hand to finger-comb his hair before reaching it out towards Jada. She latched on as a dancer about to be spun around and off the ground by her partner, practiced to look effortless.

"Mother, this is Adam. My mother." We shook hands, and I liked his grip. We agreed to meet, same place. Adam, too, had to catch a bus, while we had to get back to Rockport by train. Gladly did I leave them to stroll privately among the throngs of shoppers, meld with packs of people at food counters, waiting contentedly for a pancake-sized chocolate covered macaroon for Per, a piece of dark chocolate peanut butter fudge, without nuts, for Dom, a butter pecan yogurt shake for me. Time hung like the exotic furs on stiletto models locked behind fashion store display windows.

Adam dashed in one direction, and Jada led me down the sidewalk. "Come on," she nudged me. "We have to hurry. We have to make the last train out. I have the name of the street where Adam said we have to turn left. Then we walk until we come to a big building and we can't go any farther. We have to go through that one to get to the other side. He said the train station is attached."

The street looked deserted. I counted it a charm that we were crunched for time. We hadn't traveled many blocks before the street sign appeared, and we made the turn. Gradually the street grew lighter and a building with a bank of heavy looking wooden doors, above which was an old-fashioned marquee with rows of small bulbs showering light about it. "This must be it," Jada said as she opened one of the doors. It was more like me to throw myself into apparent chaos, not unlike the kitchen drawer that everyone has, whether it's in the kitchen or not, existing for odds and ends, reusable twist ties, uneven lengths of bakery string, ink pen carcasses needing new refills, refill cartridges that don't fit; I lived my life out of kitchen drawers everywhere, and I didn't need to impose order on minutiae to make sense of the mix. Jada did, however, having just the day before folded panties as if they could hold the shape and layered stockings, matched, the tip of the top meeting the tip of the toe.

I trusted her. We emerged into an unformed mass of hockey fans being admitted to a Bruins game. A rumbling thunder of voices, each with its own timber and pitch conjoined to carry itself across the ceiling of the hall.

"I say we cut through," Jada decided.

"We'll probably be clubbed for butting in line; let's be sure not to lose each other." I followed, lemming-like, cutting across the current of pot bellies and smoke streams. At first I politely repeated my "excuse me's." Though each body stood on its own, no one stood individually but as part of an elastic wall that stretched under pressure. Jada and I pushed ourselves through in small bursts, applying just enough force when the muscle relaxed, redirecting when it contracted. I soon accustomed myself to the medium that contained me and dispensed with language, letting my arms and legs keep me moving. All I really had to worry about was catching the end of someone's cigarette, protruding from two fingers, hidden by the flap of a suit coat or on its way to a set of brown-stained teeth. When I thought I would scream to get a breath of air, we were released from the last wall of people and were greeted by another row of glass doors. Opening them and descending steps, we recognized that we were indeed at a train station; beyond the ticket booths lay the tracks, the tracks that would lead us to Rockport. And not a minute too soon. The last train out for the night lurched forward as we boarded.

Sitting down, I felt my feet throb inside my shoes. I rubbed my leg muscles and let my back slump against the seat and my mind swell with the day's adventure. "What did you and Adam do?"

"We just walked around." The ends of Jada's lips teased, as if they might smile.

"He's cute. He looks like a runner."

"Mmm. I love the way we kiss." Jada closed her eyes to the lights of the city and did not observe their gradual thinning, the night wrapping about us like gauze through which only shapes were formed as we were being carried away, like born-agains embarking on a spiritually-charged course.

The next morning opened like spume from a fire, dirty furrowing clouds filled with the soot of an extinguished storm. Jada and I walked along the sodden beach behind the brick wall that the night before had been the ocean floor. Squiggly symmetrical ridges and corridors of sculpted miniature dunes formed patterns under our feet, each as unique as if artists were commissioned to design their own. We placed our steps so as not to mar the natural wonders made by the receding waters. Jada shot photographs, at once capturing both the panoramic mystery of earth, sea, and sky, and the tiny details of the land on which her feet made their own imprints.

We walked along docks and sailing crafts and into snug artists' galleries filled with shells and paintings of birds and fishing boats, their masts naked, moored to the ends of their docks or wharves, or piers—I knew not the appropriate term—before leaving Rockport for Essex, the antique capital of the world, toward Founders' Valley. The sun glowered from behind an almost uniform gray sky that sagged to the treetops, simmering serenely as our weekend ended.

Returned to our lives separated by a thousand miles or so, we resumed our telephone conversations, Jada singing Adam's praises as I hummed and nodded, looking across the sink and through the window to the brick wall on the other side of the courtyard, lights of the television screen flickering in a unit below. "He really cares about me. He listens to me. You know I can't talk to people about how things are; I can tell him what I need."

"That's remarkable, Jada. To establish that kind of trust. Maybe younger men are more sensitive than guys my age. How many people can really be openly and unguardedly themselves?"

"Adam can. He's what I need. I like having a boyfriend."

I smiled and pictured Adam and Jada lying on her bed, he on his back holding his bear BJ, his eyes half sleepily closed behind glasses jostled awry, she on her bellyside, propped up at the elbows with Hambone sprouting from the narrow crack between their bodies. "Yes, it is nice. I like living alone, but there is something to having a companion, to have history. He sounds like he was made for you." My hands fed glasses and saucers through the water and onto the rack. "But what I don't understand is, you told me how math majors are so conservative and now you're in love with one— one who wants to teach, at that!"

"I didn't say I was in love."

"No, you didn't, but you sure sound like it. Just be prepared when you decide you are. He may be the one. You two may decide to have sex."

"How do you know we haven't already?"

Late again. But not surprised. Or shouldn't have been; I considered her in a new frame, as I had every other time she jumped ahead of her mother, changing when I was just getting used to who she was. I felt like a puppy on ice for the first time. "Do you need to see a gynecologist?"

"I did; don't you remember? I went last summer with Kimby."

"Yes, but I mean to get some birth control."

"Mother, that's what we went for; what did you think? Kimby's been having sex with Daniel for a long time."

"What! Kimby? The person who won't go more than two miles from her home to go to college? I don't believe it!"

"Well, she has. She says they have sex about once a week."

"I still don't believe it. Kimby, proper Kimby. Does her mother know?"

"I don't know. She hasn't said. What has that got to do with it?"

"She seems to have a lot to say about what Kimby does. I guess I don't know much about people."

"Your problem is that you *do* think about people. And you think people think about people like you do. Like when you buy presents for people, you think about what they'd like. Most people just get something because they have to."

Somewhere in her statement I heard a compliment, whatever good it did me. "Yes, all those Christmases when I wrapped each gift especially for each person."

"Maybe you can do it again. Adam says he wants to come to Minnesota to visit me at Christmas."

"That would be great! We'll have to think of sleeping arrangements."

"He can sleep at Dad's in my bed. He wouldn't stay for very long. He has a test for grad school he has to study for."

I pulled out one of the four unmatched chairs in the dining room and sat. "You can have my car."

"I hope you're taking care of it! You better not have all your junk in it."

"I've been very good. I put all my school stuff in a box in the hallway."

"Why do you take all that stuff home with you? You work too hard. You should have come out here so you could clean up my dishes and do my ironing and sew me more skirts. Everyone likes the green one and wants you to make one for them. I told you; you should come out here to be a house mother."

"I'm sure! What would I do when you're off with Adam? You'd forget about me then. I wish you...only happiness." It was true, and it wasn't like wishing for more money to get furniture or pictures or a bathroom sink for the condo. And it wasn't like wishing for a body that wasn't padded with fat or wishing I had divorced earlier—much earlier—and been able to stay in the house, not for the house but for Dom, to be with Dom. There were tradeoffs in those wishes, decisions, consequences of which I wanted to change. I stretched my leg out and heard the chair creak. My castaway table and unmatched chairs were a far cry from the dining room suite Arnold and I had purchased back when we lived our life in complete and matching sets named Wedgwood and Denby and Sir Christopher, but I liked my freedom, even at the price I might be paying.

The spell broke. "There's a knock on my door, Mooie. I promised Lara I'd help her with her math."

"Okay, Honey Bunny. I've got conferences Thursday, but otherwise I'm home most nights this week. Talk to you in a couple days. Love you."

Dec. 31st

Well, it's New Year's Eve and I think I'll go to Kay's (from the American Cancer Society) party alone, as usual. I went to the movie alone today, too. That's how I'll probably spend my life—alone. Last night, after working until 9 p.m., I got mixed up driving to Steph's house and arrived too late for us to get to the movie. I was mad at myself for another negative doing in my life. Even Adam is starting to piss me off. He changed his plans—for about the fourth time!—and won't visit me until the 3rd for only two days! For $200! The more I'm away from him the more I don't think I can justify being close with him. I'm tired of trying to please him and just dealing with his fucked up doings. I feel that he has pushed me away. I don't think I can sleep with him if he can't stay committed. He's the one who wanted me to be monogamous and even brought up the idea of marrying me. And now he pulls out!? He tells me that a relationship has a risk and I should "understand" him, but I think he is using that as an excuse to not make an effort for ours.

I called him last night, which I shouldn't have, because he sent me an odd "love letter" that didn't sound like him, though he said he wrote it himself when I asked him. He thought that all was well between us, and then said he loves Debbie and Jennifer the same as he loves me! But he's jealous of my other male friends! No wonder we ended up fighting! He said that I should tell him to fuck off if I wanted to but I don't know what really I want. I couldn't sleep all night thinking of the damn two-timer and how I believe him and then he jerks me around. I wish I could just end it, but I don't want to do something so rash without working through my position and talking with him face to face. I liked the security and convenience of our relationship. We talked on the phone with each other and went on dates, though not many! Maybe he wasn't meant for me. He has to make some changes in his attitude and apologize to me for his wrongdoings. He doesn't care about money or that he doesn't wear polo clothes. He said he might teach in a high school. I *think he is rather insecure. No, I should just get it over with and deal with the pain of saying goodbye now.*

I don't think we could even be friends. He's unreliable and wishy-washy. I want someone who is responsible and trustworthy, and he has shown that he is not. I know I'm not being objective in thinking we could've been a good match, because I don't think I would want to marry him. I don't want to dislike him but I also don't want to sound like a whimpering female who has lost a perfect mate. Men! They're slime, and I have proof! I should find another man and avoid my mom and dad and I'll be able to deal with my fucking wasted life and all its difficulties.

When I go back to school it will be hard to find a new lover. I have no "starters" I can pursue. If I had some possible men in my life, it would make my life more tolerable. Having Beanie, Karen, and other friends would also help. What I want most is to feel good about myself and my decisions. Mom says I have to find my inner happiness before I find it in another person. I had better find it and fast! Why do I have such a hard time feeling good about my life? I feel like I get only a few snippets of feeling good about myself but long drawn out times of depression. I think normal people have it in the opposite ratio of shorter and smaller spurts of unhappiness. I almost always feel overwhelmed with having negative things affecting me bringing depression and thoughts of suicide. It's so ironic that other people see a strong and independent person in me. They say I am self-assured and on top of things. I must put on a real show because I don't feel any of that. It's scary to think I have a hardened shell that covers the real feelings stuffed inside. I've been shot down and wounded too many times and now my insides are rotting away in anguish.

Well, at least I have a temp job making money filing for the summer. Guess I'll have to put on my hard diamond shell and be ready for the show.

"Priss says thank you for the telephone," Jada said to my 'hello.' She and Dom bought me a portable phone to replace a wall model, but I kept it moored to its cradle on the wall between the kitchen and the dining room; I held suspect people who could make intimate connections unprotected by warm surroundings. The ceiling light fixture made a halo around the dining room table where I had been scanning a short story. I protected a fantasy that someday I'd get this teaching business down so that I wouldn't always have work to do at home, especially over a weekend, when it was hard to drum up creative juices. Whistling winter winds shimmied a loose screen in the kitchen window. Jada had returned to Mary Hillyard, bringing the old telephone to Priss, Jada's new friend in the Development Office; and, of course, she went back to Adam, about whom she was presently speaking in less than dreamy tones.

"Adam didn't do so hot on his test."

"That's too bad." I put my pencil down as if commanded to pay homage to a fallen comrade. "How important was this test?"

"It's the Physics GRE, and he says he'll be rejected from Harvard grad or another really hard school. That's what he gets mad about. Sometimes he gets so mad, he like loses control."

"So he didn't really fail. He's disappointed in himself. And maybe his parents? What are their expectations?"

"I don't think that's what matters. He talks like they don't care and he's doing what he wants to do. But I don't know if he really knows. Just a minute while I get a tissue." So often had she a drippy nose that she made her two little sniffs followed by a light swipe out of habit as much as necessity. "I wish you could talk to him about teaching. He says he wants to teach, but you should hear some of the things he says. He wants every kid to know all the stuff he's learning now. He has other weird ideas about how kids should act in school, too. I just can't see him as a teacher. He's not realistic."

"Idealism is admirable, even if it is misdefined. Most teachers learn what's age-appropriate. What concerns me is that teachers go into fields that were easy for them, so they don't break down tasks, teach how to figure the stuff out when their students don't get it."

"Yeah, see? You could tell him stuff like that." Jada's voice lightened like bubbles rising from champagne.

"If it were only that simple. People have to find out things for themselves when they need to, when they want to. The trick is to create those situations; it's called motivation."

"You and Madame. I wish I had teachers like you. You make things fun and understandable."

"You know, I'm not original; I try to apply current theory and practice."

"There you go again," Jada clucked self-righteously. "You know other teachers don't read and do half as much work as you."

"More work does not necessarily make you any better; it's what you work at. Some people believe that who we teach is ourselves. I think we should build and develop students' resources to become efficacious, to find their power."

"Can't you use regular words? What does efficacious mean?" Jada's voice came to a halt the way someone would who has decided not to run the yellow light and brakes abruptly at the crosswalk.

"Being able to do or to make happen. When people are efficacious they use their skills and knowledge to make things happen."

"Okay, I get it." The two of us listened, listened in the silence of a circle weaving itself together. Then she broke the spell: "I think Adam wants what he can't have. He has to change his attitude if he wants a relationship with me."

The red light on the answering machine flashed fretfully. "Hi, Idina, this is Kathy. We missed you today; are you all right?"... "I'm calling to tell you about our sale coming up next week. We hope you can come in and try on some of our new suits."... "This is Bethany calling. I'd be interested in going to the concert on Sunday. Should we meet at Zander's?"... "Hi, Mooie. This is your baby. Call me when you get home."

"I'm home now," I said into the phone and into Jada's ear.

"Where have you been? I called you early this afternoon." Jada's voice had the slipperiness of a melting popsicle, and I could almost see the orange smear on her chin.

"Oh, dear! I've been on an odyssey for Dom the Dictator."

"What are you talking about?"

"Dom had a paper he needed to type, and he was expecting to come over and type his paper today, but my ribbon was dry. The place I buy it is closed on Sunday, and I don't want to drive all over the city looking for a typewriter ribbon; not everyone carries them anymore. Anyway, Dom had a game so he didn't have all day anyway. So I called Jessie because I knew she was writing for her graduate classes, but she used the computer at her mother's work. She said her folks had a manual typewriter at their house and I could ask to use theirs. So I did, and off we went. Well, you can imagine how long it took Dom on that thing, so of course, I had to type it while he read it, and you know I made a few suggestions and that took even longer. By the time we got done, oh, what time was that; anyway, I had to drive him home and then I stopped for a few groceries, and that was pretty much my day. So anyway, Jessie's dad called him Dom the Dic—"

"Just a minute, Mom, someone's at my door." Distant voices mingled with my own remembered voices: Arnold's self-congratulatory pucker when he gave me the typewriter, telling me what a good deal he got on it; Jada's reprimand when I accepted it, not the electronic processor I wanted; my own telling me I'd been settling all my life.

"Oh, no, there's another one," Jada breathed, laying the phone down as she picked it up. I gathered plates from the rack—there were only two—and stacked them in the cupboard. An old-fashioned Coke glass, narrow foot and blown out bowl at the top, a little juice glass with butterflies painted on it, a squat cocktail. Everything from St. Peter Claver second-hand store. Better than being boxed up in a set like a Fischer-Price village, one wife, two children, and everything a man needs for his house on a suburban street.

"Okay, Mom, I'm back."

"What's going on?" I asked. "Do you want me to call you back?"

"No, everyone's just coming by to see if I need something. Lyn just brought me a card. Adam and I broke up."

"Oh, Jada! I'm so sorry. Why?"

"I don't know. He doesn't know what he wants. Men are so selfish. They're afraid you're going to take something away from them."

Underneath my sympathy was surprise that Jada sounded more disgusted than sorry for herself. "So when was the last time you saw him?"

"He's still around. And that's the trouble. He says he can't stay away. But he says we can only be friends."

"That's ridiculous!"

"I know it, because he also says he wants to be with me."

"Maybe you two can agree to some time apart and then talk about your feelings when you've had time to think."

"No, I don't think I want him." Her voice grew sharper, honed on a whetting stone. "He gets so mad and hits things. I'm worried about that. He doesn't control his temper very well. He comes over and goes crazy and wants to stay here. No. I don't want him that way, and he's not going to have me, either. It's his loss."

"Yes, it is. You sound like you're dealing with all this rather well. I'd want to see what I could do to work things out."

"Yeah, you'd probably say it was your fault. I have lots of support here. Everyone is being nice and understanding. I won't let him in any more. All of them say it's the right thing to do."

"Yes. I'm glad to hear you sound so strong. I know I'm not what you want right now, but you know I love you. Is there anything I can do to make things easier?"

"Yes. Keep writing me lots of letters." In the silent space I cursed my inheritance: my father's obsession with guilt and my mother's search for someone or something to blame. "He said I could keep BJ for a while." Maybe she was holding him, cuddling him as we spoke. After fights with my dad, my mother sizzled like an overheated radiator. In one of those furors, she tore up a boxful of photographs, as if the days of a life could be ripped out of a past and tossed into the fire, leaving no traces of their existence except sooty carbon that coats the interior of a neglected chimney.

The timing of this break-up, a month before spring break, coincided with Easter. Nineteen eighty-nine was one of those years in which Easter came early, much too early to herald the onset of hope. Too early, even, to stir uneasiness with death, the desolation Easter was supposed to redeem. April, the scene of too many burdens for Jada seemed distant. Gaunt March skies, not yet having had their fill of winter, stuffed their jowls with snow and vomited wet white cottontails in disregard for all the whisker-white bunnies bunched pink-eyed and puffy-soft among blooming purple and yellow flowers on greeting cards. The business of living flourished: stores advertised spring finery out of sync with the thermometer; Per was leaving for a ski trip in the mountains of California while Florida beaches beckoned everyone else; and Jada flew home, her mouth set as if she needed to concentrate all her muscles on keeping it from dropping from her face.

We stood in a ring around the luggage carousel that had begun its grinding crawl, a metal-plated caterpillar on a leash. Bags tumbled down the chute, at first in hiccoughs, then as a steady gushing of blue and green and brown suitcases, bundles and boxes dumping onto each other like dodge 'em cars at the fair. I pulled out Jada's two pieces. We tramped through the bracing evening air laden as if half-submerged and wading through a pool of cold water. Jada's coat dangled from her, one sleeve dragging like a tail from a storm cloud. In the car, I pushed the button for heat. But the chill remained.

Jada wore a bridled pout like a new spring bonnet, turning down my invitations to a museum, the conservatory, shopping. But she volunteered to pick up the wallpaper, which she liked, and watching me hang first the lining and then the patterned paper, she gave encouraging and sympathetic support, and I took the view that her muted conversations on the telephone could be the outpourings of a broken heart and that her moroseness at home was a passing mood to be turned upside down at the next good thing that happened in her life. I didn't disregard the familiarity of Jada's mood and what it could portend, but I was under a spell, the spell of chemotherapy, and didn't connect March to April and its foreboding proximity to the devastations of leukemia in earlier years. I saw the signs of deja vu in a different context: everything is never always in the same configuration as it had been before.

"Mom, will you drive me to Kimby's? I have to pick up my keys before I go back. It's snowing and slippery, and I don't feel like driving."

"Right now? I have just these pieces; then I want to clean up." I held a dripping strip of border paper over the long tray on the floor. In the early spring light, diffused through the dripping snow, what was already attached was dimmed to a flat gray.

"No," she said with exaggeration. "I have to be there between 8:15 and 8:30, that's the only time she'll be there." I was on the step stool, sliding the strip on its snotty slick glue into a straight line between the ceiling and the top edge of the shower tiles. "All week long I've been waiting for her to return them. Now I have to go pick them up because she's leaving. I knew she was going to do this to me. She's so selfish. I'm the one who did her the favor." Jada hardened her lips into thick stiff rods like wooden rollers on a hand-cranked washing machine.

"What," I asked, water falling in a sheet from the strip, "is she doing with your keys?"

"I let her use my jacket for her date with Daniel and they were in the pocket. She took them out of the pocket and when she returned the jacket, she forgot to give me my keys. She has a car; she could have driven them over here, but no, she's so busy. Not too busy to go out with Daniel."

"Where do they go?" I couldn't see Kimby wrangling in the back seat of a Dart once a week; surely she would want to have planned and made a better bed for herself.

"Movies, a hamburger. You know Kimby; nothing too spicy, and nothing that costs money."

"We could go out to eat first, if you want, though I suppose 7:30's too late for you."

"I don't want to go anyway. I'm not very hungry."

"I've noticed that. Your weight was the same when they weighed you at the clinic, wasn't it?"

"Yeah, but I feel fat. Especially next to you." She patted her belly, bulging like mine.

I looked over my shoulder at her, judging the width of her face under her permed hair, the slender fingers splayed like bent tines of a canape fork over the front of her sweatshirt. "You're not fat; but you could use some toning. Why don't you come to an aerobics class with me."

"You know I can't keep up with you."

"You don't have to. You just do what you can. If you can't jump, walk in place. I just get into it because of the music."

"And you're a goon, going to three aerobics in one day!" Jada shook her head, smiling while tsking. "What time is it?"

"I think you should go to an afternoon session. I'll ask Kathy to modify the moves for you. There, done. How do you like it?" I stepped back to look myself. "I think I'll paint some of this gray." I bent over and ran my fingers along the vanity.

"You can't ever leave things alone, can you?"

"Sure I can. But don't you think it will look nicer? Pick this lighter gray out?"

"Mm-hmm. I still like my bathroom the best. You really know how to do things."

"Oh, I just try is all. Can't be afraid to try. Let's eat, shall we?"

The car headlights shimmered in watery streams on Lawton Avenue. Whatever snow had fallen had already become mucous-slick on the black pavement. I squeezed the brake, easing toward a red light. "I got my grades," Jada said out of the darkness.

"How do you feel about them?"

"I didn't expect an A in French, but I got it so they're okay."

"Does that mean you didn't get A's anywhere else?"

"No, I got only one B+."

"Exactly. You always tell me not to expect good grades and then you get them." I lurched. "Sorry. The light turned yellow. Are you proud of me that I didn't try?" Water trickled from the roof of the car making fluid wriggles down the windshield.

"You have to take better care of this car. It's terrible how you store stuff in it. I wouldn't neglect this car if I were in charge. When was the last time you had it washed?"

I waited in the car for Jada to come out of the dorm, the keys clutched within her tightfisted hand that jutted through her pocket like a concealed weapon. Returning home, Jada watched houses, dilapidated storefronts and metal streamers of railroad tracks, dirty little snow piles go by, collecting images and thinking what? What does one think about when one knows that seeing is measured? I faced the garage door and flashed the clicker at it.

Spring break Jada had spent sorting and separating, a job made easy by already being sorted and separated into three places, what she needed for her life at school, what she needed when she was home, and what she had decided to keep as her history at the house on Lambert Lane. Her twenty years had a deliberate view of reality, divided up into past, present, and future instead of all mixed up one inside the other. She made exchanges, recalling something to life, bringing it to the condo, relegating another to the past, leaving her rubber stamps, letters of the alphabet, each pink rubber letter and animal shape washed clean of its inky imprint and lined up A to Z in her desk drawer at the house.

Movement from night to day to night was as muddy as the thickening skies and softening ground of the last days of March. Burrowed in our winter clothes, we were unaware of the unseen activity that drives the buds and forces the flowers. We held on with dreams, not noticing the changes that hindsight so clearly ridicules, until we'd be unready for the first hot day of spring, sweating in clothing that should have been stored away in moth balls. Jada had had her chemo. Her counts passed muster. Prescriptions were refilled. She had packed, and we watched for spring as the calendar days dropped away, pennies into the wishing well. The coming of April was imminent when I drove Jada to the airport on Easter morning.

April 19

Day of DOOM!! No one has to tell me. It is obvious from my blood counts that I have relapsed. I've been ignoring my symptoms a long time. That's it. I'm out of the game plan, left behind with nothing to come of me. I have a 25% chance of surviving, not LIFE, but after a successful bone marrow transplant. Everything else is just buying time. I asked Adam to come and stay with me through the night. He said he loved me and will come but not stay. Not very sensitive! He says I'll get through it. But I know I have no happy future. Typical for my life's pattern! Up shit's creek. A bottomless cesspool. I was so busy with meetings, classwork, and social activities that I was going bonkers. And now I'm so SICK. I can't believe I let it go on so long.

Jada called on a Tuesday in April. Heavy sweaters were piled on a dining room chair, gathered for dry cleaning and out-of-season storage. Mornings were still frosty; after all, it was April. No heat in a school building and no summer sun to warm us, I kept a few sweaters to wear until the long-awaited warm day.

The message her voice left on the answering machine was cryptic, like too few letters of a saying on Wheel of Fortune. She was there, leaving a ghostly message, a voice without a person, sounding even more removed from her body by being left as a tape recording, waiting to be picked up like a package delivered to your door when you're not home. It was there before me, begging me to open it. "Something is wrong."

While I waited for a voice from a real live person, I cleaned up: leftover dishes from breakfast, my unruly stack of school materials, periodicals to be read. I needed to hide them, put everything in a place, the appearance of order. Which malady is plaguing her now? So many to choose from. Dr. Lourde had investigated each anomaly, the numbness in her arms and fingers, the red eruptions on her skin, an inability to focus her mind, earaches, discharges, sending her in for CAT scans, arranging for specialists to consider the sources of these mysteries. Time would have to tell if it was a "yes" or a "no," if time did not run out, that is. Why would I consider that when her blood counts were lab-tested-good just weeks earlier?

It wasn't easy being left in the pile of delayed decisions. Dr. Silverman always knew, impetigo, measles, a viral infection, a bacterial bug, and a shot of penicillin. Come back in three days, call if it doesn't get better, here's a prescription. With this disease there wasn't a pill, a shot, or machine that would make it better; no, they made it worse, made her throw up, made her bones brittle, made the inside of her mouth spot like a field of white clover. Or made another case for Dr. Lourde to solve, a detective waiting for a lead, poising himself to pounce on that one giveaway, trusting that, without it, nothing was physically wrong. But Jada's fine sense of knowing when something *was* wrong with her own body always won out, even if neither she nor Dr. Lourde could name it, not at first. And that was the kicker, the ringer, the missing piece. I hadn't once heard Jada voice a suspicion this past month. She had just been home. She had just had the blood work, the burning chemo in her veins. It was supposed to be working even now. Yes, it was April. But then, it was almost May; we had almost made it.

The phone rang once. Jada's voice quavered. "My counts are bad," she said.

"What are you saying? What do you mean?" I felt like I had just been given a punch to the head and couldn't get the rest of my body to know what happened to it. Where was she? Why wasn't she talking to me? "Are you saying that your leukemia is back?" I ground on, letting my brain maneuver on its own while the rest of me held up the question to scrutinize the wording, personifying the disease, giving it legs and will-power and passion like some cast-out lover come back for revenge.

"I guess so. Dr. Brown called Dr. Lourde already. I have to go in right away. I've been busy all afternoon with the business office. It is so hard to get anything done! Priss is helping me get my stuff together. I'm flying home tomorrow, flight 541. It comes in at 5:18."

How could all this go on without my knowing? Receptionists knew, reservationists knew, telephone operators knew, people who had never seen Jada's name before collected bits and pieces of the most intimate information that I, the closest one to her, didn't know while I scurried about swishing Cling around the toilet, setting out fresh towels, spraying the mirror with Windex to better see myself. "Does your dad know?"

"No. Would you call him? There are so many things to do. I couldn't have got them done without Priss. She's coming back to help me pack. I just had to get stuff done for a class. I've been running all over the place. Priss had stuff to do, too."

"Yes, of course. Do you have a ride to the airport?"

"Priss said she'd take me. So did Adam. He's coming over tonight. I'm staying at Priss's. Do you have her number? It's 3972. Same area code and exchange. I still have to get to the computer lab and see Gabriella about my math. Just get everything ready. They're going to start right away."

From deep underneath the dust, the clutter, the plane tickets, and the math project, I whispered, "I'm so sorry, Jada."

Jada was alone, a thousand miles away. Surely there would be the scuttle of messengers' feet, the ins and outs of an open door while faithful friends and those curious to see how a young woman in a magnified drama would perform. Two burnished brass nude women leaned shoulder to shoulder against each other atop the ticking clock on my bookcase. With each strike, I began to accept the impact of our own separate silence.

"Yeah, so am I." Jada's voice came low and hoarse, a tugboat pulling me back, and I hung on because the silence was greater than my room and her room and the space between us, and the clock kept ticking, but I didn't hear it through the silence inside my head, throbbing, my shoulders convulsing, possessed, my stomach, choked, gripped so violently that it forced my mouth open to expel one long silent wail for no one to hear. The silence was inside Jada, too, and between us together we kept our silence separate and sanctified and secret. Everyone else was noise; and noise cannot fathom the missive between daughter and mother that they had failed, that she had failed, and that I had failed to keep the world from coming to an end.

"Will you be okay till Priss comes?"

"Other people know. They'll be here." We said our goodbye, and Jada became as unreachable as a faraway star, suspended in a void whose existence depended on faith. I drew in breath and dialed Arnold's number.

"Hi, Dom. How are you, Sugar? What're you doing?" I never called him without prior arrangement. And I never called Arnold. After hearing the score of the baseball game, I asked for him.

"Halloo," Arnold's greeting seemed to challenge.

"Jada's coming home tomorrow. Her leukemia's back."

"Okay." I imagined he was clenching his full-freckled cheeks alternately in quick spasms as the words circulated in his brain in a flurry, making lots of noise but little sense. I told him we'd know specifics by Thursday and then we hung up, but not before he repeated his line of encouragement to "hang in there." Like I was an old winter coat waiting for the reassurance of the first warm day in spring.

And then I really was alone, with only my thoughts to talk to. *You know what that means. Relapse on drugs. You know what that means. Give yourself a snort of self-pity like a quick shot of brandy and then get things in order. You will have to run on automatic pilot, so do your thinking now. What to pack for the hospital. Sheets. A roll of toilet tissue. These slippers?* I brought them out of Jada's closet. *And me: lots of turtlenecks and sweatshirts. Sweaters, too. My toiletries bag.* I had a hand project, a wedding gift for Jessie and Len. I liked holding it up after working on it each time to imprint its image, an imaginary gallery of a work in progress. *Telephone numbers. Take the book; and put stamps in it. And Per. Tell Per I won't be seeing him for a while. He'll have to wait.*

The next morning, I woke for school and made my call to Dom exactly at 6:10, just like normal, with my last cup of coffee, before I began my life as a cardboard person. Soon it would be public, my fears, my sadness, my pitiable situation, and heads down, people's eyes would search for diversion from me.

My principal was busy in her office, but as I passed I was able to interject a serious sounding request that she see me. My reading classroom, a former science room and lab, was cold, with fresh morning air circulating throughout. Recalling a teacher, a former occupant of this room, who wore a long woolen scarf around his neck and who had died of some sudden and mysterious disease, I asked the custodians to turn off the refrigeration, at least, if they couldn't turn on the heat. A well-intentioned custodian wedged three cardboard pieces into the long overhead grate spanning the room's length. I bought a space heater in front of which I sat before and after school, working in the blast of dry hot air at my shoulders.

The room bred flies in prolific numbers, all of them hatching, so it seemed, at the double windows, the most prestigious double windows in the building. Every morning I looked out through two spotted glass panes running lengthwise from above my head to just below my knees. Across the street and along the athletic field lay half a golf course beyond which, a mile away, ran a river, the Mississippi, banked deep by a lush green bluff.

Gazing out the window, I could be persuaded to believe in a lot of things. It had rained in the night, the clouds drizzling out as the morning arrived. Inside the classroom, making my customary stop at the window, I was arrested by the sight of a rainbow making its arc in the great steel blue sky. Like a shiny coin at the tip of my shoe, it could have been stepped on as I meant to hurry on with my duties. But the rainbow glinted at me, winked like a fluttering neon sign, riveted my eyes on the bands of pink, violet, and gold sloping through the bluing sky all the way downward until it reached the grassy ground just a leap away. I imagined rainbows were as mythical as their pots of gold, disappearing behind mountains, into the mist, making the promised reward impossible to reach. But here it was! The end of the rainbow was at my feet. Or nearly so. I wished for a second that I could run down the steps and out the building across the street and through the field, my arms sails toward the sparkles of gold, aqua, and magenta that kissed the tips of the green grass. But reason—or was it attitude—told me the rainbow would disappear before I got there, like so much else that began as a promise. And then I would have to wonder if that rainbow had ever even existed or if it had made a mock landing just to slap me in the face, reminding me of an end, without fanfare, glitter, or reward.

I turned my back on the window on that morning of the day I would bring Jada home. If I hadn't, I might have wept and wept and wept until there was no end, and it wasn't time for that.

Nancy was at my door right after homeroom. Things never stop, even when they must. First hour bells ring. Classes begin. Kids want attention. I stood half in and half out of the room, all the prickly hairs of my skin seeming to gather in my throat, making it dry and crackly, and my fingers felt cold through the sweater sleeves that they grabbed down about them. "Jada has relapsed," I blurted, "and I have no idea what she's going to do, but I'm very low on sick days, so I can't take the rest of the year off. I need the flexibility to come in when I can and call in when I can't."

"I'm sorry. You do what you need to; we'll adjust."

"Please, don't tell others yet; I don't want to talk to anyone about it."

I turned myself into the room, needing to focus, finding each routine new to me and requiring conscious effort to execute; I planned step by step what I would do next, asking myself what I was looking for, why I was walking toward the desk. Gratefully I acknowledged each student request for help as their hands, like gunshots, made me start toward a well-rehearsed goal. Without them, I had to activate tiny sections of my brain to make it respond consciously to what was so natural by habit and practice. But as the sun rises, the dismissal bell also rings. And there was nothing left to do but to concentrate. Hard. On everything I could find. Anything except what I would say when I accepted my daughter at the airport. The minute hand on the clock moved stubbornly forward, and as much as I prodded it along, with each glance upwards, I had to will it to dislodge itself. *It knows I'm watching; that's why it won't move.*

Then, even the distraction of forcing distraction gave way to time, and I was left to the final minutes of packing up and leaving. *In five minutes I will be there.* Five minutes of roller coasters running the length of my groin to my throat, five minutes of slapping my hand to the base of my neck as if to loosen a stranglehold, five minutes of pursing my lips, squeezing them shut to contain a curse. *No words. Hear no words. Roar, rattle, thunder, thump, thump. Say no words. Reach for the ticket, don't leave the ticket, no, leave it, no words. People walking, driving out. Coming, going, I'm coming. Here. Here I am. Find the screen, look for the gate number.*

People. They crossed in front of me. Zig-zagged around. Men in business suits. Swinging brief cases in pendulum arcs against their pants legs. Brushing, swish, swish. They were in a hurry to get home, to make it in time for supper. She'll keep it warm in the oven. The kids are hungry. Potatoes are drying out. Where is he?

Stewards spiking the heels of their shoes into the invincible inflammable impenetrable woven floor covering too tight to snag even by exposed nails of worn-down rubber pads. In tow were petite cases, their "babies," cradled in luggage strollers, wheels making straight obedient tracks behind distracted mothers, two women taking turns twisting their heads back and forth while keeping sight of their destination. They spoke in crisp syllables, timed in syncopation with their metronomic head movements. Did they share relief or even privately give thanks for another safe landing? No hijacking. No bomb. No failed engine. No mid-flight collision. No skid ending in a fireball explosion, tossing head over heels like an oil-ignited tumbleweed. Just another ordinary flight, maybe. Routine. The safety instructions, now on video, rolled through the cartridge without as much as a blipped frame. The most unusual event was that they ran out of orange juice. *Can you imagine?* Cutting down again, cutting too close.

Or was their click-clock clatter chatter sufficient code? It could have been they on the plane that Jada wished would explode, crash unannounced into the face of a mountain, all responsibility removed from herself, myself, no accountability to her, me, anyone, God. Who? Simple that way, easy. Like wishing for Arnold's fall from an icy roof. No such luck. Nothing to take your cup away from you. You gotta do what you gotta do. *And so do I.* I believed fighting for life would be worth it. Had to.

Unimaginable; I can't imagine her dead!

Selfish. She calls me selfish. No regrets: I promised myself. That's why I did what I did, do what I do. No plane crashes. Yet it does all the time. It might not be a plane plane, but the crash is a crash. Survivors fare the same as non-survivors. The duality of surviving. You might live, you know. You can dish out the orders, but you can't dish out your anger and get rid of it. No such luck. No easy death.

I picked my spot, near the mouth of the emerging passengers to see each one tread the sloping passageway from the plane. But as the stream of people thinned to a dribble, it flashed in my mind that Jada may be hobbling, unable to walk without help. She would be the last one out. Then there was no one but the representative standing at the podium.

"Are these all the passengers?" Drivers had been known to return their buses to the garage and lock them up only to later discover that a sleeping child had been left behind on a torn vinyl seat. Had they taken that precaution on the plane before folding up the accordion-like link to the passageway and locking the terminal door? He assured me that a forgotten passenger was an impossibility.

"Excuse me," I said, raising another head behind the service desk. "Would you check to see if Jada Petersen is on a flight from Hartford today? She was supposed to be on this one, but...."

"What's the name?" She reached behind the upper ledge of the desk and pulled out a clipboard.

"P-e-t-e-r-s-e-n."

Her head bent over the list, straining her eyeballs upward above her half-glasses, she asked, "Are you sure?"

"Yes, it's Danish." People always want you to be what they have in their mind.

"No, she isn't on the flight roster. Do you have the right day?"

You mean the right nightmare, I wanted to correct her. "Yes. Are there any other flights coming in today?"

She swiveled to the computer screen and tapped keys. "Yes, there's one tonight. I'm checking that now. Yes, here she is."

At home the message waited on the machine like a patient and loyal dog. "I've changed flights. I'm coming tonight at 9:14. See you later." Time loitered around me like a tarrying customer drinking another cup of coffee at closing time. I couldn't get more nervous or less; nothing changed, except the hands making their perpetual circles around the circumference of the clock on the stove. I wondered how I'd feel if I were soundly religious. I envied those people who trusted that God would take care of reality, or at least them in the throes of it. Would I have felt a relief to give up my burdens to a non-entity? What happens then? Does your mind go blank? Does a spirit replace the void like Reddi Whip in a cream puff? Sounded too easy. That stuff is mostly air, anyway, and given a little time, it escapes the cavity, leaving a flat sour soggy puddle.

Even time, the coward, ran out. With only the green and yellow digitals glowing at my dashboard, I steered the car through the almost deserted parkway, all the frenzy of daylight dissolving as I settled into the darkness of the day. Beyond the fences that cordoned the parkway from the neighborhood it gouged, rectangles of yellow on either side reminded me that children had school tomorrow and were probably brushing their teeth with sweet-tasting paste, making foamy bubbles in their bathwater, getting their pajamas on, maybe finishing their homework. Those were the ones who believed there were dues to pay for tomorrow's promise. They were the ones who subscribed to the official version of the way things work. It did not matter how their minds arranged reality; reality happened anyway.

And I was once again at the airport. This time was no rehearsal. Jada was unmistakable in the flow of people from the airplane. She wore the dress I sewed, copied from a Laura Ashley design, a slightly narrower chemise of blue print under another rose print, too thin for Minnesota's April. As she drew nearer, I could see how quickly the disease had grabbed hold. Her bare arms and face, color-faded from the voracious white blood cells crowding her marrow, betrayed her.

"Here, sit down; I'll order a cart," I said to her eyes, the crispness gone, as if closing from a startling flash of a camera. "Do you want me to take that?" "That" was her tote filled with books and papers and folders, and Hambone, his glassy eye peeking over the rim at Jada's knee. How many times has he made this trip as her faithful companion? That's really all she ever asked of anything, anyone, that it be as true to her as she to it. A baby learning to trust the world, finding milk in her bottle, her pacifier amid the sheets in her bed. Hambone, the Velveteen Rabbit in pigskin. To bed, to clinic, to college, to hospital, clutched at the neck under Jada's arm. Jada told me how the next day would begin, Arnold, Dom, and me scheduled to have our blood tested as possible marrow donors.

"Feeling a little under the weather?" the driver sympathized with soft droopy-dog eyes. I helped Jada onto the cart, her back buckling, her legs, planted steadfastly to the floor like weary old tree stumps not willing to bend with the wind, and set her bag next to her, Hambone's head nestling between the two of us. *So, Hambone, here you are again, hoarding light in your glassy eyes. Another ride, like others to start IVs, fill prescriptions, get blood, confirm to the ear what was already felt in the veins.* To some we might have looked only tired so late at night, maybe have a touch of the flu, a little flight sickness. No one could tell by looking at us that we were on a journey of the insane, on another road to a nonexistent park.

"Mom, I don't want this anymore." Another 20-year-old might toss that statement out while ridding her closet of a once-loved sweater, grown limp and baggy, its sleeves stretched wide with wear. This willful young woman, flattened under slabs of bleached blankets, was not, though tiring of a tedious task, leaving me to dispose of what she cast aside. The cancerous cells in her body had gone crazy, and if those couldn't be stopped, at least temporarily, nothing could be done whether Jada wanted it, or I wished it, or not. My once lithe and animated daughter lay fixed in the hospital bed, her feet small tipis, for the eighth consecutive day, her blanched face masking the drama that had been playing out for the past eight years, now culminating behind her opaque eyes.

I could not relieve her of responsibility, as I would have the sweater by stuffing it in the giveaway bag; nor was I able to assume the remnants of an oversized job that had been doled out to her. "I know you don't. It has gone on too long for you."

Hambone, flattened and matted, lay on his side above Jada's peachy head. They had had it. My permission was not needed. In fact, I had already given it. She was, technically, an adult and could choose freely, had chosen indirectly by following her own treatment schedule, flying home for IVs when she fit them in, not when protocol dictated, taking oral medicines by chance, not by regimen. I was still on the side of time, twenty years' worth, and she wanted me to clean my own closet of what I loved even though it no longer wore smartly on the fashion scene.

Eight days since coming home, Jada had made up her mind. She hadn't said no to the blood tests for Arnold, Dom, and me as possible donors; she hadn't said no to the insertion of a portacatheter, a small dual-capped receiver for IV needles just under the skin in the center of her rib cage. But there was the prospect of a bone marrow transplant. She was reminding me of my promise to her.

The eight days she had been home—in the hospital—were haunted by the eight years which preceded them and began early on the morning after she arrived. I had already admitted her when Arnold and Dom met me in the angular corridor outside the outpatient lab—a return to 1981 and about a thousand other blood draws. Fresh from a shower, my hair had dried into stiff gelled coils. The rest of me retained the heaviness of a short night of hard sleep, the acid smell of Arnold's cafeteria coffee rising in an oily plume making my stomach swirl.

"Hi, Dom," I said, slipping my hand along his back, wide, resembling my father, except for the hair. My father had always been bald, at least in my life. In primary school, I colored a picture of him for Father's Day. Brown suit, red tie, and skinny arms like chains hanging from a pillory is how I colored my father. In my picture, I colored my father a tie because it seemed to be what was right for a portrait, like the pictures in the stories we read with fathers who worked in offices and wore suits and ties. One thing I did not change was his bald head. I drew little black lines between his nose and his upper lip for his mustache, colored his eyes brown, and left the top of his head without hair. It was hard to imagine Dom, with all his thick brown hair, as bald, just as it was hard to imagine him as an adult, not the junior out of his high school classes to see if he could be the one to save his sister's life. Siblings were supposed to be the closest match.

I guided Dom into the lab, out of habit peeking through the window to scout the interior. Eight years I had been walking into that lab room. Eight years I had witnessed countless pokes and probes into Jada's veins. Eight years I had stood beside her, behind her, in front of her. Eight years later I stood by Dom, sitting at the table with all the tiny glass tubes lined up in their wooden rack, columns of numbers to add up, one right answer, indisputable, my hand on his shoulder because I was the mother who cared for him while he was sick, and I was the mother who took him for allergy shots every Saturday, and I was the mother who drove across the city to bandage his banged-up knee when he fell off his bike, who came when he called.

"Make a fist. Oh, that's a good one. Here, let me tie this on. Okay, make another fist. This won't hurt a bit." And then it was my turn. Eight years should have inured me. Eight years of being brave and supportive, standing by Jada's side should have cleared my head. I sat in the seat, still warm in the cool room, and obeyed the technician, letting her snap the band around my arm, feeling the needle pierce my vein. And then she—was it she?—caught me falling from the chair. I felt being lifted to my feet and was brought wobbly and slobbery to the little room with the short padded table on which Jada had lain eight years ago.

Voices, distant, indecipherable, and breathing. A sound like the shaking of a rug next to my ear drums; sharp cold on my forehead; my back, my arms stinging. Voices. Words. People speaking. *Open your eyes.* I lay, an eavesdropper through a thin wall. Dom's face, there on the other side of my knees sticking up like gables on an English house, going away from me. I lay, wanting to think, feeling ashamed of my weakness, compelled to get up, go on, prove myself strong. My arm was lifted—Dr. Lourde feeling my wrist and looking into my pupils. "Blood pressure," he said to someone behind him. "Sometimes taking blood causes a sudden drop in blood pressure." As in a nightmare, I was powerless to heed the urge to get up, and I lay. The nothingness felt so restful.

"How do you feel, Ma?"

"Help me up, slow." His long fingers lacing my arm, Dom pulled me and my eyes felt full, like a bladder that needed to empty, the pounding behind my ears like the roar of a high waterfall. I held onto the table's edge until I was sure my legs wouldn't melt underneath me and I'd drool into a pool like the Wicked Witch of the West. Leaning on Dom, I felt a chill return. But the fuzzy pinwheels were gone from around my vision, and I could stand. I looked ahead, took a step.

Trouble lines drew around Dom's eyes, but he was not shy about stating his needs, no matter how earnestly apologetic he was when he did. "You don't need me for anything else, do you? I want to get back to school." Arnold stood in the distance, looking on.

"Sure, go ahead. I'll call you when I can."

"Okay, I'm going to take Dom to school. Joe said it would take a day or so to get the results. Is there anything I can do now?"

"No, I can't think of what it would be."

Jada had been in surgery while our blood was drawn, and I turned into the waiting room where moms and dads, but mostly moms, brought their own mothers, sisters, neighbors, and children along with them, transplanting entire social centers. No one really watched the ubiquitous television set, babbling nonsense, loudly, the children running over each other's fingers with their toy cars and trucks, crying and fussing, each clan chattering continuously over the noisy distracters. Often three, four adults sat in a row and exchanged family or neighborhood stories, heads bobbing in and out of line as each had something to add. Rows of chairs squatted against the walls and cut a swath through the room. There was no not hearing the vignettes that brought people there. The whirring of human voices should have made the television noise indistinguishable background. But it was always blaring, encouraging everyone to rise above it.

In the middle of a row of chairs beyond the reception desk, unattended except for two telephones, two people sat looking seriously into each other's faces. The younger of the two, a man in a shiny taffeta-looking jacket, the kind with the name of a bar or a towing firm emblazoned on its back in gold, paid no attention to me as I walked past. "Where is she now?" inquired the woman, fitting comfortably in the scratchy blue chair. He appeared to be more accustomed to a bent-chrome-framed and vinyl-upholstered seat of an auto service center; perhaps that was why he sat forward, his legs spread apart, two columns supporting his burly arms, his worries balled up and rubbed between his thick hands, like a mass of sticky buggers he wanted to get rid of.

"I dunno. Prob'ly at her sister's. She just can't stay home and take care of 'im. I come by an' take 'im as much as I can, but you know I can't have 'im where I live. "An' I'm not home much. Sometimes I don't even come home between jobs; I jus' sleep in the car an' go off to the next."

The woman accepted his lament and, I imagined, would have lit a cigarette by way of affirmation if it weren't disallowed. Instead, her puffy finger pushed away the knitted cuff at her wrist to check the time. A spool of pink thread bounced to the floor, and I jerked to pick it up before it rolled their way and drew attention to me, an outsider, who might seem a defilement to his intense feelings for the boy of whom he spoke, the boy I assumed to be his child. I listened, not just because it was too late not to, but also because he was speaking for me, too, and I wanted to hear what I was up against.

"Last week I stopped by her apartment on my way to work?" he continued. "He was there alone with a babysitter. They din't have nothin' for supper, just some milk an' stuff. I had to go out an' git 'em some burgers an' stuff. I don't have time for that. With all this, he's goin' ta need ta be tooken care of. That just ain't goin' ta happen."

"Can't her family help?"

"Naw. You know how she is with her old lady. Her sister's the only one, an' she don't wanna have nuttin' ta do with Danny. She's busy tryin' ta do some modeling or something." The man threw open his hands, showering his seeds of turbulence in the winds. He thumped his back against the chair, impotent, letting his useless hands fall empty to his bulging jean-clad thighs. The woman nodded her frizzy head, loose skin jiggling from her lower jaw like a rooster's comb. No one else in the waiting room to catch the pods of desiccated seeds, I felt accountable to acknowledge him, or, if not him, whatever powers that had abandoned him, abandoned him as they had abandoned my own daughter. I listened like a coward, and listening made me tired. Putting my handwork down, I closed my eyes and lay my head against the wall. I was done fighting, too. Not because I didn't want to, not because I didn't feel the conviction, not because I was running away from a fight I couldn't win. I was just tired, done in, out of steam. And it was too soon to feel sad about it. Just tired. Tired of struggling against outside forces, be they researchers who had the answers in dancing tubes and figures and formulae, mutating cells and defective genes that did not succumb to the rules of order, impatient lab technicians and overworked nurses, or the monster in Jada that refused to behave. One thing was anything was everything, and they all made me tired. There, in the waiting room, tired, tired of waiting and seeing,

I began to see the end, and, tiring of waiting for its coming, I tired of tiring.

I didn't know when Jada gave in to exhaustion, but it was long before here, and it was long before I knew what it felt like to be exhausted. I didn't doze in the waiting room, though time floated through my sense of being like a leaf on a glassy-surfaced lake, and, without awareness of the details of their leaving, I became conscious that Danny's father and perhaps his grandmother were gone.

Empty, the room was desolate, a fruitless womb, the opposite to the life we hoped it would rebirth from our tattered, worn-out hopes. Realizing how tired I was, I thought of how tired Jada must have been way back even in the beginning. If she were as tired as I, she mightn't have cared quite so much that she didn't come out of surgery, wanting a little extra rest before having to get back to the fighting. She might have been so tired that she didn't want to spend the energy to do something twice—an IV poke—when it could have been done once, right the first time. She might have been so tired that she wouldn't have wanted to do any of it, so why should she want to submit? When you're tired, every push, every stab at life that failed was just a slow murder.

Jada recovered from surgery, and the rounds of medications and tests began in earnest, again. Eight years earlier, almost to the day, doctors and nurses grilled Jada as if she had been the culprit responsible for perpetrating a deadly epidemic; now she seemed a sacred sacrifice. Nurses came in deferentially. It wasn't Jada's history of being in and out of this hospital that had gained her stature. As her body wore out and she was nearly not curable, she was finally real.

"No news yet," Dr. Lourde reported on the second day, and apologized for the waiting. "I phoned for the results again, and the doctor said he ordered extra tests because you are such a difficult family." A grin grew under Dr. Lourde's mustache. "I told him, 'You didn't need to do a test to know that!'"

On the third day, he made a personal visit with the doctor in charge of matching, numbering, and coding the cells. That afternoon, Dr. Lourde entered quietly, his loafers padding softly on the linoleum floor. Jada wrestled with a knot in her shoulder and shifted uneasily. "Jada? Is your back still giving you trouble?"

"Yes," she said, squinting as she pushed herself away from the pillow. Outside the noise from the freeway construction simmered. From this side of the building, I could watch the workers and machines pound and pour, four floors, and two basements below.

Dr. Lourde grabbed the chair from the wall and brought it up to the foot of Jada's bed and sat. Eight years of experience gave him away: he had seriousness in his intentions. "I just got back from the lab where I spoke with the doc. They've done everything, even some things I couldn't think of. They still can't find a match between your brother's blood and your own." It was known almost immediately, that neither Arnold nor I had a chance of matching. Dr. Lourde maintained an even look, not a curl to his lips, even his eyebrows matching so that a pencil could have balanced on them. He went on, adding, "Even if your brother's blood had matched, you still could reject it. The body has a wonderful mechanism that keeps foreign objects out." He paused, though he did not free his gaze from Jada's face. "The best chance of surviving a bone marrow transplant is if you donated your own marrow. That's the only real guarantee that you will not reject it because it's yours."

Jada met his gaze, and from the expressions that passed between the two of them, they could have been talking about someone else's brother, someone else's blood, someone else's life. "How does that work? What would be the sense of that?" she asked.

"It wouldn't work for you because your marrow has cancer cells in it. Even though it may look clean, you know how cancer can hide out." She could donate only marrow harvested before she had leukemia, he said to me.

"How would anyone know to do that? Are they into cruel jokes?"

In contrast to his facial expression, Dr. Lourde answered melodically, "Some people can use their own bone marrow even with their cancers. It's because Jada's cancer is produced in the marrow that she can't donate to herself. If you're going to have cancer, leukemia is the worst to have."

"I'll say that!" Jada said, breaking her silence and her stony face with a dour grimace.

Dr. Lourde pulled his knee closer to his chest and continued talking with growing interest. He may have learned to keep his face emotionless, but his enthusiasm always showed in the way he talked. "With other cancers, it can be localized and isn't usually too hard to treat unless it gets picked up by the blood or lymph system and spread to other places. But leukemia is in the blood, not isolated in one area, and travels all over. You don't know where it is. And treating the blood is tricky because you need your blood and can't kill all of it."

I was listening so hard for a way out that I almost stopped listening when Jada said, "I don't want a bone marrow transplant anyway. Go through all that and I'll still have another relapse. It's not worth it."

"I think you should consider a transplant." Dr. Lourde released his leg and put both feet on the floor, bringing him closer to Jada. "Though there are some other issues we need to take care of first. One of your ovaries is about the size of a grapefruit." My mouth opened as if a tornado ripped through it. I had been so focused on the leukemia that I had forgot all of Dr. Lourde's ritualized explorations each time he examined Jada. "If it were in someone else, we would take it out. But that's too risky for you right now. I'm sending you down for an ultra sound so we can get some dimensions and see what the docs down there think. The meds we're giving you now should take care of it, but I'm going to be a little more aggressive with them and see how you tolerate them."

"Great," Jada said, deadpan. "What else is wrong?"

"Actually, we can't tell why, but there seems to be a small spot on your brain stem. Do you know where that is?" Jada nodded, the back of her head rubbing against the pillow. "It isn't in a place that presents any danger to your getting along now, so we're not going to deal with that. It could be nothing to worry about, and finding out involves too much at this stage. I don't think the docs at the U would consider it a problem. But they won't even look at your file with an ovary like that. So, let's get going, Kiddo?"

Dr. Lourde sounded more like a coach than the bearer of bleak news. Jada snorted. "I'll have so much cancer they won't be able to bury me in the ground."

"We aren't ready to bury you yet!"

Jada was launched into another quest, beginning with the radiologist's pronouncement, "Coming along nicely," as he read the spill of milky specks and smears on the screen in the dark room in which Jada, on a short examination table next to the wall, was crammed.

"Could be stars in the heavens to me. Well, that's what training is all about," I reckoned to Jada who must have been as worn with the monotony of lying as I was of standing. Scant room for patient and doctor, the room could hardly hold the machinery, which was not built tall to suit the room's dimensions, but broad at the hips, just where mine squeezed in. A huge crane-like extension blocked me from the computer screen on the other side of the metal arm. Movement in rooms like this was clumsy and fraught with danger; always on the verge of knocking an eye out on some protrusion, I stood pasted to the cold wall, trapped into a position that made me want to slide into a heap.

A smirk warped my lips as I reflected on the design idiosyncrasies we put up with in hospitals, all in the name of hope. I lived with the vinyl settee that was neither a chair nor a bed nor a couch, though it served as all three. As the days wore on, and the stakes grew higher, even the settee was a luxury. The confines of this stay became more restrictive: floor space was claimed by IV regulators on poles, a blood pressure monitor, an electronic blood sugar tester, the television and VCR on a cart; the one and only chair, wooden arms close and high, was sacrificed, pushed away, posted like a "Beware of Dog" sign at the door.

No wonder people do not want to die in a hospital. Jada had few choices for movement, contorted on a bed that bent in places regardless of the patient's body shape or size, like a figure in a Dali painting. The stiff waterproof mattress underneath all the padding we layered between her and it crackled as she twisted to find relief from the tedium of being anchored. During the eight days of Jada's incubating decision to seek a marrow transplant, she was consigned to waiting for results, for doctors, for nurses, for medicines, for days, for nights.

While we were waiting, Dr. Lourde came, pulling the chair from its place at the door, flowing past the candy-striped cotton curtain with the ease of an artist with a new canvas. "Hello, Jada, Mrs. Petersen."

"Ms. Santino," I corrected.

"Yes, I'm sorry."

"That's okay. It isn't as if you're supposed to keep up with my life."

He wedged himself between the wall and the foot of the bed, crossed his legs. He addressed Jada. "Your ovary is about half the size it was, so whatever we're doing for your leukemia is working on that. I don't think we'll have to do another ultra sound."

"Good!" Jada said, mustering some emphasis. "I didn't like drinking that dye."

"Pretty nasty stuff?"

"I didn't mind the taste so much. I just couldn't drink all of it. And then I had to pee." Her eyes were dull, her skin pasty, as if the dye had left a stain in her.

"Not a day at the park, hunh? You did well." Dr. Lourde never voiced hmms as he thought, but the sound seemed always to be there anyway, like a tune you can't get out of your head; the air bounced with the sound of breathing and the vibration of molecules bumping into each other. "As long as it's shrinking, I think the docs at the U will take your case. I know you aren't very keen on the idea of a marrow transplant, but I think it's time for you to go and have a look. We can arrange an eight-hour period without any scheduled meds if we plan it right. I'll make the arrangements for you, your mom and dad, if he wants to go."

"I've been thinking about that. How long would I have to be in the hospital?"

"Oh, I'd say about six to eight weeks." Dr. Lourde made the first statement like he was making an offer for some kind of miracle diet pill, lose sixty pounds in thirty days and don't give up eating for just $9.99 plus shipping and handling. Then he added, fast and low, details like the fast-talking announcer reciting fine print over the airwaves. "And that's after they've found a donor for you. You have to show signs of complete remission before they'll accept you."

"That means the whole summer. And what are my chances?"

Dr. Lourde gave himself room to negotiate. "I think a little longer than that. They'll want you to be ready when they're ready. There are two main concerns in a transplant. The first is rejection. Your body fights hard to keep things out of it that it doesn't recognize. And there's infection. Anti-rejection drugs will keep your immune system suppressed; and you know enough about that. It's worth a shot. Survival rate for rejection is about 20-30%." How long, I wondered, does a person study to figure out how to say one thing and make it look attractive, doable, and in saying it, hide the other ugly more awful reality without trying to deceive? But it would take me time to figure the numbers out, all mixed up mumbo-jumbo with the words and the wishes and the luck of the draw. For there was that; there always was. It worked, for some. Peg. Yes, there was Peg, and Peg had told us what Dr. Lourde was disguising, giving only one figure, not the other two, one for infection and one for yet another relapse, not counting the matching donor. It was that damned tiny print again. Without the transplant, Jada would surely die.

"I know you and I have had some differences," Dr. Lourde resumed. "We haven't always agreed, but I've always respected your intentions and hope you have mine. You're very intelligent, and you're very strong. When you make up your mind, you can make anything happen. And if you don't like what's going on, you can make life miserable. It takes a giant commitment to go through with this. I don't doubt that you can do it, if you want to. But you know the docs over there have only one goal, and that is to make it work. They'll do everything they can, and they won't ask you if it's okay or wait till you're ready. You will have to go along with whatever they think is right. And I won't be able to pull any strings for you. You'll be their patient, and I'll be out of the picture."

"Won't you be there?" Jada's question was a burst of lightning from a mass of burly black clouds.

"No; once they take over, they make all the decisions. And they have to. They can't let considerations you or I might have interfere with what needs to be done. This is serious business. Once you're in it, you can't change your mind."

Listening to Dr. Lourde was like tumbling into a deep well. I kept reaching and grabbing and scraping my feelings against rock and slime because I hadn't hit bottom yet, hoping maybe, just maybe I might be able to grasp onto something to catch me, stop the fall from the knowledge I feared. I tried to slow the doom, asked, "Jada will have been in the hospital for a long time. What if she takes a break, does a few things; can she have a transplant next year?"

Jada answered instead. "No, I wouldn't do that; I want to go back to school. Besides, I don't want a transplant. What's the point? I know I won't be able to do all the things they want me to. And I'm not going to make it, anyway." She looked so still, not like she had convulsions of perception trying to jump out of her skin.

"I know I promised to support you and your decision. I just want to look at all the options. If you knew you had another choice you may decide to try it later."

Dr. Lourde pinched the hairs of his mustache. "Mmm, I don't know about that. We couldn't keep her in remission that long. Her body couldn't survive it. And now that the cancer has spread, we're dealing with a different animal. Every time we induce a remission, the effects weaken the body and the cancer gets more resistant. This one may not hold for long. I just can't guarantee another remission."

No one came in and no one walked by; machines didn't jangle their alarms. The bulldozers and graders and jack hammers and grinders and drillers had all ceased making their thumping as if they'd all heard the knell of last resort and, in deference, made silence at once. Even the air shut down, trapping us in that room of nothing left to say.

Dr. Lourde shifted in his chair. "Well, Jada, I'll be out at the desk a while if you have any questions. Otherwise I'll see you tomorrow, okay?"

"'Kay, bye."

He and I nodded to each other, I thanking him, a small courtesy put to scrutiny as Jada deemed it disrespectful to thank someone for hurting her. We were in a new time, and words like tomorrow and later became catches in my throat, and want was a butterfly in traffic. The clock belonged to a different world, a world Jada was leaving behind. We counted time in decisions.

Dr. Lourde picked a day, a dry windy day in May, one of those days that teased to turn you topsy-turvy, hot gusts from the street grabbing the hem of your dress and pulling it up over your head, sand-filled whirlwinds grazing your shins like a stiff-bristled scrub brush. Jada and I stood outside the parking ramp, bracing each other to keep from being uplifted to the rooftops.

Our feet tapped on granite-like floors, thd-d-d thwyp, in step after a nurse who led us up an elevator and through a maze of turns and doors and passageways to where Jada would be staying, if she were to relent. When we arrived, we were the only people, surely the only people in street clothes, unable to retrace the corridors for escape, and dead-ended in a stuffy cubicle. Glassed doors to the front and to the back locked us in, and our tour nurse stood guard while pointing beyond a window almost as clammy white as the yellowing paint around it. "This is as far as we can go," she said. "Patients are in there."

Behind the glass, I saw more walls, plain and bare and stripped even of color. My suspicions rankled at the possibility that I would never get beyond this door, even with Jada on the other side, or, once in, until a turn, one way or another brought Jada out as well.

"Normally this area is quite secure." There was a round lock casing above the handle; wire mesh reinforced the glass.

"We wouldn't want to introduce any outside germs. The patients in here don't have any way to fight off infections." Dr. Lourde's admonitions about commitment and total submission to decisions made to serve a purpose and carried out by a single-minded set of doctors, like Mr. Lincoln's drummer, beating out the rhythm of courage and faith, the only survivor who refused to give up his post while all around him lay bleeding and torn carnage of war, sounded different in here, next to the battlefield.

"She can't just give up! She's got to do anything she can to stay alive," my mother insisted. Every basement she ever lived in, every second-hand piece of clothing she ever stored and wore and wore out, every thick metallic cup of old coffee she ever drank before making a new pot, every dollar she ever buried, every jar of Palm Beach cologne she used, shriveled in its foil wrappers, every threadbare towel she hung on the rack surged in me, my mother's daughter. My mother, self-preservation over comfort, economy over quality, self-subjugation over principle, couldn't understand that Jada was deciding, in fact may not consent to a marrow transplant.

I left the transplant ward with its cubicles and locks that would be Jada's life if she were to go beyond that door, and I faced a mother, my mother who was in me, and the mother who was me. No. I had picked Jada up out of her crib, desiring, needing love and acceptance, her pudgy hands hanging onto the rail, little stubs of teeth poking out of her wailing mouth, and as she nested her sticky head next to my shoulder, her face pink and strained with tears, the touch of her skin filled all my empty spaces. It was so simple then, to give her what she needed, and I promised her then as I held her and walked her and cradled her in the creaky padded rocker, that I would never, never, never, ever again desert her, forsake her to a closed room to cry alone.

We rode the elevator to a basement level where we were led to the end of the dim hall. Inside the room was an embedded metal plaque, and I assumed by the dimension and furnishings that the room was reserved for administrators and conferences. We shriveled to almost nothing in the vastness and I gravitated toward

481

the ground-level windows on the other side of which glints of light reminded me that a sun shone somewhere else, while Jada immediately took a chair at a long narrow dark wood table. I toured the perimeter, searching for a stray memo, a catalogue, a picture on the wall; nothing but stark cement that over time had absorbed the room's darkness. Overhead lights were on, but the yellow globes conspired with the windows: the room was a rainy November day. Three quarters of the way around the room, I was stopped by a simple wooden table holding an empty coffee maker, a white Mr. Coffee, too small to fill the cups of the number of people who could fill this room, and I wondered if everyone who came in here felt as despairing as I did. I retreated and sat down next to Jada.

"What are we waiting for?" she asked.

"I don't know. I guess we'll be meeting with someone. Tired?"

"Yes. And thirsty."

"I don't see a water fountain. But there must be some water around for them to make coffee. Or maybe there isn't, and that's why the coffee maker's empty." Arnold stood somewhere out of the corner of my eye until the nurse-guide reappeared at the door and hustled toward us, taking a seat at the opposite side from Jada and me, Arnold taking the seat to Jada's right, and I felt the tension of a pom-pom-pull-away line the nurse would have to break through.

"I'm sorry," the nurse started. "We were supposed to be joined by other staff, but something else interfered, so I'll do the best I can." She spoke of insurance details, which I ignored, concentrating instead on her. Her demeanor had subtly changed. Maybe as she walked and talked she could mask her tentativeness; or maybe it was just now that I was watching, noticing. Her eyes did not rest in her face; they resisted us. They wanted to be somewhere else, maybe where everyone else was, some emergency from which she was excluded, Code Blue, Long Grass, some other masked message announced over the hospital speakers that caused heads to tilt toward the firm and unhurried disembodied voice and sent white-coated persons briskly and purposefully through the corridors. Her fingers pressed and flexed, straining white digits between red knuckles, as if restraining herself from answering the alarm she couldn't until we were gone and done with.

What to do with all these numbers and facts and ifs and whens? Do all the doctors and specialists and experts come down here to this dark dingy dungeon and turn into mere statisticians, Merlins mixing numbers into magic spells that made you forget about the person upstairs, silent floors away, muffled by metal doors and locked passageways and wired glass, someone who felt thirst and pain, desire and loneliness, someone who hoped and cried and stared and cursed? I wanted to get out. I wanted to see the sun until it made black blots in front of my eyes, to feel the heat and the dry May wind that stuffed my nose with pollen. I wanted to take Jada back, back not to the beginning because the line shifts even as you toe it, but back to the hospital, Ramsey Hospital, so she could get on with living the rest of her life. My baby was going to die, and with whatever consolation I could find in her decision to die living, I was going to have to help her; I wanted to start.

She started the next day. Sitting in her bed, the bend in the mattress raising her knees slightly to relieve the pressure on her back, Jada outlined her foreseeable future to Dr. Lourde. "These are the things I want. I want to go to my friends' graduation, and then after that I want to go to a convention in July; and I want to go back to school this fall. You can give me all the stuff you want now to get me or keep me in remission or whatever, but I want you to make it so on those days I will be able to go away and not be sick. I'll do chemo for the rest of the summer, but I'm not having a transplant. Just make it so I can go back to school."

Dr. Lourde nodded his head, but he answered gravely. "I'm sorry you aren't going to try because I'd like to see you in the world in five years. But I respect your decision. You know how much it takes, and you set your limits."

"And one more thing," Jada added, her jaw set, her gaze steady, her muscles in agreement. "I'm not afraid of death. I just don't want the pain. Promise me that you'll give me everything you can for the pain."

"I can do that." Dr. Lourde paused. "Now, let's talk about those other things you mentioned. I can get you back to school in the fall, but I don't know about these others. When is graduation?"

"A week from this weekend. And the convention is in July."

"And there's Darcy's wedding, too," I broke in. "That's in June, right after the graduation."

"Hmm. I'll have to work hard on the first one. Let me do some thinking on that. I'll be here for a while if you think of anything you want right now. And I'll see you later. Goodbye, Jada. Goodbye, Ms. Santino." When he opened the door, clatter of a moving cart and staccato voices barged into the room, noises of life going on in spite of us. Lois slipped in bearing two more jelly-like bags asking, "Can I straighten your blankets for you, Jada?" She pulled and smoothed the layers of white that seemed to set Jada in place. "Tell me when you want to take a bath and we'll change the bed. What sheets did you bring this time?"

I looked at the pink butterfly pillow for an answer. "They're still in the bag. I'll get them out when she goes in for her bath."

"Just let me know when you're ready." She left quietly.

"I want to make a phone call; can you put the phone over here?" Jada asked. "Let me see if I can reach Ann. If she answers you can go for about fifteen minutes."

"Okay, Doll. Want anything while I'm out?"

"Mm-mm. But get my address book first." Before she poked at the buttons on the phone, she pointed to the stack of magazines and books on the window ledge. "And my appointment book, too." I worked my way, top to bottom, extracting first a splashy pink and yellow floral covered book and then a slim sleek spiral-bound daily planer, understatedly the color of burgundy, suitable to pull out of a brief case at a power lunch. I brought both to her, gave her a kiss on the forehead, and waited for the signal.

My bag bumping against the concrete, I wandered down the stairway. "What an irony," I said in the chamber of the stairwell, too softly to echo, too loud to ignore. "We can almost count the weeks and days and hours, and here I am spending time trying to figure out how to waste them." An immediate urge to sleep made me pull oxygen in a yawn of several stages. Sleep would be so easy. Last Sunday, I nodded to myself, I took Jada out of the hospital for a few hours between hookups. Dr. Lourde almost ordered it. Staying in the hospital for Jada was just easier, like the prospect of sleeping now.

"We can do anything, Jada. Do you want to go to a mall?" I suggested.

"I'm too tired," she answered, her voice wilting.

"We could go to a park and enjoy the fresh air. How about the sculpture garden? I could get a wheelchair and push you so you won't have to walk."

"No, just take me home." I turned right out of the parking lot and, at the top of Sibley Hill, instead of making the right turn to our condo, I drove up Cathedral Way like a tourist, driving uncharacteristically slow. I, a townie, would have been exasperated to follow myself. Bare brown stalks and thick and crusty wooden trunks still dominated the boulevard, but farther up above our heads, small green bundles made promises in the breeze. Red and yellow tulips immodestly splashing their colors like traffic signals ordering passersby to stop and notice them at the edge of lawns would soon drop their petals as spiny bushes began to flesh out, sentinels against the encroaching public. I left the car radio off, letting the rhythms of walkers, joggers, and bikers satisfy my ear for music. The sun, perched high and bright in the sky as an offering of sweet butter to the gods, beamed proudly back at us, melting all over us.

Back and forth, I drove along Cathedral Way, its cross streets, its parallels of Franklin, Walnut, Amherst, where the houses that weren't built for railroad emperors and land barons and government bosses reminded us of large families of the merchant classes. I drove until we ran out of streets and then home. Jada sat in the rocker and turned on MTV. It didn't seem enough to do something so mundane when the world was running out.

"I don't ever get to see MTV on the hospital stations, and I miss it." Jada looked at the scenes roll across the screen, a sightseer, as when she sat in the passenger seat of the car. I opened a window to the sweetness of the budding treetops below us and moved restlessly about the place, with only time to occupy my mind, music my space. As I eased into the comfort of being home, I agreed, some of the simplest aspects of living are the most satisfying.

A lot had happened since Sunday, even if it happened only the afternoon in Jada's hospital room when she declared how she wanted to spend her time on earth, and I went back into the stairwell, bumping into the thigh-high metal swinging gate, its white paint peeling, revealing brown in irregular patches, at the last landing, then trekked back up to the linen cart, stocking myself with towels and slipping my hand through the stack of blue and white hospital gowns for the softest one. I staked claim to an available tub, started the water, and went for Jada. She was sitting up, her bare feet drooping near the floor. "Perfect timing, I just started your bath water. Ready? Your dad should be here soon."

"He's coming later today. He and Dom are going to have supper in the cafeteria first."

"I wish I'd known. Maybe I could have planned something different with my time." Jada held my arm lightly, and I opened the door to the tub room and a replenishing oasis. Steam fogged the air, as water sloshed up to the edge of the tub. Jada eased into it, released into her element. I sat on the floor. "What did you find out?"

Her hands floated up to the surface. "I can stay at Priss's; she'll come and get me, or Adam will. Priss is going to talk to my instructors. I want to know what I have to do to get my credits for this semester." The repetition ached.

"So you're talking about doing that on graduation weekend, right before Darcy's wedding."

"Yes. There's an all-school reunion after graduation. I want to stay and see my friends. Adam said he'll drive me to the wedding from Mary Hillyard. Then he'll go the wedding with me, and you can get me a round trip ticket to fly into Hartford and out of Washington with you. Adam has to get back by Monday." Jada grabbed the cloth by its floating corner. I dabbed at her skin with the wet cloth and squeezed the water, rolling it down her back.

"Perfect. That means we can get a hotel room for ourselves. Will Adam need a room?"

"He can stay with us; just get an extra bed." The rest of our ritual was done to the murmurs of a body being comforted, my daubing at her white-skinned scalp, blotting her dry with the terry towel, sliding slick lotion onto her tender skin.

On her bed I spread the blue and white sheets, my favorite because they were all cotton, 100 percent, and hard to find in a world of permanent press, and sat Hambone next to the pillow.

Though she might have been refreshed from the bath, Jada's eyes slunk wearily away, to another place. I fumbled through my bag for the videos I had picked up from the video store, new to the neighborhood, just blocks from home. The owners still worked behind the counter, harkening back to the old corner grocery store days, a real mom-and-pop-eking-out-a-living story. I liked going there partly because of their seeming ingenuousness and mostly because the enterprise was independent and the selection was still small. Jada sent me with a list, typical pretty boy films with Tom Cruise or some Rob One-Movie-Flash-in-the-Pan; my latest pick was "Big." In the film, Tom Hanks, a kid in a man's body, leaves FAO Schwarz. It is the Christmas season, and the store is lavishly decked with poinsettias, foot-wide red ribbons, and glittering gold balls. In the middle of the display floor, a giant keyboard is cordoned off. Unable to control his boyish urges, the grown man leaps over the cord, his briefcase flowing gracefully along with him as if it were Fred Astaire's top hat, and skips along the keys that light up as his leather Oxfords land spritely on each one, dancing his way through a Christmas jingle to the rapture of his gathered audience, who probably wished they too could celebrate the child in themselves by letting it out once in a while.

When the scene ended, Jada, said, "I love FAO Schwarz. I could be doing stuff like that. I'm smart. I appreciate art and fine things. I'd like a job. A BMW. I could enjoy life. What a waste that I don't get to when I could really know how to live."

I assented, nodding my head, and measured my breaths, calmed my anger at her not getting the chance to grow into the adult she could be so well but trapped forever young in a body that grew old too soon, a victim of time's compression of then into nowness.

The movie ended; I set the machine to rewind and plumped Jada's pillows, adjusting the mattress and layering the sheet and blankets around her. Jada looked tired, her eyelids drooping over ocean blue eyes, the lines around them tense.

Lois, who now requested Jada for her every shift, was a familiar and welcome face after so many years of changing nurses' names and faces. Coming in to check on settings, she said, "I'm sorry I haven't been in for a while." She touched Jada's shoulder and smiled reassuringly, her butterscotch hair falling around her face. "It's been kinda busy this afternoon; I'm taking supper early 'cause we're short nurses and they asked me to stay later. Is there anything I can get for you while I'm down there?"

"No, thanks," Jada said; I shook my head. Lois vanished, and Jada, Hambone, and I were bound to the whirring clop of the machine, a clock doing double time, as if it were in a hurry to get somewhere.

"Mom, you can go if you want to, but don't forget the list of videos." Her eyes were already closed as I bent over to kiss her forehead.

"Goodbye, Darlin'; see you later." Outside the hospital door, I was smacked in the face with a feisty gust of wind. Looking out through airtight hospital windows past bricks and over gravelly roofs was an unpredictable way to read the weather. Without rattling screens or creaking trees overhead, "outside" became the whush of someone passing through the corridor or the clatter of wheels over metal tracks at elevator doors. This day whacked at me like the bloated bag of laundry, videos, a box of tissues, and a tub of Vaseline, that banged into my thigh as we both swung into the wind. I wondered what was going on in T. S. Eliot's life when he wrote his poems. This day would be tossed about as the others, scraps swirling upwards and then dropping back down, like kites that can't get off the ground. Was that all there was to our days, just so much debris caught finally against some fence, clogs in a web of holes?

At home, the hum of the dryer tossing sheets and shirts thumped thoughts. Too much; no, not enough for getting to a doctor for my allergies when I'm in a place full of doctors and for getting to work and getting the laundry done and it has to be done on time and I can't see Dom and there's no time and there's nothing but time unfulfilled and it doesn't count for anything because she's going to die and she'll never get married, live in a mansion or anywhere else or wear silks and suits and sequins, and make love, and she won't cradle tiny babies to her breast and feel sad to hear them cry and count out pennies from her leather coin purse to pay for stupid videos and I have to pretend that filling my time mattered. Time was empty, and I was filling it with nothing. I wished for the phone to ring, for Jada, who I'd left but two hours ago. Thump. She often called to hurry me back, and I felt rushed to return to her. Everything was off schedule and out of kilter, and I felt gutted, a shell waiting to be filled, and Jada the only one who could, I a nothing until she did. Thump.

These thoughts thrashed inside my head like cotton in the dryer drum; let loose, they would have pummeled anything in their way, destroying what we had been given, except that what we had been given was all we had. The thought was too great to hold. I wished to go back to the hospital, back where I didn't feel so empty.

May 14ᵗʰ

Two and one-half weeks of wasting my life in this hellhole of a hospital! My counts are super duper low because the chemo blasted my cells to hell. Infections are brewing in my blood, but, of course, all the cultures turn up no answers. I spike fevers and freak out because I think of the worst. Mom and the nurses try to calm me, but I think every one of them is something that will kill me. I feel like shit and my back has billions of knots from being in this jail of a bed so long. I'm sore and SICK! I need something good in my life and all I get to do is scream! They pump tons of antibiotics and antifungal shit into me 24 hours a day, and I take pills and liquids by the gallon, and all I get is more sick and wanting to barf. I'm still DYING but I'm not able to fucking DO IT! I'm going CRAZY! I get the chills, then sweats, then cold and hot again. My nurses and even mom drive me crazy, too. Nothing she can do will help me.

I want to get back to MHC for graduation weekend, but I have to have so-so counts and no horrible complication and key people, Adam, Lynn, and Priss, in particular, have to assure me of their support. Karen for sure will be there because she's graduating. Maybe Maureen should go out to pack up my things instead. Decisions! I hate them! I made one. I have decided not to have a bone marrow transplant. It's all or nothing, and I know I can't put out that much effort. I don't know how much longer I will live. No one grasps that I won't be back to finish school or knows how to support me. This afternoon I tried to explain to Adam what he needed to do to help me, but he didn't seem to understand that I am going to die soon. I asked Mom to talk to him about all this crap.

My friends all say they care, but why don't they show it by fucking calling and writing?! The few who do tell me to "take care" or "I'm thinking of you." Words don't mean shit without action. It's goddamn shit! I trusted people and they just fuck up on me. Adam said that I set it up that nothing would go right or feel right, but I don't think he gets it. I remember sitting by the Charles River with him on October break and he said he wished he could have been able to help me through my disease but now would stick by me thorough everything. He doesn't mean it when he says "I love you." He keeps me hanging on, but his words can't be trusted.

Oh, God! I can't bear one more day here, but the docs say it'll be another goddamn week! I don't feel as hateful of everything and everyone as I did the other times I was here. Another bad decision to have chemo. All it did was buy time, and for what! I have no friends. No lover. My body looks like shit, and I have no desire to live. It's always there—that I'm going to die. What fun is left? I won't have sex or kiss anyone passionately again. I won't get married. I'll never be free of poisons and the tubes that hitch up to my body. I'll never get another haircut.

I've been reading some entries when Adam and I started our relationship. I was rational and open. He says that I wanted more, but he was the one who wanted me. So he said! He screwed up and really fucked me over, keeping me hanging on. He's still treating me like dirt. He's seeing this Tracy girl and it makes me jealous! The world is vindictive. The bad advance and the good suffer. I don't believe I ever had a fucking chance.

The bulb above Jada's bed glowed, throwing light against dark, and the room's shadows lay flat on the surfaces like an early black and white film. I made the only noise, crackling the air as I came through the door, at first seeing only Arnold standing, arms folded, a jacket caught in front of him. "Hello," I said tentatively.

He swiveled toward me and clicked into place, saying, "Hello, Idina," in such an exerted way as to sound like he said it through clenched teeth. Dom sat, deep in the room, edging the settee.

"Hi, Dom." If he returned my greeting, it was lost somewhere in the dark, unable to find a path, overshadowed by the menacing growl that came from my right.

"Bitch." I located Jada, sitting upright in a chair, angled toward the door, in position to attack. Her eyes pierced the hazy darkness between us like a cat on the verge of pouncing, unwaveringly memorizing the position of her prey. Louder, darker, and deeper, her voice grew more threatening. "Get out of here! I don't want you here. You're a mean and selfish and fucking bitch!"

"Why are you saying that to me?" Confusion and humiliation brewed in my eyes. I looked at her face for an answer, but all I saw was blue, a blue chiseled from ice, chilling hatred.

Evil swelled in the room, filling it, straining its walls and seams and bursting with Jada's condemnation of me. "I said get out, you fucking bitch!"

"Don't say that to me, Jada. How can I come back if you say that to me?" I broke. I broke loud, and I broke high, and I broke crying.

"I don't care if you come back. I don't want you back, you bitch."

"Idina," Arnold lurched a step, but there was this space between Jada and me that was impenetrable, walled off by the malignancy emanating from her face, her stiff torso, her hands clenched bony on the edges of the chair, and he got no further.

"Jada," I begged. "Think of what you're saying. What did I do?" Arnold tried again to step in between but was stopped by the force of Jada's fury, a firestorm, burst upon burst of burning damnation.

"Bitch!" she said deafening my pleas to stop, please stop. *You are stoning me with pleasure, aborting me with a rusty wire coat hanger in some filthy back alley, leaving me to bleed to death, clotted and crusted on mangled sheets, please stop, stop.*

"Bitch!" She did not stop, and I staggered out of the room, her screams haranguing me to the stairway and echoing in my ears as I headed down. The air scalded my lungs, and I breathed in sobs and gasps. A woman entered the stairwell, stopped abruptly, staring. I went past her wrenched face, and reaching the main floor, opened the door. I walked only straight, looked only forward, fled the hospital.

Night had strangled light out of the sky and let it fall lifeless around me. I felt a glaring spotlight following me, marking me, inviting the stalkers from my past to jeer at my stumbling over the tangled wires I myself had strung across my path. How clumsy I was. I had done it all wrong, everything, feeding her, holding her, coddling her, teaching her, guiding her. I had loved her wrong.

The next day at school, like a rodent, I hugged the walls, skittering swiftly toward my destination during prep time. A colleague opened her classroom just as I was making my turn at the landing. "Idina," she called to my back. "How bad are things?" She held the door open delicately, avoiding the unpleasantness of its touch, poising her toe as if someone had spit on the floor and she was averting a slip through the slime.

"She's not going to go through with a bone marrow transplant. Her chances are too slim to be worth it to her, so…."

"Is she at home?" Katie asked from behind fashionable glasses perched on her long pinched nose.

"No, she started another round of chemo. She wants to go back to school in the…."

"Oh, I saw you walk by and wanted to check, but I have class now," she said, ducking into the classroom. How does one express the horror that one of my daughter's last wishes was to disown me? Other people could carry on affairs and keep them secret, women could hide their pregnancies and deliver babies in the bathrooms at proms and go out for the next dance. People believe what they want to, anyway, no matter how much truth they begin with. My mother expunged unpleasant memories of the past by tearing up the evidence. Change the past, make it a little rosier to remember, rip the thing in two, presto: it didn't happen. At least not that way. No regrets, I promised myself. *Is that how it goes then?*

The afternoon crept up on my thinking like the jigsaw pieces of memory to an amnesiac. There was no instant recall, just the felt knowledge that it was time for lunch, first lunch; I had last lunch. Students appeared where they were scheduled, following the paths we set out for them. Ask any one of them and they wouldn't know what room number they were going to, but they went where they were supposed to just the same. After a day's absence, they might forget their locker combinations, but they thought they knew where they were going. They arrived at my door, too, and I greeted them as they filed in.

The best that can be said for the room, other than the view from the window, was that it was spacious; the worst, other than its cold temperature, was that it was hard to decorate, make interesting. Utilitarian: lots of cupboards, large laboratory tables, gas jets and water faucets sticking out of them like oil wells on black marble plains, and white cement block walls. I displayed posters where I could, not moralistic ones about taking the first step and being a true hero, friend, learner, whatever, but posters of art work, majestic places on the earth, and playful alphabets, such as Arlene Alda's series of photographs, hanging horizontally over a sink. In twenty-six phenomena in nature, she perceived the shapes of the letters, a "v" as a limb grows from the trunk of a tree, an "o" in a bird's nest.

Built in the '60s, Parkview had solid doors without windows. We went from schools without walls to schools around halls, every one of us maintaining our own mini sovereignty when we shut our doors. I shut the door when the bell rang, the bins with fourth hour's folders were out—another habit to reinforce the work ethic; once in the room, class began, no reason to delay, clean. Kids operate better when they have routines and rituals. We were working when Mary Lou interrupted.

"Ms. Santino, you have a telephone call." Mary Lou had orders never to interrupt a class for a telephone call; take a message and put it in the mailbox was established procedure. Except for me. She notified me that she would keep the caller waiting on the line, as was requested. Like she said, she didn't give a rat's ass; she didn't want to do the wrong thing.

"Okay, thank you. I'll go down to get it." There were two telephones I could have used, both on the second floor. Down one flight, two hallways, past Andy's room, past Katie's room, past Mary's, past Scott's. I felt their pricked ears as I went past their closed doors, into the stuffy English office and storage place. Four concrete walls closed in on me, bookshelves lining every one, though evidently not enough. Brown cardboard boxes flanked the desks plunked in the middle and next to a row of cupboards. On the counter stood a coffee machine exhuming the remains of a muddy brew in snake dance swirls of cloudy steam. How many times had I punched the one blinding light in the row of buttons on a phone and listened to the sound of my world rupturing?

"Hi, This is Marilyn McKuen. Jada wanted me to call you. She and I have had a long talk. She feels very bad about last night and wanted me to ask you to come back." My shoulders dropped, relieved of a huge sigh. "I hope it's okay that I'm doing this. She was very upset today and asked to talk to me. She really does want you here."

"Of course I'll come back. It just went too far last night, and I didn't know how to stop it."

"She didn't either. She doesn't understand why she said what she did; but she is really worried that you won't come back."

"Oh, Marilyn, what am I going to do? Look at us; we can't keep our rage inside, and we can't unleash it at each other. But we're all we have. I should be helping her, and I don't know how. Tell her I'll be there sometime after I have my work done. I don't know how to do this; I feel so dumb and inadequate."

Marilyn, soft-spoken, tender, answered, "You know, she really does love you."

God, it was hard to keep the faith when I was being tested so mightily. "Thank you, Marilyn. Will you be there?"

"No, I'm leaving soon. If you ever want to talk, call me. You have my home number, don't you?"

"Somewhere, yes. Thanks." I threw my head into my hands so that anyone would think I was just tired and massaging my forehead instead of trying to recover who I was. So this is what it will be like, to "go out with a bang, not a whimper." I sat in a room, surrounded by some of the most honorable words by the greatest writers in the world, but I couldn't learn from them, not until I learned from myself. The bell rang, jolting me upright, prodding me to get back to my class, out of this crushing room.

Driving to the hospital, I arrived at Jada's door unprepared and unrehearsed, as if going naked to work. Jada's toes poked mini-mounds under her blankets, her attention caught in the crease where wall met ceiling. Though prayer seemed unlikely, I did not interrupt whatever commune she was engaged in, not even with a greeting and resumed my spot as if I had never left at all, had merely gone to the edge of the room to retrieve a dropped ball of yarn instead of to the edge of a cliff. I saw what the bottom was like, ugly, inescapable, and the ultimate horror of it mocked apologies. Her hell was worse than mine, and she hadn't even got there yet. Silence was appropriate.

We named what had to get done. I would work as many days as possible, saving every precious remaining sick day; anticipating her summer, I suggested I have a cable run into her bedroom for television viewing. "I don't want to be stuck in there," she said. "We need a couch. You'd better go out and get one now so it's there when I come home."

A couch; I had lived without the thought of one since I left two love seats behind almost three years earlier, getting by day-to-day. A couch was such an inevitable piece, like all the others that Jada's illness brought to light, a crisis pointing out the need. Always one move behind and being lightning-stricken into action is a jarring way to live, continually stunned, as if never recovering from a drugged state before being sent into the next high.

And so I bought a couch, brought Jada home, and resumed an old routine, going back to the clinic for blood work-ups, ultra scans, and IVs. A new, unfamiliar woman had replaced Krista, who sat to answer visitor questions and telephones and hand out parking vouchers at the hospital entrance. Krista had been more neighbor than receptionist, telling me about the garage sale she was having, where she and her husband were traveling on vacation, what she was making for supper that night, depending on her mood and her husband's good nature. Smiling a large-toothed smile or gathering up all the olive skin around her seepy brown eyes in a bovine-like worry, when Jada wobbled out, Krista tsked in sympathy and smiled encouragingly. The trade-off for Krista's clucking and doting was a quicker get-away from the clinic. If Krista had still been working the desk, she'd not have allowed incidents to get out of hand. But she was gone, and I dropped Jada at the hospital entrance, while I drove the half-circle drive, reentered the street and made two lefts, thereby traversing the perimeter of the parking lot to the gate that barred entrance until an attendant hand-delivered a ticket to me.

The parking lot changed in its design more often than a bird molts. What had once been the exit became the entrance; where there had been a driveway, a cement helipad was created. Back and forth, this way and that, the ways in and out adapted to the growing hospital and its services. The rules changed, too, depending on what precipitated a visit—to the hospital as a visitor or to the clinic as a patient; but before an attendant was assigned, the gate was locked in the upright position of salute. Now the skinny orange house stood with its sliding window on the passenger side of the incoming vehicle, so the newly-installed attendant had to get up and out of his comfortable chair and away from his music every time a car approached. We drivers irritated the attendants.

This attendant sprang from the narrow flat-roofed shelter and leaned his clean-featured face forward to my half-opened window. His dark eyes were set under smooth black eyebrows, and his head was flocked by hair that still showed grooves made by the teeth of his comb. Stooped over, he said confidently, "You can't park in here. It's reserved for patients at the clinic."

"But I *am* going to the clinic," I returned.

"We've been given orders not to let people park here overnight. You're supposed to park in the ramp across the street."

"I just said I am *here* for the *clinic*. Why should I have to park in the ramp?"

"I've seen you. You're staying at the hospital. We're keeping this lot for people who have appointments at the clinic."

I felt a twinge of nastiness and was tempted to go into a tirade about being watched by an amateur Big Brother, but alongside of my indignation I respected and admired his cockiness and let this thing play out pure and even. I diced each word for easy digestion. "My daughter *was* in the hospital, but she is no *longer* in the hospital. My daughter *now* goes to the *clinic.*"

"Then where is she?"

This small-time detective work was too much. I wanted to laugh at his cool and methodical attempt to snare me, but I was hooked into the inevitability of this episode. "I just drove through and dropped her off! You could have noticed *that* as long as you've made it your mission to watch *me.*"

"You'll have to move your car; someone is waiting to get in. "He walked toward the vehicle that nosed up to mine and victoriously motioned to the driver to back away enough to give me space to retreat to the parking ramp.

"Ohhh, no you don't," I said through gritted teeth. I turned the key in the ignition and removed it. Then I jerked open the car door, locked it, and slammed it shut behind me. Turning around, I glared at him, his mouth opening like a parachute.

"You can't park here. I'll have you towed!"

"You do that!" I shouted from the path I tramped to the entrance. I loved the feel of my back, the thought that people stared at it while I was extricating myself from their problem. I gave the revolving door a shove and heard it swoosh, still spinning, as I entered the lobby. "I need a manager or someone in authority! I'm here for the clinic and that guy out there won't let me park in the lot! He claims I'm staying overnight!" My arms flew, pointing at the accused, clapping my chest, sweeping at walls that separated us from the clinic. Had Krista still been there she would have shoved her chair away from her desk, her eyes growing larger behind their pop-bottle lenses, and with the strength of her experience and convictions about how to treat a friend, taken care of the matter herself.

The receptionist, who had never talked recipes or holiday bazaars with me, fumbled with her lips and reached for the telephone. Her back arched as she braced herself for action and she pushed her limp hair behind her ear. "Do you want me to call the parent representative?" She put the phone to her ear and moved her finger down a cellophane-covered list of numbers.

"I don't care who you call, but I'm supposed to be in the clinic now, not out here fighting over nonsense with some self-deluded gate-keeper. Who is he to tell me I'm not at the clinic. And, if someone doesn't come now, I'm going *to* the clinic." I felt amazingly refreshed; here was a concrete cause, one I could shout about with vindication: I was right, I had control, and I could win. Pacing back to the plate glass window to see if a tow truck had arrived yet to snatch my car, I muttered sporadically, trying to keep the steam spewing, but if anything I was cooling down like the upper crust of the lava flow, and wished a truck would come to hitch up my car and regenerate my red hot anger. Clutching my plastic bag to my belly as if it were a pouch of roos, I paced back to the desk where the receptionist pertly sat, eyes darting from me to the window to the elevator, back to me.

I was losing interest when a thin man walked with long strides down the pavement and entered the lobby. He held out a business card as he approached. "Hello, I'm Jim Matson, manager of the parking facilities. I'm sorry for the trouble. I've taken care of the matter; you can go ahead and park your car in the lot."

"Thank you! The guy's probably just trying to do his job, but I kept telling him I was going to the clinic."

"I've spoken to him. If you have any other problems, just call me."

I poked his card into my bag while he pivoted, striding away like John Wayne. I followed in his shadow, to my car, where a different attendant waited with a ticket in his hand. Too bad, I thought; the other guy didn't learn the lesson he was supposed to, not that he had to give in to me because I was the customer, "right at all times"; not that he was "just doing his job," just like he'd been told, and then got burned for it, so that'll teach ya to hang your head out on a limb; and not even a lesson in sensitivity to the kinds of issues people coming to a children's hospital bring with them. But maybe he had to learn those first before he was ready to learn what I had, that the fight we were waging did come down to every piddly little thing, and grisly hand-to-hand combats were what altogether signified the battlefield, magnificent only on the big screen.

After her release from the hospital, Jada's days and nights were filled with appointments at the clinic, meetings with Dr. Barrigan, the psychologist who listened to her dealing with the reality of her dying, and physical therapy. Once school was recessed, Per was driving to Montana to teach art to French students at a language immersion camp for the summer; he invited me to dinner on the eve of his departure.

"Is it all right if I go out to dinner with Per tomorrow night? I'd be home by eleven. You aren't planning anything, are you? I mean, with me. You'll be okay?" Jada was twenty years old and about to fly to Boston in a week; physically she was not an invalid. But I hadn't left her alone at night since her relapse.

"Yeah; okay. I have things I have to do," she said. I left the telephone numbers of both Zander and Per on the table and kissed Jada's forehead.

Trying to be normal with Per was like putting on the wrong sized clothing. He asked me how things were, but my technical answers were too big. Abbreviated, they sounded meaningless: Jada's appointment with her psychologist to talk of her approaching death being no more than a visit to the hairdresser. Then, like Cinderella, I felt the clock striking. "You don't need to drive me; I'll walk home," I offered.

"At 11:00 o'clock at night? I don't think that's very safe. Especially in this neighborhood."

"I'll be all right. I'll run and not cut through the park. I'll be home before you know it." Trotting through the unlit parking lot between Frey and Lawton, I doubted my decision. Too late to turn back now; I'd be wasting what precious minutes I had to be on time. My feet thwacked the pavement. My heart thumped, but my breathing came easy. I searched right and left, wary of movement, the flicker of any leaf, the bend of a twig.

The clean night air washed away salty specks of sweat from my face. I could see the building where I lived, my own parking lot. I dreaded coming to houses in the dark, the tense seconds of fitting keys into locks, opening doors, and worse, shutting them behind me. The time between entering and slamming shut the door felt the most vulnerable: I was a defenseless target outside, and if my attacker surged, trapped inside. If I had a 50-50 chance at the outset and nothing had happened to me yet, the odds should be next to nothing in my favor in these last few moments. But there was no comfort in almost making it, not if the greatest danger were concentrated in the last seconds. No, never safe. What I needed was to get all the way inside our unit, door shut, locked, bolted.

Early in the season, the heat of the day hadn't settled into the corridors, and I felt a shiver as moisture dried on my skin. Gently stirring air from open windows brushed me as I entered my door. Lights led me first to the living room; I turned switches off, leaving pools of darkness behind me. The kitchen, the dining room, those lights went off next. In my bedroom, Jada lay on my bed, her eyes facing the wall. "There you are. How come you're in here?" I began to undress, so I turned my overhead light off, as well.

"Why are you home so late?" She rolled and shifted, her movements making shadows in the room smoky gray.

"I'm right on time. It's five to eleven."

"You didn't have to stay so late." Her voice spread through the room like a poisonous gas leak, accumulating in corners, rising to the ceiling.

"I didn't stay late. You agreed to eleven."

Jada rose, a move that added volume and power to her voice, though it spurted in trembling ejaculations. "You didn't need to see him! You're supposed to be taking care of me! You're selfish and mean!"

"No, I don't have to see him. I don't have to see anyone. I could sit by you all the time, day and night, and I would, gladly, if that's what you want. Some people think I do now."

"Stop talking about other people. You walked away from me when I needed you the most. I'm your baby. You're supposed to help me."

"I ask you all the time, and I do what you say, and you said it was okay for me to see Per." I was down to my underwear and flung my shirt at the bed.

We had grown louder, more shrill; her sharp features cut through the motes of dimness. "You don't need to do anything. You can't do anything. You promised! I hate you!"

"What do you want from me!" I shouted back at her, at Per, at the world across the courtyard and down the street. Standing with my arms out, my palms facing her, I shouted at fate. "Should I jump out the window? Would that help?" I grabbed the elastic of my pink bikini underpants. Instead of pulling them down, I clenched and pulled as if bending open metal prison bars. The slippery cloth ripped away in my hands. "I can't help it that I'm alive. I can't undo our lives. If I could I would. If I could make one thing different, I'd sacrifice everything. I can't. I want to, but I can't." I shot my torn panties into the wastebasket and slammed shut one, then the other, window in my room.

I went to her bedroom, where the two windows, also facing the courtyard, gaped open. She shouted after me, each word pushing at me: "You're bad for making me live through this disease. You're a traitor, you're...; you should kill me instead of you—you *are* killing me by treating me so mean!" Old hotel windows do not come down easy, and each one thudded in its casing to her thunderous plaints. "And you should know! You said you'd never leave me; you promised. You have to help me."

Returning to my bedroom, I thrust my arms and head into my nightie, stopping in front of her. "Tell me, just please tell me," I begged, quietly now, my arms sticking out in supplication, "what do you want?"

"Did you ever think that sometimes I just want you to hold me?" Jada began to cry as I knelt, kissed the side of her sweaty head and cradled her as if she were the babe in my arms twenty rears ago, a baby trying, afraid, maybe, to go to sleep alone in her crib.

"Jada, I'm sorry I'm so dumb. You know I love you. We get caught in these fights, and we hurt each other, but we don't have to if I could just understand what to do."

There came a rapping at the door, an oddity that struck me not as odd at all; in night robes and loopy terry slippers, two women, the older one, though shorter, spoke evenly, almost clinically. "We live across the courtyard and heard some yelling. Is everything okay?"

"Yes." My voice was husky. Almost like telling a secret, I whispered, "My daughter has a terminal illness, and sometimes dealing with it is too much pressure."

"It sounded terrible," she said, her eyes studying me from behind black-framed glasses held in place by protruding cheekbones. "We were afraid someone might get killed. We didn't know what to do." The younger woman, standing behind the speaker, corroborated with a nod of her head. "Are you okay now?"

"Yes, thank you. Good night." I shut the door on the two women, and, walking barefoot down the hall, I tasted the words "terminal illness" as if they were vomited from my belly, sour and burning in my mouth, worse than my distempered behavior. Terminal illness had such an academic sound to it, abstracted the heart and the life and the soul from the body as being disaggregated, dashed onto slides for close inspection, made into topics of scientific journal articles. Oh, God, how was it possible to imagine, to hold the thought long enough to feel it and believe it and still go back and have to open windows and brush your teeth and go to sleep.

But that's exactly what I had to do: we both had to go on with the living parts as well as the dying parts of life. We couldn't be sure if we even wanted tomorrow, and no matter what tomorrow was, it wasn't tomorrow yet. We had to live today in defiance of tomorrow and in spite of yesterday. I turned down Jada's bed, sang to her, Hambone by her side; and I hummed and kissed her and left for my sleep, too.

If you measure your life in school years, as we did, we were one year older with the first day of summer vacation. Jada was at Mary Hillyard negotiating her senior year, her final year. She called me and reported cryptic suspicions, double crossings, and knives in the back about Family Weekend Committee. From a thousand miles away, the intrigue sounded too remote, too political, and too exclusive to grasp. I tried to connect the information with the image I had formed of Mary Hillyard, not the sophisticated suburban Wharton campus with bulletin boards and signposts boasting fliers and posters on women's issues, rape, self-defense, power, of work hard, play hard intensity.

Mary Hillyard, in its idyllic valley, wasn't like that. It had huge wealthy trees rooted firmly in the soil of a pastoral village, not stripped telephone poles plastered and replastered with blazing broadsides. It had wrought iron gates and finials that suggested cloistered sensibilities, not bulletin boards thick with angry notices. It had houses with dining rooms and white tablecloths and servers for sit-down dinners, not concrete dorms, one or two of which housed cafeteria-style-food-on-the-go for women on-the-rise. It had friendly, supportive women, not competitive, hard-driving aggressors. It had a riding stable and the rules of equine arts, not the martial arts of dealing a crippling blow to your supposed teammate. It had fooled me. Jada was fighting a coup to take over her position as co-chair of Family Weekend Committee, and the issue had reached the top hierarchy.

"I'm frustrated with what's going on. They will have careers," she said to me. "They get to do things; this is my only chance to have a leadership position. Carla had something to do with it, and I can't figure out what it is." With her name I imagined a cadre of other women riding on her skirt hem, hungry for favors, happy to serve. Maybe the whole school was like this pink petticoat deception, smarmy words as cover for an undercover fuck-you-over.

In days, Jada and Adam had to pack up his aging Datsun and drive to Washington, and conversation turned. "If we make it."

Jada warned, "I'm a little worried about his car. It's not very reliable. You should see it."

"I thought everything was set. Now you've got me worried." I was concerned more for Adam. If the car broke down, first Jada'd ride him for letting it happen; then she'd stick her thumb out and ride with another.

"Don't worry. He knows how to fix it when something goes wrong."

"Well, then, leave early so you've got plenty of time."

"You worry too much, Mother."

Entering the airport terminal and meeting with my mother, my sister Domenica and her daughter Angie, was returning to a former life. I felt the pull of old manners, old expectations, and I tried not to get in too deep where I would be sucked under by sheer force, lost in the family mystique. My mother took the seat on one side of the aisle of the airplane and handed out the other three tickets to Domenica, and Angie, and me. I sat in the middle, between them. Angie had often ridden along with Jada and Dom in the back seat, Arnold and me in the front, on trips up to Grandma and Grandpa Pope's. Angie, only six months younger than Jada, always asked questions, and Jada always had answers, while Dom slunk deeper into the cushion with a hand-held game.

Years later, her hair as red but richer and fuller around her long face, Angie was still looking for answers. "Tell me about this guy Jada's bringing to the wedding. Is he her boyfriend?"

"He used to be. He might be going with some other woman now. No, Adam promised he'd stay with her, be with her till the end. He's a nice guy. Jada says he gives in, probably had to with her. She's not too different from the rest of us, as much as she'd like to be."

Angie nodded her head and I looked up at the white pitted panel that looked like petrified tapioca pudding, square buttons inserted at intervals, my own miniature control board, wishing that by punching a few I could plug Adam into Jada's life in just the right way as to fill her last days with the love she craved.

"Idina," Domenica asked, "what does 'S-o-i-r-e-e' mean?"

"A party, an evening affair. It's French. It's pronounced 'swaray.'"

"Ooooh, soirée, huh. La-de-da." She stuck her long index finger between the pages of a thick paperback, ahemed again, and tilted forward, leaning across me to pat Angie on the thigh, spreading her mouth into a wide grin. "How ya doin' there, Angie?"

"I'm good, Ma. How are you?"

"I'm gr-reat!" Then she laughed, a laugh that matched our cousin Mary Rose, a Martin. Domenica's tight-lipped mouth came from my mother's side, too. I was filling myself up slowly, in tiny tide pools here and there, with the source of who we were; it was useless not to relent to their life-giving waters.

Punky brought us to the hotel and lay out the evening's plans. Fred had gone to the groom's party and would join us at the bar on the top floor, revolving to scope a panoramic view of Washington, D.C. The summer's day was lengthening when we stepped onto the revolving floor, the sun merely a golden reflection glancing off a glass-walled building. By the time we made the turn in our rotation, the yellow glint would be sunk. I excused myself from the large round table and went down to the lobby. Coming away from the desk, I heard clipped words of a lively conversation verging on an argument from around a corner. Jada and Adam skipped out of the hall and I stopped to hear, "I told you we'd make it on time. That was the right turn." The 'you' was Adam, but it was as clear as the ivory parquet floor beneath us that Jada was making a command performance. She flashed her eyes at me and I smiled back.

"Perfect timing," I said, leading them with me. "We're in the lounge."

They followed, but Adam ignored my interruption. "No, Jada. That wasn't the problem. We went too far north. We took the wrong turn off before we got there."

"It's been this way the whole trip." Jada's twinkling eyes rolled as they exited the elevator. Adam, his glasses slipping forward on his very serious countenance, made the perfect straight man for Jada's exaggerations. I suspected he knew his strength was in playing the part and kept the banter going as much for sport as a sense of righteousness. If it was the last word he was striving for, he'd have learned by now that he'd have as much hope as finding the Holy Grail under the hood of his car.

But you can never tell, so, entering the lounge, I said, "Well, you made it. There they are." I pointed to our table and made a flourish with my arm, sweeping the way for their grand entrance.

"Barely. You should ride in his car." Jada raised her volume over the orchestration of voices in conversations and shot a painful glance at Adam as if to emphasize the hardship she'd endured. We reached the table. "And the way he drives!"

"Now wait a minute, Jada. It wasn't that bad. And I did get you here. If you'd not have…." Adam's Boston tones made him sound much more put upon than he was, an unruffled Cary Grant playing against the rough and ready Katharine Hepburn. He had me in his baggy back pocket.

"Kind of a tense ride? Heh, heh, heh," Punky said, her eyes dealing our own life stories in episodes around the table and smiling because she knew this one best, and she knew we all knew it.

My mother looked at me, her face balled tight like a dried-up sponge. "What's the matter? What's going on?"

Punky leaned closer to her ear and said loudly, "They're having a little fight about the drive here. You know."

"What? Oh, it buzzes when it's too high." "It" was her hearing aid. "What's going on?"

"Nothing; they're just playing." She saw enough or just gave up and looked back at Jada and Adam, smiled, parting her lips to show the tips of her teeth. "Oh, yeah."

Above the rising sounds of the dance combo, growing louder as the lights in the city brimmed the lounge, Domenica flung her arm in the air as if lassoing a star and shouted an open invitation to the world. "Come on, everybody, the music's playing, let's parteee!" She broke into a full laugh and sang along to the band, "I need some good lovin'. True Love! Da-da-dotadot-da-da!" She hummed the lyrics she didn't know, bouncing her head to the beat just like she had the pom poms from her high school cheerleading days and cajoled, "Why don't you kids go out there and dance?" Crackling lights of the buildings spun around us like crushed diamonds, ice cubes rattled against glass, and voices beat like drums. Domenica was right; we had a wedding to go to, and for this weekend, it felt right to celebrate.

The early morning air was sopped with moisture, as if you could pick it up like a mop and wring out streams of water, for my run. That I could be so close to what I'd always thought of as so distant amazed me. When I arrived back to the hotel room, Jada and Adam had just left for breakfast, and then the rest of the day we took Washington by car, Adam's car. Adam knew his way around the city and wiggled his little brown beater into a spot at the edge of a corner of a park, which, Jada corrected me, was The Park. Adam went for his run while Jada and I ambled toward the back of the Capitol, and I made this observation: "I think there should be flowers. There should be impressive gardens, showy."

"I think they keep the grounds very nice." Jada spoke with an edge of defensiveness. "You always want what should be, Mother. Face reality. It isn't always pretty." As we drove to Arlington National Cemetery, I watched the city disappear into the countryside and settled comfortably in the back seat, not even making a pretense to be interested in the conversation in the front.

If Domenica waved a magic wand enchanting us with party fever the night of our arrival, it was Jada who entranced everyone at the wedding celebration. She captured hearts and stole affection so easily just by being there, totally and uncompromisingly, a presence that seemed to float by wing, no ground contact necessary. Where Jada lighted, she brought an aura, a nimbus, to the gathering. Not just once did Punky tell me of Jada's admirers, those who asked who this mystery enchantress was, wearing a short slim dress and crowned with a saucy black hat, and how did she get there? My mother and Domenica leaned together over the dinner table to wonder what had happened to Jada, as if, perhaps, she had stepped into a pair of glass slippers. I watched, enamored myself, by this goddess, my daughter, flicking diamond dust every time she clicked her heels.

The wedding party evolved into one and then several traveling parties, retaining fewer diehards with each move. Adam moved in and out of my company, trailing Jada's, as we landed at each venue. Jada had her eye on a tall dark stranger in a red Mercedes convertible, but Punky said he was smitten with another—besides himself. To Jada, if not him, she'd find another. Domenica and Angie went back to the hotel after the first stop, and Punky and Fred had also disappeared early—not in the night, in the morning. Finally at three a.m., Adam and I gave in; Jada stayed on with even later revelers than ourselves.

I rummaged at the bottom of a hand-held clutch for the room key, two pairs of shoes dangling from my fingers like hooked and strung fish, and yawned, "Why I ever thought I could wear these stupid shoes, I'll never know." I tossed the sexy-strapped high-spiked heels along with the more conservative open-toed flats I wore to the reception, to the floor. My feet ballooned and throbbed on the carpet. I had plans to immediately clean up and sink into bed. Adam stood solid, apparently not having had as many sea breezes and salty dogs as I, blocking the path I wanted to take, creases in his forehead like little furrows in a freshly planted garden. I leaned against the wall, alternately unburdening my swollen feet.

"You've been a good sport, Adam. Hanging around, especially when you don't know anybody. How'd you get over to that party room?"

"I can get along okay by myself. But it was hard for me to figure out what to do. Was I there *with* Jada? Or was I just *here* with Jada. Understand? I didn't know what to tell people because she was off with others all night. Then she'd be back and go off again." Adam spoke animatedly. I tried to follow with concern.

"She was the belle of the ball, that's for sure. I could hardly talk to anyone who wanted to talk to me, not about her. Even Max, you know, the man with dark hair, the guy I went for a walk with;

well, duh, the guy who drove us back here. He was very perceptive, noticed how she moved with a, a freedom from gravity, I guess is what I'd call it. Not abandon, but a pure joy that wasn't attached to this earth. Everyone noticed something absolutely enchanting. The navy officer, for instance, offering to give her a tour of the ship; for all I know, he'll send a fleet for her."

"That's just it! She was flirting with everybody. With me standing there. I know I came as a friend, but…." Adam's eyes went to the mirror over the dresser before finishing. "But why did she ask me to go with her?"

"I'm sure she had no way of knowing she would feel so spirited. Because, really, she wasn't flirting, at least not with people. It was like she was set free—the pure essence of Jada. She could be anyone she wanted to be. What's the point of giving up life if you're not going to enjoy living it carefree—the epitome of living? But aren't you seeing someone else?"

"Yes, but it was hard knowing what to do tonight. I didn't know if I was supposed to be her date, but then she'd run off. I spent more time with Angie than I did with her."

The light from the dressing area shining behind him intensified the concentration on his darkened face. "Well, Adam, I guess you need to figure out your own feelings about Jada. I thought you were escorting her here, but that you two aren't romantically involved. Maybe you have someone holding you back, but she doesn't." I raised my arm toward the room, crowded with predawn shadows. "Just look at us. Three of us sharing one room, with her and me in one bed. I've had too much to drink and too little sleep, and it's late. I'm tired and want to get into that bed."

"Aren't you waiting up for her?"

"Oh, my God, no! I have no idea when she'll get in, and I can hardly stay awake for this conversation. I'll never make it through my run in the morning if I don't get some sleep. I gotta go before I fall over."

"That's the other thing. I was going to drive back tomorrow but I think I'll go home now."

"At night? No, morning, at the end of a long busy day?"

"I'll be all right. It's not that far to Boston, and there are things I want to do there." Adam packed what few things were left out of his bag, and without wasting time on a shower, departed. When Jada returned, I was not aware.

We were in the car for about an hour by the time Punky pulled into her garage on a newly paved street in a newly developed neighborhood in Virginia. She kept the air conditioning on for the better part of the year, and the door closed to her back yard, fenced to keep Bandit in and the deer that came through the wooded area out. To watch Fred play with the Siberian Husky, I had either to swelter on the humid deck or shiver behind the sliding glass door.

We took the train in to Washington, toured a Smithsonian Museum, and dropped Jada for her tour at the naval compound. Jada absorbed the city and the return to Punky's quiet life at home full measure. Punky invited her to stay as long as she wanted. "I know it's a lot of extra money, but is it okay if I don't go home so early? I'd like to stay a few more days," Jada asked.

"Pick the day," I answered. My mother sat at Punky's glossy kitchen table while I set my elbows on the counter and waited for information from the other end of the telephone wire, my credit card the only clutter in sight. In my grandparents' houses, the telephone had a nook of its own, away from the washing or the cooking or the feeding, in other words away from the work. When the bell on the telephone rang, my grandmas were virtually called away to answer it and compelled to give the caller their attention. Now I was waiting on hold while on the other end a faceless woman checked her lists, and I felt uselessly unoccupied. When she reconnected herself with me, she confirmed the availability of a seat to Sibley for Jada. "Five hundred and ninety-eight dollars?" I read my VISA number into the mouthpiece, hung up and turned around. "Well, that's done."

"You shouldn't have let her get away with that." My mother's right hand gripped her empty coffee mug. Her thinly lashed eyes scowled, and the ends of her lips turned down, gathering the aging folds of her jowls. "That cost you a lot of money. $600 just because she changed her mind? You should have made her use the ticket she had."

"I'm glad she wanted to stay," I defended myself, scraping my thumb against the edge of the plastic card. "She's feeling good, for once. That's worth a little money to me." What my mother was thinking behind her weathered face, beginning to show the shift from being older to looking old, she kept unsaid, and I walked to the sliding glass door, putting my card into the pocket of my bulging leather wallet, the one Jada convinced me to buy, hoping to impose order and tidiness on my motley methods of classification. Two years old, the neat pockets curled; broken lines ran through the leather like stretch marks after giving birth, and the important flap, the one that held it all together, was unable to encompass the bulk of faded receipts, tattered coupons, and wrinkled dollar bills. "I should clean this out before Jada does." I mumbled.

Through the window, Jada watched Fred's fingers sink into a rubber ball above Bandit's upturned nose, her nostrils working in and out, her crystalline blue eyes sighting the slimy russet ball, the moment of release so ferociously in focus that whatever time was passed collapsed into this one split second for which there was no hereafter. If you could freeze one second in your life, would it be the one you thought you'd choose or would it be the one you lived, over and over without knowing it, every day?

Jada complained about inheriting my bulging belly, mushy and soft below the belly button even when I was skinny everywhere else, and Grandma M's wide calves. But Jada's hands were her own, her long slender fingers delicate filaments dancing nimbly along piano keys or poising a paint brush on canvas. They pressed tenderly on the swollen washcloth balled between her hands denting it slightly as she worked it like a wad of dough. Drops of water pinged little circles into the clearing she had made before her. All around her, the bathwater brimmed with foamy water turned yellowish-green from the gardenia bubble bath. When I poured the syrupy liquid into the falling water from the faucet, the sharpness tickled the hairs of my nose. Now the room was permeated with the sweetness from broken bubbles and dewy air pasted to my skin.

I sat on the floor against the cracked ceramic wall. When I moved in, the headiness of designing Jada's bedroom and bathroom overtook caution, and I peeled off the cosmetic coverup and stripped the 70 years of paint from the intricate pattern of the ceramic border tiles. But my dreams of retiling and installing a pedestal sink crumbled with my bank account as bills for tuition and airplane tickets came due. What was left was a room with jagged crevices running through the ceramic like earthquake fissures. The flowered wallpaper above the tiles and ceiling complimented the original toilet, the wooden built-in medicine cabinet, and the herringbone pattern on the floor. But the aged tiles and the modern sink, no.

We had returned from Washington, D.C., and that, along with her ties to the clinic and her psychologist and going to a conference in July and back to school in the fall, were the markers of Jada's summer. "Nobody believes I'm dying." Seeing Jada here, it was easy to believe she would never not be. Immersed in water from foot to neck gave medium to Jada's melancholy, and I allowed my hand to soak in it, too. "You've got to call Adam; explain to him. He doesn't understand that I'm not going to live."

"What else do you want to accomplish? Do you want to travel? Europe? France?"

Jada sat upright and rubbed her face, first her forehead, then her cheeks, until a faint rose glowed in uneven blotches at her cheekbones. The hollows under her eyes and close to her lips were tinged like old newsprint, as if she had applied make-up to age her for the stage. She raised her chin and slid the cloth down her neck, saying, "France, that's too much. Adam said he might take a cruise with me." Her skin glistened with beads of water and she dropped the cloth into the tub and spread it out, letting air bubbles ripple underneath it before sinking. "I still want to go to the CASE convention with Priss in July. I have to finish this research project for my art class. I don't really want to do anything. I just want to go on a cruise to Jamaica or somewhere with Adam. Does that sound dumb?"

"No, of course not. It's not how many things you do so much as what you want from the things you do." Philosophizing about time as if it were a commodity sounded like a self-help book full of formulaic steps, each one with a thought for the day to plug the hole of fear you woke up with. I recovered, got back to solid ground, and looked for concrete answers. "Is there anything special you want for your birthday?"

Jada dragged the cloth past her thighs and up out of the water to her chest. "A 'beemer.' Black, 325i."

"What's that? Oh, yeah, a BMW." She had shown me a magazine advertisement, using the moniker affectionately, as if it were an old love. "But what does 325i mean?"

"It's a name, like for which engine size. There's a 125, a 325, a 525, a 725, and now they've come out with a 925. That's the biggest."

"Yeah, and I bet the price is big, too. Sounds pretty fancy to me."

"A 925 is, but I don't need that; 325 is good. Stick shift."

"Well, I'll have to see about that." When my mother used that phrase, it translated to "No, but I won't say why yet." For me, I really did need to see about getting Jada a beemer. As far as I knew, cars like that were priced out of the financial means of a teacher. I massaged Jada's bent back with the nappy cloth. Debbie. Relapses. Debbie drove to treatments by herself, at least when we first met her before the last relapse when she grew the hump in her back. Who knew what other humiliations she suffered before she died. What did she do to get what she wanted? Did she just fizzle? Or was she a statement?

Or the other young woman Dr. Lourde had treated before he came to Ramsey Hospital. She'd been fighting a brain tumor, heroically. Dr. Lourde introduced us to her, she lying on a table, one arm up and laid across her forehead, and her fiancé, the young man who loved her so terrifically and wanted to marry her before she died, seated by her side, holding her other hand. She had months, maybe weeks left to life. Was he her last wish? The "last cigarette" before being dragged to the electric chair, chains of doom bound around her ankles, her wrists. One last wish to follow the last one, the one before there was time to have another last wish, to light up another cigarette and be denied. That would be greedy. Some people don't even get a first last wish. Like Akiko's son: died of internal injuries, unconscious of what they were doing to try to save him after a car accident. He died before knowing he was dying and entitled to one last wish. Or not; maybe he had been living his one last wish all his life until this last moment of it. Maybe his last last wish was a wish to stop the pain.

I sponged Jada's back and up her neck, the little knobs of her spine protruding one by one through taut skin. The bubbles had burst along the surface of the water and left islands of foam floating near the edge while Jada speared the water with her fingers and flicked fine sprays of water back onto her, runnels forming between her breasts, beads resting midway on the firm white mounds, pooling on mocha-colored nipples, supple and rounded nubs bearing the water of life. I wrung out the washcloth and slapped it over the edge of the tub. "Is there anything else you want?"

"Yeah. I want a big fucking funeral." She dropped her hands in the water.

"Oh, Jada. I will miss you so! I'm so afraid of your dying."

"Being dead doesn't scare me. It's such a waste, though! I could have lived such a good life."

"Yes; I'm sorry I haven't been able to give you what you wanted. I'm sorry about a lot of things I've done to hurt you or get in your way." I said that as I put my hands underneath her arms and she pushed herself up with her feet. As soon as she stood on the tufty soft rug, I slung the towel across her back and threw my arms around her warm body, trapping her within a cloak of pink terry. "You know how much I love you. I make too many mistakes."

"Chase says you should be honored that I can get angry at you. He says you shouldn't worry that I call you a bitch because I don't mean it at you." Her voice came breathily soft, a wisp of warm air near my ear. I released my hold, patting the towel on her skin.

"I can understand why a psychologist says that, but I sure don't feel honored when it happens. But then, what do I know? I don't even know what a 'beemer' is."

"You." Jada clucked her tongue. "How did you ever get as far as you did?"

"I don't know." Jada held on to the sink and I nudged the terry between her toes. "Just when I think I'm hot, I find out how little I know. Where's your lotion? Thirty-three years old and my ten-year-old daughter has to tell me how to pronounce victuals. Keeps me humble."

Leaning over me, she reached for the bottle on top of the toilet tank. "Eyup. That's my mom. Dumbest smart person I know. Imagine what you could have been with a different family."

"Yeah, well, that's true for all of us. You, too."

"I know. It's all your fault I have this disease." White cream made a film on her legs, forming streaks like wrinkled Saran Wrap where it hadn't been smoothed yet. "If you and Dad hadn't got married, I wouldn't have this disease. It's in your genes, you know. So it's all your fault."

"But you might have had something else if you had two different parents. In fact, you wouldn't even be you."

"Sometimes I wish that was true, too."

"I don't. But it's too bad we don't know some things ahead of time. Well, maybe we do but we don't recognize the signs. Nothing about your dad and me was right. I was even allergic to the wedding rings. Yup. Bad decisions."

"See what I said? Dumb." I opened the bathroom door to a waft of cool air, and Jada pranced, winsome and wonderful.

"You need pictures," was Arnold's greeting when he arrived to our condo. I thanked him for his gratuitous advice and led him to the living room where I wanted to point out that he was sitting on fifteen hundred dollars, half of what he paid me for everything he kept, love seats and coffee tables, dining and bedroom sets, and desks and dishes and vacuum cleaner included, not to mention Jada's piano and a tax sheltered annuity he did not declare. But it was Jada's birthday, so we lined up on the couch, all four of us, a blank wall behind us, and smiled. Jada opened presents and I served her birthday cake, Boston cream pie. As I prepared for the day, I felt pangs of guilt for not doing something spectacular. Twenty-one. Nearly impossible the word happy. But both twenty-one and happy spurred me to action. I had no idea how I'd get enough money to afford a beemer, but I trusted my decision and invited Arnold for a walk around the block.

Jada and Dom looked through the closet for a game to play, and I waited until we rode the six floors down the elevator and cleared the corner of Northern and Girard, as if Jada could hear our voices being drafted upwards through the courtyard and into the open windows before I presented my case. "You know Jada wants a BMW, don't you?"

"Yes." Arnold answered promptly.

"Well, I may have found one for her. Just what she wants. A woman is considering upgrading her lease, getting a new model. I would be able to take over her payments."

"A BMW is an expensive car."

"Yes, it is, but I'm not buying it; I'm taking over another woman's lease payments. There's only one year left of the lease, and then I'd have the option to buy."

We strolled along the shaded sidewalk, the canopy of hundred-year-old trees joining together leaving only puddles of sunlight in the street. July could hit 90, 100 degrees. This day was one of those perfect summer days that beckoned people to come out into it.

"Leasing isn't a smart thing to do, is it? I've heard of people who have to pay extra for mileage. And you're making car payments on a car you don't own."

"Arnold, I can't afford to buy one. It's taking everything I have now. But I'm not doing this as an investment. And I'm not talking a five-year commitment. I just want a car for now. I'm looking at one year only. If Jada lives longer than that, I'll deal with that then."

Arnold cleared his throat, a habit I'd learned to regard with anticipation, and fingered his hair away from his forehead, even though it was not drooping out of place. On his ring finger he wore a replacement, a chipped azure stone in a gold setting. I wondered if Arnold resorted to the once-discarded ring, reasoning that he could deal with something broken better than he could with something rejected. "How much is it?"

"Five hundred dollars a month. Nothing down, nothing else, except insurance, about $500.00 every six months. If I can, I'm getting the car. All I'm asking from you is that you insure the first half; if I know that's taken care of, I can find a way to manage the rest."

"I'm not trying to be difficult, but have you looked in the want ads for a used car?"

"I don't think you understand. I can't afford to own another car, and I don't want the responsibility of owning it. It's for Jada. A beemer. For now." We reached a corner: either we walked another block or we turned toward my home. It was a perfect place to stop and make my point, be able to say out loud for the record, just in case I had some anonymous donor or god to thank for this gift. "I can't tell you how lucky I've been with this. It's the right car, for the right time, for the right money. It's like someone knows and is doing us a favor." Arnold, looking about himself, said he'd had enough of walking, and asked as we turned back, "How will it get there?"

"She'll drive it, of course."

"Idina, she can't do that!"

I faced Arnold, who stood stunned in place, and opened my hands to ask the eternal question, "Why not? You drive places. She drove to Biwabik by herself. Besides, I can go with her and fly back if she wants. She's twenty-one, for God's sake."

"But what if something happens to her?"

"Then it does. This is the whole point of her not having a transplant. She doesn't want to live in a cubicle; she wants to do normal things, face life on the outside, live as if she weren't dying.

Normal is going back to school and, if you've got a car, driving it there. She can do what she wants; she's *going* to do what she wants. I won't tell her she can't." A squirrel leaped from the curb and stood up on its hind legs, its head photograph-still, before stretching out onto the sun-baked asphalt. I caught my breath, holding in it the warning as a brown car came speeding from the opposite direction and the squirrel stopped on all fours, its tail quivering in the air, the muscles in its legs twitching with decision, forward or back? Faster than I could think it, the squirrel made a turn around and bounded, scampering partway up a tree, clinging to the bark with its long sharp claws. I wondered how many times a day the squirrel put its life on the line, and if it stopped to think about it, how it could keep at it. "Like I said, I'm trying to get the car. It's up to you if you want to help out."

"Sure," Arnold breathed out his answer as if expelling air he'd held since we'd left. "Sounds like the lease is the best thing. Tell me when you need it." We walked in silence while I searched my emotional state for feeling relief, joy, satisfaction, some difference in attitude or way of ordering my surroundings that would tell me I'd accomplished my goal.

"That's a nice thing you're doing for her."

"It's too bad I can't buy her a man. But I'd work on that, too, if I could."

"She does want to get married. It's a shame she can't have that."

"I know, but then we'd say it's a shame she couldn't have children because then she'd want that, too. I mean, isn't that the whole thing, our wanting more of life? It *is* a shame; everything is."

Arnold dabbed beads of perspiration from his forehead as I slid the key into the heavy security door. I had given him a set of keys so that he could come to see Jada, home from the hospital, anytime without my presence. He never used them, to pick her up, to bring anything over to her. It was a fact I tried not to judge.

The Backgammon board lay open on the dining room table, black discs stacked into short towers on one side and white discs in an unruly pile on the other. Dom was in the living room, the television screen flickering white uniforms against green grass. He was about to be a senior in high school, and I knew most of his friends by name. I saw only the schoolwork he asked for help with. I called him every morning, brought him for his allergy injection every Saturday, and watched him play in baseball and basketball games. I did as much with him as many other mothers did with their sons, but we did not sleep in the same house and I did not cook his meals. He was becoming a man without me. I told myself that he would have done that even if I'd stayed in the house, for he'd already declared his break from me when he broke into adolescence. In some ways, for all his clinging to me in childhood, he'd always been a small man inside his child's body, looking manly in strong dark features. He was my baby. As I suckled him, he'd look up at me. He squirmed and squiggled in bed, hiding his head under my arm when thunder rolled and lightning struck in the middle of the night. He grasped my leg with both arms, snuggling my knee, a human walking cast, when the house filled with guests. I got him through fifth grade reading and driver's training. And now he was a man, stretched out on the new couch, just long enough for his five-foot-eleven-inch length, his head supported by two pillows and his own hand. "What're you watching, Darlin'?"

"Baseball. Team's all right." He pulled in air through his nose as if sucking up the room.

"Sitting up should help you breathe," I suggested.

"Nothing helps." The couch creaked with his shifting weight. Dom rose lazily, rubbing his hand up and down and around his nose as if it were a pinball caught between three scoring pegs rather than attached to his face. "I have to get home and take some medicine."

"Do you want to take some cake home?

Dom moved his eyebrows up and down. "Sure!" he said. I cut two pieces, the filling squishing out a thick ivory pudding, and put them into a container. "There. That ought to make you happy." I handed the cake and a kiss to Dom.

"Thanks, Ma."

"Yes, thanks, Idina. Very nice." Dishes with brown smears and pebbly crumbs scattered on the counter next to the sink, and I decided that as long as nothing better tempted me I may as well clean up.

As the water gurgled down the drain, I heard the sound of music from the living room. The volume grew louder to Madonna and I mouthed the words, "...over the borderline", as I put the China back into the hutch. Arnold must have felt magnanimous when he split the Wedgwood and the sterling flatware into six place settings of each for him and for me. He kept the whole set of Orrefors crystal, though; didn't tell me I wanted half. I hung the towel and went into the living room, bringing with me the lush red roses, a traditional gift from Arnold to Jada, and set them on a table near the windows facing eastward. The sun was sliding off to the side of the sky, hanging too heavy to keep its cheerful place after shining so intensely all day and now turned the sky an amber pink, while glinting like gold on the glass facade of a downtown building. "Look at the sky," I said to Jada. "Isn't it pretty?"

"Mm-hmm. That was a nice birthday," she said tunefully.

"I'm glad you're happy with it." Simple as the celebration was, as I reflected on our serendipitous harmony, all four of us, I concluded that that in itself had to be a fairly miraculous gift. The phone's trilling called me. "It's for you. It's Katie"

When Jada rejoined me she announced, "Katie's coming over in about an hour."

"Nice," I said. There was nothing wrong with nice. Nice was good.

The middle blimp of the summer drifted along like a tumbleweed caught by capricious desert winds grazing an artless course. I ran a short distance most mornings and worked a couple weeks writing curriculum. Except for an occasional visit such as Katie's, friends were engulfed in their new professional and graduate pursuits, or, in Kimby's case, dating Daniel, visiting Mexico, and working at her summer job, leaving Jada to spend time cleaning out.

Every time she went to the house on Lambert Lane, she threw out a little more, things that didn't matter, things that merely cluttered. The others she sorted and organized into a library to succeed her life. Cards and letters from her friends, her mom and dad, her aunts and uncles, she filed into a box. Old high school papers she pitched. Photograph albums, dolls, bears lived at our condo on her bed, in her glass curio case or on a shelf in her closet. She arranged her journals, giving me explicit orders that the only two people allowed to read them were Kimby and myself. She was prioritizing her life, separating herself from earthly trappings and distancing herself by degrees from what it meant to be alive on earth. Some decisions were not so easy to make.

At her closet, an array of items, a red woven belt that came with a pair of shorts, a clear plastic coin purse with a teddy bear printed on it, the black purse she had used until Maureen gave her the Coach bag she really wanted and now used exclusively, lay scattered on Jada's bed. She stepped into the elasticized band of a pair of white pants with red and blue stripes. "What do you think, Mom? I know they're expensive, but I don't think they look so good."

Her father had picked them up, on sale; but they belonged on someone like Grace Kelly in *High Society*. Women who owned yachts in Cape Cod, belonged to clubs in restricted areas, and divorced men for not making enough money wore these pants. "Well, they're crisp. They're not exactly what I see you wearing."

Jada added, "I don't want to hurt Dad's feelings, but I don't like them. I don't want to waste money, either." She ran her hands down the polished cloth lengthwise, the sheeny fabric sounding like slurping the last of a malt through a straw.

"Don't worry about that. If he wants to buy things for you, let him. It's his decision."

"I guess. But I don't think I'll wear them."

"Well, then, give them back." She stretched out the waistband with her thumbs, slid the pants past her hips, and leaning on the love seat, stepped out of them, and laid them on my lap.

The flow of days ran thus, sorting, relegating; visiting a friend and her baby; seeing Chase—Dr. Barrigan to me; planning wedding shower games for her cousin; going to the clinic for chemotherapy; these were the gutsy things Jada did every day. They weren't full of glamor, attending graduation, a wedding, riding in a limo to a baseball game, going to a CASE convention, which she also did, but they held the essence of living. Special events, trips, happenings were crammed into Jada's first summer of her official adulthood, enlarged in a tell-what-you-did-over-your-summer-vacation composition, in which only the big things seemed worthy enough to define time, as if the minutes of an ordinary day didn't happen, or count.

As head nurse at the clinic, Bethany rescued me more than once, providing me with a quiet room, a non-judgmental glance. Bethany flowed with musical assurance, like the swing of a cat's tail, reeking grace every time she pointed her toe. At any moment, I would not have been surprised to see her coil one arm upwards like a viper with hypnotic magical charm. She and a friend opened a dance and aerobics studio and through lessons with Bethany, I learned to value her as a friend; all the times we shared a cup of cappuccino together, we talked our talk, not clinic talk. We lived blocks away from each other, and Bethany lived alone, bearing Alexandra as a single mother in the early months of 1989. I took Jada with me to watch Alexandra. "She's a wonderful baby, very even-tempered," I said while standing at the service elevator listening to the grumbles and groans within the six-story shaft as if it were a stomach growling to be fed.

Though archaically slow, the service elevator was reportedly two seconds faster than the one in the central hall. I wasn't the one who had clocked the elevators, sending them up and down the shaft on their time trials, but if I had, I would have tried to prove that they traveled at the same velocity, but that the opening and closing of the main elevator door, hobbling slowly to the wall as if on a cane, was what accounted for the two-second difference, which is a flash compared to the duration of most events, but impressively long after you have landed and must wait useless seconds to actually arrive. I supposed the kind of people who stayed at this hotel when it was built seventy years before weren't as impatient with a few seconds' delay as we in the eighties were. And, for all of that, this summer, neither was I.

I punched the elevator button with my thumb and looked past Jada's straw hat out the window toward the treetops, at the Victorian houses they shaded. Dr. Lourde teased Jada, saying she looked like she belonged in the rice paddies in that hat, but it was perfect for her. Its rim protected her from the sun, and the bowl of the hat wasn't so large that, without hair filling the empty space, it wobbled around her head like a spinning plate on a pole. The sun streamed in from behind her making a halo around the halo of her hat on her head. Studying me under drooping eyebrows, she said "Look at you; you look younger than I do." She paused while I turned my attention to her full face. "I look so old."

Fine jagged lines, like brittle wrinkles in old paper, radiated from her eyes and mouth. Her skin had lost its resilient glow and had a flaky dryness, as if I might raise a fine chalky scatter if I blew at her. I blushed at our unnatural exchange, a real life Freaky Friday in which I, the mother, was enjoying a new fountain of pride in my body's ability to move with strength and endurance, while my daughter, prematurely aged by artificial life-sustaining drugs, was disintegrating before me. "You just had chemo. You'll get some color in a few days."

The elevator door opened, and Jada crossed the metal divide tentatively, reaching her arm out, as if feeling for a hidden obstacle. Just as we heard the click and felt the jolt of movement, the whir slowed and we braked at the fifth floor. A girl of about eight hopped on in two jumps, swinging her long tangled oak-colored hair around like a tilt-a-whirl. Her right arm poised in a frozen wave of indecision to strike the panel of buttons as if by magic one of them might take her on a ride to any place of her choosing. She flipped a glance backwards and instantly dropped her arm. I felt like one of the churlish little brats in the grocery store, wanting to yell,

"Mine!" at what she had that Jada hadn't. When the door opened at the first floor, she fled, Jada and I lagging behind.

Alexandra was spread out on a blanket in her favorite position, arms and legs stiff and straight like a gingerbread cookie. According to my astrological natal chart, I do a bit better with older children who talk and walk than I do with infants. Babies seemed to like me, anyway, so I returned the favor, pushing against their flat feet, gurgling at their bubbling mouths. I made silly faces at Alexandra and yodeled, intermittently talking to Bethany. Alexandra watched intently as I tossed my hair, zooming in and out at her. Jada sat in a chair, overlooking the two of us. "Would you like to run some errands as long as you're going to the grocery?" I asked Bethany. "Would that be okay with you, Jada?"

"Sure," she agreed. Alexandra's attention turned toward Jada.

"Actually, there are some things I could pick up at the drugstore. And that wouldn't be out of the way, if you don't mind. Alexandra loves to go outside. Maybe you can take her for a walk."

"Okay, Jada? Would you be up for a stroll?" Jada moved down to the floor and gave her fingers to Alexandra's clutch. "As long as it's short and I don't have to push."

Bethany put a bonnet on Alexandra's head before getting the stroller out of the vestibule and stocking it with baby necessities. Supplied, Jada and I started out bravely toward the front walk and to the curb at the end of the block. "Look at how she watches everything," Jada observed. "She has such big brown eyes."

"She's a striking baby. So long and sturdy. I like babies who look strong and full. You and Dom had full faces. I loved your cheeks. And you had the cutest little cleft in your chin." I dabbed my pointer finger lightly on her chin. If she had been ticklish there, she would have giggled.

"You know how Dom used to hate having food on his face? And you had to give him a wet 'washclosh' on his high chair? 'Washclosh' he called it. Did I do that?"

"Are you kidding? You loved getting into your food. Remember those pictures of you, the ones with an orange popsicle all over your mouth and down your yellow dress? And the raspberry jam? Your whole face was covered, the seeds like freckles everywhere. You would have run around all day like that; you didn't care."

"I like that picture. And that other one with me sticking my fingers into my birthday cake."

"Your dad probably has the picture of you and Dom all dressed up for him to marry you. Remember that? He was such a sucker for all your schemes."

Jada caught her breath and, probably, relished remembering the long-forgotten moment. "I thought it was pretty clever. I had to promise him a cookie if he'd kiss me on the lips."

"Jada, you weren't in charge of Dom's cookies."

"I know. But it worked. And he forgot about the cookie. What else did I do?"

"Oh, let's see. You liked washing dishes. You stood on the chair at the kitchen sink, splashing water all over the kitchen floor. I kept the bathroom door shut at the apartment because you colored the white squares of the floor and the bottom of the bowl in your potty chair with crayons. Actually, I thought that showed intelligence, but I didn't want you to think that doing it was all right." Alexandra sat still in her stroller as if listening to every word, stockpiling ideas for what she could do as soon as she was able.

Jada watched her closely. "You used to let Dom get away with stuff. He used to stand at his bottom drawer with his bottle hanging between his teeth and throw everything onto the floor."

"Funny how he could be so fastidious about food on his face yet keep his room so messy."

"Remember how packed it was?" Jada's face showed her disdain.

"All those dusty little plastic Dairy Queen baseball caps in the cardboard holder. Yeah, well, I remember how messy your room used to be, too. You made all those magic potions that spilled onto the rug and stained it. Remember going to the zoo? You loved the seals. When you got home you lay on the black footstool and raised your chest and clapped your arms like flippers pretending you were a seal."

Jada smiled. "I remember that. I always wanted to feed them, too. We bought those bags of cut up fish."

"Dom loved dogs. He crawled around the floor while we were all trying to get ready for school. 'Tend you Gramma and I be Pepper da dog.' He'd bark and paddle along after me. I put cereal in a bowl on the floor and he'd stick his tongue in it and eat it. Here, we're almost to the park. Should we find a shady spot and sit down?"

"I always heard the Redmonds call their dog Muffin, so I thought that was what all dogs were called," Jada said, adjusting Alexandra's bonnet.

Trees shaded our way as we walked the sidewalk that sliced off a triangle at the corner of the park. A large grassy rectangle studded with park benches, the park was a neighborhood front porch where mostly men, often old, gathered to sit, to visit. A bust and a plaque of the legendary Pullman car labor organizer bordered the sidewalk at the opposite end to us. Jada and I, likely the only European-Americans there, stopped at a vacant bench. Alexandra, parked between us, continued to take in the world at face value. I curled my foot on the bar of the stroller and pushed it back and forth in front of me, the spring making chirping noises as Alexandra bounced forward and back, forward and back.

"I used to take you with me everywhere. Put you in the laundry basket on top of the dirty clothes when I did the laundry, pushed you in the stroller when I vacuumed, except you cried until I picked you up." Back and forth I bounced between then and now and asked, "How're you doing, Jada, feeling okay?"

"Mm-hmm."

"She likes watching you. She likes you."

"Babies do. I don't even do anything," Jada tossed out to the lazy breeze that stroked the fine hairs on her arms.

"Maybe they sense that you don't want anything from them. It's hard to hide honesty. Kids can always tell." Jada twirled a leaf in front of Alexandra; Alexandra blinked.

"Do you think she'd like to get out?"

"We can try it. Do you want to hold her? Then she could see more." I lifted Alexandra from her stroller seat and set her on Jada's lap. Jada pointed to the flighty birds that landed on the grass in search of food and talked in Alexandra's ear. An assortment of birds pecked between the blades of grass and scattered off with another bird's landing.

"We should have brought some bread."

"We used to take you to Lyton Lake to feed the geese, too. Brought a big bag of bread. You wanted to run after them, but of course, that scared them away. I felt guilty when I didn't have more food. They'd hop about expecting more, and I felt sorry for their disappointment."

"You make it sound like they have the same feelings you do. Look, Alexandra! There's a butterfly." Jada held her breath, her arms around Alexandra's firm body. The butterfly swooped past Alexandra, flapping its large diaphanous yellow wings veined with spider-like webs of bluish brown. "There it goes! You'd like to go after it, wouldn't you?"

"I can still see that really big one at Grandma Pope's," I said, watching the butterfly dart and dip with another butterfly that appeared as if to rendezvous in the afternoon sun. I envisioned Jada in her bandana outfit, red and white pullover blouse, blue and white shorts with shoulder straps that crossed in the back. Her hair had lightened by the summer sun, probably never to grow dark again. Cropped to her ears, it flounced with her every movement, landing in a random downfall from her head.

Alexandra sat on Jada's lap like a beacon. "I used to like going to Grandma Pope's. I was so excited when I caught that fish. Dom ran up and down the dock; I think he was scared of the fish," Jada said, trying to shift Alexandra's weight on her legs.

"Do you want me to put her back in the stroller?" I asked, reminding her of the bee sting on her head that day.

"She is pretty heavy."

"Okay, Alexandra. Here we go. You're having a good time, aren't you? Nice and cool and breezy in the shade here. We're going back into the sun, though. Ready, Jada?"

Jada went to the rear of the stroller, taking it wordlessly, and pushed Alexandra back to Bethany's. "And the poem you wrote to me: 'I love you when you cook, I love it when you read a book, I love the way you make peanut butter and jelly, I even love your big round belly; I love you so much I just can't stop!'" The three of us strolled, I yearning to relive a lifetime. I laughed, remembering finding Carrie and Jada hanging upside down, swinging freely from a rafter in the garage.

"She wanted a cast just like mine," Jada recalled.

"She could have got it that way." I added, "You wanted to be a garbage man and a tightrope walker." We'd reached Bethany's.

After settling Alexandra on her blanket, Bethany returned to the kitchen. I left Jada with Alexandra and helped empty the two brown grocery sacks. "Did everything go okay?" Bethany asked, raising two cans of soup to the cupboard shelf, nearly bare except for what she was stocking into it.

"Yes, very. We went to the park and sat awhile. She sure is a good-natured baby."

"Sometimes she wakes up and doesn't even cry. If I didn't go in to check on her, she'd lie there and just look around. She loves to look at things."

"I noticed. She really likes Jada. Listen to them."

Bethany folded a bag and flattened it next to her midriff as she peeked around the corner of the wall and turned back toward me with a smile. "Jada's good with babies. Did she babysit a lot?"

"Mostly she watched a neighbor's two little girls. She'd call me up to talk if they were sleeping or to get help if things weren't going well. Once in a while I'd go over for a minute or two, keep her company. She just isn't a loner. She likes to have people around her. I'm going to miss her."

Bethany studied me as I busied myself with the rough edge of a fingernail. "Do you mean when she goes back to college?"

I wasn't ready for the question, and Bethany let the unanswered question stand undisturbed.

Through Jada's work on the Parents'—now rechristened Family—Weekend Committee, she was introduced to Priss, an officer in charge of gifts and fund-raising; she had steadily been making a place for herself in the Development Office on a work-study assignment, in Priss's home and her heart until I forgot, as they must have, the difference of a decade in their ages. Deep but without the throatiness one might expect from someone so tall and sturdy, Priss's voice belonged on stage. Or in the pulpit, embracing every carefully chosen sound, cherishing its sweetness before blessing listeners with tenderness. Not just for the love of sound did Priss take such care; she reflected before speaking. Her mind was a book of homilies, each spoken with appropriateness, her arms acceptance, filling the gaps for Jada, becoming her colleague, friend, sister, the mother at college in my stead. She was Mother Earth, The Good Witch of the North, and Ethel Merman, all in one person.

Priss respected Jada as an assistant, a competent adult, and her wish to claim a piece of the adult world, the world she would not get otherwise and arranged for her to attend the CASE conference as an alternate. While she was there, I completed the last detail and picked up the BMW I'd leased for Jada. Since I was signing the lease, I had to insure it in my name, absolving Arnold of all involvement, and now the gift was totally mine to give.

Not without a huge sigh of relief through the telephone, I told Per that Jada's BMW was safely tucked away until she came home. "Why? Aren't you going to drive it around, show it off?"

"To whom?" I asked. "Besides, I don't belong in a beemer. It's too classy. No, I'm happy with my Mazda. Though I would like a more sporty car, an RX7, or a Porsche."

In Per's silence, he had enough time to break off a hay stalk and stick it between his teeth to chew on. "How much do you think a Porsche costs?"

"Too much for me I know. But I would like one."

"How about a truck, like my Trooper? Or one of those little trucks? There's no room for anything in a sports car."

I let out a burst of air, a closet door spilling every report card and macrame wall hanging and popsicle stick rack filled with promises to mom. "When my kids were young and I had to take them places and do the groceries, I needed space. But pretty soon I won't, and I want to indulge that one thing for myself, a cute little sports car with no room for anything but two people."

Per pointed out without laughter, "That'll be the day! I've never known you without stuff in your car. You've got stuff in there from 1972. You could have a garage sale in your car."

"All right, all right. Life is messy for me. As soon as all this is over, I'll take care of it. It's been clean since Jada's been home."

"That's what I'm saying. As soon as Jada has her own car, you'll be back to the same old thing. So, what else did you do today?"

"That's it. How about you?" He and his French students had fired pots in the art tipi. That night they were going to a rodeo. I had an unfamiliar urge to find a potato farm in Idaho or a deserted ranch in Wyoming and hole up there alone, pick and choose when I would ride into town and hitch up my horse to whatever it's hitched up to and see people only when I felt like it. If I could find one of those spots, I could hide out, start a new life, heal the old.

"Well," he said after a moment's silence, "I think you should at least drive it tomorrow and surprise Jada at the airport."

"We'll see," I said, already planning how it would go before we said good-bye.

My nervousness jumbled up with eagerness; I drove without regard for others' impatience with my extra caution and parked the car carefully to meet Jada. I was sure she'd hear the little explosions of joy I was hiding, but she showed no signs of suspicion as we walked to the baggage claim. The convention, with packing and

traveling and three days of meeting schedules and keeping busy
sagged around her eyes and slumped her shoulders. Other signs,
the set mouth, her fading skin color, not really white but more
like dried clay, flat and plastic, warned that she was crashing into a
low time. "Sit down and wait," I said to her when I picked up her
suitcase from the chugging carousel. "I'll get the car and come back
in for you."

The air temperature in the shade was cool, hardly a noticeable
change from the interior of the terminal. I walked Jada along the
wide cement walkway nearly to its end until I reached the passenger
door of Jada's black BMW 325i, its hazard light flashing, and held
up the black key that would open the doors to a wish come true.
"It's yours."

Jada stood as if she didn't know in which direction to turn.
"When did you get this?"

"Yesterday. I've been so nervous! Do you like it?" I unlocked
the passenger side and tempted her with the key.

"But how?" The car gleamed before us; if we had bent over
we would have seen our own reflections, hers bewildered.

"Oh, I've been working on it. All you have to do is practice
driving it. Hills especially. Then you're set to go back to school."
The smile on my face grew weak. So, this was it. She got her wish,
the last wish I could grant her. "Do you have enough energy to
drive?" I asked, a little less selfishly, a little more gently, to a face of
exhaustion.

"No, not now." I opened the door and she slumped into the
passenger seat, looking over the soft gray upholstery, the black
knob on the shift stick, the shiny dash with round windows into
time, speed, temperature, making friends with a new companion.
The door closed after me with a firm catch, and I leaned over the
steering wheel for the ignition.

"There's only one stipulation: you have to wear your seatbelt
when you drive it." Claiming she preferred death, quick and
surprising, to the slow death she was living, Jada had broken the

habit of latching her seatbelt in spiteful revenge at the absurdity of saving a doomed life.

Two days of recovery, and Jada began her mission to drive a BMW in a manner befitting its stature. We started in our neighborhood, historically a section of the city with wealthy residents. Cathedral Way and its surrounding streets, some still paved with quaint but unevenly worn bricks, intersected rows of large Victorian homes that would have been very much at ease with a BMW parked in front of them. An editorial in the Sibley Hill newsletter disputed the notion that each house *did* boast at least one luxury car, as if dispelling that myth brought the residents down to the level of the common folk in other ways.

The streets were mostly clear and quiet in the slow-moving afternoon, as we crossed and criss-crossed a tiny section. Jada apologized at every stop, stalling and lurching ahead. "You'll get smoother every time you have to shift," I reassured her. "This is the best place to learn. We're not going anywhere, and we're not holding anyone up."

When Jada was ready for traffic, we approached Dade Street, and sure enough, she stopped at the light and flowed through the intersection in line with the other vehicles. The next day, she tackled slight inclines; and then came the true test: Sibley Hill. Having conquered that, Jada shifted from tenuous to cocky, picking up too soon. "The dealer said that it isn't good to slip into first gear before fully stopping," I cautioned. "He said people liked to do that but that it's not good for the gears."

"Okay." Jada agreed readily, for she was ready for take-off, ready to fly. It looked to me like some of the enthusiasm, some of the zest, some of the elixir of living that she had tasted at the wedding and that had waned during the conference was running through her veins again.

"Well, Jada, you're ready to go solo. One last thing. You can drive the car as often and wherever you want. But we will get charged for extra mileage, so think twice about driving other people around on errands or out to the airport, okay? I'm not saying you can't; I'm just asking you to use prudent judgment."

"Prudent. Where do you get those words? Like burgeoning. 'How is Priss's burgeoning romance going with Will?' I showed it to her and had to ask her how to pronounce it."

My role as chauffeur diminished as Jada drove to meet with Chase, whose office was in an old church building where BMWs *did* belong. She also drove to Kimby's, to Ann's, a former neighbor and friend, to meet with Brenda, a coworker at the Cancer Society from the previous summer. The glow of life grew steadily stronger, and she regained a finely spun strength and color, as if exuberance came in the color of honeysuckle pink. As the sun slid greasily across the sky, summer was tiptoeing its way out of our lives, numbering our nights together when I read to her, sang her lullabies, kissed her forehead. And she would sleep; at least I thought she did, if not peacefully, then blessedly, till morning.

Until one night. A pounding in the air, erratic but repeating, aroused my slumber. I looked out my bedroom window and, with enough light from the moon, saw only the reddish-brown rectangles of brick and darkened windows across the courtyard, but the bursts of sound, like leather-bound fists punching at a thick and heavy boxing bag drew me out of bed. I went through darkness into the living room to a different view through three windows, a triptych of the city where its heart throbbed. Capstones of buildings pierced the sky and lights on the bridge led the way across the river like stars on a runway to an enchanted land. Across the leaves of trees, undulating like an ocean of dark foamy water, green-glowing lights of the Cathedral illuminated the turrets; and the silvery lighted Capitol, its galloping golden horses, front legs raised as if being lifted by wind in perpetuity, stood barely visible at the farthest end. To the south, the sky burst with fizzling silver sparklers, red licks of flame, showers of golden glitter, blue, green, pink fragments of jewels that leaped and soared toward me and emblazoned the ceiling of the city.

There came from behind me a padding, the skid and drag of Jada's slippered feet. She sat at the couch, looking out the center window while I sat on the floor, my chin on the sill, wanting to reach out with childlike greed to catch the treasures that seemed so abundantly free for the taking. Tugging at me was the suspicion that I had sleepwalked into this dream, spellbound at the mercy of such intense and instantaneous brilliance. "These are the most beautiful fireworks I've ever seen!" I whispered.

With a finale including a volley in quick and simultaneous succession, they were over. Though a part of me wanted them back, wanted them to go on longer, especially for Jada, deep underneath was the part that knew the brilliance was in its short life; and underneath even that was the part that took what it could, knowing that having more would make the wanting worse. We sat awake and quiet, clouds of gray smoky remains shriveling in the open sky. Stars, rare appearances on any night, pierced through the drifting haze, at first apparitions of the grandeur that was gone, then bolder, burning through crisp and strong. But the thought of such far-reaching brilliance coming from a life that once was lived got trapped in my mind with *The Little Prince*. I'd been living the knowledge of Jada's brilliance without understanding it.

Jada rose from the couch, and I followed her to her bed, sat by her, at first stroking her smooth feathery hair at her crown, then placing my hand on her shoulder, for whose solace I could not say. It's all about dying; everything is. I closed my eyes to keep the thought inside my head, not because it wasn't already out in the open: I just wasn't done with it yet. Fireworks. Stars, trees, Jada. My eyes burst open. The Little Prince must be out and about this night

Too late; the fireworks of Jada's life had been lit, and it was August, when we get our first taste of autumn. If the summer had been unusually dry or cold or wet or whatever extreme that went into the jam that made for our averages in Minnesota, leaves popped out in reds and yellows here and there among balls of green foliage, turncoats to the summer month remaining to be spent. Per said it was a sign of an unhealthy tree, but I thought it was nature's forewarning, a prank to remind us that life was not free. August was a month of duplicity, sneaking in that week of nippy wet winds like a splash of cold water in the face during a peak of heated passion: the days before going back to school could be counted.

Aug 9th

I spent yesterday at the hospital. My ovary is 6 cm round—still too large. It hurt when the MRI magnet pulled at my porta-cath. Now they can't do MRIs anymore. All this scan shit is a huge waste of my time anyway. They aren't finding out why I have a headache and I have important things to do before motoring off to MHC. I hate wasting my days! I am very pressed for time and have only 20 days to decide on some goals and what I want to achieve in the time I have left to live. I find it difficult to make decisions and latch onto something to look forward to. Mom and others and I have to organize plans for me to stay involved and make small accomplishments to get me to graduation. I don't think I'll have the stamina to get through the August treatment regimen with school starting. Tomorrow I go in for ARA-C and VP16. Watching a game show would be a better way to spend my time! I will feel shitty and out of it, too. Well, I'll ask Joe if he can think of a regimen that's not so intense while I'm at school. I don't think I have the physical and emotional ability for any treatment, ever again. I have to keep my goals of graduating or at least making it through the first semester being involved and having good times in perspective. It is difficult for me to think of returning to a "normal" life because I have to also accept that I am going to die in the near future. I do not want to waste my time feeling useless and alone in a hospital or at home. I want to go to parties, have fun, take trips, chair committees, and be involved in a loving and sexual relationship. I don't think many people understand my desire to go out with a bang, and the more I have to explain my life to others, the more sure I am. Pat and I talked this afternoon about my disease and my situation. He's a nice guy and would make a good friend if he were here.

I'm excited to drive my beemer to MHC. I have the route planned and Kimby and I are planning what to do and see on the way. We could see Kris Kiersen on the Cape if she's there on the 28th. And I'll ask Lana for information on where to stay near Chicago. I'd like to stop and see Karen in Boston, but she hasn't kept in contact lately. I guess when your life is going along smoothly you don't think to keep up with others.

That reminds me. Adam hasn't called or written to me since I left school last spring. He's on the Cape with friends and his girlfriend, so I don't know how to call him either. Not talking to him for so long makes me miss him as a boyfriend and maybe have a bone marrow transplant. I would like to live and be well. I have potential to give to the world. But I can't do it now and still go back to school. So it has to wait until I graduate.

I'm still bothered by how Kimby leads her life. I shouldn't do things with her if that's how I feel, but I need her friendship, just like I need Adam. I've been thinking of how I want things to work out. I'm going to keep a notebook of what I need to do to take care of my car. I'm also thinking of who is going to get my things. I want certain things to go to the right people. Like my journals. I want Mom to get my journals. I might allow Kimby to read them if she wanted to. I do not want to be buried. I want people to support MHC as long as it stays a women's college with money contributions. I also want people to contribute towards medical research to find better treatment and a cure for leukemia. I also love Adam and want him to know that and that I want to live partly for him. And one last thing before I die. I want to know where the cancer patients are. I don't ever see them at a store or the movies or driving about town! Just at the hospital or when I worked at the Cancer Society. I want some recognition for what I have accomplished and contributed to MHC. And one last thing is to make the medical leave

*condition to be more clear and better handled for other students.
Now I will try to go to sleep.*

Dom and his father had once stopped at MHC on their way to The Head of the Charles, but sharing Jada's space in her element? She hoped Kimby would.

"You're sure?" I questioned. "Should I go ahead and buy a ticket?"

"She said her dad has a frequent flyer ticket she can use. The only thing she's not sure of is if she's staying one day or two. Her classes don't start until a week after mine, and she wants to have some time at home."

"Great. But I'll believe it when I see it."

Jada's face donned a temporary scowl. "I know. But I told her I had to know. It's not fair to Ann not to let her make plans, but she said I could tell Ann not to plan to go. It was nice of her to offer."

"I've always liked Ann and her mother; they both seemed so understanding. Say, are you hungry? I bought some Kraft Macaroni and Cheese." Jada raised her eyebrows with interest, and I pulled out the clattery stove drawer for a pan. "Is she still at the U?"

"Yes. She sells cosmetics and works at some other job, too, now."

"That's a load. But you do what you gotta do. They don't have a bunch of money laying around." I leaned against the counter and waited for the trickle of water, more like a leak than an open faucet, to fill the pan.

"Mother. I can't believe you haven't got that fixed yet!" There was next to no pressure at the kitchen faucet, and little more elsewhere. An idiosyncrasy of an old building, though hardly charming, the sluggishly flowing water became as tolerable as the slamming windows and the cracked plaster.

"I'll work on it when you go back to school, is that a deal? Ann's pretty smart and practical. She will take care of herself."

"She was going to get married, but they broke up. I think she has a new boyfriend already, and she's living at home again."

"Good. Too young to get married. Especially when you're still in school. You've got enough things to take care of."

"That's what I think, too. Why would you want to miss the fun of being in college? You'd always have to be worrying about somebody else."

"Speaking of, when are you planning on leaving?"

"I want to get there as soon as I can get into my room. If I follow the route AAA gave me, I can take three days, see some things along the way, and stay in Boston one day. I can leave on either Friday or Saturday, and Kimby can still get home in time for Labor Day weekend and the start of her school." The woven canes in the chair squealed as Jada's knee shifted under her weight.

"Charge the rooms, and I'll pay for them. Take as much time as you need. It's safer driving when you're rested."

"I know. And you know Kimby. I'm sure she'll have a schedule of how long is the right time to drive and how much she has to rest."

I nodded, turning the knob on the stove. "Just don't let little things like that bother you. It'll be hard enough being together, all day and all night. If you allow extra time, you won't have to get excited about sticking to a strict schedule."

Jada sighed, "I'm trying to get her to say exactly how long she can take for the whole trip. Then I'll know how long she'll be able to stay at Mary Hillyard."

Everything was ready to go: the strainer, the butter, the box of macaroni. I punched in along the dotted line under the top flap, making the hard little macaroni tubes rattle in their box. "It sounds exciting, stopping along the way; what are you planning to see?"

"One place I want to go to is Niagara Falls. It's not that far out of the way. But the rest depends on Kimby; I want her to make some decisions, too. I'm going over there again tomorrow so we can look at the books. I've got an appointment for an oil change and a check-up for next week, too. I think it's close enough."

"That's smart. Sounds like you're all set. I'll miss you, but I want you to go."

"Me, too." After dinner we started packing. Once brought out, the suitcase lay open on the floor like a baby bird waiting for its mother to drop more food down its throat. Most of her school clothes and all the dorm supplies she had accumulated were stored in her dorm. All that was left were what she had brought home; the suitcase, slow to fill, served instead as a beckoning call to live out the rest of her summer.

Jada drove back and forth to Kimby's bringing along her guidebooks and maps through the middle and eastern states. She came home on Tuesday and leaned her body against the heavy unit door as if a magnet on the other side were pulling her to it. The sweater coat I was crocheting lay spread out on the table. "What's the matter? Are you okay?" I asked, holding the hook in place. The pattern was complicated enough without losing track of my place in the middle of a row.

"It's Kimby!" Jada heaved, propelled from the door to the chair. The jaws of a crane wouldn't have dropped her harder. "Now she wants to go on Sunday. That doesn't give us any time for Boston. She says she doesn't want to be away so long." Worry creeped over her face, and her eyes squinted as if she were examining a minute object.

"Sounds like you two have to compromise something."

"We always do. She never can just do something. Unless it's her way, the right way. Something's always wrong and she has to change it so it fits her way. Next thing she'll tell me is that she won't stay at Mary Hillyard. I mean, what does she have to hurry back for that she can't do now? And why is it okay for her to go away to Mexico but not out East?" Green shadows filled the hollows below Jada's eyes.

"You'll work it out. Just try to be patient and see what's really bothering her about this."

Jada simmered, and I went back to the pattern under my right elbow. Spreading my work out, I discovered a mistake and needed to rework rows I'd just finished; it didn't look like the sweater would make it into Jada's suitcase.

On Thursday I worked on the sweater, playing music, thinking of all the times Jada and I sketched, adapting from pictures in books or on the television screen, for me to sew, crochet, and knit. Jada had a lot of sweaters: winter was her preferred season, though she rarely went outdoors other than to get someplace indoors again. She had ice-skated, but that was mostly indoors, too, and year-round besides. She tried skiing, but only once. Still, she preferred winter, hard, clear, predictable: it was always cold; she had only to throw a sweater over everything. Maybe it was the sweaters, not winter, that she liked. Her most recent selection required a sequence of variously crocheted stitches, which was why I was still working on the back piece when Jada exploded into the dining room and shoved the door shut with a thud.

"Well, she did it!" Jada burst, her voice as thunderous as the slam of the door. Trouble brewed around her eyes, mottling red and gray, and white. "Kimby and I had a big fight. She's not going to drive out with me."

"What!" I dropped the hook and let it dangle from a loop. Sliding the chair backwards to stand with her, I asked. "What happened?"

"After all her promises and how this time she really meant it, she was really going, now she won't go until Monday. I told her Monday was too late. If we go on Monday, we won't even get there on Wednesday, let alone stop on the way for anything. She's a bitch! I can't believe it! And I knew what was coming next, too. Then she wasn't going to stay there either. I mean, what's the point?" Jada's voice rose to impassioned stiffness.

"There's got to be a reason for her to choose Monday. Did she give you one?" I folded my arms in front of me and pivoted to follow Jada, who had begun to pace, reliving the story with every step, releasing it when she stopped.

"Yeah. Wait till you hear this! Her grandparents are having a 50th wedding anniversary party in Schafer. She says she wants to go."

"Wants to go or has to go?"

"She told me she promised them. Promised them! When? Before she promised me? They must have known about this before now! She said, 'I can't break my promise to them.'" Jada pursed her face into a prune, wrinkled and tight, an exaggerated imitation. "So I said, 'What about your promise to me? Doesn't that count?'"

"Yeah, and?"

"And you know what? This will really get you!" Jada braced herself, whether it was for dramatic effect or that she couldn't stand the shock of it herself. "She said in her, her...I don't know, you know how she is, so right and so don't-be-so-stupid, and air-headed, she said, 'You know, Jada, it's their 50th wedding anniversary, and I don't know if I'll see them again!' Can you believe it? To me!

"So I said, 'Well, if it's so important that you see them now, why not go up there *this* weekend? You're not doing anything; if it's that important for you to see them, you could go up there and visit as much as you like. Who's stopping you?'"

"What did she say to that?"

"No, she couldn't do that because the *party* is *next* weekend! *She* has to go to the *party*, and *that's* next *week* when she *promised* to go to Massachusetts with *me*. She doesn't see it as a big deal. She thinks I should be able to just go on Monday and not get so excited." Jada's arms collapsed to her sides.

"I didn't trust it from the start!" I paced figure eights at the end of the table, thinking through the puzzle. "I bet her mother told her she had to go to Shafer. How would it look if she weren't there and all that." Nodding my head, I pictured Kimby pulling her lips together, like the wrinkles folded tight around a belly button, not the juicy pucker of the discriminating gourmand. "What I don't get is how she said she'd go with you in the first place if she knew this was coming up. Unless everyone else knew and she didn't. But that doesn't make sense. No, I bet she thought if she said yes to you, she could then talk you into moving it back."

Jada stood a stone pillar around which I gravitated. The final realization, that shiver that shakes your bones, that must shake you long and hard enough so that you not only know death has clamped its wormy fingers on you was what cemented her, a sadness that oozed from her pores, a sadness that came from a well deeper than I understood until she revealed the saddest part of all. "She says she still wants to go. But she says she wants to go to see her grandparents, too, 'because,' she said, '*they may not be around that long*,' and get this, she said, '*I should understand that!*'"

"Oh, my God!" Sweat rolled cold along the hairs of the small of my back. "What did you…what *could* you say to that?"

"I said a lot of things. I told her she doesn't know how to be a friend. I told her I was tired of always having to forgive her, that I put up with too much from her. She always said she'd be there for me; she *never* was there for me; friends don't do this to their friends. I told her what I thought of her and Daniel, too. She let him use her; he fucks other women. I told her that this was the last time, her last chance. I said if she doesn't go with me, we aren't friends, and that I never want to see her again."

Jada heaved air, spewing stored venom, releasing the extra weight of carrying Kimby around with her lightening her, one less burden to keep her feet bound to the earth. She seemed surprisingly careless, though absolutely resolute, about her expulsion.

"No, you aren't friends. I'm sorry, I'm so sorry. Well, I'll go with you. It won't be the same, but I'll drive with you to Mary Hillyard. She just doesn't get it, does she? I'm just so sorry you had to listen to such, such…."

"Selfishness! I'm sorry I wasted so much time on her! I don't know why I kept thinking she'd change. She kept promising. And she did get better at some things, finally. But she just wasn't worth the effort. And now, she gets to ruin one more thing for me."

"She ruined it for herself, too. Just be glad you aren't like her, small-minded and privileged, thinking she's roughing it with her swimming pool and her mother having to actually go to work, as a substitute librarian. What I want to know is, whose idea, that's all, whose idea this was." My imagination wove threads in and around conversations, constructing a complicated scheme.

"I was thinking," Jada looked calmly back, without the fury of her previous account. "I know it's not a very nice thing to do, telling Ann no and then asking her, but Ann said she'd go if Kimby wouldn't. I'm going to ask Ann if she'll still go with me. If she won't, then you can, okay?"

"Yes. I don't care to know ahead. Just tell me what you need and I'll make the arrangements."

"Thanks, Mom. You're the best Mooie!" Jada hugged my shoulders and walked to her room, her step light, bouncing. Returning in minutes, she said she was going to Ann's house to talk over plans for driving to Mary Hillyard. I picked up the crochet hook and nudged it through the loops, glad for the lukewarm breeze that swept up from the courtyard and through the kitchen windows, flouncing the lace at the metal rod, and finding me, bent over the table, in the dining room. I savored the warmth of the last few hours of the day, letting it swirl around inside my head where anything of consequence was treated as dust and not allowed to settle. The phone rang.

"Idina, this is Roberta." Kimby's mother's voice sounded perhaps as it would if she were selling seedlings for her garden club, gathered my thoughts from their disarray and yanked them into place. "We've got to do something. Jada was over here today, and she and Kimby had a huge fight. She said some things that upset Kimby. I think this thing has gotten way out of control. You'd better talk to Jada so we can salvage this." Each word jangled, awakening my ire, one key after another, up the row of notes on a xylophone.

"In the first place, Roberta, I don't think we should or can do anything. It's their business what they do, not ours. We can't tell them what to feel. In the second, I don't disagree with Jada. Jada had every right to be disappointed and angry with Kimby. She was counting on Kimby and she pulled out."

"But Jada said some terrible things to Kimby. You should have heard her. This is serious!"

"I can imagine. But Kimby broke a promise, and that sounds pretty serious to me and deserving serious words."

"But, Idina, you don't understand. Kimby's been committed to Jada all these years, and now I don't think she'll be able to remain a friend unless we do something." I remembered the urgency to explode, to get rid of the pressure, but I had already gone cold; I was learning to be a cat, to wait, and in the waiting, to be still. Roberta said, quietly, as if her words were wrapped in a brown paper bag, "You should have heard what Jada said."

"I don't need to know what Jada said. You would say as much or more if your so-called best friend went back on a promise, maybe the last promise she could make. And for what? *Maybe* seeing her grandparents for the last time? *Maybe!* You know, it doesn't matter, it just doesn't matter what Jada said to Kimby. The point is, Kimby was not being a friend. What kind of a friend backs out on something as serious as this? It isn't just that Jada was counting on Kimby; it isn't just that Jada lost a driving partner. Kimby did more than break a promise; she treated Jada as if she doesn't matter; her campus, her last trip out, her plans for what she has left: they're nothing, they don't matter. There might be a next time for Kimby, but there won't be for Jada. Now, you tell me, would you want a friend like that? I don't think Kimby ever was a friend. She just wanted it to look that way."

The sound of a tidal wave engulfed me: it was Roberta's gasp. "Idina! You don't mean that! Kimby made a decision to be devoted to Jada!"

"Breaking this promise doesn't sound very devoted to me. Sounds more like a smokescreen to Kimby's advantage, not Jada's. The thing is, Jada's had enough—or should I say, Jada doesn't have enough time to have any more. I told you, this is their business, and it sounds to me like they've taken care of it."

"You're not making any sense! If we don't do something, this will be the end of their friendship."

"No, Roberta. I make sense. You just don't like what I'm saying. You want me to step in and control what Jada feels and says and does. Maybe you can do that with Kimby, but I can't and

I wouldn't and I won't with Jada. They're adults, and even if they weren't, they decide if it's over, not me."

"Oh, Idina." Roberta's plea echoed. "I can't talk to you. Good-bye."

"Goodbye," I said, I think, to dead space, feeling remarkably comfortable, as if, perhaps, after a bout of bloating I had eliminated the bulk or, at once grievous over the amputation of a limb, that done, enables the saving of a life.

Jada came home and announced that everything was set with Ann. "She's really excited to go. She's taking a couple days off work," Jada said as she drew nearer, unreeling her plans.

"Great. Do you know when you'll go?"

"She doesn't care; she'll go anytime. I'm bringing the books over there and we'll decide. It'll be more fun, too." Jada hovered, watching me weave the crochet hook in and out, winding wool around my fingers, twisting it in and around itself. "Ann likes to do things. She won't get too tired and have to go to bed or want to just sit in the hotel room like Kimby did in Hawaii."

"Roberta called me while you were gone. She wanted me to talk to you about your fight with Kimby. Actually, she wanted me to make you change your mind. I told her I wouldn't do that. And, anyway, I said I agreed with you."

Jada looked away briefly from following the pattern I was creating. "She called Dad, too. I went there after I went to Ann's. She told him you were being unreasonable. She wanted him to talk to you. Dad thought she was carrying this a little too far. He said, 'What do you want me to do about it? I'm not married to her anymore.' He said she was a little wacko. And, you know Dad; he doesn't want to be bothered."

"Why is Roberta involved, anyway? If your friendship matters so much to Kimby, why isn't Kimby making any calls? Well, it's too bad, anyway."

"No, it isn't. It's been going on for years. Kimby has always acted that way. We fight over it all the time. And every time *I* make up with *her*, and every time she promises to get better. I'm glad it's over. She's got one of my videos, though. I'll have to call her and get it back."

On the last Saturday in August, before the sun mustered enough strength to burn off the dew blanketing the grass, Ann's mother drove into our parking lot to the canopied entrance where Jada and I opened the trunk of her beemer and fed it two suitcases and a brown plastic bag, puffed up like a balloon and wrung shut with a twist tie. Ann took her two bags of luggage out of the car, and I fit one next to Jada's, put the other in the back seat. Phyllis crept onward, and I backed out of the car, saying "Do you want to park and see them off?"

Phyllis leaned her head out the window, her hand on the steering wheel. "No. I'll be going now. You two have a nice trip." Phyllis's eyes had the natural tendency to water, as if they were two bobbins that floated in a lake, and I couldn't tell, as Ann bent down to kiss her mother, if she was smiling or crying.

"Got everything?" I asked, trying to figure out my own emotions at this leave-taking. Jada was going to where she wanted to go; I expected Per to return from Montana that same night. Life was going on. So I continued, happy, "Got your maps? Got your money? Got your underwear?"

"Yes, Mother." Jada took quick little hops to the driver's side and amplified a sigh at my silliness.

"Well, then, let me get one last picture. Where's your camera?"

"Oh, Mom." She said and reached into the front seat.

"You love it, and you know it." I stepped backwards toward the bushes, the camera to my eye.

"Watch her try to take a picture," Jada said to Ann at the other side of the car, the front door cocked open, one foot perched on the frame, ready to board. "She gets down on her knees, and then she gets only part of you anyway." Jada chuckled through a wide smile that gleamed from underneath the shady brim of her baseball cap. "See?" she grinned back at Ann, her white teeth flashing little spears of sunlight as she swung her face back toward the camera's lens. "C'mon, Mooie. We want to get out of here today, you know. Take the picture."

"Okay. One more, just in case."

"I'm getting tired of smiling; how about you, Ann?" Jada tipped her head just a bit to squint her twinkling eyes over her sunglasses. I encased the camera and walked toward Jada who was about to step into the car.

"Wait," said Ann. "I'll take one of the two of you." She formed words the same way as her mother, each one distinct and unhurried. We stood at the car, our arms hooked around each other, Jada and I, and smiled at Ann who snapped quickly. I held onto Jada a second longer, kissed her forehead and squeezed her at the waist. We kissed each other on the cheek before I released her for good.

"Okay, schmay, we're off," Jada said over the roof of the car to Ann, herself disappearing into the vehicle.

"Have a safe trip. Call me when you get in today."

"Yes, yes," Jada said, folding her body into the car. Her slender fingers grabbed the metal flange and latched the seatbelt in place.

"Love you. And take your time," I added, my hands guiding the door shut.

"We will. Bye, Mooie!" She started the car.

"Good-bye," I called to the rolling car. The sun burst over the roof of the building as I followed Jada and Ann onto Northern Avenue. I waved behind them, stepping now and then as if keeping up in a faltering parade, until they were gone, out of sight, disappearing into the future. Then I stopped. There had to be more than a kiss and a wave. This was just too easy. Living afterwards? That will be hard.

"Stick 'em up!" shouted a man from a pickup truck as I walked a cool-down with my arms raised in the air. I laughed; an hour later Jada and I hung up the telephone, and I wanted to cry. I sat at the dining room table in my running shorts, the salty grit coating my skin, wondering if my feet felt anchored to the floor from running in the heat-saturated September afternoon or if they had been cast in the cement of wrong answers. I couldn't get up to put the phone back in place. I couldn't get up to shower. I felt I'd been dragged down through the murky river, sunk to the muddy bottom, and stuck there, every cell starved of air, fighting not to open my nostrils and my mouth. I could no longer hold my breath, and the craving to breathe was stronger than the will to live. The phone rang again. I thought it was Jada. It happened that way sometimes. I sat, anchored, knowing I had to give in, pick it up, answer it, let the water gush into my lungs. It didn't feel that bad.

But it was Beverly. "I was thinking of you and had a strong urge to see how you're doing."

"Not well!" I unleashed the hold on my bloated emotions. "How did you know to call now? I can't seem to do the right thing." I ran on and on with all I was doing wrong, misunderstanding, knowing I was leaving sentences unfinished, people unnamed, places and times out of order; but that was just it. I was as confused and disjointed in telling Beverly as I had been hearing Jada. My not grasping the suspected politics she spilled out to me made me suspect. All I knew was that ever since Jada had returned to Mary Hillyard, she had not woven herself back into college life, had hit one snag after another. Or maybe it was all one snag and the whole skein needed to be ripped out.

"Whatever it is," I said, "I don't get it. It's like my brain can't sort and categorize and put things in their places. I can't understand what's going on, and I don't say the right thing to her. I ask too many questions, looking to make sense, and she says she's told me already, but I don't remember that she told me, and I know all that's important to her, but I don't seem to get it. She thinks I'm arguing when I'm trying to get it straight. But if I don't talk, if I just listen, she says I don't care. I just make things worse every time we talk."

Beverly directed words to me like a guided missile pinning the phone to my ear. "Listen to me. You're not making things worse. You have a strong instinct about Jada. You know her. You can't let yourself doubt what you're doing. Do you hear me? I want you to know that. You're doing what you're supposed to be doing. She's counting on you. Don't let her down. Do you understand that?"

"But I do all the time. We never get to finish talking. I don't know what to think. Here I am, going on with my life, and it's all so meaningless next to hers. I feel selfish for being able to do things, for running, for seeing Per. For living. It's like she's trying to tell me something and I can't hear her or understand what she's talking about."

"She doesn't know, either, sometimes. Don't give up. You're the right thing for Jada. If you ever doubt that again, I want you to call me. I don't care what time of day or night. Do you hear me? Keep doing the things you need to do. And don't feel guilty about them. But call me!" Beverly spoke to me in a voice that reminded me of Jada's, soft without being weak, feminine without being thin; she was clear and poised, and she was sure. I wondered if brainwashing started like this.

"Okay," I agreed. My feelings had been batted about enough in just the telling, and it felt so good to stop, like the release of laughter to the passerby's mock holdup. "Thanks, Beverly. How do you know I need you when I need you?"

"I just had this strong sense that I needed to see how you were." Beverly's voice faded. I realized that I had been rubbing my forehead, covering my eyes with my hand, and after the blackness of my eyelids yielded to a spotty haze, the table at which I sat came into focus. I stretched my arm out and wanted to follow it, lie down and fall asleep.

"You're wonderful."

"Thank you. Are you okay?"

"Yeah. Just tired. You know, Beverly? All that talk about getting what you can handle? It's bullshit. I can't do this; it's too much." If Beverly had countered, said yes I could, I don't know if I'd have cried or screamed or just hung up. But Beverly agreed in her soft purring way, that, yes, it was too much, and that was enough, just enough, to go on. "Thanks for calling," I said, my brain too weary of holding onto one more thought about what could lay ahead. I closed my eyes and, rubbing around them, let another thought flourish, fill up the brain space with how alike were these two women, Jada and Beverly, who were so different. They both spoke from another realm, light years removed from me. They were like air and water reaching my rootedness in the earth.

Sept. 27th

I just talked to Mom and she helped me break out of my depression about all the things worrying me. I stress over homework and committee work and think I have to get them all done immediately. I feel people watching me and I think they are waiting for me to fuck up. But Mom said how good I was at what I am doing and that I don't have to set up a test to prove that to myself. Others like me, she said. I have to calm down and not push myself so hard. Here's where a boyfriend would come in handy. He'd help me through the bad feelings I have. I'd like one to show up soon so I could obsess over him instead of me! Pam says I'm always eating chocolate—a sure sign I need a boy friend and NOW!!

My life is full of crappy things I have to do and so many fun things I would like to do but will never have the chance. It is hard to accept my abilities and limitations. Getting married is one I really want. But that's a life over the rainbow. People think I'm bananas for wanting marriage but they don't get my situation. God! It's hard to motivate myself when I think of my conditional life. I went to the Berthe Morisot video showing last night. I saw Sharon and Jim at the reception afterwards. He remembered me and invited me to see him in Boston. I think he was serious because he gave me his card. So I think I will after the conference is over.

My grades won't be good this semester. As a matter of fact, I failed my math exam. I'm trying to not let those things stress me too much and take things as they come. My grades don't matter as much now. Maybe I should take fewer classes and get away some. I'm going to Lucy and Fred's in D.C. for fall break. I hope to see some of my favorite French Impressionist paintings at the National Gallery. And maybe visit Cheng in his apartment by the zoo. I started up Math Club again. We're working on having a volleyball game, math movies, and lectures. I want us to get information on internships and careers. I'm pumped! I have to admit that Mom is right. I do make a good leader and I'm good at getting things done. A few better committee members would help us along! I have to talk with Lynn about Parents' Weekend because I think she screwed me over. Registrations has problems because they got started before I was involved and now more and more flub-ups have accumulated. I have to talk with Adam too because I feel guilty that he has to make a sacrifice to get me to chemo. I have to arrange for everything and I don't even want the fuckin' shit!

September and my ineptness with Jada grew into October, a favorite month for me. Jada would have liked October more if she didn't suffer from the fall allergens. The dry musty leaves that marred autumn for Jada were the ones I loved to kick around as I walked. I breathed in the fruity air before it absorbed the chill of night. I drowned in the violent colors of fall—in the sky, in the leaves, in the final petals of the last hardy flowers. Vivacious pink, red, and violet stream across the glory of the setting sun; an iridescent orange moon studs the indigo evening sky; flaming crimson leaves strut among an orange, yellow, and green backdrop of plush foliage. How ironic that a perfect tree, a perfect day, a perfect pansy, is the dying breath of a lived life.

As each autumn blossomed and the winds scattered leaves to the ground, school started and a part of me was reborn. Whether I owed homage to the season and transferred it to the schoolroom or whether my discovery of a new life by schooling electrified the autumn season went deeper than reason. They both became religious, like the mingling of the Body and Blood of Christ, inseparable in sacrifice and in glory.

Going to Mary Hillyard in the fall intensified the spirit that moved through me. Massachusetts in the spring, though it throbbed life, effusing splashes of oversized pink and white flowers, trickled to predictability. But going to Mary Hillyard in the fall was like being saved, the trip itself a pilgrimage, this fall, the fall of 1989, myself a living prayer to the sanctity of Jada's purpose. Jada met me at the airport and led me, walking, no, gliding, above ground, toward her parked car. I deposited my suitcase in the trunk and got in the passenger side of Jada's shiny black beemer and felt I was entering a holy temple. She looked so peaceful, so serene, as if she weren't just a mortal exiting a busy parking lot.

Jada drove away from the curb like she'd spent half a career on making connections and meeting deadlines. She had perfected the art of doing business while driving, talking in my direction, giving the illusion of full attention to me while never letting her eye leave the roadway. She had a bed for me, as promised, her bed; she'd sleep at Priss's, and she ticked off an itinerary for me. Jada swerved into her parking place, carefully, but with just enough flair to show she'd found the limits. She was out of my class.

She and I were to drop off Hambone at Priss's while, at the same time, picking her up to meet Sharon at the trendy new restaurant in Goodrich. Inside were jungle-sized green plants surrounded by a glass dome. Though chilly outside, I was warmed by the scrunched-together tables and Spartan stumpy candles that illuminated them. We huddled toward each other and talked of school and young people and men and love. Sharon, the dean of students, was engaged to marry Jim, Priss was hot in a relationship with Will, Sharon's former flame, I was divorced and afraid to get burned again, and Jada was a tinder box looking for her lifetime love. We told a story at that table.

In the morning was the President's address, made traditionally in the amphitheater. The weak autumn sun not warming the morning hours, I shivered with damp hair and a light denim jacket, though Jada wore simply a black sweater and beige pants, tied smartly together with a black and brown belt. She sat with the rest of the Family Weekend Committee, just a few rows in front and to the left of me. When the president of the college called for audience recognition of the committee, they stood, Jada with them, and she turned her head back to me and smiled, a gesture I likened to a tip of the hat. I lined my sight on the women and focused on her, the sun's light skipping off the edges of her wispy hair, and clicked the camera. Just looking at her was relaxing, in contrast, I thought, to all of September. I had the sense that it was more than just the wading through the politics that motivated her contentment. I swelled proud that she didn't give up on herself. I treasured the privilege of being witness to Jada in her element.

The president of the college, unofficially referred to as Liz by the undergrads, shook my hand warmly and spoke glowingly of Jada's contributions to the committee's work. The reception hearkened back to my first visit, when I had been greeted as though everyone were eager for my appearance. Other bejeweled women, smelling expensive and backed up by men in cashmere, were introduced to me as though I had an endowment cached in my pocket. I had; it was Jada, whom many had met and who stood by my side, teasing me between glad-handing officers of the alumnae association. We stood united and happy to be there, me, a little scrappy with my SuperAmerica running watch and cheap sunglasses, outside on the dewy grass, cool, even though the sun was beating as hard as it could.

Adam found us meandering the children's carnival on the green, ducking the overhanging shade for sunlight. Children yelped as they chased runaway balloons down the grassy slope; their hands enveloped by adults, they trotted alongside their parents, twisting their heads to see a painted face different from their own, to follow another balloon escaping skyward. Clumps of people roamed like camouflaged trees in slow formations. I shivered, and Adam bravely gave his leather jacket to Jada, saying he could take this weather fine without it, leaving a thin cotton shirt to wrap around his wiry arms.

In return, Jada handed him her camera with the request that he snap a picture of the two of us. Jada and I stepped ahead of the tree's shadow and hugged each other in the yawning sun, glad to share our heat. Her head caught the glint of light, her sparse hair glittering in the sunshine around it. It seemed as if the sun had been following her about all day, and I, standing in her shadow, snatched a piece of her light. I smiled toward the camera; and underlying my smile was a twinge of sadness, this time for the crowning weekend, her last on Family Weekend Committee. But the bunched-up fallen yellow and orange and red leaves that rustled like the fluttering feathers of birds taking off in flight and the bald-headed moon that glared in the other side of the sky glorified our communion beyond mere sadness. I didn't want her to have this cup engraved with her name, would have gladly traded it for one with mine, but if it was to be, I would sip the sweet with the bitter.

Ahead of us was dinner with other families at a Chinese restaurant, a multicultural festival, a dance performance, before I departed, but our goodbye was here on the green. It took, like the others, its own bite. And like the others, this goodbye had all the other goodbyes inside it. She had her beemer. She had made her executive mark. She was staying on at Mary Hillyard, a trade for another chance at living longer. I might have wanted otherwise, yet because I loved her so fiercely, I wanted exactly what she had chosen. Jada had freed herself and me from the ties of dependency and taken the reins of womanhood.

Family Weekend over, so was the planning and the anticipation that propelled Jada's energy and occupied her time. Men's names were staggered in Jada's telephone conversations like game pieces on her playing board. There was Patrick in Duluth. She and he were friends from high school and began to write to each other, making plans to see each other in December when both were home on break. There was Bill. He went to Williams and would be happy if she drove there for a football game. There was Randy. He took the same math class with her at Goodrich and studied with her. She had had her fun at parties; she had flirted with pleasure and kissed with desire. Now she wanted a lasting love. Now she wanted the next thing.

I worked at my schoolwork, scattered about the table, picking at papers and folders and books as a kid would a plateful of peas and carrots. I wanted to get them all over and done with so the evening would be clear, but I could stomach them only one at a time. When the phone rang, I picked it up with a mixture of frustration and relief.

"Hi, Mooie. I made up my mind about Thanksgiving. I decided that, because I'm coming home for the conference, I'll go to New York with Jenny. Then it won't cost so much money, either."

"Jada, don't worry about the money. Just do what you want to do."

"I know, but sometimes it's hard to think. I don't want to miss your good food, but I want to see New York, too. Sometimes I get all mixed up and I forget what I'm supposed to be thinking of. So I finally just said yes." I listened, hearing again but noting it consciously for the first time, how Jada talked of being confused. She added, "Besides, there might be a man out there."

"Maybe there'll be one here when you come home in December." I had delivered her airplane tickets when I visited her at Family Weekend and was proud that Dr. Lourde had invited her to speak at a medical conference to people who crafted policy.

"Will you call the clinic for an appointment?" Jada sounded groggy.

"Didn't you do that already?"

"Maybe; I can't remember. I keep forgetting things. Well, call and see."

"Yes. I have it all figured out for the conference. If you can get up and drive me to school in the morning, you can have the car, and I'll take the bus. Have you thought about what you're going to say?"

"I have, but when I sit down to write, I can't get it out. You have to help me with it. I don't want to do it now," she added as a warning.

"Okay. Make a list or something; when you come home, I'll see what you have."

"I'm really tired, Mom. Call me tomorrow, okay?"

"Sure, Dollie. Love you." I put the phone into its cradle and decided I was tired, too.

"Okay, okay, I'm coming. Hello?"

"Hi, Mooie."

"Hi, Sugar Plum. I'm still dripping on the rug; can you wait a minute until I get my robe on?" I grabbed the lotion, too. "Okay, Jada, I'm back." Before I flipped the nozzle and tipped the bottle, I listened; she hasn't been back to school for a week, but she called every day, and every day there was another outbreak of something: this must be how the first reports in an epidemic start.

"Oh, Mooie; I don't know what I'm doing."

"Is it your math again?" Was I too light, too casual, as if this were a complaint made by an air-headed freshman fishing for compliments, not the mourning of an aficionado over the sedimentation in a bottle of vintage wine?

"I can get it right when I work on it with someone, but it gets all mixed up when I do it in my notebook. I know the formulas, but everything is all wrong."

Shivering, though my skin feels warm from the shower, I asked, "Have you talked to the professor?"

"He's really nice about it. At first he wrote red all over everything; now he writes in my notebook and tries to explain. My partner and I work on some problems together. I just can't get it to stick. It's weird because I can understand, but I can't do."

"I'm sorry, Jada. That must make you sad. You've never given up. Do you think it's the medication?"

"I don't know. I think the instructor writes his long explanations because he doesn't want me to feel bad. He knows I'm not getting it because there's something wrong on everything, but he's not making me feel like I have to keep up, either."

Whatever was supposed to sound crisp in the clock on my bookshelf made a slogging noise, slurring consonants like a drunkard. "How about that other instructor, the woman you're doing independent study with? Can she help?"

"Gabriella. She does. I go to her house, and I play with her kids. Sometimes she looks at me, and I get the feeling that she's watching me, like I'm acting weird or something." Jada paused;

before I know what to say, she said, a melancholy lilt slowing her words down, "I can't think anymore."

"Is it only math, or do you feel that way other times? You sound like you know what's going on."

"Oh...." The word trailed off to silence, a long wailing train whistle moving farther and farther away, "I don't know. I'm tired. I just can't get my math. I know it's hard anyway, but.... I have so many other things to do. Did I tell you? I'm going to Williams on Saturday."

"No, what for?" Behind my clock were two hearts, molded hand-made paper, bought and framed to hang in the center of my wall, which I hoped to fill with as many images of women that would fit. Already I had one of Jada's sketches, a full sneery-lipped and blubbery woman whose breasts look like Nerf footballs, easy to grab onto and resiliently jelly-filled, except they have long eraser-tip nipples attached to them. Underneath them are folds of fat, one tier overhanging another. I love the gestures, a practice drawing with lines drawn and redrawn. The drawing was, appropriately, mammoth.

Jada picked up her voice slowly, like starting to play a record from the off position with the needle in place. "Remember that guy, Bill? He invited me to come to one of their football games."

I brightened and felt I was catching up to speed myself. "That'll be nice. Who else is going?"

"No one. It's not really a date, but I'm working on it. I'm driving there for the game only, but I hope he asks me to stay for something else."

"How are you about driving back at night?" I tried not to sound too watchful and listened carefully.

"It's not that far. It would be better if someone went with, but if no one wants to go, I'm going alone." I wondered if I should remind her to buckle up. "I have to go now. I'm supposed to get food ready for tea. We're going to have the apples and dip. Call me tomorrow night at um, 6, between 6 and 6:30, okay, Mooie?"

"I can do that. By the way, Hon, uhh...never mind. Okay, bye. Love you."

Frost had layered everything in white, but snow was slow to follow; the ground was rock hard underfoot. On a clear sunny Saturday morning in mid-November, Per and I each ran our own pace through the trails that weave and crisscross the vast land in the Highland Park Reserve. I finished much earlier and sat in the Trooper, letting the sun penetrate the glass and warm my fleecy pullover. My journal open on my lap, I resisted writing, wondering at an uneasiness creeping through my body, a slow jog that made me shift restlessly, and studied the trees for Per to emerge. *Damn; why am I wasting this time? Jada's been bugging me to write, but I don't.* I grazed the tree line, squinting at each threshold as if, once crossed, it swallowed him whole, and now I wished it to spit him out. I checked my $9.99 watch one more time and looked up. It runs fast, so I'm not sure if he's five minutes late or ten minutes late; but I knew, because I could feel it, that he was not on time.

Then Per appeared, his elbows out on each side as if clearing his way through a pack, pitching forward from descending the crest of a stubby hill. I relaxed my muscles, but I felt no weight lifted, no baled up puff of air rushed from my chest. Danger, it seems, lurked not here, so why was I so jumpy, so wired with fear and foreboding? I didn't forget to call Dom this morning; the iron, the coffee pot, I'd left neither on. Yet I wanted to go home; something was pulling me home. It pulled like a calling: I could almost hear it. The urgency I had for Per to appear was not for him; I was being called home.

The leaves from the trees had long since changed their colors and lay brown and brittle, wasted on the brown earth. When the autumn rains pelted them, they turned to mush and the winds couldn't scrape them from the ground. They wait for snow to smother them. We drove along a road that snaked through faded grasses, once golden, then beige, the color of a well-worn carpet; and clods of hardened brown earth, some sprouting spindly shoots like candles on a cake, and bowing out around old brick houses and barns that cave in at their centers, stood humbly against encroaching developments.

Per loved to discover himself on a road he had never been on and studied the road map he held just above the steering wheel so he could read it and drive simultaneously, looking for a gray line road he'd never traversed. There were no untraveled roads left for him in this section, so he drove lazily along a ridge, cursing the suburbs' greedy hunger for land and checked the map one more time just in case he'd overlooked a way out. The Talking Heads played "Take me to the river...." It was a perfect setting for releasing the seat and staring out the window at the valley that dropped away from the pavement outside my car door.

Instead I fidgeted, fought an urge to jump out of the car and run into the valley away from the taunting, away from my nervousness. In sixth grade, Barb Walker invited me to Excelsior Park. Together we were latched into the rollercoaster, and off we climbed. Higher and higher and all I wanted was to jump out; I screamed to let me out, and Barb said, "Twenty seconds, that's all the longer this ride takes is twenty seconds." All my strength squeezed the bar down, not up, counting the twenty seconds. So high. So fast. So steep. Twenty seconds, Barb said. She kept me from jumping.

But I wasn't afraid of the height here, or the speed, the car. A vision appeared to me like a smoldering tinder that finally hits flashpoint and erupts brilliantly into flame. I saw the envelope and the unpaid bill I threw into the desk drawer. I thought there was just a lag between mailings. I had paid the premium, plus an additional amount explained as an error on the agent's part. I had forgot the bill.

The image burned everything else away, like the morning sun clearing fog. The message that the money was due and payable immediately leapt out at me in threatening bold black print. I had named my fear. Something was wrong, something about the beemer was urgent.

"Do you want to stop and pick up something to eat?" Per asked, his voice loud and jarring. It irritated me that he conversed over music, and I turned the volume down, sighing heavily.

"No. I want to get home. We must have something to eat there."

"How about the leftover pasta from last night? I'd eat that."

"Let's just get home." There, I walked quickly, way ahead of Per along the hall to my unit, the gold numbers 607 nailed on the louvered door. I heard the phone ring once, then, unlocking the door, a second time. Bumping my hip on the corner of the hutch, I interrupted the third ring.

"Hi, it's me," Arnold's voice had a familiar gritty sound. "Jada's been trying to get you all morning, so she called and asked me to try." He took a long breath. "Now, don't get excited. She's okay. But she's been in a car accident and wants you to call her right away. She was pretty upset when I talked to her."

"Was she hurt? Where is she?" The door behind me swung open, the knocker making a flapping sound, as Per came in.

Arnold cleared his throat, but his words retained the same graininess, like sand on spinach that hasn't been thoroughly rinsed. "She was taken to the hospital, but she's not hurt. They checked her over and sent her back. You better talk to her yourself."

Per was in the bathroom running a tubful of water. We lived like commuters in separate cities, he at his rented apartment in an old refurbished house on Frey during the week, spending Friday and Saturday nights at mine. In my bedroom the answering machine blinked at me, one, two, three times. Before dialing Jada's number, I played the three messages, Jada's tiny voice pleading with me to be home. I broke inside. I wasn't where she needed me, when she was scared, hurting, anxious, as I was.

Jada answered her phone, and I pictured her as a throbbing mouse clutched by the claws of a mauling cat. Escape is out of the question, but so is a swift end. She began telling her story in trembles. Her speech was weak, mumbly. "I was on my way to

Williams, and I changed lanes. I didn't even see them. I went right in front of them and hit them."

"Were you hurt? Are you okay?" My stomach rose as I imagined her spinning car, wondering how long it took for her to come to a stop. Long enough for her to have thoughts: many of them, or just one?

"No, but I was kind of hysterical, crying and screaming. As soon as they saw what I looked like, they took me to a hospital in an ambulance. They took X-rays and examined me and said I was okay. But my car. They towed my car away."

"We can always get the car fixed. As long as no one was hurt, that's what really matters."

"No. The people I hit were so nice. They were a family, a mother and father and their little girl. They tried to calm me down. I'm going to write to them and thank them. I feel terrible. My car."

"I'm sure you do. It's Saturday, so we won't be able to get anything going until Monday." I felt like crawling under the blankets and hiding. The back-and-forth long-distance arrangements seemed as daunting as if I'd have to run them on foot.

"I didn't even see the other car. I was on my way to the football game and all of a sudden I ran right into it. It was my fault.... I got a ticket for negligent driving."

"Oh, well, those things happen, too. That's why they're called accidents. And if no one is hurt, you're lucky."

"I'm sorry. I feel terrible. I didn't mean it."

"Of course not. Jada, if you're worried about me, don't be. I'm disappointed for you, but it will all work out. It'll just take some time. Are you okay now? Do you need to still talk? I don't want to let you go if you still need to talk."

"I'm okay, sleepy. They gave me something to calm me down and it's making me very sleepy. Just so you're not mad." She spoke slowly, lacking inflection.

"There's nothing to be mad about. Whatever comes will work out. I just want you to be okay."

"Okay, Mooie. I'm going to take a nap now. Pam said she'd come and stay with me for a while. Call me tomorrow."

"Okay, Darlin'. I love you."

"Bye, Mooie."

We stood around the metal-covered shelf of the Hoosier, extended all the way to display platters, and I named them as if leading a tour, the flourish of my hand stopping at each steaming dish, ending with a tradition that made our holidays, a bowl of rigatoni for Dom. One without the other was like the Fourth of July without fireworks. Or Jada. And even in her absence, I roasted a turkey, though I'd never mastered the bird, because, along with my dad's family's immigrant dishes, my mother also carried through with American fare. I took a slice of white meat in Jada's honor.

Still, I smiled, happy for her in New York, seeing the Thanksgiving parade in person, though unhappy she was not with us, filling our plates to sit at a bounteous table set for three. Dom and Per took places diagonally from each other, talking food and football, and I accepted praises for pleasing their palates and noticed the empty spot at the table, glad Jada called before dinner, where she was missed. I wished I had something less solitary than washing dinner's dishes to crowd out thoughts in my brain while Dom and Per raised an objection over the call made in the football game on television. Nevertheless, the familiarity of that tradition comforted, like steaming kitchen windows, stacking China and layering the silver; as darkness sifted through the cloudy window panes, I realized I had survived.

The linens had been wadded up and tossed next to the washing machine, ready for laundering, but assorted forks and saucers strewed the Hoosier shelf, reminders of last night's Thanksgiving dessert, pumpkin pie for Dom. Had Jada been here, I would have had another, apple or cherry, her request, my favor. I shivered and wrung my hands together, the skin dry with crepe papery wrinkles except for my fingers swollen from being too long in soapy dishwater; my fingernails had recovered, hard and thick again. I hated mornings after holidays: they're cold and they echo.

The phone rang. It was the third time Jada had called since arriving at Jenny's, and she spoke from a tomb, unable or unwilling to spark a sign of life. "Aren't you two getting along?"

"Yes," Jada answered breathily. "Jenny and I agree about everything. Her family's very nice. They'll do anything for me. I just wish I hadn't come."

"Are you doing enough things or going places?" I asked as if I hadn't already been told about Macy's Thanksgiving parade yesterday.

"Yes, they've always got something planned. We're gong to a football game tomorrow morning. That's not it. It's me. I just don't want to be here."

"I'm having a hard time hearing you." She sounded like she were stuffed among the coats in a closet.

"I can't talk loud; I don't want them to think anything's wrong."

"Oh, I know how that is, having to stick it out when you don't want to. I could cook up some reason to get you home. You could have the rest of the weekend here."

"I can't do that. I'll be okay. If I could just talk to you more often. But I can't keep calling you up all the time; they'd know something was wrong. They said I can call you as often as I want. But I don't want to hurt them. They're really so nice."

"What if I call you. Will that help?"

"I guess so. Only don't say anything about why you're calling. I don't want them to know."

"Of course not. I'll just say I need to talk to you. And don't worry about calling; just reverse the charges."

"I know. But that isn't it. I just wish I was home with you. And you could hold me."

"I miss you, too. It was strange not having you here. But, just remember, you love adventure."

"Not this one. I didn't think I'd miss you so much."

"Sugar plum, you can still come home. Catch the next flight."

"I can't do that. They're doing everything they can for me. I better go now."

"Okay; I love you, Jada."

"Love you, too, Mooie."

I called the next morning, hoping to get Jada before they left on their expedition. A woman with the voice of pancakes and sausages for breakfast, dishes done, and a pie baking in the oven answered the phone. She was doing something else while she talked, but she attended to me as if I were all that was going on. "Oh they're having a good time," she percolated. "Jenny's brother has a football game this morning, and they've gone to that. Then they're going to the shopping center for some marshmallows and things. We're going to have a little roast around the grill tonight if it's not too cold, the fireplace if inclement weather forces us indoors. Jada's a lovely person. She's so polite, and she and Jenny get along so well. They're having a wonderful time. We just love having her."

"Thank you for hosting her. Would you tell her I called, and that if she gets a chance, she can call me later. I hope it's not a bother; anytime will do. I just need to talk with her; I miss her."

"Oh, no bother at all," she said, her words like chimes in a doorbell. "I understand. I'll let her know as soon as they get in. It really promises to be a lovely afternoon here. We've been so fortunate with the weather for them to get outside."

"How lucky. It's been nice here, too. Thank you again for having Jada."

"We're glad we could. She's such a beautiful child. Jenny told us that she asked her to play the cello at her memorial service. We were very moved by that."

"Oh." My voice caught at the mention of an imagined event as if the date were set, unmoved and unmovable. "Jenny must be wonderful, too."

"Yes, we think so."

"Well, tell Jada I called. There's nothing urgent, but we're used to talking to each other."

"Yes, I'll do that. Take care now."

The lethargy that dragged through her voice in New York slithered like a snake underneath her bravado when Jada returned to Mary Hillyard. I'd felt like a piano had fallen when my insurance agent said the claim would be handled by an agent out East, relieving me, but dropping the load onto Jada. Filling out forms and making persistent phone calls fit more with her style than mine, but she seemed to be getting the runaround, toiling through back claims and congested systems.

Dec. 3rd

Yesterday's chemo was rotten! I threw up 3 times and still feel terribly weak and sick. I couldn't go to classes today because of that wicked ARA and V16. My poor baby beemer is stranded in another lot. It's probably crying for me like I am for it. I feel like it's another sign that my life is crumbling into a heap of rubble around me. I'm so sad, angry, really frustrated and really really depressed. All the things that were giving me satisfaction and purpose are now upsetting me and making life here hell. Lynn is probably the most responsible for causing my despair.

There are 17 days left in this pit before I go home. I have so much to do! I was so stressed about all the things looming over me that I had to get up from my rest. Everything is closing in on me. I have to write letters about possible employment, write a paper for history, do Complex Functions and physics homework and take the finals. I've been checking on my car and doing paperwork for the insurance. Plus there's the Morton Hall Committee work. I feel overwhelmed and without the energy and motivation to continue. I don't even feel I want to continue with my life. It's so much harder out here. It might be better for me to try to find a job at home and try to get a relationship going there. Or maybe I could live with Lucy and Fred and get a job around D.C. I have only a short time to work with!

Later on Dec 3rd

I feel MHC has already dismissed me and I shouldn't be here! Mom mailed me my sweater and some boob probably sent it to Dad's because in the directory I'm listed as on leave. It better not be lost! She should have looked at the official list! Now I have to deal with more shit! I bled a lot because of my period this morning. I was scared shitless because there was so much blood and it was everywhere. I thought of last April and why I think I should be dead. Now I have to get a dye test on my catheter at Tri County. One more scary thing. I can't do this anymore!

I have no confidence that I can accomplish anything. I need more support but I can't reach out for it. I think I scare people away, and that makes it worse. Jenny helped me see that I might still be able to reach some goals. Some other people who I can reach out to are Priss, Beanie, sometimes Pam, Ellen, Kelly, and Leslie. But I really need someone there more—a boyfriend to hold me, listen to me, love me. Someone I can love back. I need some good things in my life.

Driving to the airport, I thought about all the other trips I'd made there, so many of them charged with emotion, so many of them full of the turning points of Jada's life and, therefore, mine.

She walked mechanically, as if the knots in her back were causing her to stiffen; her face looked tight, too. She had only one bag, except for her green one with Hambone's head bobbing out of it, his two short arms sticking out ready to jump down at the first chance. Her eyes almost as glassy as Hambone's, Jada squinted in the harsh airport light. She had taken the last flight so she could attend classes. "Did you sleep on the plane?"

"No, I never sleep on an airplane. I did my math." I could see a red folder, along with other notebooks, neatly nestled in her bag. No heavy books. She had explained that they were solving problems of such complexity that one would take a chapter; at least that's how I understood it. Or didn't, for there wasn't necessarily one right way to work out a solution, a far cry beyond the math I had learned.

Travel and the drugs of chemo took a toll on her energy. Recovering, Jada sat on the rocker, her feet propped on the stool. Beads dangled and tinkled as I moved the floor lamp we both claimed as our find to her side and pulled the chain, sprinkling dusty motes about her head in the yellow light. An open notebook lay upon her thighs; a pen, standing at attention, waited for its command.

I sat on the short bench next to a wall. "What do you want to say?" I asked. She looked down at her paper. "Start anywhere."

"Nobody wanted to listen to me. But how do I say that?"

"If you mean about getting IVs and stuff.... Or maybe when you felt sick and no one believed you, is that what you're talking about?"

"Partly, but more. They didn't understand what I wanted, and they didn't try."

"Okay. So what you wanted was for people to recognize you. Charts and tests and schedules got more respect than you did. You knew your own body and what felt right and what wasn't working. You wanted to be believed."

"Yeah! That's what I mean. Joe finally did...." She looked up, finishing her thinking. "They wanted me to fit their way. They wanted me to act in a certain way to make their job easier."

"Or just doable. They were the directors, and you were supposed to be acted upon instead of an actor, a person. So you played out your person, which got their attention. You see skepticism as necessary: you look out for mistakes because you're driven to protect yourself. They talked about the disease affecting the whole person, not just the body, but they didn't seem to see you as other than a body and didn't acknowledge that you made decisions from a strong knowledge of and concern for both your body and your mind."

Jada wrote notes, then blurted. "Like Dr. Randolph. He didn't tell me what he was going to do. If he had, I might not have let him do it. And all the others, they kept saying it didn't make a difference, jumped to conclusions and got mad before finding out how I felt, and they wouldn't let me talk. But it did matter, and I didn't know how to tell them."

"No; how could you put everything into words on the spot, especially under stress and lacking information, even if you did understand all your feelings yourself? So they saw you as being a testy patient. And this isn't part of it—or maybe it's the whole point—but you didn't get your disease when you were a child and would have to do what your elders planned. Your disease was happening in a stage of your development when you needed to define your person, test your controls, become independent."

"They wanted me to be like those old people who did whatever their doctors wanted them to do, just for a few more lousy days of being sick. I mean, go there and suffer and then come home and all they do is complain about how awful it is. They call that life? Maybe for them it is, but not for me."

"Yes; that's the assumption they started with, that staying alive, not living, was the goal. And you wouldn't follow and just whine until it was over. You plain said 'stop' in ways that made them stop, or at least 'do it right.' You had expectations of them, and that surprised them. But what maybe you're trying to put into words is that if you didn't try to exert your identity—or if you had become what they wanted you to, a docile, compliant 'good little patient,' you wouldn't have been the living you, the whole person they said they wanted to treat. Oh, you would have taken your pills on schedule and weighed your food and followed your doctor's orders, kept your body alive. Then your body and your will, too, would belong to them. The behavior that made you look bitchy and difficult to them, and sometimes to me, came from the strength of your character, not the flaw. You were not going to lose your will to this mess. Take a jug to pee in when you went out? Not you.

"You couldn't be in control of fate or cells or whatever rules those things, but you could be in control of you. That was all you had, and they wanted that, too. And so what started as a battle over your body became a battle over you. The more they pushed, the more you rebelled. They had their plans and studies and notions. And then you showed up, and instead of asking themselves what they could do for you, they blamed you, sort of. I'm sure they cared about you, but the only thing that mattered was getting rid of the disease, and they saw you as preventing them from doing it."

"Yes. They assumed I wanted the same thing they did." Jada's eyes followed her pen rolling off her paper and onto the floor. "But I don't want to live if all I'm going to do is stay in bed or have people poking and cutting my body all the time. That's not living, being sick all the time and worrying about IVs and counts and everything. If they think living is so important, then they should see why it's so important to let the patient live. And they should see why it's so important to let the patient decide.

"I don't want to die. I want to live my life. I want them to understand why I made the choice I did. All they can talk about is living, as if everyone is going to live. That's not fair to make people think they can all live, because they won't. They don't ever talk about dying. They don't prepare you for it. They should prepare you for dying."

There was something in the last thing she said that wormed its way into me; I was probably the guiltiest of them all, urging her on, wanting her to want the next thing as steps up the yellow brick road. Except, except, I was her mother. I bent over, picked up her pen and placed it onto her lap. "There's your start, don't you think?"

Jada took the pen and nodded ever so slightly, still thinking, remembering. From the dining room I heard an occasional creak of the rocking chair as I imagined she shifted in the seat, constructing her notes. I didn't think I'd ever get over my anger, but I did, then, for Arnold. All those times I heard my children whimper, cough, lapse a second before inhaling, day and night while he slept through, all those times I responded, and he didn't: that primitive reptilian part of my brain paid attention to things other than what my thinking brain attended to. My instincts forged an invincible bond with my children.

The shuffling and creaking ceased, and Jada walked into the dining room, her folder at her chest, shaking her head side to side slowly. Her face turned lopsided, as if one side were disapproving, the other laughing, she asked, "Are you still doing schoolwork?"

"Yup. You know me."

December, 1989

"Well, Hambone, did I leave anything out? Have I missed something?" Of course I have. I'll never know it all, never be able to tell Jada's story; no, more than one story, a whole library of stories. Hambone feels small, like I'm crushing him by leaning my head over him in my lap. "Sorry, Hambone." I loosen my arms and cuff him on the head, trying to fluff him up. Jada is at dinner with the two doctors she met at the medical conference, seemingly the culmination of over eight years of dealing with leukemia and its awful complications, and I feel beholden to the one observer who knows more than anyone. "C'mon, Hambone, we're not to the end yet," I say, lifting myself from Jada's bed as if I am cargo in the jaws of a crane; "and I have to shower before Jada comes home."

"Jim," I repeat on the telephone. "You talk about Jim a lot. What's the deal?"

"Jim sounds pretty cute."

"Yeah, and?"

"He says he's trying to rush my claim through."

"You know, he might be slick, just trying to put you off because he doesn't know how long it'll take, either." The wind takes a swipe at the building, rattles the storm window in its frame.

"I don't think so. He doesn't say that just because I call. Sometimes he calls me. He's going to be in Minnesota over Christmas. He said he'll call when he gets in town, and we're going on a date."

"Leave it to you. Do you get any business done in your phone conversations?"

"Of course. Do you think I don't want my car back? We just find other things to talk about. You wouldn't believe how many accidents they have out here. They're behind in months. Jim says he'll try to hurry things up for me."

"Jada," I caution, remembering the long fall from high hopes. "If Jim is so easy over the phone, do you think he's the right kind of guy for you?"

"I don't care. I just want a man. Do you think he'll marry me?"

"I don't know, HonBun." A sharp crackle comes from the living room. I hope Per is watching the fireplace. If it spat out a red-hot ember, it would surely burn a hole in the carpet, or worse, the floor. "I think we should keep looking."

"Hurry up." The playfulness was gone from her tone.

"I'll do my best. I bet you miss your car."

"I do. It's a bummer without it. And I feel so bad for it all crashed and me not taking care of it."

"I hope you hear something good soon. How's your schoolwork coming? Any different?"

I listen with one ear to the crackling static in the living room, the other to a hollow echo, what I imagine it is like in an observatory. "No. I don't think I'm even passing." Jada's voice slips, goes from cold to...unattached, yes, I decide. "Priss has been helping me work on a resume. I don't have very much to put on it."

"You're a Sarah Lynch scholar, and you're in that Who's Who book; that says a lot."

"Yes," Jada sighs, I think unimpressed. "But others have internships and job experiences to put on theirs, and what do I have? I can't even say I've had a job. Not one that counts."

"What are you applying for? What are you planning to do?"

"Don't ask me that! People here are so insensitive! They ask me what I'm going to do when I graduate." Shrieks are strangled out of her.

I bumble, trying to recapture my footing, as if I could find a solid place to stand in this bed of ball bearings I've made. "Sorry, Jada, I didn't mean it in the same way." But it was said, and the scent of the words soured like a dirty dishcloth left to reek in the sink. It was just too late.

"I don't want to talk about it, okay? Just don't ask me about it. You're not supposed to be like them!"

The phone, sticky with perspiration, shakes in my hand. I flounder, cast about for something to fill the space, which between us is wide. "How's Priss? Is she still seeing Will?"

"Yes," Jada answers, subdued. "I think they're perfect for each other. He wears bow ties and drives an old car. He looks just like a professor."

"Hmm." A Volkswagen bug appears in my imagination. Priss is tall, though thin, not small-boned. I don't see her fitting in a car that small. I almost miss what Jada says next.

"I've got a pain in my back."

There's a quickening in my ears, like sound magnifying; what she said was so small that it might not have been said at all. I sift through things the physical therapist might recommend and offer, "Try standing in a hot shower. Let the water pound on it."

"No, Mom. That won't help."

"Maybe there's some medication you can take, a muscle relaxer. Do you want me to call and order some?"

"No, I have to go in for counts." She speaks slowly, as if her words are tired and the sentence droops, like a sleepy head falling forward.

"You'll be home soon; should I call and make an appointment with physical therapy?" My words come out like a rapping ruler on the edge of the desk trying to keep her awake. "What are you doing tonight?"

"I'm trying to organize stuff for our math club Christmas party. Have you got any more recipes like that fruit dip? Something easy that I can make?"

"I'll look. That reminds me. A few of us are going skiing and then coming over here for brunch. I should get some things up for Christmas; it's getting to be time."

"Don't get all the decorations out. I want to decorate when I get home."

"I'll just put a couple things out. Per said he'd take us to get the tree. What kind do you want this year?"

"A big one. I just want a big tree."

"We'll get the tallest one we can. You can decorate the whole thing."

"I better go now, Mom. I have to get over to the computer lab before it gets busy."

"Okay, Doll. I'll call tomorrow and, oh, yes, I'll look through my recipes."

"Yes, call me. Bye, Mom."

The telephone's ring wakes me in the night. A neon-like 2:02, the color of ocean water along coral reefs, illuminates the rectangular face of the clock. I interrupt, before the second ring. "I can't sleep, Mooie."

"Is it your back?" I ask with a raspy voice. It is Friday night; I haven't been asleep very long.

"Yes. And I can't sleep. I've just been laying here." I can hear the still room surrounding her. Her whispers tiptoe carefully so as not to awaken the shadows in the corners.

"Have you taken any medicine? Ibuprofen? Do you have anything to help you relax?" Mm-hmm. I did. I just need you to sing to me." I envision her lying in bed, snuggling Hambone with one arm, the telephone with the other.

I clear my throat and hear myself start on a husky note. "...my little one, little one...." Then I sing "What are little girls made of, made of? Sugar and spice and all that's nice...." I know the songs well enough to sing them in my sleep. I sing slow, I sing long, the receiver under my ear pressing hard against my head. ".... and down will come baby, cradle and all." I hum. Silence travels between us, joins us. "Hang up the phone and go to sleep, now, Jada. I love you. Here's my kiss on your forehead."

"Mmm. Night, Mooie."

On Saturday, I leave a cheer-up voice message on Jada's telephone tape. "Just calling to see how you're doing and to give you a recipe." We do not speak voice to voice, ear to ear until Sunday, when I call again. "Did you get my message? How's your back?"

"Not good."

"That's too bad. Take some Ibuprofen?"

"Yes. Sorry I didn't call back, but I've been super busy. I can't talk long. I have to work on my paper and get to the computer lab. And today's the dorm Christmas party."

"Is that the paper on the 60s and the media?"

"Yes. I really got into it. It's the first paper I felt good about writing. I understood what I wanted to say. Have you started your book about me yet?" She asks as if the truth were that I had forgot. I haven't even got to the store for the CD I want to buy her for Christmas.

"No, not yet," I say, implying that it was on my list of things to do today, like dust the furniture. "I'm glad you feel confident about the writing. I can't wait to read it."

"Well, if I don't go, you never will."

"Okay, talk to you soon."

"Bye, Mooie."

The referee's whistle and cheering crowds of a Sunday afternoon's football game come through the walls and the closed door of my bedroom. My head is propped by a couple pillows and my hands rest on my rib cage holding *Reading Today*. I doze, the purring of background television singing me to sleep. After dinner dishes and through the National Geographic television program with Per, I wait for Monday morning. I rock slowly as I watch millions of penguins make themselves into a bobbling black sea on the craggy northern landscape. He will leave when they find their happy ending. The phone rings.

"Hi, Mooie."

"Hi, Jada. How was your party?"

"Good. Everyone liked it. The punch recipe you gave me was good, too. Everyone wanted to know what was in it. Do you have any Beatles music?"

"I have one CD and a tape that Tanya made for me; why?"

"I need it for my paper. Sasha gave me some, and I've been listening to that, but I need more."

"I thought you didn't like the Beatles."

"I didn't. But now that I'm doing this paper, I'm getting to like them. I might try to work on it tonight, but I'm so tired."

"I know how serious you are about your school work, but maybe you need to sleep instead and tackle that tomorrow. Speaking of, I need to do some shopping for Christmas dinner. What kind of pie do you want? Apple? Cherry?"

"I can't think about that now. Is that okay?"

"Sure. I always get nervous too early. I asked Per to join us for dinner. That's okay with you, isn't it?"

"Mm-hmm." Jada yawns, and it comes across to me like the rippling of a blanket on a clothesline, fluttered by the wind. "I think I'll go to bed now; I'm really tired."

"Okay, Love. Talk to you soon. Love you."

"Me, too."

Dec 10th

> *I've been awake since 4 with the worst physical pain! I took codeine and 2 Tylenols and it's still very bad. I'm scared about what is causing this pain. It's 6:30 and I don't know what I should do. I need Mom. I need to be home. I need a boyfriend. I need to die instantly!*

I arrive home from school on Monday during the darkening hours, the light on my message machine blinking twice at me. SHE in Northpointe is having a sale, and the clerk wants Jada to know she could save an extra 20% on cashmere sweaters. Then Jada's voice says she thought I'd be home by now. Call her. I dial her number and leave my own message. "Hi; this is your Moo. I'm home; call me." I find the CD and tape, put them on the table in case she wants me to send them to her, though I doubt they'd get there soon enough, especially if she has already established the foundation of her paper which she is probably writing as I wait for her call.

It is Tuesday, and I am sitting next to Amelia. It has taken me a long time to get her to trust me, and in the quiet of the room with everyone working, she rereads the directions, stuck on the phrase "using the chart," and what they prompt her to do. Mary Lou's voice from the P.A. box breaks through the silken cocoon we have spun around ourselves. "Ms. Santino," she blares, "there's an important phone call from your daughter on line 11." I straighten. For a second I am stunned to immobility. She's waiting—why now?

At the bottom of the flight of steps I hear my heart knocking at my chest and take deep breaths to slow myself down. My hand twitters at the key in the lock of the small work/storage room crammed between identical brown wooden doors barricading restive students from being together, doing what they do best, socializing. Why, I wonder, do we not use their talents and inclinations instead of fighting against them, and I acknowledge that I'm avoiding thinking of possibilities for being here. The door opens into dark. The winking red square on the phone summons me like a memory of the past, and, across the gray linoleum to the desk, I follow my heart. Pressing the receiver to my ear, I hear blood flushing inside my head.

"Mom, I have to come home." Jada sounds like a pre-recorded message.

"Jada, you'll be home in days. Why do you have to come home now?" My mind jumps to her pleas for an immediate flight to Sibley with a broken leg. "Can't you wait?" I ask, screening the possibilities for something simple, a cast, a massage from the physical therapist.

"Don't you want me home?" Jada sounds hurt; no, more than that; she sounds confused. I'm confused; I hear her, but I resist what I'm being asked to do. I don't know why.

"Of course it's not that. I just don't know why you're coming home now when you've got a ticket for next week. Can't we at least check with Dr. Lourde first?" I look at the pocked concrete blocks surrounding me. What an ugly room. This whole school is ugly I think, waiting for an explanation, justification for a new ticket. I've replaced a plane ticket before; I just need a reason. What is today? Tuesday, December 12. "What is it that you can't wait?"

There is no answer, only the sound of commotion behind her while I wait in silence, wait for the clock to tick, but it doesn't; it is noiseless. Someone must have come into her room; I hear Jada speak away from the mouthpiece. Then into the phone she says, "I've got to go now. I've got a lot of things to do. People are waiting for me." I protest, but she hangs up without hearing me.

I sit, my mouth still open, to say, okay, you can come home, but no one is listening and gradually the periphery of a school in session permeates the walls. I hear a chorus of laughter bursting as one voice, fragmenting into the many voices of individuals as it dies down. Snatching my keys, I drag them over the desk and knock the light switch down. Sounds of notebook papers being mangled, chalk scratching on the board, desk legs scraping sand and grit against the floor intrude, and I feel like Alice, only I don't know if I'm too small in an oversized world or too big to fit.

I climb back to the third floor and, inside my doorway, students looking up at me as if nothing has happened, and so far as I can tell, nothing has, except that I left for a reason, and they have seen me, before and after. But before and after what? Amelia does not drop her head back to her work. Mechanically I pick up where we left off.

The passing bell rings, and I hoard my prep period, trying to gather some papers together to take home with me, but nothing seems to go with anything else. Wherever I look, I can't find what

I am seeking. Mary Lou's voice again interferes. "Ms. Santino, you have an important call."

"Who is it?" I shout back to the meshed circle in the wall. It could be a DJ trying to book a dance. World's Finest Chocolate salesman. Anyone other than Jada I don't want to talk to.

"Just a minute, I'll ask." I walk toward the speaker by the clock, watching it for news. "It's Dr. Lourde. He says he'll wait for you."

Wait for me; that's a first—his calling me is a first. "I'll be right there."

I feel the wooden rail underneath my skimming hand as I glide the steps like a swimmer splitting water, my toes splaying, bulging out the worn red leather that wraps around them. My movements are smooth, my skirt flares as I swivel my hips around the corner at the landing. I swing into the stuffy storage room again and face the same blinking light.

"Ms. Santino, I just spoke to Jada. She asked me to explain to you that she needs to come home. She's concerned that you don't want her to come home."

I am out of breath and clear my throat. *Slow down, slow down.* "Things were just getting twisted up. I just don't know what's going on. She wouldn't tell me why she needs to come home now."

"I understand," Dr. Lourde responds and pauses. He's always so careful, and I know I must listen just as carefully. "She's in a bit of pain and has taken some powerful medicine."

"Mm-hmm," I chorus. "She's been complaining about her back. In fact, I was going to call you this afternoon. But I don't know what happened. She just hung up." My face burns hot, but my shoulders shiver; streams of water run cold down my back: another one of our bumps into each other Dr. Lourde felt.

"She may not be thinking too clearly right now." I wait for the usual fastidiousness to detail, an array of possibilities, but only a tightrope links us and I get the feeling from the tone of his silence that he won't add to the weight.

"I'll call her as soon as I get home. I'd like to see what's going on. When can we come in?"

"Why don't you bring her in around 4:00 tomorrow?"

I can't sit here, not alone with my aloneness, crowded in by the walls and the books and the boxes and the clock on the wall and what if someone should come in and say how are you and what would I say and I get up and walk and instead of turning right, back up to my room, I go left, down to the corner room on the first floor and knock, then open the door a crack and peek in, my head only, I think, but who knows how much of me shows and I say to Jessie, over her students, to the other end of the room, "I'm sorry to interrupt; do you have a minute?" She nods and I hear her say something to her class as I shut the door and wait and when she opens the door she steps one foot out halfway as if she's learning a new dance but I'm the one who can't stand still and say, "Jada called a little bit ago. She's coming home today." I can't tell why I'm telling her, but I know I can tell without explaining, excusing, or asking for her to fill in the spaces. "I'm scared. I don't think it looks good." She might be waiting for more because she does not speak and I say, "I can't say what's coming up, but I'm canceling Saturday. I'm sorry."

"Sorry! Don't be. Are you okay?"

Her hand on the doorknob looks like it might move, might touch me and I lean back, a pillar whose foundation has shifted, throwing off my center of gravity and I wobble. "I'm always okay. I'm going to go tell Thomas that I won't be here tomorrow and then I'm going home. I don't know why I'm here. I just wanted to tell you."

Jessie reaches out and lightly places her hand on my arm hanging uselessly from the rest of me; maybe she wants to catch me from falling. "Thank you for telling me. I'll talk to you later." She releases me, steps back into her classroom, a rubber ball attached to an elastic string and, having stretched her limit, was pulled back to the paddle.

Except for the clap of my leather heels against the cold tiles, there is not the absence of sound in the hall, for there is a buzz from the fluorescent lights, and there is a static suggesting that somewhere just beyond a boundary someone made the airwaves bend, and there is the sound of my own thinking, a shouting through a hollow tube, and I hear it without its ever being voiced, sound in a vacuum. Just sound, the chatter of a typical 9th grader—*where am I going? how do I look? what should I do now?* Noise without substance.

Thomas is shored up at his desk sorting irregularities. He looks up and rises, expectant as always, as if I'm the one who's going to say something profound, witty, entertaining. "I need a sub for tomorrow. Jada's coming home. Something's wrong." He leads me with his open hand toward a chair, maybe the same chair I sat in with Jada on my lap. Thomas's thoughts are forming; I can see the workings on his face. I follow his bidding and now only my clenched hands rest on the soft nest of my lap. Beyond Thomas, a poster hangs above a bookshelf; the window, tall and narrow and white beyond, reveals nothing; smudges mar white plasterboard; the door stands open. The space around my eyes feels dry, stony. I notice my blinking and wonder if he can hear it.

He sits and rolls his chair in my direction, his knee jutting from behind a stack of drawers. "I don't know how you can keep up with this," he says. "It's got to be such a strain. Don't you ever want to say, 'Enough already?'"

"I don't have a choice. Whatever happens I have to deal with."

"Well, yes," he says crisply, bowing his head to the truth. His hair, thin at the top, shines gossamer filaments next to his scrubbed and glistening pink scalp. He knows immutability as well. "Some people couldn't handle it. Some people would crack."

"Sometimes I wish I could. But...." I apologize, feeling resentful. I want to keep this my way; I have to go through whatever I'm going through, and I don't want to think about or be made to feel what I can't name. Hot water wells in my eyes, stinging wet where it has been sandpapery dry. I grab both arms of the chair. "And now I have to go."

"We'll take care of everything here. Just let me know if I can do anything."

As soon as I arrive home I call Jada. "I'm so glad you called!" Sharon says. Behind her hello is a chorus of voices. A woman's question separates itself from the other voices. "Do you want me to pack this nightshirt?"

"You'll have to speak up. People are here packing, and I can hardly hear you." Her mouth sounds close to the phone and I picture her hand cupped over an ear to block out the commotion.

I feel excluded, the latecomer to this party-in-progress, and try to get involved, but they're too far ahead of me, and I must prick at the edges, try to make an opening for myself to fit in. "Where's Jada?"

"In and out. I'm worried she won't make it to the airport on time. She keeps finding something else to do. She insists on having the math club meeting. Oh, here she comes now. Talk to her. Tell her how important it is that she hurry."

I hear Jada being rallied, women's voices steering her to go this way, coaxing her to "let me take this." I imagine them pushing Jada along, trying to make her move at their tempo when she doesn't want to; I stand waiting, rocking foot-to-foot.

"Jada," I say into the phone, "I'm sorry for the misunderstanding this afternoon. I was confused. Of course I want you to be here. I'm concerned that you get home."

"Yes, Mom. Adam's coming. I haven't said good-bye to Gabriella yet." Her words come as though wading deeper into a crosscurrent.

"Okay, Doll. Do that, but listen to Sharon and Priss. They'll tell you the right things to do."

"Get that notebook and folder," Jada says away from the phone, to someone in the room. I hear a voice say she is going out to the car.

"Jada, are you listening to me?" I call, raising my voice, keeping it firm and calm.

I repeat myself louder when she doesn't respond. "I hear you." Her voice comes back limp, distant, like it's been running on a weak battery.

"What time does your flight arrive?"

"Umm. Just a minute. Where's Sharon? Who has my ticket? Go get Sharon. Ask her where my ticket is." I listen to Jada give another direction I don't understand, her mouth turned away from the phone, making sloppy sounds. Then I hear a clunk, as if I've been dropped. I am rescued; someone answers with the information.

"Thanks. Put Jada back on for a second." I wait feeling like the hot potato being tossed about.

"Yes?"

"Jada, now remember. Do what they tell you so you can get home. I'll be waiting at the airport. I love you."

"Bye," she says, and I hear the snap of the broken connection, though I feel she'd disconnected long before.

Immediately I pull out the vacuum cleaner and start searching for dust in Jada's room. I finish cleaning up the unit with a wash down in her bathroom. I chop onions and crush garlic. My eyes bulge with the pressure of repressed tears. I have an excuse to cry, but I'm not sure it's time. Tears too soon too quick will burst like a flash flood snatching everything in its raging water and get swallowed in a vastness too undefined for relief.

Per, coming in from ski practice, sniffs the aromas and sees me stirring at the stove. Gradually he has been spending more time with me during the week. I tell him we're eating dinner early because Jada's coming home. He does not question me except to ask when. That seems to be the only question that matters. I eat without much interest in either the pasta or Per's report on skiing with his team. It was cold, too cold for the golf course, and I think I have two, maybe three more hours and I wonder what I will do. After dinner and dishes, Per puts a small kiss on my cheek and leaves for his own apartment. I promise to call him when I can.

Now I am alone again. And cold. Too cold for me. For days we've been at or below zero. Icy air knifes through the window casings, and I scrunch myself into a corner of the couch in the dark drafty living room and stare out the window. An airplane skims the sky, its pinpoint lights marking its path. *Where is she now? Oh, God.... What do those people know? They're afraid, just like me, only they think they can get rid of their fear by believing it won't be their plane, that they won't crash. Yes, Jada. It wouldn't be so bad if you didn't have to think.* I shiver and squeeze both hands between my knees. *Oh, fuck. Fuck! Just fuck it! Now what?* Two flickering diamonds slide behind the south wing of my building and out of sight. Next to the window, Jada's high school graduation picture stares at me. Her slender fingers prop her face that swims in blue: blue sweater, blue tam, her eyes reflecting blue sapphires. Wherever I sit in the living room, her eyes follow me from that picture. I cock my head. Even in the unlit room, I feel them on me.

No two of my clocks are set for the same time. Per is the one who really knows what time it is, to the second. But I do not need him because I feel the heaviness of the hours as they strike me down, the minutes and the seconds pelt at what keeps escape impossible. I have won the lottery and Jada is the sacrifice. I get up from the couch and stumble into the corner of the cedar chest stuffed with saved and savored baby clothes, knocking my leg against a corner. *Okay, Jada. I'm coming.*

The airport's lighting surprises my eyes. My living room was dark. The interior of my car, the parkway were dark. My thoughts were dark, too. I squint in the glare of lights shining directly into my eyes. People are planted in the waiting area: those who greet and those who wait to depart. Tickets tucked safely away, travelers sit stoically in stationary black seats, buttressed by coats, magazines, and newspapers, a carry-on bag at their feet like a trusty dog. Waiters, those who've come with nothing, stand watching expectantly through windows, down railed ramps.

I lean against a square pillar, my arms crossed. People seem to appear in twos. Bring along someone for entertainment. Too long to go without talking. *Those two over there. How can people find so much to say that they can never be done? Why don't you do something for that screaming child? It doesn't seem to bother them. See him. Listen to him…. That's her plane.* A glob of people swell toward the rail. I hide near the post, away from the throat of the chute where everyone is disgorged from the plane.

They come, Priss and Jada, surrounded by faceless passengers, and I wonder, did she tell me Priss was coming? Why? Priss's almost black hair falls partly over her face when she turns to hear Jada, whose expressionless mouth forms words. By the time they reach me, I feel their cadence and fall into step alongside. Together we make a rank, Priss and I on either side of Jada. Except for the flicker of our eyes and the drop of our chins, we concentrate on Jada.

Thrusting my arm like a railroad crossing bar, I relieve Jada of her wool jacket, too suffocating for the plane. She hands over her green tapestry bag, and I sling my arm through the straps, Hambone's stuffed head stoutly protruding between them, his blue-rimmed brown glass eyes getting a knee-cap review of his hometown, his snout nudging occasionally my own leg. Empty-handed, Jada continues to talk and walk, but she is belabored by weight, as if a cement block has been chained to her being. We have done this before; powered by drug and what I know of her determination, she will get as far as she can before letting anyone else see the inside of her, and I accept that as I have her coat and bag, long ago becoming inured to, above, critical eyes. I walk proudly beside Jada, lumbering down the gloomy corridors, murky in contrast to the crisp darkness beyond the windows. Our eclipsed greeting we leave behind like unclaimed luggage: no fuss, no haggle, no questions, no pity: the way Jada wants it. It is normal for us. I am in a tunnel; and whether there is a light at the end, I do not see it. We speak not of the real issue, what has brought Jada home, because we are in our tunnel. We know how to do this. We are good at it. We speak normal. And I am glad for the protection of the tunnel, for now is not the time for light.

We troop our way to baggage claim, Jada jabbering, not loudly, not thoughtlessly, but not substantively, as if thought came whimsically, and having appeared, needed audience. The impetus for noise, her own voice noise is modulated by pain-numbing drugs, depressing the mechanism for speed, and her train of associations chug doggedly along on determination. I see why Jada is devoted to Priss. Probably since they left Mary Hillyard, Priss's ear has been tested. She remains, even after the three-hour trip from Hartford, patriotically attentive, nodding her head, mm-hmming, watching, engaging.

Priss bounces a sympathetic look at me, her hazel eyes flecked with light, the tips of her white teeth glowing against her faded red lips swooping up in an enigmatic smile as Jada announces, "Our airport is the best in the world. They're always so fast. Not like Hartford. And Northwest, too. Northwest is the best airline. The best I've ever flown. Look how fast we're getting our luggage." Priss and I agree, watching the carousel revolve and the baggage tumbling down into it. Priss picks out her single bag, and when Jada's two bags come, one at a time, we start for the car.

"Here, Jada." I stop, holding out her coat like a patrol flag, but she ignores my caution and keeps walking. "It's below zero; you'll need your coat," I squeeze in before she slurs into another sentence. I catch up to her at the automatic doors where we are shot by the blast of stinging cold. Even into the ramp she doesn't shiver. "Jada, really," I insist and run ahead, drop the luggage and intercept her shoulders long enough to drape her coat upon them.

The first thing Jada does inside the car is to ignore her seat belt. I leave my own unhooked in solidarity. Secondly, she tunes into radio station 99 1/2 FM, pop rock. "That song is dumb."

"Jada, I like the B-52s," Priss protests from the back seat. Must be her loyalty to California, I surmise. It is hard for me to imagine Priss being frivolous.

"Mom, you better have the place clean." I nod. "I hate it when there's no snow." I survey the peppery brown-gray patches that pass through the beam of my headlights along the thoroughfare. They look like broad flat boulders instead of dirty remains from our last snowfall. Winter had opened its jaws and clamped us into a deep freeze too cold for more snow to form. Jada turns down the blasting heater. "Our streets are always clean here. It doesn't matter how much it snows, you can always get around in Minnesota."

We reach our exit. To the right is Ramsey Hospital, which claimed too many of Jada's days over the past eight and one-half years. She points, "See, Priss, there's the hospital." Like the White House, the Vatican, Versailles, the mention of its name smacks history worthy of retelling.

I signal a turn instead to the left, up Sibley Hill, to our condominium. At the top of our climb, the sudden vision of bedecked facades and light-laced tree limbs captures Jada, and she bursts, "Mom, let's show her Cathedral Way!" Jada glows with the reflection of the stars splintered into little constellations on each tree. Buttery brick and charcoal stone mansions are swagged with greens, their stained glass doors and faceted windowpanes shattering light into spears of color. Flanking a cement walkway, two stone lions wear glittering wreaths around their necks.

Jada is quiet, transfixed, I imagine, by the greatness of the night's spectacle and the magic of the promise that the waiting would soon be over. I circle and bring us around to the Cathedral to see the site of the life-sized stable scene that is built each year onto its sloping approach. At Northern, I turn to our entrance. Inside the garage, I drop Jada and Priss near the elevator and park. Dragging her blue suitcase with the cock-eyed wheel behind me, I come into the door behind Jada and Priss in our long hallway. She is leading Priss on a tour, on her way to Jada's bedroom suite, leaping from thought to thought, as lightning bugs spew sparks haphazardly in the night, sending a signal, flashing wherever the danger of darkness threatens to settle. Priss follows, responding. She never loses her smile.

Finally to her bed, Jada drops with a bounce. "I left your bag out in the dining room," I tell Priss. She looks around, perhaps, I think, to make a place for herself.

"I just need a few things; I'll go get them," she says, on her way out.

"Help her, Mom." I follow.

"Hang your things in my closet," Jada calls from her bedroom.

Priss opens her neatly packed suitcase, removes a nightgown and a pair of pants. "It's okay, Jada; I don't need much. I'll just hang my coat." I take it to the hall closet, midway between the two women.

"Mom, set up the iron for Priss. See if she wants something ironed."

"I don't need anything ironed, Jada. These pants are fine." I come back to the dining room; Priss is holding her pants up by the cuff and says to them, "I'm wearing the same sweater back tomorrow."

"Do we have anything for Priss to eat?" I stand at the edge of the dining room between Jada's bidding and Priss's self-sufficiency feeling like a stretched slinky toy.

"I'm really fine, Jada. I don't need anything," Priss echoes down the hallway that zigs two corners before it empties into Jada's room. There is a smile in Priss's voice, an apology in her eyes.

"She's probably hungry, Mom. Offer her something to drink. And get me a glass of water, will you?"

"Okay, Darlin'." Grateful for a task I can fulfill, I twist the faucet, and Jada from her bed makes another request. She wants a cool cloth, medication, her bag of toiletries. Priss and I cross in the dining room, and in passing, she confides to me that Jada has been jumping among details, one to another, like a rock skipping along the surface, touching, never filling space and time. "Ever since leaving the hospital this afternoon, she's been finding things to say and do," Priss says secretively, and holding Jada's glass of water, I say to Priss, "I have coffee, tea, wine, water, hot chocolate, diet Coke, Mountain Dew, and beer. Tell me what you want, or be free to take anything you want." Priss smiles broadly, and I wonder if she means the Tri County Medical in Loudon, not the office of the campus doctor, and if I'd heard it earlier. Priss's clear gaze remains fixed, and she hums a kind of chant and I feel sympathy, as if there is a code to crack, and I wonder, confused, at what I know and don't know.

Jada calls, and I return to her, sitting in the same position as I have left her, as if frozen in a game of statues. Hambone is on his side behind her. Together, they look like forsaken playmates waiting to be picked up. Priss follows me; there are dark sunken half-moons under her eyes, but I see that sleep has to fight to overpower Jada. I begin unpacking. Holding up a swimsuit, I look at Jada for direction. "Put it on the shelf in the closet," she says. Atop a red flannel shirt, blue shorts lay pressed flat and folded at the center seam. They, like the swimsuit, seem out of place, and I want to ask if her dad bought tickets for a cruise but think it better to find out another time and pick up the camera nestled among lacy panties and hold it out in the palm of my hand like a communion offering. "Where do you want this?"

Jada's face becomes animated. "Take a picture of us, Mooie. I want a picture of Priss and me."

"Mmm, Jada." There is a hint of complaint in Priss's compliance, but she shakes her full-bodied hair into place, lucky compensation for being caught at a bad time.

"Come here, Priss," Jada pats the puffy quilt beside her. Priss obeys with a smile, and Jada holds her tightly. I try to frame their heads, seemingly conjoined at their ears, their smiles frozen in the camera's moment of reality, in the glare of the bright overhead light bulbs blooming from four glass tulips in the ceiling fixture.

Jada's suitcase unpacked and stored in her closet, her clothes niched among the shelves and strung along hangers, we heed our summons to bed. Priss sighs thankfully and, covering herself with the blanket she will share with Jada, turns her body to the wall while Jada, sitting on the other side, holds her arms up rigidly, like a doll with stiff limbs, and I poke them into her nightie sleeves and lead her into the bathroom. While she brushes her teeth, I heat a cup of hot chocolate, not knowing what to expect, but expecting something, listening all the while to the sound of running water, the toilet flush, anticipating the creak of the bathroom door, the call of my name.

I walk with her to her bed. "Here, HonBun," I say hoarsely in the slant of the light from the hallway. I have planned well, bringing the cushioned chair to Jada's bedside and having chocolate to drink, something to keep me awake or to soothe me to sleep, whichever the night commands, and sit carefully next to my daughter's bed. She speaks continuously, though without the effect of continuation; I hear shush-ings and hush-ings, the prattle before sleep, the frightened child inside me scared. I sing my lullabies and hum softly; gradually, reluctantly, she surrenders, as my cup cools and the chocolate settles to a dark layer at the bottom, to what I hope is the oblivion of sleep. Her breathing becomes deeper. The Victorian chair creaks when I shift. *Why didn't I recover this and the matching love seat last summer? It will never get done in time now.*

My breathing slows, in concert with Jada's steady in-and-out breath. She used to tease me at the clinic, how entrained I was with her. Others, some others, found much to criticize in that. I'm past caring, I'm tired, and tomorrow's here soon enough. Jada, I think, sleeps; I sit quietly, almost meditatively on my chair, thankful to look at her. Stunned into numbness by my acceptance of what I am doing here, what I have been doing, I do not wonder at what I would do over, were I given the chance to rechart the pathways. I must sleep, so I lift myself up, making the hundred-year-old springs agonize beneath me, and put out the lights, the last one my own next to my pillow.

Though I have not slept long, I feel drunken with sleep; I do not remember thinking or dreaming or even easing into sleep, but I know I did because I'm in the morning after. Priss and I assemble ourselves for travel in the subzero weather. Glass windowpanes are crusty white from the hand of the cold night's artist; they look enlarged, reversed negatives of jungle plants, frosted fern fans and curlicued fiddleheads. I worry about leaving Jada while I drive Priss to the airport, but, as we take our last cup of coffee, Jada calls. She is sitting up in bed, a tiny weblike impression on her right cheek, right below her eye, her sheet wrapped around the comforter and rolled down to her hips, Hambone buried somewhere beneath. After the forever-long yesterday and short night's drug-intense sleep, the hour is early for Jada. But it is no ordinary morning, either, and even though her eyes finally pulled shut, they locked up the pain inside them, and every tiny muscle in her face seems to strangle the breath out of tolerance for more. I think better of leaving her and dress her for the cold ride to the airport.

We plunge into the arctic December morning, sudden fear of Jada's vulnerability in such severe cold unnerving me, making the drive seem risky. We don't have time to park and walk Priss to her gate, and it makes good-bye easy. Priss gives Jada a final hug and waves bright-smiled and red-cheeked from the walkway at the airport entrance as the car wheezes away, shrouding Priss in a fog of crystallizing exhaust vapors. In my rearview mirror I see only the cloudy tail we drag behind us, and Jada leans forward, tackling the glove compartment. I shift my foundling worry from keeping her warm if the car broke down to preparing myself for a verbal wag of her finger at my slovenliness.

"Do you need this any more?" she queries as she holds up rectangular, red-numbered dry cleaning tickets. I shift my attention back and forth between the white lines on the parkway and the spilling contents on her lap. "How old is this?" she continues, as she industriously sorts. Rapid Oil Change receipts, a small, nearly empty plastic squeeze container of breath freshener, the cap's edge caked with fine particles from the bottom of some disused schoolbag, an unevenly folded shred of paper with scrawled titles of music heard on the car radio. She lumps a deposit slip from a defunct joint bank account and marriage and a toothpick with the disposable items. What is necessary, two maps, the car manual, my insurance card, she replaces, her self-imposed and self-composing task timed perfectly for our arrival home.

We have the rest of the day to ourselves before dipping into the deep freeze one more time to go to the clinic. Jada asks about the late hour. I conjecture a busy schedule and say I think it works out well. We could get Priss back to the airport without juggling, and I could help her take a quiet bath in her own bathtub. She accepts my offer.

I draw warm water, filling the yellowed tub to the overflow drain, adding lavender bubble bath to create plentiful honeycombs of richly scented foam. We are coming full circle from her first baths, the baths that quieted her, the baths I sudsed her, cuddled her, the baths I made her into animals with the soap bubbles, building crowns, trying her magic potions, the baths in which she, sometimes lying on her back and cupping pools of water over her belly button, imagined her *Someday* life in a mansion with a cottage in back for me.

We are into our last somedays on this cold December 13. I help Jada submerge her scarred body into the lilac-colored water and lower myself to my knees. Bending over the edge of the tub, I lather the cuddly bunnies, curly sheep, and round pigs printed on Jada's washcloth. I swirl the saturated cloth around her baby-short hair. The visibility of her scalp makes the fine wisps appear lighter than they are. I am cradling her head in my arm, and with a cup, I pour clear water over her soapy head, the water falling from her and running along my arm like silken streams spreading into a prayer cloth underneath us.

I let Jada sink into the water, submerged to her neck, her head resting on the back of the tub. Carefully, as not to irritate her translucent skin that, once dampened, seems it might rip under my touch, I avoid long abrasive strokes, lightly dabbing the cloth about her face, over her pale cheeks that cling to her cheekbones, under swollen eyelids, across her forehead, down her straight nose, and around her taut lips. As I soothe the slippery water along her neck and shoulders, gently coaxing the tightened muscles to loosen their grip, her face begins to soften.

In the warm, heavy, scented air of her bathroom, I reach under Jada's submissive body and arch her back upwards with my outstretched hand. My straining to graze her back with the whisper of a cloth draws me further forward, and I want to somersault into the water with her. Veins map her chin as if my breathing on her cooled them to blue as I glide the cloth along her back. I want to believe I can easily hug my daughter to me, as if wrapping my greedy clutch around her could rescue her from another's. But I know the power is not mine to wield and release her into the enveloping water, beginning to massage her arm, suspended weightlessly alongside her body. Jada has scars everywhere as partial payment to the cost of survival, but none so red and knotty, running like a rutted country road on her left arm. Nor one so unforgivable. Sensitive to anyone's notice, let alone touch, Jada usually withdraws her arm at once; but here, swathed in the lapping water that caresses her withering body, she gives no room to self-consciousness.

I work my way along each slender, graceful finger, decorations to the rings she loves to wear, and marvel again at the hands that were formed to bring music from the piano, sculpture from bronze. Hands meant for lofty work, artist's hands.

The dappling of the cloth in the water and my lulled breathing become muted background to Jada's murmurs and sighs, a melody of gratuitous comfort. Drawn so close to Jada, I listen to her body speak, start to hear what her body is saying. To the quiet rhythm of my daughter's bathing, I know I am kneeling at the entrance to truth, and I cannot sidestep it much longer. Still....

I stroke Jada's chest with especial care as I recall her first pain, centered there, eight-and-a-half years ago. That was in April; I dreaded April's approach as, every year, it extorted death from her, or something close to it. It was in April that Jada was diagnosed, three days after Easter. She relapsed four years later in April. Four years after that, following spring break, Jada flew home from college: she had not escaped April's cruel charge. In between those two relapses, she grew infections, her hips crumbled; those, too, in April. This is December, Christmas, Jada's favorite time, a time of birth, love, hope, not the retribution exacted from that birth, not the horror, devastation, and suffering that belong to April.

Under the weakening white-skinned suds that hide her thighs, my fingers find the staff-shaped scars, reminders of the femoral replacements that made her one-half inch taller, a quarter inch at a time, in each leg. I cannot block the pleas from my hands any longer. After all the humiliations of disease and sicknesses, invasive infections, drug side effects, operations and incisions, infiltrating chemicals, and internal imbalances, this tired and aged body of only 21 years aches for liberation from the pain and abuse of cancer's relentless onslaught and medicine's mighty but vanquished response to it. *Yes, Jada, I hear your body screaming for release; but, please, believe me, I hoped each struggle would be worth the pain, for you, and for me.*

All around, everywhere, a message blares, her confusion, her sudden inability to understand, her back pain, probably when she was unhappy in New York she was trying to tell me, or herself. And on the phone just yesterday. Dr. Lourde tried to tell me. Even Jessie and Thomas heard it, heard it from me. I can hear myself telling, but I cannot, even in the telling, hear it myself.

Something besides all the bells and warnings and signals talks to me, something louder and more powerful drowns out what I do not heed. I am listening to your warm infant body resting against my chest when I rocked you to sleep. Your smeary raspberry-jammed face. I hear you line up your stuffed animals and dolls on the pillows of my bed and pull me in to see them sleeping in a row. I hear you gasp at yourself in the mirror, a real live princess with rosy rouged cheeks and pink costume for your first ice show. I hear you (and me, too) cry watching E.T., laugh with collective and genetic vengeance through 9-5. I hear you clutch Hambone, believe the Velveteen Rabbit was real because someone loved him. I hear you call me from France in the middle of the night because you miss me and I miss you because I thought the French operator was a crank caller. I hear the games you made up, games I could never win. I hear you dancing, drawing, painting. I hear us la-la-la-ing to Mozart, the music you introduced to me. I hear the notes you wrote to me, notes promising forever love. I hear your tapes of Madonna and George Michael over and over and over until one of them wears out and breaks apart. And I hear the dying woman and her friend in Beaches and Rod Stewart singing "Forever Young," the CD I am to buy you for Christmas. I hear your disappointment when you are not chosen to speak at your high school graduation, and I hear you shriek joy when you received your acceptance letter from Mary Hillyard and you flew toward me, trusting that I would catch you. I did. I hear you start up the engine on your BMW four times at an intersection as you practiced releasing the clutch in first gear. And I hear you whisper Adam's name when your maybe love was new.

The harmony of all those songs playing in my head blocks out the discordance competing for an audience. I cup Jada's heel in my hand and see the tell-tale small red collections of blood, appearing to have been made by a red Flair marker, poking indelible dots on each successive layer of flesh on her legs, and they play for me, strumming persistently, a dirge that drowns out the sweet melody of memory. Those damning crimson spots! I hear it now. The time of my daughter's death has lost its distance.

Slathering soap around and between each of Jada's toes, I finish bathing my daughter's body. I was not aware of time passing while she was in the bathtub, but as I pat her warm body dry, I realize that an hour and a half has gone by. It could have been a lifetime.

As Jada lies stretched out on her bed, I pour pools of massage oil into my warm palms. Stroking the fragrant unction over her cleansed skin, I acknowledge where the truth leads and begin to prepare myself to follow. I lift Jada's arms to dress her in her Mary Hillyard sweatshirt; on her feet I put her hightop shoes. We are ready to go to the hospital.

The lobby is vacant—the clinic's receptionist's desk, an addition late in the course of our clinic visits, is abandoned—and not one unruly child slides down the giant plastic blocks stacked together into a play area. Dr. Lourde greets us; he is waiting for us in an empty clinic. We really are alone; I feel no one's presence behind the computer behind the counter, and I do not detect footsteps in the room behind. Heidi moved a year ago to Montana, fed up with the politics, I gathered from bits and pieces I picked up, or just needing a change. And Linda, the current clinic oncology nurse, is gone for the day. Even Barb is not to be seen. It feels as if the clinic has been cleared out of people entirely in preparation for our arrival.

Dr. Lourde, wearing his brown corduroy pants, a striped shirt, and brown loafers, leads us into the room. He shuts the door, walks to the other side of the room and stands, his back against the cupboard. We occupy the examining room alone: no one comes in to take Jada's pulse, bring in a tray topped with cellophane-wrapped syringes, Betadine pads, cotton balls and bandages. Jada is not sent to the lab or X-ray or the operating room. She lies on the table, the sweatpants drooping from her hips like the tarp of a collapsed tent. I pull a chair next to the table and sit, my chin just about level with her body. The eeriness of our isolation brings another thought to me, and I almost blurt, "You never told us when she had to refrain from eating or drinking," but, looking across Jada's hands, crisscrossing her stomach, I watch Dr. Lourde's face. He never says anything he hasn't thought about first, and I see he is ready to speak.

"How are you feeling, Jada? I hear you've had a rough time."

"I'm tired." Jada's head rests at an angle to face Dr. Lourde so that I see only the rise of her cheek, the edge of her mouth, almost lost in the blandness of her skin, the slope of her brow. "Isn't it kind of late for a bone marrow?" She puts the question out on the half beat, but hearing it, I know it fits, satisfies what has been wresting my own equilibrium.

Dr. Lourde's eyes do not blink behind his brown-rimmed glasses. The hairs of his mustache move as one when he opens his mouth to answer, and his even teeth chop out the words. "Actually I'm not going to do a bone marrow. I had a lengthy talk with Dr. Ryan and wanted to wait for him to send me some results. I didn't want to make you come in for one if you didn't need it. I'm sorry to make you wait so long, but I wanted to be sure I knew what we were dealing with." Dr. Lourde's face loses its customary determination; he reminds me of one of Per's runners: in the heat of his effort to win the race, he has sacrificed the breath he needs for the sprint; his skin pales as someone else crosses the finish line before him. "I'm very sorry to tell you this, Jada, but what's giving you so much back pain and making you tired is your leukemia. There's no doubt. Dr. Ryan knew it yesterday and told Priss so she could get you home. There would be no point now to do a bone marrow. We already know."

I concentrate on Dr. Lourde and feel salty tears trickle into the ends of my mouth, drop from my chin because they have been there all along, only I am now just tasting them. Wiping them would break something, so I sit with paralyzed shoulders. Jada cries tears herself, quiet tears, tears of the witness who finally testifies, tears that have been waiting, like mine, tears that come as an aftermath to a cataclysm too horrific to remember and still survive. I see Jada. I see her arms, I see them lift up. I see Dr. Lourde, and he comes into them, bending over her, letting her enclose him and him her. It is the first time they've broken into the circle of physical compassion.

And I cry tears by their side. I am in tears. I bathe myself in them. I sink down into them, let them flow around me, under and over me, baptize me, hold me in place. I do not make a sound. I cry tears and bite my lips between my teeth because it is not me who is dying, it is she, my baby, and as hard as it is to bear, I know it has been accepted and I am left behind.

They release each other, and Jada's face is smeared with tears, but no more come from her eyes. "I've always said I wanted you to live so I could see you as a woman," Dr. Lourde says as he withdraws. "I'm glad I waited. I like the woman you've become." Dr. Lourde backs himself to the counter again and clasps his hands together, his shoulders strong tree branches able to bend as the weight swings back and forth from them. "I know you don't want me to try to knock out the disease, but I would like you to spend a night or two in the hospital to slow it down and help you with your pain. Is that okay with you?"

Jada nods her consent, sending the last tear angling down her cheek to the paper lining and spreading into a feathery gray blotch. Dr. Lourde waits. "I don't know how it is with you and Mr. Petersen," he says to me, "but I can call him if you would like me to."

It occurs to me that Arnold may not be surprised at what I have been so clever to keep secret from myself. "No, I'll tell him." Dr. Lourde leaves, and I stand up, robotically obeying some command to move toward Jada, feeling like both of us are condemned, facing our own firing squads and, aching to keep her, I put my hand on Jada's arm; it is as much touch as I can bear.

Dr. Lourde returns and leads us out to the hall, back into the void of people in the clinic—no silent condolences—or evasions, and I feel the space bumping my shoulders. From the hospital corridor, a nurse appears with a wheelchair and steers Jada toward the large swinging doors and the room reserved for her. The walls of the hospital suction me toward the admissions office for paper work.

I am sent up to Jada on the fourth floor, but before I go, I call Arnold, and I call for a substitute. The steps are too lonely, so I ride the elevator and walk the hallway past dark rooms, past the nurses' station, festooned for the holiday season with golden garlands that flutter their skinny strands. I turn my back to the world and enter Jada's room. She sits in bed, the curtains to the window behind her still open, exposing a black picture until I get closer and see street lights and headlights below. Quickly I draw the curtains shut. Jada has nothing from home, but she doesn't seem to mind; she has Hambone and her memorized telephone numbers. They are enough for the night.

Early the next morning I am sent out for her telephone book and a fresh t-shirt. Jada orders a VCR, and I go out into breath-cracking cold for videos, torrid love stories, all of them. We play one after the other; I sit in the chair and try to keep myself warm and make no attempt to follow. I see faces, hear words, feel nothing. While a movie rewinds, I say, "Per said he'd take us for a tree on Saturday." Jada's eyes look tired, and she nods. She and I both count on Saturday for shopping and decorating. We expect Dr. Lourde to appear. We are restless. We put another movie into the machine, and my mind numbs.

Jada gets out of bed and goes into the bathroom. Hunched over, she looks more like she is slurring than walking. Dr. Lourde has kept his word: no pain. I put my stockinged feet up and cross my heels on the edge of the empty bed. My butt muscles feel relief from the shift, but I lose a lap for my hands. I tuck them under my armpits and yawn a painful yawn, pulling my neck muscles, sending my jaw into a spasm, and bringing tears to my eyes. Jada comes back into the room, crosses the TV screen, and stops, screwing her head sideways to watch a man fondle a woman. Jada resumes her journey to her bed but instead of getting in, comes around where I sit. I am about to take my legs down to let her get into bed when she places her hand at the crotch of my jeans. Her slender fingers scamper like the quick-moving legs of a spider and I feel them through the seam. "How come nobody does that to me?" she asks.

I give a start, but she keeps moving, first sitting on the bed, then swinging her body onto it. My surprise stumbles into regret. There are too many things I have to say yet, things we've not talked about. I regret that I will never be able to make up for myself, that she has nothing to look forward to, no fantasies, about dinners and breakfasts and jobs and babies and dishes to do and someone to love her and sex and time, and that I have let her down.

We have watched every movie, and Jada sends me into the hallway to scout. She is disappointed that she cannot go home yet, and a pout sets her lips downward. I agree with her; this is a petty matter, one day here or there in the hospital, or not, when all you have are days. Arnold comes, bearing a chocolate-frosted custard-filled doughnut. It is her favorite, but she lets it sit on a napkin on the bed stand. Maybe, she says, she will bring it home and eat it later. She turns sullen, and Arnold and I go in and out, trying not to get in each other's way, though the room is large, ending in a "v" as if someone tweezed a corner away from the typical square cell, extending it. But it isn't the physical space that crowds us, so I leave but want to go no place.

I come back to the floor, and Dr. Lourde is standing at the nurse's station and why Arnold is there, I do not know, but I ask Dr. Lourde when he is going to release Jada and let her go home, and he says he's not sure and then I say I need to know because I can't just show up or not show up for work but must know in advance. What I mean is I need to choose my sick days and ask him to talk to Jada, to explain to her that she should let others help her. What I really mean is that my sick leave is about to run out, so she has to let other people do some things I do, but Arnold takes me by the arm and leads me away from the desk. "Idina," he says, his head bowed, the words flowing into my ear like he's giving absolution. "You know you've got more sick pay than you think. The contract says that after you use your sick leave, you still have a hundred half-days paid sick leave." I calculate 100 days and get to somewhere in April, goddamned fucking April, and we all walk in on Jada.

Gradually the day dies, and we have nothing left to prove its life except for the uneaten custard doughnut that grows crusty and a little dusty from the blanket lint that always floats around in hospital rooms. At midnight, I sing to Jada, kiss her forehead, and go home to my own bed. The telephone rings just once. "Mom, you've got to bring me a new shirt. I'm soaking wet."

"Jada, do you know how cold it is outside?" With socks on my feet and heavy blankets heaped upon me, I feel my nose, exposed while I was sleeping, is cold and wet. I shake just remembering how quickly the cold bore through all my wraps as I walked to my car in the hospital ramp. The thought of getting up and going outside feels like the hardest thing to do now. "Can't you use one of the gowns in the hospital?"

"No; they're too scratchy. I want one of my own. You don't have to stay. Just bring me a shirt."

"You're all right otherwise?" I dress over my flannel nightie; I cannot imagine taking it off and raising more goosebumps.

"Yes. Hurry, okay? I'm all wet and it makes me cold."

Even from the heated garage, my car cannot warm the incoming air fast enough to accumulate and a film whitewashes my windows as I drive down the hill and across the parkway to the new emergency entrance where I park and flash the hazard lights. Inside, nurses behind desks along the wall look at me and make a speedy judgment. With frazzled hair and two t-shirts tucked under my arm, I could be none other than a mother. Besides, anyone out on a cold night like this is not looking for mischief.

Just an unobtrusive whirring during the busy daytime, the elevator now roars as it rises through the sleeping hospital and thunders when the door claps shut. The swishing of my sleeves rubbing against the puffy down-filled jacket herald my presence in the dimmed hall leading to Jada's room. I slow down and tiptoe in through the arrow of light that juts from the nurses' station. Jada is crouching beneath blankets and shivering. I shake out a shirt, still tinged with cold and pull off her damp nightshirt. "Do you need new sheets, too?" I ask, seeking an answer through the gray dots between us.

"No. It's not that bad. Just my shirt."

I check her water cup and plump her pillow, bouncing it upwards like a wad of pizza dough. The heating vent above hums steadily. "I'm parked in the emergency zone outside. If you want me to stay a while, I'll have to move the car. It's so cold, I didn't want to walk far." The damp shirt is lumped at the foot of her bed like a curled-up cat. "Here's an extra shirt." I point to the chair. She lies down next to Hambone and I pull the blankets up to Jada's chin.

"No, you can go. I'm going to sleep."

"Call me if you want to, but otherwise, I'll see you in the morning." I sing, I hum, I kiss Jada's forehead. "Night, Sweet."

In the morning, I wait for Jada to wake, and when she does, she wants to go home. All day we wait for Dr. Lourde to let her go. Time is a tornado snatching up events and words and people and spinning them around and around, dashing one against the morning, another against an afternoon, some to oblivion. What happens in two days, or a lifetime, spins around in a vortex of moving boundaries, and this day could be yesterday. Jada dresses for home. In her navy Mary Hillyard sweats and gray math club sweatshirt, the only thing she needs to be ready is to get her hightops on and laced. We wait. The nurse waits. Jada walks to the door and peers outwards for sight of Dr. Lourde. Otherwise she looks blankly at the flat colorless walls and sits on her bed, unfolding her body and letting the top half flop onto the rumpled sheets and blankets.

"What's taking him so long?" Jada asks, lying back on her pillow. We aren't going to a party. We aren't planning dinner; Jada hasn't eaten enough in the past three days altogether to make one full meal. But she wants to get on with what is next. I just sit. A stump. A wart. A bruise felt only when it is bumped. Nether of us lingers well. "Where is he?" Daylight sinks, dragging the overcast of gathering dusk behind it. We've wasted another day.

The door to Jada's room opens with a brush of air. The man pokes in, red-cheeked, white-bearded, his fur-trimmed jacket making little pleats where the black shiny belt cinches his middle. Though his heavy boots come up to his calves, he treads softly, as if he were shuffling through falling snow that in minutes would fill his footprints and blur evidence of his coming.

"It's okay, you can come in," I say to his hesitation. It is that time in December that the afternoon fills up with darkness like a broken ship and then drops to the ocean floor with awesome speed. We haven't yet switched on the light. He holds the door open behind him, committing himself to the room; a photographer follows behind.

"I've been looking for you," Santa says without breaking the quietness. He is at Jada's bed now. A haze fills my vision like magnified dots of a blown-up photo. "They tell me you're a very special person." He leans towards Jada as if he were a prince charming about to kiss the sleeping Snow White out of her trance and says something I do not hear. Then, while the photographer aims the camera, he says, "I'd like to have a picture with you." In the flash of a light, he bestows a kiss on the top of her head. "I have something I want to give you." Out of a bag he pulls a white t-shirt and holds it up to reveal the blue and silver wolf of the basketball team's mascot printed on the front.

I nod to Santa, who leaves the shirt at the foot of the bed while the photographer peels paper from the print that emerged from his camera. He hands the print to Santa who in turn hands it to Jada. The two walk out as gently as they arrived, making a farewell wave while Jada holds the materializing image.

"Good-bye, Santa," I say, getting up from my chair. "Oh, look at that." Leaning over Jada, I watch her and Santa take shape on the square she holds between her fingers. He stoops like a big red blister with a white beard cascading alongside Jada while she lies there, her lips a worn out rubber band between her cheeks. She regards the photograph with the same puffy eyes that look back at her. I tuck the print away in my bag.

By the time we leave the hospital, the early night of winter has dropped on us and we arrive home in the dark. "Do we have any juice?" Jada asks from the rocking chair in the unlit living room made more cavernous by the vaulted ceiling. Neither of us, it seems, wants to throw open all the house lights, so here and there little tents of light make for haziness beyond their glow. I enter the shadows in a panic. Here was another unforeseen trap. Juice? Of course not. I don't have bread or milk either. Why didn't I think to get food? I remember when my dad told me I couldn't drive my car to my own wedding in the piles of snow. Too late, I told him; the wedding was set for 1:00, and I had the starring role. He heaved a 100-pound sack of rice into the trunk of my white '65 Chevy and I headed for the church in Sibley. Twenty-three years later, the extreme cold is my concern, and I have no one to throw any protection my way. We are alone.

"I'm nervous about leaving you alone."

"If it makes you so nervous, why don't you ask Per to get it for you? Remember what you said, we have to let other people help." There is revenge tucked inside her words; I accept what is owed me.

"Guess I better take my own advice. I don't know if he's home from ski practice yet. And if he is, he'll be cleaning up. I can't ask this time. But tomorrow when he takes us for our tree, I'll give him a list of things to get us at the store. Will you be all right if I go now?" The question is stupid, but that's how I feel.

Bundled in my black coat, a scarf wound about my head, I warn, "I'll be back in half an hour, a little more." I am particularly careful, signaling early for a left turn, keeping my foot light on the accelerator. I am curiously aware of my image and its reverberation back and forth from me to others through me again, boomeranging myself into a new identity, yet remaining forever landlocked in this place of no return, a Timbuktu of consciousness.

I set the grocery bag on the table. Not finding Jada in the living room, I go through the rest of the condo. Just two more bedrooms and two baths, there are no places to hide. Jada lies on my bed. Unbuttoning my coat, I ask warily, "Do you want your juice in here?"

"No, I'll get up." She rises, my arm a hoist. I follow her hobbled walk to the living room, hanging my coat along the way. She puts a tape in the tape player and pulls the rocking chair to the edge of the rug, watches me in the dining room, pulling two jugs and a can of juices, a carton of milk and a box of instant oatmeal, maple and brown sugar flavored, out of the paper bag. I bring her a glass of apple juice on a saucer and put the rest of the groceries away. In the background, Ann Murray sings "Go Tell It On the Mountain," and even though we do not have a tree yet, I take out a box of decorations from the laundry room. The candleholder with two reindeer, butting their horns and noses together to shape a heart between them, have come unglued from their base. I dab Elmer's glue on the base. Kneeling at the table, I hold the two reindeer in place to set.

Jada watches me trying to keep my hand steady and says, "Let's go hear some Christmas music."

"I'll ask Jessie if there's any in her church. That's such a beautiful church, you'd think they'd have something. Or Holy Childhood maybe. Music's big there. You know, though, I don't recall Catholic churches having music programs at Christmas. Maybe one of the other churches on Cathedral Way." I release the reindeer, tentatively trusting them to stand on their own. Rising, I groan. It doesn't take long for kneecaps to hurt on a hard wooden floor.

"What do you think, Jada, should we get more lights like these? Or should we do all little ones this year?" I hold up a box of red metal cylinders with light bulbs on one end and a wire stringing them together through the other. They were supposed to look like candles people used to put on trees before electricity made its way into Christmas. She says nothing, and I set the boxes aside. I grab a gift box and hold up to my shoulders the heavy gray lambswool sweater for Per. "I finished the sweater." She was with me when I bought the yarn last spring.

She nods. "It looks nice," she says, but I still feel like I'm talking to myself.

I replace the sweater, folding it into a plump pillow, take out a roll of paper, and wrap the box. Then I sort through the box of trims and lay a silver wreath and red-berried plastic holly on the green foil. I look over to Jada for advice but decide it really doesn't matter and choose the silver. "There's one package. Do you want to wrap Dom's for me?" She likes to decorate packages, selecting paper, adding a sprig of holly, a bell, a pine cone, to make it as fun to get on the outside as it is on the inside. "Maybe we can get him over here on Sunday to make sugar cookies. I'll have to see what we need."

Making sugar cookies is one of our traditions. I roll them out thin and tender, sometimes too thin so that they break in the handling; those and the browned ones may be eaten from the tray; the showoff cookies I hide for company. Jada hand-places silver beads at the eyes, chocolate sprinkles for the boots, a few cinnamon hearts and multicolored pareils as gifts in Santa's bag. To Dom, taste, not appearance, is the thing, and he dumps a spoonful of sugar to cover.

The Christmas tape ends with "Oh, Holy Night," and Jada leaves me with my mess on the living room floor to go to her room. As I check my cupboards for sugar, shortening, flour, I hear her talking. I start a shopping list, knowing we'll have to compromise somewhere between cookies for old-times' sake and Jada's present energy level. Maybe half-batches of sugar cookies, snowballs for sure. Just her favorites. I'll let her decide.

"Mooie," she calls. I leave my pen and paper and my memories behind and go in to her. "I want to go to bed now. Will you get my things for me? She sits in the same place she did when Priss was here. Beneath her eyes are webs of gray. The evening has exhausted her; I bought this unit in this building because of the elevator, but I did not predict that the walk from the car to it or the walk down the hall from it to our unit could seem so long and take such effort. *I've got to remember how much energy it takes for her to even sit up for a spell, walk across the condo from one room to another.* After changing her clothes, I help Jada to the bathroom.

"Will you be okay in here alone? Or do you want me to stay?"

Jada steadies herself, one hand holding onto the sink. "I can do it. Leave the door open."

"I'll be back in a few minutes." I turn the tape player off and shove the Christmas boxes back in the laundry room. I like to have coffee ready to go in the morning, but I skip making it this time; I'll be awake before Jada, anyway. Checking that the door is locked, I turn the lights off and come back to her bathroom.

"Okay, Mooie, I'm ready." Together we walk to her bed, her arm locked in mine. "Will you sleep with me? I want you to sleep here tonight." Though it is not late, the thought of sleeping makes me instantly tired. I finish my own preparations and switch off the hallway light. Even with her blinds down, enough moonlight seeps through for me to see my way to the other side of her bed and slip between her crisp sheets already warmed by an electric blanket and thick comforter. I snuggle my shoulders into a comfortable position, and Jada rolls over, reaching her arms out for me as a child begging to be picked up or a lover beckoning her mate. I meet her embrace, and holding each other, I sing to her. I sing the lullabies I've always sung to her, every night, every night I could. "Where have they gone.... What are little girls made of.... What are little boys made of, made of? Sticks and stones, and puppy dog bones.... Rock-a-bye, Baby." I hum. I am close to her, and my breathing in and out makes the air move over her.

"Oh, Mooie, Mooie, Mooie," Jada says, as if she, too, were singing a song. "I love you."

"I love you, too, Jada. You're my baby."

607

It is still dark, and I am brought up from sleep. Jada and I are still in an embrace, our arms having not moved during slumber. "Mooie, Mooie, Mooie, Mooie," she whispers, not as a question or even a name. "Mooie," she says, as if she is choosing me.

I know I have slept, but I know I have not slept for long. "My baby, my baby," I answer back into the dark. I feel heavy, unable and unwilling to move, to pull myself up from the trance; it feels so safe holding each other and I dream of a huge wave coming over our heads and encircling us, making a shelter for us to walk through, and we do, hand in hand, holding on to one another. I wake again, and I hear Jada call again, "Mooie," as if we aren't in the dream but maybe we both are and it's hers and I say again, "My baby." The night passes through time, and Jada and I pass through the night, neither one of us moving. We hold our arms around each other, and I know I'm not dreaming and we are calling softly back and forth, "Mooie, Mooie," "My baby," a dialogue we have rehearsed all her life.

I wake up to irrepressible light through white blinds and Jada's waking. We hold each other yet, bound by some inexplicable rite. "Mooie," she says again, only once, this time.

"Mmmm. Are you ready to get up?" We let go. I make quick movements to cover myself in slippers and my long terry robe and walk around the bed to help her out and to the bathroom. Pulling the pick through my hair, I wish I had taken the time to make the coffee ready.

"Come here, quick!" It's Jada from her bathroom. I am just feet away, but there is urgency in her voice; I run. Jada is on her feet, backing away from the toilet, bent over, holding her abdomen, as if trying to keep it from spilling away from her. Her other arm grabs in front of her, but there is only air. I take the step up and catch her. "Something's wrong!" she cries, as if pain has jumped her and holds a knife to her.

"What is it? Here, let me get you to bed. I'll call Dr. Lourde."

"No! I have to get to the hospital. Something's wrong!" Her voice echoes as if it has fallen into a black hole, crying for help from a helpless place.

I steer Jada to her bed and set her on it, afraid that if she does not balance she will tip over and splinter into a thousand shards. "Okay. I'll get dressed." I run to my room and pick up yesterday's jeans.

"Hurry, Mom!"

"I'm coming," I call back to her, pulling on panties and socks.

"Hurry, hurry!" I warn myself not to forget my untied shoelaces lopping on the floor and run back to Jada, who has not moved a finger.

"We have to get something on you; it's at least 20 below." She does not want to give me her arms, so I toss the sweatshirt aside and pool the sweatpants around her ankles. "Where are your shoes? Oh, I see them." I duck for them from under the dust ruffle. As gently as I can, I pull them onto her feet and she is starting to put weight on them, economizing movement and time.

"Hambone," she says, and I snatch him along with her sweatshirt, and we start for the door. I yank our coats from the closet and put mine on as I run for my wallet and keys while Jada is out the door and on her way down the long corridor outside our unit, both arms cradling her abdomen, a weighty load pulling her downward. I run ahead and punch the elevator button. "Here, put your coat on. You'll freeze." She does not let go of her belly so I place the coat over her shoulders. We got ourselves ready in less time than it is taking to get out. To Jada, it must feel like a marathon. As she steps into the elevator, I worry that I do not get the car to her fast enough.

"Oh!" Jada cries as we drive up the ramp. The bumps of the curb, islands of iced snow, just the motion of a turn around the corner sends blades of pain through her.

"Okay, Jada, almost there, almost there. Hang on." It's another roller coaster ride, I tell myself, twenty seconds, just twenty seconds long. "Just down the hill now."

"Oh!" I stop at the ice-encrusted yellow curb at the main entrance of the hospital. Jada opens the car door and heaves herself onto the pavement, her coat falling to the seat and flopping over the frame of the car, the edge of a sleeve grazing the dirty snow. Jada shuffles, knees bent, back bent, head bent, like a crippled old woman, towards the glass doors. I push Jada's coat inside the car and shut the door she left gaping behind her. A woman in a brown security uniform walks towards me, her jaw muscles working, her arm raised in a "stop right there" motion. I look fully at her, then away after Jada, the handicapped door sliding open. Balled up in an ear-flapped bomber hat, the guard's head follows me. "I'll move it in a minute," I shout. She stops and begins to retreat.

Always, always, almost always, there's a wheelchair around to the right of the entrance. Sometimes it's tucked behind a tall leafy plant. I catch the worn rubber handgrip from under the frond of the potted plant. "Here, Jada, here. I've got a wheelchair for you!" I yank it out and chase her with it.

"Help" she pleads. "Help me!" To me she squeezes out, "It's too small."

A woman materializes from the admissions office. "We need a wheelchair that fits her. She's got to get in." I say, shoving the chair backwards on its own journey, and I catch up to Jada and the woman who holds onto her. Behind. I am always behind.

"Call Dr. Lourde," Jada spurts.

"Sit down, I'll get help." The woman goes back into her office, and I stand, holding my hand on Jada's shoulder as if to keep it from popping off like a cork in a bottle with too much gas. Two men in blue cotton shirts round the corner and rescue Jada, lifting her from the chair and leading her away toward the elevator while the woman tells me that Dr. Cung is already in the hospital and will meet her in the room. I need only to sign the insurance papers. "It's okay," she assures me, "you'll be able to go up to her in a few minutes. As soon as I find out where she is, I'll let you know."

"I'm parked at the entrance. I have to move my car." I try to shove my hands into my pockets but find they are stuffed with mittens. I pull them out, try again. My keys.

Even on a Saturday morning, all the spots in the two front tiers are taken in rebelliousness, I think, of the hospital's rule against overnight parking. I find a place in the back row, facing the street and facing the wind. Damn, it's freezing. My denim jeans are like tissue against the bite of this cold that wants to wolf me down, a mere snack for a ravenous appetite. I run to the hospital, Jada's coat muffling my hands. The woman in admissions is on the telephone. She looks up, still writing. "Room 301. That's in the Intensive Care unit." Fourth floor must be closed for the holidays becomes a random thought that rides with me up to Jada's room.

Dr. Cung and a trio of nurses surround Jada's bed like a curtain. Bags, tubes, pens drip from them, rippling in and out as if a breeze waffles the team's gear as they bend over her. I tiptoe to the closet and hang our coats. I am extraneous, in the way of traffic by the door, distracting, on my way to the other side of the room. But they do not notice me. They have a job to do, and I, having not, have to make one, like a reporter zooming in on victims of tragedy, shoving a microphone in under their dignity, leeching their privacy for a public hungry for sensationalism. I go to the surgery waiting room to call Arnold, but I can only say she is here, not why, and on to the cafeteria for a cup of coffee, which is, I say for the millionth time, bad coffee, all color and no flavor. It tastes soapy, and I drink the briny brew hot. The dishwater smell turns my stomach, and I dump the cup in the trash container. I miss being with Jada and do not want to be missing from her when she wants me.

The flurry has subsided; Dr. Cung is established in a chair next to a machine that is attached to Jada, lying quietly, her eyes closed. I want her to know I am here, but I am glad there is no sign of pain on her face, and I watch her from the window ledge. A single nurse attends Dr. Cung, silently going in and out. Arnold arrives, and he stands with a Styrofoam cup of coffee in my former spot with the same expressionless face I must have. I feel like I have been called to the principal's office without a hint as to the purpose. I don't know if I am about to receive punishment or praise, so I must be careful wearing a face that can accommodate either, at once ready to accept or deny. We stand separately like that, Arnold sipping his coffee, I stealing images, looking for clues from Dr. Cung's movements, the fold of the sheets, the white fog that swirls like little tornadoes that vanish in the air outside. Too cold for them, too. "What time is it?" I ask. Arnold, like Per, wears a watch. I can count on them for accuracy.

Arnold uses his two middle fingers to nudge the cuff of his yellow sweater from the face of his watch. "Three minutes after ten."

"I have to go out and make a telephone call. I'll be right back." I leave for the surgery waiting room, Saturday morning empty, and use the phone in the conference room. "Per, forget about the tree. I had to take Jada back to the hospital this morning. I'm here now."

"That's too bad." Per doesn't ask what is wrong, and I am relieved, for no one has told me and I have not asked myself. "What about lunch, then?"

"I don't think so. I don't know what's going on. I probably shouldn't leave."

"You're going to eat lunch somewhere, aren't you?"

"I suppose I should; I'm not really hungry, but I haven't eaten yet."

"Why don't we go over to Trident Grill. That's right by the hospital, isn't it? You'll be gone less than an hour. I'll pick you up."

"I'll see if Arnold's going to stay. If he is, I'll go. How's 12:00?" I return to Jada's room. Nothing, it seems, has changed, except that Arnold is gone, though his coat is a sign that he is somewhere nearby. A strap shackles Jada's arm to a machine, and Dr. Cung studies dials and blipping signals as if they're flirting with him. I take the chair by the window and restore myself to waiting. If thought flows, I do not pay attention to it, cannot account for my contribution to the passing of time.

Above the sound of the door's opening and closing, above the sound of rubber-soled shoes tamping on the linoleum, above the sound of Dr. Cung's shirt sleeve fabric swishing underneath his armpit, I hear Arnold's reappearance, taking breaths in and swallowing them, and forcing them out. I grow jumpy, as if I've had too much coffee on an empty stomach, yet I feel worn out and lead-footed. If I heard the word "fire," someone would have to tell me what to do. Dr. Cung slides his chair away from Jada's bed and speaks to the nurse, then to me, "Let's go out there." I follow his eyes to Arnold and gather myself to get up. He leads us to the family waiting area where Arnold and I take seats on the two-person couch. Dr. Cung sits in the blue chair and tips himself slightly toward us. He looks smaller here than he did in the room. "Jada's decided not to have a transplant, is that correct?"

I nod, wondering what that has to do with now, and Arnold says, "Correct," as if he were host of a game show and the slightest inflection would jeopardize the contestant's chances of winning.

"Am I also right in understanding that you don't want us to go to extremes to try to save her?"

I see a multiple-part question developing. I answer flatly, "Right," hearing the word smack in my dry mouth. I give a quick nod to Arnold for corroboration and run my tongue over my lips and swallow. I feel stupid and uncertain, like I have had too much to drink and have to think deliberately and ask cautiously, "What's going on?"

"Jada's suffering from internal bleeding in her abdomen. It's extremely painful and extremely dangerous. For a while it was touch and go, but we've got her blood pressure stabilized now."

A jolt charges through me; this must be what it feels to get a shock treatment, a jump start to the brain, a spasmodic moment of death, the memory of which recreates awareness. "What? You mean it's that serious?"

"That's why I've been with her all morning." Dr. Cung's gaze stares me down; he is being patient with me as I struggle to reorient myself to this new reality.

"I had no idea! I made plans to take a lunch break. Had I known, I never would have."

"Go ahead and eat lunch. As long as we keep her blood pressure under control, we can keep her comfortable. I'll be here in the hospital for a while yet this afternoon, but I won't be needing to stay with her. I just want to be sure that we aren't taking extraordinary measures that we would if, say, she were hoping for a transplant or another remission."

"I feel terrible! How can I leave her?"

"But you have to eat, Idina." Arnold's voice reaches up and grabs me, brings me down, as if I'm a balloon on a string. Dr. Cung tenses his muscles to rise. "I'll take one last look in on her before I leave."

I begin to follow, but Arnold's hand is on my sleeve. "Wait a minute." I feel myself bobbing, being jerked into a direction that opposes my instincts to soar upwards. "I know you think you can be strong, but I think you should consider a hospice."

"A hospice? No, she has to come home."

"I know. I know. It sounds like a wonderful thing to do, but I don't think you know how hard it's going to be. Not just for you, but for her. She's going to require a lot of care."

"That's probably true, but I just couldn't leave her someplace and visit. That's not what she chose to live out her life. I have to try it at home." Arnold has removed his hand, but I stay.

"Idina, you are going to need a lot of strength. At least go and eat lunch."

"I'm going back in there now. Are you going to be around for a while?"

"Yes. I've got some errands to do, but I can stay for a while, sure. We have tickets for the Minnesota Orchestra, so I won't be back tonight."

"If she's okay, then I will take a break."

I sit in the chair Dr. Cung has vacated. Not one nerve ending ripples in Jada's face, like a painting of a still lake in a windless sunset. I wonder how much she knows, how much she thinks, even while seemingly asleep, or somewhere near it. A nurse walks into the room and hands me a square of paper that reads, "Jada or Mom, call Priss."

"She said when no one answered at your house she figured you'd be here." I didn't take Jada's phone book as we fled the condo;

placing the folded note on the bed stand, in a church voice I thank the nurse. She charts.

"Would you like something?"

I shake my head. "No. Just the time." I will have to get Jada a cup of water before I go. She always likes a sip of cool water, though she hasn't shifted since I first came into the room. I regret my promise to Per, but say to her, "I'm going to go for lunch in a bit, is that okay?" I get no answer. "Your dad's here, Darlin'. I'll be back in less than an hour." I watch her in case she sits up, commands me to stay, but not even a flicker of her eyelids registers she has heard my voice. I tell the nurse at the station where I'll be and meet Per at the main entrance.

Little traffic moves slowly along the street; it is cold, it is Saturday, and people are conducting their lives elsewhere. Per's gray Trooper appears at the corner, rolls toward me like a big tank. The crunching snow under its moving wheels crackle in the frigid air. "Man, it's cold," I say over the grumbling heater when I get in. Even in the cold the interior reeks of stale sweat. He says all he has to do is take out his rollerblades, but I know the odor is permanent, like the smell of a smoky beer joint, and will never come clean.

"The high today is only six below with a wind-chill of minus 38."

"Good. Then I didn't keep you from going skiing."

"No, I'm going, but I'll go later. I'll go where it's protected by the woods. It's always ten degrees warmer in there. I shan't be skiing at the golf course. I guarantee you, though, boys on my team'll be there. Jiminee-Jesus, the wind'll be cold there!"

I shake inside my jacket and cower into it with the thought. I had told myself that I'd never complain about the cold again after Jada's convulsive reactions to a blood product and tried unsuccessfully to relieve her uncontrollable chills by laying my warm body upon hers. Hard to keep that promise when at full blast, the heater cannot gain much ground in the race it is having with the iced air it is being fed.

Per's truck slows to a stop and he tells me to "hop out"; he'll park the truck and join me. How he could go out without a thick jacket and gloves stymies me, and I accept the offer and jump down onto black covered ice that has eroded into smooth solid waves along the curb. When I get inside the restaurant door, I blot my tearing eyes.

Nothing appeals to me, not even conversation, but I order soup. It is like eating airplane food: I am filling a need greater than hunger. Per and I both look beyond each other. Behind him, tiny lights sprinkle the wreath hanging on the old brick wall.

"Tonight's the Christmas ski party at the Szandy's. I have to stop and get something to bring. Maybe some ice cream or cookies."

"What time is that?"

"About six-thirty. I won't stay very long. Probably till around 9."

"Is it okay if you go back to my place tonight? I'm staying at the hospital; but I just need you to stay at my place. Things don't feel right. Then I want to get a tree. I'll bring the tree to the hospital. Can you help me with that? Can you get it even if I can't go with you, and can you bring it to the hospital? I have to get a tree for her."

"I have to get my tree, too. I'll get it when I get mine. What size do you want?"

"Just a bitty one." I hold up my hands like a sandwich and spread them apart. "She loves to decorate the tree, and if she's in the hospital at Christmas, she has to have a tree."

Another couple sits a few booths away from us, and someone raises a yelp from the bar on the other side of the wall. I become acutely aware of the smells and sounds of a Saturday afternoon between things. Another time, another life. The sweetness of onions simmering in a soup on the stove, a spice cake just out of the oven, cooling on a rack, the flour that dusted the pan browned and smoky smelling. Droplets of sun-warmed ice turned to dribbles glistening in the window corner, a referee's whistle at a football game on TV, a giggle from a telephone conversation in the bedroom. The server sets our food before us.

I dip my spoon, folding the contents in the bowl. "You know," I say, my spoon suspended above the orange pool, "she could die." I take the soup and swallow hard. I wonder what it is like being caught in a tornado. It would have to pick you up, whirl you round and round, probably even throw you down before it could be believed. And even then it would be unbelievable.

Halfway through my soup, I say, "I'm in a hurry, if that's okay. I'd just like to get back."

"I don't need to hang around here." Per scoops up the last few bits of turkey from his plate. "I don't know about that skiing. I could take a nap. Comfort food."

"You don't take naps, remember?"

"No, I'll go skiing. I just need an hour to digest this food."

We return to an engine that has turned dead cold, finding a kind of pleasure in freezing, and resists turning its parts. "My truck isn't very happy," Per says, the breath from his mouth making little clouds. He rubs the windshield up and down with the back of his hand.

I sink my nose into my collar and chatter, though the more I try to stop my teeth from chopping, the worse it gets. "I'll call you tonight before six," I stutter. "Have a good time skiing."

He leans away from the steering wheel, and I meet his kiss. We are an odd and unlikely pair.

The hospital is as still as outdoors; no offices open, no whirring elevators with visitors bunching up in front of them, no traffic of busy people cradling papers in their arms and briefcases dripping from their hands. Jada's unit is even quieter; with the double doors to each room closed along the corridor, the only sounds are from the nurses' station, and only one nurse works at some noiseless task behind the counter.

I hang my coat in the closet and sit beside Jada and the ticking machine. It reminds me of my aunt's clock at my grandma's house, encapsulated under a glass dome, four gold serifs suspended from the calibrated timekeeping piece and driven by it, winging perpetually back and forth. I was mysteriously afraid of walking alone through the upstairs hall where it crowned the bureau, as if by watching the wonders of such exotic objects I were eavesdropping on private conversations. Click, click, click, click, the clock knew I was there.

The legs of my chair scrape the floor as I shift, the noise louder than life. Jada stirs, and I go to her. Her eyelids remain closed, and in a semi-sleeping state she rises, and I walk her to the bathroom. She leans on me, and I talk, wonder if she senses me. A nurse comes in and out, in and out, and the telephone rings. "It's Adam, Jada; do you want to talk?" She rolls to her side and I hold the receiver to her head, and she brings her hand up to it, near her ear, the other end hanging near her mouth.

"Hmm," she murmurs and pauses. "No." Her eyes are closed, as if she is taking little naps between words. "I can't talk now. I'll feel better tomorrow." She barely moves her lips, and I wonder if her words are audible through the wires. Jada's hand loosens under mine and the receiver begins to slip from her ear, her breathing hard and pronounced. I cover her with blankets to her chin.

"Priss called, too, but I don't know her number," I say, but there is no response from her faceless face, all expression erased by the loss of feeling, and a suspicion forms that Jada hadn't been aware of the words she had uttered to Adam. "Do you hear me, Jada?" A shaft of guilt for filling the room with words shoots through me: she rejects "noise" when she is sick. Would the next few months be like this, a slow wasting of time? Nothing romantic about that. People who do not want to be kept alive on machines must have witnessed people kept alive on machines. The afternoon drones with the machine clicking questions at me, picking off scabs.

Darkness drops its blanket and I pick up Jada's watch from the bedside table, rotating it in the dim light to make out the time. A couple minutes past six. But it isn't six, is it? I go to the door and look through the window at the clock on the station wall. Five here. Her watch is still on Eastern time. What is that quote? Life is what happens when you're waiting for something to happen? Something like that. Whatever are we waiting for? A nurse comes in, her eyes look wet and soft, and presents me with a piece of cake from another nurse's birthday party. Hoarsely I promise to eat it later when I am hungry.

Jada lets out a moan, a breath of air that whisks past her vocal chords, and I look for a clue. Perhaps she is dreaming, and I shiver to think we're all just a breath, time just a shadow of our waiting, we just a gasp and a sigh.

I search the face of Jada's watch for the big hand. "Will it bother you if I make a call?" I get no response and dial Per's number. His hello echoes like he's in a cave, and I tent the mouthpiece with my hand and talk into it quietly. "Did you go skiing?... No, I'm still here. Nothing's changed. She's sort of sleeping. She gets up to go to the bathroom. Do you remember when we were out at the track and some horses got Lasix?... Yes, you do. They're giving it to her to help her eliminate water and regulate her blood pressure.... Okay. I'll talk to you tomorrow."

Night prowls about Jada's room, its sticky fingers stealing precious moments. To sleep a dreamless sleep is like not living, yet I want just that. Jada uneasy under the shroud of medications, sighing the restlessness of the wind of a brewing storm just over the horizon is a negation of all that she wants to live for. I wish for her to get through this and be home. A folded bed is wheeled in and tucked into the corner by the window. I flatten it so I can lie down. Jada stirs and needs to pee; I will be getting up a lot during the night.

Then I am awakened. It has come prematurely and suddenly. Like when babies cry in the night. You don't roll over and go back to sleep; you don't walk around aimlessly banging into doors. You are instantly alert. I hear Jada before I know I am awake. She is beating the bed with her body, and I arise to see what I can do, and seeing that though there is urgency to her body movement, there is nothing apparently urgent for me to do. I have to wait this out until she calms. I am confused about the time. Have I changed her watch to Central time? It is either 11:30 or 12:30, and something is very different, about the feel of the air, about the sounds of her swishing legs, her rocking head, thumping her hands on the sheet. I am afraid not to watch her and keep a sideways eye on her while I fold up the blankets and the bed in a stack against the wall. I have not slept long, but I have slept enough.

A chill grips me, tightening my shoulders and pulling my chin down like a turtle for warmth. This morning I had no thought for later. Jada's sweatshirt lays on top of her folded sweatpants. I don't think she will use it tonight, so I pull the gray fleecy shirt over my head and thrust my fists thorough the sleeves. It will get me through the night until I can get home for clean clothes, warm clothes. And a toothbrush.

Lois comes in with a smile and a portable toilet, and I thank her for her thoughtfulness, thank her that she, of all nurses, is on this shift. "I thought this would make it easier for Jada. She won't have to walk." Jada moves about and starts to rise from her bed, as if some voice only she can hear calls her up. Lois and I each take an arm and guide her to the chair. Her face muscles work in effort to obey the drug, and her belly protrudes like a puffy marshmallow. Her arms lay on the bars along the side of the chair, and if her eyes weren't closed in a frozen face, I would have less doubt of her unawareness of her surroundings.

We sit Jada on the bed, then lifting her legs up and straightening them, Lois brings the blankets to order and empties the pot of its scant contents. Before leaving, Lois pauses at the door to smile at me. "I'm not going on break tonight. If you need me, I'll be here." I feel encouraged by her concern and stare into her absence, the blood pressure monitoring machine a metronome to the night. But wait; Lois did not check the reading on the machine, and when the other nurse stopped I cannot pinpoint. I intuit that machine readings no longer serve as indicators of the changes in Jada's body and that the waiting is different. I need to watch differently.

I need to watch Jada, fill myself with the importance of her, the shape and substance of her; I am awake to her breathing, to her spiraling eyes underneath her eyelids and the fluttering twitches around them. I feel the intensity that marks our missions, separate, yet inextricably intertwined. I'd mistakenly, obstinately believed I'd had no choice, that, had I a choice, I would not have chosen this. Yet I did choose. I chose to follow. I fell through the clutch of fear to take my place in this mission. I chose to be here in the frightful unknown, with my daughter who is on a journey I can only regard through my senses. I made the choice long ago, and I made it again and again and again today. Just as surely as Jada is not a passive passenger, so am I not just along for the ride. Nor am I going to jump out, no matter how tempting the final escape. I am here where the roller coaster has been leading all along, and I had better be ready. I think I am. I am not sleepy, though it is past midnight. I haven't eaten or drunk coffee or water or juice. I don't need to get up and move around or use the toilet or twiddle my thumbs, a nervous and somewhat archaic and annoying habit that both Per and Jada think turns me into an old fuddy-duddy. As during her birth, I can feel her writhe inside and push to move on, and I am mother for her passage.

With a powerful surge, as if yanked forward by a pulley, Jada bolts up, reaching her arms out. "Get him out of here!" she cries, her eyes open but stricken of recognizability. I look to where she appears to be looking, and I see no one in the room, but I am frightened, too. I am at the bed, her arms still stretched out, pointing, as if to a creature before her and encircle Jada, hold her, place my head next to hers.

"Okay, Jada, I'll tell him to go," I say, fearing it is come to take her. "Go, yes, go." Jada does not feel like she feels me; her arms are still stiff, though I have her in my grip.

"D over dx to the nth…. Tell them; you've got to tell them." She is urgent, her voice tearful, high and fraught.

"Yes, Jada, I'll tell them."

"No, they won't know. I'll tell you again." She repeats a formula that runs out of numbers, dwindles to unintelligible mutterings.

I rock her as an infant, comforting her with my voice. "Yes, my baby. I'll be sure they get it right. It's okay; I'm here.

"Get the Cliff notes. They have to know."

"They will; I'll tell them."

"Cosine times nx plus sin…."

I want to lead her back to the mattress but she is strong.

"It's not fair," she says, each word a blow. "I hurt all over."

"My baby, my baby, let me help you," I say in her ear, wishing I could. She is sitting stiffly, her arms still rigid. I recognize that her belly has grown larger.

"Hold on to me," she cries, and I tighten my hold; I want her to feel me, feel my strength, feel my love, trust that I will not let her fall from the edge of this cliff, not as long as I am here holding her.

"I am holding on." I say with all the conviction I have.

"I have to go. I gotta get out of here."

"It's okay, you can go." My hand cradles the back of her neck as if she were a newborn, her head about to bobble backwards. She goes limp and sags in my hold, and I guide her back to the mattress and release her but do not leave her. I sit vigilant, guarding her from whatever possessed her, a clear and present barrier to taking her, waiting, even for it to pass, or at least agree to step back and let me have her for a while longer. The birthday cake, brown and square and riddled with air bubbles on its paper plate, revolts me. I move the cake to the triangle shelf across the room.

Jada lies restlessly, rocking her head on the pillow, back and forth, back and forth, more pronounced and more urgently, as if, not being believed, she has to deny and deny and deny. Her arms make jerky attempts to raise themselves above the blankets. She takes great gusts of breath. Her legs, too, begin a kind of spastic dance that rumples the smooth blankets into a winter desert. She looks luminous in the faint light, like she is fading, yet there is a feverish feel above her, as if her body were generating a nimbus.

Something is happening, something awful and mysterious and compelling. I have no thought or desire to call for help. I covet this time alone with her and trust help to come when I need it. I watch. I watch the current of life run through her and make her jump. I watch the flow of morphine dull the sharp edges, so that I see only blurs where she wrestles with pain so intense it is all she is. I watch the tree of death send its roots down to Jada's very birth and gain its life by killing off the seed that nursed it. Jada raises herself, and I fear it will be the intruder again, hungry for its prey, getting bolder until I become mere sawdust in its way. She turns toward her left; it is the toilet she needs. Her body has learned its route. She needs me only for steadiness, though her eyes don't open. It seems a useless effort, but there is no denying the urge, and I lead her back to bed.

Jada bolts up again and peels the blankets from her right side, as if she is a toreador about to tempt the bull's charge with the sweep of the cloth. My stomach jumps ahead of me. She makes no move to get out of bed but begins to knead first her right leg, then both, as Lois comes into the room. "She's really really restless now! Tossing all the time, sitting up, and now, and now, this," I say, pointing down to her legs. "Look! Look at her legs!" I gasp at their deep purple color, a throbbing mass of ominous dark blackening under parchment white skin. I would like to tear Lois's face off to find out what is going on at Lois's sudden intake of air, the automatic flare of her wide-set eyes. We guide Jada onto the chair and then back into bed, and Lois goes to the bag of morphine. Jada is lying in bed, covered, but I am standing, looking, and Lois motions me out to the hall.

"What do you think?" Lois asks, her watery eyes on mine.

"I don't like the looks of this at all," I answer, knowing and not knowing what I have seen. My stomach churns a sour mash, and I bring my hand to my mouth.

"No." And then her voice fades from a whisper to almost nothing; I hear her clearly. "Is there anyone you want me to call?"

"Call Dr. Lourde. And her father. Call her father. And Beverly Parks. Do you know who she is? She's listed in the phone book un—"

"Yes. I know how to get her number. Are you okay?"

I nod, and we part. I go back into Jada's room, my breathing rapid, from the top of my throat. She, too, works hard at breathing, as if the air has been sucked out of the room and her lungs have to pull all the way to the door to get what they need. I sit on Jada's bed, my back to the door and do not take my eyes off her, trying not to take too much of the precious air. Her body is pushing, all the parts pulsing and surging to pass through a crowded canal. Lois returns. "Dr. Lourde is on his way. The others are coming, too." Lois stays with us, and we watch the thrashing in Jada's body.

I feel Dr. Lourde arrive. Jada rises, and I recognize her surge for the toilet. Dr. Lourde does not exit; I think that this humiliation should be repugnant but feel more appalled at the drug's power to denigrate a body's natural function into a clinical motion. He helps me put her back into bed, examining her skin and feeling her belly before covering her up and giving Lois brief instructions. He steps back again, and I take my space next to Jada. Lois returns carrying a metal container and situates it on the floor at the head of the bed. She tries to fit a plastic mask over Jada's head, but it is small, sized for a young child; and Jada, fighting or hurting, or trying to communicate, tosses so that Lois doesn't get the elastic beyond Jada's crown but lets the mask lay over Jada's nose and mouth like it has been dropped and carelessly sloughed. This humiliation, too, I want to tear away, but Jada is pulling harder at the air. I look to Dr. Lourde who explains, "We're giving her some oxygen to help her breathing." And then, to explain what he does not explain, he adds, "She can hear everything we say."

Lois backs away, and I lean in closer, my elbows on either side of Jada, my heart next to hers. "I'm here, Jada; I'm here with you. It's all right." I want her to be able to talk to me, I want to be able to hear her if what she is struggling to do is to speak.

I hear a gust, or maybe a sigh from behind. I recognize Arnold's presence and feel a weight at the foot of the bed. I don't know how I know, but I know that Beverly arrives, too. I see only Jada struggling with that nuisance of a mask that I dare not take away.

She tosses her head, fighting for air, for voice, for what? The mask comes away, and Lois's or Dr. Lourde's hands are on a chase trying to adjust it. From behind me Dr. Lourde says, "We all know what's happening here, don't we?"

My arms are around Jada and I rock with her, up together, down, her head near mine, my hands underneath, back and forth we rock. "I'm here, Jada. Your dad's here. We love you. Yes, Jada, my baby." Jada's hand fights its way up to her face and waves at the mask that covers mostly her cheek by now, hardly her nose at all. "What is it, Jada? Is that in your way? My breath?" The smile comes involuntarily to my own mouth and I shift my head so my breath goes to her ear. "You're always teaching me. You're wonderful, my baby. Thank you for everything you give us. We've all learned from you. My baby." We rock. I want to kiss her ear but I talk to her. "It's okay, Jada. I love you. Your dad loves you. Dom loves you. You're our baby. The world is lucky to have you. You're so courageous. I love you, my baby. I love you."

I hear Jada draw two short intense breaths and think, good, she can breathe again and her body tightens with a powerful surge as if she is being yanked away from me and I have to see her, look at her face and I call, "Jada, Jada?" as if I have just heard the door slam and the house shake and am asking if that is she coming home. Her pupils open like fast motion photography of a budding flower. I look into her eyes, thinking she is finally able to say something and I feel gratitude that she isn't fighting anymore, she has this gifted opportunity of consciousness; she looks alert, surprised, as if she has just come upon an idea and it is so great that she is amazed by it herself and now she gets to tell me all about it. Instead, her eyes dilate with surreal speed and open up wide, wider than I've ever seen and I think I should see the backs of her eyes but all I see is black, big deep black holes and I am looking into nothing and everything and forever. All the stiffness falls from her body and she sinks onto my arms and her head droops to the side and lays on my arm. Rusty brown blood spills from her mouth onto the sleeve of her sweatshirt on my arm and I feel its sticky warmth quickly cool.

Together with her, I lay down on the bed and blanket her, my arms still underneath her back, my head buried in the pillow next to hers. Everything is so still around me, there is no sound, no breathing, not even my own. Am I? What is supposed to happen?

In a moment, everything I have worked for is absent. I have no purpose. Nothing. I have nothing to do, nothing to lead me into the next moment, to direct my thinking, my muscles, my nerve endings. I do not know to stay, to go, what I am supposed to do. Jada's body feels empty and it is cold; it has lost all suppleness and I know Jada is not in this body nor lingers near it. I release her and stand up. I feel touch on my arm and am turned around; Beverly takes me to her but I do not bend. She is warm and soft and I think I cry into her and I make no attempt to move. I see Arnold pull her away and surround me, heave a breath so heavy I expect him to crumple but he holds onto me and my arms hang uselessly limp, and I am unable to say yes, no, I want, or I need. Prickly fibers from his red sweater scratch my chin, twitch my nose as I draw them in and I wonder why he is dressed for Christmas.

Dr. Lourde says, "You can stay in the room as long as you like," and I feel guilty for not wanting to. I have no thought to keep a 24-hour vigil in the hospital room, for I do not believe Jada's spirit would want to stay here any more now than when she was alive. Arnold lets me go. Lois is straightening the blankets around Jada's body and places Hambone where I had been. Her eyes are still open black vats until Dr. Lourde closes her eyelids. Foamy white fluid oozes from her nostrils, and Dr. Lourde puts a towel to her nose. A sound issues from her throat; Dr. Lourde explains a passage of air over her vocal chords. I look at her body that wiggled and danced and squirmed and shimmied with life and now lays there so rigidly and wonder why people would say that now she is at peace. "No," I say aloud and think to myself, no. She wanted to live with a bang, die with a bang; staying here would celebrate neither choice.

"You can leave everything. We'll take care of it," Dr. Lourde says as my eyes sweep the room. I come back to Jada, her arms like slats of lumber on the blankets on either side of the mound that is her body underneath them. She does not look like she is sleeping. I do not believe she is Jada.

"What about Hambone?" asks Lois. Hambone lived because of Jada; now she is dead.

"I want him to go with her," I say, and Arnold nods.

Dr. Lourde advises, "You'd better take him to the mortuary yourself. Everyone tries to be careful, but things get lost or misunderstood."

I go to get him but he is trapped underneath Jada's arm which does not budge as it would if she were only sleeping and I feel like a thief trying to remove Hambone because her arm is locked in the position it was put. Lois recognizes my confusion and moves Jada's arm up like a wooden barrier at the entrance to a parking lot because it does not bend at the elbow, and she hands Hambone to me. I rest my chin on Hambone's head and Beverly's arm winds around my back, the rest of her leading me out of the room, fronting me like a shield. I am afraid of seeing people. *Please, no people.* I look up. I see a clock, I see a time. I do not know it.

Beverly leads me to the sitting area and, moving together in harmony, sits me down, sitting down herself; Dr. Lourde and Arnold in tow, man comforting man, sit across. Tears don't satisfy my emptiness. I can't wish her back because I don't even know what it feels like with Jada gone; except I believe she is; I felt her leave and her leaving gutted me of will and energy, and now I am void of thinking and feeling and getting to the next minute on my own. I look robotically at my surroundings, a growing awareness of my oddity verifying the truth of my survival.

We are all four of us quiet in the predawn quiet of the hospital on a quiet Sunday morning. Dr. Lourde shifts his elbow on his knee. I hear the grating of fabric on fabric. "Ms. Santino, I want you to know I thought that was wonderful the way you helped Jada."

"Yes, it was beautiful," Arnold chimed.

"Some people fight it and make it difficult for their children to go. The way you talked to her, what you said and did helped her through. That may seem hard to hear, but you made it easier for her. I've never seen anyone do that with such grace as you did."

I nod my head dumbly, swallowing a dry tongue, unable to take credit for the accident of living and the intention of loving and what they called me to do.

"Would you like me to contact anyone?"

"Yes. Tell Dr. Silverman. And those two doctors, the ones from Chicago who were at the conference, the nurse, Pat, from the conference, if you can. They were so nice and took an interest in Jada."

"Yes, I know who they are. If there's anything else...."

Anything. Once, many times, I had an answer to that, stirring conditions and stipulations into a marshy slough of ifs and onlys, no firm footing except for a dream for tomorrow, but now we are in tomorrow and it is impossible to think of anything.

Arnold shakes his head. "Come on, Idina. I don't want you to be alone. I'll take you home with me." People rise and move about and my coat appears on my body, and I am being dragged into the present because I think of Dom and wonder where he is. We have to tell Dom. We are moving along dark morning streets, a familiar route with an unfamiliar feel, when I ask Arnold.

"I didn't wake him up. I just got a phone call to come to the hospital. No one told me why." No, I think. They never tell us. How do we know what to listen for?

The headlights make two sunbursts of yellow on the garage door as we pull into the driveway of the house I once lived in. Arnold drives into the center of the dark garage that used to hold two cars side by side and I follow him to the front door, up the steps to the closet where I hang Jada's coat next to mine. I have Jada's coat. And Hambone.

"I'll put some coffee on. You go in and tell Dom." Hugging Hambone to me, I walk a familiar route past Dom's former room. The brown, gray and white wallpaper with jocks running and jumping and hurling balls and pucks has been replaced with oversized pink Hawaiian flowers splashing a blue couch with a spindly floor lamp; it is reverted to a TV room, as it had been before he was born and Jada, Arnold, and I lived in the house together. I stride into the dark bedroom where I used to sleep. Dom's single bed has replaced mine, which had replaced ours. I am caught in circles, spiraling through my life. Jada's room is not changed.

The light from the hallway illuminates a mound of clothing on the floor and the edge of Dom's bed. I sit there taking in the warm smell of sleep and put my hand on Dom's broad back. He is a large young man, almost eighteen; every time I touch him, I feel diminished in size and wonder at his replacement in the cycle of life. "It's me," I say, waiting for him to know it is his mother talking to him and touching him. He rolls to his side and squints. The light coming around the corner of the door from the hallway is too bright for eyes that are not ready to open. "Jada died this morning."

"Oh," he makes a long scraping in his throat and takes a suffocated breath through his ignoble Santino nose. I wait for him to reach for a tissue and clear it; he is still stuffed up. Arnold is at the doorway and leans on the jamb, one arm crossed in front as a sort of wedge.

"We were there. I held her and told her how much we loved her. She died of internal bleeding."

Dom tosses his wadded tissue to the wastebasket, and instinctively, we watch to see if it drops in. "Was it from the car accident?"

"No. She was examined then. And it would have happened then, too. No. The leukemia just took over and wore her out." The justice of Jada's death by leukemia instead of all the other odds we so assiduously sidestepped is planted in little seeds and I can feel each one prick my brain as it germinates. "I'm glad you're asking questions. You'll probably have others and maybe want to talk. You know you can talk to your dad or me. But if you don't want to talk to us, it's okay, too. Just don't hold feelings in. Let us or someone know you need to talk. We all love you and want to help you."

"I'm okay, Ma."

"Yes, I believe you. But you don't know how you'll feel later. I just don't want you to feel you have to do everything alone or that you are alone. Remember when you fell on your bike and you needed me right away? You might feel like that again—it can come all of a sudden like that. I want you to call me, or someone else."

"I know. I will, Ma."

I have let my hand slip as Dom has moved around, but I have kept contact with him, and now that Arnold is not standing there I say, "You'll think I'm goofy for saying this, but, it's possible that you may hear from her. I mean, I figure anything's possible, so she might communicate with any one of us. I just want you to know that I'll believe you if you tell me she does."

"Yeah, I know. I don't think that's weird."

"Okay; do you want me to stay in here?"

"No. I'm going to try to sleep some more. I'm really tired."

"I'll be in the kitchen. See you when you get up." I kiss Dom on the forehead and follow the light to the kitchen. My whole body feels like my fingers when they're frozen: stiff, thick pegs without the sense of touch. I feel the throb inside them, but nothing outside them. Arnold pours me a cup of coffee, setting it on the glass surface of the table by the glass sliding door, the place where he used to sit. A shiver makes me hug my elbows to my rib cage. I squeeze Hambone. Is this what it feels like in space, nothing to protect me from the openness that brushes me, like the eroded side of the mountain that loses a part of itself to every encounter with its environment?

"I hope it's all right with you, but I'd like to take care of the mortuary arrangements."

"Fine. She wants to be cremated, you know."

"Yes. They'll do that. Roselawn has a special place in their cemetery for that, too. I'll make an appointment with them. I'll call St. Margaret's, too."

I sip insipid brown water. "She's not big on the church, you know. And she hasn't gone there in a long time."

"You have to have a funeral in a church. I'll call Grace and ask her to help. And flowers. We'll have to order flowers as soon as we know the arrangements. RoseAcres doesn't charge a lot of money. Insurance should cover pretty much everything. I'll handle all the bills; we'll split anything that's over."

"Fine. I can't think about that stuff now." He is tugging at me too hard; my brain feels stuck in quicksand; it is comfortable there.

Arnold exhales. "I know. Well, it's over. It was beautiful, just beautiful." The words come out like steam from a kettle while he looks down at his cup. I look for a wall, anything blank. Anything that won't add one more thought, anything that will absorb me, soak me up to nothingness. There is nothing beautiful about anything. Death is plain ugly and defiling and painful. "If only she could have got married," he muses.

"I don't think that would have been enough. How about babies? You know she couldn't have them. The only things she did have were taken away. College. Her BMW. Adam. It was all complete; she and the world were done with each other. She couldn't even have Christmas."

"I suppose you're right. We were planning a cruise after Christmas. She loved Christmas. I don't know what arrangements you have, but for the funeral, can we be a family? Sit together?"

"Of course. I hope Dom doesn't feel bad that he wasn't there when she died. He seems okay." I turn to find the time. "I have to make some phone calls. I can't sit here anymore."

"You can use the phone in the den. I've already called Maureen."

When? I must really be disoriented. How can I be here in this time? I sink into the corner of the couch in Dom's old room and dial my sister.

"Oh, no! Oh, Idina, no!"

"Yes. Arnold and I were with her. I need you to call Mother and Punky." Domenica is the only one living in the area. "Will you handle the information, see that people know to call you, not me?"

"Yes, I'll take care of that. Where are you? Are you in Minnesota?"

"Yes. I'm at Arnold's."

"On Lambert Lane? Oh, this is terrible. I didn't know it would be so soon."

"I guess it's always too soon when it happens." Tracey's parents, Beverly said, rushed her to the hospital never once foreseeing her death.

"I'm coming right over. Oh, Idina, this is awful!"

"Yeah, it is. If you do, you can drive me to get my car. I left it in the hospital parking lot."

I call Jessie, too. I want her to call Thomas and Cecilia, in Colorado. The whole day is spread ahead of me like the heavens at a planetarium. I don't know how to get to them, so I sit. Sit with Dom while he eats breakfast, turns on the television; sit with Arnold, in the kitchen, with another pot of coffee. We are as distant as stars, yet still we sit in the same frozen universe. Domenica comes, and we are with each other, though there is no small talk in the car. She doesn't ask questions, and when she drops me off at the hospital, neither of us has spilled water. I don't think I can, and when I get home, Per greets me, holds me, and I play the tape on my message machine and my mother is crying and it sounds loud and displaced, as if meant for someone else.

All day I call people, Priss, Akiko, Mike, Jeff, people who will call people who will call people. I call Jada's friends to be pall bearers, a friend to sing, Beverly to read a poem, all on Sunday. I go through Jada's closet, brushing past her pink sweater, the one that brought rose to her cheeks even when there wasn't, her polka dot cotton robe, the shorts I stacked with her swimsuit, all there and waiting for her to pluck them out of storage and onto her body. I am looking for clothing for her to wear on this final occasion. Her dressing must be perfect. There is her camel skirt, her black blazer, the outfit she wore when she spoke at the conference. I look for her blouse and am thankful she has kept it here. Do I bring nylons and underwear? I decide to include everything, for even if she is not Jada, she was, and I want to respect what was. I go back into the closet and find her jeweled hat and set that out, too. Dr. Silverman calls and the flowers he sends I place by Jada's picture. Arnold has set the church and florist meetings for Monday. Jessie will go with me on Monday night to buy a dress to wear to my daughter's funeral. I have made it through the day, much as I have every other day, focused on task; now for the night.

Dusky light blankets the living room, and I pull Hambone up to my lap. It is so wrong that I should be left to hold him, to rock him, when she is alone. I remember the times that I wanted to take her back into my body, to be the house that would keep her safe and warm and loved. My knees lock together and my head bends over Hambone making a tight womb. Things to do, things to take care of, things, things, things. No things to do. I rock Hambone and I cry.

We are waiting for Sister Paschaline at the church on Monday. I have read through Bible passages; one includes reference to a strong woman, so I choose that. Arnold asks, "Are you going to touch her body?"

"What do you mean?"

"At the funeral. Are you going to touch her body? I am."

I struggle to remember music, the music I loved and sang in church, the music I thought I'd never forget and wonder what Arnold's question might signify. There are so many customs and common understandings that I have never learned. But I am busy through the day, busy telling Sister about Jada's accomplishments, her desires and loves and character, busy ordering calla lilies, anthurium, and roses, a Christmas tree to put at the coffin, busy talking about time and food, and trying on dresses and appropriate shoes and my hair needs cutting and I have to reserve a car for Priss to drive to the mortuary when she arrives and so the question begs an answer. At the end of the day, all I can think is that I have touched Jada's body. I've touched her body for over twenty-one years when it held her alive, and I touched her as she died and her body became an emptiness, an emptiness like inside me and the end to today.

Arnold, Dom, and I stand facing Jada's coffin, staring into what is supposed to look soft and puffy and satiny. The attendant takes Hambone from me and props him against the closed half of the lid. I sigh as he watches us examine his arrangement as if perhaps she is a work on consignment and must meet our approval and maybe he senses my dissatisfaction and winds a rosary around Jada's fingers;

the crucifix hangs as if just kissed. "No, that wasn't her," I say and Arnold agrees. With his arms crossed and dropping like a fig leaf in front of him, Arnold's jowls work. "She looks good, doesn't she?"

Dom remains mute. Inside me I scream, *Good! That isn't even her! Where is her sniffle, the wiggle to her nose, the flutter of her eyelids, the stretching of her smile? You call this caky attempt to fake life good?* I turn away. This is no time to talk about her being in a better place or that death came as a blessing or now I have another angel to pray to, or any other inanity people think up to make the unacceptable dismissible. The attendant magically appears to guide us away and hides from us the practicalities of moving Jada in the heavy box into a place surrounded by flowers for public reviewal.

Dom, Arnold, and I are the last to see Jada's body—the half they allow—at the church, and I visualize Jada's glistening smile, her blue eyes with the light dancing in them, how summer sunlight streaked across her face and how she stood up, stood up when she knew the world had knocked her down. I recall her prancing gait before the firestorm of the disease crippled the litheness of her body's movement, how she undulated to the beat of the music and the rhythm of living and tell myself that I must never let this image of inertia ever outlive her animation. I breathe in the sprays of dead flowers and try to obliterate them with the delicately lingering lotions I smoothed on Jada's yielding body after a restful bath, and my arms hang dead from their sockets. I accept Jada's death and yield to this feeling of perdition: the release of her spirit. They close the lid and it goes down on everything I wanted, believed, cared about, loved, and accepted that love by itself is nothing and so it is never enough. But love with knowledge is learning how to live with its loss, and, therefore, a punishment, one worthy of the pain; it is all and more than enough.

Everyone remains in the church after the service, but I follow the casket to the car and keep walking behind the silver hearse until it leaves me behind. Outdoors we have been warned of the extreme wind-chill, but I feel nothing. From behind, someone throws Jada's coat over my shoulders.

Epilogue

Medical advances have ensured that Acute Lymphoblastic Leukemia, as some other cancers, have become more treatable over time. Had Jada been born twenty years earlier, she would have surely had a more dire prospect for survival. Twenty years later, treatment and Jada's response to it might have been different enough that she would not have endured the same side effects and complications—and outcome. Had she lived twenty years later, however, she would still have to face a prognosis and a course of treatment with no guarantees. Her story, then, would still resonate of choices, of living with integrity and dignity.

To everyone who experiences similar crises, to your self be true.

Book Group Study Questions

What feelings do you have for Jada's character? What role did her diary/journal entries play in your feelings toward her?

Mobility for Jada was compromised on several occasions throughout the course of the narrative. Discuss how that condition might be of hyper significance in a young person's view of her situation.

Jada says that her choice to die was a consequence of her desire to live. Respond to Jada's goals and conditions of living, as you understand them. How does this tension between living and dying play out in your own lives?

Beverly says that the will to live in children is strong. How is that observation embodied in this narrative?

Early on in the narrative, the reader knows of or suspects Jada's outcome. As a reader, did you have conflicting feelings as the narrative progressed? Discuss your own journey of resistance, alignment, conviction, resignation, or any other emotional response, as you read the narrative.

"Family disease" is a broad and inclusive category; yet, Jada lived a life and died a death as one, alone. Relate these concepts as they are presented in the narrative and how they apply to your experiences.

Were there sentences, insights, or passages that struck you, caused you to pause, spoke to you personally? What are they? What do you care to share about them?

In what ways is this narrative like other stories in this genre? How is it different?

What questions are left unanswered for you? Are there shortcomings in the telling of the narrative that you wished were addressed?

Evaluate the use of water as a leitmotif in *Trouble the Water*.

About the Author

*I*dina Santino grew up, taught, and mothered two children in Minnesota before moving with her long-time partner, to Tucson, Arizona, where she grandmothers, volunteers, and hikes the desert. As an educator, she has published professionally.

CPSIA information can be obtained
at www.ICGtesting.com
Printed in the USA
FSHW012350180221
78693FS